General Editor

Peter Melville Logan is Professor of English at Temple University, USA and Director of the Center for the Humanities at Temple. He specializes in nineteenth-century British literature, critical theory, the history of the novel, and the history of science. He is the author of *Victorian Fetishism: Intellectuals and Primitives* (2009) and *Nerves and Narratives: A Cultural History of Hysteria in Nineteenth-Century British Prose* (1997), as well as articles on Victorian popular culture, George Eliot, and Matthew Arnold.

Associate Editors

Olakunle George is Associate Professor of English and Africana Studies at Brown University, USA, where he teaches African literary and cultural studies, Afro-Diasporic cultural criticism, and Anglo-American literary theory. He is the author of *Relocating Agency: Modernity and African Letters* (2003) and articles in *Comparative Literature Studies, Diacritics, Novel: A Forum on Fiction*, and *Representations.*

Susan Hegeman is Associate Professor of English at the University of Florida, USA, where she specializes in twentieth-century American literature, popular culture, cultural history, and critical theory. She is the author of *Patterns for America: Modernism and the Concept of Culture* (1999) and *The Cultural Return* (forthcoming 2011).

Efraín Kristal is Chair of the Department of Comparative Literature at the University of California, Los Angeles, USA, where he is also Professor of Spanish and French. He is editor of *The Cambridge Companion to the Latin American Novel* (2005) and Jorge Luis Borges's *Poems of the Night* (2010), and the author of numerous books and articles on literature, translation studies, and aesthetics.

The Wiley-Blackwell Encyclopedia of Literature
www.literatureencyclopedia.com

The *Wiley-Blackwell Encyclopedia of Literature* is a comprehensive, scholarly, authoritative, and critical overview of literature and theory comprising individual titles covering key literary genres, periods, and sub-disciplines. Available both in print and online, this groundbreaking resource provides students, teachers, and researchers with cutting-edge scholarship in literature and literary studies.

Published:

The Encyclopedia of Literary and Cultural Theory, General Editor: Michael Ryan

The Encyclopedia of the Novel, General Editor: Peter Melville Logan

The Encyclopedia of Twentieth-Century Fiction, General Editor: Brian W. Shaffer

Forthcoming:

The Encyclopedia of English Renaissance Literature, General Editors: Garrett A. Sullivan, Jr. and Alan Stewart

The Encyclopedia of Romantic Literature, General Editor: Frederick Burwick

The Encyclopedia of the Gothic, General Editors: William Hughes, David Punter, and Andrew Smith

The Encyclopedia of Postcolonial Studies, General Editors: Sangeeta Ray and Henry Schwarz

The Encyclopedia of the Novel

Edited by
Peter Melville Logan

Associate Editors:
Olakunle George, Susan Hegeman,
and Efraín Kristal

Volume II
Lo–Z, Index

WILEY-BLACKWELL

A John Wiley & Sons, Ltd., Publication

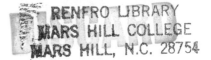

This edition first published 2011
© 2011 Blackwell Publishing Ltd

Blackwell Publishing was acquired by John Wiley & Sons in February 2007. Blackwell's publishing program has been merged with Wiley's global Scientific, Technical, and Medical business to form Wiley-Blackwell.

Registered Office
John Wiley & Sons Ltd, The Atrium, Southern Gate, Chichester, West Sussex, PO19 8SQ, United Kingdom

Editorial Offices
350 Main Street, Malden, MA 02148-5020, USA
9600 Garsington Road, Oxford, OX4 2DQ, UK
The Atrium, Southern Gate, Chichester, West Sussex, PO19 8SQ, UK

For details of our global editorial offices, for customer services, and for information about how to apply for permission to reuse the copyright material in this book please see our website at www.wiley.com/wiley-blackwell.

The right of Peter Melville Logan to be identified as the author of the editorial material in this work has been asserted in accordance with the UK Copyright, Designs and Patents Act 1988.

Wiley also publishes its books in a variety of electronic formats. Some content that appears in print may not be available in electronic books.

Designations used by companies to distinguish their products are often claimed as trademarks. All brand names and product names used in this book are trade names, service marks, trademarks or registered trademarks of their respective owners. The publisher is not associated with any product or vendor mentioned in this book. This publication is designed to provide accurate and authoritative information in regard to the subject matter covered. It is sold on the understanding that the publisher is not engaged in rendering professional services. If professional advice or other expert assistance is required, the services of a competent professional should be sought.

Library of Congress Cataloging-in-Publication Data

The encyclopedia of the novel/edited by Peter Melville Logan;
Olakunle George, Susan Hegeman, and Efraín Kristal, associate editors.
    v. cm.
  Includes bibliographical references and index.
  Contents: Introduction – v. 1. The novel A-Li – v. 2. The novel Lo-Z – Indexes.
    ISBN 978-1-4051-6184-8 (hardcover : alk. paper) 1. Fiction– Encyclopedias. I. Logan, Peter Melville, 1951– II. George, Olakunle.
III. Hegeman, Susan, 1964– IV. Kristal, Efraín, 1959–
    PN41.E485 2011
    809.3′003–dc22
                      2010029410

A catalogue record for this book is available from the British Library.

Set in 10/12.5pt Minion by Thomson Digital, Noida, India
Printed and bound in Singapore by Fabulous Printers Pte Ltd

02   2011

Contents

Alphabetical List of Entries

List of Entries by Topic

Locution *see* Speech Act Theory
Looped Narrative *see* Frame

Low Countries (Europe)

JAAP GOEDEGEBUURE

The modern novel in the Netherlands dates to the end of the eighteenth century. The examples of Samuel Richardson's *Pamela* (1740) and *Clarissa* (1747–48) inspired Betje Wolff and Aagje Deken, two female authors who lived and worked together for more than twenty-five years, to write one EPISTOLARY novel after the other. The first of these, *Historie van mejuffrouw Sara Burgerhart* (1782, *History of Miss Sara Burgerhart*), marked their greatest success and is still considered as the first PSYCHOLOGICAL novel in the Netherlands. We follow the young heroine, an orphan who is given the chance to grow up more or less independently, on her path to knowledge and virtue, taking risks by getting acquainted with a man who appears to be an unscrupulous seducer, quarrelling about religion and morals with bigoted people, but, in the end, being happily married to a righteous husband. It is clear that the authors intended to give a positive example to the young women among their readers, but their novel is still enjoyable because of its wit and its variety of characters, who are portrayed through their letters.

Whereas Wolff and Deken represent the voice of reason, Rhijnvis Feith is under the spell of sentimentalism, the other extreme of the culture of Enlightenment. His novel *Julia* (1783), whose title reminds us of Jean-Jacques Rousseau's *Julie ou La Nouvelle Héloïse*, is a lachrymose tale full of moonlight and churchyards. Its innovative qualities have, as is the case in contemporary English, French, and German novels, to do with an emancipating shift in content and characters. Narrative themes are no longer restricted to heroic events of princes and noblemen, or to the comic actions of common people (see CLASS). The leading role is emphatically taken by the citizen, now taken seriously as an individual with feelings and emotions.

THE NINETEENTH CENTURY

During the first half of the nineteenth century the Dutch and Flemish novel moved in the HISTORICAL direction, following Walter Scott. In the Netherlands the great national events of the past—especially the Eighty Years' War (1568–1648) with Spain, whose king, since Charles V, was also sovereign of the Low Countries—were told time and again. The characters of these stories are not only heroic, but also industrious, patriotic, and chaste. By being so they represent the civil virtues of the era.

Flemish nationalism, a result of resistance against the dominance of the French-speaking ruling classes in the nascent Belgian state (which broke away from the Netherlands in 1830), manifests itself in the work of Hendrik Conscience. His novels *De Leeuw van Vlaanderen* (1838, *The Lion of Flanders*) and *Jacob van Artevelde* (1849, *Jacob Artevelde*) glorify the struggle of the medieval Flemish towns of Ghent and Bruges against the French king, culminating in the famous Battle of the Spurs (1302).

Isolated among his contemporaries and unique in his literary and social opinions is Multatuli (pseud. of Eduard Douwes Dekker). Although he wrote and published many books in different genres, his fame is based on one novel, *Of de koffieveilingen der Nederlandsche Handelsmaatschappij* (1860, *Max Havelaar: Or the Coffee Auctions of a Dutch Trading Company*). The eponymous character is a thinly disguised portrait of the author, but the *Max Havelaar* story is also an act of self-justification. Part of the colonial administration in the Dutch East Indies (now Indonesia), Multatuli tried to improve the living conditions of the native people, and in so doing came into conflict with his superiors. For reasons of honor, he resigned, and vented his frustration in a book that remains a classic, not least because of its refreshing, lively, and witty style, and its capricious and fanciful structure, by which the author shows affinities with writers such as Laurence Sterne (whom he probably never read) and Jean Paul Richter. The (unreliable and ridiculed) narrator, Batavus Droogstoppel, whose acquaintance the reader makes in the first paragraph, is an Amsterdam coffee broker, who voices his antipathy to literature, saying it is nothing but lies and deceit, and of no practical use whatsoever. This harangue shows him to have the typical nineteenth-century Dutch mentality that attached great weight to such bourgeois virtues as diligence, thrift, DECORUM, and piety. The name Batavus refers to the Batavi, a Germanic tribe believed by nationalist historians to be the original inhabitants of the Netherlands (see NATIONAL); *Droogstoppel* (dry stubble) can be taken to mean a dull, boring person, someone to whom idealism and deeply felt emotions are entirely alien. Droogstoppel is indeed the antithesis of the romantic hero Havelaar, who joins battle with the corrupt and profit-seeking authorities.

Characteristic for Multatuli is his talent for satire. *Woutertje Pieterse* (1890, *Walter Pieterse: A Story of Holland*), his other major novel on which he worked for many years without finishing, is famed for the ridicule it heaps on petit-bourgeois Holland. One of its highlights is the scene in which the schoolmaster Pennewip, pedantry incarnate, proves in a discourse that Miss Laps is in fact a mammal.

FIN-DE-SIÈCLE

The next major changes in Dutch and Flemish narrative prose have to do with a radical turn toward realism. French REALISM and NATURALISM, represented by authors such as Gustave Flaubert and Émile Zola, became the new literary paradigm, although in a moderated way. The most dedicated follower of realism is Marcellus Emants, who showed serious interest in the scientific pretensions of Zola's naturalist doctrine. Some traces of naturalism, such as the belief that heredity is the cause of mental disorder, are also to be found in the novels of Louis Couperus, without doubt the most important novelist of his generation. His first novel, *Eline Vere* (1888), shows clear influences of Flaubert's *Madame Bovary* (1857). Like Emma, Eline is a woman of her time and her milieu: educated and sensitive, but shackled by the conventions and etiquette prescribed by bourgeois morals. Her romantic daydreaming clashes with reality, nourishing the neurosis which ultimately drives her to commit suicide.

In his novels Couperus steadily progresses from storytelling to social criticism. In his portrayal of the life of the upper classes he exposed their hypocrisy, prejudices, and narrow-mindedness. A highlight in this respect are the four volumes of *De Boeken der Kleine Zielen* (1901–2, *Small Souls*), a family epic which readily bears comparison with Thomas Mann's *Buddenbrooks* (1901) and John Galsworthy's *Forsyte Saga* (1906–21). Like Mann and Galsworthy, and Zola, whom he greatly admired, Couperus described the decline of the *haute bourgeoisie*.

The cultural and philosophical implications of the theme of decline turned Couperus's attention to a comparable period of history. Like other authors at the end of the nineteenth century, he was preoccupied with the decadence of the Roman Empire, a phenomenon which he and others related to the establishment of imperial rule, which destroyed republican virtues, and the inescapable law of nature that states and civilizations, just like living organisms, have a limited life span (see DEC-ADENT). He expressed these ideas in *De Berg van Licht* (1905, *The Mountain of Light*) and *De Komedianten* (1917, *The Comedians*).

THE TWENTIETH CENTURY

In the Flemish novel the realistic turn to everyday life manifests itself in a preference for rural settings. The important authors here are Stijn Streuvels (pseud. of Frank Lateur) and Cyriel Buysse. Both show their commitment with and pity for poor, exploited, and humiliated working-class people. Buysse's frank dealing with sexual taboos caused angry reactions among Catholic critics. Because of his novel *Tantes* (1924, *Aunts*), now considered his masterpiece, he was condemned as a "perverse decadent."

Streuvels is an outspoken pessimist, who depicts life as an inescapable chain between birth and death. His characters act as if they are passive prisoners of fate, unable to change or influence the eternal laws of nature. His worldview is best expressed in his EPIC novel *De vlasschaard* (1907, *The Flax Field*) and the novella *Het leven en de dood in den ast* (1926, *Life and Death in the Drying Kiln*), which is often compared with the work of Henrik Ibsen and Fyodor Dostoyevsky.

During the 1920s and 1930s narrative prose in Flanders was radically renewed under the impetus of Maurice Roelants and Gerard Walschap. These two writers were far ahead of most of their Dutch colleagues, who still worked within the nineteenth-century realistic tradition. In *Komen en gaan* (1927, *Coming and Going*), Roelants

restricted events and descriptions to a minimum while giving ample rein to the reflections of the protagonist-narrator. Walschap distinguished himself through a sharp increase in narrative tempo, which manifested itself in the schematic, quasi-chronicling nature of the factual account. Where Roelants made frequent use of dialogue, Walschap avoided it as far as possible. This latter feature has been associated with the vitalistic nature of Walschap's novels: words are much less direct than actions.

In their early works both Roelants and Walschap struggled to free themselves from Catholic dogma and the authority of the Church (see RELIGION). As the story of a love triangle that does *not* come about, *Komen en gaan* is dominated by a conflict between good and evil that issues from the Christian sense of sin. In this context Roelants's analytical and ethically oriented approach is striking. Unusually, perhaps, given the spirit of the age, there is little or no influence of Sigmund Freud's stress on the instinctual life as the basis of all action (see PSYCHOANALYTIC).

Where Roelants concentrated on a crisis-like situation in the life of an individual, Walschap tended to opt for the story of a whole life, a dynasty embracing several generations or a complete community. His trilogy *Adelaïde, Eric,* and *Carla* (1929–33) were conceived as family novels in the great nineteenth-century tradition; in style and composition, however, they are much more sober and taut. The NARRATIVE STYLE remains remarkable, recording the spoken word not as monologues and dialogues but in a form halfway between direct and free indirect speech (see DISCOURSE). The language register stands close to the spoken word and the syntax is simple. In his later novels Walschap continues this process of formal renewal.

A third innovator in Flemish prose, Willem Elsschot (pseud. of Alfons de

Ridder), was far more radical in his anticler-icalism than Roelants and Walschap. His novels are shot through with a cynical skepticism. Elsschot mercilessly exposes the nature of the petit bourgeois with his hypocrisy, selfishness, and greed. The critical and satirical tendency of his work is manifest in *Lijmen* (1924, *Soft Soap*), the story of the gentleman con-artist Boorman and his "World Review of Finance, Trade and Commerce, Art and Science." The publication with this sumptuous title is nothing but a subtle way of exposing vain businessmen anxious for publicity. Boorman usually writes an over-inflated article about their business and subsequently offloads a few thousand copies onto the company in question. In *Het been* (1933, *The Leg*), a sequel to *Lijmen*, Boorman becomes sentimental and hence falls prey to his own system. After having dumped 100,000 copies of the "World Review" on the widowed female boss of a metal works, he is subsequently moved to pity and offers compensation to the victim. She, however, proudly refuses, which leads to a fencing match to decide who will be left with the "blood money." Boorman wins, but in so doing he loses his reputation as a ruthless cynic in the eye of his subordinate Laarmans, with whom the author more or less identifies.

The Dutch author Nescio (pseud. of J. F. Grönloh) shows a kinship with Elsschot. He too was a skeptic, because of frustrated idealism. He too showed that all human effort is in vain, by demonstrating how his heroes, "little Titans" in their youth, become disillusioned and frustrated when they grow old. And, just like Elsschot, he wrote in a sober, non-ornamental style. For this reason both authors were appreciated more than ever after 1970.

DUTCH MODERNISM

Carry van Bruggen, one of the first Dutch authors who, in her novel *Eva* (1927), used the modernist "stream of consciousness" technique (see NARRATIVE TECHNIQUE), had already turned away from the realist paradigm in *Heleen* (1913). The main character's spiritual development is not described in relation to factors such as social environment and material circumstances, but the author portrays her as a self-assured individual who tries to determine her attitude toward life's great existential questions and problems.

In the context of international MODERNISM, *Het verboden rijk* (1932, *The Forbidden Empire*), by J. J. Slauerhoff, bears comparison with Virginia Woolf's *Orlando* (1927). Two characters appear in successive episodes in the story that, historically, are centuries apart. Eventually these characters, the Portuguese poet and globetrotter Luís Vaz de Camoes and an anonymous radio operator, coalesce, just as the various time levels merge. The whole is dominated by typically modernist themes such as identity and depersonalization.

Ferdinand Bordewijk combined a proclivity for the fantastic and grotesque with a compact, graphic style which displayed an affinity with German New Objectivity. But he went further than the detached registration of a world dominated by technology and urbanization; he hinted at mysterious powers active in everyday life. In this respect he has much in common with surrealist painters such as Giorgio de Chirico and René Magritte (1898–1967) (see SURREALISM).

Simon Vestdijk, author of many volumes of poetry, short stories, and essays, also wrote fifty-two novels. Among them is a fictionalized autobiography in eight volumes, the Anton Wachter cycle, which parallels Marcel Proust's *À la recherche du temps perdu* (1913–27, *Remembrance of Things Past*) and *Meneer Vissers hellevaart* (1936, *Mr. Visser's Descent into Hell*), a novel clearly inspired by the narrative technique of James Joyce's *Ulysses* (1922). First and foremost an analyst, Vestdijk dissects psychological complexes, emotions, and interpersonal relationships with almost clinical precision.

Vestdijk was also very productive as the author of HISTORICAL novels. *Het vijfde zegel* (1937, *The Fifth Seal*) centers on the life and work of the painter El Greco, with King Philip II of Spain looming in the background. The relative patchiness of El Greco's biography enabled Vestdijk to fill in the gaps with his imagination. He was to do something similar in *De nadagen van Pilatus* (1939, *The Last Days of Pontius Pilate*). Here the principal roles are played by Pilate, Mary Magdalene, and the mad emperor Caligula; in the background stands the figure of Jesus Christ.

Also semiautobiographical is *Het land van herkomst* (1935, *Country of Origin*), by E. du Perron. The novel has two story lines: one consisting of memories (see MEMORY) of a youth in the Dutch East Indies (now Indonesia) and one in which the first-person narrator, Arthur Ducroo, notes down the effect that writing has on him and what he feels and experiences in the here-and-now (early 1930s Paris). The key word is "authenticity": Ducroo/Perron is determined to reveal the truth about himself, even if it will be painful and embarrassing. But, in the end, he has to admit that as soon as one writes stories, every "I" inevitably turns into a character.

POST-WWII FICTION

After the German occupation of the Netherlands and Belgium a new generation of novelists made their appearance. Many of them wrote about the terror and violence of the Nazi period; in this respect they show an affinity with French existentialists such as Jean-Paul Sartre and Albert Camus. Willem Frederik Hermans treated the war theme in *De tranen der acacia's* (1948, *The Tears of the Acacias*) and *De donkere kamer van Damokles* (1958, *The Dark Room of Damocles*). The latter novel, which can also be read as an exciting thriller, is particularly interesting because it reveals Hermans's ambivalent attitude when it comes to philosophical questions concerning reality and truth. In his view it is impossible to decide whether someone was a hero or a villain during the war. The interests of an individual or a group are the sole criteria for such concepts as truth and justice. This is what the main character of *De donkere kamer van Damokles* experiences. A colorless figure who gets the chance to shake off his mediocrity during the German occupation by joining the resistance, he becomes so entangled in the web of espionage and counter-espionage that after the liberation he is considered a traitor rather than a patriot. Since every proof of his innocence has disappeared, the only possibility left is "to be shot while attempting to escape."

Harry Mulisch has written little that does not refer to the events of WWII. The son of a father who collaborated with the German occupying forces and a Jewish mother, he feels himself to be the personification of the war. This obsessive involvement has resulted in a number of novels which could be called milestones in Dutch postwar fiction. *Het stenen bruidsbed* (1959, *The Stone Bridal Bed*) is a forceful and convincing treatise on the problem of guilt and responsibility, showing that the hero, an American pilot who took part in the senseless bombing of the German city of Dresden at the end of the war, was guilty of a war crime. This theme recurs in *De aanslag* (1982, *The Assault*). The question here is whether an act of resistance against the Nazis was justified when it was inevitably followed by reprisals against innocent people. It is significant that Mulisch, when dealing with these problems, constantly refers to ancient

Greek myths. By connecting the recent past to MYTHOLOGY he stresses the constantly recurring chain of events, views, and traditions.

Much more embedded in the postwar here-and-now is Gerard Reve's *De avonden* (1947, *The Evenings*), which bears a striking resemblance to Sartre's *La Nausée* (1938, *Nausea*). The boredom and disillusionment of young people, whose ideals had been shattered by the horrors of the Nazi period, are depicted here in a way which evokes the grayness of the December days during which the action takes place. Reve's absurd, black humor and the stylistic mixture of the pompous and the trivial provide a counterweight to the gloom.

In Flanders Louis Paul Boon stands out as an existentialist author. In *Mijn kleine oorlog* (1946, *My Small War*) he formulated his personal creed: "I want to kick a conscience into people." The simple soldier who lets himself be conscripted for war service is the same man who lets himself be ordered about by his boss. Boon blames the authorities— the government, the administrators, the Church—for inciting the ordinary man to vice and misconduct.

Boon's masterpiece is without any doubt his diptych *De Kapellekensbaan* (1953, *Chapel Road*) and *Zomer te Ter-Muren* (1956, *Summer at Ter-Muren*). In its form this saga of "the rise and fall of socialism," as the author called it, mirrors the disintegration of twentieth-century society and the disturbed mind of modern man. The novels are a mixture of narrative, comments, fables, and more. The everyday life of the people who live in Chapel Road parallels the adventures of the protagonist of the medieval satirical epic *Reynard the Fox*, one of the canonical texts of Flemish literature.

The other major figure in postwar Flemish literature is the multi-talented Hugo Claus, who excelled as a poet, playwright, and novelist, and was also a film director and a painter. At the age of 19 he wrote *De Metsiers* (1950, *Sisters of Earth*), a somewhat torrid pastoral which owes much to the example of William Faulkner. Claus was one of the first to recognize the importance of the French *nouveau roman*. In *De verwondering* (1962, *The Amazement*) his theme is the fragmented experience of reality and the inextricable entanglement of appearance and substance, which make the conventional sequence of a story, with its beginning, middle, and end, a falsification. The main character keeps a diary on the advice of his psychiatrist, but the fragmentation of his personality increases rather than diminishes as he writes.

Claus's masterpiece is *Het verdriet van België* (1983, *The Sorrow of Belgium*), set in the late 1930s and early 1940s, the years when Flemish nationalists sympathized and even collaborated with the German occupying forces. Louis Seynave, the young hero of this novel, comes to realize that a detached, ironic smile is the only possible means of surviving the torments and frustrations arising from his adolescent problems, and from the tragicomic fate of tiny Belgium torn by the language conflict between the Flemish and Francophone parts of the nation. Claus holds up a distorting mirror to the failures and shortcomings of his compatriots.

POSTMODERN FICTION

Boon and Claus nowadays are seen as forerunners of postmodern fiction, which became dominant in the Netherlands from the 1970s on. In this decade the newly founded literary review *De Revisor* became a platform for a group of young writers, who all shared the view that reality as such exists only in so far as it can be represented in language. Skepticism and solipsism are the inevitable consequences of such an outlook; it also brings in its wake the political indifference that became widespread in the Netherlands after the euphoric years around 1968. "Imagination," a key term in the fictional and critical works of authors such as Nicolaas Matsier, Dirk Ayelt Kooiman, and Frans Kellendonk, proved worthless as a political agent after the revolutionary spirit of the 1960s had vanished; therefore it had to be returned to its original environment: art and literature. This formula has been worked cleverly and elegantly into the action of *Rituelen* (1980, *Rituals*), a truly postmodern novel for which the author, Cees Nooteboom, received positive acclaim at home and abroad. In present-day Dutch literature no one has thematized the perception of TIME so frequently and persistently as Nooteboom. In his capacity as novelist, poet, and travel writer he has for years now shown himself to be fascinated by the selective and at the same time creative ways in which we transform the passing of time— how memories are filtered in the labyrinth of our memory by the falsifying yet liberating powers of the imagination. The wonder of fiction, as Nooteboom reminds us, depends on the impossibility of recalling everything and the concomitant need to imagine. More wondrous still is that, thanks to our collective memory, we share a common past, no less selectively. In this way art fulfills the role of intermediary between our individual existence and a tradition of thousands of years, and a triangle comes into existence in Nooteboom's work between time, memory, and art. In this respect *Rituals* is a high point.

If the perception of time for Nooteboom is cause for PHILOSOPHICAL and cultural-historical reflection, other Dutch and Flemish writers perceive a challenge in the way in which *this* time, *this* moment in history, asks specific questions of us and makes specific demands on our conscience. Since the late 1990s, not by chance the decades of an "ethical turn" in literary criticism, various

writers in the Dutch and Flemish language area have wrestled with questions having to do with the eternal conflict between good and evil. Here Harry Mulisch has been at the forefront, as can be seen from his novel *De Ontdekking van de Hemel* (1992, *The Discovery of Heaven*). The core of the plot, God's action in restoring to heaven the stone tablets of the Ten Commandments, is not to be seen as an ironic story-line but an expression of concern with increasing decay in moral values. That this concern was serious became evident from a subsequent novel, *De procedure* (1988, The procedure; the title is borrowed from English), in which biogenetic manipulation forms the object of a Kafkaesque game involving crime and punishment. And in *Siegfried* (2001, *Siegfried: A Black Idyll*) Mulisch allows us to see how Adolf Hitler—as an historical concept—is "beyond good and evil": he represents the totality of emptiness, the great Nothing.

With *Siegfried* Mulisch returned to his favorite subject, WWII. In *De vermaledijde vaders* (1985, *The Accursed Fathers*) the Flemish writer Monika van Paemel connected the war theme with the persistent patriarchal power structure in Western society, the source—for her—of all evil. Later novels such as *De eerste steen* (1992, *The First Stone*), *Rozen op ijs* (1997, *Roses on Ice*), *Het verschil* (2001, *The Difference*), and *Celestien* (2004, *Celestine*), while maintaining a FEMINIST perspective, focus on the conflict between Israel and Palestine, the ethnic wars in the former Yugoslavia, overpopulation, and environmental destruction, along with other issues high on society's political agenda. It is clear that, for van Paemel, engagement is an existential matter.

A much more frivolous and sardonic attitude is to be found in the work of the Flemish writer Tom Lanoye. His trilogy *Het goddelijke monster* (1997, *The Divine Monster*), *Zwarte tranen* (1999, *Black Tears*), and *Boze tongen* (2002, *Evil Tongues*) emerged in the shadow of the scandal surrounding the pedophile murderer Marc Dutroux, an affair that shocked Belgium in the early 1990s.

Grotesquerie in theme and style is also the hallmark of the young Jewish Dutch writer Arnon Grunberg. Apparently irreconcilable opposites, such as frivolity vs. tragedy, cynicism vs. sentimentality, and horror vs. farce, express Grunberg's vision that fine words and high ideals are illusions, but that despite this vision, or perhaps because of it, we must be happy, if not in fact, then in the written word. One could sum up Grunberg's aesthetic vision in the title of one of his essay collections: *De troost van de slapstick* (1998, *The Comfort of Slapstick*). The slapstick comes into its own in his novels such as *Gstaad 95–98* (2002), *De asielzoeker* (2003, *The Asylum Hunter*), and in *De joodse messias* (2004, *The Jewish Messiah*), with the striking effect that the horrors they describe (incest, murder, rape, and in the last book, a war of total global destruction declared out of revenge by an Israeli dictator modeled on Hitler) are not palliated but rather intensified. Grunberg's reputation as a cynic who, like the cynics of Greek Antiquity, is in fact an inverted moralist, is confirmed in his philosophical pamphlet *De mensheid zij geprezen* (2001, *In Praise of Mankind*). In this variation of Desiderius Erasmus's *In Praise of Folly* (1509), war is glorified, conscience cast into suspicion, evil dispensed with ironically, and beauty brought into conjunction with cruelty and self-satisfaction. In his later work Grunberg broadens his scope; *Onze oom* (2008, *Our Uncle*), to mention one example, is set in a South American country during a war between a corrupt government and a revolutionary movement.

The cynic Grunberg's absolute opposite pole is the poet, novelist, and playwright Willem Jan Otten, the most prominent and controversial of a group of writers who returned or converted to the Roman Catholic Church. Inspired by the great cultural critic Dostoyevsky, and therefore apologetic and moralizing, and at the same time full of doubts and skepticism, Otten has expressed his opposition to the human tendency to play God that he discerns in euthanasia and genetic manipulation. He has become firmly committed to his belief in the incarnation and resurrection of Jesus Christ, a belief that he is convinced is not possible without the *coup de théâtre* of the creative imagination at the disposal of writers, artists, and actors. His novel *Specht en Zoon* (2004, *Woodpecker and Son*) treats the theme of the resurrection. It concerns a painter who is given a commission to bring a portrait back to life, but fails on account of his lack of faith.

Last is the Dutch variant of postcolonial discourse, a worldwide phenomenon of past decades. Passing reluctantly over the fact that some of the most interesting Dutch writing at the moment is being produced by first- and second-generation immigrants such as Hafid Bouazza, Abdelkadir Benali, and Kader Abdolah, I here highlight Arthur Japin, whose *De zwarte met het witte hart* (1997, *The Two Hearts of Kwasi Boachi*) gained attention on account of its story-line and its remarkable NARRATIVE STRUCTURE. The author permits one of the two princes from the West African kingdom of Ashanti, both of whom remain "hostages" at the mid-nineteenth-century Dutch court, to tell his story. This he does on the basis of existing archive material, but with an innovative tone and color. The result is a penetrating analysis of the conflict between two clashing identities: that of a displaced person in a xenophobic Europe vs. the cultivated African who will never again be able to find his roots in his country of birth.

SEE ALSO: Dictatorship Novel, National Literature, Regional Novel.

BIBLIOGRAPHY

Hermans, T., ed. (2009), *A Literary History of the Low Countries*.
Musschoot, A.M. (1998), "Netherlandish Novel," in *Encyclopedia of the Novel*, ed. P. Schellinger.

Lukács, Georg

TIMOTHY KAPOSY

Georg Lukács (1885–1971) was not only one of the founders of Western Marxism, he was one of the most important twentieth-century theorists and historians of the novel (see MARXIST, NOVEL THEORY (20TH C.), HISTORY). Born into a wealthy assimilated Jewish family in Budapest, Lukács was heralded a prodigy by his earliest educators. As a teenager, he was involved in the pragmatic and theoretical debates of fin-de-siècle Hungary, and also organized dramatic productions of Henrik Ibsen (1828–1906) and August Strindberg (1849–1912) within Budapest's factories and handicraft shops. Leaving his native soil in 1906 he enrolled first at the University of Kolozsvár, then in 1909 at Berlin University and later in Heidelberg. Lukács crossed a significant threshold of his thinking in this period: in addition to reading the texts of Wilhelm Dilthey (1833–1911), G. W. F Hegel (1770–1831), and Karl Marx (1818–83) for the first time, he was taught by luminaries Ernst Bloch (1885–1977), Georg Simmel (1858–1918), and Max Weber (1864–1920). Described in retrospect as "romantic anti-capitalism," Lukács's early writing interprets a startling range of thinkers to illustrate and critique the loss of "traditional" societies in Europe since the late eighteenth century. *A lélek és a formák* (1910, *Soul and Form*) consists of ten essays, largely metaphysical in design. Lukács's focus on artistic and critical conduct, the desire of poets, artists, and philosophers to create a semblance of reality in their work, is described in a way that shifts between a yearning for the preservation of soul amid a "lachrymose reality" and hints of social commentary. The first chapter, "On the Nature and Form of the Essay," in particular influenced many theorists of his generation, including Theodor Adorno (1903–69), and it has been taken up by contemporary theorists as well (see Butler). Examining a panorama of artists and thinkers both major—Søren Kierkegaard (1813–55), Novalis, Laurence Sterne—and minor—Stefan George (1868–1933), Theodor Storm (1817–1938)—Lukács explores the rapid emergence of modern bourgeois sensibilities and their clash with the prevailing aesthetic trends of previous eras.

Lukács's literary theory finds a more coherent and demonstrative expression in his next major work, *Die Theorie des Romans* (1920, *The Theory of the Novel*). Along with Mikhail BAKHTIN's *The Dialogic Imagination* (1975) and Ian Watt's *The Rise of the Novel* (1957), Lukács's book has been heralded as one of the century's most influential philosophical studies of the novel. Its ingenuity is attributable to two arguments. First, novelistic writing is said to consist of a singular *ontological* condition, rather than an aesthetic, historical, or psychological one. "The form of the novel," he writes, "is, like no other one, an expression of . . . transcendental homelessness" (1971b, 41). Permanently displaced from a universalized *Heimat* expressed in the cosmologies of Ancient Greece, novelistic writing emerges as the preeminent form that contends with this loss. The novel also exhibits prospects for reevaluating this condition: "The conflict between what is and what should be has not been abolished and cannot be abolished in the sphere wherein these events take place—the life sphere of the novel; only a maximum conciliation—the profound and intensive irradiation of a man by his life's meaning—is attainable" (1971b, 80).

Second, in a gesture that intimates his future conversion from a metaphysical to a historical mode of critique, Lukács uses the category of TIME to index historical shifts in novelistic genres. The narrative sequences of modern novels is interpreted by Lukács as a break with earlier narrative temporalities such as the EPIC, which, comparatively, unfolds a spatial imaginary of wandering heroes and visited lands that recounts events from a previous historical period. Lukács writes:

> [t]he normative attitude towards the epic, according to Goethe and Schiller, is an attitude assumed towards something completely in the past; therefore its time is static and can be taken in at a single glance. The author of an epic and his characters can move freely in any direction inside it. ... Only the complete disorientedness of modern literature poses the impossible task of representing development and the gradual passing of time in dramatic terms. (1971b, 122)

Lukács's deceptively complex insight that "we might almost say that the entire inner action of the novel is nothing but a struggle against the power of time" (1971b, 122) was immensely influential for critics attempting to understand the synthesizing and/or discordant effects of artistic expression, the artifacts it produces, and the time and place of its genesis. Walter Benjamin (1892–1940), for instance, wrote in a letter to Gershom Scholem (1897–1982) that *The Theory of the Novel* "astounded" him because of its ability to "[proceed] from political considerations to a theory of cognition" (355).

On 7 Nov. 1917, Lukács walked to the Deutsche Bank in Heidelberg and placed all his writings in a safe-deposit box, thereby bringing to an end his tacit intellectual preoccupations. Soon thereafter, with reports of the Russian Revolution fresh in his mind, he returned to Budapest and joined the Hungarian Soviet Republic, becoming People's Commissar for Education and Culture. The regime was eventually defeated, which caused him to flee to Vienna. While there he met, among others, Italian Marxist Antonio Gramsci (1891–1937), and he reformulated the fundamental political principles of his thought.

Lukács's next major intervention, *Geschichte und Klassenbewußtsein* (1923, *History and Class Consciousness*), is considered by many his masterpiece. This study is most influential today as a work of capitalist epistemology. His landmark concept of "reification" is described as a process in which capital shapes all aspects of social life (see CLASS, IDEOLOGY). Building upon Marx's problematic of commodification, Lukács reinterprets capital as having a broad set of consequences throughout daily life. Social formations and their products appear natural, their contingencies and antagonisms are effaced or rendered inexistent in the commodity's genesis. Therefore the consciousness accompanying class divisions— i.e., its de facto legitimacy—is countervailed in Lukács's account by the consciousness of the proletariat, or those who produce the "qualitatively determined unity of the product" (1971a, 88). Class consciousness is thus conceived by Lukács not as an empirical experience of a single group of people but as a *zurgerechnetes* (imputable) type of awareness of social inequality that is deeply antagonistic with the attempt to make capitalist economies and cultures appear natural. This work would come to prominence once again after its republication in the late 1960s, with a critical preface by Lukács, and deeply influence a generation of cultural critics and theorists of the novel, most significantly among them, Fredric Jameson.

After a hostile reception to this work—for which Lukács would offer a brilliant polemical defense that was published for the first time in 1996—his political and theoretical orientation would undergo another major shift. *Der historische Roman* (*The Historical Novel*), which he wrote in Moscow during the winter of 1937–38, exemplifies his more complex dialectical interpretation of literature as contextualized by and narrating the forces of its social totality. A dynamic interpretation of the role of literature in the political movements of post-Napoleonic history—"the contradictions of human progress" (1962, 344)—he marks the differences in the genre between both earlier historical dramas and the proto-modernist fictions of Flaubert that emerge after the failed revolutions of 1848. "What matters . . . in the historical novel," he writes, "is not the re-telling of great historical events, but the poetic awakening of the people who figured in those events. . . . It is the portrayal of the broad living basis of historical events in their intricacy and complexity, in their manifold interaction with acting individuals" (1962, 42–43). In the opening of his preface to this work, Jameson describes it as "perhaps the single most monumental realization of the varied program and promises of a Marxist and a dialectical literary criticism" (1962, 1).

In his later work on the novel, Lukács turns primarily to a theorization of REALISM. Consonant with the formulations of class consciousness in his earlier work, he describes realism as a narrative practice that enables its practitioners to express the interrelation of economic and political forces within a particular social totality. This sets the ground for a clash with advocates of modernist writing, chief among them Bertolt Brecht (1898–1956), Adorno, and his teacher, Bloch.

Lukács's influence in cultural theory and literary criticism is impossible to avoid. Any thorough study of capitalist reification and totality or novelistic forms must engage his work. Edward Said, perhaps the most insightful literary interpreter of Lukács's trajectory, has argued for a fidelity to Lukács's "inducement to insurrectionary action" and argued against tempering his ideas into mere interpretative devices. For Said, Lukács's "Marxism . . . regulated an interchange between the individual or group intellect and brute actuality; it did not overcome barriers; it dissolved them by formalizing them almost infinitely, just as (paradoxically) proletarian consciousness truly existed when a dehumanized atomism had both dismembered and postponed all human solidarity" (65–66). In the contemporary field of modern and world literature, Franco Moretti, Roberto Schwarz, and Jameson, among others, employ the lessons of Lukács's theories. For Moretti, *The Theory of the Novel* and Lukács's writings on realism from the 1930s stand alongside Eric Auerbach's *Mimesis: The Representation of Reality in Western Literature* (1946) and Pascale Casanova's *Republique mondiale des lettres* (1999) as theories of the novel invaluably shaped by political constraints of their day. A disavowal of this political complication and gravity, prevents us from understanding Lukács's critique of the narrative modes mediating our perception of capitalism, and reverses the most valuable direction in which Lukács's work leads: aesthetic qualities of novels need to be interpreted not as hermetic codes to be deciphered unto themselves, but as complex articulations of the socioeconomic situation. Jameson argues for a deep consistency throughout what is too often perceived as Lukács's disjointed oeuvre: "Lukacs's work might be seen as a continuous and lifelong meditation on narrative, on its basic structures, its relationship to the reality it expresses, and its epistemological value when compared with other, more abstract and philosophical modes of understanding" (1971, 163).

BIBLIOGRAPHY

Adorno, T. (1991), "Essay as Form," in *Notes to Literature*, vol. 1, trans. S.W. Nicholsen.

Benjamin, W. (1966), *Briefe*, ed. T. Adorno and G. Scholem.

Butler, J. (2009), "Introduction," in G. Lukács, *Soul and Form*, trans. A Bostock.

Corredor, E.L. (1997), *Lukács After Communism*.

Jameson, F.R. (1971), *Marxism and Form*.

Kadarkay, A. (1991), *Georg Lukács*.

Lukács, G. (1962), *Historical Novel*, trans. H and S. Mitchell.

Lukács, G. (1963), *Meaning of Contemporary Realism*, trans. J. and N. Maunder.

Lukács, G. (1970), "Narrate or Describe?," in *Writer and Critic, and Other Essays*, trans. A.D. Kahn.

Lukács, G. (1971a), *History and Class Consciousness*, trans. R. Livingstone.

Lukács, G. (1971b), *Theory of the Novel*, trans. A. Bostock.

Lukács, G. (2000), *A Defence of History and Class Consciousness*, trans E. Leslie.

Moretti, F. (2003), "More Conjectures," *New Left Review* 20 (Mar./Apr.).

Said, E. (2002), *Reflections on Exile and Other Essays*.

M

Maghreb *see* North Africa (Maghreb)

Magical Realism

DANIEL BALDERSTON

In a conversation with novelist Cormac McCarthy, filmmaker Ethan Coen asks McCarthy whether he ever rejects ideas because they are too outrageous. McCarthy replies: "I don't know, you're somewhat constrained in writing a novel, I think. Like, I'm not a fan of some of the Latin American writers, magical realism. You know, it's hard enough to get people to believe what you're telling them without making it impossible. It has to be vaguely plausible" (L. Grossman, 2007, "What Happened When," *Time,* 29 Oct.). This quotation neatly catches an equivalence that has come to exist between the most commercially successful works of Latin American literature and magical realism, a concept contested by Latin American writers since it was first imported from German art criticism in the late 1920s. A concept that was for a time (mostly in the 1960s and 1970s) used to sell some forms of Latin American writing is now a straitjacket, resented by most Latin American writers, because it constrains a vast literary tradition.

The term "magical realism" was first used by Franz Roh (1890–1965) in 1929 to describe certain currents in German art after expressionism. It was used early by Arturo Uslar Pietri and Miguel Ángel Asturias, and then vigorously challenged by Alejo Carpentier. In 1949 he coined a competing term, *lo real maravilloso* (the marvelous real), in several essays and prologues, as a way in which the Latin American writer, in contradistinction to the surrealists, can find the marvelous in the real. While not as influential, Carpentier's term is set out somewhat more clearly. Magical realism became a dominant critical term through Ángel Flores's "Magical Realism in Spanish American Fiction" (1955) and Luis Leal's 1967 essay of the same name, in which Leal argues with Flores about what the term means and whether Franz Kafka is crucial as an influence. The corpus of both Flores and Leal includes such writers as Jorge Luis Borges and Ernesto Sábato, though they are no longer thought of in this regard.

The concept, however confused, became indelibly associated with Gabriel García Márquez's epic novel *Cien años de soledad* (1967, *One Hundred Years of Solitude*). From there the term became largely the property of publicists and journalists; literary critics despaired of finding a coherent concept in magical realism. It certainly does not define a dominant tradition in Latin American writing since the 1970s. However, it has been used to promote the writing of Asturias, Jorge Amado, Isabel Allende, Márcio Souza, Laura Esquivel, Demetrio Aguilera Malta, and others. Although there is no consensus regarding the term's meaning, magical realism has influenced writing beyond Latin America, as in the work of Salman Rushdie.

In the most important recent book on Latin American writing of the 1960s, Diana

Sorensen writes against magical realism. Though sympathetic to García Márquez's novel, Sorensen considers its core structural motif: the transformation of the real (ice, for instance, at the beginning of the novel) into the unreal, and the magical (the rain of yellow flowers, levitation, magic carpets) into the natural. According to Sorensen, this was not typical of the writing of the period. Nor was it read sensitively by the publicists for magical realism. The failure to be sufficiently "magical realist" contributed to the lack of global success of such Latin American writers as Juan Carlos Onetti, José Donoso, Clarice Lispector, and Juan José Saer, as well as a group of younger writers who have called themselves the "McOndo" generation as a way of distancing themselves from the flights of fancy associated with García Márquez's imaginary town.

SEE ALSO: Genre Theory, Modernism, National Literature, Realism.

BIBLIOGRAPHY

Bowers, M. (2004), *Magic(al) Realism*.
Parkinson Zamora, L. and W. Faris, eds. (1995), *Magical Realism*.
Sorensen, D. (2007), *Turbulent Decade Remembered*.

Mainland Southeastern Asia *see* Southeast Asian Mainland
Manga see Graphic Novel
Maqama see Arabic Novel (Mashreq); North Africa (Maghreb)
Maritime Southeastern Asia *see* Southeast Asian Archipelago

Marxist Theory

PHILLIP E. WEGNER

The question of the novel has long been central to Marxist theory. Karl Marx "was a great reader of novels," noted Paul Lafargue, and he "admired Balzac so much that he wished to write a review of his great work *La Comédie Humaine* as soon as he had finished his book on economics" (Baxandall, 150). Conversely, some of the most important and influential contributors to the theorization and history of the novel arise from Marxist theory. This is in part because Marxist theory develops during the peak of the novel's cultural importance; and in part, because of the central role of narrative in Marxist theory.

To understand Marxist theory presupposes a larger question about the nature of Marxism itself. Although many answers have been offered, an especially useful one is that proposed by Fredric Jameson. Marxism is less doctrine or unified theory than a *problematic*, "not a set of propositions about reality, but a set of categories in terms of which reality is analyzed and interrogated, and a set of essentially 'contested' categories at that" (1983, "Science Versus Ideology," *Humanities in Society* 6(2–3):283). Marxism is the science (a continuously evolving, axiom producing, and totalizing epistemological project) of the capitalist mode of production, and dialectically invested in both IDEOLOGY and economics—expressed as the binaries of superstructure and base, subject and object, idealism and materialism, freedom and determinism—with the issue of social CLASS at its center. Finally, the political questions of conflict and struggle, and the transformation of our understanding, institutions, and ultimately our world, form a practical horizon that "always interrupts the 'unity of theory' and prevents it from coming together in some satisfying philosophical system" (Jameson, 2006, "First Impressions," *London Review of Books* 28(17):7).

What draws together the great variety of Marxist theory is the question of the relationship of the novel, as both particular works and a larger institution, to its historical situation. How the novel relates to that historical context—reflecting, critiquing, dissimulating, intervening in, shaping—is the substance of debate among the tradition's major figures. The answers range between viewing the novel as a mere epiphenomenal (superstructural) reflection of more fundamental economic realities (base), to seeing it as a concrete expression of a class worldview, to taking it as a significant force in both shaping capitalist society and its ultimate overthrow. As a result, Marxist theory has produced rich and diverse contributions to our understanding of the novel.

Although suggestive reflections on the novel are scattered throughout Marx and Engels's writings, one of the first explicit statements is to be found in Friedrich Engels's Apr. 1888 letter to novelist Margaret Harkness. There, Engels defines REALISM as implying "besides truth of detail, the truthful reproduction of typical characters under typical circumstances" (Baxandall, 114). He then praises Honoré de Balzac, who offered a "complete history of French Society" and, even more importantly, who despite "his own class sympathies and political prejudices . . . *saw* the necessity of the downfall of his favorite nobles" (Baxandall, 115–16). This short essay establishes a significant line of development of Marxist theory as it encourages a reading of the form and content of novels against the grain of an author's conscious political affiliations. Vladimir Ilich Lenin (1870–1924), for example, writes of the way Leo Tolstoy's novels reflect their author's "epoch" (Eagleton and Milne, 42); and Engels's notion of "typicality" reappears in Georg LUKÁCS's work on the historical novel, work Jameson calls "perhaps the single most monumental realization of the varied program and promises of a Marxist and a dialectical literary criticism" (Lukács, 1983, 1).

It is in the struggles for socialism that the practical questions of literature's role come to the fore. One of the most influential statements in this regard is Leon Trotsky's *Literature and Revolution* (1924), which argues that a proletarian revolution must also produce a new art and culture. While critical of the Formalist and Futurist schools (see FORMALISM), Trotsky is far from offering a blanket dismissal of MODERNISM, and is equally cautious of demands for a doctrinaire realist proletarian literature, arguing that these are "dangerous, because they erroneously compress the culture of the future into the narrow limits of the present day" (205).

The two most important early Marxist theorists of the novel, LUKÁCS and BAKHTIN, also arise out of the political and cultural ferment of the Russian revolution. Lukács produced his first major work, *The Theory of the Novel* (1916), before his encounter with Marxism. Influenced by Georg Wilhelm Friedrich Hegel (1770–1831) and Søren Kierkegaard (1813–1955), Lukács constructs an ideal typology of the genre that he famously describes as "the epic of a world that has been abandoned by God" (1971, 88). The novel thus struggles to give "form, to uncover and construct the concealed totality of life" (1971, 60). Lukács's pioneering genre study, *The Historical Novel* (1937), takes a more materialist approach, tracing out the conditions that enabled Walter Scott to found both the genre and its new historical sensibility. Part of the originality of Lukács's study is his suggestion that any genre has moments of vitality followed by decline, the latter occurring for this quintessential bourgeois genre after the revolutions of 1848. Lukács's later work expresses a deep hostility toward modernism (though he too was critical of socialist realism as well), arguing for the greater political potentialities of classical realism. This would put him in conflict with a number of his contemporaries, including Bertolt Brecht, Walter Benjamin, Ernst Bloch, and Theodor Adorno (their debates are reprinted in Bloch, et. al, *Aesthetics and Politics*, 1977).

Bakhtin's approach to the novel is a different one, at once deeply populist and sympathetic with modernism, and this put him at odds with the Soviet Union's increasingly rigid literary establishment. For Bakhtin, the novel is deeply rooted in popular culture's satirical traditions, and is distinguished from classical genres such as the epic in that it offers a stylized expression of the rich "polyphony" or "heteroglossia" of different groups and classes, each locked in "dialogic" struggle with its competitors. In the "English comic novel," for example, "we find a comic-parodic re-processing of almost all the levels of literary language, both conversational and written, that were current at the time" (1975, 301). The study of the novel thus needs to be a "sociological stylistics" exposing "the concrete social context of discourse" (1975, 300).

The closing of the revolutionary horizon, the onset of the Great Depression, and the rise of Fascism created a climate less propitious to the development of Marxist theory, although the 1930s did see important reconsiderations in Granville Hicks's *Great Tradition* (1932) and V. F. Calverton's *Liberation of American Literature* (1932) of the CLASS dimensions of American literary history, and scathing critiques of British literature by Christopher Caudwell in *Studies in a Dying Culture* (1938). This was also the moment of Kenneth Burke's influential theorization of literature as "symbolic action" (see Frank Lentricchia, 1983, *Criticism and Social Change*). The postwar moment witnessed an institutional reluctance to engage in Marxist theory, although even here important interventions appear. These would include C. L. R. James's *Mariners, Renegades and Castaways* (1953), a study of Herman Melville's fiction, as a diagnosis of capitalist modernization and its tendency toward totalitarianism; and Adorno's formulations in *Notes to Literature* (1991) and other works of a modernist aesthetics whose

political import lay in its thoroughgoing negativity.

The political, cultural, and theoretical ferment of the 1960s saw a revival of the fortunes of Marxist theory. In addition to reconsiderations of earlier interventions, three distinct trends can be identified. First, Lucien Goldman develops a Marxist sociology of the novel whose central problem is "that of the relation between the *novel form* itself and the structure of the social environment in which it developed, that is to say, between the novel as a literary genre and individualistic modern society" (Eagleton and Milne, 209).

Secondly, Louis Althusser's structuralist Marxism provided an impetus for original work (see STRUCTURALISM). Pierre Macherey developed a strategy of "'symptomatic reading' which enables us to identify those gaps and silences, contradictions and absences, which deform the text and reveal the repressed presence of . . . ideological materials" (1966, *A Theory of Literary Production*, viii). A decade later, Terry Eagleton further expands upon the Althusserian turn, reading the literary text not as the expression of ideology but as "a certain *production*" of it (1976, *Criticism and Ideology*, 64). However, Eagleton soon turned from structuralism, something evident six years later in *The Rape of Clarissa* (1982), a study that combines historical materialism with poststructuralist theories of textuality, psychoanalysis (see PSYCHOANALYTIC), and feminism (see FEMINIST).

Finally, evolving out of a left humanist tradition and contributing significantly to the development of British cultural studies, Raymond Williams also produced a deeply influential body of scholarship. Williams argues that novels give voice to what he calls "structures of feeling," "meanings and values as they are actively lived and felt" (1977, 132). For example, in *The English Novel from Dickens to Lawrence* (1970), Williams explores how the nineteenth-century novel registers a crisis in the sense of nation and "knowable community"; and his masterpiece, *The Country and the City* (1973), maps how a tradition of British literature extending from sixteenth-century country-house poetry through contemporary global fictions both reflect changes wrought by the Industrial Revolution and register emerging sensibilities before they enter into explicit public discourse.

The most elaborate contemporary statement of Marxist theory is to be found in the work of Jameson. Questions of the novel and narration already play a central role in his *Marxism and Form* (1971). However, his most influential theorization of the novel occurs in *The Political Unconscious* (1981), a work whose opening motto, "Always historicize!" (9), signaled a turn in the 1980s from formalism to deeper attention to concrete situations out of which cultural texts emerge. Bringing together the seemingly antithetical strains represented by Lukács and Althusser, and supplementing these with insights drawn from psychoanalysis (see PSYCHO-ANALYTIC) and STRUCTURALISM, Jameson develops a threefold hermeneutic that reads any text in terms of their "symbolic acts," "ideologemes," and "ideology of form" (1981, 75–6). His deeply dialectical approach also challenges readers to be sensitive to utopian figurations in novels.

The publication of *The Political Unconscious* opened a richly productive period in Marxist theory. At the forefront of this new work stands Michael McKeon's *The Origins of the English Novel, 1600–1740*. McKeon sets for himself the task of explaining "how categories, whether 'literary' or 'social,' exist in history: how they first coalesce by being understood in terms of—as transformations of—other forms that have thus far been taken to define the field of possibility" (4). McKeon shows how the "simple abstraction" of the novel comes into being as the culmination of a centuries-long debate over the two intertwined sets of epistemo-logical and social concerns, "questions of Truth" and "questions of Virtue." The novel emerges as the negation of both the authority of established texts and the aristocratic code of behavior found in the chivalric romances.

This moment also witnessed a new centrality of GENDER in Marxist theory that reconfigures in significant ways traditional understandings of CLASS. For example, Rachel Bowlby's *Just Looking* (1985) explores how naturalist novels stage the spectacular growth of modern consumer society and its effects on class and gender identity (see NATURALISM). Nancy Armstrong's *Desire and Domestic Fiction* challenges the portrayal of women novelists as victims by showing how their work participates in the triumph of middle-class culture. The novel was so successful in this political work precisely because it presents itself as domestic, feminine, and apolitical. Bruce Robbins's *The Servant's Hand* (1986) further complexifies the analysis of nineteenth-century British novels by looking at the crucial role played by the figure of the servant.

Franco Moretti, building upon the work of Lukács, has also been a major figure in the recent development of Marxist theory. His *The Way of the World* explores the mediatory role of the BILDUNGSROMAN in nineteenth-century Europe and the development of "youth" as "a value in itself" (177). In *Modern Epic* (1996) and *Atlas of the European Novel, 1800–1900* (1998), Moretti offers highly original contributions to the "spatial turn" in theory, examining how the novel, in its thematic, formal, and institutional dimensions, reflects and furthers global transformations wrought by capitalist modernity.

Other recent work in Marxist theory has also increasingly turned to questions of imperialism, postcoloniality, and globalization. Edward Said's *Culture and Imperialism* (1993) is a landmark in this regard. Gayatri Chakravorty Spivak, who forged a Marxist theory informed by feminist theory, subaltern studies, and deconstruction, maps out "the vicissitudes of the native informant as figure in literary representation" (1999, *Critique of Postcolonial Reason*, 112). Peter Hitchcock's *Dialogics of the Oppressed* (1993) deploys the critical resources made available by Bakhtin in a nuanced reading of postcolonial women's novels. Kojin Karatani's *Origins of Modern Japanese Literature* (1993) explores the role of the innovations in the novel form in the modernization of Japan; Mary N. Layoun's *Travels of a Genre* (1990) looks at the twentieth-century migration of the novel into Greek, Arabic, and Japanese cultures and its role in debates between the "modern" and "tradition;" and Jean Franco's *Decline and Fall of the Lettered City* (2002) investigates the effects of the Cold War on the Latin American novel.

Marxist theory has also provided a significant impetus to an engagement with popular novels. Drawing upon Brecht, Darko Suvin developed a theory of SCIENCE FICTION "as the literature of cognitive estrangement," and hence as one of the great modernist genres (1979, *Metamorphoses of Science Fiction*, 4). Jameson has famously argued for the need to think about the specificity and originality of such forms as science fiction and "Third-World literature" (see Jameson, 2005, *Archaeologies of the Future* and 1986, "Third World Literature in the Era of Multinational Capitalism," *Social Text* 15:65–88). In *Delightful Murder* (1984), the political economist Ernest Mandel has written about ideology and form in the "crime story"; and Michael Denning has explored the ideological work of British spy thrillers in *Cover Stories* (1987) and nineteenth-century American dime novels in *Mechanic Accents* (1987) (see DETECTIVE). All of this work, as well as a wealth of recent studies by a new generation of scholars, shows that Marxist theory continues to be an indispensable resource for developments in the study of the novel.

BIBLIOGRAPHY

Armstrong, N. (1987), *Desire and Domestic Fiction*.
Bakhtin, M.M. (1975), *Dialogic Imagination*.
Baxandall, L. and S. Morawski (1973), *Marx and Engels on Literature and Art*.
Eagleton, T. and D. Milne, ed. (1996), *Marxist Literary Theory*.
Jameson, F. (1971), *Marxism and Form*.
Jameson, F. (1981), *Political Unconscious*.
Lukács, G. (1971), *Theory of the Novel*.
Lukács, G. (1983), *Historical Novel*.
McKeon, M. (1987), *Origins of the English Novel*.
Moretti, F. (1987), *Way of the World*.
Trotsky, L. (1924), *Literature and Revolution*.
Williams, R. (1973), *Country and the City*.
Williams, R. (1977), *Marxism and Literature*.

Mashreq *see* Arabic Novel (Mashreq)
McKeon, Michael *see* Marxist Theory; Novel Theory (20th Century)

Melodrama

WEIHSIN GUI

A genre of theater that emerged in late eighteenth-century France, melodrama is distinguished by spectacle and sensationalism, intense and extravagant displays of emotion and affect (often through the use of stage tableaux), polarized characters who are hapless victims, dastardly villains, and virtuous heroes, highly schematized plots centered around family secrets, domestic scandals, or calumnious mysteries, and the ultimate revelation and resolution of such affairs when the forces of good triumph over evildoers. Peter Brooks's important study (1976, *The Melodramatic Imagination*) points to French playwright François-René

Guilbert de Pixerecourt (1773–1844) as the founder of this genre. But the influence of melodrama extends beyond the stage onto the pages of the modern European and Anglo-American novel, exemplified by Honoré de Balzac's *Le Père Goriot* (1835, *Father Goriot*) and Henry James's *The Wings of the Dove* (1902). Responding to modernity's desacralization and loss of tragic vision (see MODERNISM), the melodramatic imagination in the modern novel underscores the theatricality and excess of fictional representation. This dramatic excess locates and articulates the "moral occult," namely "the domain of spiritual forces and imperatives that is not clearly visible within reality," but has to be revealed (Brooks, 20). James's characteristic dense and sinuous prose, and his portrayal of female protagonists like Isabel Archer in *The Portrait of a Lady* (1881), can be read as the work of a melodramatic imagination. Similarly, Balzac's combination of literary realism and theatrical melodrama may be thought of as subversions of the prevailing social conventions underpinning these GENRES.

In nineteenth-century Britain, the adaptation of many novels for the theater created more intersections between melodrama and the novel, exemplified by Wilkie Collins's *The Woman in White* (1859) and Charles Dickens's *Great Expectations* (1861). Dickens in particular is noted for his adaptation of GOTHIC villains for novelistic melodrama and his externalization of private emotions, which helped popularize the novel as a cultural form that both instructs and entertains a mass audience. The rise of sensation theater later in the century was concomitant with the emergence of sensation novels such as Mary Elizabeth Braddon's *Lady Audley's Secret* (1862) and Ellen Wood's *East Lynne* (1861). Winifred Hughes (1980, *The Maniac in the Cellar*) traces its roots to the traditional ROMANCE, the gothic novel, and the Newgate novel of

crime and prison houses (see DETECTIVE), but argues that melodrama is key to understanding the sensation novel's combination of romance and REALISM, and how its heightened affect and exaggerated style react against the prosaicness of mainstream DOMESTIC fiction. However, sensation novels' focus on female propriety, marital relations, and family connections suggests a form of domestic melodrama that problematizes rather than rejects the family as an ambiguous and contested space.

In the U.S., sensationalist writing in popular city novels contributed to a growing consciousness of nation and empire in the nineteenth century. The melodramatic imagination has been an important part of historical and contemporary representations of RACE in American popular culture, ranging from novels such as Harriet Beecher Stowe's *Uncle Tom's Cabin* (1852) to the media coverage of O. J. Simpson's trial in 1995 (L. Williams, 2001, *Playing the Race Card*). Outside the U.S. and Britain, melodrama also played an important part in late nineteenth- and turn-of-the-century fiction in Spanish America and Japan. Colombian writer Soledad Acosta de Samper's *Los Piratas de Cartagena* (1886, The pirates of Cartagena) used sensational swashbucklers and beautiful heroines to dramatize the conflict between different political forces in the nation-building process (N. Gerassi-Navarro, 1999, *Pirate Novels*). Novels such as Natsume Sōseki's *Gubijinsō* (1907, Poppies) drew on melodrama's moral polarization and sentimental domesticity to represent social and ideological struggles during Japan's sweeping Meiji Restoration (see IDEOLOGY). Furthermore, reading melodrama as a sensational mode of representation rather than a strictly defined genre has enabled analyses of different types of narratives. Ann Cvetkovich (1992, *Mixed Feelings*) draws attention to sensationalist rhetoric in Karl Marx's discussion of commodities in

Capital, while Anna Maria Jones (2007, *Problem Novels*) shows how certain strands of Victorianist criticism are also marked by literary sensationalism.

BIBLIOGRAPHY

Ito, K. (2008), *Age of Melodrama*.
John, J. (2001), *Dickens's Villains*.
Kirby, D. (1991), *Henry James and Melodrama*.
Prendergast, C. (1978), *Balzac*.
Pykett, L. (1992), *"Improper" Feminine*.
Streeby, S. (2002), *American Sensations*.

Memoir-Novel *see* France (18th Century)

Memory

EDWARD J. DUPUY

> How great, my God, is this force of memory, how exceedingly great! It is like a vast and boundless subterranean shrine. Who has ever reached the bottom of it?
>
> (Augustine, *Confessions*)

Without memory, the narrative act, let alone any other artistic form, would seem an impossibility. Like a piano keyboard, the "boundless subterranean shrine" provides for infinite arrangements—now in one key, next in another—and like the music created, memory patterns, disrupts, suggests, reveals, conceals, creates, destroys, invites, and puts off. It recollects the known, calls forth the unknown, animates selfhood, or challenges the very notion of self. As such it comes as no surprise that memory is the sine qua non of novels and novel writing, in whatever epoch. Memory can be hailed in the early modern, serve as the object of recovery in the modern, or be denied in the postmodern. In every period, however, it remains, positively or negatively, a focal point for novels and novelists.

MEMORY IN LITERARY HISTORY

Each era in literary history displays a characteristic understanding of memory, and so it is possible to speak of an evolution of memory. The transition from epic tale to renaissance drama to the early novel, for example, suggests a radical transformation of memory. The epic poet recited from memory the accounts of the great deeds of founding cultural figures. The poet told of defining wars replete with national heroism and individual honor. Western myths of the classical era recount origins, *in illud tempus* (in that time), of good and evil, of creation, and even of time itself (see MYTHOLOGY). All this transpired first in the oral tradition, through the power of memory. It might even be possible to speak of that era possessing a collective memory, the shared consciousness of time, and thus history and culture through the recounting of story, legend, and myth. The world of myth exemplifies circular time, the eternal recurrence of events that frame time, space, government, and everything that moves under the sun. Thus Plato could say in the *Timaeus* (360 BC) that time is the "moving image of eternity" and that memory is the recollection of what has already been known in eternity but forgotten in time. And the later Greek ideal expressed by the Stoics manifested not a reveling in time but an endurance of its repetition.

Juxtaposed with our postmodern world, however, one might find the Greek view unfathomable. The denizens of the West, from the dawn of the modern era to the present day, would be hard pressed to speak of a shared consciousness or collective memory—except perhaps in the puzzling connection between novel, novelist, and reader during the act of reading, or in other forms of linguistic exchange. Instead of collectivity or the possibility of a shared recollection, the contemporary consciousness revels in difference, individuality, its own creativity, or in the case of Samuel Beckett, the impossibility of positing an "I."

William Shakespeare can be viewed as a transitional figure between a Western culture that shared its foundations of meaning and origins through recollection in memory and the radical disjunction of memory and collectivity. In that sense he best expresses the early modern period and he anticipates the fragmentation of consciousness (1603–6, *King Lear*), the will to power (1601–7, *Macbeth*; ca. 1603, *Othello*), and a radical deracination and doubt (1599–1601, *Hamlet*), all decidedly contemporary issues. He writes of the deeds of the great, to be sure (Hamlet, King Lear, Macbeth), and in so doing he both defines history and recounts it. As the problematic Henry V tells Katherine: "Dear Kate, you and I cannot be confin'd within the weak list of a country's fashion. We are the makers of manners ..." (ca. 1599, *Henry V*, V.ii.269– 71). In these simple lines of wooing, Henry at once recalls the place of the king in his age and heralds an age rife with individual definitions of manners, and one could say, of time and history as expressed through a deracinated and individual memory.

THE RISE OF THE NOVEL AND THE AUTOBIOGRAPHY

It may come as no surprise that the novel arises soon after Shakespeare's genius. Ian Watt, for his part, argues that in order for the novel to rise as a literary form it was necessary that the ordinary activities of ordinary individuals become notable. Hamlet may be the Prince of Denmark, but he is also very much an individual who battles with the memory of loss, the vicissitudes of history, and the call to act in time. In these attitudes, he presages the contemporary world. Hamlet could very nearly stand in for William Faulkner's Quentin Compson, who in both *Absalom, Absalom!* (1936) and *The Sound and the Fury* (1929) tries to piece together the fragmented history of his past,

of the American South, and, one might say of history itself. And it is no secret that Faulkner borrowed the title of the 1929 work directly from Shakespeare's *Macbeth:* "[Life] is a tale told by an idiot, full of sound and fury, signifying nothing" (V.v.26–28).

Quentin is no epic hero, prince, or person of remarkable stature. Nor, for that matter, is his "idiot" brother Benjamin (Benjy). And yet their story bears the truth of Watt's argument about the novel—that it steps into the literary landscape to tell of the ordinary deeds of everyday people. *The Sound and the Fury* carries within it elements of the picaresque, the early example of the novel that tells in episodic form of the wanderings of the *pícaro*, or rogue, an "ordinary" person if ever there was one. While Quentin's section in Faulkner's remarkable novel is exceedingly stylized, the success of that section rests partially on Quentin's picaresque wanderings around Boston—and his dark wanderings in memory—ending at the fateful bridge spanning the Charles River.

In order for the *pícaro* to find an audience, however, and in order for the novel to gain a foothold, a transition of memory and history must also have taken place. Georg LUKÁCS calls the novel "the epic of a world that has been abandoned by God." By this I take him to mean that the novel emerges in response to the demise of cyclical time and as a result of the perils of linear and unrepeatable time. And Walter Reed says that the novel "opposes itself to other [traditional] forms of literature," and that this opposition finds expression clearly in the novel's audience—"not a community of listeners attending to an epic 'song' ... Rather, [the novel's audience] is a solitary, anonymous figure, scanning a bulk of printed pages, out of a sense of nothing better to do" (Reed; see also Dupuy).

It is the individual, both as character and audience, which the novel depicts. Furthermore, it is ordinary events in time and memory that the novel recounts. Time, memory, and the novel are thus inextricably joined. It is not surprising that at the same time novels were finding their way into the hands of solitary readers, autobiography also arises (see LIFE WRITING). It is as though memory and the individual have been cut loose from the stays of cyclical and epic time, and they seek mooring through the literary forms of the novel and autobiography that uniquely address self and memory. Georges Gusdorf has noted that one of the "conditions and limits" of autobiography involves a radical new awareness of time—a self bereft of the mythic structures that held the "terrors of history" at bay. Much the same could be said for the novel. Memory and history find themselves freed (and threatened) in the early modern period with its newfound awareness of the linearity, the nonrepeating quality, of time and history. The novel and autobiography emerge at once to express it and to quell the nascent unease such a realization evokes.

MEMORY IN AUTOBIOGRAPHY

Autobiography is an important consideration here, because the person who takes the time to write his or her life must use memory to do so. If a person's life could be charted on a time line, then the autobiographer stops at a point on that line to look back in memory and fashion the story. James Olney, perhaps the greatest of the students of autobiography, has noted that in writing his first book, *Metaphors of Self* (1972), he wanted to explore ways writers transform experience into literature. In that sense, he did not consider the work a strict study of autobiography, which he did not try to define. Instead he looked at consciousness, time, and memory, and the interplay of those with a written text. Olney considers what a novel, a series of poems, an entire oeuvre, or a self-proclaimed autobiography might say about the "self" who produced them. (And

what they might say to the reader about time and memory—and his or her experience of "self.") Taken even further, what might they say about the age in which the works were produced, and the "self's" understanding of itself in that age? These are the questions Olney explored in his first works. In his later works, and particularly in his magisterial *Memory and Narrative* (1998), he refines and deepens that search to include not only time and memory, but also their correlate: narrative. And he chooses three giants—Augustine, Rousseau, and Beckett—as his signposts in the vast history of literature, but he makes several intermediate stops along the way to consider works that might traditionally be considered "autobiography," and many others that may not.

In this landmark volume, Olney notes a consistent pairing in Augustine of remembering and confessing, recalling and narrating, recollecting and telling: "a single activity of dual dynamic, recalling a story backward and telling it forward" (1998). The dual dynamic, furthermore, recapitulates Augustine's tripartite understanding of time—the present of time past (memory), the present of time present (awareness), and the present of time future (anticipation). The act of narration involves all three inasmuch as the recitation is held in anticipation, moves through recitation itself, and then is "stored" again in memory for another telling. For Augustine, memory provides the link, the continuity and stability of being across time. Memory connects past experience and present consciousness and thus allows for what Augustine considered a stability of "self."

By the time Samuel Beckett appears on the scene, however, such continuity and stability are called radically into doubt. Augustine would say the past is present in memory and is thus in some sense, verifiable. Beckett suggests that the past is so removed from the present that it cannot possibly be verifiable, and therefore the *I* that presumably supplies the continuity across time is likewise suspect. Hence, Beckett, "like other writers of our time, has altered the terms . . . by calling into doubt, in the most radical way, memory's capacity to establish a relationship to our past and hence a relationship to ourselves grown out of the past" (Olney, 1988). Augustine's vast "subterranean shrine" that allows a subject to say "I remember" in a present consciousness is not available in the same way to Beckett. For Beckett, there remains only the infinite regress of memory and narrative, the endless attempt, as in *Krapp's Last Tape* (1958), to try to tell from memory, and to try to remember the attempt at telling in memory the trying to tell and trying to remember— and then musing at the consistently failed attempts.

St. Augustine set the stage for hundreds of years—leading to Jean-Jacques Rousseau— for Olney, a transitional figure who in his emphasis on his absolute uniqueness as expressed in feeling and memory, sets the stage not only for the Romantics who would follow him, but also for the unverifiable memory of Beckett. If Augustine formulated the triad of memory, self, and God, then Rousseau not only reduces the terms to memory and self, but those terms are further reduced to feeling: "I have need of no other memories; it is enough if I enter again into my inner self." That inner self dwells in memory, but memory is a function of feeling. Rousseau sets out in his *Confessions* to tell the "history of his soul." That "history" is the history of his feelings. Though they be unverifiable, their "truth" rests on their uniqueness such that Rousseau presents himself as having no parallel either before or after.

While I have shown memory's relation to the rise of the novel and of autobiography, and while I have followed James Olney in his tracing of the major stages of memory and narrative, I have avoided mention of T. S. Eliot and Marcel Proust, two other giants in whose works memory is not only an agent but also a theme. Eliot's *Four Quartets* (1943), among others, and Proust's *À la recherche du temps perdu* (1913–27, *Remembrance of Things Past*) stand also as seminal works in the evolution of an understanding and expression of memory, Eliot for passing through the remembered gate at Little Gidding, for example, and Proust for the tremendous outpouring of narrative arising from a remembered sensate experience.

I suggested early on that memory is the sine qua non of novels and novelists. Faulkner stands as a colossus among writers of the American South, a region haunted by memory, as many commentators note. Yet Eudora Welty, Robert Penn Warren (both in his poetry and novels), Richard Wright, Thomas Wolfe, Maya Angelou, William Styron, Alice Walker, Toni Morrison, and Walker Percy, among many others, all trouble over the question of memory and self, time, and history. Among many others on the world stage, Wole Soyinka's *Ake* (1981), Nathalie Sarraute's *Enfance* (1983, *Childhood*), Maxine Hong Kingston's *The Woman Warrior* (1976), Ronald Fraser's *In Search of a Past* (1984), and Primo Levi's *Il sistema periodico* (1975, *The Periodic Table*) all offer unique expressions of memory and its problematic role in relation to time, consciousness, and "self." In contemporary novels, too, memory finds its place. That place may or may not be expressed as the vast storehouse of Augustine, the unique feeling of Rousseau, or even the radical disconnection of Beckett. But memory is there, in all its ineffable and inexhaustible nature.

SEE ALSO: Narrative, Psychological Novel.

BIBLIOGRAPHY

Cox, J. (1989), *Recovering Literature's Lost Ground*.
Dupuy, E.J. (1996), *Autobiography in Walker Percy*.
Eakin, P.J. (1985), *Fictions in Autobiography*.

Eakin, P.J. (1999), *How Our Lives Become Stories*.

Gusdorf, G. (1980), "Conditions and Limits of Autobiography," trans. J. Olney, in *Autobiography*, ed. J. Olney.

Lukács, G. (1971), *Theory of the Novel*.

Olney, J. (1972), *Metaphors of Self*.

Olney, J., ed. (1998), *Memory and Narrative*.

Reed, W. (1981), *Exemplary History of the Novel*.

Watt, I. (1957), *Rise of the Novel*.

Metafiction

WEIHSIN GUI

Metafiction is often used to describe *avant-garde* works by American and British writers published from the 1960s up to the early 1990s, and is considered an important component of postmodernist literary style. The term was introduced by American novelist William H. Gass to describe writing "in which the forms of fiction serve as the material upon which further forms can be imposed" (25). Elaborating on Gass's definition, Patricia Waugh glosses metafiction as writing "which self-consciously and systematically draws attention to its status as an artefact in order to pose questions about the relationship between fiction and reality" (2). The increasing presence of metafiction in literature during this period is connected to sociopolitical changes in the U.S. and Britain, such as the civil rights and feminist movements and the introduction of French structuralist and poststructuralist theories of language and signification into the Anglo-American academy (see STRUC-TURALISM), as well as the translation into English of works by South American writers such as Jorge Luis Borges's *Ficciones* (1944, *Fictions*) and Gabriel García Márquez's *Cien años de soledad* (1967, *One Hundred Years of Solitude*). Some features of metafiction include self-reflexiveness about the writing process, anxiety and uncertainty regarding the authenticity of representation, and playfulness and irony in narrative voice, as

well as the authorial manipulation of linguistic signs and systems. Peter Ackroyd's *Chatterton* (1987), John Fowles's *The French Lieutenant's Woman* (1969), William H. Gass's *Omensetter's Luck* (1966), Iris Murdoch's *The Black Prince* (1973), and Vladimir Nabokov's *Pale Fire* (1962) are important examples of metafictional novels from this period.

However, some of these metafictional features are found in narratives written before the twentieth century, such as Miguel de Cervantes Saavedra's *Don Quixote* (1605, 1615) and Laurence Sterne's *The Life and Opinions of Tristram Shandy* (1759–67). This anachronism points to metafiction's analytical usefulness that extends beyond the time period described above. As a critical term, metafiction interrogates the boundaries between literary fiction and scholarly criticism, foregrounds yet circumscribes authorial power, implicates the reader in the production of the text's narrative, and questions the novelistic conventions of linearity and realism that became predominant during the eighteenth and nineteenth centuries. Linda Hutcheon discusses a specific form of historiographic metafiction that combines both descriptive and analytical aspects; novels such as J. M. Coetzee's *Foe* (1986), Salman Rushdie's *Midnight's Children* (1981), and Graham Swift's *Waterland* (1983) blend historical realism with metafictional qualities to suggest "that to re-write or to re-present the past in fiction and in history is, in both cases, to open it up to the present, to prevent it from being conclusive and teleological" (110). In African American literary studies, metafiction often marks writers' self-conscious negotiations with the history of colonialism and slavery as well as American and African folklore and cultural myths, evidenced by novels such as Rita Dove's *Through the Ivory Gate* (1992), Charles Johnson's *Middle Passage* (1990), and Toni Morrison's *Tar Baby* (1981). Metafiction is also an important mode of writing in modern

Spanish novels, ranging from Cervantes's *Don Quixote* to Miguel de Unamuno's *Niebla* (1914, *Mist*) and Juan Goytisolo's *Juan sin Terra* (1975, *Juan the Landless*), with a gradual transformation from narratorial intrusion and the demystification of fictional conventions into a self-referential commentary on the power of the authorial imagination and the art of creating fiction.

BIBLIOGRAPHY

Gass, W.H. (1970), *Fiction and the Figures of Life*.
Hutcheon, L. (1988), *Poetics of Postmodernism*.
Jablon, M. (1997), *Black Metafiction*.
Marshall, B. (1992), *Teaching the Postmodern*.
McCaffery, L. (1982), *Metafictional Muse*.
Scholes, R. (1979), *Fabulation and Metafiction*.
Spires, R. (1984), *Beyond the Metafictional Mode*.
Waugh, P. (1984), *Metafiction*.

Metaphor *see* Figurative Language and Cognition; Rhetoric and Figurative Language

Mexico

DEBORAH COHN

In 1996, five Mexican authors issued what they called the *manifiesto crack* ("crack manifesto"). Ricardo Chávez Castañeda, Ignacio Padilla, Pedro Ángel Palou, Eloy Urroz, and Jorge Volpi were all born in the 1960s and had come of age in the shadow of writers such as Julio Cortázar, Carlos Fuentes, Gabriel García Márquez, and Mario Vargas Llosa, who rose to prominence throughout the West in the 1960s as part of the movement known as the "Boom" in the Spanish American novel. The choice of "crack" for the more recent movement deliberately echoed the use of the term "Boom" to designate the tremendous success of García Márquez and his contemporaries. But the label also implied a rupture, namely the authors' re-

jection of MAGICAL REALISM, a mode initially associated with García Márquez that had, by the 1990s, become both popular and commercially successful, and that readers and publishers alike had come to expect of Latin American writers. Instead, the writers advocated a return to more demanding novels, looking to their Mexican forebears, Spanish American models, and to European classics. At the same time, they asserted their right to not write about Mexico or Latin America, often setting their work in Europe and drawing heavily for their subject matter on European intellectualism.

By rejecting both magical realism and the assumption that novels by Mexican authors must also be about Mexico, the "crack" writers were, in effect, redefining expectations of the Mexican novel. But if the move away from Mexico as a subject suggested a break from tradition, it was, in fact, part of the longstanding pendular movement in Mexican literature between two conflicting tendencies: nationalism, where writers were expected to take the nation's social and political situation as their subject; and cosmopolitanism, which sought to open Mexican culture up to foreign influences in an effort to bring the nation into sync with the Western world (see NATIONAL).

THE NINETEENTH-CENTURY NOVEL

The tensions between Mexico's autochthonous and European heritage are evident in José Joaquín Fernández de Lizardi's *El periquillo sarniento* (*The Itching Parrot*), Mexico's—and Spanish America's—first novel. Published in installments in 1816, while Mexico was still struggling to achieve independence, it describes life in late eighteenth-century colonial Mexico, focusing on the shifting social landscape, including the rise of capitalism and the concomitant emergence of the bourgeoisie. The novel draws on the PICARESQUE for its structure and themes, narrating, in episodic form, the apprenticeships and (mis)education—as well as the ultimate repentance—of Pedro Sarniento (see BILDUNGSROMAN). The novel also conveys Fernández de Lizardi's support for Mexican independence in its critique of the Spanish colonial administration, as well as its satire of the corrupt and incompetent professionals whom Sarniento meets.

After achieving independence in 1821, Mexican politics entered a turbulent period of revolving-door presidencies and civil wars. From the 1860s on, Ignacio Altamirano, a writer and politician of indigenous descent, used his work to help model a path for building the nation. *El zarco, episodios de la vida mexicana en 1861–1863* (1901, *El Zarco, The Blue-Eyed Bandit*), is what Doris Sommer has labeled a "foundational fiction": the story of a romance between characters representing conflicting races, classes, and/or interests in the new republic that must be brought together in "marriages that provide a figure for apparently nonviolent consolidation" and thereby serve as models for hegemonic projects of national consolidation (6). Set during the early years of the presidency of Benito Juárez (1806–72), an Indian who set in motion a number of liberal reforms, *El Zarco* tells the story of Nicolás, an indigenous blacksmith in love with a white woman of a higher class, who eventually marries Pilar, a *mestiza* woman of humble origins. Nicolás's qualities as a model citizen and his relationship with Pilar offer a contrast to and way out of the contemporary social and political upheaval.

THE NOVEL OF THE MEXICAN REVOLUTION AND ITS SUCCESSORS

The presidency of Porfirio Díaz (1877–80, 1884–1911) emphasized modernization and development, but extended the material benefits of progress to very few. Francisco Madero (1873–1913) wrested power from Díaz in a struggle that set off the Mexican Revolution, which lasted until 1920, devastating the nation's infrastructure and land, and claiming thousands of lives. In 1915, while the fighting still raged, Mariano Azuela, a doctor who had fought alongside Pancho Villa (1878–1923), published *Los de abajo* (*The Underdogs*) in serial form (see SERIALIZATION). (The work was republished as a novel in 1925.) The novel follows the rise of Demetrio Macías, who becomes a war hero even though he does not understand what he is fighting for, and his subsequent fall as he and his men become mirror images of the corrupt and violent government troops whom they had once fought. *Los de abajo* offers a biting critique of the corruption, disorganization, and lack of ideals behind the Revolution and the increasing violence and opportunism that characterized it.

Azuela's novel initiated the literary tradition known as the *novela de la Revolución* (novel of the Revolution), a largely realist genre (see REALISM) that dominated Mexican narrative through the 1940s. Authors such as Martín Luis Guzmán (1928, *El águila y la serpiente, The Eagle and the Serpent*; 1929, *La sombra del caudillo*, The Shadow of the Caudillo); Nellie Campobello (1931, *Cartucho Cartucho*); Gregorio López y Fuentes (1931, *Campamento*, The Encampment), and others used the genre, in conjunction with large measures of history, biography, and autobiography, to scrutinize the players and power dynamics that had wrought so much violence, as well as the troubles of the post-revolutionary order (see LIFE WRITING). The 1947 publication of Agustín Yáñez's *Al filo del agua* (*The Edge of the Storm*) was a turning point in the nation's narrative, for it fused the novel of the Revolution, which was nationalist in content and realist in style, with the stylistics and thematics of Euro-American MODERNISM, which was making inroads into Spanish American fiction at the time. Set in a small town on the eve of the civil war, *Al filo del agua* uses poetic techniques and interior monologues to convey the repression and stagnation of life in the town, both of which are shattered by the outbreak of the Revolution. As the war takes place offstage, with only its effects narrated, the novel represents a fundamental shift away from the genre, in which the Revolution was traditionally a protagonist.

In 1955, Juan Rulfo published *Pedro Páramo*, in which voices from the grave narrate fragments of the rise of the eponymous *cacique* or local boss, whose violence and abuse paralyzes the town of Comala. Páramo's rise to power dates to the years of Díaz's regime and his downfall takes place in the aftermath of the Mexican Revolution, but is not a product of its reforms. His trajectory thus allegorizes the failure of the Revolution to bring about change. The novel draws deeply on Octavio Paz's exploration of Mexican character in his seminal essay, *El laberinto de la soledad* (1950/1959, *The Labyrinth of Solitude*). At the same time, the polyphonic structure and themes (e.g., patriarchy, failed paternity, revolution, and the rise of a new social order) are often compared to the work of William Faulkner, in particular, to *Absalom, Absalom!* (1936).

In 1958, Carlos Fuentes took the Mexican literary scene by storm with *La región más transparente* (*Where the Air is Clear*), which drew on John Dos Passos's cinematographic technique and collective protagonist, and which was as much about post-Revolutionary Mexico City as it was about its myriad characters. Over the next few years, Fuentes's fame grew both in Mexico and internationally, and he was instrumental in promoting the Boom in Europe and the U.S. *La muerte de Artemio Cruz* (1962, *The Death of Artemio Cruz*) condenses the first 150 years of Mexican independence into the history of Artemio Cruz and his family. The novel is narrated in first-, second-, and third-person voices from the deathbed of the patriarch and newspaperman, whose life is emblematic of the post-revolutionary order. It is an inversion of the traditional "life of" story that also pays homage to Orson Welles's movie *Citizen Kane* (1941). The novel also engages with Paz's ideas about Mexican history and his vision of *lo mexicano* (Mexicanness). Like Rulfo's *Pedro Páramo*, *Artemio Cruz* proffers a biting critique of the failure of the post-revolutionary period to bring about change in Mexico. The later novel offers its only hope in the death of Cruz, which coincides with the Cuban Revolution and the hope for political autonomy that it inspired throughout Spanish America. Over the years, Fuentes has maintained a high profile with novels such as *Terra Nostra* (1975, *Terra Nostra*), *Cristóbal Nonato* (1987, *Christopher Unborn*), and *La frontera de cristal* (1995, *The Crystal Frontier*). He has continued to address Mexico's efforts to incorporate its pre-Columbian heritage and to find a place for itself on the world stage. And he has drawn heavily on New-World chroniclers such as Bernal Díaz del Castillo (ca. 1495–1584), using the epic mode of their work to undergird his own, and seeking in parallel fashion to describe the New World and put it into global circulation.

THE 1960s: COUNTERCULTURE, WOMEN'S WRITING, AND OTHER NEW DIRECTIONS IN THE MEXICAN NOVEL

Over the years, other directions can be seen in the trajectory of the Mexican novel. In the 1940s, activist-intellectual José Revueltas published *El luto humano* (1943, *Human Mourning*) and *Los días terrenales* (1949, Earthly days), which use PSYCHOLOGICAL analysis and interior monologues to explore CLASS consciousness in the context of a labor strike and the author's tumultuous relationship with the Communist Party, respectively. The late 1950s and 1960s also bore witness to the emergence of a variety of other voices. Jorge Ibargüengoitia's *Los relámpagos de agosto* (1964, *The Lightning of August*) joined *Pedro Páramo* and *Artemio Cruz* in offering a scathing demythification of the Revolution and other national myths while adding a dimension of satire, humor, and irreverence to the treatment of the former. Ibargüengoitia, along with Salvador Elizondo, Juan García Ponce, and others, were among a group of young writers who dominated the nation's cultural media and were outspoken in their advocacy of cultural internationalism. Their work was experimental and deeply interiorized, sometimes imbued with a sense of altered mental states and often marked by strong erotic tendencies.

Several women writers, most notably Rosario Castellanos, Elena Garro, and Elena Poniatowska, also begin to make a name for themselves during this period. Each of these writers took on the Revolution and its aftermath through the lens of the experiences and social restrictions of female protagonists: Castellanos's *Balún Canán* (1957, *The Nine Guardians*) dealt with indigenous uprisings following post-revolutionary agrarian reforms in Chiapas; Garro focused on the *guerra de los cristeros* (Cristero war) of the late 1920s in *Recuerdos del porvenir* (1962, *Recollections of Things to Come*); and Poniatowska was one of the leaders of the new wave of testimonial writing in Spanish America with *Hasta no verte, Jesús mío* (1969, *Here's to You, Jesusa!*), which narrated the experiences of Josefina Bórquez in the Revolution and throughout subsequent decades of Mexican history.

The countercultural movement of the late 1960s is noticeable in the works of the writers known collectively as *la onda*, which began in the mid-1960s and included writers such as José Agustín (1964, *La tumba*, The Tomb) and Gustavo Sáinz (1965, *Gazapo, Gazapo*), most of whom were born between 1938 and 1951. Their work was profoundly marked by the social upheaval and changes of the 1960s: they rebelled against Mexican culture, looking instead toward Western ideas of modernity, U.S. rock music, and popular culture, and they became deeply involved with the U.S. anti-establishment movements. According to Rachel Adams, *la onda* "was a crucible where transnational popular culture met uneasily with the politics and aesthetics of Mexican nationalism ... [and where] middle-class teenagers aligned themselves with an international counterculture" (59, 60). Despite a shared interest in cosmopolitan literary and cultural movements, however, *la onda* writers broke from older cosmopolitanists by refusing to engage with master narratives of national identity and history and by espousing popular culture's modes and models. Margo Glantz's 1971 anthology, *Onda y escritura, jóvenes de 20 a 33*, both theorized *la onda* and brought additional prominence to the writers. In addition to being an important critic of Mexican, U.S., and European literature in her own right, Glantz also went on to write an autobiographical narrative, *Las genealogías* (1981, *The Family Tree*), as well as several works of fiction (e.g., 1996, *Apariciones*, Appearances and 2002, *El rastro, The Wake*), and has received numerous literary prizes and academic fellowships.

The debate over the relationship between literary nationalism and cosmopolitanism was forever changed with the massacre of student protestors by the police and army in Mexico City's Plaza de Tlatelolco on 2 Oct. 1968. Carlos Monsiváis, one of the nation's preeminent cultural critics, and Poniatowska used literary journalism and strategies akin to the U.S.'s "new JOURNALISM" to chronicle these events in their testimonial works, *Días de guardar* (1970, Days of observance) and *La noche de Tlatelolco* (1971, *Massacre in Mexico*), respectively. *Mexicanidad* ("what it means to be

Mexican"), a master narrative of Mexican literature since the 1930s, ceased to hold center stage, and writers began to focus instead on the question of socialism, revolution, or democracy; on the role of women; and on popular culture. Women writers who came of age in the 1960s, including Carmen Boullosa, Laura Esquivel, and Ángeles Mastretta, began to publish in the 1980s, to significant popular acclaim. They, too, engaged with Mexican issues such as the Revolution (e.g., Esquivel's 1989, *Como agua para chocolate*, *Like Water for Chocolate* and Mastretta's 1986, *Arráncame la vida*, *Mexican Bolero*), the Conquest (e.g., Esquivel's 2006, *Malinche*, *Malinche*), and Mexico's colonial past (e.g., Boullosa's 1994, *Duerme*, Sleep), but with irreverence and humor as part of their toolkit for challenging patriarchal narratives of national history. Along with *la onda*, their work moves away from the master narratives of Mexican history, but also—along with contemporary "post-Boom" writers in Latin America—from the totalizing and experimental works of the Boom.

The "crack" generation of the 1990s shared the Boom's embrace of cosmopolitanism and likewise sought to take formal and aesthetic risks. Perhaps the best-known "crack" novel to date is Volpi's *En busca de Klingsor* (1999, *In Search of Klingsor*), winner of Spain's prestigious Biblioteca Breve prize. The novel is a thriller set in postwar Germany about a U.S. physicist who embarks on a military mission to find the head of Nazi atomic research; it is a meditation on the nature of science as well as a search for truth and a study "of the human tendency to construct artificial patterns of order" (Swanson, 98) that is reminiscent of the stories of Jorge Luis Borges, an important precursor of Boom writers. Like Borges, "crack" writers refused to be confined to their national tradition, claiming instead the world as their patrimony. As Volpi once stated, "We don't search for our national or Latin American identity in literature. We use literature as a base for expression" (qtd. in LaPorte). This is not to say that the nation is not a concern for "crack" writers. But whereas many Mexican writers of the 1950s and 1960s sought to demonstrate that their literature was inextricably interwoven with both the nation's autochthonous cultural traditions and Western influences, and drew on cosmopolitanism to open Mexican culture up to new influences, today's "crack" writers and their contemporaries presuppose a modern national identity and full participation in a global cultural arena. Rather than Mexican writers, then, they aspire to be known, above all, as writers.

SEE ALSO: Dictatorship Novel, Ideology, Latina/o American Novel, Regional Novel.

BIBLIOGRAPHY

Adams, R. (2004), "Hipsters and *jipitecas*," *American Literary History* 16(1):58–84.

Bruce-Novoa, J. (1991), "La novela de la Revolución Mexicana," *Hispania* 74(1):36–44.

Brushwood, J.S. (1966), *Mexico in its Novel*.

LaPorte, N. (2003), "New Era Succeeds Years of Solitude," *New York Times*, http://www.il. proquest.com/proquest/ (NYT ProQuest), 4 Jan., consulted 17 Dec. 2009.

Pereira, A., ed. (2000), *Diccionario de literatura mexicana*.

Rutherford, J. (1996), "The Novel of the Mexican Revolution," in *Cambridge History of Latin American Literature*, ed. R. González Echevarría and E. Pupo-Walker, 2 vols.

Sommer, D. (1991), *Foundational Fictions*.

Sommers, J. (1968), *After the Storm*.

Steele, C. (1992), *Politics, Gender, and the Mexican Novel, 1968–1988*.

Swanson, P. (2005), "The Post-Boom Novel," in *Cambridge Companion to the Latin American Novel*, ed. E. Kristal.

Volpi, J., E. Urroz, and I. Padilla (2000), "Manifiesto Crack," *Lateral. Revista de Cultura*

70, http://www.lateral-ed.es/tema/
070manifiestocrack.htm
Zolov, E. (1999), *Refried Elvis*.

Mimesis *see* Novel Theory (19th Century);
Story/Discourse
Modern Analytic Novel *see* Psychological
Novel

Modernism

ROBERT L. CASERIO

The term modernist in the early twentieth century came to mean an iconoclastic response to long-established conventions. (The meaning partly derives from a turn-of-the-century adjective for rebellion against orthodox religious authority.) In the HISTORY of fiction, the modernist novel stands out for the ways in which its content subverts traditions of social order and moral conduct. Complementing the subversive aims, modernist fiction disruptively experiments upon inherited forms of representation, and opposes ordinary or clichéd uses of language and ideas.

In line with such disruption, the Spanish philosopher José Ortega y Gasset, in *The Dehumanization of Art* (1925), defines modernism in terms of abstraction and dehumanization, both of which undermine literary REALISM. Literary realism, according to Ortega, asks its audiences to identify with the persons and experiences it represents, and to overlook the artifice inherent in aesthetic representations. In contrast to the objects of literary realism, an object of modernist art "is artistic only in so far as it is not real. . . . Art has no right to exist if, content to reproduce reality, it uselessly duplicates it." The modernist, Ortega asserts, is "brazenly set on deforming reality, shattering its human aspect, dehumanizing it" (1968, trans. Helen Weyl, 10, 48, 21).

James Joyce's *A Portrait of the Artist as a Young Man* (1916) exhibits thematically and formally a characteristically modernist re-

bellion. Its Irish hero refuses to pay service to the conventional assumptions about life, conduct, and meaning that are defined by church, country, and family. Those assumptions require, he discovers, factitious or worn-out constraints on liberty (he feels those constraints operating even in anti-imperialist, nation-centered politics in Ireland). Joyce's employment of fictional form and verbal ingenuity complements the hero's rebellion. Flouting readers' assumptions about storytelling, Joyce undermines narrative itself. By intensively joining free indirect DISCOURSE with a prose equivalent of visual impressionism, and by scrupulously avoiding clichéd language, Joyce's "portrait" appears to be a prose version of lyric poetry more than a novelistic tale. The innovative development directs a reader to attend to Joyce's verbal and formal inventiveness. In Joyce's hands the art of the modernist novel becomes its leading story line, one that competes with, and exceeds, the traditional novel's investment in characters and events.

To be sure, one must beware of accepting definitions such as Ortega's or practices such as Joyce's without qualification. Joyce's *Finnegans Wake* (1939), which deforms English and seeks to invent a new language altogether, and which certainly shatters fiction's immediately recognizable human interest, matches what Ortega describes; yet Joyce's *Portrait* and *Ulysses* (1922) carry on the conventions of literary realism—especially in their evocation of characters with whom readers are invited, all humanistically, to identify—even as they undo those conventions. Nevertheless, paradoxical simultaneity of antithetical aims is an additional hallmark of the modernist novel—and exemplifies a characteristic irony that Ortega also ascribes to modernism.

DISRUPTIVE INNOVATIONS

The modernist novel celebrates deliberate estrangements from established orderings of life and its meanings. The hero of André Gide's *L'Immoraliste* (1902, *The Immoralist*) willfully yields to antisocial impulses that he discovers in himself. He colludes with a criminal family that poaches on his landed property (which he renounces); and he ruthlessly abandons his mortally ill wife, preferring to explore his bisexual impulses with natives of French colonial Algiers. Henry James's *The Golden Bowl* (1904) represents a complex adultery—between its heroine's husband and her stepmother—without bowing to conventional moral judgments about irregular liaisons; instead, James's narrative replicates the amoral intelligence with which the four parties to the adultery work out their passions. D. H. Lawrence's *Women in Love* (1920) includes a male protagonist who calls marriage "the most repulsive thing on earth" and asserts that "You've got to get rid of the *exclusiveness* of married love. And you've got to admit the unadmitted [sexual] love of man for man" (chap. 25). The heroine of Dorothy Richardson's series of novels, *Pilgrimage* (1915–67), declares that women "*can't* be represented by men. Because by every word they use men and women mean different things" (1927, *Oberland*, 4:92f.). Refusing patriarchal and masculinist domination, the heroine allies herself with socialism and the suffrage movement. True to rebellious modernist inspiration, however, she also later revolts against socialism and feminism, because she considers that progressive political movements, no less than conservative ones, obscure, and betray, her vital experience of being "an unknown timeless being, released from all boundaries, … yet still herself" (1931, *Dawn's Left Hand*, 4:364).

To complement the transgressions and transcendences that characterize the content of literary modernism, modernist novels undo narrative's reliance on discernible events. James's stories can pivot on what one of his unfinished novels calls "the force of the stillness in which nothing happened" ("Sense of the Past," bk. 2). Gertrude Stein writes that it is necessary "to stand still" in order "to live"; standing still now must replace "what anybody does" as inspiration for "a new way to write a novel" (*Lectures in America*, 1935). Hence Stein's *Three Lives* (1909) and *The Making of Americans* (1925) replace choice and change, actions on which the structure of stories usually depend, with what Stein (converging with Richardson) identifies as changeless "being existing."

Ulysses might illustrate such novelty. It invokes a likeness to the event-filled EPIC *The Odyssey*, but *Ulysses* reduces epic events to the minute thoughts and routines of ordinary persons on one ordinary day. The gigantic artifice of multiple styles wherewith Joyce represents trivial or banal phenomena in *Ulysses*, and not what "happens" in the novel, is what matters. (The novel's most discernible event is a wife's act of infidelity, but her action is superficial compared to her emotional fidelity to her husband, and to Joyce's evocation of her static being.)

Given the modernist novel's distance from events, it can appear to undo differences between action and description, or between the novel and the essay. The essayistic meditations on history that constitute Thomas Mann's *Der Zauberberg* (1924, *The Magic Mountain*) paradoxically result from its hero's withdrawal from the historical world, and from eventfulness itself, into a timeless space. Similarly replacing narrative with essayistic and descriptive components, Marcel Proust's *À la recherche du temps perdu* (1913–27, *Remembrance of Things Past*) evokes a panoramic social transformation, yet celebrates, despite the temporal extent of a "story" that requires seven volumes to encompass, a surmounting of change and time. When the modernist novel does bring actions to the forefront of what it pictures, it is likely to do so in a way that, in line with "dehumanization," strips them of coherent or intelligible motivation, as is the case in Gide's *Les caves du Vatican* (1914, *The Caves of the Vatican*). Its hero murders a man gratuitously, for the sake of exhibiting the accidental nature of all human deeds and the arbitrariness of moral or religious codes that purport to justify actions.

Narration depends upon chronology, and novelists have always used narrative as a time machine, enabling them to move at will back into the past and forward into the future. Modernist fiction adapts this time machine to its own ends, experimenting with temporality, and even smashing the engine—perhaps as a complement to the changed status of events in modernist storytelling. Joseph Conrad's *Nostromo* (1904) tells the history of a South American republic. But with unprecedented audacity the narration leaps backward and forward, simultaneously compressing years and elongating moments, and involving past with present and future, in a way that makes it hard for a reader to grasp history (as Conrad models it) in terms of sequential relations of cause and effect. What can history be said to tell if such relations, as well as the character of TIME, are made uncertain? *Nostromo* makes them uncertain, partly to substitute for them the preeminence of the geography that Conrad invents for the novel. The suggestion is that a modernist vision values atemporal places and spaces more than historical relations (see SPACE, TIME). An even more audacious subversion of chronology organizes Ford Madox Ford's *The Good Soldier* (1915), which implies that the erotic passions portrayed in the novel are impervious to time, and confound historical accounting.

Virginia Woolf's novels exemplify modernist fiction's struggles with time. Mrs. Ramsay in *To the Lighthouse* (1927) might be Woolf's delegate in the text because she represents an author-like way of weaving persons and things into unified relation, endowing them thereby with a story and a history. Yet Mrs. Ramsay also longs for moments of being that are dissociated from relation and time, "immune from change." Woolf allows the longing to be brutally contradicted. Killing off Mrs. Ramsay, time appears in the narrative as a starkly antirelational force, decentering and dissolving the novel's unity. Woolf's *The Years* (1937) and *Between the Acts* (1941) continue to dramatize attempts to diminish time's dictatorial regulation of life and narrative. A bold diminution of the regulation is John Dos Passos's *U.S.A.* trilogy (1930–36). Dos Passos traces multiple characters' lives, but does so simultaneously and discontinuously, rarely (and only momentarily) conjoining them. Collaged juxtapositions replace storytelling's conventions. *U.S.A.*'s subversive form complements its underlying allegiance to political anarchism, an IDEOLOGY with which modernism has an affinity.

Modernism transforms character and characterization no less than events. The English modernist Wyndham Lewis's fictions represent character as an absurd phenomenon (for Lewis, "absurdity ... is at the root of every true philosophy," as he writes in "The Meaning of the Wild Body"). Persons are absurd, because their minds at are odds with their bodies, which Lewis describes as machine-like contraptions. "Men are necessarily comic: for they are all *things*, or physical bodies, behaving as *persons*." Characterizations of the protagonists of Lewis's *Tarr* (1918) and *The Revenge for Love* (1937) evoke the pathos of this comedy. D. H. Lawrence's fiction presents another innovation. "You mustn't look in my novel[s] for the old stable *ego*—of the character," Lawrence explains. His characterizations represent inchoate centers of flux, "according to whose action," he says, "the individual is unrecognizable" (1962, *Collected Letters of D. H. Lawrence*, ed. H. T. Moore, 44). Woolf's *Jacob's Room* (1922), about a young man who is killed in WWI, constructs Jacob's life history as a collage of sketchy experiences and fleeting ideas that constitutes an essentially unformed person, a near-blank in life and narrative as well as in death. Woolf suggests that none of us is more formed a character than Jacob. The Russian modernist Andrei Bely, in *Peterburg* (1916–22, *Petersburg*), presents character as a perpetual masquerade. Uncanny dislocations of personality result. One of Bely's protagonists is described thus: "he ... was not [he], but *something* lodged in the brain, looking out from there ... *until it plunged into the abyss*" (chap. 3). The abyss provides a paradoxical standpoint for Bely's unsettling narrator, himself a masquerader or confidence-man. Modernist narrators are typically shape-shifters, as experimental in essence as the characters they chronicle. The narrator of Alfred Döblin's *Berlin Alexanderplatz* (1929, *Alexanderplatz, Berlin*) takes on multiple personalities, becoming by turns everything from an external observer to the protagonist to the advertisement hoardings of Berlin.

TRAGIC AND COMIC VISIONS

Realist novels explain human sorrow by assigning its causes to history; naturalist novels explain it by assigning its causes to biology (see NATURALISM). The explanations suggest possibilities of remedy. Modernist novels do not adopt therapeutic explanations. Hence modernist fiction presents its readers with tragic visions that are unusually stark (see COMEDY). *Nostromo* evaluates global capitalism's betrayal of republican governments and of the working classes as an historical outrage; but it also distances itself from approval of any political ideology, and thereby suggests that "history" and "politics" are tragically illusory frameworks of life. Eros as another source of irremediable tragic illusion is explored in *The Good Soldier*. Its narrator believes that sexual love, even in the case of "normal," respectable people, makes experience "all a darkness" of underlying motives. Franz Kafka's stories and novels witness an equivalent obscurity. His *Der Prozeß* (1925, *The Trial*) features an everyman figure whose life is a senseless undergoing of prosecution for unspecified crimes. Modernism's tragic sense of life is summed up in the hero of Mann's *Dr. Faustus* (1948), a modernist composer. His atonal music, representing modernism's break with convention, is indifferent to harmony and melody. To secure the greatness of his art despite its apparently unmusical basis, the composer appears to make a pact with the devil, from whom he accepts his own dehumanization as the price of his achievement.

Tragedy is not the whole story of modernist fiction, however. With characteristic dissonance, it renders comic visions side by side with tragic ones. In *Del sentimiento trágico de la vida* (1913, *The Tragic Sense of Life in Men and Peoples*) the Spanish modernist man of letters and novelist Miguel de Unamuno argues that tragedy and comedy are two sides of the same coin; "passionate uncertainty" as to which of them most matters is vivifying. The critic Edwin Muir (and first translator of Kafka into English) in *We Moderns* (1920) believes that "tragic art is more profound than morality" because it stimulates "the desire for expression. ...When [the desire for expression's] rule is ... obeyed Life reaches its highest degree of joy and pain, and becomes creative. This is the state which is glorified by the tragic poets" ("The Tragic View," 226–27). The creative vitality that Muir describes manifests itself as a comic radiance in modernist novelists whose subject matter promises to be tragic. William Faulkner's *As I Lay Dying* (1930) transfigures poverty, death, deception, and insanity, making them simultaneously comic and tragic, by virtue of Faulkner's modernist will to forge innovative forms of expression for them.

Lawrence's *St. Mawr* (1925) diagnoses the social world it represents as "a new sort of sordidness," alienated from "inward vision and . . . cleaner energy." The novel uses Lawrence's modernist ego-dissolving characterization to express an alternative: a world that will be more alive, "a further created being," supervening upon civilization's tragic arrest.

SEE ALSO: Definitions of the Novel, Historical Novel, History of the Novel, Georg Lukács, Narrative Perspective, Novel Theory (20th Century), Psychological Novel.

BIBLIOGRAPHY

Adorno, T.W. (1997), *Aesthetic Theory*.
Caserio, R.L. (1999), *Novel in England 1900–1950*.
DiBattista, M. (2009), *Imagining Virginia Woolf*.
Eysteinsson, A. (1990), *Concept of Modernism*.
Gass, W. (1979), *Fiction and the Figures of Life*.
Kern, S. (1987), *Culture of Time and Space*.
Levenson, M. (2005), *Modernism and the Fate of the Individual*.

Modernismo see Caribbean; Central America; Southern Cone (South American)
Moretti, Franco see History of the Novel, Marxist Theory, National Literature

Mythology

WILLIAM BLAZEK

In Don DeLillo's 1985 novel *White Noise*, a sociologist explains the postmodern significance of television: "It's like a myth being born right there in our living room, like something we know in a dreamlike and preconscious way. I'm very enthused, Jack" (51). The passage hints at several of the issues involved in considering the place of mythology in studies of the novel: whether or not it is possible to have a modern myth, how relevant oral storytelling (from which myths are born) is to literary fiction, and what role the preconscious or unconscious self has in either mythology or literature (see PSYCHOAN-

ALYTIC). Perhaps the fact that a contemporary novelist such as DeLillo can reconfigure the novel form through references to mythology and some of its key tenets suggests the enduring importance of myths to human perception and the writer's imagination. Moreover, the novel, especially in the twentieth century, provides examples of the variety of functions served by mythology in the shaping of modern fiction. Depending on how the parameters of myth are defined and on how they are applied to literature, a case could also be made that myth is such a basic and vital aspect of human nature that it infuses the novel structurally, linguistically, and thematically.

Opposing views point to the incompatibility of myths and literature. Northrop Frye (1912–91), one of the main advocates of mythology's crucial stake in the workings of literature and criticism, accepts that the ancient sources of myths appear in muted and degenerated form in literature and that the evolution of literary forms from Greek drama and epic poetry to Romantic poetry and realist fiction also marks the decline of mythology's significance, although he sees a cyclical return to myth in the ironic mode of modernist texts (see MODERNISM). For the Victorian anthropologist Edward B. Tylor, myths concern the external world and have no symbolic, and therefore no immediate literary, value. The twentieth-century American critic Richard Chase (1914–62) considers myths to have been almost completely superseded by literature. Another case against the synthesis of mythology and literature is made by Walter Benjamin (1892–1940), who blames the evolution of the print industry for the loss of an oral storytelling tradition and the wholesome communities that it sustained. In particular, he explains, "The earliest symptom of a process whose end is the decline of storytelling is the rise of the novel at the beginning of modern times," and claims, rather unjustly, that the novel "neither comes from oral tradition nor goes into it" (87; see HISTORY). Whether literature is understood as leftover myth or the novel as the chief culprit in the decline of myth's storytelling foundations, the relationships outlined here are clearly fraught with controversy, not least because the purlieus of myth are so wide-ranging, and the measurement of mythology's value to the novel depends on how myth is defined and understood by writers, critics, and readers.

THEORIES OF MYTH

Difficulties in defining the meaning and importance of mythology stem from the various ways myth has been applied to different fields of study, notably ANTHROPOLOGY, psychiatry, sociology, and literary criticism.

Anthropology, in the pioneering work of Tylor and James G. Frazer (1854–1941), centers on the dynamic roles and rituals associated with primitive mythology, exploring both the social experience behind mythic beliefs and the symbolic importance of fertility rites and burial practices, for example. Frazer's *The Golden Bough* (1890–1915) catalogs a large number of nature myths, taboos, festivals, customs, and folk practices. The author draws from ancient Egyptian, Greek, and other European traditions in order to prove the intricate practice but also the extinction of magic and religion among what he calls "the primitive savage" (374) and "rude races" (254) before the supremacy of modern science. For Frazer and his follower Jessie L. Weston (1850–1928), myth was a remnant of the past. Nevertheless, Weston's analysis of the Grail legend, *From Ritual to Romance* (1920), proved a key text in the early twentieth-century revival of interest in myth associated with T. S. Eliot's *The Waste Land* (1922). A literary critic with a deep understanding of anthropological theory and practice, Eliot became the dominant force

in promoting a particular elite version of modernism, in large part because his literary art and criticism were linked to contemporary debates about mythology and ethnography. These debates ranged from Frazer's myth-and-ritual inheritors among the Cambridge Hellenists, most notably the classicists Jane Harrison (1850–1928) and Gilbert Murray (1866–1957), to the opposing views of Franz Boas (1858–1942) and Bronislaw Malinowski (1884–1942), founders of the modern science of ethnography and the "functionalist" method of fieldwork, initially among tribal cultures. (Malinowski's *Argonauts of the Western Pacific* was published the same year as *The Waste Land* and James Joyce's *Ulysses*.) The authority of Eliot's vision enabled him to project in his generous and self-serving 1923 review of *Ulysses* that Joyce's "mythical method" would replace traditional narrative and prove "a step toward making the modern world possible for art" (1975, *Selected Prose of T. S. Eliot*, ed. F. Kermode, 178).

Sigmund Freud (1856–1939) found the mythic patterns of Greek drama useful paradigms to explain the symbolism of dreams and to develop theories in psychoanalysis about the role of parents and siblings in the formation of sexuality and the psyche. His rival Carl G. Jung (1875–1961) took a more comprehensive view of the ways that myth might release the potential of the unconscious. He proposed a theory of archetypes, motifs that run through ancient and modern myths—sky gods, for example, are expressed in stories of Zeus or flying saucers. Jung identified the source of archetypes as the "collective unconscious," which he described as the "common psychic substrate of a suprapersonal nature which is present in every one of us" (2). While Jung's interest in mythology was aimed at explaining how archetypes might aid psychological wellbeing, his exhaustive research into mythic symbols and structures influenced literary critics such as Frye and the American "myth and symbol" school. It also seemed to validate the mythological subject matter chosen by leading modernist novelists such as Thomas Mann and Joyce.

From the mid-twentieth century, Joseph Campbell (1904–87) assimilated Jung's theory of archetypal images and popularized the study of myth beyond the confines of anthropology and psychiatry. Emphasizing the myth of the heroic quest, Campbell claims in his seminal early work *The Hero with a Thousand Faces*:

> It would not be too much to say that myth is the secret opening through which the inexhaustible energies of the cosmos pour into human cultural manifestation. Religions, philosophies, arts, the social forms of primitive and historic man, prime discoveries in science and technology, the very dreams that blister sleep, boil up from the basic, magic ring of myth. (13)

This overarching assertion was further developed in Campbell's later writings, such as *The Masks of God* (1959–68) and the television series and book entitled *The Power of Myth* (1988), in which he extols the eternal and universal qualities of myth. The romantic appeal of Campbell's work is described by Robert A. Segal as "fetching" but the theories as being flawed because of their circular arguments, under-analyzed evidence, and mystical nature (138–41). Nevertheless, the generosity of Campbell's vision of oneness between humans, animals, plants, and sky finds parallels in myth and symbol literature criticism with its tendency to find in narrative texts a wealth of mythic imagery and designs.

The French sociologist and philosopher Roland Barthes (1915–80) would also interpret myths as universal forces, but his aim in *Mythologies* (1957) is mainly to alert readers to the ways that political and social hegemonies can manipulate myths to stultifying effect. Through insightful observations of contemporary life, he develops a way to understand the mechanisms of myth through its historical layers of meaning—investigating through semiology how, for example, a picture of a black French soldier saluting comes to represent imperial France (see IDEOLOGY, STRUCTURALISM). "Signified" objects and concepts combine with verbal, visual, and auditory "signifiers" to form "signs" that can be read by the semiologist in Barthes's system, one that aims to liberate the mind to see the world more clearly. Semiology can therefore defend individuals from the passive conservatism promoted by constricting ideologies that manipulate myths in order to dominate and control. Barthes asserts that myth "establishes a blissful clarity" (143) that simplifies the complexities of history, and that "the very end of myths is to immobilize the world" (155). "[N]othing can be safe from myth" (131), he warns, and thus the myth-reader or semiotician serves as a kind of sociolinguistic Knight Templar to protect the oppressed. Barthes essentially views myth as a danger to the good of modern communities. He pays little attention to other theories of mythology and usually ignores ancient myths in his analyses. Myth as it features in ideology is his predominant concern, and in that regard he is closely in tune with literary critics who acknowledge the inextricable ties between ideology and myth in literature.

NORTHROP FRYE: MYTHOLOGY, IDEOLOGY, AND CRITICISM

Northrop Frye, although open to the most wide-ranging applications of myth to literary study, was keenly aware of the ideological attachments to mythology in practice. In *Myth and Metaphor*, he calls literature "the mythological imagination at work in the world" (1991, ed. R. D. Denham, 91). Furthermore, he notes two principal features of the social function of myth: it provides "a vision of the cosmos, constructed from human concern" and it will "be seized on by whatever establishment or pressure group is in power" (252). In a manner related to both Campbell and Barthes in their reaction to modern political and social norms, Frye defines the role of his profession: "I see it as the essential task of the literary critic to distinguish ideology from myth, to help reconstitute a myth as a language, and to put literature in its proper cultural place as the central link of communication between society and the vision of its primary concerns" (103).

One of Frye's major contributions to this task was to identify key modes of literary myth, first defining myth as "*mythos*, story, plot, narrative" (*Myth and Metaphor*, 3). From that formal basis he identifies core mythic narratives such as the journey and return, the attendant features of those narratives (including metaphorical associations with nature and the seasons, symbols of death and rebirth, or temporal and spatial shifts that might reflect natural cycles or visionary dreams), as well as mythic symbolism and archetypes. With regard to the latter, he explains how "Moby Dick cannot remain in Melville's novel: he is absorbed into our imaginative experience of leviathans and dragons of the deep from the Old Testament onwards" (*Anatomy*, 100). In his efforts to rescue primary myths from the secondary influence of ideology, Frye observes that primal concerns for a supply of food, sexual reproduction, and communal dwelling can be found in myth's influence on literature across millennia. Examples include archetypically significant scenes in Charlotte Brontë's *Jane Eyre* (1847) following Jane's flight from Rochester and the night she spends alone outdoors, without food or the means to ask for it. Mythic omen and prophesy could be associated with the technical use of foreshadowing (prolepsis) in Leo Tolstoy's *Anna Karenina* (1875–77). While Frye most often draws his examples from British drama and poetry—most frequently William Shakespeare, William Blake

(1757–1827), and John Milton, with special reference to the Bible—he gives space to the novel in his work on myth and literature. His exemplars include Herman Melville, Marcel Proust, and Joyce, notably *Finnegan's Wake* (1939), which reveals "the turning cycle of life, death, and renewal" (*Myth and Metaphor*, 372). Frye's critical studies illustrate that "a work of literature has a structure of myth and a texture of metaphor" (*Myth and Metaphor*, 127). The cultural critic Marc Manganaro examines the authority gained by the rhetorical skills and the comprehensive nature of the work of comparative anthropologists and critics including Fraser, Eliot, Campbell, and Frye, but also notes the conservative strain within these efforts to build a unified system for literary criticism and mythology, a program that cannot escape inherent ideological objectives (1992, *Myth, Rhetoric, and the Voice of Authority*).

THE MYTHOLOGICAL NOVEL

Two critical texts that focus entirely on mythology and the novel are John J. White's *Mythology in the Modern Novel* (1971) and Michael Palencia-Roth's *Myth and the Modern Novel* (1987), and both attempt to explain the resurgence of mythological themes and subject matter, especially in British and European literature, following WWI. A need to reassess the foundations of European culture after the war is one explanation, along with a concurrent rejection of mimetic narrative, the influences of Freud and Jung on the novel's range of psycho-mythic referents, and the imaginative potential offered in playing myth and archetypes against the everyday experiences of modern life. White lists sixty-six entries in his bibliography for "Mythological Novels and Novels with Other Preconfigurations," a term he uses for mythic structures and metaphors in the modern novel (242–45). Among the texts he examines are Mann's *Joseph und seine*

Brüder tetralogy (1933, 1935, 1943, *Joseph and his Brothers*) and *Doktor Faustus* (1947, *Doctor Faustus*), Joyce's *Ulysses* ("the archetypal mythological novel," 30), John Updike's *The Centaur* (1963), Bernard Malamud's *The Natural* (1952), Hermann Hesse's *Demian* (1919), Alberto Moravia's *Il disprezzo* (1954, *Contempt*), and Alain Robbe-Grillet's *Les Gommes* (1953, *The Erasers*). An updated compendium would include texts by ethnic American writers such as Sandra Cisneros, Louise Erdrich, Maxine Hong Kingston, N. Scott Momaday, Toni Morrison, and Amy Tan, novelists who draw upon classic American mythology. Other writers to be added might include Cormac McCarthy (for his reassessments of the frontier myth), writers who use global myths from native or immigrant sources, and writers who mix elements of traditional native or religious myths with the contingencies of contemporary existence.

White focuses on novels that retell classical myths, reference mythology within contemporary settings, or allude to myths. He expresses reservations about an uncritical acceptance of archetypes as central to the mythological novel, acknowledging how Frank Kermode and René Welleck distrust such notions as racial memory in the aftermath of the Holocaust during WWII (78, 104). Palencia-Roth's work is more open to the ideas of Frye and Campbell in incorporating archetypes within his definition of the mythological novel. This inclusiveness allows him to investigate recurrent patterns with mythic associations in three texts, each of which represents one of three types of mythological novels: Gabriel García Márquez's *Cien años de soledad* (1967, *One Hundred Years of Solitude*), a mythification novel; Mann's *Joseph und seine Brüder* (1933, *Joseph and his Brothers*), illustrating demythification; and Joyce's *Ulysses*, a novel about remythification. There are certainly naïve and overzealous examples of archetypal criticism: the American myth and

symbol critics R. W. B. Lewis, Leo Marx, and Henry Nash Smith earned notoriety as well as opprobrium. Nevertheless, a willingness to discern archetypal structures and imagery in the novel has its rewards for the discerning reader.

Creation, flood, journey, and hero myths are the foundational stories for many texts; but on another level an awareness of archetypes and symbols that relate to human sexuality, nourishment, shelter, community, and consciousness all give life to the novel. Furthermore, to associate the writer with the prophet and visionary, as Frye suggests (*Anatomy*, 56, 139), or to connect the experience of reading with a form of eternal time (Palencia-Roth, 86), contributes another dimension to the interpretation of mythology's integral relationship with the novel. Miguel de Cervantes's *Don Quixote* (1605, 1615) undermines the myth of a golden age of chivalry, yet the characters' testing journey is mirrored by the adventure of the reader in following their stories through the construction of the narrative, balancing ideology and myth, rationality and emotion, reality and imagination.

SEE ALSO: Magical Realism, Reading, Religion.

BIBLIOGRAPHY

Barthes, R. (1957), *Mythologies*, trans. A. Lavers.
Benjamin, W. (1968), "The Storyteller," in *Illuminations*, trans. H. Zorn.
Campbell, J. (1949), *Hero with a Thousand Faces*.
Chase, R. (1949), *Quest for Myth*.
Frazer, J.G. (1922), *Golden Bough*, abridged ed.
Frye, N. (1957), *Anatomy of Criticism*.
Jung, C.G. (1969), *Four Archetypes*, trans. R.F.C. Hull.
Palencia-Roth, M. (1987), *Myth and the Modern Novel*.
Segal, R.A. (1999), *Theorizing About Myth*.
White, J.J. (1971), *Mythology in the Modern Novel*.

N

Narratee *see* Reader

Narration

EDWARD MALONEY

The term narration is most commonly understood as the act of telling a story. But there are other relatively common understandings: a synonym for an entire narrative; a description of the verbal medium of narrative fiction; a rhetorical device different from argument, exposition, or description; and as the binary opposite of dialogue. For the purposes of this entry, I will limit myself to a discussion of narration as *the production of a narrative*, including how a narrator tells a story, the context and situation in which this recounting takes place, and the complex dynamics involved in any telling. This definition follows Gérard Genette's tripartite division of narrative into discourse, STORY, and narration. Genette separates narrative discourse (*récit*), from the events the discourse purports to recount (*histoire*), and at the same time separates the discursive text from the act of telling (*narration*) that produces the narrative. Despite the usefulness of Genette's distinction, later narratologists often combine the concepts of discourse and narration under the heading "narrative discourse," highlighting the presentation of a story from the story itself. Because of its central role in the presentation of any story, narration involves a number of narrative techniques employed in narrative fiction (e.g., perspective, voice, etc.) and

their related concerns and distinctions. Of course, the novel is not a homogeneous category, and novelists have often pushed the limits of narrative convention in order to produce desired effects. Consequently, our understanding of narration should follow novelistic practice rather than legislate it.

SHOWING VS. TELLING

In *The Rhetoric of Fiction* Wayne Booth argues against the modernist dogma that showing is superior to telling, contending instead that both showing and telling need to be assessed in relation to the needs of individual novels. Nevertheless, Booth's argument underscores the classical distinction between mimesis and diegesis, i.e., the speech of characters as represented by the poet (mimesis) and the speech of the poet (diegesis). In mimesis, the poet seems to record speech as it happens, creating the illusion of showing the actions as they unfold. In diegesis, the poet mediates the events and actions through paraphrase and (re)telling. In the novel, quoted text (meant to indicate the direct representation of speech) and interior monologue (meant to represent the unmediated thoughts of a character) are sometimes seen as mimetic and outside of narration. Booth, Genette, Bal, and others have suggested, however, that pure mimesis in narratives is always an illusion, and that any representation of speech by characters is a narrative act

The Encyclopedia of the Novel   Edited by Peter Melville Logan
© 2011 Blackwell Publishing Ltd

mediated by a narrator. In Jane Austen's *Emma* (1815), for example, the extensive quoted dialogue is always framed by the narrator's diegetic commentary. Novels that eliminate or efface the narrator and rely on dialogue both to show and to tell can be understood as efforts to escape to eliminate diegesis in favor of mimesis.

WHO SPEAKS?

The first step in understanding the narration in any novel is to address the question, "Who speaks?" In order to identify the complex dynamic involved in answering this question, many narrative theorists have proposed to distinguish among the real author, implied author, and narrator(s). Following the work of Booth, Genette and others, Seymour Chatman identifies the following components of narrative communication:

Narrative text

The implied author is one of the more controversial concepts in narrative theory. Booth develops the implied author as a way of distinguishing between the real author and the persona "he" constructs when writing a narrative, a persona that is visible to the reader in the narrative text as the agent who establishes the cultural and ethical norms of the text. While the debate about the implied author and his or her various relations to the real author and the narrator are outside the scope of this entry, the very distinctions among the three agents of telling indicate that narration is not the direct transmittal of a story

from author to reader. Despite the debate about the value of the concept of the implied author, narrative theorists generally agree that authorial communication in the novel is mediated through the narrator. The author—narrator relation can vary across a wide spectrum. At one end of the spectrum, the narrator may be virtually indistinguishable from the (implied) author, and, at the other end of the spectrum, the narrator may be a fully developed character who has almost nothing in common with the (implied) author. Regardless of where the narrator exists on the spectrum, the answer to the question who speaks, begins with a discussion of the narrator.

One of the initial distinctions we commonly make about a narrator is whether she is a character in the story. In common usage, we often talk about the point of view of a narrator as a way of describing this relationship, and narrators have been referred to as first, third, and occasionally second person, depending on their role in the story. As Genette points out, the problem with this taxonomy is that it conflates voice (who is speaking) with vision or perception (who is seeing or perceiving), which Genette calls focalization. Genette goes on to develop more precise taxonomies of each phenomenon. With voice he separates the question of the narrator's participation in the story from the question of the narrative level at which the telling occurs. With participation, he distinguishes between homodiegetic (participating) and heterodiegetic (non-participating) narrators. With level he distinguishes among extradiegetic (one level above the main action), intradiegetic (within the main action), and hypodiegetic (one level below the main action). Thus we might have a narrator, such as Conrad's Marlow in *Heart of Darkness* (1899) who participates in the story he recounts (homodiegetic), but whose retrospective telling to his audience on the Nellie is extradiegetic.

In addition to issues of the relationship of a character narrator to the story she is telling, character narration also raises the issue of reliability. Reliability is an especially complicated issue since in most cases of character narration the only direct voice we have in the story is of that character/narrator. How can we determine whether the person telling us the story is to be trusted and in what ways? Perhaps the most important use of Booth's concept of the implied author is in helping us determine the reliability of narration in such cases. If we assume that the implied author establishes the ethical and cultural norms of the narrative, the reliability of the narrator then can be judged in relationship to those norms. This is not always easy, as debates about the reliability of the governess in Henry James's *The Turn of the Screw* (1898) and about the sincerity of Humbert Humbert's condemnation of himself in Vladimir Nabokov's *Lolita* (1965), among many other examples, suggest. It is also possible for narrator to be reliable about some things and unreliable about others. James Phelan has developed a useful taxonomy of reliability, arguing that narrators can be reliable or unreliable reporters of events, interpreters of knowledge or perceptions, or evaluators of ethical or moral issues. In this respect, a narrator may be unreliable because she misreports events. Or, as in the case of *Lolita*, a narrator may report the events accurately, but misregard the ethical values that the implied author has established.

WHO SEES?

Genette identifies different types of focalization, depending on the focalizer's relationship to the story (internal, exter-

nal), whether the focalization is fixed, variable, or multiple, and how the focalizer's intellectual, ethical, and psychological beliefs affect what the focalizer is able to see (Rimmon-Kenan). Consider the opening lines to Jane Austen's *Emma* (1815), where the narrator's particular focalization allows her to comment on Emma Woodhouse's character and qualities: "Emma Woodhouse, handsome, clever, and rich, with a comfortable home and happy disposition, seemed to unite some of the best blessings of existence; and had lived nearly twenty-one years in the world with very little to distress or vex her." Novelists often indicate that the perspective of the focalizing agent is not the same as that of the perspective of the narrator. For example, in Joyce's *A Portrait of the Artist as a Young Man* (1916), the narrator is external (heterodiegetic) and above story level (extradiegetic), but the focalization is through the eyes of Stephen Dedalus: "Once upon a time and a very good time it was there was a moocow coming down along the road and this moocow that was coming down along the road met a nicens little boy named baby tuckoo" (chap. 1). Here we see (i.e., hear) primarily through the perspective of Stephen, even as the voice appears to be a blend of Stephen's and that of someone telling him this story. As the novel progresses, the narrator's focalization grows and changes with Stephen. By the end of the novel Stephen's voice ultimately takes over that of the narrator's in the form of Stephen's journal. The meeting of voice and vision at this moment of the novel highlights Stephen's artistic hopes as he goes off to "to forge in the smithy of my soul the uncreated conscience of my race." In this way, the trajectory of the narration is crucial to Joyce's conveying Stephen's movement toward becoming an artist.

ORDER AND TIME

Novels often imitate nonfiction forms such as the history or biography (Rabinowitz). In this respect, novels are generally understood to recount events that have already taken place. Following Genette, Rimmon-Kenan identifies four classifications of narrative tense representative of different ways that narratives relate to the time of the story. The first, "ulterior" or "prior" narration, is the recounting of events that have already happened. This is the most common form of narration, and we find it in novels such as Austen's *Emma*. The second, anterior narration, is "predictive" or "subsequent," and suggests future happenings, such as those in prophecies. In some narratives, the actions and narrative occur "simultaneously," and in a fourth type of narration, "intercalated" or "interpolated," the telling and action are not simultaneous but impact each other throughout the narrative. An epistolary novel such as Richardson's *Clarissa* (1747–48) employs intercalated narration. These types of temporal narrations are often associated with the verb tenses used in the narration. Ulterior and intercalated narrations are most often told in the past tense, though sometimes the historical present is used. Anterior narration is most often told in the future tense, but may involve some form of the present or past tense as well, while simultaneous narration is told in the present tense.

The time of narration is also related to the order in which events are recounted. Genette's story plane assumes that outside of narration there exists a story that happened in chronological order. How this reconstruction takes place is often affected by the order in which events are told, and can have a significant impact on issues such as suspense and narrative expectations. Narration can reconstruct the story in chronological order or it can employ anachronisms such as flashback (analepsis) and foreshadowing (prolepsis), and the more complex narratives often play with a combination of narrative order and time. For example, in William Faulkner's *Absalom, Absalom!* (1936), Quentin Compson's narration does not order events chronologically. Rather, Quentin unfolds the narrative in sequences that require his narratee (Shreve) and the reader, to piece together details about the Sutpen family and the true story of their history.

SELF-REFLEXIVITY

Finally, it is worth noting that the many of the issues of narration so far discussed have become central concerns of the novel in the twentieth and twenty-first centuries. This type of self-reflexive or metafictional work highlights that act of telling as part of the story (see METAFICTION). In John Fowles's *The French Lieutenant's Woman* (1969), for example, the narrator acting as an author not only interrupts the flow of the narration to explain his as plight as the writer of the novel we are reading, but by the end of the book becomes a character in the novel, watching the events unfold much like the reader. This metafictional attention to narration is not new, of course, and we need simply go back to Cervantes or Sterne to see that narration is not only a complex subject but one that has long occupied writers' imagination and attention.

BIBLIOGRAPHY

Austen, J. (1815) *Emma*.
Bal, M. (1997), *Narratology*, 2nd ed.
Booth, W. C. (1983), *Rhetoric of Fiction*, 2nd ed.
Chatman, S. (1980), *Story and Discourse*.
Genette, G. (1980), *Narrative Discourse*, trans. J. Lewin.

Joyce, J. (1916), *Portrait of the Artist as a Young Man*.
Phelan, J. (2005), *Living to Tell About It*.
Rabinowitz, P. (1998), *Before Reading*.
Rimmon-Kenan, S. (1983), *Narrative Fiction*.

Narrative

H. PORTER ABBOTT

For the question "What is a narrative?" the commonest response is "a story," and for narrative in general, "the telling of stories." But the subject is more complicated than this. Story is indeed essential to narrative and is generally understood as having the core properties of an event or events, proceeding chronologically in time, and being conveyed through some medium. But almost immediately differences of opinion arise regarding the first of these core properties. For some scholars only one event, however meager ("The gourd bounced off the wall"), is needed to qualify as a story. It extends the concept of story to almost any instance of discourse involving a verb of action, but at the cost of including many that would not earn the status of a "story" as the word is commonly used. Its advantage is that it identifies a specific cognitive gift—the ability to represent events in time—without which there would be no stories at all, much less narratives.

All other definitions of story are more exclusive, though they all involve this universal building block. In some definitions, for the event to qualify as a story it must result in a change of state ("The gourd fell apart when it bounced off the wall"). For others a succession of at least two events is required ("The gourd fell apart when it bounced off the wall. Night fell as the sun slipped below the horizon"). Still others require that the events be causally connected ("The gourd fell apart when it bounced off the wall, revealing a perfect diamond that began to glow and slowly rise from the scattered fragments"). Many also require human characters and at least some human agency ("An aged shaman threw the gourd against the wall, causing it to fall apart. The assembled throng gasped as a perfect diamond slowly rose, glowing, from the scattered fragments"). And finally, there are those for whom a story is fully legitimate only when its events follow an arc from equilibrium to disruption and back to equilibrium ("The first star of heaven was born when the last Shaman of the Dark Nights threw a gourd against a wall, causing it to fall apart. The assembled throng gasped as a perfect diamond slowly rose, glowing, from the scattered fragments. Steadily it rose, gathering speed, until at last it came to its rightful place in the sky as the Evening Star").

Wherever one draws one's defining line, it is clear that for each succeeding example above there is an increase in "narrativity," i.e., an increase in the sense that one is apprehending a story. The advantage of narrativity's "scalar" rather than absolute quality is that, on the one hand, it reflects a reality of the experience of narrative and, on the other, it helps avoid tying the term "narrative" down in ways that are more arbitrary than useful. Narrativity includes, but should not be confused with another scalar feature of narrative, William Labov's concept of "tellability," which registers the extent to which a narrative has point, i.e., the extent to which it forestalls the "so what?" response. Narrativity also plays a key role in how we designate longer texts like epics and novels in which narrative elements are intermixed with stretches of description, discussion, poetic rhapsodizing, and other non-narrative modes that interrupt the sequence of events. They earn their status as narrative because there is a sufficient arc of connected action, a sufficient degree of narrativity, to earn that status. This is often a judgment call. Herman Melville's *Moby-Dick* (1851), for example, includes a great deal of non-narrative material, yet has a sufficient narrative arc to persuade most readers that it is a novel. Søren Kierkegaard's *Frygt og Bæven* (1843, *Fear and Trembling*), by contrast, is less a novel than an apologue, in which philosophical exposition predominates. While a text like Walter Pater's *Marius the Epicurean* (1885) seems to straddle the line between narrative and philosophical exposition.

CONSECUTION AND CONVEYANCE

So far, we have been focusing on the core element of the event or events, as a key component of any story and the variable element of narrativity in the way events are rendered. But, looking at the second core element of story, the consecution of its events, another complication arises. For where story events always proceed in chronological sequence, they can be narrated out of chronological sequence. In our minds, we restore the proper sequence, even if it is given to us in reverse ("The Evening Star is a perfect diamond. It soared to its rightful place in the heavens from the remnants of a gourd that fell apart when the last Shaman of the Dark Night threw it against a wall"). This is an aspect of narrative that has been compounded by the digital resources of hypertext narrative, where readers themselves may choose different combinations of narrative bits (lexia) to get from one end of the narrative to the other.

This is also a key reason why narrative cannot be the same thing as story. In consequence, most narrative theorists divide narrative into at least two components: the chronological sequence of the events and the sequence in which they are conveyed. Russian formalist critics of the 1920s called the first of these the *fabula* (story) and the second the *sjuzhet* (sometimes translated as "plot") (see FORMALISM, STORY). For some

theorists it is the complex interplay of these two sequences, the story and the way it is plotted, that is at the heart of the narrative experience. Generally in English, the broader and more inclusive term "discourse" is used instead of "plot" or *sjuzhet*, in which case, to adapt the words of Seymour Chatman, narrative can be defined as the "story-as-discoursed" (43).

This brings us to the third core element of story: that it is always conveyed in some way. We never encounter an unmediated story, never experience it in the way we experience events in life, but always as inflected by the medium through which it is conveyed and by an array of other elements of the discourse, like the order in which events are recounted, the amount of time given to a particular event, the number of times an event is recounted, the eyes through which we see the story, the voice by which we hear it, the sensibility of the narrator, the style deployed. Whether theorists lump all of these mediating factors under the single umbrella term of "narrative discourse" or keep them in separate bundles of concern as medium, plot, narration, or style, they lend their combined effects in broad or subtle strokes as they convey the story.

There are several consequences of the separation of story and discourse. One is that, increasingly, scholars have released the concept of narrative from the necessity of a narrator. The distinction between stories that are told and stories that are enacted is a venerable one that goes back to Plato's distinction in *The Republic* (ca. 380 BCE) between diegesis and mimesis. Some narratologists would still insist that the distinction is significant enough to justify requiring that a narrative have a narrator. But others argue that media like staging and filming, with the elements of directing, acting, camerawork, editing, etc., do essentially what narrators do: convey a story. The separation of story from discourse also means that stories are "transposable" (Chatman, 20). Stories are told and retold, enacted and reenacted, painted and repainted. The same story can be rendered in prose, in film, and on stage. The life of Christ and numerous other stories of the Bible and MYTHOLOGY have been rendered in all three and in painting as well. There are a host of other media to which stories can be transposed, including ballet, comics, mime, and electronic media.

Another consequence of this separation of story and discourse is that a story seems always to precede the discourse. The logic here is that there must already be a story for it to be conveyed. For this reason most stories are told in the past tense. They are all in their way history, either fictional or nonfictional. The absolute necessity of this has been challenged by Dorrit Cohn (107) in the example of "simultaneous narration" in fiction when it is rendered in the first person ("I throw the gourd against the wall and watch it burst into fragments"). In this mode of narration, Cohn argues, there is no temporal gap between the words and the experience they give voice to. Jonathan Culler has made the larger claim that any story can be said to come after the discourse, since there is no story until the discourse generates it. Moreover, expectations that are aroused by the discourse can play an irresistible role in determining the story's course of events (169–87).

THE RECOGNITION OF NARRATIVE

Human beings have probably been telling stories for at least 120,000 years. For most of this time, what people thought about the art of storytelling, like most of the stories themselves, is lost to us. But from the earliest recorded commentary up to the 1960s, the analytical reflection on narrative has been largely genre-specific, as it was in Aristotle's *Poetics* (ca. 335 BCE), which focused not on

narrative per se but on the essential properties of tragedy and COMEDY. Narrative as a phenomenon transcending genre fully emerged as a subject of disciplined study in the 1960s with a constellation of brilliant work by Roland Barthes, Algirdas Julien Greimas, Claude Bremond, Tzvetan Todorov, and others. Christened in 1969 by Todorov as "narratology," the field was arguably a last efflorescence of the European structuralist tradition. As such, it took as its model Saussurean linguistics, which had already been applied to narrative in the 1920s by the Russian formalists Viktor Shklovsky, Boris Tomashevsky, and Vladimir Propp, whose *Morphology of the Russian Folktale* (1928) was to be a major influence (see FORMALISM; STRUCTURALISM).

The Anglo-American prehistory of narrative theory was also formalist but was confined largely to the novel. It was also less scientist and more oriented toward the craft of fiction, beginning with Henry James's essay "The Art of Fiction" (1884) and running through work by Virginia Woolf, E. M. Forster, Percy Lubbock, Cleanth Brooks, Robert Penn Warren, William K. Wimsatt, and Kenneth Burke. This work was not displaced by the structuralist onslaught in the 1960s but rather absorbed into the discourse on narrative, along with an array of its own concerns such as repetition, central reflectors, narrative voice, point of view, perspective, showing versus telling, and characterization. Perhaps the most powerful American influence on the future development of narrative theory, however, was Wayne Booth's *Rhetoric of Fiction* (1961), which itself was a critique of the formalist tradition out of which it came. For Booth, authors had an obligation to their readers to achieve a certain moral clarity, and the formal concepts he introduced (the implied author, reliable and unreliable narrators) were keyed to this concern for the transaction between the novel and its reader. Booth's rhetorical and ethical concerns have been richly developed by narratologists in the intervening years. More broadly, the work on narrative that has evolved from the 1970s to the present has built a host of other contextual considerations (historical, cultural, social, psychological, ideological) onto its formalist base, while extending its domain into the cognitive inner space of audiences and authors, and outward to narrative modes far from the realms of art.

Though there are those who argue that at some point narratology's structuralist base must give way entirely if we are to progress in our understanding of narrative (Gibson), the implicit near-consensus for now appears to be that with continual adaptation the base will prove strong enough to support a poststructuralist or "post-classical" narratology (Herman, 1999). At the same time, disciplines across the academic spectrum, as well as professional fields like law and medicine, have experienced a "narrative turn," as more and more researchers explore the many and pervasive roles that narrative plays in almost all aspects of life.

NARRATIVE LIMITS

As the study of narrative has expanded our understanding of both its internal complexity and the extent to which it can be found in areas far removed from traditional storytelling, much attention has been given to the question of limits. How much actually happens in the narrative transaction, and where does narrative give way to other modes of expression?

Narrative space

Narrative both tells of events as they transpire in time and is apprehended through time. Narrative desire, intensified through the management of suspense and retardation, is always looking forward to what will happen next. Accordingly, definitions of narrative have emphasized the element of time, TIME much of the classical work on narrative has implicitly and sometimes explicitly assumed that the anti-type of the narrative arts are the spatial arts (painting, sculpture). But, on the one hand, though this may be true of portraits and still-lifes, it neglects the narrative element in much of the representational art in spatial modes. A painting of St. George and the dragon, a sculpture of St. Sebastian, an eighteenth-century genre painting of a girl with a broken pitcher, are each moments in a story in progress. This was an insight that the German aesthetician and dramatist Gotthold Lessing formulated more than 200 years ago in his treatise on the *Laocoön* (1766), but it was largely neglected during the structuralist development of narrative theory.

On the other hand, narrative itself is not so much a purely temporal phenomenon as it is what Mikhail BAKHTIN called "chronotopic" or temporal-spatial. Like the Russian formalists, Bakhtin first developed his theory of the chronotope in the 1920s, and like their theories it, too, lay comparatively dormant until the 1960s. But it is now common to speak of the "storyworld" that a narrative creates, and that grows larger and more complex as a narrative advances in time. In the example above, each advance in narrativity is accompanied by a corresponding increase in our sense of a world with its own inhabitants and geography (indeed, universe), as well as the inner space of thought and feeling that goes on in its inhabitants. Just as we are conscious of ourselves inhabiting an actual world and imagining all kinds of "possible worlds," so a narrative fiction has its own actual world in which fictional people imagine a proliferation of possible worlds (Doležel; Ryan). The common feeling of being "immersed" in fiction or "transported" by it is a feeling of being in a whole other world.

Narrative and abstract expression

The psychologist Jerome Bruner has made the case for two modes of thinking that "are irreducible to one another" (11): narrative and argument. The former deals with human beings in particular situations, the latter with abstractions. Bruner's distinction echoes a common opposition of narrative and abstraction. For Herman, this is the deep difference between narrative and scientific discourse: "Science explains how in general water freezes when ... its temperature reaches zero degrees centigrade; but it takes a story to convey what it was like to lose one's footing on slippery ice one late afternoon in December 2004, under a steel-grey sky" (2007, 3). Though there can be stretches of abstract discourse in the longer narrative genres like the novel and autobiography, it is the sensed preponderance of narrativity that keeps any particular text from being shifted to another, non-narrative, genre. An interesting borderline case is narrative allegory in which each character stands for an abstraction, like Beauty, Strength, and Knowledge in the medieval play *Everyman*. Call it "narrativized abstraction," but watching the play, the audience becomes immersed in the story. It is the particularity of Everyman and his personal engagement in his quest that makes this immersion possible. Authors have at times named their characters with abstract labels, as Charles Dickens did when he named the schoolmaster in *Hard Times* (1845) Mr. M'Choakumchild. But despite the way Dickens telegraphs the idea the schoolmaster stands for, it is his capacity to develop him as a particular character that brings him to life in a way no abstraction can.

Narrative, poetry, and the lyric

Poetry and narrative have also been frequently referred to as opposites. But probably a majority of all narratives ever told or written have been in poetry, not prose—this would include all the great epics, medieval romances, ballads, European drama up through the Renaissance, and even some novels (David Jones's *In Parenthesis*, 1937; Vikram Seth's *The Golden Gate*, 1986). A much more defensible opposition is between narrative and lyric. Lyrical poetry is by definition devoted to the expression of an emotion, whether grief (elegies), veneration (odes), or love (most sonnets). And though lyrics may contain micro-narratives and even undergo a shift in mood (in effect, a change of state), as in the last quatrain or sestet of a sonnet, by and large they tend to be static evocations of emotion rather than vehicles for a story. Here again there are borderline cases like Jeanette Winterson's short work "The White Room" (2002) or Ann Beattie's "Snow" (1983), where it is difficult to say whether it is narrative or lyric that predominates.

Narratives and games

A number of other contrasting modes to narrative have been proposed—description, exposition, meditation, instruction—but with the explosion of digital and internet resources, and the hybridization of narrative games, considerable attention has lately been given to the question of how games and narrative differ, if indeed they do. On the face of it, they seem to be distinctly different, a narrative being essentially a representation of an action and a game being a rule-bound contest involving one or more players. A narrative conveys a story that seems to preexist its conveyance; a game is not conveyed but unfolds in the present. A narrative differs from life in the actual world by existing in an imagined storyworld, a game happens in the actual world but differs from life by its containment within arbitrary rules and its unambiguous production of winners and losers.

But "text adventures" and role-playing games (RPGs) take place in a narrative environment. In varying degrees there is a story, apprehended by players who in turn participate through fictional creatures (avatars) they control. With on-line multi-user RPGs, game masters stay several "plot points" ahead of their players, so a story can be said to precede its apprehension in narrative time, though it is "read" through an active process of search and discovery. Moreover, in some multi-user RPGs, much of the action in the story (or game) world is a kind of improvised story production carried on independently by the players' avatars. Finally, though there are electronic games and on-line RPGs that operate like a competitive sport with a premium on winning, the game aspect of many multi-user RPGs is more like play than sport, taking place in a community atmosphere where "winning" or achieving some kind of goal is less important than having a good time.

The hybridization of narrative and game in multi-user on-line RPGs poses a fascinating challenge to assumptions that are built into customary definitions of narrative. Is the story "conveyed," or are clues to it simply lying about, waiting to be discovered, and are players more like detectives, unraveling a mystery that has taken place in a storyworld now belonging to the past? Conversely, to what extent is the story as given subsidiary to the storylines that the avatars make up as they go along? If achieving the goal set by the game masters coincides with the full comprehension of the story behind the game, do these two ideas remain conceptually distinct? Or does their conjunction correlate with the feeling one has when finishing a novel—a kind of victory in a solitary game in which the object is to overcome one's ignorance of what happened? Finally, if much of the action is improvised on the spot in a series of unre-peatable acts in real time, how different is this from what happens in actions of life itself which are also, in effect, consumed as they are made?

The postmodern narrative

It is difficult to generalize about postmodern narratives, because their range of experimentation is so great, but it is safe to say that many of them challenge our narrative expectations. Some of these involve the violation of narrative levels (metalepsis) as when the author enters his or her novel as a character (John Fowles's *The French Lieutenant's Woman*, 1969) or the reader is made a character in the novel (Italo Calvino's *Se una notte d'inverno un viaggiatore*; 1979, *If on a Winter's Night a Traveler*); some induce a permanent confusion about what happens in the story (Alain Robbe-Grillet's *Dans le labyrinthe* (1959, *In the Labyrinth*); some develop forking paths in which worlds contradict each other (Peter Howitt's film *Sliding Doors*, 1998); some even lack characters (Samuel Beckett's *The Unnamable*, 1953). There are many more postmodern modes of deliberate narrative frustration, almost all of which challenge narrative theory. In his study of "extreme narration," Brian Richardson has argued that "the essence" of such fiction "is to elude fixed essence" (140) and has called for a revaluation of narrative theory from the ground up to address their extraordinary departures from narrative normality.

NARRATIVE POWER: PLOTS AND MASTER PLOTS

The power of narrative to rouse an audience was certainly recognized long before Plato banned the poets from his republic because of their ability to wield that power. For Plato, the storyteller's art could override reason and on that account alone, he recommended limiting its use to martial themes when they were needed to defend the republic. For Plato's student, Aristotle, it was precisely the emotional appeal of narrative that gave it cathartic and restorative powers, and a way of lodging wisdom in the heart that abstract reasoning could never achieve. Between them, Plato and Aristotle established two poles within which much of the discussion of narrative effects has played out ever since.

The power of narrative has often been keyed to the way stories conform to one or another plot or story type. "Plot" is a term used in several incompatible ways, but in this sense a plot is a skeletal story that is repeated in one variation or another in any number of distinct narratives. The fact of its repetition is in itself an indication of its power to catalyze strong emotional responses. Some plots in this sense of the word are more universal than others. Narrative versions of the quest story, for example, can be found across cultures and throughout recorded history, from the *Odyssey* (ca. eighth century BCE) to *Saving Private Ryan* (1998). Archetypal theories of story types see in them a reflection of universal structures of the human imagination, as in Northrop Frye's four "generic plots": the comic, the tragic, the romantic, and the ironic (see MYTHOLOGY). As a general rule, however, the more particularized the plot, the more likely it is to be the property of a distinct culture and to deal with issues that are of critical importance to that culture. In many such instances, the plot is a defining feature of a GENRE (literary kind), as in the Jacobean revenge tragedy, the medieval romance, or the saint's life. Genres that have no defining plot, like the novel or the ballad, often have a number of subgenres that are to some degree plot bound: the bildungsroman, the Harlequin romance, the Horatio Alger story, the vampire novel.

The term "master plot" (often used in the discourse on film in the sense of story type) includes a connotation of the ideological power that can be embedded in a popular cultural plot (see IDEOLOGY). The story of Abraham Lincoln (1809–65), from his birth to his presidency, conforms to a master plot that orchestrates major elements of American mythology—the democratic belief that anyone, however impoverished in his origins (the gender is part of the myth), can rise to the highest social position, through the application of his native gifts, hard work, and steadfast determination. Much narrative theory taking FEMINIST or minority viewpoints has stressed the ways in which such stories work to obscure, marginalize, or contain segments of the population by the kinds of roles that come with those plots. Nancy Miller, for example, has shown how the role of "heroine" in plots common to the eighteenth-century novel strictly limited the range of agency and favorable plot paths for women characters. This stood in sharp contrast to the range of behavioral options and power open to the "hero." But it is also possible to achieve rhetorical power by working against received treatments of cultural types and their culturally scripted roles. Much of the immense impact of Richard Wright's *Native Son* when it was published in 1940 derived from the way it took a frightening cultural master plot—the story of sexual and deadly force visited on a white woman by a black man—and opened it up to an inside view that disallowed the narrow psychology sustaining the cultural story.

Our dependency on plots to organize and make sense of events has been extended by Hayden White to the entire domain of historiography. In this view, the writing of history (as opposed to the mere chronicling of one event after another) is inevitably a process of "emplotment," the shaping of what has happened in time according to the requirements of one or another plot drawn from the cultural repertory. This is a cognitive operation, however, that must be concealed from consciousness in order for history to succeed as nonfiction. The necessary illusion of history as a plot-free apprehension of reality, harmonizes with Jean-François Lyotard's concept of the *grand récit* ("master narrative"). This is the overarching "meta-narrative" that permits storytelling to pass as knowledge. The Enlightenment idea of progress through the application of reason and a disciplined process of empirical testing and verification, for example, is in Lyotard's view the master narrative that permits science to pass as an objective encounter with reality rather than a narrative art. As might be expected, the views of White and Lyotard have been the subject of intense debate.

Master plots of human development were fundamental to the work of Freud, Jung, and other early architects of PSYCHOANALYTIC theory and practice. With an event structure keyed to traumatic moments of early childhood, and a powerful posttraumatic determining power, such plots were assumed to be universal and thus to be the deep structures of stories endlessly recurring in dreams, literature, and the other arts. Freud's master plot of male development took its name from the most famous of Greek tragedies, Sophocles's *Oedipus Rex* (ca. 429 BCE) and therapy itself became a mode of narrative inquiry. More recently, Bruno Bettelheim focused on the critical role fairy tales play in childhood development, while psychologists like Jerome Bruner, Katherine Nelson, Oliver Sacks, Bettelheim, the historian Carolyn Steedman, and others have, in their different ways, featured the developmental importance of situating oneself within one's own narrative (see LIFE WRITING).

In these and many other ways, the power of narrative in our own lives and in almost every aspect of culture and society, has been intensively researched and, no doubt, will continue to be.

BIBLIOGRAPHY

Bakhtin, M.M. (1981), *Dialogic Imagination*, ed. M. Holquist, trans. C. Emerson and M. Holquist.

Barthes, R. (1977), "Introduction to the Structural Analysis of Narratives," in *Image Music Text*, trans. S. Heath.

Booth, W. C. (1961), *Rhetoric of Fiction*.

Bremond, C. (1973), *Logique du récit*.

Bruner, J. (1986), *Actual Minds, Possible Worlds*.

Chatman, S. (1978), *Story and Discourse*.

Cohn, D. (1999), *Distinction of Fiction*.

Culler, J. (1981), *Pursuit of Signs*.

Doležel, L. (1998), *Heterocosmica*.

Frye, N. (1957), *Anatomy of Criticism*.

Gibson, A. (1996), *Towards a Postmodern Theory of Narrative*.

Greimas, A. J. (1983), *Structural Semantics*, trans. D. McDowell, et al.

Herman, D. (1997), "Scripts, Sequences, and Stories," PMLA 112:1046–59.

Herman, D. (2007), "Introduction," in *Cambridge Companion to Narrative*, ed. D. Herman.

James, H. (1956), "The Art of Fiction," in *Future of the Novel*, ed. L. Edel.

Labov, W. (1972), "Transformation of Experience in Narrative Syntax," in *Language in the Inner City*.

Lyotard, J.-F. (1979), *Postmodern Condition*, trans. G. Bennington and B. Massumi.

Miller, N. (1980), *Heroine's Text*.

Propp, V. (1968), *Morphology of the Russian Folktale*, trans. L. Scott, 2nd ed.

Richardson, B. (2006), *Unnatural Voices*.

Ryan, M.L. (1991), *Possible Worlds, Artificial Intelligence, and Narrative Theory*.

Todorov, T. (1968), "La Grammaire du récit," *Langages* 3(12):94–102.

White, H. (1987), *Content of the Form*.

Narrative Form *see* Time

Narrative Perspective

MICHAEL BELL

If narrative perspective, in its most general meaning, is the angle from which the subject is viewed, then it is clearly one of the most significant factors governing a novel's representation of its world. Indeed, it can on occasion virtually constitute the subject of the narrative. Henry James, for example, records that the "germ" of *The Spoils of Poynton* (1897) was given him as a reported situation in which a wealthy, cultured widow, with a much-loved only son and a house full of beautiful objects, faced the prospect of passing the inheritance to a pushy, philistine daughter-in-law. The situation only came alive for James's novelistic imagination, however, when he imagined it from the viewpoint of a new, invented character, a young woman of intelligent sensibility and deeply in love with the son, who, for those very reasons, is unable to use the sharp elbows of her rival. Through her consciousness, the very crudeness of the external situation as James first heard it is transmuted into an anguished internal drama.

In the case of James's novel, the initial process of creative exploration and the final dramatic realization of the narrative are at once highly self-conscious and consummately achieved, but precisely the success of such an achievement can disguise the difficulties and complexities that are involved in the notion of narrative perspective. For although "perspective" is in the first instance a visual term, it has metaphorical senses extending through several levels, from the dramatic to the moral and the philosophical. For that reason it is helpful first to distinguish the technical aspect of narrative perspective from these possibly more important, yet also more elusive, dimensions.

By the technical aspect here is meant the literal "point of view" of the narration, which can be to some extent concretely, even linguistically, defined: a story may be told, for example, in the first person, or the third person, or in "free indirect speech," known in French as *style indirect libre*, and in German as *Erlebte Rede* (see DISCOURSE).

"Point of view" in this sense has become an acknowledged term of art for literary critics and, while such narrative choices are clearly important for the writer and the critically reflective reader, they can be analytically misleading and critically distracting owing to the widespread impact of what might be called the "technical fallacy." The modern literary academy was largely founded in the period of early twentieth-century MODERNISM, and was decisively influenced by the self-conscious concern for technique in writers like Henry James and James Joyce; the generation of writers in whom the novel itself achieved a fully recognized status as an artistic GENRE. Explication of such technique became a central activity in the teaching of literature and, because it is technical and demonstrable, it is eminently teachable even where neither the teacher nor the students have a profound literary responsiveness or demanding critical sense. The outcome is a recurrent overinvestment in the notion of technique, as if the NARRATIVE TECHNIQUE as such could produce the moral intelligence of the work, or provide an adequate locus for a critical understanding of it. Mark Schorer's influential essay "Technique as Discovery" (1948) and Wayne Booth's much later *The Rhetoric of Fiction* (1961) variously exemplify this tendency. Both attempted a reading of D. H. Lawrence's *Sons and Lovers* (1913), seeking to expose the weakness of the novel as a failure to maintain a consistent point of view with respect to the central character, Paul Morel. Many years later both revised their perception of the novel as they came to realize that, despite its possible faults in this regard, Lawrence was actually attempting a more subtle, and shifting, relation to his material and his characters. In other words, there is, indeed, a problem of moral perspective in *Sons and Lovers*, a certain *parti pris* for Paul Morel, but consideration of the novel's narrative technique, while a significant part of the necessary analysis, does not adequately catch the nature of Lawrence's struggle with his material. Of course, this remains a matter of judgment in any given instance, but the general point is that the technical point of view is not necessarily a complete index of the narrative's overall moral perspective, and on occasion these might even be at odds whether through artistic failure or through deliberate irony. What follows, therefore, are some classic but varied instances of the importance of narrative perspective.

As the *Sons and Lovers* case suggests, the especially difficult instances for the control of narrative perspective are likely to be those in which a highly personal, individual emotional condition is of the essence. This was evident in one of the early, and formative, European novels, Johann Wolfgang von Goethe's *Die Leiden des jungen Werthers* (1774, *The Sorrows of the Young Werther*). Goethe's novel arose partly from his own experience of romantic attraction to a young woman betrothed to his friend, but it was also a critical reflection on the contemporary fashion of sensibility, the excessive value placed on feeling; a fashion which was associated especially with the influence of Jean-Jacques Rousseau. The narrative is made up of a series of letters written by Werther up to the point of his suicide and, in contrast to other EPISTOLARY novels of the period, the reader sees no replies to Werther's letters so that the narrative reinforces his moral and emotional self-enclosure. The novel was a great popular success, but readers overwhelmingly identified with Werther and sympathized with his fate as a romantic tragedy rather than as the moral warning that Goethe intended. Indeed, this was the conventional, and approved, response to the literature of sensibility at the time. Readers were invited to identify with figures of virtue in distress. Accordingly, Goethe modified the text and

gave weight to an editorial figure who not only assembles the letters but gives a third-person conclusion to the narrative. But Goethe's difficulty, apart from the possible seduction of his own autobiographical involvement in a similar situation (see LIFE WRITING), was that the intensity of Werther's emotional subjectivity is necessary to the story. Without that, the critical perception of him would have no point, or be merely banal. Goethe needed to be fully inside the contemporary man of feeling in order to subject him to an immanent critique. Not surprisingly, perhaps, Goethe's next novel, *Wilhelm Meisters Lehrjahre* (1796, *Wilhelm Meister's Apprenticeship*), is narrated in the third person and with an overt irony in the manner of Henry Fielding's *Tom Jones* (1749). Yet despite this radical change, the final balance of approval and critique in the story of Wilhelm's education also remains highly elusive, albeit now for quite different reasons. As the defining instance of the BILDUNGSROMAN, the novel enacts a belief in fruitful, perhaps necessary, error on the part of the hero and, more importantly perhaps, it celebrates the elusiveness of authentic individual development to general moral judgment. Hence Goethe's ironic narrative perspective tends to suspend rather than enforce authorial judgment.

George Eliot admired Goethe's novel and defended its trusting naturalism against Victorian charges of amorality. She saw a deeper and more intrinsic morality at work in it and, although Eliot herself was more overtly moralistic than Goethe, she strove, within her own conception, to achieve something comparable by extending the moral sympathies of readers (see REALISM). Hence the dramatic highlights of her novels, and their overall NARRATIVE STRUCTURES, often turn on sympathetic connections across widely different human types. The two parallel narratives of *Daniel Deronda* (1876), for example, are held together by the purely sympathetic connection between Gwendolen Harleth and Daniel Deronda; a connection that is the more pointed for their lacking a shared narrative or the motive of sexual attraction. Likewise, Dorothea Brooke's generous visit to Rosamund Vincy, while believing her to be the successful rival for Will Ladislaw's love, is one of the cardinal moments of *Middlemarch* (1871–72). Moreover, in one of her famous reflections, Eliot explicitly thematizes the narrative perspective of her novel as an extension of the reader's moral sympathy. Having drawn the reader into the process of Dorothea's idealistic and dutiful acceptance of the dreadful pedant Edward Casaubon as her husband, the narrator starts chapter 29 with an abrupt turn to ask, "why always Dorothea? Was her point of view the only possible one with regard to this marriage?" And Eliot goes on to show that the pitiful, insecure, repressed Casaubon has his own particular anguish. In another famous aside, in chapter 15, the narrator contrasts the narrative perspective of *Middlemarch* with that of Henry Fielding. Whereas Fielding is imaged as the theatrical spectator who sits in a fixed position in his armchair and yet can expose all of the action as a matter of leisured generalization, Eliot's narrative has to follow more minutely the hidden, "interwoven" connections of the action and characters. The moral or psychological correlative of this difference is that whereas Fielding, like many of his contemporaries, tended to contrast virtue with conscious villainy and hypocrisy, Eliot was concerned rather with the subtle forms of self-deception. Hence, while Eliot's moralism is very different from Goethe's naturalism, it has a comparable elusiveness of final judgment.

The great nineteenth-century novels, such as Eliot's, tend to be multi-perspectival. They show the lives of selected individuals, many of them perhaps unknown to each other, while also building up an image of the social and historical whole by which these lives are conditioned. This latter aspect involves a more elusive kind of narrative perspective understood now as the total worldview or social interpretation produced by the symbolic rhetoric of the work. Charles Dickens, for example, does this through powerful images such as the law in *Bleak House* (1853). Also, within his Shakespearean comic subplots, his minor characters act as expositions of themes left implicit in the major characters. The effect is like an engineer's exploded diagram revealing the internal relations of a complex system. By contrast, Honoré de Balzac typically gives a sense of underground connections which can never be brought fully to light but only glimpsed in characters such as Vautrin, the underworld villain who passes for an honest citizen. Leo Tolstoy, meanwhile, creates a sense of natural process to which the characters must intuitively attune themselves, as Konstantin Levin learns to do in *Anna Karenina* (1877), or else suffer the consequences essentially from the process itself. By the end of the century, however, writers were less confident in such overall models of the world or society and the increasingly deterministic, scientistic conception known as NATURALISM seemed too limited. Another important factor here is the growing awareness of CLASS as a difference in moral understanding. The confident moral perspective of Fielding was a class confidence, so that although his narrative encompassed all levels of society, it did so from an essentially genteel perspective. By contrast, for a late nineteenth-century writer like George Gissing even the poetic wholeness of the Dickensian novel began to seem untenable.

Accordingly, the modernist generation sought different modes of imaginative wholeness and some of them produced remarkable fictions based on a double narrative perspective (see MODERNISM). On the one hand, the fiction of Joyce, Lawrence,

Marcel Proust, or Virginia Woolf was highly subjective in its representation of the world through the processes of individual consciousness. Yet at the same time the very elements that pass apparently randomly through this consciousness are constructing, for the reader, an aesthetic or mythic whole which provides the ultimate narrative perspective of the book. In this line of modernist fiction, the world is typically not so much an external given to be mimetically represented, as a construction of the human mind for which the construction of the book is a direct analogue or working example. The human mind, that is to say, does not create material existence, but it transposes it into what Ranier Maria Rilke called the *bedeutende Welt*, the interpreted or meaningful world. Hence, the dual narrative perspective of these modernist works respects both the immediate randomness of experience for the character and the secret, world-creating order of the whole.

The ambition for a novel to create a narrative perspective out of its own substance rather than by reflecting an independently given worldview had its first powerful articulation in the proto-modernist Gustave Flaubert. In a famous letter, he spoke of the desire, albeit an impossible one, to write a book about nothing, a work suspended purely by its own style. Of course, as T. S. Eliot (1888–1965) pointed out, the nineteenth-century notion of "art for art's sake" was, if taken literally, either banal or incoherent. Otherwise, it is the image of a moral attitude to life, as Flaubert evidently understood, and for him it represented a famous ideal of impersonality *vis-à-vis* the subject matter of the work. Flaubert's posture of narrative indifference is both genuine and a feint: in its refusal of a conventionally sentimental response it invites a reflective compassion from the reader, and a major element in that reflection is an atheistical awareness of the indifferent universe which

this narrative posture represents. Flaubert drew especially on premodern literary models, models predating the eighteenth-century's sentimental turn which so strongly governed the formation of the European novel, and he would have appreciated one of world literature's most startling uses of narrative perspective. Toward the end of Geoffrey Chaucer's *Troilus and Criseyde* (ca. 1385), the departing spirit of the dead Troilus pauses at the outermost sphere of the medieval cosmos and looks back, with a new detachment, on the world it has just left behind. This is a Flaubertian moment *avant la lettre*.

It is evident, then, in all these novels that narrative perspective is not a readily isolable aspect but a subtly total outcome of the work's subject, structure, and style. For that reason, the question of narrative perspective throws some light on a radical problem posed by Henry James. Much as he admired their achievement, James deprecated what he saw as a lack of artistry in the "loose, baggy monsters" of his nineteenth-century predecessors such as George Eliot. He spoke of the novelist's need to draw a bounding line, which must not seem merely arbitrary, around the potential infinity of relations that extend outward from any novelistic subject. Laurence Sterne's *roman-fleuve*, *Tristram Shandy* (1759–67, is the classic comic enactment of this difficulty. Where does the story of a life start, where does it finish, and what does it include? Where the understanding, or the meaning, of a life are in question, even birth and death are conventional rather than intrinsic limits. But that is to conceive the question too externally, perhaps, as one of imposing limits. The image of perspective as the ordering of visual representation developed in the European Renaissance has a different implication. Perspective is an internally intrinsic way of organizing not just what we see but what we infer without seeing.

The perspectival standpoint determines the limits of the vision or of what needs to be represented. Of all novelists, James had perhaps the most conscious sense of how narrative perspective governs by an internal, organic logic the process of shaping and selection by which the work is created.

SEE ALSO: Adaptation/Appropriation, Closure, Cognitive Theory, Frame, Story/Discourse.

BIBLIOGRAPHY

Booth, W.C. (1991), *Rhetoric of Fiction*, 2nd ed.
Chamberlain, D.F. (1990), *Narrative Perspective in Fiction*.
Cohn, D. (1978), *Transparent Minds*.
Hühn, P., W. Schmid, and J. Schonert, eds. (2009), *Point of View, Perspective and Focalization*.
James, H. (1978), *Art of the Novel*.
Scholes, R. and R. Kellogg (1996), *Nature of Narrative*.

Narrative Structure

KATHERINE SAUNDERS NASH

Narrative structure is the set of relations among the constituent parts of a narrative, as well as between those parts and the narrative as a whole. Narrative structure has proven a vital if elusive object of study for narrative theorists, in part because of the relationship between structure and narrative competence. Narrative competence is the intuitive grasp of conventions and distinctions that allows audiences to recognize certain productions as stories, to identify the essential units of those stories, and, with those units in mind, to read, retell, paraphrase, expand, evaluate, and interpret the stories. It means recognizing sequences such as, for example, a rags-to-riches plot in different forms: a film, a pantomime,

a comic strip, a novel. Narrative competence permits audiences even with widely divergent backgrounds, in dissimilar contexts, to have similar intuitions about stories, and often to agree on basic—and even complex—rules by which stories operate.

As an outgrowth of FORMALISM and STRUCTURALISM, narratology (a term used here interchangeably with narrative theory) sought from its inception in the 1960s to explain narrative competence by determining a system of units and rules that underlies all narratives, the structure of relations on which the meaning of human productions is predicated. As Roland Barthes puts it, rather starkly, in his "Introduction to the Structural Analysis of Narratives," "[E]ither a narrative is merely a random collection of events, in which case nothing can be said about it other than by referring back to the storyteller's (the author's) art, talent, or genius ... or else it shares with other narratives a common structure which is open to analysis." Without that common narrative structure, Barthes declares, story production and reception both would be "impossible" (1966, 82). Study of narrative competence was, at least in the early years of narratology (known as its "classical" phase), inseparable from analysis of narrative structure. This entry will examine the progressive understanding of narrative structure afforded by narratology, first in its classical and then in its postclassical phases. As the notion of narrative competence has evolved, so has the concept of narrative structure.

DEEP AND SURFACE STRUCTURES

One salient feature of most early models of narrative structure is their reliance on binaries. Structuralism borrows several key concepts from Saussurean LINGUISTICS, chief among them the distinction between *langue* and *parole* (see STRUCTURALISM, POSTSTRUCTURALISM). *Langue* is a system, a network of rules underlying a language, whereas *parole* is the individual manifestations of that language in speech and writing. This binary operates by distinguishing an abstract concept from a specific iteration of that concept. Noam Chomsky's "competence" and "performance" (1965, *Aspects of the Theory of Syntax*) operates in the same way, as do several of the binaries used to describe narrative structure. For instance, theorists such as Algirdas Julien Greimas differentiate a narrative's immanent level, at which story is an abstract and autonomous concept, a sequence of events, from its apparent level, which is that story mediated and manifested in a particular text. Whereas immanent versus apparent emphasizes a hierarchy of accessibility (signaling the structuralists' interest in comparing deep and surface levels, as discussed below), Gérard Genette's distinction between *histoire* (story) and *récit* (text) discards the structuralists' sense of hierarchy and focuses instead on juxtaposing virtual stories with actual written expressions of those stories. The Russian formalists' pairing of *fabula* (fable) with *sjuzhet* (plot), by contrast, emphasizes the process of selection and design, particularly sequential arrangement; *sjuzhet* is the strategic organization of certain events in a particular order (i.e., not necessarily the original chronology), whereas *fabula* is the complete story, the story-world in its totality: all possible settings, characters, and a chronology of all events, from which the *sjuzhet* is selected. In all three binaries, the first term (immanent level, *histoire*, *fabula*) represents a plentiful and inclusive entity that has the potential to give rise to a multitude of unique iterations (apparent level, *récit*, *sjuzhet*).

In the 1960s, 1970s, and early 1980s, narratologists strove to characterize narrative structure as scientifically as possible. Setting aside questions of hermeneutic interpretation, theorists tried to determine what all and only narratives have in common, to offer taxonomies of narrative rules, and, ultimately, to establish narrative grammars. To accomplish these goals they needed to codify rules by which narrative structure operates on both surface and deep levels. Vladimir Propp's formal analysis of nearly two hundred Russian folktales provided one influential model of surface narrative structure. From that analysis he derived a total of thirty-one functions, or significant constituent events, which appeared recurrently throughout the folktales in regular sequences, though no one story contained all thirty-one functions. Propp's analysis reveals three central insights: (1) that certain functions always appear together, always in the same order; (2) that functions are more fundamental to narrative structure than characters, since the characters performing the functions change from one story to the next; and (3) that functions, as invariable components of a narrative, are crucially different from variable or inessential ones. On the last point Propp's work parallels Boris Tomashevsky's distinction between bound (or plot-relevant) and free (non-plot-relevant) motifs, Barthes's (1966) nuclei and catalyzers, and Seymour Chatman's kernels and satellites.

Claude Lévi-Strauss's theory of mythic structure became the basis for understanding deep narrative structure. According to him, analyzing myths selected from different cultures can reveal insights into the way narrative competence operates worldwide. By treating myths as *parole*, and individual cultures' variations on those myths as *langue*, one could deduce that the same four-part homology underlies all myths (A is to B as C is to D) and that, owing to that deep structural unity, people from dissimilar cultures could nonetheless understand one another's myths (see also Culler).

Greimas, expanding on both Propp and Lévi-Strauss, proposes an actantial model to represent both deep and surface structures. Actants are fundamental roles in a narrative trajectory, located at a narrative's deep level, whereas actors populate the narrative's surface level. Greimas's original actantial model includes six actants: subject, object, sender, receiver, helper, and opponent. The actors who fulfill those roles, however, might vary in number and scope: several actors might occupy a single actantial role, and several actantial roles might apply to a single actor.

Like any other semiotic system, the hierarchical model of narrative structure begs the question of how deep structures are converted into surface structures to produce meaning. To answer this question, some narratologists worked toward establishing narrative grammars, which would enumerate the finite number of rules governing the combination and functioning of narrative units, explaining the production of all possible narratives. Narrative grammars are designed to explain how narrative structure and narrative competence are interdependent within a given context of semiotic conventions. Grammars depend in part on paradigmatic and syntagmatic analysis. Paradigmatic analysis examines deep structural units that may be substituted for one another in static, logical equations, but which are mutually exclusive (e.g., Greimas's semiotic squares). Syntagmatic analysis pertains to coexistent surface structural units (e.g., Propp's functions or Greimas's actors) that may be grouped together according to a variety of temporal or causal principles. Greimas, for instance, proposes three kinds of syntagms: performative (tests and struggles), contractual, and disjunctional (related to departures, returns, and displacements). Other types of narrative grammar include structuralist models that focus on the syntax and semantics of plot (Pavel), generative-transformational models that account for both story and discourse (Prince), and story

grammars that draw on research done by cognitive psychologists and specialists in artificial intelligence (Mandler and Johnson). By the mid-1980s, however, most narratologists and linguists alike concluded that the grammars produced to date had inadequate explanatory power. In the field of narratology, the rise of interest in discourse and plot dynamics reflected a widespread desire for a more supple theoretical model of narrative competence.

POSTCLASSICAL STRUCTURES

Early models of narrative structure focus more on story than on discourse, more on what the narrative depicts than on how it is depicted (see STORY). While they do not exclude discourse-related topics, such as the ordering of events in the *sjuzhet*, they demonstrate the structuralists' heavy reliance on the assumption that a story and its rendering are separable. As the field of narratology gained momentum and moved beyond its structuralist origin, many followed Genette's example in theorizing extensively and productively about narrative discourse, particularly order, duration, frequency, mood, and voice. Chatman's model proved particularly influential in the evolution from classical to postclassical concepts of structure, as he demonstrated that story and discourse may both be mapped on a single diagram of narrative structure. Chatman brings together structuralist units of narrative content (such as events, existents) and Genette's work on narrative expression. He demonstrates that content and expression, though theoretically separable, are functionally interdependent, and that our understanding of narrative structure must reflect that. Further, he depicts structure as a process of transmission (see diagram in NARRATION). Two of the postclassical phase's major innovations appear in this model: the inclusion of audience in the structure itself, and a shift from models of narrative structure as essentially static to fundamentally dynamic.

Whereas classical (structuralist) narratology identifies structural units by their generic function, postclassical narratology concentrates more closely on the relationships those units have to one another and to the reader. Moreover, what constitutes a structural unit changes considerably after the heyday of structuralism. The structure of a narrative comes to be seen as something that unfolds progressively through the act of reading, rather than as a stable construct independent of the reader's vantage. Theorists such as Edward Said, Susan Winnett, and Peter Brooks consider plot to be of primary importance in dynamically structuring both the narrative and the reader's experience, though they differ respectively on whether the wellspring of a plot's energy appears at its beginning, middle, or end. (Brooks's model of end-driven narrative structure takes up the old challenge of explaining deep structure: he posits a correspondence between plot dynamics and Freud's theories about desire and the death drive.) Elements that create suspense, delay, divagation, and indeterminacy figure prominently in postclassical narrative structure, particularly as they are deployed to amplify readerly desire. Theorists such as Wolfgang Iser and Meir Sternberg demonstrate the importance of information gaps as structuring devices that encourage the implied reader to fill in blanks, anticipate further developments, and retrospectively assess meaning in the course of reading. Poststructuralists, on the other hand, look not for unity but for instability and open-endedness, declaring that if structure exists anywhere, it resides in the reader's mind. Barthes's (1974) theory of writerly texts posits a vital interplay between the reader's reversible, revisable interpretations and "textual signifiers," each identifiable by one of five codes (hermeneutic, semiotic, proairetic, symbolic, and cultural). The writerly text allows a reader to paraphrase her reading comprehension through a series of labels as she decodes the text, but more importantly, it permits her to revise some labels as her reading progresses.

As theoretical approaches to narrative have multiplied in recent years, maintaining consistent terms and definitions has become increasingly difficult. However, two major methodologies appear poised to establish long-lasting criteria for understanding narrative structure through narrative competence: COGNITIVE and rhetorical narrative theories. Cognitive narratologists study the neurological processes involved in narrative competence, including but not restricted to perception, memory, language use, and knowledge. Research in psychology and artificial intelligence has yielded useful data about how we mentally structure our reading experience (e.g., Fludernik; Herman; Jahn), including the use of our theory of mind, or mind-reading abilities (e.g., Zunshine). Marie-Laure Ryan applies semantics and AI to her theory of the way we mentally construct storyworlds. And theorists such as Alan Palmer study cognition in fictional minds, rescuing characters' sophisticated thought processes from the rather coarse categories to which they had been consigned by structuralist analysis.

The rhetorical approach defines narrative as a communicative act—"Somebody telling somebody else on some occasion and for some purpose(s) that something happened" (Phelan)—and examines the nuanced roles of both speaker (real author, implied author, narrator) and audience (real reader, authorial audience, narrative audience, narratee) (Rabinowitz, 2006). James Phelan posits that narrative is structured according to its progression, which he defines as the simultaneous development of plot dynamics—including the mimetic, thematic, and synthetic dimensions of character construction—with the development of readerly dynamics: the audience's cognitive, affective, ethical, and aesthetic experiences as they arise from the audience's sequence of interpretive, ethical, and aesthetic judgments. Readerly judgments, especially those that occur early in a narrative, are necessarily revisable—not, as for Barthes, because of textual indeterminacy, but because the experience of reading fiction is based on a recursive relationship, constantly unfolding, among author, text, and reader. The rhetorical model of progression draws on Wayne C. Booth's theories about the way authors implicitly and explicitly shape their readers' desires in fiction, and on Rabinowitz's (1987) demonstration that narrative and textual features activate expectations we already have before reading a given text. Rabinowitz shows that our mastery of the tacit rules by which narratives operate corresponds not to a *langue* of narrative structure but to a vast set of conventions shared by authors and readers alike.

BIBLIOGRAPHY

Barthes, R. (1977), "Introduction to the Structural Analysis of Narratives," in *Image-Music-Text*, trans. S. Heath.

Barthes, R. (1974), *S/Z*.

Booth, W.C. (1983), *Rhetoric of Fiction*, 2nd ed.

Brooks, P. (1984), *Reading for the Plot*.

Chatman, S. (1978), *Story and Discourse*.

Culler, J. (1975), *Structuralist Poetics*.

Fludernik, M. (1996), *Towards a "Natural" Narratology*.

Genette, G. (1980), *Narrative Discourse*, trans. J. Lewin.

Greimas, A.J. (1983), *Structural Semantics*.

Herman, D. (2002), *Story Logic*.

Iser, W. (1974), *Implied Reader*.

Jahn, M. (1997), "Frames, References, and the Reading of Third-Person Narratives," Poetics Today 18: 441–68.

Lévi-Strauss, C. (1968), *Structural Anthropology*.

Mandler, J.M. and N. Johnson (1977), "Remembrance of Things Parsed," *Cognitive Psychology* 9:111–51.

Palmer, A. (2004), *Fictional Minds*.

Pavel, T. (1985), *Poetics of Plot*.

Phelan, J. (2007), *Experiencing Fiction*.

Prince, G. (1973), *Grammar of Stories*.

Propp, V. (1968), *Morphology of the Folktale*.

Rabinowitz, P.J. (1977), "Truth in Fiction," *Critical Inquiry* 4:121–41.

Rabinowitz, P.J. (1987), *Before Reading*.

Ryan, M.-L. (1991), *Possible Worlds, Artificial Intelligence, and Narrative Theory*.

Said, E.W. (1975), *Beginnings*.

Sternberg, M. (1978), *Expositional Modes and Temporal Ordering in Fiction*.

Tomashevsky, B. (1965 [1925]), "Thematics," in *Russian Formalist Criticism*, ed. L. T. Lemon and M. J. Reis.

Winnett, S. (1990), "Coming Unstrung," PMLA 105: 505–18.

Zunshine, L. (2006), *Why We Read Fiction*.

Narrative Technique

JAMES PHELAN

Narrative technique is the umbrella term for the multiple devices of storytelling. In the terms of narratology's distinction between story and discourse or the what and the how of narrative, narrative technique is a rough synonym for discourse. Narrative technique is so central to our understanding of storytelling that, throughout history, theorists of narrative in general (e.g., Aristotle in the *Poetics*, ca. 335 BCE) or the novel in particular (e.g., Henry Fielding in his Preface to *Joseph Andrews*, 1742) invariably comment on it. But ever since Henry James wrote his Prefaces to the New York edition of his novels (1909–10), theorists have paid increasing attention to the subject, as they have proposed and debated various ways of achieving a more adequate understanding of its workings. Here I will focus on four key concepts: transmission, temporality, vision, and voice.

NARRATIVE TRANSMISSION

Seymour Chatman (1978), building on the work of Wayne C. Booth (1983), Gerald Prince, and Gérard Genette (1972, 1980), among others, developed an influential model of communication that traces transmission from author to reader through the textual intermediaries of the implied author, narrator, narratee, and implied reader (see diagram in NARRATION).

"Implied author" is Booth's term for the version of herself that the real author constructs through her choices in writing the narrative; the "narrator" is the teller of the tale; the "narratee" is the audience (characterized or uncharacterized) addressed by the narrator; and the "implied reader" is the ideal audience addressed by the implied author.

Not surprisingly, Chatman's model has been contested in various ways. Some theorists, including Genette (1988), argue that the implied author is an unnecessary concept. Some, including Phelan (2005), endorse the concept but argue that it should be located outside the text in order to signal the implied author's role as the agent who produces the text. Others, including Richard Walsh, adopt a "no narrator" position, arguing that the author is the teller unless the novel employs a character narrator (2007, *Rhetoric of Fictionality*). There is more consensus about the audience side of the model, but Peter J. Rabinowitz has made a strong case for the explanatory value of the "narrative audience" as distinct from the narratee (1976, "Truth in Fiction," *Critical Inquiry* 4:121–41). Whereas the narratee is a textual construct identifiable through the teller's address, the narrative audience is a role the real audience takes on as it assumes an observer position in the storyworld and regards the characters and events as real. In a novel with a characterized narratee, the concepts of narratee and narrative audience nicely complement each other. In Emily Brontë's *Wuthering Heights*, Nelly Dean tells her tale to Lockwood, the outsider who does not believe in ghosts, while the narrative audience listens in and concludes that in this world ghosts roam the moors.

The various disagreements with Chatman's model nevertheless reinforce its value as a useful starting point in analyzing narrative technique. A more significant objection is that the model neglects the role of characters as independent agents of transmission because it subsumes dialogue under the narrator's reporting to the narratee. One task for the future, then, is to remedy this flaw in the model.

TEMPORALITY

Genette (1980) offers what is still the most influential analysis of techniques for representing time, as he compares time in the story to time in the discourse under the rubrics of *order, duration,* and *frequency.* Order refers to the relation between the chronological sequence of the story events and the sequence in which they appear in the discourse. In some novels there is a close match, but in others the discourse significantly rearranges the story order by means of analepsis (flashback), as in Nelly's narration in *Wuthering Heights* (Emily Brontë, 1847) or prolepsis (flashforward) (as in chap. 3 of Ian McEwan's *Atonement* (2001), when the temporal location of the narration suddenly jumps from 1935 to "six decades later.") Duration refers to the relation between the length of time an event takes and the amount of space given to it in the novel. The events of many years can be narrated in a single sentence, and an event that takes a few seconds can be narrated over many pages. Frequency refers to the relation between the number of times an event occurs and the number of times it is narrated. Singulative narration recounts once what happens once: "Reader, I married him" (Charlotte Brontë, 1847, *Jane Eyre*); iterative narration recounts once an event that occurs many times: "Every morning the world flung itself over and exposed itself to the sun" (Zora Neale Hurston, 1937, *Their Eyes Were Watching God*). Repeating narration reports multiple times an event that happens once, as in Joseph Heller's revisiting of the scene of Snowden's death in *Catch-22* (1961).

David Herman (2002, *Story Logic*) has built on and revised Genette's work by noting that not all novels allow us to specify fully the temporal relations between story and discourse. In such cases we have what Herman calls "fuzzy temporality." Brian Richardson (2007, *Unnatural Voices*) goes further and argues that Genette's model does not work well for what he calls the "unnatural narration" of novels that eschew mimesis in favor of other effects and that deliberately frustrate any efforts to find a clear sequence of story events.

VISION

Genette (1980) astutely observes that the term "point of view" conflates two different concepts, voice (the answer to the question, "who speaks or tells?") and vision ("who sees or perceives?"), an observation that paved the way for more precise understandings of author—narrator—character—audience relationships. Genette proposed a taxonomy of three kinds of vision or what he called focalization, based on the ratio between the narrator's knowledge and characters' knowledge. In zero (or free) focalization, the narrator's knowledge exceeds that of the characters (e.g., the first

chapter of *Bleak House*). In internal focalization, the narrator's knowledge is equal to the character's knowledge (e.g., James's center of consciousness narration). In external focalization, the narrator's knowledge is less than the character's knowledge because the narrator does not have access to the character's consciousness (e.g., Dashiell Hammett, 1930, *The Maltese Falcon*—Genette's example).

Virtually all theorists accept Genette's initial distinction between vision and voice, but many have sought to improve his specific account of vision. Mieke Bal, for example, pays more attention to the agent and the object of focalization. This attention reduces Genette's three types of focalization to two: that by the narrator (zero and external focalization) and that by the character (internal focalization). Other theorists such as Chatman (1990) object to regarding both narrators and characters as focalizers since that conception violates the boundary between story (the realm of characters) and discourse (the realm of narrators). Still other theorists such as Phelan and Manfred Jahn side with Bal rather than Chatman. Phelan (2005) suggests that rather than basing a taxonomy of focalization on ratios of knowledge between narrator and character we should base it on the possible combinations of their visions and voices: narrator's focalization and voice; character's focalization and voice; character's focalization, narrator's voice; narrator's focalization, character's voice; and blends of vision and voice as in much free indirect discourse. Jahn emphasizes that focalization can vary along a spectrum from weakly to strongly located, and that it can be either on-line (about objects immediately within the perceptual frame) or off-line (about objects outside that frame). Jahn also notes that perception is not simply visual, a point that Herman has developed in suggesting that theorists replace the term focalization with the term conceptualization, which would include the cognitive activities associated with all aspects of our embodied human experience. Like Herman, Alan Palmer moves beyond focalization as he emphasizes what he calls the thought-action continuum and the way representations of characters' consciousness can be indicated by descriptions of behavior as well as thought (2010, *Social Minds in the Novel*). In addition, he calls attention to novelistic representations of intermental (or group) thinking, and, thus, identifies the "social mind" of many novels.

VOICE

Genette (1980), with characteristic insight, points out that a taxonomy of narrators based on grammatical person is imprecise because any narrator can use the first-person. He proposes an alternative model, his Diegetic Family Tree, that seeks precision by attending to the crisscrossing branches of (1) the narrator's participation in the action (participants are homodiegetic and nonparticipants heterodiegetic) and (2) location along various narrative levels. The level at which the main action takes place is the diegetic; narration at that level (e.g., Nelly's telling to Lockwood) is intradiegetic; narration above (about) that level (e.g., George Eliot's narrator's telling to the uncharacterized narratee in *Middlemarch*, 1871–72) is extradiegetic; and narration embedded within the diegetic level (a character narrating a story told by a different character) is hypodiegetic. Thus, different combinations of participation and level are possible: the *Middlemarch* narrator is heterodiegetic—extradiegetic, while Jane Eyre's retrospection marks her as homodiegetic—extradiegetic. A character who narrates a story about others (e.g., Sam Spade's account of Flitcraft in *The Maltese Falcon*) is heterodiegetic-in-

tradiegetic, while one who narrates a story about himself (e.g., the Man of the Hill in Henry Fielding's *Tom Jones*, 1749) is homodiegetic-intradiegetic.

Mikhail BAKHTIN work on voice goes beyond concerns with form to those of IDEOLOGY. His core principles are that any use of language always carries with it some ideological force and that the novel is the genre characterized by the interaction of multiple voices and their attendant ideologies (heteroglossia). More particularly, he examines what he calls double-voiced discourse, narration in which a single utterance contains two voices. In the first sentence of *Pride and Prejudice* (1813), "It is a truth universally acknowledged that a single man in possession of a good fortune must be in want of a wife," Jane Austen juxtaposes the voice of someone such as Mrs. Bennet who would utter the statement as gospel, and that of someone such as Mr. Bennet, or of course Austen herself, who would utter it ironically and thereby undermine the ideological values implicit in the first voice.

Bakhtin's concept of double-voicing connects nicely with Booth's concept of distance as a key variable in our understanding of the relationships among authors, narrators, and audiences. In Austen's sentence author, narrator, and implied reader stand together as they distance themselves from the ideology of the literal statement. In unreliable narration, on Booth's account, implied author and implied reader stand together as they distance themselves from the narrator. Phelan (2005) has extended Booth's model by observing that because narrators perform three main functions—reporting about facts, characters, and events; interpreting those entities; and evaluating them—they can be unreliable by underreporting or misreporting, underinterpreting or misinterpreting, and underevaluating or misevaluating. In addition, Phelan (2007a) argues that any one kind of unreliability can either increase or decrease the interpretive, affective, or ethical distance between narrator and implied reader, and, thus, the effects of unreliability can range along a spectrum from strong bonding at one end to extreme estranging at the other.

FEMINIST theorists combine Genette's interest in the formal dimensions of voice with Bakhtin's interest in its political and ideological dimensions as they consider the gender politics of technique. Robyn Warhol (1989, *Gendered Interventions*) analyzes direct address by heterodiegetic narrators to their narratees in nineteenth-century British fiction and finds a pattern of "engaging" addresses by female authors and "distancing" addresses by male authors. Susan S. Lanser (1992, *Fictions of Authority*) argues that narrative authority is a function of both the rhetorical and social properties of any given voice, and she analyzes the various strategies—and the attendant risks—that women authors have employed to claim or to eschew authority in different cultural and historical contexts. Alison Case (1999, *Plotting Women*) identifies and explores the formal and political dimensions of "feminine" narration in the eighteenth- and nineteenth-century British novel, i.e., narration by a narrator, male or female, who is unable either to plot or to preach, unable to shape the tale into a well-designed configuration with a central thematic point.

CONCLUSION

The careful study of narrative technique that began with James continues to develop as theorists carry out such projects as exploring the links between technique and ethics (see Booth, 1988; Newton, 1995, *Narrative Ethics*; Phelan, 2007a) and analyzing the various phenomena of unnatural narration. Since narrative technique is so central to the art and power of the novel and since nove-

lists themselves continue to invent new ways of telling stories, we can expect the past century's close attention to narrative technique to continue into the foreseeable future.

BIBLIOGRAPHY

Bakhtin, M.M. (1981), "Discourse in the Novel," in *Dialogic Imagination*, trans. C. Emerson.

Bal, M. (2009), *Narratology*, trans. C. van Boheemen, 3rd ed.

Booth, W.C. (1988), *Company We Keep*.

Booth, W.C. (1983), *Rhetoric of Fiction*, 2nd ed.

Chatman, S. (1990), *Coming to Terms*.

Chatman, S. (1978), *Story and Discourse*.

Genette, G. (1972), *Figures III*.

Genette, G. (1980), *Narrative Discourse*, trans. J. Lewin.

Genette, G. (1988), *Narrative Discourse Revisited*, trans. J. Lewin.

Herman, D. (2009), "Beyond Voice and Vision," in *Point of View, Perspective, Focalization*, ed. P. Hühn, W. Schmid, and J. Schönert.

Jahn, M. (2007), "Focalization," in *Cambridge Companion to Narrative*, ed. D. Herman.

Phelan, J. (2005), *Living to Tell about It*.

Phelan, J. (2007a), "Estranging Unreliability, Bonding Unreliability, and the Ethics of *Lolita*," *Narrative* 15: 222–38.

Phelan, J. (2007b), *Experiencing Fiction*.

Prince, G. (1973), "Introduction à l'étude du narrataire," *Poetique* 14:178–96.

Narratology *see* Narration; Narrative; Narrative Structure; Narrative Technique; Story/Discourse

Narrator

PAUL McCORMICK

Narrator refers to the mediating agent through whom an author presents a narrative. To the question, who tells?, the answer is always "the narrator." (However, there is a minority position that argues for versions of the "no-narrator theory," explained later.) But importantly, it is not always the answer to the other key question of narration in a novel, through whose perception do we understand the story? That is a question of point of view or focalization, for the narrator may tell the story not through his or her own perspective, but rather through those of characters in the story's world.

Authors assign narrators specific features in order to achieve specific effects, and much research about narrators entails distinctions among their possible features. In fact, a more specialized definition of a narrator is: a collection of various features (traits, beliefs, ethics, linguistic habits, and ultimately functions) assigned by an author to a designated storyteller. Distinguishing among different types of narrators allows readers to better understand the selection of features from which authors can choose and why they select and combine certain features. In general, two critical concepts have proven particularly useful in conceptualizing the possible relations among those features and effects: the Proteus Principle and the concept of narrative situations. Meir Sternberg's Proteus Principle states that "there are no package deals in narration" because there are "many-to-many correspondences between linguistic form and representational function" (1982, 112). With respect to narrators, the Proteus Principle indicates that any particular narrative feature may lead to a wide range of narrative effects because the effects depend not just on that feature but also on many other elements of narrative. In a way, the Proteus Principle helps to qualify and balance the concepts of narrators and of narrative situations as previously developed in classical studies by Gérard Genette and Franz Stanzel. For Stanzel, a narrative situation conceptualizes narrators as bundles or arrangements of different features relating to their identity, point of view, and degree of intrusion.

While different features can lead to different effects, understanding how different features are often bundled together allows readers to compare the similarities and differences among different types of narrators and offers a point of reference for generalizing about the sort of effects authors have historically achieved with different combinations of narrator features.

Accordingly, this entry begins by describing two fundamental ways of distinguishing among narrators: identifying a given narrator's participation in STORY and the level of her narration in relation to the primary action-level (Genette, 227–62). Then, the article uses three sections to discuss Stanzel's three narrative situations: authorial, figural, first-person—and some larger issues related to each.

NARRATOR PARTICIPATION AND NARRATIVE LEVELS

A fundamental distinction of novelistic technique is whether a given narrator is participatory (and physically present) or non-participatory (and physically absent) in the story she is telling (see NARRATIVE TECHNIQUE). In the past and less frequently today, this distinction was often roughly made by both authors and critics who relied on a grammatical opposition between "third-person" and "first-person" narrators. However, as Genette points out, this grammatically based taxonomy is too imprecise because any narrator can use the first-person and almost all use the third. Genette suggests that a better way of making the appropriate distinction is to distinguish between narrators who are able to participate in the narrated action (homodiegetic) and those who are not (heterodiegetic). In addition to participation, Genette identifies narrative levels as another key variable influencing a narrator's telling. Here, I prefer the term *external narrator* to replace heterodiegetic narrator (third-person) and *character narrator* to replace homodiegetic narrator (first-person).

The distinction between external and character narrators is essential because it is tied to their respective epistemological privileges. The storyworld non-participation of external narrators can correlate to a privileged and even unworldly knowledge of characters and events; e.g., some external narrators have full and unmediated access to the interior mental and emotional states of several characters. In contrast, the realistic conventions of character narration usually demand that these narrators restrict their reports to what they witnessed or can retrospectively infer from their experiences in the storyworld. Character narrators can be very knowledgeable indeed, even with respect to the inner lives of other characters. However, character narrators' special knowledge of the inner workings of other characters must be justified (i.e., motivated, naturalized) or readers may suspect their claims of knowledge. In contrast, it is a literary convention that external narrators may have complete and reliable access to the inner lives of characters without explanation (see DISCOURSE). If an external narrator quotes a character's thought, readers typically take the quotation as wholly accurate.

The concept of narrative level places acts of narrating (and thus individual narrators) and narrated stories in relation to the entire narrative of which they are parts. There may be many narrating acts and many narrated stories in one novel, and consequently many narrative levels and narrators, which narrative theorists have proposed various terminologies to describe and analyze. Here I draw primarily upon Genette's model to outline a procedural approach for placing narrators on narrative levels. The first step is to determine whether a narrator is an external narrator or a character narrator. The

second step is to identify the primary action-level of a novel, often called its diegesis in reference to Genettian vocabulary. For example, Genette uses the term extradiegetic to signal a narrator once-removed from this primary action-level, and intradiegetic to signal a narrator telling a story on that primary action-level. However, I prefer to speak in terms of *remove* from the primary action-level while retaining Genette's concepts. For example in Gustave Flaubert's *Madame Bovary* (1857), Rodolphe's seduction of Emma Bovary is part of the primary action-level (pt. II, chap. 9); this narrative level should be distinguished from the one occupied by the external narrator; it should also be distinguished from the world and actions described in *Lucie de Lammermoor*, an opera which Emma attends (pt. II, chap. 15). The third step is to ask whether the narrator is narrating the main level of action at one remove (a narrator at one-remove) or if the narrating act occurs at the same level as the primary action-level (a narrator at zero-remove). In other words, at how many removes is a particular narrator from the novel's primary action-line?

Once these first three steps are completed, readers can execute the final step of identifying what level a particular external or character narrator occupies. For example, George Eliot's external narrator in *Middlemarch* (1871–72) operates at a single remove from the primary action-line (external narrator at one-remove). While Joseph Conrad's Marlow functions as a character-narrator in *Heart of Darkness* (1902), he also narrates at one-remove because he retrospectively narrates the novel's primary action-line (character narrator at one-remove). Both external and character narrators can also narrate at zero-remove. For example, in James Joyce's short story, "The Two Gallants" (1914), Corley narrates on the same narrative level as the primary action-line when he tells Lenehan how he first seduced the maid he will meet later, so Lenehan is a character narrator at zero-remove from the primary action-level (but one-remove from his story about the maid). Compare this to the "Hades" episode of Joyce's *Ulysses* (1922) when Martin Cunningham tells Mr. Power that Rudolph Virag poisoned himself (6:529). Martin was a non-participant in the story of Virag's suicide, but it occurs on the same narrative level as his current ride to the cemetery. So in this instance, Martin Cunningham functions as an external narrator at zero-remove. These four combinations of narrative features are Genette's version of narrative situations because they represent four common combinations of types of narrators and narrative levels. However, Genette notes that other options exist in novels with multiple narrative levels. For example, narrators can be several times removed from the primary action-line (e.g, narrators at twice-remove). In addition, several narrators can exist at the same narrative level, as in the first three narrators of William Faulkner's 1929 *The Sound and the Fury* (serial narrators). In each case, however, the primary action-line (the diegesis) is the baseline from which all distinctions regarding narrative level are made.

EXTERNAL NARRATORS AND THE AUTHORIAL NARRATIVE SITUATION

The negative correlation between story participation and story knowledge is strong enough that the two most famous studies of narrators differ on what primarily defines an external narrator: Are narrators of novels like William Makepeace Thackeray's *Vanity Fair (1848)*, Anthony Trollope's *Barchester Towers* (1857), and Henry Fielding's *Tom Jones* (1749) defined by their non-participation in the story or by their unworldly knowledge (omniscience)? Generally, as in

this entry, the distinction between participation and non-participation is held to distinguish external narrators and character narrators, respectively. But when Franz Stanzel offers his classic definition of the authorial narrative situation, he has good reason to discuss a prototypical external narrator (his "authorial" narrator) as one whose unworldly knowledge or omniscience is her primary trait. In his model, the opposite of an authorial narrator is not a character narrator, but a limited point of view. Certain external narrators like those of *Vanity Fair* and *Tom Jones* do seem to flaunt their omniscience to the point where it becomes their dominant characteristic, and controlling the knowledge of both characters and readers is crucial to authors' narrative techniques. However as Dorrit Cohn (1978) notes, unworldly knowledge means that the narrator exists out of the world, that in some sense the unworldly perspective of Stanzel's authorial narrator means that she is also Genette's non-participatory narrator. Still, there are gradations of omniscience among external narrators who are primarily defined by their non-participation in the storyworld. While non-participation/participation is key to discerning between external narrators and character narrators, the difference between Genette and Stanzel reminds us that non-participation is often bundled with privileged knowledge, to varying degrees.

Traditionally called "omniscient narrators" in Anglo-American literary criticism are the external, once-removed narrators like those of *Vanity Fair*, *Middlemarch* or Leo Tolstoy's *Voyná I mir* (1865–69, *War and Peace*) that offer "inside views" of many characters in the storyworld, often commenting on the narrative world and reporting not just characters' actions, speech, and writing, but also their emotions and cognition. As Stanzel observed, these narrators were particularly popular in nineteenth-century Euro-American novels and less popular in the twentieth century. However, Stanzel prefers the term "authorial narrator" to refer to such narrators, and the terminological value of "omniscient narration" has been recently contested. Detractors of the term consider it a sloppy analogy with untenable theological freight because we do not know the characteristics of any deity to make the comparison (e.g., Culler); however, its supporters note that many authors have made the same analogy of "godlike" powers and that some external narrators do exercise unusual and even divine knowledge as mediators of the narrative world (e.g., Olson). Salman Rushdie's novel *The Satanic Verses* (1988) offers a good example of a contemporary author having some fun with the concept of omniscience when his external narrator says, "I know the truth, obviously. I watched the whole thing. As to omnipresence and -potence, I'm making no claims at present, but I can manage this much, I hope. Chamcha willed it and Farishta did what was willed. Which was the miracle worker? Of what type—angelic, satanic—was Farishta's song? Who am I? Let's put it this way: who has the best tunes?" (pt. 1, sec. 1). Although sometimes, as in the case of *Satanic Verses*, the connection between some narrators and omniscience deserves exploration, most external narrators offer inside views of only selected characters.

Stanzel's term *authorial* narration also suggests how the greater epistemological privilege enjoyed by external narrators and removed narrators (once-remove or more) can conventionally signal closer proximity between the implied judgments, norms, and ethics of the author and those of the narrator. But this also helps to explain why twentieth-century authors tend to use external narration less frequently than nineteenth-century authors. In the middle of the twentieth century, Percy Lubbock used the terms "showing" versus "telling" to discuss the same distinction as it pertains to the novel. For Lubbock, the journals of Henry James revealed a prescriptive difference between the two: showing is always preferable to a narrator telling. What Lubbock meant was that a story should be presented as if unmediated by the presence and opinion of a narrator, that a dramatic style of presentation was best. However, Wayne Booth made two influential observations in reply, first, that an omniscient narrator who uses intrusive commentary to comment upon the story is often just as appropriate and artistic for a particular story, and second, that strictly speaking, showing in the novel genre is impossible anyways because some agent must mediate or narrate the action. Today, the distinction between direct and indirect speech and thought representation is not prescriptive but descriptive and often analytically so: identifying whether speech and thought is represented directly or indirectly can often provide important information about the narrator, including the specific relations between the narrator and a given character.

Narrators represent and communicate ethics, history, and politics as well as epistemology when authors select and combine their features. When Mikhail BAKHTIN's influential scholarship was first widely received in the U.S. in the 1980s, it became clear that a specialized formal study of narrators could be strengthened by studying the historical and ideological inflections of narrators and their discourses (see IDEOLOGY). As Brian McHale puts it, "Of course, it is precisely his insistence on historicizing language, on restoring it to its place in a historically contingent social realm, that has made Bakhtin so congenial to so many varieties of historicist and contextualist theory in our own time" (63). For example, FEMINIST narratologists have made significant contributions to "the study of narrative structures and strategies in the context of cultural constructions of gender" (Warhol, 21) with a Bakhtinian-inflected dual interest in history and form. Many of these studies have broad implications for the study of narrators. For example, Susan Lanser (1992) has shown how women writers can use the authority conventionally granted to external narrators to establish their discursive authority but also to question the origins of that authority. Robyn Warhol has made an influential distinction between external *distancing* narrators who discourage the actual reader from identifying with the narratee (the textual recipient of the narrator's telling), and external *engaging* narrators who encourage actual readers to identify with the narratee. Building upon the foundational work of D. A. Miller and Gerald Prince, respectively, Warhol has recently detailed how classifying and attending to what narrators do not narrate, what she calls "the unnarrated," often reveals much about authorial purpose, social norms, and GENRE identification. A wide variety of historical approaches, including those of feminist narratology, have helped to clarify the implications of various narrator features for actual authors and readers.

External narrators can be dramatized to different degrees, and often they do not self-identify their GENDER, RACE, ethnicity, SEXUALITY, etc. Ungendered narrators pose an additional practical problem for literary criticism—how should one refer to the narrator if she or he is left ungendered and unnamed, as in Austen's *Emma* (1815)? As a result, many scholars follow what has become known as Lanser's rule: In the absence of any text-internal clues to the narrator's sex, use the pronoun appropriate to the author's sex. Assume that the narrator is male if the author is male, and that the narrator is female if the author is female (Lanser, 1981, 166–8). This rule is not without its complications, for it adds personal qualities to the narrator that the author apparently did not specify, and disambiguates what the author may have left purposely ambiguous. All the same, it is sometimes awkward to discuss a hypothetical narrator, which is why I alternate between he and she in this article. Lanser's rule makes for easier practical reference and also sets a standard that can be challenged in appropriate cases.

However, the existence of such a rule evokes more significant questions, especially for external narrators. For example, should narrators be interpreted anthropomorphically when there is little textual support for such an interpretive decision? In other words, should one assume that external narrators are always somehow human and attribute to them full human qualities? And why always assume the presence of a narrator (human-like or not) instead of attributing the narration directly to the author (implied or otherwise)? The answers to these questions can depend upon the particular narrative in question: e.g., on the degree of the narrator's consciousness of their narration, whether the narrator offers commentary and judgment, and whether the narrator's voice is distinctive. Toward one end of the continuum one could place external narrators yet personal narrators like those of *Vanity Fair* or *Tom Jones*, and on the other end, some of the more impersonal external narrators of Ernest Hemingway's "The Killers" (1927), John Dos Passos's *The Big Money* (1936), or Alain Robbe-Grillet's *La Jalousie* (1957, *Jealousy*).

But answers also depend upon readers' assumptions about narrators. The claim that there is always a narrator in every story largely derives from the assumption that literary narration is a kind of speech or communication act, in which someone must necessarily speak to someone else. That is why many communication models are symmetrical, with an implied author speaking to an implied reader, a narrator speaking to a narratee, and the real author speaking to the real reader, as in the influential communicative model developed by Seymour Chatman (see diagram in NARRATION). Conversely, the claim that there need not be a narrator—called the no-narrator theory—often derives from linguistic analyses in which acts of speech and thought are traced to certain grammatical agents—all of which must exist in the narration's syntax because expressivity is located in grammar (e.g., Banfield). From this perspective, the concept of voices is subordinated to deictic centers, linguistic centers of consciousness whose use of directional and temporal words like "here" and "then" spatially and temporally situate them in the storyworld (see SPACE, TIME). Some no-narrator approaches argue that the narrator is not always an inherent element of narration, while Richard Walsh argues more radically against any necessary qualitative distinction between narrators and characters: "The narrator is always either a character who narrates or the author" (505). POSTMODERN and experimental texts often seem to delight in raising theoretical as well as hermeneutic questions about a narrator's humanity or gender, and recent studies of "unnatural" narrators have brought the possibility of non-anthropomorphic narrators to the fore (e.g., Richardson; Alber). In general, it seems likely that individual authors differ on whether or not their narrators are always anthropomorphic beings, just as readers and theorists do.

REFLECTORS AND THE FIGURAL NARRATIVE SITUATION

The type of narration in which the narrator seems most withdrawn, covert, or absent is often reflector narration, or what Stanzel calls the figural narrative situation. Narratives using this mode of narration can appear to have no narrator at all because the story is told through the perspective of a single character without his or her knowledge. Examples of reflector narration include Joyce's *The Portrait of the Artist as a Young Man* (1916) and James's *The Ambassadors* (1903). At first, such novels seem to have neither an external nor a character narrator because the narration offers the ostensibly unmediated thoughts of only one character, but those thoughts are presented in the third person. As Käte Hamburger once noted, it is only in literature that the I-originarity of another's self can be presented in the third person as if from their very own perspective. And in chap. 1 of Joyce's *Portrait*, for example, we see this I-originarity in the third person without the intrusive presence of an external narrator when we read sentences like, "He had to undress and then kneel and say his own prayers and be in bed before the gas was lowered so that he might not go to hell when he died" (30). But although we thus gain unworldly access to Stephen's thoughts, the third-person syntax reveals that it is not Stephen who tells the story.

But while for some critics this novel may have no narrator, most would say that novels like *Portrait* are narrated by external narrators but reflected through the consciousness of a particular character. In other words, the "voice" is that of an external narrator who is looking through Stephen's "vision." Reflector narration is an important subset of external narration, but it is a subset: the narrator is an external, covert narrator who is merely choosing to perceive the world as reflected through a character's consciousness (see NARRATIVE PERSPECTIVE). For authors, the advantages of reflector narration are several. First, readers may be more willing to identify with a character who is not consciously crafting his identity through the narrative. Whatever Stephen's faults, we know he is not performing for the authorial audience. Second, the author may restrict her ideal reader's knowledge more naturally, i.e., with less sense that the author is tricking her. This explains why Stanzel locates the figural narrative situation next to limited point of view. For example, because we see through Strether's consciousness, we are more apt to learn about the affair between Chad Newsome and Mme. Vionnet only when he does, toward the novel's end. Third, the ostensibly "unmediated" access can allow a fuller exploration of changing and unusual minds because it puts the reader's focus on the consciousness and not the mediator (see PSYCHOLOGICAL).

CHARACTER NARRATORS AND THE FIRST-PERSON NARRATIVE SITUATION

A character narrator is defined by her participation in the narrative she actively mediates; or as Stanzel puts it in his description of the first-person narrative situation, the realms of existence of the character and the storyworld must be identical. However, the degree of a character narrator's participation can vary considerably, from narrators who mostly observe the primary action line like Conrad's Marlow in *Lord Jim* (1899–1900) to narrators who are the protagonists of the primary action line like Brontë's eponymous Jane Eyre. In addition, character narrators vary in terms of artistic control and self-consciousness (Sternberg, 2008) because authors motivate their narrators in different ways—i.e., they can choose from many possible explanations for why the narrator delivers the narration, or offer no explanation at all. So although all character narrators lead double lives as narrators and characters, as a narrating-I and an experiencing-I, authors may emphasize

a character narrator's life as a character, her function *qua* narrator, or attend equally to both.

One challenge of character narration is that the author must communicate to the authorial audience through the character narrator's story to his narrative audience. From this perspective, character narrator is an "art of indirection" because the author must communicate indirectly through the limited perspective and realistic communicative frame of the character narrator's story to a dramatized or undramatized narratee that cannot be the actual reader (Phelan). Accordingly, rhetorical narratologist James Phelan has made an influential distinction between "disclosure functions" and "narrator functions." A character narrator's disclosure functions involve the information of all kinds that the author wants to indirectly reveal to the actual reader. Narrator functions involve all the information that the narrator directly gives to her narratee. The value of this distinction is that it can explain why narrators sometimes offer their narratee information that he or she would presumably already know, what Phelan calls "redundant telling": because the author needs to disclose that information to the authorial audience. Similarly, sometimes character narrators do not reveal their full relevant knowledge immediately, what Phelan calls "paradoxical paralepsis," because the author needs to keep that information hidden, perhaps for plot tension. In short, the distinction between disclosure functions and telling functions helps readers consider the author's purposes for the character narrator's discourse.

As Wayne Booth first articulated, the personalization of character narrators especially evokes the question of (un)reliability: In what ways do the norms, values, and judgments of the narrator resemble or diverge from the implied author as recoverable from the narration? (Un)reliability remains a significant subject of study with respect to character narrators. Much debate focuses on the definition and utility of the implied author as a way of studying (un)reliability. For example, some critics define the implied author as a purely textual construct, others as a streamlined version of the real author. Still others argue that the implied author concept is not a useful way of understanding unreliable narration. In general, the implied author concept takes significant importance in the author-centric approaches that seek to know the author's intention (McCormick). This research has shown that character narrators can be (un)reliable with regard to their facts, interpretations, or judgments (Phelan, 50) and their reliability can change at different points in the narrative discourse. In contrast, reader-centric approaches emphasize that the hypothesis of unreliability is only one way that readers can account for anomalies in the text, especially if they don't center their reading on authorial intention (Yacobi). In general, unreliability studies intersect with many other questions, including the historical reception of texts, how readers make textual judgments, and author/reader relations, and so will likely continue to be a rich area of research in the future.

Just as (implied) authors have various relations with their character narrators, narrating-I's have various relations with those versions of themselves living in the primary-action level, the experiencing-I. Cohn (1978) makes a valuable distinction between "consonant" narrators, who identify with their experiencing-I, and "dissonant" narrators, who claim moral and intellectual distance from their former selves. For Cohn these categories can apply to external narration as well, but her terms are especially valuable to discuss character narration, and particularly when the experiencing-I is the protagonist of the primary-action level, as in J. D. Salinger's *The Catcher in the Rye* (1951) or Dickens's *David Copperfield* (1850).

Another important relationship involving character narrators is that between a narrator and the communities they may represent. Bakhtin discusses how the speech register of a particular character or narrator may represent an entire community of people who use the same kind of ideologically inflected language. Susan Lanser (1992) has shown that in novels like Sarah Orne Jewett's *The Country of the Pointed Firs* (1896), the narrator can situate herself inside the community she seeks to represent, and to some extent become an "I" that speaks for "we." Such communal voices are interesting similarities and differences from those novels that actually use "we" to represent a particular community, like in Conrad's *The Nigger of the Narcissus* or the opening of Gustave Flaubert's *Madame Bovary*. (For more on "we" narration, see Richardson, 37–60; and Margolin, 591–618.)

FUTURE STUDY

Recent studies of narrators have brought much needed attention to the use of simultaneous narration, camera-eye, and "unnatural" narrators of all types, including those in novels and short stories of dubious or limited narrativity. In addition, second-person narration is a particularly interesting case of "unnatural" narration because it does not fit cleanly into any of Stanzel's or Genette's categories (Fludernik 1996, 226; Richardson, 28). These are promising research topics for the future, as are studies of narrators in postcolonial novels and in different genres and media.

SEE ALSO: Editing, Formalism, Linguistics, Narrative Structure, Rhetoric and Figurative Language, Speech Act Theory, Story/Discourse.

BIBLIOGRAPHY

Alber, J. (2009), "Impossible storyworlds—and what to do with them," *Storyworlds* 1:79–96.

Bakhtin, M.M. (1981), *Dialogic Imagination*, ed. C. Emerson, and M. Holquist.

Banfield, A. (1982), *Unspeakable Sentences*.

Booth, W.C. (1983), *Rhetoric of Fiction*, 2nd ed.

Chatman, S. (1990), *Coming to Terms*.

Cohn, D. (1978), *Transparent Minds*.

Cohn, D. (1981), "The Encirclement of Narrative," *Poetics Today* 2:157–82.

Culler, J. (2004), "Omniscience," *Narrative* 12(1): 22–34.

Fludernik, M. (1996), *Towards a "Natural" Narratology*.

Genette, G. (1980), *Narrative Discourse*.

Hamburger, K. (1973), *Logic of Literature*, trans. M. J. Rose.

Lanser, S.S. (1981), *Narrative Act*.

Lanser, S.S. (1992), *Fictions of Authority*.

Lubbock, P. (1921), *Craft of Fiction*.

Margolin, U. (2000), "Telling in the Plural," *Poetics Today* 21(3):591–618.

McCormick, P. (2009), "Claims of Stable Identity and (Un)reliability in Dissonant Narration," *Poetics Today* 30(2):317–52.

McHale, B. (2008), "Ghosts and Monsters," in *Blackwell Companion to Narrative Theory*, ed. J. Phelan and P. Rabinowitz.

Miller, D.A. (1981), *Narrative and its Discontents*.

Olson, B.K. (1997), *Authorial Divinity in the Twentieth Century*.

Phelan, J. (2005), *Living to Tell About It*.

Richardson, B. (2006), *Unnatural Voices*.

Stanzel, F.K. (1984), *Theory of Narrative*, trans. C. Goedsche.

Sternberg, M. (1978), *Expositional Modes and Temporal Ordering in Fiction*.

Sternberg, M. (1982), "Proteus in Quotation-Land," *Poetics Today* 3:107–56.

Sternberg, M. (2008), "Self-Consciousness as a Narrative Feature," in *Blackwell Companion to Narrative Theory*, ed. J. Phelan and P. Rabinowitz.

Walsh, R. (1997), "Who is the Narrator?," *Poetics Today* 18(4):495–513.

Warhol, R. (1986), "Toward a Theory of the Engaging Narrator," *Papers of the Modern Language Association* 101(5):811–18.

Warhol, R. (2008), "Neonarrative; or, How to Render the Unnarratable in Realist Fiction and Contemporary Film," in *Blackwell Companion to Narrative Theory*, ed. J. Phelan, and P. Rabinowitz.

Yacobi, T. (2001), "Package Deals in Fictional Narrative," *Narrative* 9:223–9.

National Literature

IMRE SZEMAN

Even as it was in the process of being established at the end of the eighteenth and early nineteenth centuries, the productivity and function of the concept of "national literature" was already being questioned. National literature and its apparent opposite—world literature—find their origins in German Romanticism. The intimate, organic connection between land, language and people (captured in the concept of *Volksgeist*, or "national spirit") that lies at the heart of all understandings of national literature owes a great deal to the ideas of Johann Gottfried von Herder (1744–1803); the first expression of the concept of a *Weltliteratur* (world literature) was made by Herder's contemporary, Johann Wolfgang von Goethe. This origin of opposites from the same conceptual terrain is less surprising than it might seem. From our contemporary perspective, it is all too easy to imagine that the idea of national literature has been gradually superseded by ideas of world literature, global culture, and cosmopolitanism—the xenophobia and false limits of the national giving way over time to the borderless imaginings that we (too quickly) assign to contemporary cultural production. But in literature the "world" was always already a category that unsettled the assertion of the national. Goethe's scattered comments on world literature show how the consolidation of a number of discrete national-literary fields immediately opens up its opposite: the possibility of encountering numerous literary traditions as a form of enlightened training in both difference and the common humanity thought to be expressed incompletely in each national form.

Despite these uncertain foundations, the idea of national literature has proven to be remarkably durable—perhaps the single most durable literary-critical concept, having changed little in its core precepts over more than two centuries, and continuing to be the predominant form into which literatures and literary study are institutionally organized throughout the world. Fundamentally, "national literature" expresses the belief that one of the most significant elements in shaping literary expression—and thus guiding literary criticism in its analysis of texts as well—is the national SPACE or culture out of which it originates. That a political form—the nation—would be imagined as having such a decisive impact on aesthetics and culture is directly related to the powerful IDEOLOGICAL work that the idea of the nation has performed since it began to be used in at the end of the eighteenth century. In *Treatise on the Origin of Language* (1772), the unfinished *Outline of a Philosophical History of Humanity* (1776), and other works, Herder argued that it was essential to see that there were deep connections between geography and history, and as a consequence, the development of languages and cultures as well. For Herder, specificities of place and historical experience gave rise to linguistic (see LINGUISTICS) and cultural differences to which of necessity linguists and historians had to carefully attend. They also gave rise to *Volk* (distinct peoples) shaped by these specific circumstances, each of whom would find representation in discrete political forms. In Herder's thought, there is a conflation between RACE, culture, language, and nation; as he writes, "every nation is one people, having its own national form, as well as its own

language" (166). Long held as one of the structuring assumptions of modernity, this equation of land, language, and people in the form of the nation has continued to shape geopolitics and culture even in the global present, a time that is often imagined as being post-national by definition.

What has always been most ideologically suspect about the concept of the nation lies in its powerful inversion of historical cause and effect. Herder's aim in his account of the development of the *Volk* was to insist that languages and cultures had to be seen as expressions of particular people at a particular time. This attention to the specifics of history challenged universalistic accounts of social development and pointed to the necessity of analyzing peoples and cultures on their own grounds, as opposed to through a temporal measure of universal human development. On its own, this insistence on the importance of material reality and on the interrelation of mind and matter expresses a significant development in social and cultural historiography. At its most productive, the concept of national literature draws attention to the ways in which material realities shape literary expression. However, by making "nation" and "people" into organic, universal concepts as opposed to understanding them as historical and political ones, Herder and other early theorists of the nation made each into natural, necessary forms in ways that have proven surprisingly difficult to shake.

The idea that the natural "container" or "unit" of cultures is the nation is a political invention. States do not develop organically out of the material of national cultures at the end of a long process of emergence—the effect of a cause that begins in the soil of geography. Rather, states *invent* nations as a way of legitimating and giving material and imaginative substance to those geographic spaces over which they claim sovereignty (Gellner; Hobsbawm). The end result of the governing fiction of the nation—i.e., that it represents the political expression of a real as opposed to an essentially arbitrary isomorphism between land and culture—has played an essential role in virtually every instance of human conflict and deprivation over the past two centuries. Belief in nation and national culture has enabled wars of sovereign states against one another (through a logic of "us" versus "them" and the necessity of defense of one's homeland), justified internal suppressions of all manner of differences, legitimated zones of inclusion and exclusion along arbitrary geographic borderlines, and produced particularly vicious attacks on those groups, such as Roma and Jews, who are imagined as being peoples without their own "home" nations.

As a primary example of the distinct form of the cultural expression of a people, the idea of national literature has played a central role in legitimating the myth of the nation. The development of literature as a category (and the rise of the novel in particular) from the end of the eighteenth century occurs alongside the emergence of the nation as a political form. As Terry Eagleton and others have argued, "literature, in the meaning of the word we have inherited, *is* an IDEOLOGY" (19). Those written works that qualified as literature were thought to express universal values of order, propriety, Reason, and Progress. This made literature into a tool of CLASS politics that could be used to "raise up" philistine middle and lower classes who lacked proper, "cultivated" values; as "national literature," these same texts were taken to exemplify national greatness and intellectual achievement, highlighting both specific national characteristics (e.g., the pioneer spirit of Americans, French intellectualism) and the capacity of a nation's people to generate these universal Enlightenment values. As instruction in literature became institution-

alized in universities at the end of the nineteenth and the beginning of the twentieth centuries, a canon of representative literary texts was developed which had the dual function of training a nation's subjects in national values and beliefs (Baldick), and managing colonial subjects through immersion in the "universal" values of the literature of colonizing countries (Viswanathan). Also, as Benedict Anderson has influentially shown (1991), the novel in particular makes an important *formal* contribution to the creation of nations. By introducing the possibility of social simultaneity—the ability for of a spatially extended community to believe they all belong and exist together as one social body—the novel helps to create "imagined communities."

In literary criticism, the body of what might be considered to constitute various *theories* of national literature consists largely of attempts to challenge the ideological work of the nation, both on its own and in conjunction with the categories of literature or the literary. What has made this task complex and confusing is that even if at their core both "nation" and "literature" are political inventions, over time each category has produced real objects with material and imaginative substance. When Fyodor Dostoyevsky is described as a Russian writer, Wisława Szymborska (1923–) as a Polish poet, or Ivo Andrić as a Bosnian writer, the national designations are provided as more than markers of citizenship; "nation" is offered as an immediate contextual entry point into how each writer is to be read and understood. The borders of (for instance) European nation-states have been changing even up until the present (e.g., Andrić was a Yugoslavian writer when he received the Nobel Prize for literature in 1961). Nevertheless, the concerted political and sociocultural activity of state and people within the borders of nations with centuries-long genealogies (such as France or the U.K.) has created "imagined communities" that are far from contingent. On the level of literary training and practice, the institution of national canons and of national literary markets has produced the conditions for the production of literary texts that draw on national narratives and see themselves as speaking to specific national audiences. The challenge and difficulty for those theories of national literature that want to suspend the priority of the category—the way in which it has "in the last instance" come to define literary production and criticism—is to be able to simultaneously insist on the fiction of the category of national literature while also being attuned to the substance that this fiction continues to have.

There have been three major areas of debate over the concept of national literature within contemporary literary criticism: (1) debates over the constitution of national literary canons; (2) the difficult and contradictory genesis of postcolonial national literatures; and (3) a range of proposals that insist on the transnational or global character of all literary production.

The establishment of national literary canons played an important role in training in literary studies, and in representing and reproducing national verities and virtues to those audiences who were being constituted as national subjects. Since the late 1990s we have witnessed significant challenges to existing national canons throughout the world, most famously in the 1980s and 1990s in the U.S. The charge against U.S. literary canons was that they were unrepresentative of the true multicultural character of U.S. society and history (Morrison). By failing to include literary work by women, African Americans, Hispanics, Native Americans, and other minority groups, the canon functioned to maintain older forms of class privilege and power. The ensuing "culture wars" over U.S. multiculturalism did help to make canons more diverse,

despite concerted efforts by conservative commentators (most notably Allan Bloom) to preserve the core texts of the old Western canon. The culture wars were fought both against a general Western canon of texts (from Plato to T. S. Eliot), as well as against national canons, such as those that might be used in an introductory class on (U.S.) American literature. While it was recognized that national literary canons were artificial inventions, arguments about canons were rarely posed as arguments against the category of national literature as such, as much as about the specific composition and representativeness of national literatures.

To a degree not often appreciated, many of the important issues and themes raised within postcolonial literature and criticism relate to the problems of the category of national literature. In virtually every postcolonial situation, whether in decolonized countries in Africa or Asia, "settler countries" such as Canada and Australia, or "developing" countries in South America riding the global wave of cultural nationalist sentiments that followed WWII, the challenge for both writing and theory came from the contradictions and paradoxes of establishing national literatures in these states (Szeman). The issue in postcolonial countries was also one concerning canons. Following the pattern established in Europe, it was imagined that new nations—whether new by virtue of becoming independent modern states for the "first" time (e.g., Jamaica, Nigeria, India), or as a result of increasing confidence in and hopes for national self-definition (e.g., Brazil, Canada, Australia)—required of necessity their own national cultures, including national literatures that would define and shape the nation. The creation of these literatures took a variety of forms, from nativist assertions of the need for writing in African languages (as in the work of

Ngũgĩ wa Thiong'o) to critical anxieties over lack of established national canons in countries such as Canada, and the consequent activity of creating them rapidly and from scratch (Lecker). The fiction of national literatures was hardest to sustain in these circumstances in the postcolony, in part because of the clear artifice of the nation itself in countries produced as a result of colonial misadventure rather than through centuries of the development of land, language, and people (e.g., Nigeria, which contains myriad languages, ethnicities, and peoples). The category of postcolonial literature for this reason has from its inception productively unsettled the Eurocentric idea of national literature; the category of the "postcolonial" challenges the limits of the national and points toward the necessity of considering literary developments on a global scale.

In the era of globalization, it is Goethe's *Welt* rather than Herder's *Volk* that has dominated attempts to map literature into its contexts and circumstances. Though literary studies remain organized into national literatures, the literatures studied within this framework now often focus on multiple, extranational spaces and imaginations (e.g., within the U.S., ASIAN AMERICAN literature, LATINA/O literature). Comparative literature (see COMPARATIVISM), which has implicitly relied on national spaces across which to deploy its critical strategy of comparison, has set out in new directions, best exemplified in Gayatri Spivak's arguments for a transnational literary criticism in *Death of a Discipline* (2003). Most intriguingly, scholars such as Franco Moretti (1998) and Pascale Casanova (2004) have sought to reimagine literary geography entirely, by looking past the nation to the spatial coordinates of literary genre, reading publics, and marketplaces, and to the place of cities in the development of fiction.

SEE ALSO: Anthropology, Comparativism, History of the Novel, Regional Novel.

BIBLIOGRAPHY

Anderson, B. (1991), *Imagined Communities*, rev. ed.
Baldick, C. (1987), *Social Mission of English Criticism*.
Bloom, A. (1987), *Closing of the American Mind*.
Casanova, P. (2004), *World Republic of Letters*.
Eagleton, T. (1983), *Literary Theory*.
Gellner, E. (1983), *Nations and Nationalism*.
Goethe, J.W. von (1973), "Some Passages Pertaining to the Concept of World Literature," in *Comparative Literature*, ed. H-J. Schulz and P. Rhein.
Herder, J.G. von (1800), *Outlines of the History of Man*, trans. T. Churchill.
Hobsbawm, E. (1990), *Nations and Nationalism since 1780*.
Lecker, R. (1995), *Making It Real*.
Morrison, T. (1992), *Playing in the Dark*.
Moretti, F. (1998), *Atlas of the European Novel, 1800–1900*.
Ngũgĩ wa Thiong'o (1986), *Decolonising the Mind*.
Spivak, G.C. (2003), *Death of a Discipline*.
Szeman, I. (2003), *Zones of Instability*.
Viswanathan, G. (1989), *Masks of Conquest*.

Naturalism

DONNA CAMPBELL

The term *naturalism* refers to a late nineteenth-century and early twentieth-century literary movement whose practitioners used the techniques and theories of science to convey a truthful picture of life. The characteristics of naturalism include a carefully detailed presentation of modern society, often featuring lower-class characters in an urban setting or a panoramic view of a slice of contemporary life; a deterministic philosophy that emphasizes the effects of heredity and environment; characters who act from passion rather than reason and show little insight into their behavior; and plots of decline that show the characters' descent as the inevitable result of the choices they have made. The critic George Becker once defined naturalism as "pessimistic materialistic determinism" (35), but its elements are more complex than that phrase would suggest. For example, David Baguley identifies naturalistic novels as those that treat sociological or scientific subjects, often to expose individual or cultural pathologies, through a combination of dysphoric plots of decline and minutely detailed settings; they also "undermine parodically the myths, plots, idealized situations, and heroic character types of the romantic and the institutionalized literature to which they are opposed" (21). In its frank presentation of violence and SEXUALITY, naturalism broke free from earlier and more genteel conventions of REALISM and revealed a vision of life previously considered too brutally graphic for middle-class audiences. It tested the limits of what publishers would print and what audiences would read, thus setting a new standard for serious fiction and paving the way for later authors (see PUBLISHING).

The origins of naturalism lie in the biological, economic, and psychological discoveries of the nineteenth century, all of which relied on the intensive application of scientific empiricism. The most significant of these discoveries were the evolutionary theories of Charles Darwin (1809–82) and Herbert Spencer (1820–1903). In *On the Origin of Species* (1859), Darwin reported his observations of the manifestations of hereditary traits in successive generations, and in *The Descent of Man* (1871) he described the processes of sexual selection in animals. Such theories gave credence to the naturalists' belief that a submerged, primal animal nature revealed itself in human beings when the veneer of civilization was shattered by the stress of extreme circumstances. Another naturalistic idea borrowed

from evolutionary theory is Herbert Spencer's phrase "survival of the fittest," which naturalist authors embraced as an interpretive paradigm for their study of the desperate lives of the poor. Among the first to understand the potential that these scientific ideas had for fiction was Émile Zola, whose preface to *Thérèse Raquin* (1867) is generally considered the earliest naturalist manifesto since it expresses Zola's intention to subject his characters to scientific study. A more complete statement of naturalism is his *Le Roman expérimental* (1880, *The Experimental Novel*), which elaborated on the idea that the experimental method should be applied to characters in novels: "Naturalism, in letters, is equally a return to nature and to man; it is direct observation, exact anatomy, the acceptance and depiction of what is." The twenty-volume Rougon-Macquart series of novels follows this pattern as Zola traces several generations of inherited character traits, such as a propensity toward alcoholism, avarice, prostitution, or obsessive behavior. For example, one descendant of the Macquart family, Gervaise Coupeau of *L'assommoir* (1877, *The Drunkard*), shows the lack of self-awareness and the impulsive behavior of a typical naturalistic character; her son, Paul Lantier, is plagued by an obsessive need to paint and repaint his masterpiece in *L'Oeuvre* (1886, *The Masterpiece*); and her daughter, Nana, slips into prostitution and dissolution in *Nana* (1880). As is evident in Zola's attacks on dysfunctional social and industrial systems in *L'assommoir* and *Germinal* (1885), naturalism often implies a social critique, yet promoting reform was not the goal; as his *Roman expérimental* admonished his readers, "like the scientist, the naturalist novelist never intervenes." The idea that art should be morally impersonal and that the depiction of evil actions need not be automatically followed by scenes of punishment stirred outrage, since it violated the principle that a failure to punish evildoers would influence readers to imitate the actions they found on the page. What Zola saw as objectivity, the critics saw as immorality, and despite Zola's protestations that "it is not possible to be moral outside of the truth," naturalism was routinely vilified as indecent and immoral.

EUROPE

The furor over Zola and naturalism spread throughout Europe and Latin America during the 1880s and 1890s, following a consistent pattern of condemnation of naturalism's supposed excesses by some critics and the adoption of its principles by novelists and dramatists who saw it as a means of expressing social truths. In France, the birthplace of the movement, the ranks of naturalists included Edmund and Jules de Goncourt, whose novel *Germinie Lacerteux* (1864) traces the descent into death of a servant who leads a double life of devotion to employer and after-hours dissipation; and Guy de Maupassant, whose first novel *Une Vie* (1883, *A Woman's Life*) and short stories such as "Boule de Suif" (1880, "Butterball") exemplify naturalistic principles. The line between realism and naturalism was less firmly drawn in Spain, but Benito Pérez Galdós 1886–87, (*Fortunata y Jacinta*, 1881, *La desheredada*; 1881, *The Disinherited Lady*), Leopoldo Alas 1884–85, (*La Regenta*, *The Regent's Wife*), and especially Emilia Pardo Bazán wrote novels with naturalistic elements such as a frank treatment of sexuality, factory scenes, investigations into the plight of the working poor, and indictments of hypocritical social institutions. Pardo Bazán's novels *Los pazos de Ulloa* (1886, *The Son of a Bondwoman*) and *La Tribuna* (1882, *The Tribune of the People*) depict a family in decline and the lives of the working-class urban poor, respectively, yet she disavowed Zola's determinism in her influential series of essays *La cuestión palpitante* (1883, *The Burning Question*).

In Italy, Giovanni Verga's *I malavoglia* (1881, *The House by the Medlar Tree*) and Luigi Capuana's *Il Marchese di Roccaverdina* (1901, The Marquis of Roccaverdina) are examples of *verismo,* a variant of naturalism opposed to some of naturalism's vulgarity but committed to its ideal of objective representation and the erasure of the author's intrusions into the text. Gerhard Hauptmann's drama *Die Weber* (1892, *The Weavers*) and Thomas Mann's *Buddenbrooks* (1900) typify German naturalism, although according to Lilian Furst, the latter is only "the closest approximation to a native German naturalist novel" (1992, "Thomas Mann's Buddenbrooks," in *Naturalism in the European Novel,* ed. B. Nelson, 244), given the dominance of forms other than prose fiction in Germany at that time. In England, debates over naturalism became conflated with those over CENSORSHIP, the New Woman, and the frankness of the New Fiction (Pykett), for there as elsewhere naturalism was seen as a threat to propriety and the established social order. After publishing "Literature at Nurse" to protest the prudery of English booksellers who would not stock his earlier realist works, George Moore wrote *Esther Waters* (1894), a sympathetic treatment of a housemaid who becomes pregnant out of wedlock and refuses either to give up her child, or, in the tradition of romantic fiction, to die of shame at having borne it. Unlike Moore, Thomas Hardy dismissed the influence of Zola on his novels, yet *Tess of the D'Urbervilles* (1891) and *Jude the Obscure* (1895), emphasize naturalistic elements, adding the pressures of rigid class structures to those of biological determinism as forces opposing the individual will.

THE AMERICAS

Zolaesque naturalism was also an important literary movement in Latin America, where naturalistic novels directly confronted issues of class, race, and social upheaval. Argentina's Eugenio Cambaceres explored classically naturalistic sexual themes in *Sin Rumbo* (1885, *Without Direction*), but his treatment of immigration in *En la sangra* (1887, In the Blood) departs somewhat from naturalist practice to express anxieties about the large influx of Italian immigrants into the country. Like Zola, the Mexican novelist Arcadio Zentella protests the abuses of a social system—in *Perico* (1886), the hacienda system—and Federico Gamboa's *Santa* (1903) features as its title character a prostitute, a common feature in naturalist novels such as Stephen Crane's *Maggie: A Girl of the Streets* (1893) and Zola's *Nana*. Turn-of-the-century Brazilian naturalists include Aluísio Azevedo, Júlio Ribeiro, Adolfo Caminha, Raul Pompéia (1888, *O ateneu, The Boarding School*), and Manoel de Oliveira Paiva (wr. 1897, *Dona Guidinha do Poço*, Dona Guidinha of the Well). As David T. Haberly notes, Brazilian naturalists not only responded to great social changes, such as the emancipation of African slaves in 1888 and the proclamation of the Republic in 1889, but also treated sexual themes in stronger terms than did their European counterparts: "Nothing comparable to the most extreme examples of Brazilian Naturalism, Júlio Ribeiro's *A carne* [1888, Flesh] or Adolfo Caminha's 1895 novel of interracial homosexuality *Bom crioulo* [*The Black Man and the Cabin Boy*], could have been published and marketed in England or the United States before the middle of the 20th century" (88). Another novel with a racial theme, Azevedo's *O mulato* (1881, *The Mulatto*), is generally considered the first Brazilian naturalist novel; his *O cortiço*

(1890, *The Slum*) addresses not only race, but, like novels by Zola and Crane, topics such as female sexuality, slum life, prostitution, and suicide.

Outside of France, naturalism had its most lasting impact in the U.S., with Crane, Frank Norris, Jack London, and Theodore Dreiser acknowledged as naturalist writers and others such as Edith Wharton, Kate Chopin, and Paul Laurence Dunbar writing for a time in a naturalistic vein. Of these figures, Norris provided the most extensive explanation of naturalism for American audiences. Norris believed that naturalism was not simply a more extreme form of realism but revealed a different kind of truth. Contending that genteel realism "stultifies itself" and "notes only the surface of things" (1166) by striving for accuracy rather than an essential truth, Norris claimed that naturalism, being essentially romantic rather than realistic, could "go straight through the clothes and tissues and wrappings of flesh down deep into the red, living heart of things" (1165) and portray a truth inaccessible to realism.

For many naturalist authors, including Crane, Zola, Dreiser, and Dunbar, the setting for discovering the "red, living heart of things" was the modern city. The city in naturalism is at once an urban jungle, a site of spectacle, a space of sexual desire and capitalist exchange, a testing ground for adaptation, and a place of transformation in which identity can be dissolved, reshaped, or lost; in novels featuring female characters, the theme of the city as contributing to prostitution is common. For example, Crane's *Maggie* describes the brief, poverty-stricken life of Maggie Johnson, whose dreams of romance crumble before the reality of prostitution. The city erases one identity—her name—as it gives her another, for as a prostitute, she is only an anonymous "girl of the painted cohorts of the city" (chap. 17). Lacking Maggie's revulsion against selling herself, Zola's character Nana gleefully embraces the life of the streets as a child in *L'assommoir* before turning to acting and prostitution in *Nana*. The city that had drained individuality from Maggie supplies multiple identities for Dreiser's Carrie Meeber of *Sister Carrie* (1900), who, like Nana, takes to the stage and makes a living from the admiring gaze of men in the audience. Her ability to adapt to her surroundings stems from a desiring self: she is both stimulated by the city and never satisfied by what she finds there. In Dunbar's *The Sport of the Gods* (1901), a desire for city pleasures destroys the family of Berry Hamilton, whose daughter, like Carrie, takes to the stage, and whose son, a kept man, kills his wealthy lover. In naturalistic fiction, the only certainty that the city affords is that it will be an overpowering force for transformation, and, in keeping with the pessimism of most naturalistic fiction, the change will not be for the better.

Heredity, for the naturalists, was not a simple biological construction or chart of descent; rather, it included ideas of inheritance since proven false, such as atavism, the reversion of the individual to type, or to an earlier state of the RACE through unconscious race memories; the inheritability of acquired characteristics; and hierarchical distinctions among desirable racial characteristics, with minute differences in ethnic identity used to characterize "races" such as Anglo-Saxons. The themes of reversion to type and the brute within were particularly common in naturalistic fiction. For example, the protagonist of Frank Norris's *McTeague* (1899) struggles between his better self and a brutish nature that propels him into sexual experience, drunkenness, and violence. After he kills his wife, McTeague meets his end in Death Valley, urged on by an "obscure brute instinct" that hints at a prehistoric, apelike past (chap. 21). Jack

London's *The Call of the Wild* (1903) also illustrates a reversion to ancestral type: "instincts long dead [become] alive again" as Buck rediscovers the forgotten lessons of his wolf ancestors and finally answers the call of the wild (chap. 2). Kate Chopin's *The Awakening* (1899) shows Edna Pontellier shedding portions of her constructed persona as a well-to-do wife and mother in favor of an identity as an artist and as a sexual being, a transformation symbolized by her pleasure in swimming. In each case, the "call" of heredity is wordless, felt or heard within the body and processed by the "primitive" rather than the rational brain (see ANTHROPOLOGY). In establishing the primacy of the physical, emotional self and granting its dictates legitimacy, the naturalists theorized that by understanding primitive, impulsive human actions they would be better able to identify the primary rules of human behavior.

THE TWENTIETH CENTURY

Although the classic phase of naturalism ended before WWI, novels influenced by naturalism were published throughout the twentieth century. The theories of William James and, later, Sigmund Freud and Carl Jung increased understanding of powerful PSYCHOLOGICAL forces such as habit, obsession, sexual desire, and the collective unconscious, and they added psychological determinism to the social and material determinism of classic naturalism. In the U.S., Sherwood Anderson's *Winesburg, Ohio* (1919) combined a modernist simplicity of style with a subject matter in which psychological repression and the social constraints of the small town contributed to the characters' predetermined fates. Decades later, the Depression-era (1930–39) fiction of John Dos Passos, James T. Farrell, and John Steinbeck infused the determinism of classic naturalism with a social critique and political consciousness born of the times. Steinbeck's *The Grapes of Wrath* (1939) is naturalistic in its study of the deterministic forces arrayed against its migratory family, the Joads, but its overt politicizing makes it more akin to the proletarian novel of social protest than to classic naturalism. Like Ellen Glasgow's *Barren Ground* (1925) and Edith Summers Kelley's *Weeds* (1923), it focuses on rural subjects; in this way, it recalls the "neo-naturalism" of Latin American fiction of the 1930s, which brought naturalist methods to the study of the land and its "foundation myths" (Morse 47). Using naturalism to explore racial tensions in the U.S., Richard Wright's *Native Son* (1940) and Ann Petry's *The Street* (1946) chronicled urban despair and posited racism as a determining environmental force, with Petry's Lutie Johnson, like Wright's Bigger Thomas, as a character driven to violence by the incessant degradation and constricted opportunities she suffers. Although some writers, including Don DeLillo and Joyce Carol Oates, continued to employ naturalistic themes well into the twentieth century, the rise of MOD-ERNISM and postmodernism, with their emphasis on subjectivity, or the critique of pure scientist objectivity, rendered naturalism a diminished rather than a vital force in the literary landscape.

SEE ALSO: Decadent Novel, Ideology, Modernism, Romance, Surrealism/Avant-Garde Novel.

BIBLIOGRAPHY

Baguley, D. (1992), "The Nature of Naturalism," in *Naturalism in the European Novel*, ed. B. Nelson.

Becker, G., ed. and intro. (1963), *Documents of Modern Literary Realism*.

Bueno, E.P. (1995), *Resisting Boundaries*.

Carsaniga, G. (2003), "Literary Realism in Italy," in *Cambridge Companion to the Italian Novel*, ed. P. Bondanella, and A. Ciccarelli.

Haberly, D.T. (1997), "Aluísio Azevedo, 1857–1913," in *Encyclopedia of Latin American Literature*, ed. V. Smith.

Howard, J. (1985), *Form and History in American Literary Naturalism*.

Lehan, R. (2005). *Realism and Naturalism*.

Morse, R.M. (1996), "The Multiverse of Latin American Identity, c. 1920–c. 1970," in *Ideas and Ideologies in Twentieth-Century Latin America*, ed. L. Bethell.

Norris, F. (1986), "A Plea for Romantic Fiction," in *Frank Norris*, ed. D. Pizer.

Papke, M.E., ed. (2003), *Twisted from the Ordinary*.

Pizer, D. (1984), *Realism and Naturalism in Nineteenth-Century American Literature*, rev. ed.

Pykett, L. (1992), "Representing the Real" in *Naturalism in the European Novel*, ed. B. Nelson.

Neorealism *see* Italy; Realism
New People Novel *see* Russia (18th–19th Century)
Newspaper Novel *see* Journalism
Nonfiction Novel *see* Journalism; Fiction

North Africa (Maghreb)

NOURI GANA

The Maghreb is the name that Arab writers and geographers gave to the region north of the Sahara which, for Europeans, corresponded to Barbary or Africa Minor, and for Ibn Khaldoun, to the Berber zones before the seventh-century Arab conquest. Nowadays, the term is much more specific but not fully unequivocal. As opposed to the Mashreq (i.e., the place of the rising sun), which covers all Arab lands east of Egypt, the Maghreb (i.e., the place of the setting sun) refers to the westernmost fringes of the Arab world in northwestern Africa. At the height of Arab Muslim rule in the medieval Mediterranean, the Maghreb used to denote not only northern Africa but also Sicily and

Spain. Given that the word Maghreb in Arabic comes from the root *gharb* ("west"), it has at times been used sweepingly in reference to different regions west of the Arab peninsula. Hence, the association between the Maghreb and the West in the Mashreqi imagination has enjoyed an enduring resonance throughout Arab history and did not fully diminish after either the collapse of Arab rule in Europe nor of European rule in the Maghreb.

Because it is the Arabic word for Morocco, Arabic writers have reserved the expression *al-Maghreb al-Aqsa* for Morocco and *al-Maghreb al-Kabir* for the Greater Maghreb. Whether in English or French, the word Maghreb is synonymous with what is called in Arabic the Greater Maghreb. As to what specific countries (should) constitute the Maghreb, or the Greater Maghreb, this remains an unresolved issue, continually rehearsed by scholars depending on their own political, disciplinary, and methodological approaches and purposes. Sometimes the Maghreb is used interchangeably with the whole of North Africa (at times with and at others without Egypt in the mix); most commonly, however, the geopolitical reach of the term is considerably narrowed down to include only Morocco, Algeria, and Tunisia—the three countries whose common colonial experience has been thought, particularly among Francophone scholars in the U.S. and elsewhere, to have fostered their decolonial affinities and solidarities and, later, postcolonial ties to their former colonizer, France. While it is understandable why Libya, being a former Italian colony, is left out of this Francophone trio, the reasons why Mauritania, a former French colony, has been routinely overlooked have never been fully accounted for.

On 17 Feb. 1989, the leaders of Algeria, Libya, Mauritania, Morocco, and Tunisia met in Marrakesh and officially signed a treaty creating *Ittihad al-Maghreb al-Arabi*, the Union du Maghreb Arabe (Arab Maghreb Union, or UMA). Although UMA is still a frail geopolitical and economic entity, it has gone a long way toward promoting fraternal and cooperative relations between the five Maghrebian countries. Bilateral relations between, for instance, Libya and Tunisia, on the one hand, and Algeria and Morocco, on the other, underwent various crises from the 1970s onward before they improved by the late 1980s. The abortive union between Tunisia and Libya in 1974 wrecked interstate relations between the two countries for several years. The dispute between Algeria and Morocco over the fate of the Western Sahara (which was abandoned by Spain in 1975) resulted in a breaking-off of diplomatic relations between the two countries for a dozen years. The Western Sahara question deteriorated into a continual cold war between Algeria and Morocco, resulting in UMA's patent failure to make any substantial progress in establishing a common economic market in the Maghreb. Economically, the member states of UMA compete among themselves for partnership with Europe rather than partner each other against European hegemony. Culturally, the Maghreb is thriving: many pan-Maghreb projects such as Nessma TV are now bringing into dialogue the dialects and cultures of UMA member countries.

NOVEL FORMATIONS

The Arabic novel owes its beginnings, in good part, to East—West intellectual and crosscultural encounters and exchanges through, among other factors, travel, colonial contact, and translation. While the different motives behind these encounters can be discerned retrospectively through, for instance, the lenses of Orientalism or

Occidentalism, the literary and cultural entanglements they (must have) produced remain hardly mappable into a master historiographical narrative from which a genealogy of the novel proper can be reconstructed. Early Arab literary narratives—such as the eighth-century *Kalila wa Dimna*, a volume of animal fables of Indian origins, which Ibn al-Muqaffaʻ translated from Persian into Arabic; the *maqamat* or chivalric tales of Hamadhani and Hariri in the tenth and eleventh centuries, respectively; the twelfth-century philosophical tale *Hayy Ibn Yuqzan* (*Ibn Tufayl's Hayy Ibn Yuqzan*) by the Andalusian physician and philosopher Ibn Tufayl; and, particularly, *Alf layla wa-layla* (*The Thousand and One Nights*), an authorless narrative that spans geographies and centuries—had variably informed the rise of the novel in Europe from Miguel de Cervantes Saavedra's *Don Quixote* (1605, 1615) and Daniel Defoe's *Robinson Crusoe* (1719–22) to Laurence Sterne's *Tristram Shandy* (1759–67) and beyond. The early Arab novels (at least in their ostensibly formless or searching forms in the second half of the nineteenth century) were, in turn, informed by the gradual development, translation, and dissemination of the novel in and outside Europe from the eighteenth century onward. As such, the novel emerges less as the property of one geopolitical or sociocultural sphere of production and influence than as the materialization of transformational and generative entanglements—really, the crystallization of transcultural and transnational collaborative endeavors.

The Arab novels that emerged in the second half of the nineteenth century were wittingly or unwittingly inclined to reconcile between the westward and eastward or inward strains and constraints by which they were shaped and to which they in turn gave concrete shape. This *bidirectional impulse* has largely animated the various novels

of this period, namely: Kahlil Khoury's *Oui ... idhen lastu bi-Ifranji* (1859, *Yes ... So I am not a Frank*); Salim al-Bustani's *Al-Hiyam fi Jinan al-Sham* (1870, *At a Loss in the Levantine Gardens*); Francis Marrash's *Ghabat al-haqq* (1865, *The Forest of Truth*); Ahmad Faris al-Shidyaq's *Al-Saq ala al-saq* (1855, *Leg upon Leg*); and Muhammad al-Muwailihi's *Hadith Isa ibn Hisham* (1907, *Isa ibn Hisham's Tale*). In addition to Khalil Gibran's *Al-Ajniha al-mutakassira* (1912, *Broken Wings*) and Muhammad Husayn Haykal's *Zaynab* (1914), almost each of the above novels has at one point or another been claimed as the first Arabic novel, which goes to suggest that the Arabic novel emerged from several rehearsals and multiple beginnings rather than from one single origin. Given that the very Arabic word *riwaya*, which is now used exclusively in reference to the "novel," has traditionally conjured up a tangle of narrative genres such as *hadith* (prophetic tradition), *sira* (prophetic biography), *hikaya* (tale), and *maqama* (in which authorial transmission or *riwaya* of speeches, stories, reports, and news, or *akhbar*, is central), it might not be unfair to contend that the Arabic novel owes its early formation not only to the appropriation of the novel genre from Europe—a widely accepted view by Edward W. Said and Mohamed Berrada, among others—but also, and more importantly, to the revival and transformation of traditional narrative genres in the wake of Napoleon's 1798 expedition into Egypt and the Arab world's firsthand encounter with industrialized imperial Europe.

The pioneers of the Arabic novel were part and parcel of the experimental ventures of the nineteenth-century *nahda*—the largely intellectual movement that sought to revive and reinvigorate Arab culture by assimilating European modernity and resurrecting forgotten Arab modernity (following, as it were, three centuries of

Ottoman rule). Little surprise, then, that Nasif al-Yaziji, al-Shidyaq, al-Muwailihi, and Hafiz Ibrahim, to name only a few, returned to the *maqama* in order to write novels. While for Abdelfattach Kilito al-Muwailihi's *Hadith Isa ibn Hisham* concludes the transition of Arabic prose from the *maqama* to the novel, ridding the latter from the stylistic adornments and constraints of the former, it can be argued that the Arabic novel has not fully abandoned all the formal aspects of the *maqama*. Elias Khoury's experimental novels, for instance, rely heavily on episodic narration across orality and textuality, and Ahlam Mosteghanemi's trilogy is an exercise in *saja'*, or rhymed prose, weaving together idiomatic neologisms and elaborate rhetoric across poetry and prose. It might be the case that the colonial scramble for the Arab world in the long nineteenth century pushed some Arab novelists to turn to traditional forms of expression such as the *maqama* as acts of resistance to European cultural hegemony, but the fact remains that the Arabic novel as such never quite flourished at the time when major parts of the Arab world had been under unchallenged colonial rule. Poetry, that oldest form of Arab literary expression, continued to reign supreme. It was not until decolonial struggles gained momentum across the Arab world that Arab novelists felt warranted not only to appropriate the novel as a form of decolonial expression but also the very language of the colonizer itself. This is most noticeably the case with the Maghreb, whose placement in the Arab Muslim world and submission to a very long French (and, to a lesser degree, Italian and Spanish) colonial domination produced a rich tradition of novel writing, along with some of the most compelling debates about the postcolonial or Third-World novel in relation to questions of language, ethnicity, modernity, culture, nation, decolonization, and a host of other issues.

TWILIGHT COLONIALISM, DECOLONIAL NOVELISM

The novel in the Maghreb emerged de facto during the decolonial struggles that started to take shape in the early twentieth century and gained momentum after WWII. Much like Jurji Zaydan, Salim al-Bustani, Farah Antoun, and Numan Abduh al-Qasatili, all of whom variably turned to the past glories of Arabs and Muslims to write HISTORICAL novels writ large, the pioneers of the novel in the Maghreb were no exception to this overall trend that accompanied the rise of the novel in Egypt and the Levant in the late nineteenth century. In addition to translations from French, Spanish, and Russian (e.g., Leo Tolstoy was introduced to Tunisian Arabic readers in 1911), the beginning of the Maghrebian novel occurred in Tunisia at the hands of writers of historical novels or social romances, including Saleh al-Souissi, *Al-Haifa wa Siraj al-Lail* (1906, Haifa and Siraj al-Lail); Al-Sadiq al-Rizgi, *Al-Sahira al-Tounisiyya* (1910, literally, The Tunisian enchantress); and, particularly, Ali al-Dou'aji—*Jawla hawla hanat al-bahr al-mutawassit* (1935, A Tour around the Mediterranean Taverns). This early generation of Tunisian and Maghrebian novelists wrote at the crossroads of narrative genres, particularly at a time when what is now called "novel" used to mean *qissa tawila* (long story) as opposed to *qissa qasira* (short story). If we abide by this distinction—and bear in mind the many lost or unpublished novelistic manuscripts as a result of the colonial clampdown on Arabic writings and publications at the turn-of-the-century Maghreb—a long list of pioneering novelists may be drawn up, including Zine al-'Abidine Al-Senussi, Sliman al-Jadawi, Muhammed al-Habib, Muhammed Fahmi Ben Sha'ban, and Hasan Hosni Abdelwaheb, who wrote *Amiratu Gharnata* (The Princess of Granada) as early as 1905.

A much more bold development of the novel in the Maghreb takes place in the 1930s and 1940s—the two decades that consolidated the decolonial struggles that would bring about the demise of colonialism by the late 1950s and early 1960s from the entirety of the Maghrebian countries. In Tunisia, the Neo-Destur (or New Constitutional) party led by Habib Bourguiba appealed to the masses and became the center for the broad-based Tunisian independence movement *Jama'at tahta al-sur* (literally, against-the-wall group), which brought together a heterogeneous number of intellectuals, helped raise awareness about the colonial condition through regular meetings and debates organized in a popular café; Abu al-Qasim al-Shabbi (1909–34), one active member of the *Jama'a*, wrote "Iradit al-hayat" (The will to life), a poem that became a rallying cry against oppression across the Arab world; several periodicals, newspapers, and magazines offered timely outlets for translations of European fiction and for the creative output of several early Tunisian novelists from al-Dou'aji to al-Bashir Khrayyif. Apart from al-Dou'aji, whose narrative skills would inspire generations of Tunisian writers, Mahmoud al-Messadi helped found a singular tendency of novelism in the Maghreb that remains unequalled to this day. Educated at the Sorbonne and immersed in the Arabic literary heritage, al-Messadi wrote unclassifiable novels, cutting across several genres, including *quissa, hadith, maqama*, drama, and Islamic existential philosophy. *Al-Sudd* (The dam, wr. 1939–40, pub. 1955) is an inimitable work whose elegant language (using *saj'*), imagery, and rhetorical power combined to make it into an exceptional phenomenon in the history of the Arabic novel. Like al-Shabbi's poem, *Al-Sudd* dramatizes human will, creativity, and transformational generative powers; it is a subtle allegory of empowerment in the

face of the colonial policies of *francisation* that would diminish Arabic literacy in certain parts of the Maghreb. Like *Al-Sudd*, *Haddatha Abu Hurayra Qal* (*Thus Spake Abu Hurayra*) and *Mawlid al-Nisyan* (*The Genesis of Forgetting*) were all written in the 1930s and 1940s, partly serialized in the literary review *Al-mabahith*, but not published in full until the early 1970s. By this time, however, not only would al-Messadi have become the minister of culture in post-independence Tunisia and devoted himself fully to the reformation (and Arabization/Arabicization) of the educational system, but he would have already passed the torch to several other budding novelists. While his intellectual vision and influence cannot be overstated, al-Messadi's writing style constitutes a rare trend in modern Arabic literature.

In the 1960s and 1970s, the Tunisian novel developed further along the historical and social realist lines of prose fiction inaugurated by al-Rizgi and al-Dou'aji at the turn of the twentieth century. Three of the more notable novelists of this period are without a doubt al-Bashir Khrayyif, Muhammad La'roussi al-Matwi, and Muhammad Salih al-Jabiri. While he wrote numerous short stories and novels and published to great acclaim his historical novel, *Barq Al-Layal* (which is a knight's name—literally, "lightning of the night") in 1961, Khrayyif is more commonly known for *Al-digla fi 'arajiniha* (Dates in their Branches). Published more than a decade after Tunisia's independence, the novel takes place in the south of Tunisia in the 1920s and chronicles the beginnings of syndicalism and the nationalist movement by focusing on the multifaceted struggles of the mineworkers, inventing, in the process, a language that vacillates seamlessly between Arabic *fusha* in narration and Tunisian *darija* in dialogue. Similarly, al-Matwi's novels of this period—*Halima* (1964), and, particularly, *Al-Tut al-murr* (1967, *Bitter Blueberries*)—are mostly situated in the south and stage both the struggle against colonialism as well as the misery of subaltern Tunisians. Al-Jabiri is an accomplished critic, novelist, and playwright. In addition to *Al-Bahru yanshuru al-wahahu* (1971, *The Sea Scatters its Driftwood*) and *Laylat al-sanawat al-'ashr* (1982, The Night of the Decade), his acclaimed debut novel *Yawm min ayyam Zamra* (1968, *One Day in Zamra*) sheds light on the popular uprisings against French rule even while it brings into relief the treason of local collaborators. Other novelists of this period who engaged with the question of national self-determination in tandem with the emancipation of women and other related issues such as the clash between the country and the city, migration, and experimental socialism include Abdel Qader Ben Shaikh in his *Wa Nasibi min al-Ufuq* (1970, *My Share of the Horizon*), Mustafa al-Farsi in *Al-Mun'araj* (1969, *The Curve*), Muhammad Rached al-Hamzawi in *Bududa mat* (1962, *Boudouda Died*), Omar ben Salem in *Waha bila zilal* (1979, *Shadeless Oasis*), and Al-Bashir Ben Slama in *Aisha* (1981). Of note also are the plethora of novels produced by, among others, Hammouda Karim al-Sherif, Abdelmajid ben Attia, Abdelaziz al-Sa'dawi, Abdelrahman Ammar, Muhammad al-Mokhtar Janat, Muhammad al-Dib ben Salem, Mohsen ben Diaf, Moheddine Ben Khalifa, and Muhammad al-Hadi ben Saleh. I would be remiss here not to mention such influential short-story writers as Hind Azzouz, Hasan Nasr and, particularly, Ezzeddine al-Madani, whose social realist and experimental style has been crucial to several Tunisian novelists who started writing after independence.

In the two decades that followed independence, the preoccupations of the Tunisian novel revolved around largely didactic and decolonial aims: it exposed sociocultural ills such as witchcraft, alcoholism, gambling, hypocrisy, and ignorance and engaged with (as well as mobilized Tunisians to engage with) the colonial legacy and its sedimentations. The same could be said about the novel in Morocco in the period that followed its independence in 1956. What is somewhat puzzling is that the Moroccan novel did not begin in earnest until the mid-1960s—when Abdelkrim Ghallab published *Sab'at Abwab* (1965, *Seven gates)* and, particularly, *Dafanna al-Madi* (1966, *We Buried the Past*) and *Al-Mu'allim Ali* (1971, *Master Ali*)—even though the conditions for an earlier beginning were present: Morocco did not become a French protectorate until 1912, more than thirty years after Tunisia submitted to a similar fate; therefore, it must have had access to Arabic sources of information from the Mashreq without the interposition of the kind of colonial censorship policies that were in place in Tunisia and Algeria. Be that as it may, there have been a few rehearsals of novel writing before Ghallab, which include autobiographical or semibiographical attempts by al-Tohami al-Wazzani (1942, *Al-Zawiya;* The Hermitage—literally, The Corner or The Cell), Ahmed Abelsalem al-Baqqal (1956, *Ruwad al-majhoul*; *Pioneers of the Unknown*), and Abdelmajid Benjelloun (1956, *Fi al-tufula*; *On Childhood*). The latter's novel resembles Taha Hussein's *Al-Ayyam* (1933, *The Days*) in its autobiographical and sentimental strain but lacks the critical maturity and satiric portrayal of Morocco that marks the autobiographical novels of Mohamed Choukri and Muhammad Zafzaf. In addition to Mubarak Rabi' and Ghallab, it is with Choukri and Zafzaf that the Moroccan novel reaches the stage of social realism and becomes a vehicle of nationalist, political, and ideological aspirations, disenchantments, and harsh criticisms (particularly in the wake of the 1967 Arab nationalist setback and the successive 1971 and 1972 coups that sought to dethrone King Hassan II). No wonder, then, that Choukri and Zafzaf wrote novels that were routinely censored in Morocco and elsewhere in the Arab world because of their searing portrayals of social reality.

In the 1980s, the Moroccan novel tended toward experimentation in narrative form and theme and moved beyond the molds of social realist fiction and traditional styles of storytelling. Authors as various as Abdallah Laroui, Muhammad al-Haradi, Muhammad Ezzeddine al-Tazi, Al-Miloudi Shaghmoum, Muhammad al-Ash'ari, Mohamed Berrada, and Bensalem Himmich, among others, variably made use of stream of consciousness, polyphony, flashback, prolepsis, allegory, folktales, dreams, fantasy, history, mysticism, and philosophy in order to rediscover reality through mirrors rather than portray it through mimetic realism (see NARRATIVE TECHNIQUE). The same can be said about a number of Tunisian novelists in the 1980s, including Muhammad Tarshouna, Slaheddine Boujeh, Salimi al-Habib, and Aroussia al-Nalouti. There might not be much here that is specifically Moroccan or Tunisian about these techniques of novel writing beyond their local appropriations, but it is a feat of the Maghrebian novel that it compressed neatly the otherwise long stages of development of the European novel from REALISM to postmodernism. This accomplishment has been achieved on a smaller scale in Libya and Mauritania partly because both countries possess few (albeit important) novelists and partly because they are located on the outskirts of the Maghreb and, in the case of Mauritania, on the outskirts of both the Arab world and Black Africa.

Libya is the only country in the Maghreb to have submitted to Italian rather than to French rule and for the shortest period of time (1912–51). Yet, because Italian colonialism was averse to literacy (e.g., Musso-

lini built no schools), the emergence of the novel was retarded till the early 1970s (if we discount Huseen Zafer Ben Moussa's 1937 *Mabrouka* and Muhammad Farid Syala's 1961 *I'tirafatu Insan*, or *Confessions of a Human Being*, because of the controversies surrounding their publication, circulation, and censorship). Other post-independence novelists include Muhammad Ali Omar, who published two novels between 1962 and 1964, but the real beginning of the Libyan novel occurs after the dissolution of the monarchy during the 1969 revolution and with the foundation of the Union of Libyan Writers (which, ironically, transformed writers from forces of rebellion to advocates of the revolution), the establishment of new publishing houses, and the rise of such internationally acclaimed novelists as Al-Sadiq al-Nayhum, Khalifa Hussein Mustapha, Ahmad Ibrahim al-Faqih (a.k.a. Ahmed Fagih), and, particularly, Ibrahim al-Koni, whose novels brought Tuareg and desert culture to a worldwide readership, consolidating a trend of Maghrebian Sufi literature that was inaugurated by the writings of al-Messadi and carried on by several other novelists, particularly in Morocco, Algeria, and Mauritania.

Mauritania is arguably the only Maghrebian country in which the novel is a true latecomer. Obtaining its independence in 1960 (albeit, ironically, not abolishing slavery until 1980), Mauritania remained true to its reputation as "the land of a million poets" (with poetry writing undertaken not only in classical Arabic (form) but also in Fulani, Wolof, and Soninke) until 1981 when Ahmed Ould Abdelqader, an accomplished poet himself, took it upon himself to pioneer the Mauritanian novel. He published *Al-asma' al-mutaghayyira* (*The Changing Names*) in 1981 and *Al-qabr al-majhoul* (*The Unknown Grave*) in 1984; both novels were critical of the Ould Daddah one-party system (1960–78), servility to France, and the vision of "Greater Mauritania," which brought the country to near-collapse. While Tène Youssouf Guèye and Di ben Amar published novels in French in the 1980s, it was not until Moussa Ould Ebnou published *L'amour impossible* (Impossible Love) in 1990 and *Barzakh* in 1994 that the Mauritanian novel reached a stage of maturity in terms of its narrative form and thematic content. Ould Ebnou's novels bring into intimate collision philosophy and literature, myth and history, social realism and politics, and, above all, SCIENCE FICTION and mysticism (the former is a rarity in Arab literature and the latter a mark of the Maghrebian novel, according to Ghazoul). What is important to stress here is that Ould Ebnou wrote both novels in French first and then Arabicized—not translated—them himself under the titles of *Al-hub al-mustahil* (1999) for *L'amour impossible* and *Madinat al-riyah* (1996) for *Barzakh*.

MULTILINGUALISM AND ITS DISCONTENTS

While in all the UMA member states discussed above the novel first appeared in Arabic, in Algeria it appeared in French. More than a dozen novels were published in the first half of the twentieth century by, among others, Seddik Ben El-Outa, Caid Ben Cherif, Abdelkader Hadj Hamou, Said Guennoun, Assia Zehar, Djamila Débèche, and Taos Amrouche. These pioneering novelists were critically neglected not only because they wrote in French but also because they wrote under the influence of the variably assimilationist or atavistic Latinism as well as Orientalist racism of colonialist French writers, namely Louis Bertrand, Robert Randau, and Louis Lecoq. Unlike these early novelists who were variably fascinated by and assimilated to French culture,

the generation of Francophone novelists that emerged in the 1950s—including Mouloud Feraoun, Mouloud Mammeri, Mohammed Dib, Kateb Yacine, Assia Djebar, and Malek Haddad—had a strong commitment to Algerian independence and dramatized the experience of alienation, identitarian crisis, and anger against colonization. Many of these novelists and several others—namely Nabile Farès and Rachid Boujedra—went on to write in the following decade novels expressive of popular disenchantment and discontent with the FLN (National Liberation Front), whose transition from a revolutionary organization to a political organ was marred by cumulative factionalism and serial military dictatorships. It was not until the early 1970s when dozens of novels had already appeared in French that the Arabic novel emerged with the publication of Abdelhamid Ben Hadduga's *Rih al-janoub* (*The South Wind*) in 1971 and Tahir Wattar's *Al-zilzal* (*The Earthquake*) in 1974. In the decade that followed, a record number of more than sixty Arabic novels were published, including novels by the now canonized Wasini Laraj and Rachid Boujedra. By the early 1990s, Algeria would see the spectacular birth of its first Arabic woman novelist, Ahlam Mosteghanemi, whose *Dhakirat al-jasad* (1993, *Memory in the Flesh*) continues to be one of the most sold and widely read novels in the Arab world.

The delayed start of the Arabic novel in Algeria had been routinely attributed to the cultural and linguistic longevity of French settler colonialism from 1830 to 1962 and beyond; it should equally be attributed to the precolonial lack of centers for teaching Arabic and Islamic civilization such as the Zaytuna Mosque in Tunisia (founded in 732) or the Qarawiyin Mosque in Morocco (founded in 859), both of which ensured the endurance and cultivation of Arabic throughout the French colonial era. It is worth noting here that both Ben Hadduga and Wattar studied in the Zaytuna Mosque because of the lack of the infrastructure for teaching Arabic in colonial Algeria, where Arabic was legally a foreign language. Not unexpectedly, the FLN was eager after independence not only to make up for such a lack, but also to embark on a process of cultural Arabization and linguistic Arabicization which would fuel debates about language, ethnicity, and national identity among Arabophone, Berberphone, and Francophone communities in Algeria and across the Maghreb. Kateb Yacine, who famously claimed that he wrote in French to tell the French he was not French, would abandon French shortly after independence and devote himself completely to creating drama in the Algerian dialect; Malek Haddad would also reject French only to withdraw into silence for the rest of his life, given that he could not write in Arabic (and, hence, becomes, in the eyes of Mosteghanemi, "a martyr of the Arabic language"); Rachid Boujedra, however, would successfully switch to writing in Arabic after fulfilling his contractual obligations and producing six novels in French; in 1981, he published *Al-tafakkuk* and translated it into French as *Le Démantèlement* (1982, The Dismantling). During the Algerian civil war between the army-led government and FIS (Islamic Salvation Front) in the 1990s, the choice of the language of expression was not inconsequential, since Francophone writers and journalists were routinely targeted for assassination (e.g., Tahar Djaout and Youssef Sebti) and forced into exile (e.g., Boujedra, Djebar, Mammeri, and Rachid Mimouni).

The joined-up forces of Arab nationalism ('*uruba*) and Arabicization (*ta'rib*)—which promised the political unity of the Maghreb and the Mashreq on the basis of the extraterritorial bonds of language, culture, and history—sought to eradicate French from public life and restore Arabic throughout the Maghreb and particularly Algeria where

a *fatwa* (a religious decree or ruling) against teachers of French went hand-in-hand with a massive recruitment policy of teachers of Arabic from the Mashreq. Although it was officially reduced to a foreign language—and although Algeria routinely declined membership in the *Organization internationale de la francophonie*—French has continued to dominate daily and weekly newspapers, education, and government (Abdelaziz Bouteflika's first national speech in April 1999 was in French), which leaves largely unfulfilled the promise of national unity on the basis of language (all the more so given the Berber resurgences and defiance of the post-independence clampdown on Amazigh studies and indigenous languages). Since the imposition of Arabic as the national language, the Francophone Algerian novel has flourished beyond expectations, as if Algerian novelists were energized by the paradox of writing in the colonizer's language—really, a language whose semblance of underdog status in postcolonial Algeria only matched its legitimizing and marketing powers in Paris. Boudjedra, the *enfant terrible* of the Algerian novel, reverted back to writing in French in the wake of the Algerian civil war and in such nonfiction works as *FIS de la haine* (1992, The FIS of Hatred) and *Lettres algériennes* (1995, Algerian Letters). Surely, the Algerian civil war has provoked a novelistic insurgency of sorts, yet it is Paris that provided the incentive: many exiled Francophone novelists such as Yasmina Khadra, Malika Mokeddem, and Leila Sebbar produced their novels at a secure distance from the events in Algeria and catered for the thirst for knowledge about the war that had struck the French public sphere and which the publishing industry capitalized on.

The Francophone Algerian novel has derived its legitimacy, at least in part, from its marketability. Yet it does not suffice to write in French to be marketable. With few notable exceptions (Tahar Ben Jelloun, Driss Chraibi, Abdellatif Laâbi, Abdelwahab Meddeb, Mustapha Tlili, and Albert Memmi), the Moroccan and Tunisian Francophone novel has generally garnered less attention than its Algerian counterpart. In fact, during the Algerian civil war, Orientalist and marketing calculations combined to valorize the Francophone Algerian novel (almost beyond measure) and simultaneously ignore the Francophone Tunisian and Moroccan novel produced at the same time. The same scenario replayed itself in the wake of 9/11, when not only the Francophone but also the Anglophone world became thirsty for knowledge about Islam and Islamism. Several Francophone novelists (e.g., Slimane Benaissa, Zahia Rahmani, Salim Bachi, and Yasmina Khadra) felt warranted in writing 9/11 novels because of their vicarious or firsthand experiences of the Algerian civil war. I do not wish to undermine the value of these novelists or their novels, but any discussion of the novel in the Maghreb must confront at the outset the technologies of literary value which are inevitably entangled with questions of language, geopolitics, and marketing.

Despite the ideologies of Arabization and Arabicization, the multilingualism of the Maghreb has challenged the continuum of language and nationalism (see NATIONAL), yet by no means should it undermine the politics of language choice, particularly when such politics is dramatized, displaced, or resolved at the level of narrative poetics as is the case, most notably, in Assia Djebar's and Abdelkebir Khatibi's novels. Today, the novel in the Maghreb is truly multilingual, yet with profound power asymmetries between Arabic, French, Berber, and English. Hence, multilingualism is also another word for competitive or insulated monolingualisms, particularly made worse by the lack of translations between languages. For instance, while the Tunisian novelistic tradition is the oldest in the Maghreb, not even a handful of novels have—at this time, one decade into the twenty-first century— been translated from Arabic into English.

In addition to the Arabophone and Francophone novel, which continues to flourish consistently, the Maghrebian novel is consolidating itself in France with the emergence of such immigrant and *Beur* (French *verlan* slang for Arab) novelists as Leila Sebbar, Mehdi Charef, Azouz Begag, Farida Belghoul, Faïza Guène, Tassadit Imache, Akli Tadjer, and *harki* (Algerian soldiers loyal to France) novelists like Zahia Rahmani, Dalila Kerchouche, and Brahim Sadouni. Maghrebian novelists such as the Moroccan Anouar Majid and Laila Lalami, the Tunisian Sabiha al-Khemir and the Libyan Hisham Matar have written successful novels in English; indeed, Matar's *In the Country of Men* was shortlisted for the 2006 Man Booker Prize. Other immigrant Maghrebian novelists have taken up writing in a multitude of languages, including Italian (Nassera Chora, Abdelmalek Smari, and Amara Lakhous), Spanish (Najat El Hachmi and Saïd El Kadaoui) and Dutch (Fouad Laroui and Abdelkader Benali). If anything, the multilingualism of the Maghrebian novel might attest to the attenuation of the politics of language, which might, in turn, be a price willingly paid—provided the Maghrebian novel begins to be approached comparatively rather than exclusively from a French and Francophone perspective, which is the ongoing practice in North American universities, or from an equally exclusive Arabophone perspective, which is largely the case in departments of Arabic across the Arab world.

BIBLIOGRAPHY

Allen, R. (2007), "Rewriting Literary History," *Journal of Arabic Literature* 38:247–60.

Berrada, M. (2008), *Al-riwaya dhakira maftouha.*

Dobie, M. (2003), "Francophone Studies and the Linguistic Diversity of the Maghreb," *Comparative Studies of South Asia, Africa and the Middle East* 23(1–2):32–40.

Ghazoul, F.J. (1997), "Al-riwaya al-sufiya fil-adab al-magharebi," *Alif* 17:28–53.

Hassan, K.J. (2006), *Le roman arabe (1834–2004).*

Johnson, R.C., R. Maxwell, and K. Trumpener (2007), "*The Arabian Nights*, Arabo-European Literary Influence, and the Lineages of the Novel," *Modern Language Quarterly* 68(2): 243–79.

Kilito, A. (2006), "Qissa," in *Novel*, ed. Franco Moretti, vol. 1.

Laroussi, F. (2003), "When Francophone Means National," *Yale French Studies* 103:81–90.

Mortimer, M., ed. (2001), *Maghrebian Mosaic.*

Omri M.-S. (2008), "Local Narrative Form and Constructions of the Arabic Novel," *Novel* 41 (2–3):244–63.

Said, E.W. (2003), "Arabic Prose and Prose Fiction After 1948," in *Reflections on Exile and Other Essays.*

Sakkut, H. (2000), *Modern Arabic Novel*, 6 vols.

Salhi, Z.S. (1999), *Politics, Poetics and the Algerian Novel.*

Northern Europe

JAN SJÅVIK

The novel of the Nordic countries has its roots in the medieval Icelandic sagas, the oral narrative tradition of the Scandinavian countries, and the continental European literary tradition. As modern Scandinavian literary culture gradually developed under the influence of such forces as the Lutheran reformation and the Humanist tradition, texts written in the vernacular languages gradually replaced the Latin writings of medieval priests and monks. The antiquarian concerns of some of the major Scandinavian humanists, few though they were, led to a renewed interest in the literary monuments of the high Middle Ages that were preserved primarily in Icelandic manuscripts, and the works of Snorri Stur-

luson and other medieval saga writers began to be studied and translated into the modern Scandinavian languages. The oral literature of the Nordic countries later became the object of similarly enthusiastic attention.

It may seem paradoxical, however, that one of the earliest Scandinavian fictional narratives of any length was not written in the vernacular. Ludvig Holberg wrote his novel *Nicolai Klimii Iter Subterraneum* (1741, *Journey to the World Underground*) in Latin in order to escape possible legal consequences, for his narrative is highly critical of contemporary European political institutions, including the Danish absolute monarchy, whose subject he was. It tells the story of one Niels Klim, who enters a cave near the city of Bergen, Norway, and discovers a new and different world hidden inside the earth. Niels travels extensively in this world, encountering a variety of peoples and countries that together offer a kind of fun-house reflection of Holberg's contemporaries.

Scandinavia had only the rudiments of literary and cultural institutions prior to 1850, and only a limited number of novels were produced. Under the influence of German GOTHIC fiction, the Norwegian Maurits Hansen published a number of rather hastily written tales full of villains, ruins, supernatural occurrences, and strange coincidences, but also governed by an idealist worldview. His Swedish contemporary Carl Jonas Love Almqvist shared a similar attraction to Romanticism's dark side, but his best work is marked by early literary realism, as in his short novel *Det går an* (1839, *Why Not?*). This work also has a strong FEMINIST slant, as its protagonist, Sara Videbeck, is a glazier who privileges economic independence over conventional marriage. A certain REALISM coupled with Romantic idealism is also found in the novels of the Dane Hans Christian Andersen, most of them written in the 1830s and 1840s, before he became famous for his shorter fiction. The Swede Fredrika Bremer wrote a number of novels dealing with middle- and upper-class life; one of them, *Hertha, eller en själs historia* (1856, *Hertha*), points forward to the feminist concerns of the second half of the century.

THE GOLDEN AGE, 1850–1900

The second half of the nineteenth century is the Golden Age of the literature of the Nordic countries, when a substantial cohort of writers created works that stood at the forefront of European writing. While the dramatic work of such writers as Henrik Ibsen (1828–1906) and August Strindberg has withstood the test of time better than that of the Nordic novel of the period, many more novels than plays were written, and the audience of fiction was generally larger than that of drama. Gradually a class of professional novelists—both men and women—arose. Most of these writers were on the left in both politics and the cultural debate and subscribed to a view strongly advocated by the Danish critic Georg Brandes (1842–1927), that the primary mission of contemporary literature was to debate current issues. The most important such issue in the Scandinavian novel of this period was the proper place of women both in the home and in society, but this body of literature also debates other matters, including religion, a favorite target of Scandinavian realists and naturalists (see NATURALISM). In tandem with the emphasis on depicting modern life there was also a modernization of style and narrative technique.

Throughout the 1850s the idealism of the Romantic era was clearly on the wane in the novels of Northern Europe. Camilla Collett wrote about the plight of upper-CLASS daughters in Norway's first truly modern novel, *Amtmandens Døttre* (1854–55, *The District Governor's Daughters*). While critical of contemporary society, Collett uses a fairly traditional NARRATIVE TECHNIQUE and speaks in a genteel tone. Her fellow Norwegian Amalie Skram, who wrote about women of all social classes, is, by comparison, both bitter and angry, and is motivated by a naturalistic worldview. The Swede Victoria Benedictsson was particularly clear-sighted with regard to women's economic position, as demonstrated by her novel *Pengar* (1885, *Money*). Several works by the Norwegian Jonas Lie dealt with women's issues, e.g., *Familjen paa Gilje* (1883, *The Family at Gilje*), in which a talented young woman rejects marriage in favor of economic independence, and *Kommandørens Døtre* (1886, *The Commodore's Daughters*), the title of which evokes that of Collett's earlier book.

One of the most significant stylistic innovators in the 1850s was the Norwegian Bjørnstjerne Bjørnson, who drew on both the oral style of the medieval sagas and such oral literature as legends and folktales in several peasant tales, *Synnøve Solbakken* (1857), *Arne* (1859) and *En glad Gut* (1860, *A Happy Boy*). These works eschew such traditional narrative devices as long declarative sentences, the use of fictional diary entries, and apostrophes to the reader, and Bjørnson's narrative style became widely imitated across the region. His concern with rural life found a parallel in the best-known novel written in Finnish, *Seitsemän veljestä* (1870, *Seven Brothers*), by Aleksis Kivi, which tells the story of a group of young men who leave civilization behind and take refuge in the woods for several years.

Religion is a major theme in the work of the Dane Jens Peter Jacobsen, who in *Niels Lyhne* (1880) examines the power of inherited RELIGION over the mind of an avowed atheist. The book's eponymous protagonist sacrifices greatly for his unbelief but finally turns to God in prayer, receiving no answer. The Norwegian Alexander L. Kielland mercilessly satirizes both the established state-church and low-church pietistic religion in several works, among them *Garman & Worse* (1880) and *Skipper Worse* (1882), a prequel to the former. Arne Garborg, another Norwegian, attacked the use of religion in the education of children and youth in his novel *Hjaa ho Mor* (1890, Living with Mama), in which he touched on the connection between religion and the physical abuse of children. His later novel *Trætte Mænd* (1891, *Weary Men*) offers an ironic depiction of the relationship between religion and sexuality, a theme that had also been discussed in *Hjaa ho Mor*.

Around 1890 the foremost novelists of Northern Europe abandoned their focus on social themes and centered their attention on the interior life of human beings (see NOVEL THEORY, 19TH C). Strindberg, the Swedish dramatist who also wrote a number of important novels, anatomized his first marriage in *Le plaisyoyer d'un fou* (1888, *The Confessions of a Fool*), which was originally written in French. *I havsbandet* (1890, *By the Open Sea*), which extolled the qualities of a Nietzschean superman, also showed, however, that the mind's irrational forces are an ever-present danger. The Dane Herman Bang offered portraits of both personal and familial decline, while in Sweden Selma Lagerlöf memorialized the past of her home district—including some of its distinctive inhabitants—in *Gösta Berlings saga* (1891, *The Story of Gösta Berling*).

The most significant novelist of the Scandinavian countries is Knut Hamsun, who almost singlehandedly created the modern PSYCHOLOGICAL novel through the publication of four works that probe the human subconscious, *Sult* (1890, *Hunger*), *Mysterier* (1892, *Mysteries*), *Pan* (1894), and *Victoria* (1898). Hamsun's early protagonists are troubled individuals whose actions are motivated by irrational forces which they do not themselves fully comprehend, but which the author tries to allow the reader to decode. Hamsun's approach to psychology was intriguing to many of his contemporaries, and he became a significant early contributor to the movement later to be known as MODERNISM.

NEOREALISM AND MODERNISM

The dominant style in the twentieth-century Nordic novel is psychological realism, coupled with modernist themes and motifs. Echoes of the great nineteenth-century realists are also to be found, particularly in a pervasive concern with social and historical developments. For example, Hamsun turned away from the experimental psychology of his earliest novels in such works as *Børn av tiden* (1913, *Children of the Age*), *Segelfoss by* (1915, *Segelfoss Town*), and *Markens grøde* (1917, *Growth of the Soil*), in which he offered a historically based—and utterly scathing—critique of modernity. The Danes Johannes V. Jensen and Hans Kirk also exemplify this turn, the former in the psychological study *Kongens Fald* (1900–1901, *The Fall of the King*), as well as in a six-volume cycle entitled *Den lange Rejse* (1908–22, *The Long Journey*), which tells a Darwinian story of life from before the Ice Age to the height of the industrial period. Kirk interrogated the nature of religious life in *Fiskerne* (1928, *The Fishermen*, 1999), a collective novel that was influenced by both Marxism and Freudianism as it portrayed a group of fishermen and their families (see MARXIST). The Swede Selma Lagerlöf memorialized the past of her home district in the aforementioned *Gösta Berlings saga*. Psychological realism was an important feature of many HISTORICAL novels as well, as, for example, the *Kristin Lavransdatter* trilogy by Sigrid Undset, which consists of the volumes *Kransen* (1920, *The Bridal Wreath*), *Husfrue* (1922, *The Mistress of Husaby*), and *Korset* (1922, *The Cross*), and has been translated into over seventy languages.

Scandinavia's most important theorist of modernism is Pär Lagerkvist, who was active as a poet and dramatist as well as a novelist. In his semi-allegorical novel *Dvärgen* (1944, *The Dwarf*), he attempts to explain the rise of evil in twentieth-century Europe. The Norwegian Cora Sandel, on the other hand, focused on such modernist themes as the development of the artist and the role of the city. A trilogy consisting of the volumes *Alberte og Jakob* (1926, *Alberta and Jacob*), *Alberte og friheten* (1931, *Alberta and Freedom*), and *Bare Alberte* (1939, *Alberta Alone*) details her own development, particularly during her life in Paris during the 1920s. The Dane Tom Kristensen interrogated the theme of personal identity in *Hærværk* (1930, *Havoc*), which is set in Copenhagen in the 1920s and presents the self-destructive behavior of the author's alter ego.

THE NORDIC NOVEL AFTER WWII

WWII was a traumatic experience for all of Scandinavia, but particularly for Denmark and Norway, which were occupied for five years, and also for Finland, which saw much conflict. The events of the war figure in a major way in the postwar novel. In Finland, Väinö Linna wrote the pacifist *Tuntematon Sotilas* (1954, *The Unknown Soldier*), which tells the story of a platoon of machine-gunners during the Continuation War (1941–44). In Norway, Jens Bjørneboe investigated both the war experience as such in the novel *Under en hårdere*

himmel (1957, *Under a Harder Sky*), in which the treatment of collaborators was discussed, and in a number of novels that dealt with the problem of evil in a more general sense. Sigurd Hoel offered an analysis of the psychological background for collaboration in *Møte ved milepelen* (1947, *Meeting at the Milestone*), while Tarjei Vesaas discussed the war in allegorical terms in *Huset i mørkret* (1945, *The House in the Dark*, 1976). The Icelander Halldór Laxness detailed some of the war's consequences for his homeland in *Atómstöðin* (1948, *The Atom Station*).

While the Scandinavian novel had generally had a progressive bent, a significant radicalization took place in the late 1960s and early 1970s, when many novelists became strongly interested in Maoism as well as engaged in opposition to the Vietnam War (1955–75) and the increasing power of multinational corporations. The documentary novel became widely used as a means of furthering leftist causes. The Norwegians Edvard Hoem and Tor Obrestad both presented fictionalized attempts to bring about a Marxist—Leninist revolution in Norway, while the Swedes Per Olof Sundman, Per Olov Enquist, and Sara Lidman wrote about various historical persons and topics.

During the last two decades of the twentieth century, the Nordic novel became strongly influenced by postmodernist ideas and techniques. Kjell Westö masterfully mixes elements of high and low culture in *Drakarna över Helsingfors* (1996, *Kites above Helsinki*), which traces the development of capitalism in Finland. Kjartan Fløgstad uses similar narrative devices in his novels, including *Dalen Portland* (1977, *Dollar Road*), which details the development of the hydroelectric industry in western Norway. The Dane Peter Høeg uses elements of the crime novel (see DETECTIVE) in his very successful *Frøken Smillas fornemmelse for sne* (1992,

Smilla's Sense of Snow) and *Kvinden og aben* (1996, *The Woman and the Ape*), a critique of the scientific mindset. In Sweden, P. C. Jersild both reimagines the course of human history and parodies the writing of history in *Geniernas återkomst* (1987, The return of the geniuses). Elements of METAFICTION and MAGICAL REALISM remain important in the novel of Northern Europe.

SEE ALSO: Epic, History of the Novel, Mythology, National Literature, Romance.

BIBLIOGRAPHY

Algulin, I. (1989), *Contemporary Swedish Prose.*
Bisztray, G. (1976), "Documentarism and the Modern Scandinavian Novel," Scandinavian Studies 48:71–83.
Gustafson, A. (1940), *Six Scandinavian Novelists.*
Laitinen, K. (1984), "The Finnish War Novel," World Literature Today 58:31–35.
Magnusson, S. (1968), "The Modern Icelandic Novel," Mosaic 1:83–93.
Mawby, J. (1978), *Writers and Politics in Modern Scandinavia.*
Rees, E. (2005), *On the Margins.*
Schoolfield, G. (1962), "The Postwar Novel of Swedish Finland," Scandinavian Studies 34:85–110.
Sjåvik, J. (2004), *Reading for the Truth.*
Sjåvik, J. (2006), *Historical Dictionary of Scandinavian Literature and Theater.*

Nouveau roman *see* Description; France (20th Century)

Novel Theory (19th Century)

NICHOLAS DAMES

There was little that went under the name of "novel theory" in the nineteenth century in Europe; indeed, the first real use of the term

"theory" in connection with the novel form came late in the century, with the 1883 publication of the German novelist Friedrich Spielhagen's *Beiträge zur Theorie und Technik des Romans* (*Essays on the Theory and Technique of the Novel*). This absence of an easily identifiable nineteenth-century "novel theory" has led most contemporary scholars to decide that before the twentieth century the novel had not been truly theorized. Most histories and anthologies of "novel theory" begin no earlier than the critical works of Henry James, assuming that the twentieth century was the period that belatedly attempted to understand the genre that the nineteenth century unreflectively generated (see NOVEL THEORY (20TH C.)). This is a mistake born of the nineteenth century's very different labels for, ideas about, and locations of theorizing the novel form. To excavate the novel theories of the nineteenth century, we need first to reorient our sense of where, in literary and cultural space, they could be found.

Whereas twentieth-century novel theory appeared in the form of well-shaped, often academic books, starting with Georg LUKÁCS's 1920 *Theory of the Novel*, nineteenth-century versions tended more often to be journalistic in mode, scattered across the print runs of such important venues as the *Contemporary* in Russia, the *Fortnightly Review* or *Blackwood's* in Britain, or the *Revue des deux mondes* in France. Other locations were prefaces to controversial novels, such as those by Edmond and Jules de Goncourt, Guy de Maupassant, and Émile Zola; theories of aesthetic sensation, such as *The Gay Science* (1866) by the British critic E. S. Dallas (1828–79); physiologies of consciousness, such as *The Emotions and the Will* (1859) by the eminent British psychologist Alexander Bain (1818–1903); and the relatively new genre of the national literary history, such as Hippolyte Taine's (1828–93) *Histoire de la littérature anglaise* (1864, *History of English*

Literature), David Masson's (1822–1907) *British Novelists and Their Styles* (1859), or Charles-Melchior de Vogüé's 1886 *Le roman russe* (*The Russian Novel*). By contrast, the most eminent critics of the period, such as France's Charles Augustin Sainte-Beuve (1804–69), or Britain's Matthew Arnold (1822–88), shied away from offering any general account of the novel as either a genre or a cultural phenomenon. While most literary historians have focused on the writing of actual novelists, the novel theorists of the nineteenth century were just as likely to be journalists or occasional critics; and they were often interested in psychological science, particularly physiological psychology, one of the nineteenth century's most prevalent theories for human receptivity (see REVIEWING). Insofar as the discipline of literary studies had not yet been institutionalized in universities, the study of the novel was an amateur pursuit, often borrowing from disciplines (the natural sciences, psychology, evolutionary biology) that were more securely institutionalized. And given the novel's unparalleled popularity, nineteenth-century theorists of the novel were more willing than their twentieth-century offspring to confront not just a restricted set of acknowledged masterpieces but rather the cultural phenomenon of the novel as a whole. What the student of nineteenth-century novel theory finds, in fact, is that the century's haphazard but nonetheless suggestive accounts were attempts to confront what seemed like a new object of knowledge: the novel as a cultural medium, and novel reading as a strange cultural practice.

UNDERSTANDING THE MEDIUM: NOVEL READING

It is in Britain that what might be called the early "media studies" of the novel began, with the attempt to differentiate the novel from its great generic predecessor, the drama. As early as Edward Bulwer-Lytton's 1838 "On Art in Fiction," the distinctiveness of the novel is ascribed to the way it is consumed: in private, by oneself, as opposed to the public setting of the drama. For Bulwer-Lytton, the novel is not just a new literary genre but what we would today call a new medium: a culturally significant rearrangement of communicative possibilities between producer and consumer. The pertinent result of this rearrangement is a different set of affective relations; the drama concentrates on public and universal passions, while the novel, Bulwer-Lytton insists, appeals to "those delicate and subtle emotions, which are easily awakened when we are alone, but which are torpid and unfelt in the electric contagion of popular sympathies" (145). Two elements of Bulwer-Lytton's analysis are characteristic of much of the writing done in Victorian Britain on the novel form: its value-neutral acceptance of solitary reading, and its preference for a language of affect, or kinds of feeling. A study of communicative relations—or, how solitary reading uniquely configures the possibilities of aesthetic experience—leads inevitably to a study of the reader's receptive states (see COGNITIVE).

As a result, psychologists and physiologists began to take an interest in the reading of fiction. Bulwer-Lytton's description of the novel reader's "delicate and subtle emotions" would be the terrain of much mid-Victorian work, as critics and psychologists attempted to be more precise about what those subtle emotions are, and how they are created. Britain was, from the 1840s until the late 1870s, at the forefront of European work on the physical and psychological laws of nervous receptivity, known more generally as "physiology," and many of the important practitioners of physiology turned their attention to novel reading as an important case study of how the mind receives and processes stimuli. The most influential practitioner of this school of novel theory was G. H. Lewes (1817–78), the polymath author, literary critic, and physiologist, as well as George Eliot's partner. In a series of pivotal articles written in the middle decades of the century, as well as a collected series of lectures published in 1865 as *The Principles of Success in Literature*, Lewes proclaimed that the proper task of the critic was to understand how the visible forms of a literary genre work to produce certain affective results in the reader. Lewes's word for this causal connection was "construction": the ways in which authorial workmanship—most importantly in plotting—produces certain kinds of readerly receptivity.

Other important mid-century critics followed suit. The second volume of E. S. Dallas's *Gay Science* offered an account of the novel as the genre of mass identity, in which the workings of plots to prohibit heroic action produce in the reader a feeling of sympathetic identification, in which we see ourselves mirrored by average, ordinary protagonists. Alexander Bain, in his magisterial *The Emotions and the Will*, described the novel as "the literature of plot-interest," in which the mechanics of plot produce a distinctive psychological mechanism called "engrossment." In France, Émile Hennequin's (1859–88) *La critique scientifique* (1888, *Scientific Criticism*) called for an *esthopsychologie* of the novel, which, Hennequin predicted, would understand the novel as the genre that best produced standard, comparable, invariable responses in its many different readers. As late as the 1890s critics were still turning to Lewes's idea of "construction" as a methodological goal; the British critic Vernon Lee (1856–1935), in articles like her 1895 "On Literary Construction," made a case for novelistic technique as the micro-management of a reader's attention and sympathy. The emphasis on

a reader's physiological and cognitive reception of the novel, and on what those receptions might say about novelistic form, was a primarily British methodology that nonetheless runs through much of nineteenth-century speculation on the form.

REALISM

What British physiological criticism was not particularly interested in was mimesis: how the novel form managed to produce the illusion of reality. Yet the question of the novel's particular brand of mimesis, eventually to be called REALISM, emerged as an important one in the second half of the century. The word realism itself dated only from the late 1840s and early 1850s in France, and was initially applied to visual art; but by the 1860s and 1870s it was a central term in the debates over what, exactly, the methods and aims of novelistic mimesis might or should be. While the nineteenth-century debate over realism was often bewilderingly complicated, two central positions nonetheless emerged over the course of the century. Both could derive ultimate authority from G. W. F. Hegel (1770–1831), whose analysis in the *Aesthetics* of "the rich detail of the phenomenal real world" in Dutch painting provoked two radically different interpretations (173).

The first interpretation was generally associated with domestic realism of the British variety (see DOMESTIC). It explained realism as a particular subject matter: the homely, the everyday, the ordinary, like the *topoi* of the Dutch painting Hegel had praised. George Eliot, in her 1859 *Adam Bede*, argued openly for the Dutch preference for the homely and ordinary, and issued a quasi-religious call for attention to the ordinariness around us. Eliot's emphasis falls here on the quotidian aspect of what Hegel had praised; to the extent that any subject matter was shocking, unfamiliar, not corroborated by a reader's everyday experiences, it left the realm of "realism." By contrast, a muscular and more radical version of realism advanced on the Continent, where the stress was laid less on subject matter than procedure: realism as a practice of detail. Maupassant's description, from the preface entitled "Le Roman" to his 1888 novel *Pierre et Jean*, is characteristic: "The most insignificant thing contains some little unknown element. We must find it. . . . Make me see in a single word how one cab-horse is distinct from the fifty others in front of it and behind" (Maupassant, 1979, "The Novel," in *Pierre and Jean*, trans. L. Tancock, 33).

Yet the emphasis on detail had an embedded subject matter. In practice, "detail" meant not the detail of Hegel's Dutch paintings—the inanimate surround of comfortable bourgeois life—but the hidden details of lower-CLASS existence, the details that respectable readers are shielded from, knowingly or otherwise. From Edmond and Jules Goncourt to Zola, the stress on a detailed realism meant a firm downward movement of the novel's gaze: toward the unattractive facts of the lives of the urban proletariat. "This book," the Goncourt brothers proudly wrote in the preface to *Germinie Lacerteux* (1864), "comes from the street" (25). Although aligned with the precision of science, realism-as-detail had an inescapably political dimension, which led Anglo-American critics to denounce its reality as partial. The powerful American critic William Dean Howells (1837–1920) responded angrily to the French notion of realism as an exposé, lamenting "the ugly French fetich [*sic*] which has possessed itself of the good name of Realism to befoul it" (W.D. Howells, 1959, *Criticism and Fiction*, 128). Yet radical novelists outside of France, such as George Moore, George Gissing, and Frank Norris, worked against their national traditions by explicitly following the French model (see NATURALISM).

It remained for later novelists working in the realist mold, such as Henry James, to attempt idiosyncratic reconciliations of both versions of realism. The debate, however, persists to the present, particularly in commentary surrounding daringly "realist" film and television narratives (see ADAPTATION).

THE VANISHING AUTHOR

If the debate over the meaning of novelistic mimesis had no clear winner, one central question within nineteenth-century novel theory did: the relation between authorial voice and realism. The position that eventually became an accepted truism was that a properly "realist" or "real" mimesis (the terms were often used interchangeably) needed a guiding authorial presence to vanish. Realism became aligned here with the supposed objectivity of photography and science, and—in the nineteenth-century understanding—both scientific objectivity and photographic truth were notable for erasing the shaping hand of either scientist or photographer. In one sense this claim on behalf of the entirely transparent authorial function was an old one, and continually reiterated throughout the century in a set of different metaphors. Honoré de Balzac, in the 1842 "Avant-Propos" to his *Comédie humaine* (human comedy), described himself as merely a "secretary" transcribing social reality without distortion. In his 1880 manifesto "Le Roman expérimentale" ("The Experimental Novel"), Zola claimed for the novel the status of an observational science. These were, however, epistemological and not technical claims for the novel; they attempted to erase the distinction between science and novel and were not tied to any particular formal feature of novelistic prose.

This began to change in the 1880s, when several key publications generated a particular aesthetic approach to realist transparency. With the publication of Friedrich von Spielhagen's *Beiträge zur Theorie und Technik des Romans* (*Theory and Technique of the Novel*) in 1883, the correspondence of Gustave Flaubert in 1883 in part and in 1887 in whole, and James's "The Art of Fiction" in 1884, this aesthetic approach had a series of foundational texts. It also had a recognizable term: *impassibilité*, or "indifference," "impersonality." Spielhagen's collection emphasized the author's responsibility to objectify every possible idea through a character's speech. James's seminal essay complained about the shattering of the mimetic illusion created by authorial intrusions of the kind beloved by Victorian novelists. For both critics, the contemporary novel was lamentably deficient in proper technique; unlike the work of British physiological novel theory, Spielhagen and James were openly prescriptive, not merely descriptive. Similarly, both Spielhagen and James made novelistic objectivity not a result of a scientific outlook, as in Balzac or Zola, but instead the outcome of a difficult aesthetic process in which the merely personal voice would be renounced.

Flaubert's letters, however, were even more influential. They provided this movement for aesthetic objectivity with memorable formulations and slogans. "An author in his book must be like God in the universe, present everywhere and visible nowhere," one important declaration ran (173). Flaubert's proclamations were explicitly aesthetic—or, as above, theological—rather than appeals to scientific practice. One result of the Flaubertian shift away from scientific objectivity was to purge novel theory of the taint of radicalism; as a practice, *impassibilité*, unlike Zola's realism, had no obvious political connotations. Whereas Zola's *roman experimentale* was freighted with the legacy of scientific rationalism and leftist politics, Flaubert's aesthetics, as limned from his letters, were a matter of purely aesthetic hierarchies. The danger for Flaubert was not, it seemed, political quiescence, but the novel's usual lazy discursivity. Absent this tendency to preachiness, the novel might move up the hierarchy of artistic forms.

Such, at least, was the lesson gleaned from Flaubert, and the openly expressed desire of Spielhagen and James. And such was the birth of what would be a twentieth-century mode of novel theory: FORMALISM. Spielhagen's idea of objectification through character became, in James's later criticism, the pivotal idea of "point of view," the mechanism through which the author is eliminated from the scene of narration (see NARRATIVE PERSPECTIVE). In later theories of the novel this would become the famous distinction between "showing" and "telling." What late nineteenth-century formalism did to novel theory, however, was even more significant than sidestepping the political questions that Balzac and Zola had made prominent. It occasioned a fundamental reorientation of the whole question of the novel's meaning and function. What had been a study of the novel as a medium, rooted in a consideration of novel reading, became an author-centered theory—albeit one that sought to best understand how the author might disappear. A consideration of the novel as a force in the world, a cumulative impact of numberless novels, was replaced by the careful, precise consideration of a smaller set of representative, canonical novels (Flaubert's most prominently) in order to proclaim the novel's true, proper aesthetic. With this pivotal reorientation, a new century of novel theory began.

SEE ALSO: Definitions of the Novel, History of the Novel, Psychological Novel.

BIBLIOGRAPHY

Bulwer-Lytton, E. (1838), "The Critic—No. 2: On Art in Fiction," *Monthly Chronicle* 1:138–49.

Dames, N. (2007), *Physiology of the Novel*.

Flaubert, G. (1980), *Letters of Gustave Flaubert, 1830–1857*, trans. F. Steegmuller.

de Goncourt, E. and J. (1980), *Préfaces et Manifestes Littéraires*, ed. H. Juin.

Hegel, G.W.F. (1975), *Aesthetics*, trans. T. M. Knox, vol. 1.

James, H. (1984), *Essays on Literature, American Writers, English Writers*.

Spielhagen, F. (1883), *Beiträge zur Theorie und Technik des Romans*.

Wellek, R. (1965), *History of Modern Criticism*, vol. 4.

Yeazell, R. (2007), *Art of the Everyday*.

Zola, E. (1893), *Experimental Novel and Other Essays*, trans. B. Sherman.

Novel Theory (20th Century)

KENT PUCKETT

What characterizes novel theory in the twentieth century? In the broadest terms the phrase "twentieth-century novel theory" refers to any and all thinking about the novel over the course of those hundred years. Insofar as the novel emerged in the eighteenth and nineteenth centuries as a distinctly authoritative literary form, novel theory is the large and disparate effort to account for the rise, shape, and limits of the novel as a literary form and as a historical phenomenon. However, if the novel has encouraged many kinds of critical response, there are a few key concepts that give the field of novel theory thematic and intellectual coherence. Oddly enough, one of the most important of these concepts comes from someone who had relatively little to say about the novel: the German sociologist Max Weber (1864–1920).

THE DISENCHANTMENT OF THE WORLD

In his 1918 lecture "Science as a Vocation," Weber argues that "disenchantment" marks the modern world: "The fate of our times is characterized by rationalization and intellectualization and, above all, by the 'disenchantment of the world'" (1918, *From Max Weber,* ed. H. H. Gerth and C. W. Mills, 155). What gives modern life its character is an absence of meaning, a meaning that in other times counted on the public presence of the divine, the absolute, or the supernatural. If older, less complicated societies could look to "gods and demons" to give life its significance, to make life readable, coherent, and clear, the loss of that supernatural presence leaves the modern world in a state of alienation. The disenchantment of the world, which is for Weber an effect of the increasingly rationalized nature of knowledge production under capitalism, is not simply a theological problem. It is rather the very condition that separates the past from the present and that makes the seemingly fruitless and certainly anxious search for meaning a defining quality of modern life.

Weber's thesis encouraged others to ask what was and still is a central critical question: If modernity is characterized by its disenchantment, what aesthetic form is best suited to represent that modernity? Although there are different answers to this question, in poetics, philosophy, popular culture, and so on, many have seen the novel as the form especially suited to represent the experience of modernity. In fact, we can see the influence of Weber's thesis in otherwise unrelated kinds of novel theory. In order to trace out some of the ways in which novel theory can be understood as a response to a disenchanted modernity, it is useful to focus on three representative questions that novel theorists have asked. First, what is a novel if we take the novel as modernity's representative form? Second, when does the novel emerge and in relation to what specific social, political, or economic conditions? And, third, how does the novel represent its world?

EPIC AND NOVEL

A text that comes closest to embodying Weber's thesis is also one of the most important within the field of novel theory. Georg LUKÁCS's *The Theory of the Novel*, first published in 1916, was written while he was a member of Weber's circle. Lukács defines the novel in relation to EPIC, an earlier form that he associates with "integrated civilizations," claiming, "Happy are those ages when the starry sky is a map of all possible paths—ages whose paths are illuminated by the light of the stars. Everything in such ages is new and yet familiar, full of adventure and yet their own" (29). Because these ages organize themselves around the presence of what he calls a "transcendental locus," they are experienced as coherent, harmonious, and legible totalities (29). And the epic, by which Lukács means the great Greek epics, is the form that best represents the experience of that total form of life.

The novel, modernity's answer to the epic, is similarly interested in representing totality. However, because inhabitants of the modern world cannot count on or refer to the presence of any transcendental center or foundation, since the world has become too big and thus too complicated, its totality "is bound to be a fragile or merely longed-for one" (60). As a result, the novel is the form of "transcendental homelessness," a form caught between the urge to produce and the impossibility of producing the world as a meaningful and whole thing (61). Lukács then goes on in discussions of Miguel de Cervantes, Honoré de Balzac, Johann Wolfgang von Goethe, Gustave Flaubert, and others to account for the ways in which the novel approaches its compensatory, second-order totalities at the level of technique, including, for example, the novel's management of character, description, and time.

While Lukács's historical account of the novel's appearance might seem overly schematic, his distinction between epic and novel exerts tremendous influence over subsequent novel theory. In the 1930s, the Russian literary critic Mikhail BAKHTIN reworked Lukács's temporal distinction into a strategic, political, and structural opposition between the official, "monologic" form of epic and the subversive and even anarchic "dialogic" form of the novel. What produced the melancholy of homelessness in Lukács becomes for Bakhtin a salutary opportunity for linguistic and social resistance. Walter Benjamin (1892–1940), the MARXIST literary and cultural critic, argues in "The Storyteller" (*Illuminations*, ed. H. Arendt, 1936) that the novel's rise coincides with a developing print culture and the consequent decline of epic modes of storytelling. What characterizes the novel is its response to the increasingly bewildering experience of modern life: "To write a novel means to carry the incommensurable to extremes in the representation of human life. In the midst of life's fullness, and through the representation of this fullness, the novel gives evidence of the profound perplexity of the living" (87).

In *Deceit, Desire, and the Novel* (1961), critic and philosopher René Girard sees the novel as structured by what he calls "mimetic desire," the shared desire that two or more characters have for the same object. Where earlier forms organized their quests around divine, otherworldly, or magical objects, which he calls "external," the modern novel is characterized by the everyday, ordinary, "internal" quality of its objects of desire. Once the space between desire and everyday life collapses, values become contingent, enigmatic, and changeable. More recently, we can see the influence of both Lukács and Weber in Franco Moretti's *The Way of the World* (1987), which argues that the novel, and especially the BILDUNGSROMAN, represents an attempt to recapture the effect of totality in the modern world through the narrative assimilation of the solitary individual into his or her society. The novel's usual plots, which include familiar moves toward knowledge, marriage, and death, are a response to a world that is wide but not whole.

THE RISE OF THE NOVEL

If Lukács's opposition between epic and novel can seem overly stark, Ian Watt's *The Rise of the Novel* offers a more fully developed but nonetheless related description of the specific conditions that led to the rise of the novel in eighteenth-century England. Just as Lukács draws on Weber's sense of a disenchanted world in order to account for the novel's historical appearance and aesthetic function, so too does Watt understand the rise of the European novel as coincident with certain fundamental aspects of modern life, including increased "economic specialization" under capitalism, the new centrality of the city to national life, and the appearance of "an ideology primarily based, not on the tradition of the past, but on the autonomy of the individual" (61, 60). As the middle classes escaped from the crush and din of cities into newly developing suburbs, a complex notion of privacy emerged. First, a desire for privacy arose as a reaction to the alienating complexity of urban life. Second, it became a value represented by new kinds of architectural, domestic, and often feminized spaces such as the home and the boudoir. Third, privacy emerged as the newly self-conscious experience of a personal, interior, and essentially private psychic life. It is in response to the appearance of this new set of values, particularly social privacy, gendered domesticity, and psychological interiority, that the novel rises to cultural prominence

as the aesthetic form best able to represent those values. As a result, the individual consciousness, the persistence of character over time, and an attention to the specificity and texture of everyday life become important aspects of what Watt identifies as the novel's ultimate generic achievement: formal REALISM.

Certain strands of novel theory have followed, while also revising and complicating, Watt's compelling but arguably reductive story of the novel's development from Daniel Defoe, Henry Fielding, and Samuel Richardson through Jane Austen, Henry James, and others. In *Desire and Domestic Fiction*, Nancy Armstrong retells the novel's story in order to foreground the productive centrality of women who both wrote novels and were, as its heroines, the novel's most regular subject. Armstrong draws on the work of French philosopher Michel Foucault in order to argue that a gendered culture of the novel both represented and, in fact, helped to produce the modern subject as a gendered subject: "the modern individual was first and foremost a woman" (8).

In *The Novel and the Police*, D. A. Miller makes an argument about the relation between the form of the novel, whose moment of greatest cultural authority he locates in the Victorian novel, and the development of the modern subject. Also invoking Foucault, Miller argues that the novel, so often seen as a playful and potentially subversive escape from the seriousness of the social, is in fact a form that not only participates in the invention of liberal individuality but also actively disciplines its readers into good subjects: "the point of the [novel], relentlessly and often literally brought home as much in the novel's characteristic forms and conditions of reception as in its themes, is to confirm the novel-reader in his identity as 'liberal subject'" (x).

In another attempt to revise Watt, Michael McKeon complicates the history of the novel and its contexts in *The Origins of the English Novel, 1600–1740*. Rather than seeing the novel's rise as the unbroken movement toward the end point of Watt's formal realism, McKeon argues that the novel is, instead, a dialectical form that derives its character from the embodied tension between the residual excesses of ROMANCE and an emergent formal realism: "one central problem that Watt's unusually persuasive argument has helped to uncover is that of the persistence of romance, both within the novel and concurrently with its rise. And behind this lurks a yet more fundamental problem, the inadequacy of our theoretical distinction between 'novel' and 'romance'"(3).

ASPECTS OF THE NOVEL

If novel theory is interested both in what the novel is and in when it appeared, it is also interested in the way particular aspects of its form are suited to the work of representing its world. There have been many efforts to account for the novel as an analyzable formal system. We could look to the novel theory contained in and inspired by Henry James's essays and his prefaces to the 24-vol. New York Edition of his novels (1907–9), in which James works to pinpoint the right relation of character to plot, realism to romance, and showing to telling (1934, *Art of the Novel*). In *Aspects of the Novel* (1927), E. M. Forster addresses novel basics such as "story," "people," and "plot." He also coins the familiar distinction between flat characters, which "are constructed round a single idea or quality," and round characters, which have "more than one factor in them" (67). Arguing against the Jamesian emphasis on showing over telling, Wayne Booth shows in *The Rhetoric of Fiction* that the novel is in the first place a communicative act, an act of telling, dependent on relations between a

number of sending and receiving positions present in every narrative, including the implied author, implied reader, and the narrator.

We should turn finally to a distinction that has been central to the analysis of the novel and that can once again be understood in relation to Weber's thesis: the distinction between story and discourse (see STORY). If the term *story* names the "what" of a narrative or novel (i.e., the events that are to be represented), then *discourse* names the "how," or the order, point of view, and pace in which those events are presented. Early twentieth-century Russian Formalists, including Viktor Shklovsky, Boris Eichenbaum, and Vladimir Propp, first introduced the distinction between *story*, or *fabula*, and *discourse*, or *sjužhet* (see FORMALISM). It has proven to be a powerful way into the novel as a system. A number of structuralist and narratologist theorists of the novel have since adopted the terms *story* and *discourse* (see STRUCTURALISM; NARRATIVE).

In *Narrative Discourse*, Gérard Genette builds on these concepts in order to offer a general theory of narrative. He argues that "analysis of narrative discourse ... constantly implies a study of relationships: on the one hand the relationship between a discourse and the events that it recounts ... on the other hand the relationship between the same discourse and the act that produces it" (26–27). Genette breaks down the analysis of the novel into questions of tense, mood, and voice in order to show that it is the necessary difference between story and discourse that makes the novel so generative a form. And Roland Barthes's *S/Z* builds on an exhaustive analysis of Balzac's "Sarrasine" (1830) in order to account for the plural nature of all novelistic discourse. He demonstrates that to read a novel is to apply pressure to the ways in which it only appears as a natural, singular, finished totality: "the work of commentary, once it is separated from any ideology of totality, consist precisely in *manhandling* the text" (15).

In these works and others, it is the distance between discourse and story, between a representation of a world and the world itself, that leads to the restlessly original force of the novel. That distance is also the way in which the melancholy that Lukács associates with the novel finds its best formal expression. Story, the ultimate meaning of things, is always available to us only through its second-order representation in discourse. Always marking that distance, the relation between story and discourse is the novel's melancholy.

THE NOVEL IN THE TWENTY-FIRST CENTURY

It is clear that much novel theory in the twentieth century focuses on a relatively restricted canon of European novels, particularly those by authors such as Goethe, Balzac, Stendhal, Austen, and Leo Tolstoy. However, as novel theory moves into the twenty-first century, critics are looking beyond its usual temporal and geographic borders. What will happen to novel theory as our understanding of the novel as a historical and a national phenomenon shifts and expands? In what way has the possibility of a world literature exposed limits to novel theory? These questions and others must at last remain subjects for other entries.

SEE ALSO: Genre Theory, History of the Novel, Modernism, National Literature, Novel Theory (19th Century); Religion.

BIBLIOGRAPHY

Armstrong, N. (1987), *Desire and Domestic Fiction.*
Bakhtin, M. (1981), *Dialogic Imagination.*
Barthes, R. (1974), *S/Z*, trans. R. Miller.
Booth, W.C. (1983), *Rhetoric of Fiction*, 2nd ed.
Genette, G. (1980), *Narrative Discourse.*
Lukács, G. (1971), *Theory of the Novel.*
McKeon, M. (1987), *Origins of the English Novel.*
Miller, D.A. (1988), *Novel and the Police.*
Morretti, F. (1987), *Way of the World.*
Shklovsky, V. (1990), *Theory of Prose.*
Watt, I. (1957), *Rise of the Novel.*

Novel, Definitions of the *see* Definitions of the Novel.

Novel, History of the *see* History of the Novel

Novela de la tierra *see* Latina/o American Novel; Regional Novel

Novella *see* Defintions of the Novel

Orientalism *see* Race Theory
Oxymoron *see* Figurative Language and
Cognition

P

Paper and Print Technology

SYDNEY J. SHEP

Although the novel is often considered a Western genre, South and East Asian literature was populated by many comparable antecedents in print, be they HISTORICAL romances, fictional narratives, extended short stories, or hybrid literary forms. In China, the rise of vernacular fiction from the fourteenth century paved the way for *Hung-lou-meng* (1791, *Dream of the Red Chamber*), attributed to Cao Xueqin. This DOMESTIC novel, with its enormous cast of characters and detailed observation of mid-eighteenth-century court life, loves, and society, is considered one of China's four great classical novels, along with *Shuihu zhuan* (1614, *The Water Margin*) and *Sanguo yanyi* (1552, *Romance of the Three Kingdoms*), by Luo Guanzhong, and *Xiyou-ji* (1592, *Journey to the West*), by Wu Cheng'en. It circulated privately in scribal form—a common practice– until 1791, when it was first printed using movable type.

Once the Chinese *kanji* script arrived in Japan and was naturalized, written literary production gained momentum. The classical novel of the early eleventh century, also considered the first modern novel, was Murasaki Shikibu's work *Genji Monogatari* (ca. 1010, *The Tale of Genji*), which competed for literary shelf space with *Makura no Sōshi*

(ca. 1000, *The Pillow Book*), also by a court authoress, Sei Shōnagon. By the Edo period (1603–1867), the importation of Chinese vernacular fiction influenced the work of Ihara Saikaku, whose racy novels of the 1680s set in the brothels, teahouses, and theaters of Tokyo's red-light district were complemented by *ukiyo-e* (floating world) woodblock prints (see fig. 1). The reopening of Japan to the West during the Meiji period (1868–1912) resulted in rapid and significant exposure to European literary practices and markets. During a relatively short period of time, Japanese writers began to write fluently and concurrently in prose styles of the Enlightenment, Romanticism, NATURALISM, and REALISM. A similar pattern occurred in China with the efflorescence of the modern novel during the late Qing dynasty (1895–1911). Novels were translated and exported to the West; writers such as Yasunari Kawabata and, later, Kazuo Ishiguro and Gao Xingjian, won prestigious international awards. The impact of the Cultural Revolution (1966–76) in China and the subsequent centralized control of print and digital media resulted in a thriving underground and domestic publishing industry and a surge in both novel writing and reading. Postwar Japan witnessed the development of the internationally significant GRAPHIC NOVEL genres, *manga* and *anime*.

Until and even after contact with the technological apparatus of the West, the

The Encyclopedia of the Novel Edited by Peter Melville Logan
© 2011 Blackwell Publishing Ltd

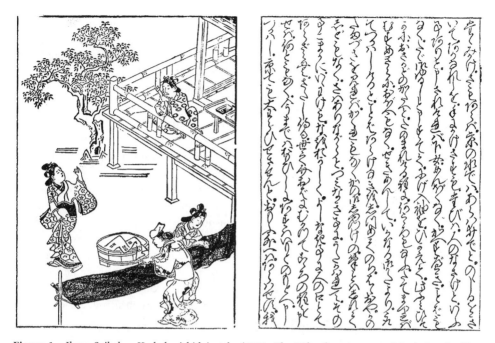

Figure 1 Ihara Saikaku, *Koshoku ichidai otoko* (1684, The Life of an Amorous Man), 8 vols., illus. Hishikawa Moronobu. The National Diet Library, WA9-10. Used with permission

production of Asian literature was a self-sufficient economy based on manuscript copying and book-block or xylographic printing and fed by centuries of papermaking expertise. The simplicity of equipment and materials fostered an almost unlimited capacity for cheap REPRINTS and the ease of rebinding the softback, multivolume works extended their life in harsh tropical environments. The shape, size, and paperback form also engendered different reading habits as well as the construction of different reading spaces for the consumption of fiction. The complexities of Indic, Arabic, and East Asian scripts have always proved problematic for moveable type (see TYPOGRAPHY). The enormous number of characters required and the need for diacritical marks, combined with capital investment and production exigencies, often paled by comparison with the commercial efficiencies of the traditional manuscript and book-block economies. Western mission-

aries prioritized the printing of religious and educational works in the vernacular, and advocated for the production of printing types. Many secular works were printed with these types, although the popular print of nineteenth-century India, for example, frequently resorted to chromolithography to overcome the limitations of moveable type. Even the famous Bengali poet, novelist, musician, artist, and social reformer, Rabindranath Tagore, privileged the manuscript as the embodiment of spiritual and literary worth, and retained an ambivalent relationship to letterpress printing all his life.

The development of the novel in the West coincided with and was facilitated by profound changes in the technologies of book production. The industrialization of papermaking and printing processes in the late eighteenth and early nineteenth centuries, coupled with the advent of new readers, new markets, changed legislative frameworks, and faster transport systems, paved the way for the efflorescence of the genre. The second phase of industrialization in the late nineteenth and early twentieth centuries broadened the global reach of this print form. Finally, the advent of digital technologies has thrust the novel into the domain of hypertext and multimedia, reshaping both its creators and readers.

MAKING PAPER BY HAND

Before the invention of the Fourdrinier papermaking machine and rotary machine presses, the novel was a luxury item manufactured in small editions for limited audiences, and priced well beyond a worker's average weekly wage. Whether available in one or two volumes, or the classic three-decker or three-volume form, its paper was handmade in single sheets, the type composed by hand from foundry type, the text printed on a two-pull wooden platen or single-pull iron handpress, and the final work bound by hand. These craft technologies and the traditions and institutional structures that surrounded them shaped the look, feel, and market for early novels. Daniel Defoe's *Robinson Crusoe*, for example, first appeared in octavo format in 1719. The paper was rag-based, produced in laid sheets made by an English mill, and taxed per ream at the source. The physical traces of the mold and deckle appeared in the watermark and any uncut edges; the papermaker's characteristic "shake" could be detected in the variable thickness of the sheet. The text was composed letter-by-letter and space-by-space from upper and lower typecases by several compositors in W. Taylor's print-shop at the Sign of the Ship in Paternoster Row, London, who deciphered and interpreted the manuscript hand, and worked with the pressman to pull galley proofs. Once corrected, the pages were imposed, locked up, and printed on the handpress, where they were worked off by the pressman and beater at a rate of 250 sheets per hour. The presswork alone for an edition of one thousand copies could take anywhere from two to three months to be completed on two presses working continuously. If sold folded rather than flat, the printed sheets were gathered and sewn into flimsy, paper-covered boards with a paste-on label—a temporary solution—awaiting the purchaser to commission his or her own bespoke binding. The finished article, with its leather, blind or gold tooling, edge-gilding, and armorial bookplate, would be read with paper knife in hand in a comfortable armchair near a sunny window or by a candle, and finally reside in a private library of considerable prestige and conspicuous value.

MECHANIZED PAPERMAKING

The demands of an increasingly literate reading public meant that popular forms of print such as newspapers and the periodical press were at the forefront of technological change. A prototype papermaking machine was brought to England by its inventor, Nicolas-Louis Robert (1761–1828), and was patented in 1801. After some modifications by Bryan Donkin (1768–1855), a viable machine was installed at the Frogmore Mill (Hertfordshire) in 1804. Using a continuous web of woven wire, this Fourdrinier machine, named after the papermaking brothers who invested in the project, was connected at one end to a vat of continuously agitated furnish distributed onto the web, and at the other end, to a series of rollers for draining, pressing, and drying. By 1807, more paper could be produced in a day from this endless web than was possible in a one-vat hand paper mill. However, demand soon outstripped supply as linen rags required for the best quality papers were in short supply and alternative fibers suitable for mechanical production, particularly straw and esparto grass, became the focus of attention. Although wood-based papers would not be commercially produced until the end of the nineteenth century, the experimental work of Matthias Koop in 1800 laid the foundation for the second phase of paper industrialization. Cheap newsprint and paperback novels could not have been realized without the emergence of wood pulp, which guaranteed papers at once regular, reliable, and anonymous.

PRINTING INNOVATIONS

As paper production was being mechanized, so too was printing. Throughout the later eighteenth century, numerous attempts were made to retrofit existing wooden platen presses to operate with greater efficiency and ease. Charles Stanhope (1753–1816) worked with his engineers on a cast-iron handpress, hoping to increase the size of sheet which could be printed in one pull as well as the impression strength, evenness, and quality. The Stanhope Press went into production in 1800, followed quickly on both sides of the Atlantic by the Columbian and Albion, among others. However, these machines were expensive and still relied upon single sheets to be hand-fed and hand-pulled; they did not increase the speed of printing sufficiently to change the industrial landscape. Around 1810, a German émigré based in London, Friedrich Koenig, experimented with a steam-driven platen press and automatic inking mechanism. Soon he shifted his energies to the cylinder or rolling press more commonly used by copperplate engravers. In late 1814, *The Times* of London, which underwrote Koenig's invention, printed off 1,100 sheets per hour and announced a new era in newspaper production. Improvements thereafter resulted in the Applegarth

vertical rotary printing machine with multiple feed stations and a fourfold increase in production. By 1850, *The Times* achieved a remarkable twelve thousand impressions per hour, increasing this figure to twenty thousand per hour eight years later using a ten-feeder horizontal rotary press developed by R. Hoe & Co. of New York. When paper duty was finally abolished in 1861, web-fed presses that printed on both sides of a continuous reel of paper were one of the crowning achievements of industrialization.

The irony attendant upon the invention of the power presses was that they remained predominantly the domain of the large newspaper corporations, unaffordable to the small printer with his limited capital, short print runs, and diverse product lines. Although some larger printing houses such as William Clowes Ltd. adopted steam presses in the 1830s, book printing was still primarily the province of the handpress up until mid-century, when the Wharfedale (1856) was introduced. However, the new power presses enabled publishers to rethink their production strategies, develop new advertising and distribution networks, and create new business models. Furthermore, the development of mechanical type-casting in America in 1838 made type more affordable and available for large projects. Refinements to the stereotyping process provided a welcome solution to the biggest hurdle in print production: typesetting. Until the invention of hot metal machines for composition setting such as the Linotype (1885; see fig 2) and the Monotype (1896), stereos enabled text to be handset once in metal, a mold made from plaster of Paris (1784), or later, papier-mâché or flong (1828–29), and any number of flat or curved plates cast on demand. Type was no longer redistributed, thus requiring a complete resetting for a new edition, or left standing awaiting the risky speculation of a future printing. Flongs could be stored indefinitely, brought out for casting when required, and did not tie up precious capital. Consequently, the single largest expenditure apart from paper was soon reduced, placing the notion of production inextricably linked to volatile consumer demand within easy reach of the printer. Furthermore, the portability of the lightweight flong molds resulted in texts circulating the globe through stereo exchange and lending networks, feeding the market for REPRINTS sustained by, amongst others, Harpers in New York, the Galignani Brothers in Paris, and Tauchnitz in Germany.

CONSEQUENCES FOR THE NOVEL

Novels were the beneficiaries of these new technical developments driven by the newspaper and periodical press. Given the increasing speed and scale of production, plus opportunities for repurposing content as publishers moved to capture market share through SERIALIZATION, part publication, and other commercial strategies, novels evolved into an exemplar of commodity culture. The works of Harriet Beecher Stowe, Alexandre Dumas, and Charles Dickens, for instance, gained greater international market penetration through serialization, dramatization, TRANSLATION, and merchandise tie-ins. The production of editions suited to specific markets and new spaces of reading was also made possible by the industrialization of print. Lending LIBRARIES such as Mudie's (founded 1842) were both a driver sustaining artificially high pricing of the three-volume novel and a captive market for editions of the most recent popular novels. They also provided the impetus for the development of publishers' cloth, and case or library bindings to ensure maximum durability and longevity.

The railway and the concomitant development of commuter reading spawned the railway bookstall, and their owner-publishers, such as W. H. Smith in London (1848) or Louis Hachette in Paris (1853), controlled supply and drove demand. The railway novel or "yellowback" with its distinctive mustard-plaster, soft-cover binding was introduced in 1855, paving the way for the mass-produced paperbacks of the 1870s that led, in turn, to the Penguin publishing phenomenon established in 1935. The paperback format enabled the publisher Philipp Reclam in Leipzig, for example, to manufacture user-pay, coin-operated book dispensers to supply cheap, standard editions for readers in railway stations, hospitals, spas, and on board ships, thus bypassing the bookshop entirely and heralding a new kind of book-on-demand economy. The colonial edition enabled a hungry novel-reading public around the world to partake of the latest fiction at discount prices, in a climate of competitive wholesaling and asymmetrical COPYRIGHT legislation, which controlled novelists, printers, publishers, booksellers, and their markets. In all of these examples, the economics of print and of publishers' design decisions affected availability and price; the gradual miniaturization, portability, and standardization of novels were linked to a reduction of price achieved through mechanized production methods, larger print runs, low production costs, and volume sales.

By the turn of the twentieth century, the industrialization of photography and lithography provided new opportunities for technological advancement in the printing industry. The offset press, developed by Ira Washington Rubel in 1903 and mass produced by the Harris Automatic Press Co. of Cleveland, Ohio, adapted lithographic principles and adopted various improvements in ink, paper, and plate manufacture for high-volume commercial printing. Since the 1950s, it has remained the printing press of choice for quality book printing and reprographics, facilitated by direct

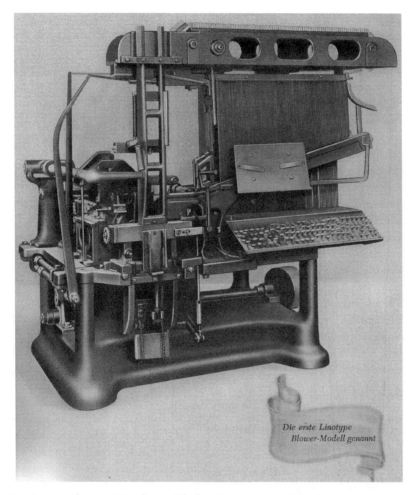

Die erste Linotype
Blower-Modell genannt

Figure 2   Linotype Blower, 1886. The world's first linecasting machine, the Blower was produced by Ottmar Mergenthaler (1854–99) in the U.S. The machine was later renamed "Linotype" (short for "Line of type"). Image courtesy of Linotype GmbH

computer-to-plate technology. Digital presses cannot yet compete with offset presses in terms of scale or quality, but are quickly narrowing the gap. Phototypesetting or cold type, first introduced in the 1940s, replaced hot metal by the 1970s and, in turn, was rendered obsolete by digital type. The development of the personal computer, the font menu, and software programs for design, illustration, and desktop or on-line publishing has put the control of production and dissemination firmly within reach of the author.

Just as early novels such as Laurence Sterne's *Tristram Shandy* (1759–67), with its marbled or black pages, or Samuel Richardson's *Clarissa* (1748), l with its psychological typography, constitute a metanarrative of book production, so too do contemporary e-novels play with the bits and bytes of their material form. While hypertext fiction and cyber-novels do not rely on print and paper, they employ many comparable readerly strategies and paratextual cues to fashion a cyberworld where the reader is now a fully immersive, multimedia participant, if not equal partner, a multimodal writer. At the same time as the e-book and internet permeate our culture, the book object remains an important constituent element. Printed novels in octavo format with pseudo-deckle or uncut edges join expensive hardbacks with faux embossing and tooling. Reading clubs abound, airport bookshops market prizewinning novels in multiple languages and filmic covers, and lending libraries purvey the latest bestsellers. Novels are repurposed into films, graphic novels, stage plays, musicals, and computer games. The markers of the chronological development of the novel can now be seen existing simultaneously in the contemporary world.

SEE ALSO: Adaptation/Appropriation, Authorship, Editing, Illustrated Novel, Publishing, Reviewing.

BIBLIOGRAPHY

Clapperton, R.H. (1967), *Papermaking Machine.*
Dagnall, H. (1998), *Taxation of Paper in Great Britain 1643–1861.*
Eliot, S. and J. Rose, eds. (2007), *Companion to the History of the Book.*
Fraser, R. (2008), *Book History through Postcolonial Eyes.*
Gaskell, P. (1995), *New Introduction to Bibliography.*
Hills, R.L. (1988), *Papermaking in Britain.*
Kornicki, P. (2001), *Book in Japan.*
Rummonds, R.-G. (1997), *Printing on the Iron Handpress.*
St. Clair, W. (2004), *Reading Nation.*
Watt, I. (1957), *Rise of the Novel.*

Paratext *see* Frame

Parody/Satire

FRANK PALMERI

Satiric narratives have been crucial for the development of novelistic forms in the West; Miguel de Cervantes Saavedra's *Don Quixote* (1605, 1615) provides the paradigmatic instance of this relation between satire and novel. Nevertheless, satire stands in a vexed relation to novelistic forms. They may be closely related, but there is a general consensus that satires such as Jonathan Swift's *Gulliver's Travels* (1726) differ from novels in their typical plot, treatment of character, and mode of representation: generally, the interior life of characters in satires is not available as it is in most novels; satires also tend to conclude inconclusively, without a change in the condition of the world that led to their composition (Kernan); finally, satires do not provide the same level of verisimilitude in the detailed depiction of objects (but may employ long and wildly heterogeneous lists instead). Although these distinctions may seem well established, they would not be accepted by Mikhail BAKHTIN, one of the foremost theorists of novelistic forms, whose extremely expansive understanding of novels encompasses almost any long fictional narrative (except epic), including ancient Greek romances, thousand-page-long seventeenth-century French romances, and satires such as François Rabelais's *Gargantua* and *Pantagruel* (1532–52), as well as eighteenth-, nineteenth-, and twentieth-century novels of contemporary life, bildungsromane, and historical novels. Bakhtin considers the romances and psychologically realistic narratives to belong to one line or tradition of the novel and parodic satires to be characteristic of a second line. Individual fictional narratives can be placed along a spectrum on which the two types approach each other: William Makepeace Thackeray's *Vanity Fair* (1848) is a novel with strong and sustained satiric implications, while Gustave Flaubert's *Bouvard et Pécuchet* (1881) is a satiric narrative with some novelistic features.

PARODIC SATIRE AND NOVELISTIC FORMS

This strong relation between satire and novels results from the crucial role that parody plays in satiric narrative. It would be more accurate to speak of parodic satire, rather than pure satire, at work in many or even most satiric narratives, because the capacities of narrative representation complicate the kind of unidirectional attack on a single object that is characteristic of poetic satire. Parody introduces ironic distance between an implied meaning and the overt statements of a narrative voice, or of any characters who participate in a dialogue or dramatic situation, and the irony may move in various directions in different chapters or parts of a long narrative. Parodic usage does not employ conventions straightforwardly, but aslant, with a difference. Without an overt statement of position having been made, the distance emerges between the previous form or position and the parodic implication, which usually carries a critical and satiric charge. Thus, in *Don Quixote*, the actions and speeches of the impoverished knight who takes literally the values and conventions of romances of adventure that had been popular for several centuries reveal the gap between the world of those conventions and the early modern world in which he expects to find them. Moreover, if the strategy of the first chapters of pt. 1 is to show the inadequacy of the conventions of the older literary and social form, successive chapters critique the modern by comparison with the ideals of another time, without offering the possibility of return to such a past. Finally, after numerous episodes, intrusions of other genres, a shift to a metanarrative level in pt. 2, and the multiplying of ironies almost beyond reckoning, *Don Quixote* concludes as the knight emerges from his delusion only soon thereafter to die: the narrative moves beyond satire toward novelistic form (see METAFICTION).

Perhaps even more insistently than the first part of *Don Quixote*, the *Satyricon*, written by Petronius (ca. 60 CE, in the reign of Nero), was probably composed almost entirely of parodies interwoven with parodies. On the evidence of the hundred-page fragment that survives (perhaps one-eighth of the original), Petronius parodically satirizes declamatory rhetoric, and especially the conventions of epic poetry. The curse of Priapus that afflicts the narrator, Encolpius, parodies the curse of Poseidon that prevents Odysseus's successful homecoming. In addition, satire of the outrageous nouveau-riche dinner host Trimalchio turns against those who consider themselves superior to him, Encolpius, and his crowd of hollow con-men, leaving readers without a position to occupy (Palmeri, 2003). Although Petronius's narrative did not lead to a tradition of novelistic forms in antiquity, it does demonstrate that novels could be constituted by adopting a thoroughly irreverent and leveling relation to epic, as well as other high, serious forms.

Like the *Satyricon*, Rabelais's *Gargantua* and Swift's *Gulliver's Travels* open up new ways of thinking through the use of parodic satire, and both stand in a close relation to later novelistic forms. Through his folkloric giants, Rabelais mocks the narrow learning of the medieval scholastics and celebrates a new world of thought to be explored through the rebirth of the classical languages and literatures; but he also undercuts the self-importance of the high Renaissance through his praise of drink and exuberant celebration of the functions and products of the body. Rabelais's encyclopedic learning, combined with his earthiness, opened up wide prospects for European novelistic prose. *Gulliver's Travels* parodies and satirizes travel narratives, but does not authorize a return to a classical Stoic ethics, such as might have been embodied by the Houyhnhnms and their passionless reason. Swift's satire of narratives such as Daniel Defoe's *Robinson Crusoe* (1719–22) also implies a critique of the emerging culturally dominant constellation of empiricism, capital growth, and colonialism (McKeon), and prepares the way for such eighteenth-century comic novels as Henry Fielding's *Joseph Andrews* (1742) and *Tom Jones* (1749), Tobias Smollett's *Roderick Random* (1748) and *Humphry Clinker* (1771), Laurence Sterne's *Tristram Shandy* (1759–67), and Denis Diderot's *Jacques le fataliste et son maître* (1796, *Jacques the Fatalist and His Master*) (Paulson).

Jane Austen's *Northanger Abbey* (1818) satirizes the gothic novel, associated with women readers, but like Rabelais and Swift she also points to the limitations of a presumed alternative, in this case the male-dominated genre of historical narrative. Distinguishing her narrative from GOTHIC and from history, she clears a space for a form that can accurately represent modern social and individual experience: the comic novel of contemporary manners, the form that Austen explores and makes her own in her later works (see COMEDY). Thus, in all these instances, the satiric parody of literary, cultural, and/or social forms clears the way for new forms of thought and literary practice, even if a clear novelistic tradition does not proceed directly from the narrative satire.

Although the satiric critique of established institutions often carries progressive political implications, the form may also express a more conservative ideology. Austen, for example, is moderately conservative in her implied attitude toward property, the social hierarchy, and marriage, although she also contests many reigning pieties concerning gender. Among other satiric novels by women from the same period, Elizabeth Hamilton's *Memoirs of Modern Philosophers* (1800) adopts a more hard-edged conservative position than does Austen, while Elizabeth Inchbald's *Nature and Art* (1796) implies a radical and ironic critique of most English social institutions.

NONPARODIC SATIRE

Characteristic of conservative satires, Hamilton's *Modern Philosophers* almost entirely lacks a parodic or ironic dimension: non-parodic satires generally tend to be more unidirectional and less interested in opening up new possibilities in form and thought. However, as Bakhtin observes, by the nineteenth century in Europe and North America, the more psychological line of the novel and the more satiric line became less distinct, as many novels included elements of each, and as irony broke off from and often replaced satire and parody. Austen's later novels illustrate this point: they are not parodic or strongly satiric, yet a knowing irony attends characters, plot, and dialogue, and the narrator's formulations raise questions about some accepted opinions and established hierarchies.

Vanity Fair is a late example of a strongly accented satiric novel in England and France, where, for almost the next half-century, satire played only an episodic and subordinate role in European novels. The late novels of Charles Dickens, for example, usually contain some recurring objects of satire, but even where the satire is strongest, as in *Bleak House* (1853) and *Little Dorrit* (1858), it remains episodic, subordinated to novelistic concerns such as the revelation of characters' identities and relations, and the final disposition of protagonists in marriage. Similarly, Anthony Trollope's novels, such as *The Eustace Diamonds* (1873) and *The Way We Live Now* (1875), often satirize elements of contemporary social life, raising questions about the condition of women, the conditions of publishing, the established

Church, and the stock market; still, however liberal and fair-minded such questions might be, the novels do not seriously undermine conventional proprieties and hierarchies of value in mid-Victorian England. Thus, if in some major periods and instances, satire can serve a generative function for novelistic forms, in other circumstances, satire serves only as a subordinate and accompanying element of an established novelistic form.

Victorian novels did not break out of this bind, this marginalizing inclusion of satire, until the 1890s, but Samuel Butler's *Erewhon* (1871) provides an anticipatory, early instance of one direction satire would later take in its satiric representation of a utopian society. Here, the strange country the narrator discovers seems at first to have utopian possibilities, although its laws and values soon prove to be based on what seem to be bizarre inversions of common sense and rationality: sick people are treated as criminals, while those who have violated laws are sentenced to medical treatment. It turns out that this culture in fact bears a strong resemblance to the culture of England. Finally, having realized the illogicality and bankruptcy of all the major institutions of Erewhonian and English society, the narrator implies that there is nothing to be done but to conform, observing the customs of the country and the code of a gentleman.

Butler's work and others, such as Flaubert's *Bouvard et Pécuchet*, anticipate the return of satiric narrative to prominence in the twentieth century; in fact, there has been an explosion of satiric fictions and forms since the turn of the twentieth century in modernist, postmodern, and postcolonial varieties, in speculative fiction, and in various subgenres. A series of dystopian novels has registered satiric critiques both of communist and of capitalist utopian visions (see SCIENCE FICTION). Works in this

strain include some novels that had a great impact on twentieth-century fiction and culture: Evgeny Zamyatin's *My* (wr. 1920–21; pub. U.S. 1924, *We*), Aldous Huxley's *Brave New World* (1932), George Orwell's *1984* (1949), Ursula Le Guin's *The Dispossessed* (1974), and Margaret Atwood's *The Handmaid's Tale* (1985). The first half of the twentieth century also saw a large number of satiric novels make use of animals to communicate their satiric vision. Among such works can be numbered Natsume Sōseki's *Wagahai wa Neko dearu* (1906, *I Am a Cat*), Anatole France's *L'Île des Pingouins* (1908, *Penguin Island*), Mikhail Bulgakov's *Sobach'e serdtse* (wr. 1925; pub. U.K. 1968, *Heart of a Dog*), Lao She's *Mao Ch'eng Chi* (1932, *Cat Country*), Karel Čapek's *Válka s mloky* (1936, *War with the Newts*), and Orwell's *Animal Farm* (1945). Expanding the ancient form of the animal fable to novelistic length, these works disguise their satiric critique in order to evade censorship or attack. The allegorical nature of such works, in which the animals' behavior resembles that of humans, aligns them with satiric allegory, another longstanding combination of forms, which can be allied with a religious vision, as in both Apuleius's *The Golden Ass* (second century CE) and Wu Cheng-en's *Xiyou ji* (1592, *Journey to the West*).

POSTCOLONIAL AND POSTMODERN SATIRIC NOVELS

Not only can long narrative satires prepare the ground for novelistic forms, but also novellas and short stories: Nikolai Gogol's tales, especially "The Nose" (1836) and "The Overcoat" (1841), prepared the way for Fyodor Dostoyevsky's novels by focusing satirically on characters who experience extreme states of deprivation and debasement. Gogol's "Diary of a Madman" (1834) also provided a model for Lu Xun, whose own "A Madman's Diary" (1918), *A-Q zhengzhuan* (1921, *The True Story of Ah Q*), and other narratives represent twentieth-century China as a society whose people have become so morally and psychologically degraded that it is barely possible to retain both one's decency and one's sanity among them. Similarly, the tales of Jorge Luis Borges, such as those in *Ficciones* (1944, *Fictions*), opened the way for novels of MAGICAL REALISM—notably Gabriel García Márquez's *Cien Años de Soledad* (1967, *One Hundred Years of Solitude*), but also the Boom in Latin American fiction in the 1960s and 1970s. Borges's melding of fictional and nonfictional elements, fantasy and essay, utopia and history, proved well suited to expressing the sometimes phantasmagoric history and reality of previously colonized societies, as can be seen also in works such as Salman Rushdie's *Midnight's Children* (1981). Rushdie's novel not only provides a history of India in the twentieth century through its allegorical and fantastic protagonist, the son of an English father and a poor Hindu mother raised in a well-to-do Muslim family; it also parodies famous English novels as it demonstrates the fantastic nature of history. In this latter effort at historical representation often outside the constraints of realism, Rushdie is joined by many authors of satiric historical novels in the last half-century, among them E. L. Doctorow, John Barth, and Günter Grass. The satiric novels of Thomas Pynchon—*V.* (1963), *Gravity's Rainbow* (1973), *Mason & Dixon* (1998), and *Against the Day* (2006)—all of them constructed almost entirely of parodies, perhaps most clearly demonstrate the possibilities for increased cultural self-understanding opened up by the satiric historical novel, a distinctive postmodern genre. The conjunction of parody and satire in fiction is still generating new and important novelistic forms.

BIBLIOGRAPHY

Bakhtin, M.M. (1981), *Dialogic Imagination*, trans. C. Emerson and M. Holquist.
Elliott, R.C. (1960), *Power of Satire*.
Frye, N. (1957), *Anatomy of Criticism*.
Guilhamet, L. (1988), *Satire and the Transformation of Genre*.
Hutcheon, L. (1985), *Theory of Parody*.
Hutcheon, L. (1988), *Poetics of Postmodernism*.
Kernan, A. (1965), *Plot of Satire*.
McKeon, M. (1987), *Origins of the English Novel*.
Palmeri, F. (1990), *Satire in Narrative*.
Palmeri, F. (2003), *Satire, History, Novel*.
Paulson, R. (1967), *Satire and the Novel in Eighteenth-Century England*.

Performativity *see* Speech Act Theory
Periodicals *see* Serialization
Perlocution *see* Speech Act Theory

Philosophical Novel

DAVID CUNNINGHAM

The philosophical novel can be minimally defined as a GENRE in which characteristic elements of the novel are used as a vehicle for the exploration of philosophical questions and concepts. In its "purest" form, it perhaps most properly designates those relatively singular texts which may be said to belong to both the history of PHILOSOPHY and of literature, and to occupy some indeterminate space between them. Today the term is often used interchangeably with the more recent concept of the "novel of ideas," though some theorists have sought to establish a clear division between the two (Bewes).

Among better known (and relatively uncontentious) examples of the form are works such as Voltaire's *Candide* (1759), Jean-Jacques Rousseau's *Julie, ou la nouvelle Héloïse* (1761, *Julie, or the New Héloïse*),

Thomas Carlyle's *Sartor Resartus* (1833–34), Fyodor Dostoyevsky's *Brat'ya Karamazovy* (1880, *The Brothers Karamazov*), and Jean-Paul Sartre's *La Nausée* (1938, *Nausea*). However, an extremely wide and disparate range of canonical novels, from Jane Austen's *Pride and Prejudice* (1813) to George Eliot's *Middlemarch* (1871–72), have also been read by critics in such terms (McKeon, Jones), and it is clear that, as a genre, the philosophical novel is marked by an exceptional plasticity. Certainly, to the extent that it is not identifiable with any specific formal or technical quality—equally embracing, for example, the epistolary novel and science fiction, omniscient narrators and interior monologues—the attempt at any precise generic definition would seem inherently problematic.

ENLIGHTENMENT NARRATIVES

Although the extent of their direct influence upon Western European literary developments remains disputed, an important precursor to the philosophical novel is to be found in Arabic fictional narratives. Of particular significance is Ibn Tufail's *Hayy ibn Yaqzān*, written in the twelfth century. An early example of the desert-island story, *Hayy ibn Yaqzān* utilizes fictional narrative for explicitly pedagogical and didactic purposes, as a means of explaining, and dramatizing, philosophical-theological ideas. The book was newly translated into Latin in 1671 as the *Philosophus Autodidactus*, followed by English, German, and Dutch translations at the beginning of the eighteenth century, and is thought to have influenced Daniel Defoe's *Robinson Crusoe* (1719–22). It also bears comparison with a text such as Rousseau's *Émile* (1762)—anticipating the latter's use of novelistic form to elaborate a philosophy of education, in a manner

which was itself to exert a crucial influence on the later BILDUNGSROMAN.

It is in the context of the development of eighteenth-century Enlightenment philosophy, particularly in France, however, that the philosophical novel most clearly assumes its modern shape. Ian Watt notoriously claimed that eighteenth-century French fiction "stands outside the main tradition of the novel" (33), as opposed to that "inaugurated" by Defoe, Samuel Richardson, and Henry Fielding. Yet this *exception culturelle* might equally be regarded as a function of the unique centrality of the philosophical novel to the early French novel's development, constituting an alternate tradition to its Anglophone counterpart. In a later 1754 commentary on his *Lettres persanes* (*Persian Letters*), originally published in 1721, Montesquieu writes: "Nothing has been more pleasing in the *Persian Letters* than finding there, without expecting it, a sort of novel [*roman*]" (qtd. in Keener, 136). Although not quite the first epistolary fiction, Montesquieu's early use of that form lends it some distinctive characteristics, as he makes clear: "[I]n ordinary novels digressions may be permitted only when they form a new story themselves. The author should not add passages of philosophical discourse because . . . that would upset the nature and purpose of the work. But in a collection of letters . . . the author has the advantage of being able to join philosophy, politics, and morality with a novel" (qtd. In Keener, 137). Significantly, the *Lettres persanes* is thus marked, formally, by the extent to which philosophical reflection and social comment tend to predominate over characterization or narrative momentum (see EPISTOLARY).

The legacy of such openness to directly philosophical "digressions" may be located in a number of later eighteenth-century fictions such as *La nouvelle Héloïse* and the

Marquis de Sade's *Aline et Valcour* (1788, *Aline and Valcour*). Yet, tellingly, if the fictional and narrative works of Rousseau, or, say, Denis Diderot, are often regarded by critics as occupying a somewhat liminal position with respect to the mainstream history of the novel, it is because, in their apparent privileging of discursive reflection over plot or characterization, they are generally seen as belonging more properly to the history of philosophy itself.

By contrast, other eighteenth-century novels such as *Candide* or Samuel Johnson's *Rasselas* (1759) are much more clearly organized around "a single motivating [philosophical] doctrine [which] generates a parable that illustrates it" (Anderson, 172). These works are less distinguished by the heavy presence of philosophical discourse within the fabric of the text than by their specific use of novelistic technique to give "concrete" imaginative form to a set of more or less "abstract" theoretical propositions. Often close to allegory in this respect, characterization and plot are not so much downplayed in such novels, as they are used as a kind of literary means to implicitly philosophical ends. Characters thus tend to be constructed so as to embody specific intellectual positions, while fictional situations are deployed as illustrative of particular philosophical dilemmas.

Candide and *Rasselas* also conform to BAKHTIN's theorization of the novel as acquiring its productive dynamic from the parodying of other GENRES—in this case, the "genre" of philosophy itself. Similarly to Jonathan Swift's slightly earlier comic deflations in *Gulliver's Travels* (1726), a novel such as *Candide* is, above all, parodic and satirical in its approach to the intellectual positions it engages, Voltaire's central target being a somewhat caricatured version of Leibnizian "optimism." The capacity of the novel to give concrete and particular form to philosophically lofty ideas is thus deployed here to largely negative effect, as the theory that all is for the best in the best of all possible worlds" is violently confronted with the reality of the actual world Candide encounters (see PARODY).

FROM ROMANTICISM
TO THE NOVEL OF IDEAS

Although it has had a far greater influence on the philosophy *of* the novel than on the philosophical novel itself, one key legacy of French Enlightenment narratives is to be found in early German Romanticism. Friedrich Schlegel's famous declaration that the *roman* (novel) is (or should be) a "romantic book"— a specifically modern fusion of "poetry and prose, inspiration and criticism" (1991, *Philosophical Fragments*, 31)—takes much from his readings of Rousseau and Diderot, as his 1799 "Letter about the Novel" makes clear, and is also manifested in a handful of novels attempted by the Romantics themselves, including Friedrich Hölderlin's *Hyperion* (1797–99), Novalis's *Heinrich von Ofterdingen* (pub. posthumously, 1802), and Schlegel's own *Lucinde* (1799). Alongside the French philosophical novel, the major reference point for these works is Johann Wolfgang von Goethe, in particular *Wilhelm Meister's Lehrjahre* (1795–96, *Wilhelm Meister's Apprenticeship*), of which Schlegel wrote an enthusiastic 1798 review. Initially, Novalis, too, praised Goethe's famous BILDUNGSROMAN as a work of "practical philosophy" and thus "true art," but his later misgivings concerning its focus on the quotidian particulars of contemporary bourgeois reality—"unpoetic to the highest degree, as far as spirit is concerned"— are perhaps more revealing as regards the philosophical novel's immediate fate (1997, *Philosophical Writings*, ed. M. M. Stoljar, 158).

Nineteenth-century REALISM did not prove especially conducive to the philosophical novel, for obvious reasons given its emphasis on the empirical and everyday. Many canonical works of realism certainly have strong philosophical elements within them—George Eliot's novels, for example, exhibit an obvious influence of the German thought of which she was herself a translator—but these are rarely presented as dominant concerns. The exception to the rule here would appear to be the Russian novel, although, arguably, this is because of the exceptional nature of its relationship to the "foreign imports" of both Western European realism and post-Enlightenment philosophy (F. Moretti, 1998, *Atlas of the European Novel 1800–1900*, 195–97). In Leo Tolstoy's *Voyná i mir* (1865–69, *War and Peace*), characters not only become the focal point for a complex exploration of different systems of belief, but, in its later sections, the novel increasingly incorporates philosophical and essayistic forms of discourse into the prose itself. Such direct argumentation is further combined in Dostoyevsky's *Zapiski iz podpolya* (1864, *Notes from Underground*) with a more thoroughgoing construction of the novel as a vehicle for putting to "the test of life" particular contemporary ideas—in this instance, Russian nihilist and utopian socialist thought—a model which Dostoyevsky was radically to extend in a progressively ambitious series of works that followed.

Importantly, Dostoyevsky's novels have come to be among the first since early German Romanticism to be accorded serious attention *as* philosophy. The "Grand Inquisitor" story recounted by Ivan in *Brat'ya Karamazovy* has, for example, frequently been anthologized and discussed as a significant philosophical argument in its own right. However, to treat such sections in isolation as minor philosophical treatises is to remove them from what Bakhtin describes as their specific "polyphonic" or "dialogic" context, which constitutes Dostoyevsky's most significant contribution to the modern philosophical novel's development. For the latter is generally less concerned with using the novel for the elaboration of a preconceived or "monologic" philosophical position than with the deployment of narrative as the means by which divergent ideas may be brought into (a frequently unresolved) conflict with each other in the work.

MODERNISM

The philosophical novel arguably returns to much greater prominence in so-called "high" modernism. Works such as Robert Musil's *Der Mann ohne Eigenschaften* (1930–42, *The Man without Qualities*), Marcel Proust's *À la recherche du temps perdu* (1913–27, *Remembrance of Things Past*), or Thomas Mann's *Der Zauberberg* (1924, *The Magic Mountain*) are, for example, readable as varieties of philosophical novels in the degree to which they directly interpolate often lengthy philosophical reflection into the prose of the novel itself, whether via first-person narration or dialogue. At the same time, early twentieth-century novels that sought to elaborate (often idiosyncratic) philosophical ideas frequently did so, implicitly, as a means of responding to a perceived historical "crisis," as in D. H. Lawrence's *Women in Love* (written during WWI, pub. 1920). If such extensive incorporation of philosophical discourse recalls the eighteenth-century French philosophical novel, however, writers such as Musil or Mann tend to be far less systematic in their elaboration of any identifiable philosophical proposition, and more concerned, in the wake of Dostoyevsky and Tolstoy, with constructing and meditating upon a confrontation between ideas as a means of representing the contemporary.

Although, in practice, the two overlap, a somewhat different type of philosophical novel might be identified in novels such as Hermann Hesse's *Siddhartha* (1922), Sartre's *La Nausée*, or Albert Camus's *L'Étranger* (1942, *The Outsider*). While both their literary tone and variant philosophical sympathies are radically different from those of a novel like *Candide*, such works still tend to conform, in broad terms, to that Voltairean model of the philosophical novel organized around a "motivating doctrine [which] generates a parable that illustrates it" (Anderson, 172). By contrast, a rather different manifestation of the philosophical novel would be identifiable in Franz Kafka's *Der Prozeß* (1925, *The Trial*) or Samuel Beckett's *Trilogy* (1951–53). Here it is less a question either of direct philosophical reflection, in the manner of *Der Mann ohne Eigenschaften*, or of the quasi-allegorical elaboration of a preexisting philosophical "content" by literary means, than of the degree to which such novels may be read as exploring a series of fundamental philosophical questions at the level of literary form itself. As Theodor Adorno argues, while in Sartre philosophical problems tend to be "diluted to an idea and then illustrated" (though this is perhaps less true of *La Nausée* than of the plays), in Beckett and Kafka "the form overtakes what is expressed and changes it" (241). In Beckett, this is complicated by a network of philosophical allusions that, while making his writing seem to "offer itself generously to philosophical interpretation," go on, as Simon Critchley puts it, apparently "to withdraw this offer by . . . reducing such interpretation to ridicule" (143). As such, recent readings of Beckett have often stressed the fundamentally parodic character of his allusions, recalling, in their own way, the satirical eighteenth-century philosophical novels of Voltaire and Johnson.

CRITICAL ISSUES

For many critics, as Proust once remarked, a novel that too obviously trumpets the explicit "idea" behind its construction is akin to an artwork with the price tag left on. English Showalter's judgment that a writer like "Sade" has more interest because of his ideas than because of his talents as a novelist" (477) is, then, fairly typical of the opposing claims of literary value and philosophical originality or rigor that are often evoked in debates surrounding the philosophical novel. Adorno, for example, criticizes both Sartre, for using literature as a mere "clattering machinery for the demonstration of worldviews" (242), *and* Musil, for a predominance of "thinking" at the expense of properly novelistic narration (see S. Jonsson, 2004, "A Citizen of Kakania," *New Left Review* 27:140).

From a different perspective, however, it is the novel's very concrete sensuousness and attentiveness to everyday experience that has been said, by some, to lend it a special intellectual significance with regard to characteristically philosophical concerns. Hence Showalter argues that the novel may actually have been "the best medium" for a thinker such as Rousseau "to express his thought . . . [insofar as] the autonomy of . . . fiction nullifies the philosopher's tendency to sterile systems and abstract perfection" (476–77). It is not surprising, therefore, that the specific philosophical position with which many of the more successful early practitioners of the philosophical novel, such as Voltaire or Johnson, are associated is one that favors empiricism and a skepticism toward abstraction *per se*.

Finally, an obvious issue raised by this brief account concerns the degree to which the philosophical novel—in its loose, traditional, generic definition—has historically been, or remains, a European or "Western" form. Certainly the usual examples proposed of contemporary novels within the genre, such as Milan Kundera's *Nesnesitelná lehkost bytí* (1984, *The Unbearable Lightness of Being*), have tended to be by somewhat self-consciously European writers. Of course, there are obvious instances of the philosophical novel to be found within the North American tradition, stretching back to the nineteenth century—from Herman Melville's *Moby-Dick* (1851) to the works of William T. Vollmann and others today. Equally, there are many twentieth-century Japanese novels, like Kenzaburō Ōe's *Man'en gannen no futtoboru* (1967, *The Silent Cry*), strongly influenced by existentialism, or his *Atarashii hito yo mezame yo* (1983, *Rouse Up, O Young Men of the New Age!*), that could be read as examples of the form. Surprisingly, while, for example, various of Jorge Luis Borges's hugely influential short stories have often been understood as belonging to the broad tradition of the *conte philosophique*, critical consideration of the Latin American novel during the Boom period has rarely engaged any of its canonical works as instances of the philosophical novel, even if the writings of Alejo Carpentier or Isabelle Allende would certainly seem open to such interpretation.

More generally, attempts to locate examples of the genre beyond "the West" entail the perhaps difficult question of how far the modern European conception of "philosophy" itself can be projected onto other traditions of thought. This would clearly be an issue in assessing whether, for example, various instances of the modern Indian novel's engagement with Hindu thought should be read as belonging strictly to the philosophical novel tradition. Nonetheless, it is fair to say that there are, at the very least, strong parallels to be found in the case of works such as R. K. Narayan's *The English Teacher* (1945), with its semiautobiographical exploration of grief and enlightenment, or Raja Rao's *The Serpent and the Rope* (1960) and *The Chessmaster and His Moves* (1988), both of which draw extensively upon Vedantic thought.

SEE ALSO: Definitions of the Novel, Figurative Language and Cognition, Ideology, Intertextuality

BIBLIOGRAPHY

Adorno, T.W. (1991), "Trying to Understand Endgame," in *Notes to Literature*, vol. 1, trans. S. Nicholsen.

Anderson, P. (2006), "*Persian Letters*," in *The Novel*, vol. 2, ed. F. Moretti.

Bakhtin, M. (1984), *Problems of Dostoyevsky's Poetics*, trans. C. Emerson.

Bewes, T. (2000), "What Is 'Philosophical Honesty' in Postmodern Literature?," *New Literary History* 31: 421–34.

Critchley, S. (1997), *Very Little . . . Almost Nothing*.

Jones, P. (1975), *Philosophy and the Novel*.

Keener, F.M. (1983), *Chain of Becoming*.

McKeon, R. (1979), "*Pride and Prejudice*," *Critical Enquiry* 5(3): 511–27.

Schlegel, F. (2003), "Letter about the Novel (1799)," in *Classical and Romantic German Aesthetics*, ed. J.M. Bernstein.

Showalter, E. (1972), "Eighteenth-Century French Fiction," *Eighteenth-Century Studies* (17.5)3: 467–79.

Watt, I. (1972), *Rise of the Novel*.

Photography and the Novel

DANIEL A. NOVAK

The invention of photography (literally "light-writing") was perhaps the most important revolution in representation for the nineteenth and twentieth centuries. The development of the Victorian and modern novel—indeed, one might say modernity itself—is coterminous with the invention and development of photography and eventually film. As Michael North argues, "the very existence of a modern period, broken away from the time before, is to some extent the creation of photography, which has made all time since the 1840s simultaneously available in a way that makes the years before seem much more remote" (3). For the first time in human history, we were confronted by images made (seemingly) without the intervention of the human hand or human bias—an object more like an emanation of the thing itself than a representation. Because of this, the photograph had profound implications for how novelists imagined (and reimagined) the act of writing, depicting, and narrating, as well as how they negotiated the relationship between writer and world. Moreover, this impact was not limited to writers who considered themselves "realists" or even part of a movement like NATURALISM, but rather extended to literary movements that developed in response to REALISM, such as MODERNISM and postmodernism. Photography produced a sustained meditation on many of the concerns at the heart of novelistic fiction: point of view, framing, context, representation, identity, desire, and the nature of the human body itself. If one thinks about the most influential texts in the HISTORY of the novel, from Charlotte Brontë's *Jane Eyre* (1847) and Charles Dickens's *Great Expectations* (1861) to F. Scott Fitzgerald's *The Great Gatsby* (1925) and William Faulkner's *The Sound and the Fury* (1929), so many of them were written in the shadow of photography—what Nancy Armstrong refers to as "fiction in the age of photography."

Photography is at once an idea–one might even say ideology, in the spirit of Karl Marx's famous comparison of IDEOLOGY to an image in a camera obscura—and a specific set of technologies. But, it is important to remember that throughout the nineteenth century photography was never one technology, with each format and process having important implications for how we understand photographic meaning, production, circulation, and reception. As Geoffrey Batchen (1999, *Burning with Desire*) points out, the "desire" to photograph predated 1839 (Daguerre's announcement of the invention of photography), with experiments dating back to the beginning of the nineteenth century. But we conventionally associate the invention of photography with two figures: Louis J. M. Daguerre (1787–1851) in France and Henry Fox Talbot (1800–77) in England. Talbot began his experiments in 1834 but did not patent his "calotype" or "talbotype" paper process until 1841. Yet, while we refer to both of these methods as "photographic," their different technologies represented a crucial difference in how we understand the relationship between photography and reproducibility. Daguerre's method was a direct positive process, in which an image is developed on a silver-coated copper plate itself coated with light-sensitive chemicals, producing a *unique* and unreproducible image. In contemporary photographic terms, the daguerreotype was more akin to a Polaroid than a traditional film camera. Talbot's process would be closer to what we think of as photography today—the negative/positive process with the capability to produce multiple reproductions.

At the same time, while enormously different, taken together, the daguerreotype and the calotype embody what we can refer to as the "photographic imaginary," which broadly consists of two key ideas: (1) the idea of an objective, mechanically produced image free from human intervention (what Talbot calls the "pencil of nature") and (2) the idea of an image that can be endlessly reproduced, that, as Walter Benjamin (1892–1940) argued in his essay "The Work of Art in the Age of Mechanical Reproduction" (1936), is *designed* for reproducibility and for which there is no "original" (*Illuminations*, 224). Photography in this last sense represents a revolution not just in how we understand representation but also how we understand the relationship between original and copy. By 1851, with the invention of collodion (a material that was used to coat a glass plate and hold the light-sensitive chemicals), the promise of endless reproducibility became an industrial reality with millions upon millions of photographs being made, sold, and circulated. The development of the roll-film camera, popularized by Kodak in the late nineteenth century, finally extended the power of image making to the masses.

Given that photography was a key shift in how writers thought of the act of representation as well as a fact of everyday experience, it is no surprise that photographs and photographers littered nineteenth-century novels and are almost ubiquitous in those of the twentieth century. Some novelists (to name just a few), like Lewis Carroll, Émile Zola, Jack London, Eudora Welty, and Wright Morris, even took to photography themselves. Yet, beyond being a subject for novels, photography acted as a metaphor for writing. Nineteenth-century realists like Dickens, William Makepeace Thackeray, Gustave Flaubert, and Honoré de Balzac were praised for their "photographic" style. Mark Twain argued that novelistic characterization was like a "composite photograph ... the blending of more than two or more real characters" (Rabb, 108). And this metaphor worked both ways, as photographs were praised for being "as good as a new novel" (E. Y. Jones, 1973, *O.G. Rejlander*, 15).

But photography could also be deployed to denigrate novels, either for not being realistic enough or for being too focused on the fragmentary and material. George Henry Lewes (1817–78) condemned the photographic "detailism" in Victorian literature; by littering the text with "unessential details" writers ended up making their texts both incoherent and unrealistic (1885, *Principles of Success in Literature*, 100–101; see DESCRIPTION). Such criticisms stretch into the twentieth century with theorist Georg LUKÁCS (1885–1971) condemning entire literary movements like Naturalism and Modernism by associating them with a fragmentary "photographic" style (1948, *Studies*, 60, 143–45; 1962, *The Meaning of Contemporary Realism*, 45). Writing in 1856 about Dickens's style, George Eliot uses the photograph to signify a form of representation that fails to go beyond surfaces: "But while [Dickens] can copy Mrs. Plornish's colloquial style with the delicate accuracy of a sun-picture ... he scarcely ever passes from the humorous and external to the emotional and tragic, without becoming as transcendent in his unreality as he was a moment before in his artistic truthfulness" (1963, *Essays of George Eliot*, ed. T. Pinney, 271). The photograph's accuracy—its tie to the material and the visible—here is what prevents it from representing the *invisible* subjects treated by novelists: thoughts, emotions, desires.

And yet, at the same time, writers were claiming that these invisible emotions, secret desires, and hidden tendencies were precisely what photography had the power to make visible. Holgrave, Nathaniel Hawthorne's daguerreotypist in *The House of the Seven Gables* (1851) famously exposes Judge Pyncheon's "unamiable" self: "There is a wonderful insight in Heaven's broad and simple sunshine. While we give it credit for depicting the merest surface, it actually brings out the secret character with a truth that no painter would ever venture upon, even could he detect it" (91). Even if, as

Stuart Burrows has argued, Judge Pyncheon's character was never actually secret, never needed to be exposed by the power of photography (35), we are left with a vague sense of photography's association with a kind of gothic knowledge–an association often used to satirize photography as a "dark art" carried out in mysterious darkrooms. Holgrave's claim that photography has the power to photograph the interior of the subject finds its technological and historical reflex in efforts to visualize invisible ideas, from emotion and morality to ghosts and fairies. Scientists, phrenologists, and the police harnessed the medium to create images of the insane and the criminal body. Charles Darwin (1809–82) made extensive use of (often staged and manipulated) photographs in his *Expressions of Emotions in Man and Animals* (1872). Others, like William H. Mumler (1832–84), turned the lens on even more inaccessible realms, claiming to have captured ghostly visitations. Even a writer firmly aligned with the deductive reasoning of his master detective Sherlock Holmes–Sir Arthur Conan Doyle–famously believed in the authenticity of photographs of fairies.

So thoroughly was photography integrated into literary perception, that by 1901, French novelist Émile Zola argued that "You cannot claim to have really seen something until you have photographed it" (Sontag, 87). While novelistic interest in the photograph overlaps with the equally important advent of film in the late nineteenth century, the still image remained enormously influential and important for MODERNISM, not only because of its continued association with the objective and real, but also because of its fragmentary, abstract, and context-less qualities. Henry James (who collaborated with photographer Alvin Langdon Coburn) theorized literary form as a kind of lens–the "apertures" in the "house of fiction" in his introduction to *Portrait of a Lady* (1881): "The pierced aperture, either broad or balconied . . . is the 'literary form'; but they are, singly or together, as nothing without the presence of the watcher" (7). Christopher Isherwood went further, collapsing the "watcher" and the lens, writer and camera: "I am a camera with its shutter open, quite passive, recording, not thinking" (1939, *Goodbye to Berlin*, 1). Isherwood's yearning for a kind of writing without writing is summed up in James Agee's remarks in his collaborative phototext with Walker Evans *Let Us Now Praise Famous Men* (1941): "If I could do it, I'd do no writing at all here. It would be photographs; the rest would be fragments of cloth, bits of cotton, lumps of earth . . . plates of food and of excrement" (10). If Agee invested the photograph with the same kind of material immediacy and authenticity as the "lumps of earth" and other pieces of his subjects, others, like John Dos Passos in his fragmented and montage-like "Camera Eye" sections of *U.S.A.* (1930–36), associated the camera with a new kind of abstract, mechanical perception that, as North argues, in its detachment was paradoxically aligned with a subjective point of view (146; see NARRATIVE PERSPECTIVE). The fact that photography is looked to as a model and metaphor for realistic, omniscient narration as well as stream-of-consciousness and avant-garde narrative styles (see NARRATIVE TECHNIQUE) shows not only how enduring and attractive, but also how flexible the idea of photography still remains for imagining the visual, narrative, and conceptual work of the novel.

PHOTOGRAPHY AND CONTEMPORARY LITERARY CRITICISM

As we have seen, photography was being linked to literature in general and the novel in particular from its inception, and critics have continued to focus on the camera as metaphor for narrative point of view. Examples include Alan Spiegel's *Fiction and the Camera Eye* (1976) and Carol Shloss's *In Visible Light* (1987). However, it is only relatively recently that the study of photography and literature became a field in its own right. Much of this is due to the rising interest in critical theory and interdisciplinary research in general, and the relationship between the visual and verbal in particular. The work of Walter Benjamin and Roland Barthes has played and still plays an important role in how photography is understood, as has the work of John Berger, Susan Sontag, and W. J. T. Mitchell. Critics have been especially drawn to Barthes's *Camera Lucida* (1981), with its account of the photograph's historicity (its ability to record what "has been there") and its melancholy and strange temporality (it records what will no longer be there).

But, while photography is still used as a way to understand narrative point of view and literary realism, the past decades have seen an increased interest in reading literary realism alongside photography as a material artifact and cultural practice embedded in complex social, technological, political, scientific, textual, and economic histories. Critics like Carol Armstrong in her *Scenes in a Library* (1998) have explored the way in which photography was bound up with textuality and the book—literally in the form of the ILLUSTRATED book and conceptually as a form of "written imagery" (3). In *Framing the Victorians* (1996), Jennifer Green-Lewis historicizes the image of the photographer in Victorian literature by tracing how photographers were figured and represented themselves in Victorian photographic journals. Miles Orvell analyzes the intersections of photography, consumer culture, advertising, and literature to trace the shift in the discourse of realism

from the nineteenth to the twentieth century—from a "culture of imitation" (based on familiar and "typological representation") to a "culture of authenticity" (based on a mechanical objectivity that would change how we see the world) (198).

More broadly, critics have theorized the relationship between literature and material photographic culture. In *Confounding Images* (1997), Susan Williams usefully outlines a methodology for reading literature and photograph which recognizes both how the photograph "affected American literary culture" but also how literary culture "affected popular conceptions of the daguerreotype" (3). Nancy Armstrong (1999) extends this reciprocal relationship into a reevaluation of literary realism itself. She theorizes a circular, reciprocal relationship between literary and photographic culture in which "fiction and photography had taken up a mutually authorizing relationship" (247), together defining what readers would consider "real" in the textual and visual realm.

Along the way, critics interested in realism have turned to photography, its cultural history, and the language in which it was described as a way of understanding a variety of novelistic preoccupations that intersect with realism, including RACE, nation (see NATIONAL), SEXUALITY, GENDER, surveillance, and power. Allan Sekula's essay on "instrumental" uses of photography to identify the unfit or deviant body by the police and the state in "The Body and the Archive" (1986) and John Tagg's *The Burden of Representation* (1993) have influenced a number of studies that employ the theories of Michel Foucault to understand the relationship between realism and social control. For example, Jennifer Green Lewis has chapters devoted to photographs of the criminal and insane body. Ronald Thomas's *Detective Fiction and the Rise of Forensic Science* (1999) reads novels from Dickens to Raymond Chandler in the context of photography's associations with surveillance and detection (see DETECTIVE). Others, like James Ryan, Catherine Lutz, Jane Collins, and Kobena Mercer, have explored the relationship between photography and colonialist ideology.

Most recently, however, scholars have explored the ways in which photography was associated with a way of seeing that was not reducible to the kind of instrumental realism discussed in earlier studies. Katherine Henninger argues that the critical habit of seeing the camera as "inherently a 'master's tool'" or an instrument of the "male gaze" functions as a kind of "ideological fantasy" dependent on accepting photography's "realism" as "natural" and ignoring photography's "radical indeterminacy" (116–17). Henninger locates this indeterminacy in contemporary Southern women's literature and its use of the "fictional photograph"—the photograph described in language. For Henninger, translating the photographic object into language has the effect of foregrounding "the cultural dynamics of vision and visual representation" (9) and opens a space for resisting patriarchal (see FEMINIST) and racist ideologies (see IDEOLOGY).

Others, such as Daniel A. Novak, argue that, while some Victorian writers associated photography with objectivity, they also aligned it with fiction and the unreal. Rather than a process that recorded accurate "likenesses" of individuals, photography was seen as a medium that effaced particularity and individuality. In this context, he reads the often spectral, abstract, and typological figures in texts considered part of Victorian "realism" not as failures of realistic representation but as figures aligned with photography and photographic discourse. Along the same lines, Stuart Burrows argues that "the relationship between photography and American fiction is one

not *of* likeness but *about* likeness" (19). For him, photography embodied a flattening of difference and redundancy that rendered American identity and history both homogenous and "endlessly reproducible" (11). Like Novak and Burrows, Richard Menke (2008, *Telegraphic Realism*) associates photography more with the abstract than the real; he places photography in the context of the nineteenth-century invention of disembodied and immaterial "information." Finally, North points to the ways in which photography transformed both vision and writing itself but in unexpected ways: "Photography is itself a kind of modern writing ... neither linguistic nor pictorial but hovering in a kind of utopian space between, where the informational utility of writing meets the immediacy of sight" (4). For North, the shifts in perception *away* from realism and even the visible itself that we associate with modernism started with the invention of photography in the nineteenth century.

This rich and diverse body of critical work on photography and literature—even and especially work that reaches back into history—forms the contours of a field that will only become more important for understanding our contemporary culture, a culture that increasingly accesses text in a digital and visual environment.

SEE ALSO: Adaptation/Appropriation, Graphic Novel, Intertextuality, Memory, Novel Theory (19th Century).

BIBLIOGRAPHY

Armstrong, N. (1999), *Fiction in the Age of Photography*.
Barthes, R. (1981), *Camera Lucida*.
Burrows, S. (2008), *A Familiar Strangeness*.
Green-Lewis, J. (1996), *Framing the Victorians*.
Henninger, K. (2007), *Ordering the Façade*.
Mitchell, W.J.T. (1994), *Picture Theory*.

North, M. (2005), *Camera Works.*
Novak, D.A. (2008), *Realism, Photography, and Nineteenth-Century Fiction.*
Orvell, M. (1989), *The Real Thing.*
Rabb, J., ed. (1995), *Literature and Photography.*
Sontag, S. (1977), *On Photography.*

Picaresque Novel

ALOK YADAV

Picaresque is a critical construct used since the nineteenth century to refer to both a specific novelistic genre and a wider fictional mode. In its narrower usage, the term refers to a genre of fiction centered on the life of a *pícaro* or *pícara*. Scholars have built up a normative conception of this genre, according to which the picaresque novel consists of a retrospective first-person narrator writing an episodic and open-ended narrative about his or her life as a rogue, one who hails from a low or dishonorable background and travels from place to place in a struggle for survival (see NARRATIVE PERSPECTIVE). The *pícaro* seeks a secure toehold while living by his or her wits in an exploitative, corrupt, urban world.

The picaresque novel flourished in late sixteenth- and early seventeenth-century Spain, and was transformed as it spread during the later seventeenth and eighteenth centuries to other European countries, especially England, France, and Germany. Since the nineteenth century, the picaresque is also evident in Russia, the U.S., and Latin America, but by this point it is easier to talk of a picaresque mode manifest in a wide range of novels than it is of the picaresque novel as a distinct genre. After its initial emergence, the history of the picaresque novel is both one of generic disintegration and of modal consolidation, a complex dynamic addressed below in two parts: (1) Spanish origins and (2) generic transformations.

SPANISH ORIGINS

The picaresque novel is generally seen as an early modern innovation, a new cultural form that emerged in Golden Age Spain and which played a significant role in the subsequent development of the novel. However, the genre draws on many antecedents, ranging from such Spanish works as *La Lozana andaluza* (ca. 1528–30, *Lozana, the Lusty Andalusian Woman*) by Francisco Delicado, *La Celestina* (1499) by Fernando de Rojas, and the *Libro de buen Amor* (1330, *Book of Good Love*); to medieval buffoon literature, the Arabic genre of the *maqāma*, and folk materials such as trickster tales; to narratives from antiquity, including Apuleius's *The Golden Ass* (ca. 100–200 CE) and Homer's *Odyssey.*

Generally considered the first picaresque novel, the anonymous *La vida de Lazarillo de Tormes* (1554, *The Life of Lazarillo de Tormes*) was followed, after a forty-year gap, by the immensely successful *La vida de Guzmán de Alfarache* (1599–1604, *The Life of Guzman de Alfarache*) by Mateo Alemán, and then by other novels that participated in the picaresque vogue, such as Francisco López de Ubeda's *La pícara Justina* (1605, *The Rogue Justina*), Alonso Jerónimo de Salas Barbadillos's *La hija de Celestina* (1612, *Celestina's Daughter*), Vicente Martínez Espinel's *Marcos de Obregón* (1618), and *El buscón* (1626, *The Swindler*) by Francisco de Quevedo y Villegas. Many of these works have a complicated relation to the generic construct of the picaresque novel. *Marcos de Obregón* and *El buscón*, for example, have been described as subverting the genre, but they all exploit and respond to the new kind of fiction popularized by *Guzmán de Alfarache*, contributing to the development of a generic tradition even as they modify it.

Much modern criticism investigates the relationship between social reality and cultural form in the emergence of the picaresque novel. The form is understood as engaging in a social critique of the caste society of Golden Age Spain—especially the marginalization of *conversos*, or "new Christians," deriving from Jewish or Muslim families—and offering a critical response to the emergence of commercial modernity and the subsequent hollowing-out of traditional systems of value. According to José Antonio Maravall, the identity of literary *pícaros* is constituted not simply by their low condition but by their rejection of the notion that the social status into which one is born constitutes one's destiny for life.

Scholars emphasize the fact that picaresque novels have been written from different ideological perspectives and that they offer a range of views on the making of a *pícaro* and the legitimacy of his or her social ambitions. Some picaresque novels blame the *pícaros'* heredity or intrinsic nature, while others view them as products of their degraded environments and closed social opportunities. Some picaresque fictions blame the *pícaros'* social ambition as the impulse behind their knavery, while others validate their ambition to escape miserable circumstances.

Attention to the ideological diversity of picaresque novels has not prevented scholars from positing a generic construct of the genre in terms of a constellation of supposedly characteristic features across three dimensions: the character of the protagonist, the formal structure of the narrative, and the typical storyworld inhabited by the characters. Although it is difficult to confine the actual diversity of picaresque novels within this generic construct, it nonetheless informs scholarly discussion of the topic and provides a useful lens for examining individual works (Dunn).

The protagonist of a picaresque novel typically hails from a low, dubious, or disgraced family background and is quickly orphaned or expelled from the family home. From this point on, the *pícaro* exists as a lone individual burdened with the shame of his or her family background and engaged in a struggle for survival. The protagonist exists in a world of fraud, deceit, theft, and exploitation, and experiences physical hardship in the form of hunger, filth, and violence. He or she survives more through tricks and stratagems than penurious labor. Purveyors of fictions and narrators of their own stories, *pícaros* might be said to have at least as much affinity with actors and writers as with the criminals and delinquents whose kin they become.

Picaresque novels are as interested in the social world inhabited by the protagonist as they are in the figure of the *pícaro* or *pícara*. Although they hail from a low milieu, they move among the respectable as servants, apprentices, or beggars, and harbor aspirations to join this world. As a result, picaresque novels shine a spotlight on this other world as well. Indeed the encounter between the *pícaro* and respectable society forms a central part of the narrative interest of the picaresque novel and gives it much of its satiric edge by revealing the respectable world as operating under a more organized form of the exploitation, theft, and fraud that characterizes the *pícaro's* low milieu.

In picaresque novels, the characteristics of the *pícaro* and his or her world are also typically accompanied by certain narrative structures. Lacking any secure place in the world, *pícaros* are itinerant figures, moving from place to place and from master to master. The vagrancy of the *pícaro's* life results in the episodic and open-ended plot structure. It is a life lived at hazard, and the episodic plot embodies this chanciness by not offering the reassurances of a providential order or comic plot.

Moreover, the *pícaro* is not only the protagonist but also the retrospective narrator of the action. The distance between the persona of the narrator and the younger self whose actions he or she narrates serves as the basis for an important dynamic in picaresque novels. From the narrator's relationship with the protagonist it may not be entirely clear whether it is the *pícaro* or the *pícaro*'s society which is being held up for the reader's critical examination. The *pícaro*'s experiences as protagonist may be harsh, but they are rarely inflected as tragic; rather, they are often presented in the mode of coarse comedy, grotesque or scatological humor, or as farce.

Interpretation of picaresque novels is inherently tricky due to the narrative's status as the testimony of a liar. The reader is left to assess the ways in which the narrative might be unreliable, ironic, or elliptical (see NARRATIVE STRUCTURE). Moreover, picaresque novels often make use of self-conscious, multilayered narration with an intrusive narrator, a present narratee, direct address to the reader, extensive commentary, self-reflexive references, and allusions to other literary works. Older criticism tends to emphasize the "realistic" texture of picaresque novels and their engagement with the quotidian, even as it makes assumptions about the "simple" and "primitive" nature of these narratives. Recent criticism emphasizes the discursive complexity of the genre.

GENERIC TRANSFORMATIONS

The immense popularity of *Guzmán de Alfarache*, and the concomitant revival of interest in *Lazarillo de Tormes*, served to establish the picaresque, but almost immediately the genre began to be appropriated or elaborated in diverse ways. Peter Dunn argues that "after *Guzmán* there is no unified, coherent picaresque genre" (265). This is in part because the picaresque novel does not develop in isolation from but as a counter-genre to other genres and discourses. These include the chivalric romances, sentimental novels, Moorish novels, pastoral novels, Counter-Reformation religious discourse, popular mystic literature, autobiography, confessional writings, Renaissance humanist discourses about the dignity of man, and the quixotic mode inaugurated by Miguel de Cervantes Saavedra.

The relational identity of picaresque novels has a double effect. Their oppositional, counter-generic stance gives them certain similarities of outlook and method, despite the variety of genres and discourses they engage, but at the same time this very diversity of counter-generic engagements has the effect of pulling the genre in various directions and transmuting it into a variety of successor forms. This latter process was exacerbated as the picaresque novel was translated and adapted in other European countries. The general effect elevated the social identity of the *pícaro* and turned the protagonist, in this respect, "into an 'anti-pícaro'" (Sieber, 59).

In Spain, as elsewhere, the genre was transformed along several different lines. In one direction, the adventure element came to the fore and the picaresque novel shifted into "the picaresque adventure stories of Salas Barbadillo and Castillo Solórzano" (Bjornson, 70). Indeed, the major picaresque fiction in Germany, *Der abentheuerliche Simplicissimus* (1668, *Simplicius Simplicissimus*) by Hans Jakob von Grimmelshausen, is seen as both an example of the *Schelmenroman* (picaresque novel) and the *Abenteuerroman* (adventure novel). Where the element of itinerant travel became most prominent and expansive, the picaresque novel modulated into the peripatetic novel, often in exotic settings (e.g., James Moirer's *The Adventures of Hajji Baba of Ispahan*, 1824). In a third direction, the focus on *pícaras* led to works like Daniel

Defoe's *The Fortunes and Misfortunes of the Famous Moll Flanders* (1722).

Along another trajectory, the picaresque novel modulated into the BILDUNGSROMAN (novel of formation). The social aspirations of the *pícaro* are more successfully realized in later adaptations as the picaresque novel grows into the novel of social ascension, as in the major French picaresque novel, *L'Histoire de Gil Blas de Santillane* (1715–35, *The Story of Gil Blas de Santillane*) by René Lesage, and in British works like Tobias Smollett's *The Adventures of Roderick Random* (1748). The picaresque itinerary through different scenes in a given society leads directly to the object narratives of the eighteenth century, in which a nonhuman protagonist functions as a window onto various social milieus in a given society (Aldridge). In the nineteenth century the panoramic dimension of the picaresque novel gave rise to the survey of customs and manners in the *costumbrismo* genre in Latin America, while the itinerant plot of the picaresque novel fed into the road-trip fiction of the twentieth century.

There has been a neo-picaresque revival in the twentieth century, anticipated by Mark Twain's *The Adventures of Huckleberry Finn* (1884), and continuing with such works as Thomas Mann's *Die Bekenntnisse des Hochstaplers Felix Krull* (1911–54, *The Confessions of Felix Krull*), José Rubén Romero's *La vida inútil de Pito Pérez* (1938, *The Futile Life of Pito Perez*), Camilo José Cela's *Nuevas andanzas y desventuras de Lazarillo de Tormes* (1944, *New Fortunes and Misfortunes of Lazarillo de Tormes*), and Günter Grass's *Die Blechtrommel* (1959, *The Tin Drum*).

The Spanish picaresque flourished in the transitional space between the breakdown of traditional paternalistic notions of honor, including the social obligations of patron and client, and the reconceptualization of "selfishness" into the utilitarian social ethic of the bourgeois era. Eighteenth-century European adaptations of the picaresque novel function as part of this transformation of materialism and egotism into a kind of social ethic. Thus the picaresque drama of exclusion and social contempt was transformed, among other ways, into a narrative of social ascension. But the renewal of the picaresque novel since the late nineteenth century resonates powerfully with earlier picaresque social contexts. The proletarian narratives of the 1930s and the situations evoked in some contemporary postcolonial novels revive a picaresque sensibility in response to conditions of social exclusion and degradation. In works such as Uzodinma Iweala's *Beasts of No Nation* (2005) and Aravind Adiga's *The White Tiger* (2008), modern picaresque returns us to a world in which society functions not as an enabling structure for human life and livelihood, but as an oppressive structure or an anarchic chaos that reduces people to the condition of homeless and vicious *pícaros*.

The difficulties of a generic conception of the picaresque, combined with the literary-historical complexity of the neo-picaresque revival in the twentieth century, have given rise to attempts at a modal conception of the picaresque that is much sparser and more malleable. It addresses characteristics of the protagonist and his or her fictional world "in which disharmony, disintegration, and chaos prevail" (Wicks, 45), but it does not imply any of the conventional assumptions about narration or plot (e.g., first-person narration, episodic plot). As a result, a modal conception of the picaresque applies to a much wider range of novels than the generic conception. The modal conception of the picaresque helps secure its status as an addition to what André Jolles calls the "permanent inventory" of fictional possibilities (quoted in Wicks, 41).

SEE ALSO: Character, Class, Genre Theory, History of the Novel, Intertextuality, Life Writing, Modernism, Plot.

BIBLIOGRAPHY

Aldridge, A.O. (1972), "Fenimore Cooper and the Picaresque Tradition," *Nineteenth-Century Fiction* 27:283–92.

Alter, R. (1964), *Rogue's Progress.*

Bjornson, R. (1977), *Picaresque Hero in European Fiction.*

Dunn, P. (1993), *Spanish Picaresque Fiction.*

Eisenberg, D. (1979), "Does the Picaresque Novel Exist?" *Kentucky Romance Quarterly* 26:203–19.

Guillén, C. (1971), *Literature as System.*

Maiorino, G., ed. (1996), *Picaresque.*

Maravall, J.A. (1986), *Literatura picaresca desde la historia social.*

Parker, A.A. (1967), *Literature and the Delinquent.*

Rico, F. (1984), *Spanish Picaresque Novel and the Point of View.*

Sieber, H. (1977), *Picaresque.*

Wicks, U. (1989), *Picaresque Narrative, Picaresque Fictions.*

Plot

K. M. NEWTON

Plot is one of the oldest of critical terms, since it is a translation of Aristotle's *mythos* in the analysis of tragedy in his *Poetics* (ca. 335 BCE). For him it meant "the organization of events" (11), and is the most significant of the six elements that he argues constitute tragedy; it is the "most important thing of all" (11) and the "source and ... soul of tragedy" (12). He emphasized the need for a coherent relationship between the incidents that combine to produce a tragic drama in order that the action of the play is not episodic but exists as an organic whole. Intrinsic to his concept of tragedy is "effecting through pity and fear the purification of such emotions" (10) and plot functions as the most important formal element in achieving this (see COMEDY).

Though Aristotle's concept of plot is highly formalist, it has influenced the novel, but it should be remembered that the origins of the novel derive more from narrative modes such as epic and romance than from dramatic modes such as tragedy (see FORMALISM). As Erich Auerbach has argued, the development of narrative from the classical period onward can be persuasively discussed in terms of the representation of reality. In the first chapter of his study *Mimesis*, entitled "Odysseus' Scar," he suggests that the basis of the representation of reality in Western literature is to be found in two ancient and opposed types of narrative: the Homeric epics and the Bible. In their representation of reality, the one turns away from plot, the other embraces it. Auerbach claims that "the element of suspense is very slight in the Homeric poems; nothing in their entire style is calculated to keep the reader or hearer breathless. ... What [Homer] narrates is for the time being the only present, and fills both the stage and the reader's mind completely" (3–4). The scar on Odysseus's leg is the subject of a digression because nothing should be left in an "unilluminated past" (4). In representing external phenomena or psychological processes, "nothing must remain hidden and unexpressed ... the Homeric style knows only a foreground, only a uniformly illuminated, uniformly objective present" (5). This is because "delight in physical existence is everything to [the Homeric poems], and their highest aim is to make that delight perceptible to us" (10).

In contrast, biblical narrative is dominated by plot in which suspense plays a significant role. For example, "in the story of Abraham's sacrifice, the overwhelming suspense is present" (8). Whereas in Homer the past is absorbed into the present, thus abolishing history as difference, in the Bible story "time and space are undefined and call for interpretation," so that "Abraham's actions are explained not only by what is happening to him at the moment, nor yet only by his character ... but by his previous history" (9). In a Homeric narrative like *The Odyssey*, "this 'real' world into which we are lured, exists for itself, contains nothing but itself; the Homeric poems conceal nothing, they contain no teaching and no secret second meaning," while in contrast "[w]hat [the Biblical narrator] produced ... was not primarily oriented toward 'realism' (if he succeeded in being realistic, it was merely a means, not an end); it was oriented toward truth.... The Bible's claim to truth is not only far more urgent than Homer's, it is tyrannical–it excludes all other claims" (11–12).

For Auerbach, these narratives are opposed in style and in their assumptions about the nature of reality (see REALISM). In the Bible, in his reading of it, reality must be part of a narrative structure and interpreted if truth is to be revealed; the meaning or significance of events and human speech cannot necessarily be taken at face value, as they are in Homer, if they are to be understood. The plot of the biblical narrative gives meaning to the world even if that meaning is dependent on a theological conception of truth. Homer's narrative, according to Auerbach, being unconcerned with truth or meaning beyond the experience of physical existence, thus lacks the intellectual basis of biblical narrative. But does the Bible not sacrifice experiential reality in incorporating it within a structure of plot and framing it within a single concept of truth? Is it not also open to the objection that reality is distorted by its theological agenda? It is only with the emergence of the novel in the modern era, Auerbach goes on to suggest, that a narrative form is created that aspires to overcome the opposition between the Homeric and the biblical representation of the real. But can it be done persuasively? Can the limitations of each approach be overcome?

An overview of the eighteenth-century novel shows that its dominating drive is to represent in narrative social reality and the human experience of it. But in giving that narrative a structure that goes beyond narrating a story as a mere sequence of events through the construction of a plot, can a convincing representation of reality be created? Novelists from the eighteenth century onward can be seen as grappling with this problem, at a conscious or unconscious level. In *Moll Flanders* (1722), Daniel Defoe's method is to use first-person narration in which the narrator tells the reader the story of her life. Because the narrator is telling her own story, it stands in place of a plot that connects events and incidents, as the consciousness and personality of the narrator give them significance, Moll being at the center of all that is narrated. Yet is first-person narration enough in itself to transform mere story into plot and overcome the objection that the narrative is essentially episodic? In the epistolary novel, identified with Samuel Richardson in the novels *Pamela* (1740–41) and *Clarissa* (1747–48), the characters still narrate in the first person but in letters which relate to specific experiences and to the personal problems and issues that derive from them. Suspense is built into the narrative, especially *Clarissa*, as the reader does not know what is going to happen next and how threatening situations will be resolved. This provides a plot structure, but one which is integrally connected with the tangible experiences of Clarissa Harlowe, the most important letter writer in the novel, so that it appears that there is no separation between plot and character. The intensity with which the letters are written gives the experiences being recounted a powerful sense of presence even if they are not happening precisely at the time of writing. Another advantage of the epistolary form over Defoe's first-person narration is that more than one character can be brought into play as the letters are exchanged, and provoke responses from the recipients.

Henry Fielding rejected Richardson's method. In *Tom Jones* (1749) he constructed a narrative in which virtually every character or incident is incorporated into the novel's much admired plot, with the narrator represented as a historian writing about real events, thus giving the narrative credibility. Jones's experiences are described in detail but the narrator can also distance himself from them and reflect on the wider issues they raise. This became an influential narrative form for mid-Victorian novelists. That there was doubt in this period as to whether novels could legitimately claim to represent reality with any authenticity is strongly suggested by Laurence Sterne's *Tristram Shandy* (1759–67), which satirizes any attempt to create a plot that can make sense of reality, thus mocking the novels of both Richardson and Fielding. Another significant development was the reaction against realism with the emergence of the GOTHIC novel in the later eighteenth century. Though not rejecting realism as such, it introduced fantasy and the supernatural, and is particularly notable for making plot the central element in the narrative through emphasizing suspense and mystery, with the result that complexity of character and theme become subordinated to plot.

Jane Austen famously mocked the gothic novel in *Northanger Abbey*, published posthumously in 1818, but probably written in 1798–99. Austen is not generally seen as a major innovator but her fiction can be seen as being aware of and, at a formal level, responding to the work of her eighteenth-century predecessors, especially in regard to her handling of plot. Like Fielding, she uses third-person narration, but her narrator is not a historian and there is little of Fielding's general reflections on life and the world. The novel is narrated at the time the action is happening and point of view is primarily focused on the main character without judgment from a future perspective being explicit. This means that the plot is not organized in such a way as to give the reader at a first reading knowledge superior to that of the main character. Even though narration is in the third person, the use of free indirect speech—which merges third-person narration with the character's point of view in her own language—gives the reader a strong sense of empathy with the character and defers judgment (see DISCOURSE). Austen also exploits her reading of gothic fiction by making suspense or a situation that does not seem open to resolution integral to her plot, most obviously, as in *Pride and Prejudice* (1813), whom the heroine shall marry, given that the obstacles in the way of a satisfactory marriage might seem insuperable. The ambiguity of reality is also a feature of the Austen plot. In *Emma* (1816), the eponymous heroine is continually misreading events and the behavior of other characters, partly motivated by the limits of her life and the influence of romantic ideas on her mind. The reader, however, knows no more than Emma, which leads to a more active involvement in the novel's plot since the reader has to interpret the same ambiguous events and actions as Emma. For this reason, *Emma* can be compared to a DETECTIVE story. An advantage of this approach to plot is that, as in Richardson, there is no separation between character and plot. Emma's mistakes and misjudgments constitute the plot and at the same time reveal her character both to herself and to the reader. This leads to ethical reflections on Emma's part and potentially also on the part of the reader. A well-known critical comment of Henry James has strong application to Austen: "What is character but the determination of incident? What is incident but the determination of character?" (1988, 174). It is likely that Austen, in her use of a single plot and a restricted point of view, was a more significant influence on him than he was prepared to admit.

For mid-Victorian novelists Austen's fiction was seen as too narrow in scope for their purposes. Walter Scott famously contrasted her "exquisite touch" with his "Big Bow-Wow strain" (Southam, 155). Scott's creation of the HISTORICAL novel expanded the horizons of fiction and was a major influence on French social realism of the first half of nineteenth century, notably in the novels of Stendhal and Honoré de Balzac. These influences may have affected Victorian novelists in England, for they adopted a new approach to plot, one which they no doubt believed could best represent the more complex social world of the mid-nineteenth century. In contrast to Austen's use of a single plot with the point of view confined to one character, the multi plot novel was created, with Charles Dickens, W. M. Thackeray, George Eliot, and Anthony Trollope being its best-known exponents.

Eliot's *Middlemarch* (1871–72), for example, begins like an Austen novel with the upper-middle-class heroine, Dorothea Brooke, living in a small community and, like Austen's Emma, prone to perceive reality in the light of her imaginative constructions. In the Austen plot, the heroine's mistakes and misinterpretations are eventually overcome or resolved and the audience has the expectation of there being a happy ending in marriage with a man who eventually proves to be a worthy husband. *Middlemarch* confronts the reader with a more uncertain world. In Eliot's version of the Austen plot misinterpretation can have serious, even disastrous, consequences, and happy endings are not assured, and even if they occur the reader is likely to feel some disquiet. The Dorothea Brooke plot is just one of several in this novel, and others soon emerge, notably that relating to Lydgate. He is a doctor and scientist and through him the novel's scope is greatly widened. The multi-plot in *Middlemarch* leads to the narrator with a limited point of view, as in Austen, being replaced by a dominant Fielding-influenced narrator who can move from representing the points of view of several characters to standing apart from all the characters and reflecting or commenting on the action and its implications. Readers can be pulled up sharp in their sympathetic perception of Dorothea by the narrator's intervention in chap. 29: "But why always Dorothea? Was her point of view the only possible one with regard to this marriage?" This is disingenuous on the narrator's part, as the plot up to this point has encouraged the reader to see things from Dorothea's point of view, and in this radical departure the reader is exposed to the idea of the relativity of points of view in regard to how reality is perceived and interpreted, and thus to the need for the novel to have multiple plots in order to create a more complex conception of the real.

The multi-plot novel is open to the objection that it is episodic and irreconcilable with the Aristotelian conception of how plot should function, though novelists like Dickens, Eliot, and Trollope could have argued that they were following Shakespeare's practice with regard to plot rather than classical models. They also attempt to avoid the episodic by the use of structural and thematic links between different plots in order to create narrative unity. In Dickens's *Little Dorrit* (1857) the various spheres of the novel are connected both literally and metaphorically by a recurrent prison-motif reinforced by patterns of imagery, though hardly any commentators on the novel at the time seem to have noticed this (Collins, 2003). In *Middlemarch* the narrative draws attention to parallels between the various plots in the titles of the Books that make up the novel, such as "Waiting for Death" and "Three Love Problems." The deaths of Casaubon and

Featherstone, which affect all of the plots of the novel, have been seen as Eliot's using "coincidence" as a formal device to create narrative unity (Hardy, 1959). This might suggest that linking of these deaths belongs to "story" in itself as a sequence of events, but it is the narrator who creates thematic connections between the deaths by organizing the narrative through plot to highlight parallels between events that another observer would not necessarily see. The various plots are designed by the narrator to give structure to the narrative and this organization is not independent of the narrator's perceiving and interpreting mind.

Despite the intricacy of the structure of multi-plot novels such as *Middlemarch*, Henry James criticized them for lacking form, which made them irreconcilable with his concept of art. In a review, he famously said, "*Middlemarch* is a treasure-house of details, but it is an indifferent whole" (qtd. in Haight, 81). He believed that for form to function authentically in the novel there must be only a single plot governed by one dominating point of view. In a more general attack on the multi-plot novel, mentioning specifically Thackeray's *The Newcomes* (1853–55) and Leo Tolstoy's *Voyná i mir* (1865–69, *War and Peace*), he wrote, "But what do such large loose baggy monsters, with their queer elements of the accidental and the arbitrary, artistically *mean*?" (1988, 84). James was an influence on an important strand of the modernist novel in which plot is increasingly downgraded (see MODERN-ISM). James's later novels become more and more complex in their organization and use of language. A crude summary of novels such as *The Wings of the Dove* (1902) or *The Golden Bowl* (1904) reveals that these novels do have plots but that the plot has little importance in itself. In the more experimental novels written during the modernist period, such as those by James Joyce and Virginia Woolf, plot is—if not dis-

carded, which may be impossible—minimal at best. Modernist novels look toward other means of organizing narrative. The downgrading of plot reaches perhaps its highest point in Woolf's *To the Lighthouse* (1927), where both historical and personal events that would have been crucial to the plots of earlier novels are merely mentioned in passing. In the very short second section of the novel, the dominant character of the first section, Mrs. Ramsay, dies; WWI takes place, in which her son is killed; and her daughter dies in childbirth. All of these, of course, have effects, but they are of little interest to Woolf at the level of plot.

One reason for the retreat from plot in modernism and in later fiction influenced by modernism may be that novelists tended to share James's view that it was futile for the multi-plot novel to try to capture something as multifarious as reality or the many aspects of society, and that if the novel was to succeed as art it had to aspire to "organic form"—"I delight in a deep-breathing economy and an organic form" (1937, 84)—in order to achieve an authentic artistic unity. But perhaps a more important reason is that just as plot-driven gothic romance emerged in the later eighteenth century as an alternative to the dominant realist mode, in the latter half of the nineteenth century the "Sensation Novel" challenged the dominance of social realism, and a more radical division than was apparent in the past began to develop between "literary" and "popular" fiction. Plot dominates the novels of "sensation" writers, particularly the devices of suspense, surprise, and intrigue, which keep the reader turning the pages to discover what will happen next and how problematic situations will be resolved, albeit with a sense of certainty that they will be. Trollope, in his *Autobiography*, first published posthumously in 1883, contrasts the kind of novel he as a mid-Victorian realist tried to write with the plot-dominated fiction written by Wilkie Collins—"with Wilkie Collins … it is all plot" (156)—the best-known sensation novelist:

> When I sit down to write a novel I do not at all know and I do not very much care how it is to end. Wilkie Collins seems so to construct his, that he not only, before writing, plans everything on, down to the minutest detail, from the beginning to end; but then plots it all back again.... One is constrained by mysteries and hemmed in by difficulties, knowing, however, that the mysteries will be made clear and the difficulties overcome at the end of the third volume. Such work gives me no pleasure .... (159–60)

Trollope had used intrigue and suspense in the plots of his own fiction but almost regarded them as mere expedients to keep the plot going and the reader interested. In chap. 30 of *Barchester Towers* (1857), the narrator writes of Eleanor Bold: "How easily would she have forgiven and forgotten the archdeacon's suspicions had she heard the whole truth from Mr. Arabin. But then, where would have been my novel?" He creates suspense and then dissipates it; the reader is assured in chap. 15 that "it is not destined that Eleanor shall marry Mr. Slope or Bertie Stanhope." Trollope's narrator is well aware that what most readers of novels may want is to be kept in suspense, at least until near the end of the novel, but pretends that they are too high-minded to need such devices in order to be interested in the characters and their situations.

Novelists like Dickens, Eliot, and Trollope were able to take the novel seriously as literature but also appeal to a wide audience. Plot remained central, together with devices like suspense and surprise, but it did not break free from character, theme, or style. In the late nineteenth and early twentieth centuries, there is a serious split in the reading public for fiction: the novel that aspires to be "literary," with its downplaying of plot and page-turning devices, becomes the interest of

a minority. The great majority of novel readers in the late nineteenth century and beyond, however, read fiction in which plot is overwhelmingly important, such as the sensation novel (see MELODRAMA) and gothic fiction—Bram Stoker's *Dracula* (1897) being the best-known late nineteenth-century example of the latter. The popular novel becomes increasingly associated with plot-dominated genres such as crime and detective fiction, horror, fantasy, and family sagas. This situation continues, as is apparent from bestseller lists. Bestselling novels seldom win literary prizes, which generally go to the kind of "literary" fiction that underplays plot in favor of linguistic inventiveness, imaginative sweep, or narrative experiment. The winners of such prizes can sell many copies, but hardly compete with the plot-driven bestsellers of genre fiction. Edmund Wilson perhaps articulated the attitude of those who favored the novel with literary aspirations over plot-dominated fiction in a 1945 essay in *The New Yorker*: "Who Cares Who Killed Roger Ackroyd?"

However, in the latter part of the twentieth century this picture changed somewhat when the influence of postmodernism on fiction saw the revival of plot as a central element in novels with literary aspirations. A significant factor was that many novelists had studied literature as an academic discipline, and this academic background created a self-conscious awareness of literary styles, conventions, and genres, and their historical development (see HISTORY). Narrative in particular had been subject to particularly powerful academic study. Russian FORMALISM had made significant contributions: Vladimir Propp's study, *Morphology of the Folktale* (1928), set out to demonstrate that the plots of folktales were variants on the same set of structural elements, and Viktor Shklovsky devised the terms *fabula* and *juzhet* to differentiate between the basic elements of narrative, *fabula* being events or incidents in the order in which they happened, and *juzhet* the arrangement of those to create a plot or narrative structure to serve literary ends. These ideas were influential on French structuralists—who used as equivalents for the Russian terms *histoire* and *récit* (usually translated as "story" and "discourse")—with Algirdas Julien Greimas, Roland Barthes, and especially Gérard Genette making significant contributions to what came to be called narratology. American theorists such as Wayne C. Booth and Seymour Chatman also made important contributions to narrative theory (see NARRATIVE; STRUCTURALISM).

Barthes was the most polemical of these theorists, especially in his attitude to realism and plot in the novel. His study *S/Z* (1970) analyzed the realist text and saw it as consisting of lexies or minimal functional units which are governed by a set of codes. Two of these codes related to plot: the "proairetic" code organizes action in order to create suspense while the "hermeneutic" code operates in terms of mysteries or enigmas within the narrative and defers their resolution. Barthes was generally hostile to the REALIST novel which, as he saw it, claimed to represent reality truthfully but in fact constructed, on the basis of a set of codes, what was an inauthentic version of reality rooted in IDEOLOGY. He advocated a break with "readerly" realism in favor of "writerly" experimental fiction which operated independently of such codes. The other structuralist critics were less political than Barthes and tended to confine themselves to how the elements of narrative functioned without drawing political conclusions. Poststructuralist critics were critical of the use of value-laden binary oppositions in narratology: Jacques Derrida questioning the opposition between story and discourse and Barbara Johnson, a former student of the leading American deconstructionist, Paul de Man, destabilizing Barthes's opposition between the readerly and the writerly text.

The postmodern novel arises out of this critical and theoretical background, since an awareness of narratological theory becomes part of the content of fiction. In contrast to fiction influenced by modernism, the postmodern novel does not as a matter of principle try to discard plot or at the very least reduce it to a minimum. Plot is used, but with the consciousness that it is a fictional device and therefore not to be seen as reflecting reality in any straightforward sense. In much postmodern fiction plot operates in terms of various sets of conventions which are open to PARODY or pastiche (Hutcheon). It can still be integral to the pleasure of the text even if there is skepticism about any claim that it can offer privileged insight into the nature of reality.

It could be argued that some pre-twentieth-century novelists, even if deprived of narratological theory, also used plot with a proto-postmodernist awareness that it constructed the world rather than reflected it, even if they would have resisted the extreme skeptical view that there is a radical discontinuity between the structure of narrative and reality. In her essay, "Notes on Form in Art" (1868), George Eliot stresses that the structure of works of art is imposed by the mind on the world: "And what is structure but a set of relations selected and combined in accordance with the sequence of mental states in the constructor, or with the preconception of a whole which he has inwardly evolved?" (356–57). The passage in chap. 27 of *Middlemarch* in which events are compared to scratches on a pierglass expresses the same idea: when the light of a candle is held against the scratches they appear to be concentric but examined without such a light being applied "[i]t is demonstrable that the scratches are going everywhere impartially." This is applied to the ego of any character, but it also must apply to the creation of a complex multiplot novel.

Trollope sometimes goes further than this and was attacked by Henry James for doing so: "when Trollope suddenly winks at us and reminds us that he is telling us an arbitrary thing, we are startled and shocked in quite the same way as if Macaulay or Motley were to drop the historic mask and intimate that William of Orange was a myth or the Duke of Alva an invention." For James, it is "suicidal" for a novelist to break the realistic illusion by revealing that the novelist has made up or manipulated the plot to serve his or her own purposes; if the novel is to have credibility it must "relate events that are assumed to be real" (qtd. in Smalley, 536). But for Eliot, Trollope, and many novelists associated with postmodernism, to reveal that plot constructs the world it brings into being and to mock some of the devices that novelists have used does not necessarily undermine fiction's claim to represent reality. Any representation will be an interpretation, as James was very well aware, even if at the time of writing his essay on Trollope he believed novelists should cover this up. Trollope's claim to be one of the major realist novelists of the nineteenth century has been unaffected by his occasional playfulness, and novelists associated with postmodernism have been able to produce novels in which plot plays a strong role without undermining their claim to be serious novelists writing literary fiction. Though there have been different attitudes toward plot by novelists, as long as the novel survives as a form it seems certain that it will always have a part to play.

SEE ALSO: Adaptation/Appropriation, Closure, Philosophical Novel, Serialization.

BIBLIOGRAPHY

Aristotle (1996), *Poetics*, trans. M. Heath.
Auerbach, E. (1957), *Mimesis*, trans. W.R. Trask.
Barthes, R. (1990), *S/Z*, trans. R. Miller.
Booth, W.C. (1961), *Rhetoric of Fiction*.
Brooks, P. (1984), *Reading for the Plot*.
Chatman, S.B. (1978), *Story and Discourse*.
Collins, P. (1980), "*Little Dorrit*: The Prison and the Critics," *Times Literary Supplement*, 18 Apr.: 445–46.
Derrida, J. (1979), "Living On," in H. Bloom et al., *Deconstruction and Criticism*.
Eliot, G. (1992), *Selected Critical Writings*.
Garrett, P. (1980), *Victorian Multiplot Novel*.
Genette, G. (1980), *Narrative Discourse*, trans. J.E. Lewin.
Haight, G.S., ed. (1966), *Century of George Eliot Criticism*.
Hardy, B. (1959), *Novels of George Eliot*.
Hutcheon, L. (1988), *Poetics of Postmodernism*.
James, H. (1937), *Art of the Novel*.
James, H. (1988), *The Art of Criticism*.
Johnson, B. (1980), *Critical Difference*.
Prince, G. (1982), *Narratology*.
Smalley, D., ed. (1969), *Trollope*.
Southam, B.C., ed. (1976), *Jane Austen*.
Trollope, A. (1999), *Autobiography*.
Watt, I. (1963), *Rise of the Novel*.

Psychoanalytic Theory

FLORENCE DORE

Psychoanalytic readings of narrative fiction advance the idea that the novel's most important feature is its depiction of human subjectivity. The psychoanalysts who have most influenced literary studies believe that reading, whether clinical or literary, reveals the unconscious dimension of the human mind in particular. Scholars of the novel who employ psychoanalytic theory, accordingly, presuppose that the principal function of the novel is to describe the unconscious. Psychoanalytic study of the novel can be said to have originated in 1907 by none other than the founder of psychoanalysis himself, Sigmund Freud (1856–1939), but psychoanalytic theory did not become established as a preferred method for analyzing novels until the mid-1970s, following the introduction of French psychoanalyst Jacques Lacan's (1901–81) theories into literary studies. In what follows, I will explain why Lacan had such a tremendous influence on novel theory. Lacan is known for his revision of the Freudian conception of the unconscious, and this change in psychoanalytic theory turns out to have overlapped, historically and theoretically, with narratologist Roland Barthes's (1915–80) influential revision of the idea of the author. In the 1970s Lacanian theory was taken up by literary scholars interested in Barthes, and in combination, psychoanalytic theory and narratology created a significant conceptual approach to understanding the novel as a genre (see NOVEL THEORY, 20TH C.). Two of the three psychoanalytic readings Dorothy Hale identifies as crucial to the development of novel theory—by literature scholars Peter Brooks ("Turning the Screw of Interpretation") and Shoshana Felman ("Freud's Masterplot: Questions of Narrative")—were published in Felman's 1977 collection, *Literature and Psychoanalysis*. Of these early psychoanalytic readings influenced by Lacan, I will focus on Brooks's to demonstrate the particular version of psychoanalytic theory that would qualify it as a movement in novel theory.

In their elaboration of theories about the human mind over the course of the twentieth century, Freud and Lacan were above all concerned with the clinical redress of neurosis, but each saw the analysis of novels as relevant to this project because both saw the novel as a privileged site for the analysis of the human mind. Freud wrote two studies of novels, "Delusions and Dreams in Jensen's *Gradiva*" (1907) and "Dostoevsky and Parricide" (1928); and although between 1975 and 1976 Lacan gave a yearlong seminar on James Joyce's novels–published posthumously as *Le Sinthome* (2005, The Symptom)—he published just one novel analysis during his life, the 1965 "Homage to Marguerite Duras, on *Le Ravissement de Lol V. Stein*." In each of these readings, we can find versions of the famous declaration by Freud in his reading of Dostoyevsky's *Brat'ya Karamazovy* (1880, *The Brothers Karamazov*): "Before the problem of the creative artist, the analysis must, alas, lay down its arms" ("Dostoevsky and Parricide," 177). Lacan referred to his analysis as "superfluous" to Duras's novel (1998a, 141), and in relation to his reading of Joyce noted his "embarrassment where art—an element in which Freud did not bathe without mishap—is concerned" (1978, ix). Reading novels seems to have clarified for both analysts that the novel's purpose was to describe the human mind, and in each case, the analyst saw himself as striving to achieve with theory what the novelist achieves with writing. These disavowals themselves may seem superfluous, until we consider them from the point of view of novel theory. Freud and Lacan study the human mind, but their statements of insufficiency where novel writers are concerned also implicitly theorize the novel: if novelists are the superior analysts, then novels reveal what psychoanalysis reveals. Although Freud and Lacan understood their readings of novels to be advancing their ideas about human subjectivity, they were, as importantly, contributing to the definition of the novel as principally concerned with those ideas.

THE NOVEL AND THE UNCONSCIOUS

Hale describes psychoanalytic theory not as a clinical method but instead as a branch of novel theory in its own right. In her assessment, psychoanalytic theory furthered STRUCTURALIST and poststructuralist theories of the novel; she demonstrates that psychoanalytic theorists drew from and advanced the idea that novels depict, engage, and create what is in effect a Lacanian model of human subjectivity. As she puts it, poststructuralists implicitly theorize the novel as offering a "partial and incomplete" (197) subject, and the influential psychoanalytic studies of the novel in the 1970s take this psychological model as the basis for their readings. This "partial and incomplete" subject Hale identifies turns out to distinguish Lacanian psychoanalytic theory from its Freudian origins, and Lacan's revision altered the way novels are read. This change can be gleaned in the contrast between Freud's reading of the unconscious in Wilhelm Jensen's novel *Gradiva* (1903) and Lacan's in *The Ravishment of Lol V. Stein* (1964). Freud's "Delusions and Dreams in Jensen's *Gradiva*" (1907) suggests that the novel's main character, Norbert Hanold, will find what we might understand as a kind of psychological coherence—what Freud understood as a reasonable view of himself and the world—once his delusion is cured. In particular, Norbert is delusional, Freud says, because he has repressed erotic feelings for his childhood friend Zoe Bertgang; as a result, he can see Zoe only as a statue come to life. For Freud, the image of Pompeii in the novel symbolizes the "disappearance of the past combined with its preservation"

(1907, 45) in Norbert's mind, and thus perfectly illustrates the theory of repression. Freud's reading of the novel is based on the postulation that Norbert's unconscious can be plumbed, and it presumes that delusions can be alleviated. In Freud's reading, then, the novel portrays a coherent subject who is temporarily fractured, and in the end restored to himself. In his later analysis of *Brat'ya Karamazovy*, which he reads as a "confession" (1928, 190), Freud similarly advances this kind of subjective coherence in his assessment of the novel as evidence of the author's masochism—a symptom of a resolvable disturbance in Dostoevsky's unconscious (1928, 178).

By 1977, Brooks and Felman would explicitly oppose this kind of psychoanalytic reading, and advocate instead for what Brooks called a "psychoanalytic criticism of the text itself" (299). The kind of psychoanalytic reading these critics envisioned for novels entailed recognition of an unconscious dimension, but in narrative itself, and both declare the insufficiency of readings that simply extract repressed material from the unconscious of authors, readers, or characters. Brooks offers a brief analysis of Charles Dickens's *Great Expectations* (1861) in which he identifies a broad narrative unconscious, one that explicitly replaces an idea of the unconscious in a discrete subject. Brooks's essay compares the Barthean idea that narrative is driven by a desire for meaning at ends to the Freudian death drive, and in making this comparison he theorizes that plot is a force that slows progress to those ends. One basic feature of plot, he observes, is repetition, and Brooks understands narrative repetition as a "binding" (289) of disparate temporal moments that resembles the repetition caused by trauma. In *Great Expectations*, he argues, a textual desire for the end moves through repetitions of what he describes as the "primal scene" of Pip's "terrifying" encounter with Magwitch

(1977, 298). In Freud's conception of the primal scene (1918, 1925, "From the History of an Infantile Neurosis," *Complete Works* 17), the analysand's delusional fear of wolves is a symptom of his repressed sexual identifications, but for Brooks the primal scene is an effect of the structural operations that create both narrative and life. Brooks does identify the primal scene as involving a discrete subject, Pip, but here the primal scene is simply an occasion for the discharge of an "energy" (298) that precedes and generates the character, Pip. To perform the new, preferred kind of psychoanalytic criticism in a reading of Dickens's novel, according to Brooks, the kind that avoids finding an unconscious in characters, readers, or authors, one has to "show how the energy released in [*Great Expectations*] by its liminary 'primal scene'... is subsequently bound in a number of desired but unsatisfactory ways" (298). For Brooks as for Freud, repetition is a form of mastery, but in the new kind of psychoanalytic reading, it must not be understood as the character's attempt to master trauma. In accordance with Brooks' theoretical refusal of coherent subjectivity, he sees repetition as instead a mastery belonging to a disembodied, abstract agent—what both he and Felman understand as "text."

A PSYCHOANALYTIC NARRATOLOGY

Brooks argued that the "possibility of a psychoanalytic criticism" would now rely on "the superimposition of the model of the functioning of the mental apparatus on the functioning of the text" (300). But why did he think that psychoanalytic criticism would be impossible without his intervention? What has happened to invalidate psychoanalytic readings of novels that discover the unconscious in characters and authors? One reason psychoanalytic readings no lon-

ger seemed valid to Brooks is that he was also influenced by one of the inventors of narrative theory, the structuralist Roland Barthes. In *S/Z*, his 1970 reading of Honoré de Balzac's novel *Sarrasine* (1830), Barthes redefines the novel as text, and evokes a domain of signification that resembles the unconscious Brooks sees as preceding authors, characters, and readers. Hale explains that structuralist narratology, the "science" of reading narrative that Barthes was largely responsible for inventing, "builds itself around" the "linguistic law" (193) identified by the Swiss linguist Ferdinand de Saussure (1857–1913), and she clarifies that narratology emerged as "the logical next step in the Saussurian project" (189). For Barthes, indeed, it is the structural operations of signification defined by Saussure that allow for his definition of the novel as a "galaxy of signifiers" (1974, 5), and we can find traces of this emphasis on linguistic law in Brooks's reading of *Great Expectations*. Among the repetitions Brooks identifies in Dickens's novel, significantly, is the palindrome in the name Pip: "Each of Pip's choices ... while consciously life-furthering, forward oriented, in fact leads back, to the insoluble question of origins, to the palindrome of his name" (298). Brooks sees the repetition of psychoanalysis as emanating from the same circularity that snares the character's "consciously life-furthering" choices, those forward movements that actually lead backward. This repetition, for Brooks, is an operation generated by the laws of language identified by Saussure— operations that can be identified even at the level of the name, Pip. For Barthes, moreover, the new structuralist idea of the novel as text entails a recognition of the author as similarly a collection of signifiers–as in this sense "dead." Writing, he argues, is "a neutral, composite, oblique space where our subject slips away, the negative where all identity is lost, starting with the very identity of the body writing" (1974, 142). What Barthes called the "death of the author," we might say, can be understood as the birth of language, and it turns out to have coincided with the death of the coherent Freudian subject. Brooks perceived older modes of psychoanalytic criticism as no longer tenable because he embraced these ideas.

The advent of what I will call psychoanalytic narratology, the theoretical model of psychoanalytic reading I have been tracing in Brooks, came from an apparent perception among literary scholars that Lacan and Barthes were theorizing the same thing. And, in point of fact, psychoanalysis was revolutionized by the same Saussurean ideas that fueled the creation of narratology. It was the theoretical compatibility of these two projects that led to the establishment of psychoanalytic theory as a preferred mode for understanding the novel. Like Barthes, Lacan was heir to Saussure's ideas, but if for the narratologist LINGUISTICS offered a way to reimagine the author, for Lacan it provided the theoretical basis for a sweeping redefinition of the human subject. And Brooks's narratological reading of linguistic repetition in the novel is clearly indebted to Lacan, who himself similarly emphasized puns in his reading of Joyce's *Finnegans Wake* (2005). We can see the compatibility of these approaches in a comparison of "Death of the Author," Barthes's landmark essay of 1968, and Lacan's "Signification of the Phallus," first given as a lecture ten years earlier. Barthes's theory of the text is rooted in the belief that language creates the author—not the other way around—and the Lacanian conception of the incoherent subject relies on the same reversal. As for Barthes, "it is language that speaks, not the author" (1974, 143), so for Lacan, it is "not only man who speaks, but in man and through man that it [*ça*] speaks" (2007, 578). For both of these theorists subjectivity emanates from language, and for Lacan this meant that the

unconscious is an aspect of the subject's irresolvably alienated, incoherent condition.

Turning now to Lacan's analysis of Duras's novel, we can see how his theoretical model of subjectivity leads to the kind of novelistic reading Brooks preferred. Cautioning against what he terms the analytic "pedantry" of postulating an authorial unconscious (1998a, "Homage," 138), Lacan finds in Duras's novel instead the linguistic structure that generates all subjects—Duras, his reader, her reader, himself. Because Lacan understands all of these subjects to exist in a common linguistic realm, his reading identifies not repressed material in the unconscious of a single subject, but the laws structuring all. In his analysis of Lol's dress, this perception leads Lacan to figure his own reading as a "thread" (1998a, 139) that will "unravel" something in the novel, and to suggest that he pulls this "thread" from a "knot" involving the reader (ibid.). Because his reading of the dress is a "thread," and because readers are implicated in the "knot" he unravels, all subjects relevant to his reading can be understood to inhabit the same quasi-fictional dimension as Lol's dress. Quite unlike Pompeii, Freud's image of burial that makes of the unconscious a depth, the dress is for Lacan a cover into which analysis itself collapses, and in his reading depth is altogether eradicated. Lacan asks: "What is to be said about that evening, Lol, in all your passion of nineteen years, so taken with your dress which wore your nakedness, giving it brilliance?" (ibid.). Here, in the reversal— the dress wears the naked body instead of the other way around–Lacan intimates the idea of subjectivity that we might identify as the most basic feature of psychoanalytic reading after Saussure. In Freud's reading, the unveiling of Norbert's unconscious undoes his delusion, and he thus returns to a coherent version of himself. In Lacan's reading, characters emerge as instead constitutively defined by that which seems to cover their inmost depths—and the idea that such a return to coherence might be possible is the delusion. For psychoanalytic critics who follow in Lacan's wake, the novel's function is to reveal this fracture, to identify in the novel the same linguistic operations that generate human subjects. In the conception of the novel that Lacan and Barthes inaugurated, authors emerge as beings who are, if dead, somehow also especially attuned to the operations of language, and therefore, it seems, to humanity itself.

BIBLIOGRAPHY

Barthes, R. (1974), *S/Z*, trans. R. Miller.
Barthes, R. (1977), "Death of the Author," in *Image, Music, Text*.
Brooks, P. (1977), "Turning the Screw of Interpretation," in *Literature and Psychoanalysis*, ed. S. Felman.
Felman, S., ed. (1977; 1982), *Literature and Psychoanalysis*.
Freud, S. (1907 German [1917 English]), "Delusions and Dreams in Jensen's *Gradiva*," in *Standard Edition of the Complete Psychological Works of Sigmund Freud*, trans. and ed. J. Strachey, vol. 9.
Freud, S. (1908 German [1925 English]), "Creative Writers and Day-Dreaming," in *Standard Edition of the Complete Psychological Works of Sigmund Freud*, trans. and ed. J. Strachey, vol. 9.
Freud, S. (1928 German [1929 English]), "Dostoevsky and Parricide," in *Standard Edition of the Complete Psychological Works of Sigmund Freud*, trans. and ed. J. Strachey, vol. 21.
Girard, R. (1965), *Deceit, Desire, and the Novel*.
Hale, D.J., ed. (2006), *Novel*.
Irwin, J.T. (1975), *Doubling and Incest/Repetition and Revenge*.
Jameson, F. (1981), *Political Unconscious*.
Jones, E. (1949), *Hamlet and Oedipus*.
Lacan, J. (1978), *Four Fundamental Concepts of Psycho-Analysis*, ed. J.-A. Miller, trans. Alan Sheridan.
Lacan, J. (1998), "Homage to Marguerite Duras, on *Le Ravissement de Lol V. Stein*," in *Critical Essays on Marguerite Duras*, ed. B.L. Knapp, trans. P. Connor.
Lacan, J. (1998), *The Seminar of Jacques Lacan: Book XX: Encore 1972–1973*, trans. B. Fink.
Lacan, J. (2005), *Seminaire XXIII*, ed. J.-A. Miller.
Lacan, J. (2007), "Signification of the Phallus," in *Écrits*, trans. B. Fink.
Lydon, M. (1998), "The Forgetfulness of Memory," *Contemporary Literature* 29(3):351–68.

Psychological Novel
ATHENA VRETTOS

The psychological novel is traditionally understood as a genre of prose fiction that focuses intensively on the interior life of characters, representing their subjective thoughts, feelings, memories, and desires. While in its broadest usage the term psychological novel can refer to any work of narrative fiction with a strong emphasis on complex characterization, it has been associated specifically with literary movements such as nineteenth-century psychological REALISM, twentieth-century literary MODERNISM, and the "stream-of-consciousness" novel, and with narrative techniques such as free indirect DISCOURSE and the interior monologue. The term psychological novel also refers to works of prose fiction that draw upon contemporary psychological theories (see PSYCHOANALYTIC), and recent studies of the psychological novel have focused on historical convergences between the two fields.

ORIGINS AND DEVELOPMENT OF THE GENRE

Because the term is so flexible, there is little consensus about the origins of the psychological novel. Some trace the GENRE back to the earliest origins of the novel itself; others cite influences ranging from Miguel de Cervantes Saavedra's *Don Quixote* (1605, 1615) to genres such as the historical ROMANCE, the sentimental novel, the EPISTOLARY novel, and the spiritual autobiography (see LIFE WRIT-ING). Some of these diverse influences can be seen in psychological novels from the first half of the nineteenth century, including James Hogg's *The Private Memoirs and Confessions of a Justified Sinner* (1824), which makes extended use of the doppelganger, or alter ego, and Stendhal's realist BILDUNGSRO-MAN *Le Rouge et le Noir* (1830, *Scarlet and Black*).

Regardless of its origins, by the second half of the nineteenth century the psychological novel was flourishing. Fyodor Dostoyevsky's novels constitute particularly influential examples of the genre; his intense psychological portrayals of suffering and despair were precursors to twentieth-century existentialism, and his fictional legacy extends to authors as diverse as Marcel Proust, Albert Camus, Jean-Paul Sartre, Franz Kafka, James Joyce, Virginia Woolf, and William Faulkner. Leo Tolstoy was also crucial in the development of the psychological novel. His detailed observations of the inner lives of his characters had an impact on both nineteenth- and twentieth-century practitioners of the genre. Anticipating modernist portrayals of subjectivity, both Tolstoy and Dostoyevsky embedded internal monologues—direct representations or thought- quotations from the mind of a character—in the omniscient NARRATIVE STRUCTURE of their fiction.

Tolstoy's intimate and psychologically complex characterizations were echoed in a wide range of nineteenth-century novels that not only developed narrative techniques for the representation of human interiority, but also reflected and contributed to psychological debates of the period. As recent critics have demonstrated, nineteenth-century psychological novels explored new theories of emotion, attention, habit, selfhood, memory, trauma, consciousness, and the unconscious. In particular, authors such as George Eliot and

Henry James were central figures in the growth of the psychological novel and the rise of psychological realism in Britain and America. Both authors drew upon their knowledge of the rapidly developing field of psychology to explore the inner lives and unspoken motives of characters in works such as Eliot's *Middlemarch* (1871–72) and James's *Portrait of a Lady* (1881). Their close family connections with two of the most respected psychologists of the period—George Henry Lewes (1817–78) was unofficially married to George Eliot, and William James (1842–1910) was Henry James's brother—further shaped Eliot's and James's engagements with contemporary psychological theories. Tracing the psychology of characters through the use of free indirect discourse and omniscient third-person narration, their narratives move subtly in and out of the minds of different characters to convey their feelings, thoughts, and perspectives, and to suggest the intricate relationship between mind and body, internal motivations, and external actions. In the process, Eliot and James (like many of their contemporaries) put into practice some of the principles of nineteenth-century physiological psychology, which emphasized the material basis of the mind. James's later novels are characterized by experimentation with points of view, interior monologues, and unreliable narrators. In works such as *The Turn of the Screw* (1898), *The Ambassadors* (1903), and *The Golden Bowl* (1904), James's indirect and often elusive prose style conveys what Sharon Cameron has called the "omnipresence of consciousness" (1989, *Thinking in Henry James*, 5). These works exemplify not only James's intense psychological focus, but also his experimentation with narrative techniques that link him to both the discourse of late Victorian psychology and the developments of modernism.

James's later writings emerged in the context of a fin-de-siècle ethos that offered challenges to traditional values and literary forms, as well as a rapidly changing psychological and literary landscape. This period included the rise of the DECADENT movement, which championed both sexual and aesthetic experimentation, and the French Symbolist movement, which challenged the capacity of conventional language or realist literature to convey the sensation of consciousness. Instead, the Symbolists sought a condensed, highly symbolic language that emphasized images, dreams, and the imagination. The symbolist experimentations of such writers as Stéphane Mallarmé and Édouard Dujardin were important inspirations for Joyce and other modernist writers. Another contributor to this experimental period, the Norwegian author Knut Hamsun, published psychological novels such as *Sult* (1890, *Hunger*) and *Pan* (1894) that depict characters suffering from suicidal isolation and deep skepticism. Employing narrative techniques such as flashbacks and fragmentation, Hamsun's novels were vital influences on modern continental fiction.

CRITICAL EMERGENCE
OF THE GENRE

Although it did not become a standard part of the critical lexicon for identifying fictional genres until the end of the nineteenth century, the term "'psychological novel" first entered the English language as a literary insult when Eliot, in 1855, criticized "'psychological' novels ... where life seems made up of talking and journalizing" ("Charles Kingsley's Westward Ho!"). By the end of the century the term was used to describe Eliot's own fiction, and it appeared regularly in encyclopedias and critical histories of the English novel, with whole chapters devoted to the genre. In these early definitions of the psychological novel authors such as Charlotte Brontë, Elizabeth Gaskell, and George Meredith were frequently included along with Eliot and James, as was the popular French novelist and critic Paul Bourget, whose influential *Essais de psychologie contemporaine* (1883, *Essays in Contemporary Psychology*) viewed literature and psychology as inextricably linked. However, an entry on the psychological novel from *The New International Encyclopedia* of 1903 declared, somewhat prematurely, that "for the time being, psychology seemed to have run its course in English fiction" (209).

FIN-DE-SIÈCLE PSYCHOLOGY
AND THE EXPERIMENTS OF
MODERNISM

While some styles of psychological realism had, indeed, begun to decline in popularity by the early twentieth century, the psychological novel was far from having "run its course." In a 1907 lecture later published as "Creative Writers and Day-Dreaming," Sigmund Freud (1856–1939) identified the psychological novel as a distinct genre in which "the hero—is described from within. The author sits inside his mind, as it were, and looks at the other characters from outside. The psychological novel no doubt owes its special nature to the inclination of the modern writer to split up his ego, by self-observation, into many" (150). Drawing upon psychological theories of memory and consciousness, the psychological novel eventually became central to the development of literary modernism. The emergence of the memory sciences in the latter half of the nineteenth century, including French philosopher and psychologist Henri Bergson's (1859–1941) identification of *mémoire pure* (i.e., "pure memories" that are experienced involuntarily rather than intentionally recollected), coincided with a steadily increasing literary interest in portraying the unpredictable vagaries of memory and consciousness that had begun in the final decades of the nineteenth century. William James's analysis of "desultory memory" and Lewes's coinage of the term "stream of consciousness" corresponded to literary attempts to replicate the experience of consciousness—to convey its paradoxical combination of continuity and change—through language. Early twentieth-century writers such as Marcel Proust, James Joyce, Dorothy Richardson, William Faulkner, and Virginia Woolf fused their experiments in literary form with these new understandings of the mind. For example, in the multi-volume À la recherche du temps perdu (1913–27, Remembrance of Things Past), Proust explores "pure" or involuntary memory—including, most famously, the role of the senses in triggering memories. Early twentieth-century psychological novels were frequently narrated from within the minds of individual characters, employing first-person narration combined with interior monologue to trace the intrusions of fugitive memories, thoughts, associations, and perceptions in the experience of consciousness. In addition to Proust's semi-autobiographical fictional memoir, Richardson's multi-volume Pilgrimage (1915–38), Joyce's Portrait of the Artist as a Young Man (1914–15) and Ulysses (1922), Woolf's Mrs. Dalloway (1925) and To the Lighthouse (1927), and Faulkner's The Sound and the Fury (1929) all experiment with portraying the evanescence of thought, thereby developing the literary form that author May Sinclair first described in a 1918 review of Richardson's fiction as "a stream of consciousness, going on and on" ("Novels of Dorothy Richardson"). Although these literary attempts to reproduce the experience of consciousness drew most directly upon the theories of Bergson (1896,

Matter and Memory) and William James (1890, Principles of Psychology), they also coincided with (and, in the later works, drew inspiration from) Freud's revolutionary theories of selfhood and the unconscious.

Although Proust, Richardson, and Joyce all published their groundbreaking narratives in the years between 1913 and 1915, Joyce's Portrait offered the most radical departure from previous fictional forms. Immersing the reader in the fragmented thoughts and memories of a child, Joyce's opening language provides no explanatory critical framework, no traditional narrative frame, no recognizable entry point—only the abrupt immediacy of mental perceptions and sensations (see CLOSURE). Even more than the publication of Portrait, however, the appearance of Joyce's Ulysses in 1922 reconceived the psychological novel through its revolutionary linguistic rendering of the mind (see LINGUISTICS). Tracing the "labyrinth of consciousness" through three central characters, and transpiring within the period of a single day, Ulysses has been hailed as "the fountain-head of the modern psychological novel" (L. Edel, 1972, The Modern Psychological Novel, 2nd ed., 75). If Ulysses offers an immersion in the playful fluidity of waking consciousness, Joyce's notoriously elusive final novel, Finnegans Wake (1939), probes the nocturnal, unconscious mind, weaving a dense linguistic tapestry of dream associations and allusions, puns and portmanteau words that assault the boundaries of the psychological novel's coherence and form.

CRITICAL AND POSTMODERN REACTIONS

May Sinclair predicted that such "stream-of-consciousness" narratives would constitute the future of the novel, and indeed this version of the psychological novel, which also has been termed the "novel of introspection," "the subjective novel," and, in France, the "modern analytic novel," became one of the defining experiments of literary modernism. Sinclair declared that the twentieth-century novelist "should not write about the emotions and the thoughts of his characters. The words he uses must be the thoughts—be the emotions" ("The Future of the Novel"). Leon Edel later described this as the difference between subjective states being "reported" and being "rendered" (19).

However, over the course of the twentieth century, there were numerous critiques of the psychological novel, the most famous of which is MARXIST literary critic Georg LUKÁCS's claim that the genre sought "to achieve an idealist and reactionary separation of the psychological from the objective determinants of social life" (1983, *Historical Novel*, 240). Lukács observed that as a result of this separation, "all social criticism disappears." Others have complained that the psychological novel is overly intellectual, devoid of action, or lacking in subtlety. Carl Jung (1875–1961) objected that the psychological novel "does too much of the work for the reader. Its psychology is self contained and explained by the author," leaving nothing for the psychologist to interpret (1930, "Psychology and Literature"). More appreciative critical studies, especially of the modernist psychological novel, flourished in the 1950s and 1960s and helped to define the genre (Edel, Friedman).

Although early twentieth-century writers and critics often framed modernist versions of the psychological novel in opposition to their nineteenth-century counterparts, more recent critics have reevaluated this relationship to find a wide-ranging and complex narrative engagement with contemporary psychological issues in both periods. Recent critical approaches to the psychological novel range from rigorous narratological analyses of the literary presentation of consciousness (Cohn) to historical and theoretical studies of the close relationship between fiction, psychology, and neurology in different eras (Bourne Taylor; Davis; Matus; Ryan; Shuttleworth; Stiles). This latter approach, in particular, has generated an array of critical analyses of the relationship between fiction and psychology, especially in the nineteenth century. Sally Shuttleworth, for example, has demonstrated the extensive use of phrenology, physiognomy, associationist psychology, and the rhetoric of the self-help movement in Charlotte Brontë's fiction, and has explored the intersecting embodiment of memory in Victorian psychology and the novel. Jill Matus has explored early theories of trauma in the nineteenth century, especially in the work of George Eliot and Charles Dickens. Other studies of the intersections between psychology and the psychological novel have ranged from detailed studies of individual authors, such as Nancy Paxton's examination of the dialogue between Eliot and Herbert Spencer on issues of psychology, evolution, and gender, to broad studies such as Nicholas Dames's exploration of forgetting, nostalgia, and theories of memory in *Amnesiac Selves* (2001), and his analysis of the relationship between reading, literary form, and the nineteenth-century neural sciences in *The Physiology of the Novel* (2007).

By the middle of the twentieth century, the central role of the psychological novel in literary modernism had inspired a range of postmodern reactions that challenged both the form of the "stream-of-consciousness" narrative and its predominant focus on characters' subjective, psychological experiences. Though notoriously slippery to define, postmodernism's often playful metafictional pastiches of prior literary forms frequently include the use of deliberately superficial characters—characters that are intentionally flat, ghostly, or cartoon-like—in part to interrogate the conventions and assumptions of the modern psychological novel. Thomas Pynchon's *The Crying of Lot 49* (1966) and *Gravity's Rainbow* (1973) and Don DeLillo's *White Noise* (1985) are examples of this postmodern trend. There are still, however, numerous examples of the psychological novel in contemporary fiction, as we see in Mark Haddon's *The Curious Incident of the Dog in the Night-time* (2003), which merges the psychological novel with both the DETECTIVE novel and the diary to portray the world through the eyes and mind of an autistic teenager. Such fusions of the psychological novel with other genres suggests that contemporary authors are finding creative new directions for the future of the psychological novel and should make critics wary of prematurely pronouncing its decline at this new turn of the century.

SEE ALSO: Cognitive Theory, Mythology, Time.

BIBLIOGRAPHY

Bourne Taylor, J. (1988), *In the Secret Theatre of Home.*
Campbell, M. and S. Shuttleworth, eds. (2000), *Memory and Memorials, 1789–1914.*
Cohn, D. (1978), *Transparent Minds.*
Davis, M. (2006), *George Eliot and Nineteenth-Century Psychology.*
Matus, J. (2008), "Historicizing Trauma," *Victorian Literature and Culture* 36:59–78.
Paxton, N. (1991), *George Eliot and Herbert Spencer.*
Ryan, J. (1991), *Vanishing Subject.*
Shuttleworth, S. (1996), *Charlotte Brontë and Victorian Psychology.*
Shuttleworth, S. and J. Bourne Taylor, eds. (1998), *Embodied Selves.*
Stiles, A., ed. (2007), *Neurology and Literature, 1860–1920.*

Purana *see* Ancient Narratives of South Asia

Publishing

DAVID FINKELSTEIN

The age of print and publishing begins with the development of the printing press by Johannes Gutenberg (fl. 1390–1468) in Mainz, Germany in about 1450. Adapting techniques and equipment used in agricultural settings (e.g., the grape press), by 1456 Gutenberg had begun producing multiple copies of texts in printed form, including a 42-line Bible, some grammatical works, a papal indulgence, and at least one broadside astrological calendar. Within a few years of its first use, this new technology for making books had spread throughout Europe (see PAPER AND PRINT).

Printing proved a lucrative business: books became valuable commodities, requiring the development of a sophisticated network of production, sales, and distribution. The late medieval book trade had centered on local markets and needs. The age of humanism, an increase in literacy in the 1600s, and the expansion of literary culture to embrace literature, however, saw printing and publishing expand to become international in scope. From the 1470s, printing spread outward from Germany, appearing in Buda in Hungary in 1473, Cracow in Poland, and Prague in Bohemia within the next two or three years. In Spain book publishing arrived in Valencia in 1473, then Madrid in 1499. Printing appeared in Lisbon in 1489, Scandinavia in 1483, Constantinople in 1488, Salonika in 1515. In England, William Caxton (ca. 1422–91) set up a printing press at Westminster Abbey in 1476, and in Scotland the first book was printed in Edinburgh in 1508 (Finkelstein and McCleery, 55).

NINETEENTH-CENTURY INNOVATION

Until the early 1800s, the general format for the production of books in Western Europe followed basic, established business patterns. Early printers combined the roles of printers, publishers, and booksellers in one, buying rights to works, then printing and profiting from the results. As trade increased to include international links, these roles began to be separated, and by the early nineteenth century, Western European publishers had begun devolving production work to printers, illustrators, and other related production specialists. The technological innovations accompanying the Industrial Revolution in nineteenth-century Britain enabled it to become a world leader in book production and dissemination, producing books faster and less expensively than its continental rivals.

The introduction of the steam-powered press in London in 1814, a Koenig press imported from Germany by *The Times* newspaper for its daily printing work, sparked its integration into general publishing activity. This, along with advances in mechanical typecasting and setting, stereotyping, and innovations in the reproduction of illustration, led to less costly and faster-produced books (see ILLUSTRATED NOVEL, TYPOGRAPHY). Industrialized societies across the world saw the need for a better-educated, certainly literate, workforce to service new processes and occupations. In Britain the Education Acts of the 1870s cemented the growth of literacy so that by the turn of the twentieth century the vast majority of the population constituted the market for books (Feather). Book publishing became a boom industry.

Such industrialization of printing and publishing systems went in partnership with the general industrialization of business across Britain and then Western Europe. Mechanization increased market potential and forced publishers to adapt quickly to survive. As Robert Escarpit notes, "faced with a developing market, printing and bookselling underwent a major change, as nascent capitalist industry took charge of the book. The publisher appeared as the responsible entrepreneur relegating the printer and bookseller to a minor role. As a side effect, the literary profession began to organize" (22–23).

NEW BUSINESS MODELS

British printers and publishers were among the first to adopt new business models to match new technological opportunities, turning themselves into large, predominantly family-run corporate enterprises. These included Macmillan, William Blackwood & Sons, John Murray, William Chambers, Smith, Elder & Co., and William Longman, almost all founded within the first twenty years of the nineteenth century. Their national dominance would translate into international success as they expanded into the colonial markets that emerged from the 1870s onward. Such success encouraged the free flow of books beyond national borders. Britain and its empire, it can be argued, was the first transnational, globalized economy to emerge as a beneficiary of the advances supported by industrialization. From the 1830s onward Britain's innovations would be copied in other European states and further abroad, with a resulting sea change in trade practices by the mid-nineteenth century. In tandem with such changes an increasingly literate reading audience demanded new products to read, allowing profitable firms to expand and dominate local and national markets. Among the most important to develop in Europe and the U.S.

were Hachette in France; Samuel Fischer and Bernhard Tauchnitz in Germany; George Putnam, Houghton Mifflin, and Harpers & Co. in the U.S.; Gyldendals in Denmark; and Norstedts and Albert Bonnier in Sweden (Gedin, 34–39; Hall, 44; Chartier).

The rise of the novel as a cultural signifier during the nineteenth century was closely linked to such changes. The number of titles produced by these internationally positioned publishers rose dramatically, in line with a growth in readership and the establishment of well-provisioned commercial bookshops, circulating library networks such as the renowned Mudie's Circulating Library, public libraries, and retail distribution outlets such as the British railway bookstall networks founded by W. H. Smith in 1842, John Menzies in 1857, and the French network founded by Hachette in 1853 (see LIBRARIES). It is estimated that the number of general book titles published in Britain per decade rose roughly from 14,550 in the 1800s to around 60,812 in the 1890s; at the peak of book production, fiction accounted for about a third of the titles listed in contemporary book-trade journals (Eliot, 294, 299).

Popular titles could achieve substantial sales in their own right. While a bestselling novel of the 1800s might have had a combined print run and sales of up to 12,000, by the 1890s popular titles were achieving print runs and sales of 100,000 in various editions within the first five years of publication (Eliot, 294). Popular demand for fiction was met in various ways, including SERIALIZATION in high-quality monthlies, "illustrated" magazines, mass-circulation weeklies, and through syndication in metropolitan, regional, and provincial newspapers. Thus in newspaper and periodical spaces, readers would encounter poetry and fiction in conjunction with fashion, news, opinion, and reportage, a mélange that also engaged and satisfied general reading expectations. Equally, readership interest would be pi-

qued and encouraged by the increasing use of advertising in popular journals and in the end pages of novels and other publications.

As the nineteenth century progressed, more and more titles were published and publishers' niche subjects grew in diversity. In Britain roughly one hundred new titles were published each year up to 1750, growing to six hundred by 1825, and to six thousand by the beginning of the twentieth century—at its close new titles topped the hundred thousand mark (Feather). The century also saw experiments with new formats such as the popular series, large quantities of books published at low prices and intended for mass consumption. These were often a means of enabling access to novels that had first appeared in expensive formats: for much of the century, novels were first published in three-volume form, to be accessed mainly through the commercial circulating libraries that dominated book distribution throughout the century. A year after their initial appearance many of these would then be reprinted in the cheaper one-volume form, thus establishing a precedent that still holds true in current book-publishing patterns.

European print communication practices as reconfigured during this period were subsequently exported to other countries, with colonial powers in particular establishing print networks in overseas possessions so as to service didactic and governing needs. At the same time, such international print production and communication systems also proved susceptible to hierarchies and divisions, part of a "distinctive, determinate set of interlocking, often contradicting practices" (Feltes, 17). Literary value, COPYRIGHT, and the commercial worth of books increasingly became linked to commercial potential, creating a niche for intermediaries such as literary agents to filter and promote the "raw" material needed by publishers.

INTELLECTUAL PROPERTY RIGHTS

Integral to business success was the management of rights in the texts produced. In 1709, the first U.K. Copyright Act created a template soon adopted in other countries, enshrining in law the principle that copyright in a work belonged to its author. This permitted some authors to demand greater sums when selling their works to publishers. The publication of books on subscription, a popular method of financing publication before 1709, was one method of copyright management, but by the mid-nineteenth century had been superseded generally by contracts offering outright sale of copyright to the publisher. The professionalization of AUTHORSHIP throughout the nineteenth century, which gained impetus as further outlets for literary work opened up, saw contractual arrangements changing, with most publishing contracts by the end of the century offering writers sliding-scale royalty figures based on numbers of copies sold.

However, while copyright could be enforced within the one country, it did not have any international status. For British and English-language publishing, this resulted in a voracious and unchecked pirating of works in the U.S. and elsewhere that drew the ire of many authors and their representatives. Not until the Berne Convention of 1886 was approved did international copyright protection become universal, later strengthened by the Universal Copyright Convention of 1952. In the U.K., the Copyright Act of 1911 incorporated references to non-print media by adding clauses guaranteeing the protection of copyright to visual and oral media. This in turn provided a secure basis both for the development of work in such media and for the adaptation of an author's work for non-print sources (Finkelstein and McCleery, 62–63).

INTO THE TWENTIETH CENTURY

Such changes in nineteenth-century legal statutes, technology, business practices, and social formations created circumstances by which printed texts, manufactured more quickly and at increasingly cheaper costs, could be sold to more people, generating larger profits for publishers and allowing individual authors to claim more profits from work produced. Much remained static during the first half of the twentieth century, though the introduction in Britain of inexpensive Penguin paperback books by Allen Lane (1902–70) in 1935 was a key moment in the history of book production. Penguin books drew on previous experiments in paperback production, paying close attention to visually rich covers, marketing and selling in nonconventional; outlets such as retail shops and direct sales, and offering new, original titles in paperback rather than hardback. Their success opened the way for a mass-market explosion in paperback publishing: in the U.S., for example, Robert de Graaf founded Pocket Books in 1939, marketing populist titles with bright covers for a mass readership, while in Britain Penguin faced competition from Pan Books and Panther, established after WWII to tap similar mass-market interest.

Such developments were part of a shift in book publishing to a position strongly dependent on mass market literary taste. As Richard Ohmann comments, "publishing was the last culture industry to attain modernity. Not until after World War II did it become part of the large corporate sector, and adopt the practices of publicity and marketing characteristic of monopoly capital" (22). To increase economies of scale, from the 1960s onward publishing houses merged with other media operators to form large, often trans-national conglomerates. The general traits and practices of family-run and family-focused publishing houses began to be replaced by international corporate organizations that joined together different media areas (books, television, film, music) under one umbrella.

But publishing in the twentieth century also saw exponential rises in global book production. It has been estimated that in 1850 annual world book production totaled 50,000; in 1952 it had risen to 250,000 titles; by 1963 it equaled 400,000; in 1970, 521,000 (Escarpit, 57–58; Milner, 70; Zaid, 21). Of such production, four language groups (English, French, German, Spanish) dominate, accounting for between 34 and 36 percent of these titles (Escarpit, 61–62). The increasing domination of large global corporations has also involved a shift in the control and shaping of international book markets, particularly in the Anglophone world. In the nineteenth century Britain was the dominant player in innovative publishing terms; by the late twentieth, power and influence had shifted towards U.S.- and continental European-based players (Finkelstein, 338).

These players instituted significant technical developments that shaped contemporary book markets. Thus we have seen an important shift away from fiction to non-fiction titles as the commercially dominant part of a publisher's list, with what Robert Escarpit has called "functional books," particularly textbooks, providing "powerful testament to the commercial significance of the captive market delivered to the book trade by the systems of higher and secondary education" (Milner, 70). Furthermore, books are increasingly marketed and distributed through a range of nontraditional retail outlets that have their origins in earlier initiatives (such as newsagents, supermarkets, department stores, and book clubs), so expanding the availability of fiction and books beyond specialist bookshops. Equally important has been the place of online retail spaces such as Amazon.com in supporting book sales and distribution in sections of the world that have access to new media and the internet. Finally, audiences have been exposed to more texts worldwide as a result of the adoption of the paperback as a significant publishing format for new books. Pundits have been predicting the death of the book for some time now, but the strength of sales and the reach of texts beyond national borders in such fashion suggest that books may yet survive as important communication tools in the increasingly globalized media and information world of the twenty-first century.

SEE ALSO: Adaptation/Appropriation, Editing, Graphic Novel, History of the Novel, Journalism, Reading Aloud, Reprints, Reviewing, Translation.

BIBLIOGRAPHY

Chartier, R. (1981), "L'ancien regime typographique," *Annales E.S.C.* 36:191–209.

Eliot, S. (2007), "From Few and Expensive to Many and Cheap," in *Companion to the History of the Book*, ed. S. Eliot and J. Rose.

Escarpit, R. (1966), *Book Revolution*.

Feather, J. (2006), *History of British Publishing*, 2nd ed.

Feltes, N.N. (1986), *Modes of Production of Victorian Novels*.

Finkelstein, D. (2007), "The Globalization of the Book, 1800–1970," in *Companion to the History of the Book*, ed. S. Eliot and J. Rose.

Finkelstein, D. and A. McCleery (2005), *Introduction to Book History*.

Gedin, P. (1982), *Literature in the Marketplace*, trans. G. Bisset.

Hall, D.D. (1996), *Cultures of Print*.

Milner, A. (1996), *Literature, Culture and Society*.

Ohmann, R. (1998), *Selling Culture*.

Zaid, G. (2004), *So Many Books*.

Purana *see* Ancient Narratives of South Asia

Qissa *see* Arabic Novel (Mashreq)

Queer Novel

ROBERT L. CASERIO

"The queer novel" addresses a complex object. The phrase points to fiction in which characters are identified as gay or lesbian or bisexual or transgendered, and in which same-sex love is prominent. But that is only one meaning of the phrase. Scholarly use of the term "queer" intends to undo our certainties about erotic desire and our definitions of agents of desire, even when eros and its agents are denominated as gay or lesbian. Hence "the queer novel" comprehends more than "gay fiction" or "lesbian fiction," more than fiction by gay or lesbian authors, even though it takes inspiration from the same-sex eros that religion, law, and society might identify as unnatural or abnormal. Identification of what is "abnormal" overlooks the arbitrariness and instability of the institutionalized conventions on which "normality" is based. "Heterosexuality" is also an unstable category or identity, itself a queer business. As Sigmund Freud declares in 1915 in a footnote to the first of his *Three Essays on the Theory of Sexuality*, "the exclusive sexual interest felt by men for women is . . . a problem that needs elucidating and is not a self-evident fact." Eros is unruly; attempts to regulate it are costly. "The requirement . . . that there be a single kind of sexual life for everyone," Freud

protests in *Civilization and Its Discontents*, "disregards the dissimilarities, whether innate or acquired, in the sexual constitution of human beings" (chap. 4).

The novel has always occupied itself with dissimilarities in humanity's erotic constitution; designating a subspecies of fiction as "queer" perhaps is redundant. If, however, we take the queer novel most obviously to mean an alternative to representations of opposite-sex eros, in the nineteenth century the genre originates in German Romantic fictions about male–male love by August, Duke of Saxony-Gotha, and by Heinrich Zschokke. In France, Honoré de Balzac's output includes *La fille aux yeux d'or* (1835, *The Girl with the Golden Eyes*), about a lesbian liaison; and three novels (1837–49) that feature a compelling homosexual master criminal (and eventual head of the Paris police), Jacques Collin. Balzac is not claimed as a gay writer, but the queer novel is alive in him. In North America, Herman Melville's novels imply sexual encounters between men: *Moby-Dick* (1851) includes a fantasy of male group masturbation and idealizes—significantly for future developments of queer fiction—a correlation between homosexual eros and radical democracy.

Oscar Wilde's *The Picture of Dorian Gray* (1891) initiates the queer novel in English and Irish fiction. Wilde's protagonist, who can be interpreted as bisexual, is ultimately punished for his departures from norms. His punishment might represent Wilde's submission to the legal and social conventions

The Encyclopedia of the Novel   Edited by Peter Melville Logan
© 2011 Blackwell Publishing Ltd

that, as a result of his trial for sodomy in 1895, condemned him to prison for two years. Yet when Wilde emerged from prison he did not recant his eros. And *The Picture of Dorian Gray* invests with homoerotic desire for Dorian the artist who paints the magical picture. The portrait painter is sympathetically rendered. If Dorian is punished by his maker, Wilde, it is in part because Dorian ruthlessly kills the blameless artist.

Homophobia (both external and internalized) has been said to dictate unhappy fates for same-sex love in queer novels written before Stonewall-era liberation (i.e., 1969 and after). Evidence of this view adduces multiple censorships: E. M. Forster's self-suppression of his novel *Maurice* (1913) because it asserts the happiness of a male couple; legal prosecution of A. T. Fitzroy's *Despised and Rejected* (1918), a WWI "coming-out" novel about a friendship between a lesbian and a gay conscientious objector; and the trial for obscenity of Radclyffe Hall's *The Well of Loneliness* (1928), in which the heroine, a novelist, loses her beloved Mary to heterosexual marriage, and swears thereafter to martyr herself to her queer "kind." Her kind demand that she use fiction to "acknowledge us ... before the whole world," to "give us also the right to our existence," even if service to the demand "tear[s] her to pieces" (chap. 5, §3).

In the face of such unhappy outcomes, one must keep in mind that realism and naturalism in fiction, of which Hall's novel is a mixture, tend to represent defeats of eros, no matter what its variety. The Brazilian novel *Bom-Crioulo* (1895) by Adolfo Caminha explicitly recounts a rivalry between a black gay sailor and a white Portuguese woman for the sexual possession of a cabin boy. The rivalry is disastrous; but the disaster is caused by naturalism's fatalistic view of eros, rather than homophobia.

Moreover, by the time of the trial of *The Well of Loneliness*, queer eros in fiction is more affirmed than stories of fatality or legal suppression suggest. Mikhail Kuzmin's Russian novel *Krylya* (1906, *Wings*), an experiment in modernist impressionism, unfolds the increasingly joyous sexual self-discovery of its young protagonist. In the U.S., Edward Prime-Stevenson's *Imre* (1906) also vindicates homosexual romance. In England fictions by Frederick Rolfe and Ronald Firbank maintain Wilde's vital influence. Rolfe's *Hadrian the Seventh* (1904) imagines a chaste but homosexual pope, who blesses a male–male union between his chamberlain and a failed candidate for the priesthood. Firbank's *The Flower beneath the Foot* (1924), about an imaginary European nation-state, exhibits routine lesbian love affairs, a boy-loving former prime minister, and gay migrant workers from North Africa. Such content in Rolfe's and Firbank's fictions was not prosecuted. Also not prosecuted was Virginia Woolf's *Orlando*, about a time-conquering transgendered protagonist, published in the same year as *The Well of Loneliness*. In France the prestige of the novels of André Gide and Marcel Proust, both of whom portray queer figures, commenced before WWI; the English translation of Proust's *Sodome et Gomorrhe* (*Cities of the Plain*), revealing the homosexuality of multiple leading characters, appeared the year before *Orlando* and *The Well of Loneliness*.

MULTIPLE ORIENTATIONS

The queer novel acquires intensity in the first half of the twentieth century by becoming the joint product of writers whose sexual orientations are diverse. Among English-language novelists whose lives conform outwardly to "heterosexual" practice but who produce "queer" fiction we might include such canonical modernists as Joseph Conrad, Dorothy Richardson,

James Joyce, and D. H. Lawrence. They, like their gay and lesbian fellow-writers (Gide's 1902 *L'Immoraliste, The Immoralist*, is exemplary here), write novels that are scrupulously detached from, or downright subversive of, regulatory norms. The norms they distance themselves from include traditional moral distinctions; fixed definitions of what is male and female; and the conventional respect accorded monogamy and family. Conrad's "The Secret Sharer" (1909) dramatizes a virtually amorous male–male intimacy between a ship's captain and a criminal he hides in his closetlike shipboard quarters; Richardson includes in her thirteen-novel *Pilgrimage* (1915–67) a love affair between her heroine and a fellow suffragette; Joyce's *Ulysses* (1922) and *Finnegans Wake* (1939) include fantasies or scenes of transgendered people and polymorphous eros (including male–male incest); Lawrence in *Women in Love* (1921) creates a protagonist who believes that marriage "'is the most repulsive thing on earth. . . . You've got to get rid of the exclusiveness of married love. And you've got to admit the unadmitted love of man for man'" (chap. 25). The belief appears to be seconded in Willa Cather's *The Professor's House* (1925). In Germany, Thomas Mann's novels, like their author, question the undermining of conventions, yet simultaneously make it heroic, as in his *Doktor Faustus* (1947, *Doctor Faustus*), where Faust is a bisexual modernist composer. Modernist fiction's subversive alliances across sexual orientations continue in representations of homosexuality, bisexuality, and transgendered people to be found in novels by Marguerite Yourcenar (her 1951 *Mémoires d'Hadrien, Memoirs of Hadrian*, exalts the Roman emperor who made his adolescent male lover into the object of a world religious cult), Iris Murdoch (*The Bell*, 1958; *The Red and the Green*, 1965), Brigid Brophy (*In Transit*, 1969), Hanif Kureishi (*The Buddha of Suburbia*, 1990), Pat Barker (the *Regeneration*

trilogy, 1991–95), Jeannette Winterson (*Written on the Body*, 1992), and John Banville (*The Untouchable*, 1997).

RELATION TO POLITICS

The diverse sexualities that produce queer fiction often have been inspired by egalitarian motives, including beliefs (especially before WWI) that homosexual love democratically levels class and gender distinctions. Accordingly, the queer novel develops, during the middle and the latter parts of the twentieth century, along lines that exemplify queer love's continuing political vocation. Its vocation seems certain in mid-century fiction by John Horne Burns and James Baldwin. Horne Burns's *The Gallery* (1947), about the Allied liberation of the Italian peninsula in WWII, delivers excoriating political criticism of U.S. neo-imperialism by pairing the army's exploitation of "liberated" Naples with its repression of gay love among military men. Baldwin's *Another Country* (1962) undertakes to articulate intersections of American racial, sexual, and gender categories in order to forge an adequately complex model on which to base social and political progress.

An irony attends the development of queer fiction's democratic calling, however. For better or worse, it can loosen alliances among sexual orientations, and thereby reify the meanings of "gay," "lesbian," or "straight." The paradoxical result makes the queer novel less comprehensively queer. For example, in Christopher Isherwood's career, the protagonist of *The World in the Evening* (1954) is bisexual; a secondary character is a gay man who predicts the vociferous queer identity and activism of 1969 and after. The secondary character's exclusively homosexual identity becomes primary by 1976, in Isherwood's *Christopher and His Kind* (a mix of novel and memoir). Isherwood's post-Stonewall consciousness insists on the uniquely separate character of gay men, on the basis of which he equates queer love's political tendency with an egalitarianism that is antinationalist and cosmopolitan. A complementary identitarian and political turn is exemplified by the Manx-born novelist Caeia March in *Three Ply Yarn* (1986), which proposes exclusive lesbian love and identity as the ultimate political weapon against patriarchy and androcentrism.

The politicizing use of fiction by novelists and readers as a vehicle for claiming a "right to our existence" was intensified in the 1980s by the AIDS pandemic and the scapegoating of homosexual men as the alleged "source" of the plague. In developing that use of fiction, however, criticism of celebrations of subversion enters the queer novel, perhaps as a result of post-Stonewall activists' practical engagement with state powers. Angus Wilson's *Hemlock and After* (1952) predicts the criticism: its gay protagonist believes that he must cede some of his unconventional liberty in order to share the benefits and the responsibilities of public life. Alan Hollinghurst's AIDS-era novels elaborate the gist of *Hemlock and After*. *The Swimming-Pool Library* (1988) casts a cold eye on gay men's capacity for self-destructive treachery and lack of solidarity; it also shows (*pace* Isherwood and despite cosmopolitanism) that gay white male citizens of imperialist nations easily exploit colonialized or postcolonial gay men. Hollinghurst's *The Line of Beauty* (2004) suggests complicity between Thatcherite betrayals of public and global welfare and a gay man's self-indulgent innocence about national and international politics. Queer politics, Hollinghurst suggests, must avoid the pitfalls that his novels illustrate.

But while one vital tradition of the queer novel remains attached to politics, another—perhaps more directly continuous with modernist fiction—withdraws from it, as if restlessly searching for alternatives that are utopian, or forever beyond social articulation, or even beyond language. The philosopher George Santayana's novel *The Last Puritan* (1936) suggests that his closeted queer hero's tragedy is the hero's political impulse: a "wish to govern" that, essentially puritanical, blights eros. The heroine of Djuna Barnes's *Ladies Almanack* (1928), Dame Musset, sees struggles for gay rights—including a right to marriage—as already out of date, a reactionary limit on queer possibility. Barnes's cultivation of verbal opacity in *Nightwood* (1936) seeks to resist co-optation of eros by stock responses and clichés that might seek to "govern" sexual passion; James Purdy's novels (1956–92) are in line with Barnes's resistance. Jean Genet's novels (1941–52) dramatize the contention that legitimate social order and homosexual criminal life are mirror images of each other. They imply that political interventions cannot break through the deadlocked symmetry. A similar skepticism informs the fiction of the American anarchist Paul Goodman, an admirer of Genet. Goodman's *Parents' Day* (1951) represents the hopes but also the limits, due to sexuality's incalculable force, of the aims of progressive political and educational collectives. William Burroughs's novels (1959–71) invoke homosexual desire as a resource with which to destroy narrative and generic coherence and thereby to disclose alternative visions of experience and language; but they are visions that outdistance politics. The same might be said of the exilic consciousness that informs the queer eros of Juan Goytisolo's "Count Julian" trilogy (1966–75). Cuban novelist José Lezama Lima's *Paradiso* (1968) uses verbal and formal opacities to protect its investigation of same-sex anal erotism from censorious response and political interference. The fiction of Lezama's junior colleague Reinaldo Arenas, bitterly disillusioned by the hostility to homosexuality of Castro's "progressive" Cuba, refuses all political allegiances.

A recent trend in the U.K. has produced reimaginings in fiction of the sexual culture and experience of writers who, representing a spectrum of erotic diversity, stand at the origins of the modern queer novel: Wilde, Henry James, and Joyce, especially. Maureen Duffy's *The Microcosm* (1966), although reaching further back in time, is an avatar of this mode, which includes work by Jamie O'Neill, Colm Tóibín, and Sarah Waters.

SEE ALSO: Gender Theory, Sexuality.

BIBLIOGRAPHY

Caserio, R.L. (forthcoming), "Queer Modernism," in *Oxford Handbook of Modernisms*, ed. P. Brooker, et al.
Dean, T. (2000), *Beyond Sexuality.*
Edelman, L. (2004), *No Future.*
Wachman, G. (2001), *Lesbian Empire.*
Woodhouse, R. (1998), *Unlimited Embrace.*
Woods, G. (1998), *History of Gay Literature.*
Woods, G. (forthcoming), "Novels of Same-Sex Desire," in *Cambridge History of the English Novel*, ed. R.L. Caserio and C.C. Hawes.

Quixotism *see* Fiction; Iberian Peninsula

R

Race Theory

EVA CHERNIAVSKY

Let us start with what "race theory" is not. It is not a unified body of analytic work, nor does the signifier *race* name a singular object of investigation that would remain consistent across different theoretical traditions or schools of inquiry. If we can say anything at all about "race theory" in general, it is that the work of theorizing race remains fundamentally bound up in the effort to historicize the production of race as an epistemological category, as well as to address the centrality of race to the production of modern epistemologies; to situate racial tropologies within the wider discursive fields of modernity (discourses of gender, class, nationalism, empire, and mass culture, for example); and to chart the manifold articulations of racial epistemologies and discourses to institutionalized social practice— to the material conditions of raced bodies and raced subjects. In other words, if there is anything that "race theory," in general, might tell us at the outset, it is that race is less an object than a field of inquiry—an inquiry into processes of racialization at the center of modern knowledges, discourses, and institutions.

What this means for the student of the novel is that the matter of race neither begins nor ends with the matter of racial "content"—of explicitly racialized themes or characters. The nineteenth-century real-ist novel, its critics tend to agree, variously engages the conditions of modernity, including the emergence and consolidation of industrial capitalism; the social and political ascendance of the bourgeoisie; the logic of the contract as the central principle of social relations (the Social Contract; wage labor); the effects of urbanization and the stranger sociality of the industrial metropolis; the sacralization of home and domestic relations as the scene of authentic human feeling and sympathies; the emergence of commodity culture and new prospects for the mass dissemination of social norms; and the turn to education and reform (e.g., the public school and the prison) as central institutions of social regulation through induced self-surveillance. Among the *leitmotifs* of the classic realist novel, then, we number the possibility and limits of individual autonomy and self-determination in a world of material inequality and ubiquitous social constraint; the relations between the propertied classes and the dispossessed as they comprise a (putatively organic) national people; the tensions between progress (civilizational advance) and the atomizing, alienating effects of urbanization and industrial production; and the division of urban space and social life into public and private domains that alternately enable and circumscribe self-interest and mobility on the basis of gender and age. All of these enumerations are partial and fragmentary but intended to sketch the broad social canvas on which the

The Encyclopedia of the Novel   Edited by Peter Melville Logan
© 2011 Blackwell Publishing Ltd

realist novel is drawn, in order to situate, in turn, this essay's main critical preoccupation with the racial grammar of the novel. Rather than locate the question of race in segregated *topoi*, or in explicitly raced (nonwhite) protagonists, this essay draws on some of the germinal scholarship in postcolonial and ethnic studies to suggest how the defining concerns of the realist novel—with individualism, freedom, property, progress, national identity, domesticity—are inextricably bound up in racialist thought and practice.

RACE AND EUROPEAN MODERNITY

Edward Said's watershed *Orientalism* (1979) in many respects set the stage for the subsequent wealth of inquiry into the fundamentally racialized character of European modernity (see MODERNISM). The organizing contention of Said's study is that the conceptions of "the Orient" and "the Oriental" wrought in the contexts of European imperial expansion and colonial rule are projections (fantasies of an "other") that bear essentially no relation to Asian peoples as culturally heterogeneous, historical subjects, except—and the weight of this exception can hardly be overstated—insofar as the fiction of the "Orient" authorized and enabled forms of regulation, coercion, and expropriation with all too real, material consequences for the colonized (see IDEOLOGY). Orientalist discourse, Said argues, rehearses a structuring opposition of Orient to Occident, in which the backwardness, the arbitrary tyranny, the irrational customs, and the stasis of the former serve as the screen on which the progress, political emancipation, enlightened reason, and human advancement of the latter are writ large. The stake in Orientalism, then, is the legitimation of modern European national identities, political institutions, legal norms,

governance strategies, scientific protocols, moral sensibility, and cultural ethos (see NATIONAL). While Orientalist discourse so insistently associates the racial difference of the colonized with atavism, irrationality, and the retrenchment of human possibility, this version of an Orient is original and proper to Europe, Said contends, and to a specifically modern cultural imaginary. At the same time, his work demonstrates, Europe is not self-contained, as its self-conception is forged along its peripheries, in relation to racially differentiated cultures and peoples.

In the intervening decades, a rich and diverse array of scholarship has extended and elaborated Said's critical remapping of European modernity in ways that account for the iterations of European epistemologies, institutions, and discourses within European settler colonial contexts (particularly the U.S.) and that consider as well the wider terrain of imperial and colonial imaginaries, as these encompass Africa, the African diaspora, the indigenous peoples of the Americas, Australia, and the Pacific. In Paul Gilroy's influential work, for example, the deportation of captive African labor appears not as an anomaly, not as an exception to the processes of human advancement with which it is oddly and embarrassingly contemporaneous, but rather as a fundamentally modern instance of the large-scale displacement and mobilization of human populations. Gilroy's understanding of the slave's Atlantic passage thereby interrupts the more familiar conjugation of labor migration with urbanization (loss of tradition but also release from traditional social bonds) and industrialization (alienation, but also emancipation from forms of indentured agrarian labor). Rather, in his account, chattel slavery indexes the imbrication of modernity and its meta-narrative of progress (emancipation from customary servitude) in institutionalized practices of racial terror: the internment, surveillance, and prostration of racialized human populations.

RACE, GENDER, AND DOMESTICITY

Other important scholarship on race and modernity attends specifically to matters of gender and domesticity in ways especially relevant to the realist novel, as well as to modernist fiction that both defamiliarizes the terrain of the realist novel (shatters its illusionism) *and* retains many of its preoccupations with the formation of individual consciousness and the scales of interior life (home, psyche), posed over and against mass culture and the alienating conditions of the industrial metropolis (see MODERN-ISM). For example, in *Imperial Leather* (1995) Anne McClintock elucidates the relation of the privatized nuclear family to the modern nation as imperial power. In her account, the family resolves a structuring contradiction in the temporality of the nation, which is at once future-oriented (nations develop and progress) and backward-looking (however modern, nations always lay claim to an origin, or essence, expressed in an abiding national character or traditions). Within this fractured temporal scheme, the family embodies the timelessness of national life (a national essence preserved outside historical time) that guarantees the continuity of the nation as a public, political order advancing on futurity. At the same time, the trope of family also functions to secure the progressive character of imperial nations on the world stage by temporalizing racial and cultural difference. Within the discourse of the "family of man" born of comparative anatomy (and other forms of racial pseudo-science), cultural difference is constituted as racial difference arrayed along an evolutionary scale, with "European" man at the apex of this "family

tree," the avatar of humanity in its most developed form, and the "lower" races ranged along the lower branches of the diagram, which represent anterior, "primitive" levels of human development. Thus on the national scene, family appears ahistorical (natural) and continuous, but in the imperial context, British, French, or American family domestic relations, for instance, stand as the mark of progress measured against the backward sociality of "primitive" peoples. McClintock's analysis permits us to understand how family life signifies at once social reproduction and civilizational advance within the national literary traditions of imperial states.

This work has both enabled and been enabled by specifically literary scholarship on the novel that has argued for the centrality of race and empire to metropolitan narratives, which often pay little overt attention to these themes. Gayatri Chakravorty Spivak's account of Charlotte Brontë's female BILDUNGSROMAN, *Jane Eyre* (1847), for example, makes an important intervention into other critical reading practices (feminist and Marxist, in particular) that privilege the novel's engagement with questions of GENDER and CLASS exclusively (see FEMINIST, MARXIST). Empire appears to dwell on the margins of this novel: in the figure of the planter's daughter, Bertha Mason, whose madness and abandon is only the direst expression of her Creole family's degenerated state; and in the aborted prospect of Jane's attachment to St. John Rivers and missionary toil in India, an environment that would, the novel assures us, swiftly bring on her demise. But the novel's concern with forging a social context for the female individual, Spivak contends, is imbricated in a racialized imperial imaginary. Thus the elaboration of women's identity beyond childbearing and sexual reproduction, she argues, is staked on middle-class women's capacity for "soul-making," the cultivation of morally advanced human sensibilities, which authorizes women within the space of the bourgeois household but also crucially aligns them with a broader social mission. It is this delineation of social mission that opens the colonies as a field of self-realizing moral labor for British women such as Jane Eyre, and Spivak's point, broadly sketched, is that white women's emergence within the wider discourse of the "white man's burden" enables their self-cultivation as individuals (as legitimated actors within civil society) only insofar as colonized women remain excluded from this gendered norm. The "native female" is both the object of white women's imperial benevolence and the sign of a racialized, gendered atavism (one that can infect even white settlers' daughters, such as Bertha, born and bred in the morally toxic environment of non-white populations in the colonies).

THE "RACIAL GRAMMAR" OF THE NOVEL

Toni Morrison pursues a similar line of argument in *Playing in the Dark*, where she traces the centrality of an "Africanist presence" in canonical U.S. fiction, a black figure lurking on the fringes of realist and modernist novels, less a character possessed of his (or her) own interiority than an icon of what lies beyond the discursive world of the novel—an icon for what the text cannot assimilate. For Morrison, the identities of the novels' protagonists (and identifications of their readers) are formed over and against this mute and peripheral presence, whose exclusion, she suggests, is therefore rightly understood as constitutive of the identities, social formations, histories, and futures on which the novels center. Like Spivak, and in line with other critical work less specifically focused on literary practice, Morrison thus points us to what I call, in a

phrase adapted from Hortense Spillers, the "racial grammar" of the novel, by which I mean the ways that the fundamental preoccupations of the novel with gendered personhood, family, generation, progress, mobility, loss of tradition, and new forms of attachment (including, centrally, attachment to one's self, or self-possession) are defined along an axis of racial differentiation in relation to forms of nonpersonhood, degeneration, atavism, and dispossession that are explicitly and insistently racialized within the context of modern imperial and colonial world-making. Thus as Morrison insists, novels where "black" protagonists appear largely incidental, or peripheral to the narrative, fundamentally require such figures as the mainstay of their own coherence: the intelligibility of their characterization, the transparency of their narrative conventions.

Conversely, one might argue, novels where nonwhite characters figure prominently as the subjects of the narrative are routinely split off or displaced into nominally discrete literary categories. As Harryette Mullen provocatively points out, for example, the act of racial "passing," although conventionally framed as deception, is nothing other than the effort to move from margin to center that reads as the exemplary pursuit of cultural assimilation when performed by European immigrants, who shed their pasts and traditions so as to attain to an authentically (white) "American" identity. From this perspective, the genre of the "passing novel" is narratively indistinguishable from the American bildungsroman, except insofar as it represents the trajectories of racially disqualified protagonists, whose passing recapitulates all too closely the normative employment of the self-made "American." Mullen's argument further reminds us how the classic American novel, from Horatio Alger's *Ragged Dick* (1867) to F. Scott Fitzgerald's

The Great Gatsby (1925) and beyond, is always and necessarily racialized, that is, concerned with the reproduction of whiteness, or in Étienne Balibar's suggestive phrase, the "fictive ethnicity" of the nation (96).

By thinking in terms of "racial grammar," I aim to insist at once on the power and tenacity of novelistic convention and on its contingency: grammar is abiding, and challenges to grammatical usage routinely incur the stigma of bad usage, but grammar is *not* intractable and in point of practice is continuously assailed by the forces of colloquial innovation. Henry Louis Gates, Jr.'s influential work on the African American literary tradition opens one important critical vantage point on the question of discursive innovation, through his account of "signifyin(g)" as an African-derived practice of repetition with a difference. "Signifyin(g)" mobilizes the instability of language understood as a system of differential meaning (words mean only in relation to other words, to the totality of signifiers in the language), in order to dislodge a particular term from the matrix of related signifiers in which it is conventionally embedded. "Signifyin(g)" thus entails re-functioning familiar idioms and tropes in such a way as to interrupt the meanings that normally accrete to them and, in so doing, to more or less subtly disorient the reader. To cite just one example of literary "signifyin(g)," I note that certain novels of racial uplift, such as Frances Harper's *Iola Leroy* (1892), signify on American citizenship, recirculating a familiar rhetoric of "good citizenship" but also disrupting its relation to a series of related signifiers, including especially *whiteness*, in a manner to reposition the African American as the exemplary subject of civic participation. Alongside "signifyin(g)," recent criticism and fiction has explored a wealth of narrative strategies for redrawing the boundaries of family, home, public, private, and nation, and reimagining the

kinds of subjects who move within and across these narrative domains (see Lee; Layoun; McClintock et al.). If the defining motifs of the novel are racialized (quite apart from explicitly racial content), then, reciprocally, a rescripting of these motifs— e.g., in novels that rewrite women's relation to nationalism, or that refuse linear temporalities (clean distinctions between past and future, origins and telos), or that dismantle distinctions between authentic and assumed identities, or that trace connections between freedom and terror— is vital to the work of racial critique and to revising, however incrementally, the racial grammar of the novel.

SEE ALSO: African American Novel, Asian American Novel, Latina/o American Novel.

BIBLIOGRAPHY

Balibar, É. (1991), "The Nation Form," in *Race, Nation, Class*.
Gates, H.L., Jr. (1988), *Signifying Monkey*.
Gilroy, P. (1993), *Black Atlantic*.
Layoun, M. (2001), *Wedded to the Land*.
Lee, R. (1999), *Americas of Asian American Literature*.
McClintock, A., A. Mufti, and E. Shohat, eds. (1997), *Dangerous Liaisons*.
Morrison, T. (1993), *Playing in the Dark*.
Mullen, H. (1994), "Optic White," *Diacritics* 24: 71–89.
Said, E. (1979), *Orientalism*.
Spillers, H. (2003), "Mama's Baby, Papa's Maybe," in *Black, White, and in Color*.
Spivak, G.C. (1985), "Three Women's Texts and a Critique of Imperialism," *Critical Inquiry* 12: 243–61.

Reader

MICHAEL SCHEFFEL

Generally related to a text-based literary culture, the term *reader* is connected in academic usage to various concepts of literary criticism and theory. In a narrowly defined sense it is used to refer to (1) the empirical reader, the individual historical recipient of a written or printed text. Thus, taken as a group, empirical readers constitute the author's "public" who, as the final link in the chain of literary communication, also influence the production of literature. Accordingly, the historical figure and reading habits of the empirical reader have been the subject of studies ranging from behavioral and cognitive psychology to the sociology and history of reading. Clearly distinct from the empirical reader is (2) the fictional reader, who belongs to the explicitly imagined world of many literary texts and whose profile and reading habits is a major theme of world literature. Literary criticism and theory use the term *reader*, however, not only to refer to the real or imaginary recipient of a text, but in a broader sense to pinpoint various aspects of writing connected with the addressee. Here the reader is generally a more abstract construct embodying various roles or functions in the process of literary communication; but precise definitions of the concept differ so widely that a consistent typology, let alone a single theory or model covering all usages, is hardly possible. Nevertheless, two concepts can be broadly distinguished: first (3) the fictive reader, understood as the counterpart to the figure of the narrator within the fictional framework, and second (4) the implied reader, a figure of varying profile and indefinable ontological status that functions as the (ideal) conceptual addressee of the text.

THE EMPIRICAL READER

The earliest culture of individual reading known to us developed in the Hellenistic period (fourth and third centuries BCE), not as a substitute but parallel to the communal reception of texts read aloud to a group of listeners, whose popularity had spread during the seventh and sixth centuries BCE. From Antiquity to the Middle Ages reading *alta voce* (aloud) was, in fact, the norm for aesthetic, cultic, or religious (as opposed to purely pragmatic) reading activities. (This changed only with the development of literary prose: novels, for example, were from the very beginning read silently, whilst poetry and drama were still as a rule read aloud right into the eighteenth century.) After the fifth or sixth century CE in Europe the activity of reading lapsed entirely for some six centuries, and written culture became the prerogative of the monastic schools. The twelfth and thirteenth centuries saw a renewal of writing, and from the fourteenth to the fifteenth century the nascent urban culture of Europe brought with it a growth in literacy. Not until the sixteenth century, however, did this show signs of developing into a bourgeois reading culture in the modern sense, and only in the context of the eighteenth century. Enlightenment was a culture of individual reading generally established—with considerable national differences. Its basis was the shift from the received tradition of cyclical or repetitive reading of the Bible and other religious and devotional writings to the "one-off" reading of secular texts, pride of place among them being taken by the bourgeois novel. In the course of the eighteenth century an expanding book market, reading societies, and lending libraries began to supply an increasing volume of reading material to a public progressively differentiated on gender lines, with men predominantly reading newspapers, periodicals, and factual texts and women fiction and belles-lettres. Numerically speaking, the empirical reading public in Europe remained small: at the time of German Classicism (ca. 1800), regular (i.e., at least one book per year) readers of belles-lettres in Germany amounted to hardly one percent of the adult population. Technical innovations in paper manufacture and book production during the second half of the nineteenth century, along with new methods of distribution (e.g., peddling) of newspapers, periodicals, and tracts, brought considerable price reductions and led to a corresponding surge in the number of empirical readers. This stabilized into the typical pattern of twentieth-century industrialized countries, with a good third of the population reading books regularly (i.e., several times a week), a third reading occasionally or rarely, and almost a third not reading at all. The continuous growth of the new media since the end of the twentieth century has introduced further changes. Reading and the use of the new media are now functionally interdependent, and the polarization between regular readers who are at the same time literate users of other media and occasional or nonreaders is currently becoming more acute.

THE FICTIONAL READER

In various guises the figure of the reader and his/her reading matter has played a role in literature ever since classical Antiquity. Far from functioning in a naively realist sense, however, this figure (i.e., the fictional reader) serves as a mirror opening up critical discussion of the many forms of literature and its reception—a meta-level reflecting and stimulating reflection on the poetological issues of the day. Thus the motif of reading has often been used to hold certain types of literature and reading attitudes at arm's length. Lucian's *True History* (ca. 180 CE), for example, opens with the I-narrator presented as a reader of Homer's *Odyssey* (eighth century BCE) and other works of "the ancient poets, historians and philosophers,"

whose impact has induced him to write his own "tale of lies." In Canto V of Dante's *Inferno* (1307–21, *Divina Commedia*; *The Divine Comedy*) we find the first tale of a couple veritably seduced by a literary text: Francesca and her husband's brother Paolo, who fell tragically in love after reading the romance of Lancelot together. The dangers of emotional identification with literature are subsequently treated in many texts of world literature, and the fictional reader finds famous expression in figures ranging from Don Quixote, driven to deeds of adventure by reading knightly tales, to Madame Bovary, who attempted in vain to find in extramarital love the happiness peddled in the cheap novels of her day. Both Sir Launcelot Canning's *Mad Trist*, read by the I-narrator to his friend Roderick Usher in Poe's *The Fall of the House of Usher* (1839), and the "yellow book" (i.e., J.-K. Huysmans's 1884 *À Rebours*; *Against Nature*) held in such esteem by Dorian Gray in Oscar Wilde's *The Picture of Dorian Gray* (1890), exemplify the way in which authors have linked the fictional reader with the motif of the book within the book. Finally, the figure of the fictional reader offers an opportunity in many novels for reflection on the complex interweave of relations between writing, reading, and life. The technique of implanted narrative used in some epistolary novels or journals like Johann Wolfgang von Goethe's *Die Leiden des jungen Werthers* (1774, *The Sorrows of Young Werther*) or Irmgard Keun's *Das kunstseidene Mädchen* (1932, *The High Life*) is particularly effective in this respect. Mention must also be made of works such as André Gide's *Les Faux-Monnayeurs* (1925, *The Counterfeiters*) and Aldous Huxley's *Point Counter Point* (1928)—tales of an author-reader at work on his own manuscript that embody the fluid interface of life and literature in the form of a novel about writing and reading a novel.

THE FICTIVE READER

The fictive reader differs from the fictional reader in being a more or less abstract construct extrapolated from the text rather than a specific figure within it. As a critical concept, the fictive reader functions as the extradiegetic addressee of a fictional text, the fictive counterpart of its (equally fictive) narrator; as such it is part of the imaginary world created in and by the sentences of the text. Like the narrator, the fictive reader can be presented explicitly or implicitly. Explicit presentation involves the use of second-person (singular or plural) pro-nouns and grammatical forms, or such third-person conventions as "the gentle reader." Constructed in this way and en-dowed with widely varying levels of concrete detail and characterization, the image of the addressee can shadow that of the narrator throughout a text. In Laurence Sterne's *Tristram Shandy* (1759–67), for example, or in many of Fyodor Dostoyevsky's narra-tives, the fictive reader is constantly present as listener-recipient conceived in the tradi-tion of oral storytelling. On the other hand, works that present a fictive reality as if it were historical and "objective" will rarely contain explicit indications of a recipient: examples from the nineteenth-century re-alist tradition are the novels of Gustave Flaubert, Émile Zola, or Theodor Fontane. An interesting case from the point of view of narrative theory is Italo Calvino's *Se una notte d'inverno un viaggiatore* (1979, *If on a Winter's Night a Traveler*), which plays on (and with) the border between fictional and fictive reader, telling the story of a man and a woman engaged in the activity of reading and responding to the very novel that creates them.

Explicit presentations of the fictive reader are generally concerned with a single person, but in older texts, from Ludovico Ariosto's *Orlando furioso* (1532, *Mad Orlando*) to eighteenth-century novels like Christoph Martin Wieland's *Don Sylvio* (1764), the figure is often conceived as a member of a group, allowing the narrator to address various individuals from that group in turn. Conceived as a single person, the fictive reader is most often presented as the friend or privileged partner of the narrator; a further variant is the type of the insulted or ironized fictive reader.

Reconstructed via a critical reading of the text, the implicit fictive reader is the product of the need for a counterpart to the narrator, an addressee without whom no communi-cation could occur. All texts, in fact, contain implicit information about the intellectual and emotional norms of their putative ad-dressee, whether linguistic, epistemic, ethi-cal, or social—even if only in the narrator's apparent anticipation of a certain pattern of behavior and response. Flaubert's novels, for instance, project a rather passive and silent fictive reader, whereas Dostoyevsky's suggest one that actively asks questions, utters objections, and expresses doubts.

THE IMPLIED READER

Whilst the fictive reader, as the narrator's addressee, clearly belongs to the imaginary world created in and by the sentences of a fictional text, the implied reader, as the author's addressee, is a construct external to that fiction. Prescinding from the widely differing approaches of literary theory to the task of definition, the implied reader can be meaningfully conceived as a func-tion or instance determined by textual features, and as such strictly distinct from any concept the historical author may have had of a real or ideal reader (in the sense of an "intended reader").

Although already latent in Wayne C. Booth's concept of the "implied author," the concept of the implied reader was introduced into literary research as a term in its own right by Wolfgang Iser in the 1970s. Together with H. R. Jauss and other German scholars, Iser founded the school of *Rezeptionsästhetik* (reader-response criticism) that raised awareness of the role of the reader in any explication of the process of literary communication. It is important for an understanding of Iser's approach to realize that the concept of the implied reader is part of a comprehensive theory of aesthetic response. A basic assumption of this theory is that from the pragmatic point of view the sentences of a literary fiction represent utterances divorced from any real situational context, and that from a formal point of view they contain many gaps. Iser uses the construct of the implied reader to grasp the presuppositions within the text for the many and varied acts of meaning-making actually performed by its possible readers. His implied reader is in this sense "a structure inscribed in the text" that determines the "conditions of reception" of the literary work and thus serves as a foundation for the reader's "initial orientation" and subsequent "realization" of the text. Compatible with Iser's approach is Walker Gibson's idea, already mooted in the 1950s, of a "mock reader": a construct, determined by the text, embodying the role taken by the real reader in the process of reading. Iser's idea was further refined by Umberto Eco's anthropomorphic text-based concept of a *lettore modello* ("model reader") that—like Stanley Fish's "informed reader" and Jonathan Culler's "competent reader"—possesses knowledge of all the codes required for an understanding of the text, as well as the cognitive competence and readiness to complete the steps constituting the process of understanding. In practice, the reader who sets out to pinpoint such a presuppositional construct via a process of textual analysis must first have understood the text. Thus, sooner or later, the concept of

the implied reader inevitably encounters the hermeneutic problem of understanding.

BIBLIOGRAPHY

Bray, J. (2009), *Female Reader in the English Novel*.
Culler, J. (1975), *Structuralist Poetics*.
Eco, U. (1979), *Role of the Reader*.
Fish, S. (1980), *Is There a Text in This Class?*
Goetsch, P. (2004), "Reader Figures in Narrative," *Style* 38:188–202.
Iser, W. (1974), *Implied Reader*.
Iser, W. (1978), *Act of Reading*.
Nelles, W. (1993), "Historical and Implied Authors and Readers," *Comparative Literature* 45:22–46.
Prince, G. (1971), "On Readers and Listeners in Narrative," *Neophilologos* 55:117–22.
Rabinowitz, P.J. (1977), "Truth in Fiction," *Critical Inquiry* 4:121–41.
Tompkins, J.T., ed. (1980), *Reader-Response Criticism*.
Travis, M.A. (1998), *Reading Cultures*.
Wilson, D.W. (1981), "Readers in Texts," *PMLA* 96: 848–63.

Reading Aloud

PATRICIA HOWELL MICHAELSON

The development of the novel is often linked to the practice of silent reading. Previously, readers typically read only a few texts, such as the Bible, "intensively" and often aloud (Engelsing). Silent reading gave access to a wider range of texts, which might be read only once and in private. Silent, solitary reading has been seen as essential to the novel's appeal to its early readers (Hunter). But reading aloud has never disappeared: novels have been read aloud since the genre developed, both in the family and, especially in the nineteenth century, in professional performances. The oral performance of literature was a part of the school curriculum in Britain and the U.S. well into the twentieth century. Professional recording of books began in the 1930s as an aid for the blind; today, a burgeoning market for audiobooks supplements that for printed novels.

Eighteenth-century critics of the novel often expressed anxiety about how easy it was for young, undereducated readers (women, in particular) to be corrupted by the novel's individualist values. Reading silently and alone, they claimed, not only kept young readers from more important duties, but made them more susceptible to the novel's negative effects (Pearson, Flint). Samuel Johnson's characterization of novel readers as "the young, the ignorant, and the idle" (*Rambler*, 1750) and Gustave Flaubert's Madame Bovary, a century later, are iconic examples of this idea. In modern times, reading alone may still be viewed as a private indulgence, a break from the daily routine and a chance to experience idealized romance (Radway).

The practice of reading novels aloud, by contrast, makes reading a part of family or social life. Samuel Richardson's *Pamela* (1740) was read aloud, famously, in villages where the literacy rates were low. In middle-CLASS homes, family reading provided an experience that was shared, interrupted for discussion, and mediated by comments on the text. Reading became a performance, in which the reader could act out the parts of the narrator and the various characters. This entry will discuss, first, the eighteenth-century British "elocution movement," which theorized reading aloud; second, the practice of reading novels aloud; and lastly, the changes brought by twentieth-century media.

THE ELOCUTION MOVEMENT

In Britain, beginning in the 1760s, elocutionists like Thomas Sheridan brought attention to the oral performance of texts. In keeping with classical rhetoricians, Sheridan argued that texts were "dead" until performed by the living voice; his focus was on persuasion in the public spheres of church and politics (see RHETORIC). In his *Lectures on the Art of Reading* (1775), Sheridan analyzed the church service almost line by line, criticizing the usual reading and marking emphases and pauses so the performer would properly convey the text's meaning. Another elocutionist, John Walker, taught that a grammatical analysis would lead to proper pronunciation. Still others, like John Burgh, championed the expression of emotion as part of the art of persuasion.

The elocutionists' ideas were popularized in anthologies used for teaching reading in schools, which were widely available through the nineteenth century in Britain and the U.S. (The American "McGuffey Readers" are perhaps the best known.) The anthologies often include prefatory instructions for reading aloud, generally borrowed from elocutionists like Sheridan or Walker. The section on "Pronunciation, or Delivery" from Hugh Blair's *Lectures on Rhetoric and Belles Lettres* (1783) was another favorite. This text frames its rules as part of two main goals of reading aloud. For the text to be understood, the reader must speak loudly, distinctly, slowly, and with correct pronunciation. To please and move the audience, the speaker uses proper emphasis, pauses, tones, and gestures. Proper emphasis was highlighted by the elocutionists, since emphasis could alter meaning, as in the example, "'Do you *ride* to town today?' 'No, I walk.' 'Do you ride *to town* today?' 'No, I stay in the country.'" Pauses, too, were seen as a kind of emphasis, drawing attention to significant points. Elocutionists criticized the artificial tones that some readers used and recommended using the tones of everyday speech. The use of gestures in reading was more controversial, with some authors offering diagrams of gestures and formal rules for expressing various emotions, and others dismissing gestures as overly theatrical.

Later in the nineteenth century, elocution became associated with exaggerated and stilted performances, often taught as the "Delsarte system." The close attention to the author's meaning, so important to the earlier elocutionists, was abandoned in favor of melodramatic gesture. However, the concern for authorial intention was revived in the twentieth century under the names of "oral interpretation" or simply "interpretation." Teachers like S. S. Curry early in the century, W. M. Parrish in the 1930s, and Don Geiger in the 1960s all argued that preparing a literary text for a reading was the best way to develop a deep understanding of it. Elocution has been primarily an Anglophone phenomenon. In 1877, Ernest Legouvé lamented the French lack of interest in reading aloud and closed his treatise on reading with a call to imitate the Americans "by making the art of reading aloud the very corner-stone of public education" (1879, *Art of Reading*, trans. E. Roth, 145).

READING NOVELS ALOUD

While the elocutionists explicitly focused on reading in the church or in public speeches, and the school anthologies offered examples of famous speeches from history and from drama, as well as short pieces in prose and verse, the ideas of the elocutionists did influence the reading of novels. Jane Austen, for example, was well aware of the elocution movement; its influence on reading the church service is discussed in *Mansfield Park* (1814, vol. 3, chap. 3). Austen's letters and novels provide many examples of reading aloud in the family circle, with comments on the quality of the reading. In her novels,

Austen sometimes marked her text for the oral reader, who, unlike a reader of the church service, would probably not have prepared the reading in advance: her use of italics and paragraph breaks suggest points where the reader might emphasize or pause (Michaelson).

As a mixed genre, novels demanded a range of reading styles. The elocutionists had urged readers to "personate" the author of a speech they were reading; this facilitated the reader's primary job, to convey the author's meaning to the audience. But readers of novels should personate the author only in narrative sections; in the dialogues, they should portray the various characters. Reading aloud becomes a kind of acting. Gilbert Austin wrote that readers of novels should hurry through "mere narrative." "Interesting scenes" demand more careful, impressive reading, while dialogue should be read as if it were drama (1806, *Chironomia*, 206). John Wilson noted that even a given description must be read differently, depending on which character is speaking (1798, *Principles of Elocution*).

These elaborations reimagine the novel as theater. Authors planning for an oral performance, then, might minimize narrative in favor of dialogue, leading to livelier reading. In preparing his own texts for his popular public readings, Charles Dickens tended to abbreviate narrative while making characters' speech more inflected by dialect. Dickens noted emphases, as well as tones and gestures, in his prompt books. He maintained the line between reading and acting, remaining behind his reading desk, but reviewers called him "one of the best of living actors" (Collins, lvi; see also Andrews).

Reading novels aloud alters the audience's experience of the text. The reader is an intermediary between text and audience, not only interpreting the text through his or her voice, but also abridging the text in some places and stopping to comment in others. In her diary of 1798, Frances Burney says of her husband reading *Gil Blas* to their son, the "excellent Father judiciously omits or changes all such passages as might tarnish the lovely purity of his innocence" (1976, *Journals and Letters*, 6:801). The risk that the solitary reader might enter too deeply into the illusion is obviated. The text is shared, interpreted, and contextualized in the family. In addition, reading aloud within the family reinforces social bonds and hierarchies: the reader might be a father surrounded by his family, a husband reading to his wife in bed, reinforcing their intimacy, or a paid companion reading to amuse her patron (as Jo does in Louisa May Alcott's *Little Women*, 1868).

NEW MEDIA

The new media developed in the twentieth century (radio, TV, analog and digital recording) largely displaced reading aloud as an everyday family entertainment, with one notable exception: the ritual of parents reading bedtime stories to young children. As in earlier periods, reading to children performs multiple functions as a means of education and a way of strengthening relationships, and as before, the parent selects the text, interprets it, and interrupts it for discussion. In present-day adult settings, reading novels aloud is often in the context of a special event, like marathon readings of James Joyce's *Ulysses* (1922) or authors reading from their own work. The actor Patrick Stewart performed Charles Dickens's *A Christmas Carol* (1843) on stage during the holiday seasons in the 1990s and into the new century, harkening back to Dickens's practice, to great acclaim.

New media may have aided the demise of family reading, but they enabled the development of audiobooks. Thomas Edison had predicted as early as 1878 that book recordings would be one future use for the phonograph. Beginning in 1930s, recordings of books were made for the benefit of the blind, both in Britain and in the U.S. The BBC also broadcast "story hours" on the radio for a more general audience. A mass market for recorded books developed in the 1970s, when cassette players became standard equipment in American cars, and their use was closely tied to long drives and/or daily commutes. The American audiobooks industry describes its typical consumer as someone who reads widely and who sees audiobooks as one way to fit more reading in. In the early twenty-first century, audio versions of novels are usually released at the same time as the print publication. The reader is either an actor or, less commonly, the author, and the text is usually abridged. Audiobooks are considerably more expensive than the printed book. Downloadable digital formats and rental programs may make the price more competitive and may help develop a younger and wider listening audience.

SEE ALSO: Adaptation/Appropriation, Dialogue.

BIBLIOGRAPHY

Andrews, M. (2006), *Charles Dickens and His Performing Selves*.

Bartine, D. (1989), *Early English Reading Theory*.

Collins, P. (1975), *Charles Dickens*.

Engelsing, R. (1974), *Bürger als Leser*.

Flint, K. (1993), *Woman Reader, 1837–1914*.

Hunter, J.P. (1990), *Before Reading*.

Michaelson, P.H. (2002), *Speaking Volumes*.

Pearson, J. (1999), *Women's Reading in Britain, 1750–1835*.

Radway, J. (1984), *Reading the Romance*.

Realism

DEAK NABERS

Realism served as the dominant mode of nineteenth-century novelistic discourse. Although the representation of reality has played at least some small role in many literary movements and projects, the term "literary realism" generally identifies a historically specific set of literary techniques and ambitions. Emerging in France in the 1830s in the work of Stendhal and Honoré de Balzac, realism received its first theoretical elaborations in the 1840s and 1850s in the work of French authors Champfleury and Louis Edmond Duranty and the English critic John Ruskin (1819–1900). The mode flowered across Europe from the 1850s through the 1880s: in France in the work of Gustave Flaubert; in England in the work of George Eliot and Anthony Trollope; in Russia in the work of Leo Tolstoy and Ivan Turgenev. By the late nineteenth century, literary debate in the U.S. revolved around realism, which heavily influenced the work of Mark Twain, Henry James, and William Dean Howells. "The great collective event in American letters during the 1890s and 1890s," Walter Berthoff explains, "was the securing of 'realism' as the dominant standard of value" (1). Constructed out of an awkward mix of paradoxically linked commitments and bearing a complicated and multivalent relationship to nineteenth-century social order, realism has invited a long history of critical speculation. Its exact specifications have repeatedly resisted simple definition.

REALISM'S PROJECT

Realism's early practitioners tended to present the enterprise in disarmingly matter-of-fact terms. "Realism is nothing more and nothing less," Howells claimed, "than the truthful treatment of material" (966). Revolving around "simple honesty and instinctive truth," it could be "as unphilosophized as the light of common day" (966). The narrator of Eliot's *Adam Bede* (1859) announces, in chap. 17, that her "strongest effort" is simply "to give a faithful account of men and things as they have mirrored themselves in my mind." If this meant that she would have to present an uninspired clergyman rather than a saint full of "truly spiritual advice," then so be it. "I would not, even if I had the choice, be the clever novelist who could create a world so much better than this," she explains. "I am content to tell my simple story ... dreading nothing, indeed, but falsity." In *Mimesis*, an extraordinarily influential mid-twentieth-century account of the "representation of reality in Western Literature," the German philologist and literary historian Erich Auerbach identifies the "modern realism" of the nineteenth century as, quite simply, "the serious treatment of everyday reality" (491).

Of course, as Auerbach himself demonstrated in great detail, nineteenth-century realists were not the first authors to aspire to the "truthful treatment of the material" in their works. They were hardly unique in preferring "truth" to "falsity." Authors had been representing reality as long as they had been producing literature. Nor was the realist suspicion of inherited cultural fictions like the infallibility of the local clergy especially unconventional, at least in formal literary terms. By the mid-nineteenth century the novel form itself had long been associated with what Fredric Jameson calls "the systematic undermining and demystification, the secular 'decoding,' of those preexisting inherited traditional or sacred narrative paradigms which are its initial givens" (152). In order "to convince us of his essential veracity," writes Harry Levin, "the novelist must always be disclaiming the fictitious and breaking through the encrustations of the literary" (71). So the distinctiveness of what Auerbach calls modern realism hinged less on the new realism's commitment to representing reality than on the particular kind of reality it represented. Realism's "truthful treatment" of the world was less decisive than its interest in reality in its everyday form.

The nineteenth-century realist's everyday reality was the social world of the bourgeoisie, and to treat it seriously was to focus, first, on the domestic intricacies that constituted the lived experience of middle-class life and, second, on the complicated interconnections between social practices and economic necessity which gave rise to bourgeois subjectivity. Auerbach contends:

> The serious realism of modern times cannot represent man otherwise than as embedded in a total reality, political, social, and economic, which is concrete and constantly evolving. . . . [The realist author] not only . . . places the human beings whose destiny he is seriously relating, in their precisely defined historical and social setting, but also conceives this connection as a necessary one: to him every milieu becomes a moral and physical atmosphere which impregnates the landscape, the dwelling, furniture, implements, clothing, physique, character, surroundings . . . and fates of men, and at the same time the general historical situation reappears as a total atmosphere which envelops all its several milieux. (463, 473)

The "necessary connection" between "furniture," "implements," and the like and the "fates of men" places a great deal of pressure on the emblems of everyday life in which the realist novelist tended to traffic. Eliot may well claim that she is content to depict "monotonous homely existence" so

long as she can avoid falsity (chap. 17). But from Auerbach's perspective it is not enough for her accounts of "flower-pots," "spinning wheels," "stone jugs," and "all those cheap common things which are the precious necessities of life" merely to be truthful (Eliot, chap. 17). They must also be suggestive.

Necessity is as important here as reality. The American author Ambrose Bierce once jokingly declared that realism is "the art of depicting nature as it is seen by toads. The charm suffusing a landscape painted by a mole, or a story written by a measuring-worm" (1911, *Devil's Dictionary*, 206). And Lionel Trilling once noted that in the cruder forms of realism, reality "is one and immutable, it is wholly external, it is irreducible. . . . Reality being fixed and given, the artist has but to let it pass through him, he is the lens in the first diagram of an elementary book on optics" (4–5). But the realist's topical immersion in quotidian details generally occasioned a thematic elevation of those details to a higher plane of importance. According to George Parsons Lathrop, writing in 1874, realism "sets itself at work to consider characters and events which are apparently . . . most . . . uninteresting" only so as to "extract from these their full value and true meaning." Realism "reveals," he continued; "where we thought nothing worthy of notice, it shows everything to be rife with significance" (321–22).

It is for this reason that the Hungarian literary critic Georg LUKÁCS praises Balzac as much for his commitment to what Lukács calls "abstraction" as for his attentiveness to "material problems" (44, 51). One could treat "everyday reality" "seriously," to return to Auerbach's terms, only by rendering it something more than the merely everyday, more than the simply immutable and irreducible external world. "The concrete presentation of social interconnections,"

Lukács insists, "is rendered possible only by raising them to so high a level of abstraction that from it the concrete can be sought and found as a 'unity of diversity'" (44). For Lukács the "very depth of Balzac's realism" does not derive from his attention to the quotidian. It instead "removes his art ... completely beyond the photographic reproduction of 'average' reality" (60). The novelistic representation of Eliot's "vulgar details" depends, paradoxically, upon a "passionate striving for the essential and nothing but the essential"—upon, indeed, a "passionate contempt for all trivial realism" (69). Hence the structural ambivalence at the heart of the realist enterprise: simultaneously embracing and rejecting the trivial, the realist novel privileges the concrete over the abstract even as it derives the abstract from the concrete.

Despite all of its posturing against literary conventions, realism was itself quickly recognized as a set of conventions. As Michael Davitt Bell explains, "realism involves not a rejection of style (if such a thing were even possible) but a particular *use* of style" (20–21). Realism was a specific and historically inflected mode of writing as well as an impulse to tether writing more closely to the empirical world, and in many respects its status as a literary mode proved more commanding and durable than any of its actual representational powers. The "descriptive fabric" in Flaubert's fiction, French literary theorist Roland Barthes maintains, is significant not in its careful conformity to the actual facts of the worlds the fictions represent, or what Barthes calls "conformity ... to ... model," but rather in its conformity to the "cultural rules of representation" that allow certain details to stand in for the quotidian world and for that world's meaning in relation to bourgeois social life as a whole (144–45). Flaubertian realism, and realism more generally, thereby hinge on what Barthes calls a *"referential illusion"* (148). Those details that "are reputed to *denote* the real directly" in realist fiction instead merely imply or *"signify"* the real (148). Eliot's references to stone jugs do not reproduce stone jugs. Instead they enact a drama in which quotidian objects like stone jugs come to stand for reality. Such details, Barthes suggests, "say nothing but this: *we are the real*" (148). The "contingent contents" of reality constantly give way in realist fiction to their aesthetic "effect" (148). Realism's modesty and deference before the real merely mask its deeper ambitions and aggression: realism does not represent reality so much as redefine it.

REALISM'S POLITICS

If literary historians have generally agreed that realism is the preeminent literary mode of the bourgeoisie, they have come to widely divergent conclusions about what realism had to say about bourgeois social life and about how it participated in the various social developments it documented. Realist fiction would seem to give expression to all of the complications of the CLASS most clearly identified with the capitalist marketplace and its processes of what the Austrian economist Joseph Schumpeter calls "creative destruction" (81). There is a straightforward sense at least in which realism casts itself as an oppositional and disruptive discourse. In substituting grimy details for exalted ideals, it cannot help but make the ideals look somewhat dishonest. When Eliot not only represents an uninspired clergyman but also goes so far as to identify the "precious quality of truthfulness" with such mediocrities, she raises the prospect that the virtues of the Victorian clergy might be largely illusory (chap. 17).

Even when realists set out to affirm social ideals rather than undermine them, moreover, literary historians detect crucial countervailing crosscurrents coursing through their work. Lukács acknowledges that Balzac was so politically conservative that the author could not properly understand the social and economic forces he represented in his novels: "Balzac did not see this dialectic of objective economic evolution and, as the legitimist extoller of the aristocratic large estate that he was, he could not possibly have seen it" (38). But for Lukács, Balzac's "deep understanding of real conditions" inevitably led him to a critical stance his own political sympathies would have precluded:

> But as the inexorable observer of the social history of France he did see a great deal of the social movements and evolutionary trends produced by [the] economic dialectic of the smallholding. Balzac's greatness lies precisely in the fact that in spite of all of his political and ideological prejudices he observed with incorruptible eyes all contradictions as they arose, and faithfully described them. (38–39)

In this schema, insofar as realism is simply identified with the suspension of the ideological it is also simply identified with the cause of social transformation (see IDEOLOGY). To represent capitalism is to represent its contradictions, and to represent its contradictions is to point the way to a better future. Realism itself enlists its practitioners in the cause of a reform they need never outwardly endorse.

"Incorruptible eyes" mark an almost impossibly high standard for a social critic, needless to say, and the notion that the mere recognition of capitalism's contradictions will necessarily generate a brighter future might now seem unduly optimistic. But literary historians following in Lukács's wake have often located emancipatory tendencies in realism without needing to trace them to such suspect origins. For Jameson, realism's basic focus on the domain of the contingent detail, its dramatization of the relationship between the contingent and the necessary, leads it to challenge the notion that the bourgeois order is in any way inevitable. Jameson does not think that Balzac's representation of "social movements" and "evolutionary trends" itself entails a critique of the "economic dialectic of smallholding" (Lukács, 38). But he does think that the author's "narrative register" presents accounts of these movements and trends which "offer" them "to us as merely conditional history" (169). Balzac's narrative techniques "transform the indicative mode of historical 'fact' into the less binding one of the cautionary tale and didactic lesson," and what Jameson considers the "tragedy" of capitalist development is thereby "emptied of its finality, its irreversibility, its historical inevitability" (169). Noting capitalism's contingency might seem less immediately subversive than revealing its contradictions, but in both schemes, Lukács's and Jameson's alike, realism opens capitalist social order to the prospect of radical redefinition.

But, just as Schumpeter's famous formulation associates capitalism as much with centripetal creative authority as with centrifugal destructive effect, realism seems to offer a conservative tug to accompany its critical push. "The realist writer," explains Leo Bersani, "is intensely aware of writing in a context of social fragmentation" (60). But for Bersani, realism does not expose this fragmentation or glory in the prospects for political transformation it might seem to offer; instead, it mitigates its effects. Social fragmentation appears in realism only against the backdrop of a deeper sense of order: "The realistic novel gives us an image of social fragmentation contained with the order of significant form—and it thereby suggests that the chaotic fragments are somehow socially viable and morally redeemable" (60). If Lukács's realism makes radicals even out of the ideologically conservative, Bersani's realism renders the seemingly radical nothing more than the agents of social order. The point is not that realist novels represent a conservative and staid social world; it is rather that they "serve" in the production and maintenance of that world, and that they do so even when they would seem to be dwelling on bourgeois society's least stable features. Realism's iconoclastic surface merely obscures a "secret complicity between the novelist and his society's illusions about its own order" (63).

Critics operating under the influence of the French historian Michel Foucault have extended this point. D. A. Miller notes that the realist novel often seems to take the maintenance of bourgeois social order as its explicit subject matter. As he puts it, "discipline" and the institutions through which it is disseminated—schools, police stations, courts, orphanages, and the like— provide the realist novel "with its essential 'content'" (18). But Miller also insists that the realist novel does not merely represent discipline in its various modes of nineteenth-century operation. It also "*belongs to the disciplinary field that it portrays*," which means that the realist novel's thematic embrace of instability will always coincide with its formal resolution of the putative crises it addresses (21). The realist author "inflects 'the social problem novel,'" Miller explains, "so that any 'problem' is already part of a more fundamental social solution: namely, the militant constitution and operation of the social field as such" (116). Realists may well tend to be skeptical about the value of this conservative process, but even when they go as far as to condemn militant efforts to maintain social order, they nonetheless participate in them: "Whenever the [realist] novel censures policing power, it has already reinvented it, in

the very practice of novelistic representation" (20). For Bersani and Miller, the realist novel would seem to reaffirm social order in the act of challenging it, but for Lukács and Jameson it challenges the social order in the act of reaffirming it.

In one respect, this divergence of opinion simply marks yet another chapter in the longstanding and interminable critical battle over the extent and limit of art's critical relationship to the broader culture from which it emerges. But in another respect the two sides seem less to be arguing with one another than emphasizing different features of the same essentially double-edged structure: all four critics distill realism from a complicated play of fragmentation and retrenchment. We should hardly be surprised to find curious combinations of stability and subversion in a privileged representational form of a socioeconomic system whose "essential" mode of functioning, at least according to Schumpeter, depends upon "incessantly revolution[izing] . . . *from within*" (83).

REALISM'S LEGACIES

Toward the end of the nineteenth century, realism gradually fell from its preeminent position in the European and American novel, as it was displaced first by NATURALISM and later by MODERNISM. The naturalism arising from the works of Émile Zola, Thomas Hardy, Stephen Crane, Theodore Dreiser, and Frank Norris was in many respects an evolutionary outgrowth of realism. However, there are important differences between the two projects. While the realist focused on what Lukács called "social interconnection" and the various forms of "necessity" to which it gave rise, the naturalist often seemed to dwell on more purely physical and scientific forms of connection and necessity. "We picture the world as thick with conquering and elate humanity," explains the narrator of Crane's "The Blue Hotel" (1898), a story set in a Nebraskan blizzard, "but here, with the bugles of the tempest pealing, it was hard to imagine a peopled earth. One viewed the existence of man then as a marvel, and conceded a glamour of wonder to these lice which were caused to cling to a whirling, fire-smote, ice-locked, disease-stricken, space-lost bulb" (1984, *Crane: Prose and Poetry*, 822). The shift from realism's "defined historical and social setting" to naturalism's heavily marked biological world of disease and lice is significant. At worst, it might mark a departure from the various forms of contingency that so appeal to Jameson. If realism revealed that "evolutionary trends" had their origins in "social" developments over which persons might exert some control, naturalism might seem to restore to such developments their "finality," "irreversibility," and "historical inevitability." As Lukács would make the point, insofar as Zola's "most sincere and courageous critique of society" proceeded from a "'scientific' conception" that led him to "identify mechanically the human body and human society," that critique remained "locked into the magic circle of progressive *bourgeois* narrow-mindedness" (86–87). Whether this is an entirely accurate account of the way in which naturalists addressed the relationship between biological and social forms remains an open question. The naturalist identification of social order with biological necessity is often highly provisional: when "The Blue Hotel" ends by raising the question of whether its events result from individual acts or a social "collaboration" (827), Crane represents that collaboration both as something like a social choice ("We, five of us, have collaborated in the murder of this Swede," 827) and as a collective process so impersonal as to be almost wholly naturalized (the murder was

merely "a culmination, the apex of a human movement," 828). And in light of this uncertainty the continuities between naturalism and realism are likely to take on a greater salience. Naturalism may have complicated realism's resolutely social calculus with potentially extrapersonal factors, but it nonetheless retained, and indeed extended, realism's persistent interest in exploring the ways in which human subjects might be said to be "embedded," to use Auerbach's term, in a "total reality" or "physical atmosphere" (463, 473).

If naturalism can be configured as an organic development of realist considerations and principles, however, modernism would initially seem to involve an outright rejection of them. Realism openly proclaims its dependence upon representational transparency. It is "done with the conviction," writes Auerbach, "that every event, if one is able to express it purely and completely, interprets itself and the persons involved in it far better and more completely than any opinion or judgment appended to it could do" (486). Modernism would seem to hinge on more formal and self-referential considerations. "The positivist aesthetic of the twentieth century," writes art and cultural critic Clement Greenberg, "refuses the individual art the right explicitly to refer to anything beyond its own realm of sensations" (274).

But there is a sense in which even modernist self-referentiality is little more than an extension of the simple realist premise that successful art consists in "the truthful treatment of material." When Eliot claims to present life as it is and not as it "never [has] been and never will be," she offers not the world itself but "men and things as they have mirrored themselves in my mind" (chap. 17). Art cannot offer the world. It can only offer art: images, pictures, representations. This is why Howells can find himself in the odd position of celebrating realism precisely because it sustains "the illusion in which alone the truth of art resides" (967). From this vantage, modernist FORMALISM emerges as a way of avoiding the illusions of art, even, or especially, the illusions of realistic art. Presenting only itself, in its formal and material specificity, the modernist novel completes the realist project of avoiding deception as much as it abandons it. Greenberg would note that even as the formalist imperatives of modernist aesthetics seem to "override . . . nature almost entirely," nature remains "indelibly" "stamped" even on the most abstract modernist works: "What was stamped was not the appearance of nature, however, but its logic" (272). The art that abandons realist representational ambitions, namely the appearance of nature, nonetheless carries out the realist aesthetic ambition of presenting reality in the logic of nature, or the reality of the aesthetic object itself. Perhaps this is why the realist considerations remain a vital part of the novelistic practice of many leading modernists, such as E. M. Forster, Joseph Conrad, John Dos Passos, Ernest Hemingway, and Willa Cather.

In the wake of modernist innovations, realism remains an important, if not central, feature of novelistic discourse. Realism may have ceased to be the hallmark of formally ambitious fiction, but it nonetheless served as something like the early twentieth-century novel's default form. In addition, the realist project would loom large in a number of important twentieth-century literary movements. A vigorous social realist movement emerged in the 1930s and 1940s among American writers, such as John Steinbeck, Richard Wright, Nelson Algren, William Attaway, Betty Smith, and Wright Morris. The 1920s saw the first theorizations, in the work of Franz Roh, of MAGICAL REALISM. Dedicated to the notion that a proper realism would discover seemingly supernatural or mysterious properties inhabiting the empirical world, or that, to use the terms of Alejo Carpentier, "the strange is commonplace, and always was commonplace," magical realism flourished, among other places, in the Latin American novel of the second half of the twentieth century, shaping in various ways the work of such major novelists as Carpentier, Juan Rulfo, Julio Cortázar, Gabriel García Márquez, and Carlos Fuentes (104).

Realism survived even the mid-twentieth-century rise of postmodernist aesthetic ambitions. According to Tom Wolfe, "by the mid-1960s the conviction was not merely that the realistic novel was no longer possible but that [modern] life itself no longer deserved the term *real*" (1989, 49). But by the mid-1980s many leading American writers were associated with the practice of what editor Bill Buford calls "dirty realism." His description of the fiction of writers like Tobias Wolff, Raymond Chandler, Richard Ford, Jayne Anne Phillips, and Frederick Barthelme almost directly follows Auerbach's account of "the modern realism" of the nineteenth century. What Auerbach called the "foundations" of modern realism—namely "the rise of more extensive and socially inferior human groups to the position of subject matter for problematic-existential representation, on the one hand; on the other, the embedding of random persons and events in the general course of contemporary history, the fluid historical background" (491)—remain foundational in Buford's dirty realism, comprising as it does "unadorned, unfurnished, low-rent tragedies about people who watch day-time television, read cheap romances, or listen to country and western music ... drifters in a world cluttered with junk food and the oppressive details of modern consumerism" (4). All the same, by the end of the twentieth century it was very difficult to argue with the contention of *Partisan Review* editor William Phillips (1907–2002) that realism had become "just another formal device, not a permanent method for dealing with experience" (qtd. in Wolfe, 1998, 50). Wolfe may well have been right: "The introduction of detailed realism into English literature . . . was like the introduction of electricity into machine technology. It raised the state of the art to an entirely new magnitude" (Introduction, 1). But having lifted the state of the art to that new magnitude, it gradually ceased to define it.

SEE ALSO: Definitions of the Novel, Genre, History of the Novel, Marxist Theory, Novel Theory (19th Century), Novel Theory (20th Century).

BIBLIOGRAPHY

Auerbach, E. (2003), *Mimesis*, 50th ed., trans. W.R. Trask.
Barthes, R. (1987), *Rustle of Language*.
Bell, M.D. (1993), *Problem of American Realism*.
Bersani, L. (1976), *Future for Astyanax*.
Berthoff, W. (1965), *Ferment of Realism*.
Buford, B. (1983), "Introduction," in *Granta 8*.
Carpentier, A. (1995), "The Baroque and the Marvelous Real," in *Magical Realism*, ed. L. Parkinson Zamore and W.B. Faris.
Eliot, G. (1859), *Adam Bede*.
Greenberg, C. (1949), "The Role of Nature in Modern Painting," in *Collected Essays and Criticism*, vol. 2, ed. J. O'Brian.
Howells, W.D. (1889), "Editor's Study," *Harper's New Monthly Magazine*, Nov.: 962–67.
Jameson, F. (2002), *Political Unconscious*, 2nd ed.
Lathrop, G.P. (1874), "The Novel and Its Future," *Atlantic Monthly* 34:313–24.
Levin, H. (1957), "What Is Realism?" in *Contexts of Criticism*.
Lukács, G. (1972), *Studies in European Realism*.
Miller, D.A. (1988), *Novel and the Police*.
Schumpeter, J.C. (1942, 2008), *Capitalism, Socialism, and Democracy*.
Trilling, L. (1950), "Reality in America," in *Liberal Imagination*.
Wolfe, T. (1973), "Introduction," in *New Journalism*.
Wolfe, T. (1989), "Stalking the Billion-Footed Beast," *Harper's Magazine*, Nov.: 45–56.

Recognition *see* Closure
Referentiality *see* Fiction
Reflector *see* Narrator

Regional Novel

CAREN S. LAMBERT

The regional novel is based on the idea that there is a connection between a region and the literature it produces, whether one understands region to mean a distinct physical environment (from the Latin *regionem*, "boundary or district") or a part of some larger political entity (from *regere*, "to direct or to rule"). The traditional understanding of regional identity is grounded in eighteenth-century political philosophy concerning national identity, which assumes that material circumstances (climate, quality of soil, topography, natural resources) shape individual inhabitants in similar ways, producing patterns of social, economic, and political behavior. These shared patterns of behavior, in turn, form both the nation's institutions and its cultural expressions. Its theoretical basis goes back at least as far as Montesquieu's *De l'esprit des lois* (1748, *The Spirit of the Laws*), a comparative study of legal and political institutions in which he asserts that the "empire of the climate is the first, the most powerful of empires" (ed. D. W. Carrithers, 1997, 294). It continues in the work of German Romantic thinkers such as Johann Gottfried Herder (1744–1803), who maintained that folk thought was the organic root of national spirit, or William von Humboldt (1767–1835), who asserted that language is the expression of the genius of a people.

The theories of Montesquieu, Herder, and von Humboldt do not allow for nations large enough to contain significant variations in environment, folk, or language. In other words, they do not allow for regions. In Montesquieu's opinion, what we think of as regional boundaries were also the natural boundaries for nations and their cultures. Nations that contained too much variation would find "the government of the laws" becoming "incompatible with the maintenance of the state" (278). When you have a nation as large and topographically varied as the U.S., as Alexis de Tocqueville (1805–59) puts it in *Democracy in America* (1835), the "sovereignty of the Union" is no longer natural, but instead "a work of art" (1966, trans. G. Lawrence, 167). The nation becomes, as Benedict Anderson describes it, an "imagined community," while regions remain tangible and immediate (1983, *Imagined Communities*). Regions within the imagined nation, however, are still thought of as organic, coherent, rooted in the land, and characterized by homogenous geographies and populations.

Authors who speak from this traditional regional perspective often present the region as in danger of being destroyed by national and global influences and in need of being preserved in literature. As Thomas Hardy explains in his "General Preface" to the Wessex Edition of his *Works* in 1912, his goal was to "preserve . . . a fairly true record of a vanishing life." The American poet and critic Allen Tate (1899–1979) famously described the regional literature of the Southern Renaissance (1929–53) as "a backward glance" which the South gave as it stepped into the modern world, integrating with national culture and relinquishing its regional character (1945, "The New Provincialism," *Virginia Quarterly Review*). Characters in such regional works experience what Ian Duncan calls the "collapse of a traditional distinction between horizons of knowledge," between the immediate and tangible region and the distant and intangible world, as region is assimilated into nation (2007, *Scott's Shadow*, 228). Publish-

ers and readers who understand regional writing in this way tend to judge works by their supposed authenticity, by whether they are "true" to some preexisting sense of a place. For instance, the African American author Charles Chesnutt first gained popularity for his Southern dialect writing in *The Conjure Woman* (1899), which reworked the Uncle Remus stories of Joel Chandler Harris. In later novels such as *House behind the Cedars* (1900), when Chesnutt turned to criticism of race relations in the region, he largely lost his reading audience.

The difficulty with this traditional, environmentalist conception of regions and their literature is that although regions may be rooted, regional cultures and their cultural products are mobile. Another way of conceptualizing region that takes into account not just physical circumstances but also cultural flows can best be understood using a combination of nineteenth-century literary criticism, late nineteenth- and early twentieth-century anthropology, and late twentieth-century cultural geography. The idea that literature reflects cultural flows has its origins in *Histoire de la littérature anglaise* (1863, *History of English Literature*) by the French critic Hippolyte Taine (1828–93). As Brad Evans points out, Taine presents literature as "a material artifact of the history of a people's origins and migration, of cross-cultural contact, conflict and acculturation, of the permanency and change of their character" (2005, *Before Cultures*, 89). Later in the century, anthropologists including Franz Boas (1858–1942), Melville Herskovits (1895–1963), and Fernando Ortiz (1881–1969) also began to move away from Matthew Arnold's (1822–88) idea of a singular Culture comprised of the best that has been thought and said, and toward cultural relativism and a conception of plural cultures. Together, Taine and the anthropologists offer a useful formulation for understanding literature both in the colonized Americas and the imperial nations of Europe, which did not contain a singular folk and to which cultural artifacts often traveled independently of the folk with which they originated. From the 1970s on, cultural geographers such as Henri LeFebvre (1901–91) have drawn upon cultural theory, anthropology, sociology, and philosophy to move beyond the organic assumptions of traditional regionalism and to discuss the way in which cultures produce the spaces they inhabit for specific ideological ends.

This second regional perspective presents regional identity as something continuously being created rather than naturalizing that identity. Regions emerge from a continuing negotiation between nature and cultures in the minds and actions of their inhabitants. Regional culture and cultural products are syncretic rather than pure, mobile rather than rooted. Literary works that belong to this cultural regional tradition tend to have faith in the positive, transformative power of new influences and the continuing flexibility of regions. They often attempt to negotiate some form of improved community for the future. George Washington Cable's *The Grandissimes* (1888) is an example of this second type of regional novel. It captures the moment at which the once Spanish, now French, colony of Louisiana passes into American hands and the mixing of languages, cultures, and races that occurs at what would seem to be a triumphant moment of standardization and nationalization.

The regional novel resembles the provincial novel, but there are important distinctions between the two which keep the categories firmly separated. As Franco Moretti points out, the term "provincial" derives from the *provinciae* of Rome in which people were subjects but not citizens. The "provinces are 'negative' entities, defined by *what is not there*," while regions are filled with highly specific cultural content (2005,

Graphs, Maps, Trees, 53). Hence provincial settings are interchangeable while regional settings are not. The greater the number of metropolitan centers a country has, the less likely it is to have a strong provincial literature. Regional novels flourish in the U.S., where provincial literature is basically absent. Both provincial and regional novels are found in the U.K., where the provinces tend to be closer to London, like the Midlands in George Eliot's *Middlemarch: A Study of Provincial Life* (1871–72). Places that are farther afield, like the Wales of Richard Llewellyn's *How Green Was My Valley* (1939), are able to differentiate themselves into regions. In the Russian tradition, Anne Lounsberry argues that provincial literature such as Nikolay Gogol's *Mertvye dushi* (1842, *Dead Souls*) dominates because highly centralized autocracy quells regionalism.

HISTORICAL DEVELOPMENT

Regional novels tend to emerge at moments of crisis within a given national tradition. They offer a means of negotiating between local, national, and international identities at moments of national expansion or disintegration. As Doris Sommer puts it, regionalism provides a distinct voice to culturally or linguistically identified groups inside unwieldy or porous nations (1999, *The Places of History*). American critics such as Judith Fetterley and Richard Brodhead have suggested that regional writing provides an outlet for the voices of women and ethnic or racial minorities who are otherwise excluded from the national literary dialogue. The balance of power in the national culture and the position of the nation within the larger international order determines who chooses to speak from a regional perspective at any given moment.

Regional novels from the eighteenth and nineteenth centuries most often belong to the genres of historical fiction or realism. In this period, regional novels typically include ethnographic description of manners, traditions, and folklore; written imitations of dialect; an attention to landscape and natural forms; some account of the workings or structure of the local economy; and details of local history. They often have a frame structure with a narrator speaking standardized language and characters using various phonetically rendered regional and/or racial dialects. At times the narrator is a native speaking from within and concerned with the preservation of regional traditions and community in response to social conflict, fragmentation, or alienation. In other instances, the narrator is a native who feels intellectually detached from the region. In a third variation, a detached narrator comes to the region as a cultural tourist and presents it as something exotic and entertaining, ventriloquizing the local inhabitants rather than authentically representing them. In the latter two categories, the narrator typically depicts the region in order to criticize and perhaps even reform it.

The regional novel in English has its origins in Irish and Scottish regional fiction produced as Great Britain confronted the problem of how to subsume various national identities into that of a single modern imperial state. Maria Edgeworth's depiction of Irish character, speech, and folklore in *Castle Rackrent* (1800) established many of the conventions of regionalism discussed above. Walter Scott noted his debt to Edgeworth, in the 1829 preface to *Waverley*, in which he wrote about the Scottish border regions. After a mid-century move toward the provincial novel, British literature returned to regionalism in the 1870s. Writers from this period at times used regionalism as a refuge from contemporary conditions, as in the escapist historical romance of R. D. Blackmore's *Lorna Doone* (1869) or the nostalgic tone of the Scottish Kailyard writer

J. M. Barrie. Other authors adopted the regional novel in order to challenge contemporary conditions, as in Thomas Hardy's ironic reworking of Scott's historical regionalism, in *The Mayor of Casterbridge* (1886).

With the rise of Scott, British regional novels became part of global literary culture, influencing not only European traditions but New World literatures as well. Regionalism as a genre was rooted in the Old World and yet flexible enough to be transplanted to the New World, providing romantic nationalists in the Americas with a model for producing colonial literatures with national potential. Representing New World difference became a cultural declaration of independence. David Jordan argues that the Latin American *novela de la tierra* is a richer regional tradition than that found in North America and one with no pejorative connotations, unlike "local color" in the U.S.

Scott's novels were widely read in the nineteenth-century U.S., where the lack of international copyright laws meant that they were less expensive than domestically produced literature, making regionalism a form readily available to American authors. They helped pave the way for the earliest regional writings of Augustus Baldwin Longstreet, George Washington Harris, and Bret Harte, which were short stories in dialect drawing on native traditions of southwestern humor and the tall tale as well as later full-fledged Southern regional novels such as Mark Twain's *The Adventures of Huckleberry Finn* (1885). Feminist critics trace a different trajectory for the regional novel in the U.S. beginning with Harriet Beecher Stowe's *The Pearl of Orr's Island* (1862), which the nineteenth-century regional writer Sarah Orne Jewett identified as a formative influence on her own writing. Regional writing in the U.S. reached its height in the period following reconstruction, from 1877 through 1900, mostly thanks to the publication of short regional writings in periodicals including the *Atlantic Monthly, Harper's, Century,* and *Scribner's.* Critics such as Richard Brodhead and Amy Kaplan emphasize the way in which depicting the "foreign" regional helped to familiarize it and contributed to the reconstruction of the nation after the Civil War.

Twentieth-century regionalists use more experimental forms but retain their careful attention to distinctive local patterns of speech and their familiarity with local traditions and knowledge. The decision of the American modernist Willa Cather to dedicate her first novel, *O Pioneers!* (1913), to Sarah Orne Jewett shows one of the most prominent American modernists specifically thinking of herself as part of a regional tradition. Consider the combination of pioneering modernist form and detailed portrayal of local life in James Joyce's *Ulysses* (1922) or William Faulkner's *As I Lay Dying* (1930). In South America, the late nineteenth and early twentieth centuries saw the rise of avant-garde regionalists such as José Eustasio Rivera in Colombia, Romulo Gallegos in Venezuela, and Ricardo Güiraldes in Argentina. The magical realism pioneered later in the twentieth century by Gabriel García Márquez also has a strong regional bent. Examples of postmodern regionalism include works by the Mexican writer Carlos Fuentes, such as *La region más transparente* (1956, *Where the Air Is Clear*) and *Las buenas conciencias* (1959, *The Good Conscience*), and the Western novels of Cormac McCarthy, such as *Blood Meridian* (1985).

SEE ALSO: Anthropology, Dialect, Historical Novel, Intertextuality, Magical Realism, Modernism, National Literature, Naturalism.

BIBLIOGRAPHY

Brodhead, R. (1993), *Cultures of Letters.*
Dianotto, R. (2000), *Place in Literature.*
Draper, R.P., ed. (1989), *Literature of Region and Nation.*
Fetterley, J. and M. Pryse (2003), *Writing Out of Place.*
Foote, S. (2001), *Regional Fictions.*
Jordan, D., ed. (1994), *Regionalism Reconsidered.*
Joseph, P. (2007), *American Literary Regionalism in a Global Age.*
Kaplan, A. (1993), "Nation, Region, Empire," in *Columbia History of the American Novel,* ed. E. Elliott.
Karem, J. (2004), *Romance of Authenticity.*
Lounsberry, A. (2005), "'No, this is not the provinces!' Provincialism, Authenticity, and Russianness in Gogol's Day," *Russian Review* 64: 259–80.
Lutz, T. (2004), *Cosmopolitan Vistas.*
Snell, K.D.M., ed. (1998), *Regional Novel in Britain and Ireland, 1800–1990.*

Religion

VINCENT P. PECORA

Received wisdom of the twentieth century tells us that the concepts "religion" and "novel" are mutually exclusive. That the novel is a powerful reflection and instrument of secularization is a truism. As Jack Goody writes, at the start of what may be the most ambitious anthology so far to circumscribe the novel transnationally, "The modern novel, after Daniel Defoe, was essentially a secular tale, a feature that is comprised within the meaning of 'realistic.' The hand of God may appear, but it does so through 'natural' sequences, not through miracles or mirabilia. Earlier narrative structures often displayed such intervention, which, in a world suffused by the supernatural, was present everywhere" (1:21). The division in European fiction for Goody—as for so many before him—is between, on the one side, mythic classical ROMANCES, such as Apuleius's *The Golden Ass* (ca. 100–200 CE), the saints' lives of the Middle Ages, and exemplary tales such as John Bunyan's *Pilgrim's Progress* (1678), and on the other side naturalistic fictions such as Daniel Defoe's *Robinson Crusoe* (1719–22), which often elaborated upon current events and assumed the characteristics of print reportage (see JOURNALISM). (In such accounts, it is important that the etymology of *novel* is "news," the sort of diplomatic information that appeared in broadsheets in the late fifteenth century along with the printing press, but eventually included stories like the shipwreck of Alexander Selkirk and other castaways.)

THE SECULARIZATION THESIS

Whether one looks at Goody's account or at those of Ian Watt, Michael McKeon, or Benedict Anderson, one finds a well-engrained family of ideas: the fifteenth-century advent of printing (see PAPER AND PRINT) coincided with the scientific revolution and the rationalized religion of the Protestant Reformation, which eventually enabled the invention of the nation-state, civil society, and capitalism during the eighteenth-century Enlightenment. The novel appears in the English-speaking world at the crossing of what Hans Blumenberg called an epochal threshold separating the religious worldview of medieval Catholicism and a secular, or least Protestant, worldview defined by an unknowable divinity, an inward spirituality, and a desire for worldly achievement, individual self-assertion, and instrumental morality. This is the story of Western secularization, and even in globally focused projects it determines how the novel is understood. Most of it could be traced to Max Weber, who also subtly inflects how we interpret historical changes

within the novel. Franco Moretti calls "fillers" the expansion of mundane passages of conversation or description in the realistic novel in which nothing seems to happen; Honoré de Balzac's *Illusions perdues* (1837–43, *Lost Illusions*), George Eliot's *Middlemarch* (1871–72), and Thomas Mann's *Buddenbrooks* (1901) are apparently full of them. "Fillers are an attempt at *rationalizing the novelistic universe:* turning it into a world of few surprises, fewer adventures, and no miracles at all" (1:381). By this measure, we could say that all of Henry James is one long filler. People still go to church in Henry Fielding; Laurence Sterne adapted his own sermons for *Tristram Shandy*. But the thesis of the secularizing novel pays little attention to such topical embellishments. Since the novel, in this view, is the aesthetic exemplification of the deists' universe of the *deus absconditus*, it is not surprising that scholars like Martha Nussbaum (who sees the novel as the elaboration of secular moral philosophy) and Lynn Hunt (who locates the invention of compassionate human empathy—surprisingly for those familiar with the great world religions—in eighteenth-century EPISTOLARY novels such as Samuel Richardson's *Clarissa*, 1747–48) describe the novel as the foundation of modern secular morality.

This last claim heaps much ethical, political, and metaphysical weight onto the shoulders of what is after all a mere literary convention, and might suggest that for many of its early readers, the novel was a secular substitute for diminishing religious feeling—or what Blumenberg calls a "formal reoccupation" of now "vacant" theological "answer positions" (69). In fact, the Weberian interpretation of the GENRE is to be found less in Weber himself than in his contemporary interlocutor, the Hegelian (and later MARXIST) philosopher Georg LUKÁCS. For the early Lukács, the novel was the supreme representation of nostalgia for the "immanence" of meaning once supplied by religion. Lukács's novel is a secularized epic, and he specifies what "answer position" the novel has come to reoccupy: "The novel is the epic of a world that has been abandoned by God" (88). The novelist's irony, "with intuitive double vision, can see where God is to be found in a world abandoned by God" (92). Lukács subtly reworks the perspective of G. W. F. Hegel, who elaborates the novel—most obviously the BILDUNGSROMAN of Johann Wolfgang von Goethe's *Wilhelm Meisters Lehrjahre* (1795–96, *Wilhelm Meister's Apprenticeship*) and its sequel—as exemplifying the unfortunate way irony dominates modern culture (see MODERNISM). What was fatally missing in the novel, Hegel claimed, was *earnestness*, which means that the novel lacks all capacity for EPIC achievement or forms of understanding that transcend the quotidian pursuits of everyday life. Lukács turned Hegel's criticism of the novel's formal failing into a melancholy commentary on its spiritual homelessness. "The novel is the form of the epoch of absolute sinfulness," Lukács wrote, and the novel's irony negatively illuminated culture's profound longing for a world redeemed from its sublunary bad faith and emptiness (152).

Erich Auerbach produced the great and still unparalleled *summa* of the novel's career as the genre of secularization. Auerbach's focus is narrative form broadly conceived, including drama and verse. But it is the novel that occupies most of his attention after Miguel de Cervantes Saavedra's *Don Quixote* (1605, 1615), and that most fully embodies Auerbach's primary thesis. Yet this thesis depends on a notion of secularization more evident in Lukács (and throughout Hegel's work) than in the later criticism of Watt, McKeon, Moretti, et al. Auerbach's sympathetic, nonsystematic perspective is the final product of the long development of Christian human-

ism in Europe, beginning in what Auerbach discerns as the mixture of styles and the imaginative sympathy granting tragic sublimity to the lowest social orders in the Gospel of Mark (a sympathy absent in Homer, Tacitus, and Petronius, and generally available only in stylistically appropriate comedy throughout Antiquity). Auerbach rooted this stylistic confusion in the story of Christ's human incarnation amid the humblest of circumstances and in the earlier Jewish idea of universal history in which the sublime and everyday could be united (as in the story of Abraham and Isaac). Auerbach regarded the nineteenth-century novel's "revolution against the classical doctrine of levels of style" (or "DECORUM," for Horace") as simply one revolt among many in the Western literary history (554). Auerbach made clear "when and how this first break with the classical theory had come about. It was the story of Christ, with its ruthless mixture of everyday reality and the highest and most sublime tragedy, which had conquered the classical rules of styles" (555). The demise of the stylistically hierarchic thus accompanies—or rather, generically records and compels—the demise of the spiritually hieratic. As has been the paradoxical case for numerous historians and sociologists of religion, the story of secularization that becomes the story of the novel actually begins for Auerbach with the story of Christ.

RELIGION, ROMANCE, AND REFORMATION

Alternatives to this history of the novel as secularization—implying either a break with the religious past (as in Goody) or a translation of religious into secular motifs (as in Auerbach)—have long been available. G. A. Starr and J. Paul Hunter emphasize the religious sources of Defoe's seminal novel—the first in broadly Christian terms, the second as Puritan (Bunyanesque) guide—in which spiritual quest, pilgrim allegory, and typological thinking predominate. For them, *Robinson Crusoe* (1719–22) is as much spiritual autobiography as proto-capitalist adventure—a conflation that would hardly have surprised Weber. Though neither Starr nor Hunter places "romance" at the novel's rise, they nevertheless highlight characteristics of *Robinson Crusoe*—the work often considered the model for the "realistic" novel—that reflect the techniques of romance writing. A genre with classical origins and the mythic motifs (see MYTHOLOGY) of quest, ritual, archetype, and symbolic (or allegorical) action, romance becomes for others the template that rivals Lukács's epic. Northrop Frye's use of romance illustrates elements in the modern (post-Defoe) novel that remain anchored in religious tradition. Margaret Anne Doody emphasizes not only the generic continuity of classical and medieval romance (from Heliodorus, Apuleius, and Petronius to Giovanni Boccaccio and François Rabelais) with the modern novel (especially that of Cervantes, Richardson, Balzac, Charles Dickens, and Thomas Mann), as well as the contributions of African and Asian sources to romances of the Roman Empire, but also the self-serving nature of the distinction itself within English novels and criticism.

It is not trivial that the English novel putatively spawned by worldly travel and the quotidian entertainment of the *news* would appear to diverge from the older European tradition of the *roman* (a word meaning romance, fiction, and novel, and not only in the Romance languages but in German as well). For whatever one thinks of Doody's debunking of the English claim to have invented the novel, the classical tradition of romance fed seamlessly into Roman Catholic (and often Platonic) traditions of romance in medieval and Renaissance literature. Even when he confronts the

grotesque satire of Christian idealism in Rabelais, Auerbach is careful to point out that Rabelais's stylistic olio is an imitation of late medieval sermons, which were "at once popular in the crudest way, creaturely realistic, and learned and edifying in their figural Biblical interpretation," as well as a product of Rabelais's experience with the earthy, mendicant life-world of the Franciscans (271). (Auerbach's point evokes that Rabelaisian modernist James Joyce, whose sermon in *A Portrait of the Artist as a Young Man* (1916), lifted with scrupulous meanness from an actual Catholic sermon manual, is a later version of what Auerbach means.)

By contrast, from the English Reformation emerged a sober anti-Platonism, a rejection of the vivid imagery of medieval Catholic cosmology (as found in Dante), and the tailoring of the spiritual-amorous quest (filigreed with colorful symbolism in a verse romance like Guillaume de Lorris and Jean de Meung's *Roman de la Rose*, mid- to late thirteenth century) to fit the far more pedantic and ham-handed allegory of *Pilgrim's Progress*. Despite Defoe's affinity with Bunyan, a national Protestantism bequeathed to the English novel a far less *romance*-oriented and religiously oriented sensibility. Even when bitterly satirized, religious feeling is elaborated by the French novel in striking, exotic, and intimate detail. Nothing in Jane Austen, Dickens, or George Eliot—despite the latter's Dorothea Brooke in whom, unlike her uncle, "the hereditary strain of Puritan energy ... glowed alike through faults and virtues" (Eliot, 6)—remotely approaches the religion haunting Gustave Flaubert's Emma Bovary. And nothing in the English novel would allow a reader to understand what Flaubert does with religion in *Trois contes* (1877, *Three Tales*), *Salammbô* (1862), and most of all in his dramatic novel, *La tentation de Saint Antoine* (1874, *The Temptation of St. Anthony*), on which Flaubert labored throughout his life in the face of his friends' ridicule. By 1876, Richard Wagner's mythic opera cycle, *Der Ring des Nibelungen*, and his retelling of the Grail legend, *Parsifal*, were being embraced on the Continent. Despite the undeniable Christianity of his sensibility, Dickens's characters no longer go to church, even on Sundays, and they almost never discuss religion.

THE RETURN OF THE REPRESSED

Unsurprisingly, the two-volume, 2,000-page English version of Moretti's *The Novel* devotes only trivial, passing remarks to the greatest religious novel yet written— Fyodor Dostoyevsky's *Brat'ya Karamazovy* (1880, *The Brothers Karamazov*), of which the "Grand Inquisitor" chapter is the single most important literary reflection on religion in modernity, a text equal to (and perhaps influencing) the late writings of Friedrich Nietzsche. Dostoyevsky's engagement with Russian Orthodoxy is very different from Flaubert's with Roman Catholicism, but one cannot discount the roles of these two writers in creating the formal and thematic foundations of the twentieth-century novel. Lukács pointed beyond the bitter disillusionment of Leo Tolstoy's realism toward the future impact of Dostoyevsky, who he claimed "did not write novels," and who promised an escape from the "age of absolute sinfulness" (152–53; see DEFINITIONS). Apart from vexed questions about the persistence of romance, the European novel after (or despite) the flowering of NATURALISM in the nineteenth century, and the concomitant rise of symbolism in poetry, recovered much that was central to religious sentiment and its mythic, archetypal, symbolic, and allegorical machinery: Joris-Karl Huysmans's *À rebours* (1884, *Against Nature*; stimulated by Flaubert's religious exoticism, and called fatal to nat-

uralism by Émile Zola), Oscar Wilde's *The Picture of Dorian Gray* (1890), Thomas Hardy's *Tess of the D'Urbervilles* (1891) and *Jude the Obscure* (1896), André Gide's *L'Immoraliste* (1902, *The Immoralist*; which Gide traced to Dostoyevsky, about whom he wrote at length) and *La Symphonie pastorale* (1919, *The Pastoral Symphony*), Joyce's *A Portrait of the Artist as a Young Man*, *Ulysses* (1922), and *Finnegans Wake* (1939) (in all three of which there is not one "filler"), Mann's *Der Tod in Venedig* (1913, *Death in Venice*), *Der Zauberberg* (1924, *The Magic Mountain*), and *Doktor Faustus* (1948), Albert Camus's *L'Étranger* (1942, *The Stranger*), *La Peste* (1948, *The Plague*), and *La Chute* (1957, *The Fall*), and most perplexingly yet deeply religious of all, the entire corpus of Franz Kafka (1883–1924). In praising *Das Schloss* (1926, *The Castle*), Mann called Kafka "a religious humorist"; the phrase may be applied broadly to the novelists of Kafka's era (x). (That much of this modernist work reveals powerful homosexual impulses may be one interesting consequence of the novel's rejection of the earlier Protestant, everyday sobriety that Moretti emphasizes.) This may be the revenge—or better, the Heideggerian *Verwindung*, the spiritually distorted return—of religious romance (see Vattimo, 172, 179; Pecora, 20–23). Its effects can be felt to the end of the century, in the MAGICAL REALISM of Gabriel García Márquez, whose deeply Marxist *Cien años de soledad* (1967, *One Hundred Years of Solitude*) is simultaneously profoundly shaped by the syncretistic peasant Catholicism of fictional Sulaco, and of Salman Rushdie's *The Satanic Verses* (1988), a novel (perhaps a romance?) in which Islam is given a formal and thematic centrality— always the Achilles' heel of satire—never before seen in English novels. It may yet turn out that the quotidian, rationalized, often Protestant, and apparently secular novel that began with Defoe came to a halt with Zola, and that "the novel" as so many continue to see it will soon be understood as no more than a two-century aberration in literary history.

SEE ALSO: Comedy/Tragedy, Gothic Novel, History of the Novel, Novel Theory (20th Century), Realism.

BIBLIOGRAPHY

Anderson, B. (1983), *Imagined Communities*.
Auerbach, E. (1974), *Mimesis*, trans. W. Trask.
Blumenberg, H. (1985), *Legitimacy of the Modern Age*, trans. R. Wallace.
Doody, M.A. (1997), *True Story of the Novel*.
Eliot, G. (1968), *Middlemarch*.
Frye, N. (1976), *Secular Scripture*.
Goody, J. (2006), "From Oral to Written," in *Novel*, ed. F. Moretti, 2 vols.
Hunt, L. (2008), *Inventing Human Rights*.
Hunter, J.P. (1966), *Reluctant Pilgrim*.
Lukács, G. (1971), *Theory of the Novel*, trans. A. Bostock.
Mann, T. (1974), "Homage," in F. Kafka, *Castle*, trans. W. and E. Muir.
McKeon, M. (1987), *Origins of the English Novel, 1600–1740*.
Moretti, F. (2006), "Serious Century," in *Novel*, ed. F. Moretti, 2 vols.
Nussbaum, M. (1992), *Love's Knowledge*.
Pecora, V.P. (2006), *Secularization and Cultural Criticism*.
Starr, G.A. (1965), *Defoe and Spiritual Autobiography*.
Vattimo, G. (1988), *End of Modernity*, trans. J. R. Snyder.
Watt, I. (1957), *Rise of the Novel*.
Weber, M. (1992), *Protestant Ethic and the Spirit of Capitalism*, trans. T. Parsons.

Reprints

MEREDITH L. McGILL

Distracted, perhaps, by novels' own claims to novelty—what Ian Watt has identified as the form's primary criterion of "truth to individual experience ... which is always unique and therefore new" (1957, *The Rise of the Novel*, 13)—or by the novel's long association with the news, ephemera, and fashion (see JOURNALISM), literary critics often fail to account for the role of reprinting in the history of the GENRE. Bibliographers and collectors overwhelmingly privilege first editions, despite the fact that later editions were often more valued by authors, printers, and readers, owing to the correction of errata. (Benjamin Franklin's witty epitaph for himself imagines his body reissued after death "In a new and more elegant Edition/Revised and corrected/By the Author.") Even Franco Moretti's experimental, quantitative account of the rise and fall of the novel across a number of national traditions measures only the production of new novels, not reprinted ones (2005, *Graphs, Maps, Trees*). Despite the emphasis critics place on first editions, the small print runs of novels in the 1700s and early 1800s, which James Raven estimates averaged 500–750 copies, suggest that any novel that gained significant purchase with readers in this period did so by virtue of successive waves of reprinting. Taking reprinting seriously as a factor in the history of the novel can illuminate the cultural life of individual works—both the pace of a novel's initial acceptance by its readers and the strength and nature of its explanatory power long after the time in which it was written. Reprinting also helps to explain how the fortunes of the genre have been tied to expanded literacy and the demand for cheap reading (see PUBLISHING). Along with TRANSLATION, ADAPTATION, and abridgment, reprinting is one of the primary ways in which publishers target new audiences for novels. Although we have become accustomed to tight control over intellectual property, throughout most of the novel's history the uneven global distribution of intellectual property rights allowed for significant experiments in unauthorized reprinting (see COPYRIGHT). NATIONAL literary traditions have been more influenced by reprinted foreign novels than nationally framed literary criticism is generally willing to acknowledge.

A tremendous amount of what we ordinarily think of as printing is, technically, reprinting, defined as the resetting of type—i.e., printing not from manuscripts, but from already printed texts (see TYPOGRAPHY). Prior to the development and popular use of stereotype and electrotype technologies in the early 1800s, publishers who sought to profit by publishing multiple editions of a work were forced to incur the considerable cost of recomposing the text (see PAPER AND PRINT). While pages that were difficult to set up, such as title pages, might be left in standing type in anticipation of further printings, publishers frequently found themselves scrambling to meet unanticipated demand for a particular work, hiring compositors to reset the text not long after the first edition had left the printshop. The history of reprinting of a particular novel can offer a good index of the time lag between initial publication and popular acceptance. For instance, Daniel Defoe's *The Life and Strange Surprizing Adventures of Robinson Crusoe* (1719–22) was reprinted three times in the four months following its initial London publication, with three more editions following in the next six years, along with numerous abridgments, sequels, and translations. By contrast, Raven estimates that close to two-thirds of English novels first published between 1770 and 1800 never saw a second edition.

A history of reprinting can also offer considerable insight into a publisher's projections for a work. For instance, while Nathaniel Hawthorne's publishers assumed that *The Scarlet Letter* (1850) would do well, printing an uncharacteristically large edition of 2,500 copies, popular demand for Hawthorne's controversial "Custom House" introduction outstripped supply, prompting Ticknor & Fields to reset the type and to reprint another 2,500 copies within two months of the first publication. Still unaware that they had an incipient classic on their hands, Ticknor & Fields neglected at this time to invest in stereotype plates, and thus were forced to pay to reset the type for a third time just four months later when they finally stereotyped the book.

Reprinting is fundamental to the internal dynamics of the printshop, testifying to publishers' careful calculations about supply and demand for printed works. It has also long been a crucial factor in the regional, national, and international circulation of print. It was Scottish reprinters such as Alexander Donaldson (1727–94) who forced the courts in *Millar v. Taylor* (1769) and *Donaldson v. Becket* (1774) to define the nature and limits of British copyright law. English publishers largely ignored Scottish reprinters, who supplied their home market with cheap reprints of English texts, until Donaldson brazenly opened a shop in London in 1763, undercutting London booksellers by as much as 30–50 percent. The copyright case that bears Donaldson's name served as a turning point in British law, establishing copyright as a statutory right of limited duration (rather than a perpetual right under the common law), instantly transforming many of the most valuable English works from private into public property. The sudden availability for reprinting of texts by long-dead authors such as William Shakespeare and John Milton, and more recent texts by Daniel Defoe, James Thomson, and Henry Fielding arguably helped popularize the very notion of classic texts in English. In the wake of *Donaldson v. Becket*, literary works with expired copyrights joined early modern steady-sellers such as the Bible, catechisms, and primers as books that could be freely reprinted in a variety of editions for a wide range of potential readers. The first successful English reprint series was John Bell's *Poets of Great Britain* (1777–92), which ran to 109 volumes and sold for one shilling and sixpence each. This venture was soon followed by reprint series that featured English and foreign novels, such as James Harrison's *The Novelist's Magazine* (1779–88) and John Cooke's *Select Novels* (1793–95). Harrison's series of 23 volumes, which sought in its format and title to capitalize on the connection between the genre of the novel and the currency of the magazine, printed entire works by Fielding, Samuel Richardson, Oliver Goldsmith, Tobias Smollett, Laurence Sterne, and Eliza Haywood, along with translated continental fiction by authors such as Voltaire and Johann Wolfgang von Goethe. Cooke's pocket-size sixpenny volumes and Harrison's series helped consolidate a canon of respectable novels by making selected works affordable for readers outside the bounds of the circulating libraries (see LIBRARY).

Reprinting works that had fallen out of copyright protection had by the nineteenth century become an important segment of the trade, enabling both highbrow ventures such as the handsomely bound, fifty-volume series *The British Novelists* (1810), prefaced by a substantial introductory essay on the history of the novel by Anna Letitia Barbauld, and remainder-dealer Thomas Tegg's cheap, unreliable reprints and abridgments aimed at the very bottom of the market. Over the course of the nineteenth century, the success of Tegg's reprints, and of cheap publication in England's breakaway American colony, helped to put downward pressure on the notoriously high price of English books and to widen the circle of novel-readers. After the thriving Irish reprint trade was brought under British copyright by the Act of Union (1800), closing down a vexing source of

cheap texts illegally smuggled back into England and opening the Irish market to English publishers, many of the most successful Irish publishers and tradesmen emigrated to the U.S. Irish reprinters brought to the new republic both well-honed publishing and marketing strategies and an acute sense of the vulnerability of provincial reprinting to the forces of centralized capital.

In the U.S., the publishing system was defined by reprinting from the Copyright Act of 1790 well into the twentieth century. The same law that granted copyright to American citizens and residents explicitly denied such rights to foreign authors, bestowing on American publishers an extraordinary license, that of the unrestricted republication of foreign texts. The American legal rejection of foreign authors' rights proved a boon for the circulation of British novels, which in many cases first achieved mass readership outside the boundaries of Great Britain. For instance, Clarence Brigham has noted over a hundred editions of *Crusoe* published in America between 1774 and 1830. Boston, New York, and Philadelphia publishers famously competed to be the first to reprint Walter Scott's *Waverley* novels (1814–28), setting type as soon as packet ships carrying the latest novel arrived on the docks. The success of the *Waverley* series helped American publishers establish the size of the market for popular novels. The competition to capture market share led publishers such as Carey and Lea of Philadelphia and Harper Brothers in New York to develop more efficient and ambitious printing and distribution systems, paying Scott and his publisher for advance sheets of the novels and nurturing contacts with booksellers in far-flung Southern and western cities.

By the 1840s, American authors and some publishers began to push for the passage of an international copyright law, but their efforts were blocked by tradesmen, chief among them newly unionized typographers, who argued that stereotype technology, when combined with copyright, would give London publishers too much power over the American market. When literary nationalists protested that American authors could not compete with the flood of cheap reprints of popular British novels, members of the print trades responded with a canny analysis of the politics of book distribution, arguing that, with the backing of an international copyright law, heavily capitalized London publishers could potentially print off large American editions from British-made plates, greatly benefiting from economies of scale. Opponents of the law worried that international copyright would enable London publishers to supply books to the American market at high prices without the risk of underselling, maintaining a stranglehold on American reading. Reprint publishers contrasted the democratizing virtues of the frequent resetting of type with the dangers of centralized media, arguing that reprinting allowed for local control over the circulation of print and for a more equitable distribution of profits. In their view, multiple American editions of foreign works were not excessive or inefficient, but proof of the general diffusion of knowledge and of the benefits of competition between and among small-entrepreneur publishers. Instead of viewing the burgeoning reprint market as a sign of colonial dependency, those opposed to international copyright claimed that national values were instantiated in processes of production. One identified an American book by its physical appearance—by its cheap paper and closely set lines of type, enabling a novel that had been published in three expensive volumes to be compressed into two or one—and not by its contents or by the nationality of its author.

For most of the 1800s, international copyright advocates' appeals for the regulation of the book trade through universal respect for authors' rights were no match for the realities of a decentralized American literary marketplace—the difficulty of transporting printed matter between and among scattered cultural centers; the new nation's appetite for high-culture works in mass-culture formats; and the profits to be made in an uncertain, expanding market by publishing works that had already proved popular with readers. While supporters of an international copyright law chiefly sought to bring order to the transatlantic book trade, opponents defended a system that served the publishers of newspapers, magazines, and pamphlets, as well as books. Reprinting occurred across a variety of formats: poetry and tales that were first published in expensively bound gift books reappeared as filler in local newspapers; entire novels were closely printed in double-columned pages and sold for as little as $12\frac{1}{2}$ cents; and elite British magazines were reprinted in their entirety or mined for essays that were reassembled into regionally published, eclectic magazines.

While American opposition to internal copyright was successful in blocking proposed laws and treaties, it did not prevent the consolidation of publishers' power. Faced with potentially ruinous undercutting, reprint publishers developed a system of de facto copyright known as "courtesy of the trade," in which a newspaper announcement of the intent to publish a foreign work informally carried the weight of a property claim. This kind of gentlemanly agreement enabled reprint publishers to invest considerable sums in stereotyped editions of foreign authors' collected works without the threat of competition. Publishers secured informal rights in foreign texts by advertising their association with a particular author and by voluntarily sending payments to foreign authors (or their publishers) to establish goodwill, to obtain advance sheets of their books, and for the right to produce authorized editions. Such extra-legal arrangements, enforced by campaigns of retaliation when printers broke with the custom of voluntary restraint, continued to regulate the reprint trade throughout this period, despite the fact that they were unenforceable at law.

The profits to be made through authorized or unauthorized reprinting of British novels were substantial, so long as rivals could be kept at bay. During the depression of 1837–43, weekly newspapers such as *Brother Jonathan* (1842–43) and *The New World* (1840–45) engaged in cutthroat competition, reprinting popular British novels and French novels in translation on enormous folio newspaper sheets and in quarto size as "extra issues," sold to enhance circulation of the periodical. These newspaper supplement-novels were printed in the tens of thousands, hawked on street corners, and circulated at favorable rates through the mail. While competition from better-capitalized book publishers and changes to the postal code ultimately brought an end to the cheap weeklies, they successfully demonstrated the viability of cheap printing on a massive scale—aiming for narrow profit margins on high-volume sales—in a widely literate and expanding nation. On his 1842 tour of the U.S., Charles Dickens was both thrilled and horrified to discover the extent to which unauthorized reprints of his novels had preceded him.

Dickens had included the humble and oppressed in his novels as objects of sympathy, but cheap American reprints of his fiction enabled them to be drawn into the orbit of literary culture as actual or potential readers. Dickens was warmly welcomed by his American audience: statesmen and literati staged lavish banquets in his honor, and every stage of his trip was covered obsessively by local newspapers. But the tour became something of a public-relations disaster as Dickens's insistence on speaking publicly on behalf of an international copyright law was met with incredulity and suspicion. Dickens seemed unaware that his popularity was a function of the system of reprinting he continued publicly to attack, while many Americans interpreted his advocacy of international copyright as mercenary and ungrateful. Dickens's encounter with his American readers left him with an acute sense of vulnerability to the mass public which sought to embrace him.

Although in advocating foreign authors' rights Dickens thought he was championing both his own cause and that of American novelists, crowded out of the market by foreign competition, reprinting did not simply hinder the growth of the American novel. Even as publishers such as Harper Brothers built substantial enterprises publishing uncopyrighted texts, they began to make different kinds of investments in the American texts that, thanks to copyright, they controlled outright. In addition to stimulating book production in the early republic, American copyright law's uneven disposition of property rights did much to shape the distinctive character of American publishing. Authorized editions, complete with frontispiece portraits and facsimile signatures, became a popular way for reprint publishers to distinguish their editions. Other publishers attempted to discourage rivals by saturating the market with editions at every conceivable price point. Philadelphia publisher T. B. Peterson and Brothers, for example, advertised thirteen different octavo editions of Charles Dickens's works bound in seven different styles, two different illustrated editions, and a "People's Duodecimo," available in eight different binding styles; prices ranged from $9 to $75 for a complete set. Reprinting also conferred a new kind of value on illustrations. While type could easily be reset, engravings were more difficult and expensive to reproduce, enabling publishers to secure property in their texts by investing heavily in ornamental plates, a practice that Hugh Amory has called "proprietary illustration."

Reprinting shaped the course of numerous American novelists' careers, as authors such as James Fenimore Cooper, Nathaniel Hawthorne, Harriet Beecher Stowe, and Mark Twain sought to acquire de facto international copyright by carefully coordinating the publication of their works at home and abroad. Until the mid-1800s, it was widely assumed that prior or simultaneous publication of an American work in Great Britain would be enough to confer British copyright. However, in *Jeffreys v. Boosey* (1854) the House of Lords determined that a foreign author needed to travel to Britain in order to claim copyright protection. This ruling produced a wave of British reprints of American works and a number of strategically timed trips to London by American authors so that they could claim copyright on newly printed novels. When the House of Lords amended this ruling in 1868 to extend copyright to foreign authors who resided anywhere in the British dominions, many American novelists chose to travel to Canada during the time of their books' London publication so as to acquire what came to be known as a "Canadian copyright."

Although for much of the nineteenth century American publishers were caricatured as ruthless pirates of foreign works, British and European publishers also derived great benefit from the lack of international copyright. French publishers Galignani & Baudry, which specialized in providing British tourists with cheap editions of the latest London books, reprinted numerous novels by James Fenimore Cooper, themselves often copied from British reprints. German publisher Bernhard Tauchnitz (1816–95) published hundreds of volumes of British and American works

in a numbered series for circulation throughout the Continent, paying authors nominal sums for the right to advertise these volumes as "author's editions" or "copyright editions" (some of which were actually covered by copyright in select European nations in the wake of the 1846 Anglo-German copyright agreement and other bilateral treaties). Many authors considered having a novel reprinted by Tauchnitz to be a mark of international recognition. The standardized, plain style of Tauchnitz editions made them easily recognizable across Europe, the series itself a hallmark of affordability, portability, and literary quality. Although merely a cheap reprint, the Tauchnitz edition of Nathaniel Hawthorne's *The Marble Faun* (1860) was frequently rebound by Italian booksellers as a keepsake, including numerous photographs of artworks and landmarks mentioned in Hawthorne's Rome as well as blank pages for tourists to paste into the novel photos they had purchased or taken on their trip (see PHOTOGRAPHY).

By far the most impressive and consequential example of an American novel's European career was the popular reprinting of Harriet Beecher Stowe's *Uncle Tom's Cabin* (1852). Stowe's novel was a runaway bestseller in the U.S., with over three hundred thousand copies sold in the first year of publication, but its domestic sales paled next to the novel's success in Great Britain, where over a million copies were reportedly sold within a year of publication. The circulation of *Uncle Tom's Cabin* in Britain far exceeded that of Scott's or Dickens's novels, and its rapid translation into numerous European languages was taken as a sign of the persuasiveness and power of the abolitionist movement. The novel's success tested the norms of copyright in the U.S., where the Supreme Court ruled in *Stowe v. Thomas* (1853) that Stowe's copyright in her work did not extend to its German translation. The novel also opened American publishers' eyes to the potentially enormous foreign market for American fiction.

American fiction was well represented in numerous British and European reprint series: Richard Bentley's "Standard Novels" (1831–55) included novels by Cooper and Charles Brockden Brown; Henry Bohn's "Standard Library," launched in 1846, included numerous works of fiction by Washington Irving; George Routledge's "Railway Library," begun in 1848, provided cheap editions for British railway passengers, including novels by Hawthorne, Herman Melville, and Susan Warner. Routledge was successful enough to establish a branch in New York in 1854 to manage his publication of American works, including a series of dime novels called "Beadle's American Sixpenny Library." British publishers developed similar reprint series designed for the colonial market. John Murray published the "Colonial and Home Library" between 1843 and 1849, aiming "to furnish the settler in the back-woods of America and the occupant of the remotest cantonments of our Indian dominions with the resources of recreation and instruction at a moderate price." This short-lived series failed in the U.S. largely due to competition from cheap domestic reprints, but it also suffered by neglecting novels in favor of more edifying works: Melville's *Typee* (1846) and *Omoo* (1847) were published as nonfiction alongside other travel narratives, works of history, and biography. When Macmillan began its "Colonial Library" series in 1886, targeted at the growing ranks of Indian readers as well British officers and expatriates, it made a point of emphasizing fiction. Trial and error established that the real profits in India were to be made through the simultaneous printing of popular British novels (with sheets set aside to be shipped to the Subcontinent) and not through reprinting. And yet Macmillan's Colonial Library was nonetheless centrally shaped by the tradition of cheap reprinting: the series was self-consciously designed as a colonial version of the Tauchnitz editions and motivated by the desire to short-circuit the importation into India of cheap American reprints of British novels. Macmillan's aim in publishing cheap editions for sale in India, Australia, and New Zealand was to secure colonial markets for British publishing without threatening the higher price of books in Britain; many of these books included on their title pages the proviso "Only for sale in India and the Colonies."

Throughout the 1800s, international copyright was governed by a patchwork of bilateral treaties, allowing for considerable experimentation in the interstices of these agreements. Britain signed reciprocal copyright agreements with a number of German states in 1844, with Prussia in 1846, with France, Belgium, and Spain in 1852, with Sardinia in 1861, Venice and Mantua in 1867, and Rome in 1870. Under the leadership of Victor Hugo, the French Association Littéraire et Artistique Internationale drafted the Berne Convention for the Protection of Literary and Artistic Works, creating a legal and administrative framework for the international protection of literary property. Great Britain, Germany, France, Belgium, Spain, Italy, Switzerland, Tunisia, and Haiti adopted the Berne Convention in 1887. The mounting numbers of international copyright treaties made the U.S.'s refusal to enter into such arrangements seem anomalous; by the 1880s, the tide was turning in favor of an international copyright agreement of some sort. In 1878, the British Copyright Commission tendered a blistering report on the obscurity and inconsistency of British law, strongly recommending that Great Britain accept American protectionist demands that copyrighted foreign works be manufactured in America. In brokering the

Chace Act, which became U.S. law in 1891, American copyright advocates acceded to the demands of the International Typographical Union, which insisted that foreign works could be copyrighted only if they were produced from type set or plates made within the borders of the U.S. This provision remained in force through the 1950s, when both Britain and America ratified the Universal Copyright Convention (1952), a treaty that eliminated trade protections.

In the wake of the Chace Act, British publishers expanded their American operations while British authors began to demand higher royalties, expecting increased profits from American editions. British publishers had to make careful calculations about costs, however; where the risk of reprinting was low, it was often more economical to forgo international copyright, to publish the book or print the sheets in England, and to settle for whatever profits might be made from exporting the British edition. As the U.S. became a net exporter of literary and cultural works, American publishers began to seek more uniform international treatment of their properties, but disagreements concerning fundamental aspects of the Berne agreement, such as minimum terms, registration requirements, and moral rights for copyright holders (including the "right of paternity," or attribution, and "right of integrity," or protection against distortion or intentional destruction of a work) kept the U.S. from joining the largest and most important multilateral copyright agreement. So long as the U.S. remained outside the Berne Convention, American publishers fell back on a familiar nineteenth-century strategy for securing rights, approximating international copyright protection through the simultaneous publication of literary works in the U.S. and in a Berne country such as Canada. After significant changes in American copyright law in 1976 and 1988,

the way was paved for the U.S. to join the Berne Convention in 1989. Because the Berne agreement lacked enforcement mechanisms, however, in the 1970s the U.S. government began to attach the protection of intellectual property to trade agreements. As of 1994, membership in the World Trade Organization (WTO) requires countries to accept nearly all the conditions of the Berne agreement.

While popular novels were at the center of nineteenth-century debates over international copyright, the rights to software, digital music, and video have taken center stage in late twentieth- and early twenty-first-century disputes about intellectual property. Although reprinting is still a factor in publishers' calculations about the marketing of novels, unauthorized reprinting has gone underground as all but a few countries participate in the WTO. Popular novels such as J. K. Rowling's *Harry Potter* series (1995–2007) continue to be pirated in China and India, however, and many publishers worry that the illegal digital distribution of novels over file-sharing sites will threaten the small margins they earn on all but the most popular titles. Nevertheless, the extension of intellectual property rights across ever-wider geographical spaces and their extension in time has worked to curtail the practice of reprinting. The gradual increase in the length of terms of copyright, driven in part by the demands of international treaties and in part by increasing corporate interest in controlling global rights to creative works, has made the experience of a popular novel coming out of copyright and becoming part of the public domain an unfamiliar one. The U.S. Copyright Extension Act (1998), popularly called the Sonny Bono Act, protects works for the duration of the author's life plus 70 years, while works of corporate authorship are granted copyright for 120 years after creation or 95 years after publication, whichever comes first.

If recent legal and diplomatic developments have clamped down on unauthorized reprinting, copyright advocacy groups such as Creative Commons, which established a system of licenses to permit creators to reproduce, adapt, and distribute their work, and digital entrepreneurs such as Google Books have succeeded in putting reprinting right back at the center of controversy. Google's ambitious plan to digitize and make accessible the holdings of entire libraries threatens the very premise of copyright—controlling distribution by restricting copying—insofar as it requires that digital copies be made before the question of rights is determined. Google has maintained that the digital reproduction of works in the public domain and of copyrighted books that are out of print is necessary for these works (or brief selections from them) to show up in online searches. It proposed that, rather than delaying scanning until owners could be found for indeterminate or "orphan" works, copyright holders be permitted to opt out of its scheme (well underway, with over seven million books scanned by 2008), preventing the online display of already digitized books. In this scanning project, expanded access to print in digital form and the profits to be derived by copyright holders through Google's search algorithm both depend on unauthorized reprinting on a massive scale. It remains to be seen whether mass-digitization projects such as Google Books will force changes in a law designed for the protection of printed works, or whether the inflexibility of copyright law will produce creative workarounds in print and digital publishing.

SEE ALSO: Authorship, Censorship, Class, Editing, National Literature, Reading Aloud, Reviewing.

BIBLIOGRAPHY

Altick, R.D. (1998), *English Common Reader*.
Barnes, J.J. (1974), *Authors, Publishers, and Politicians*.
Brigham, C.S. (1958), *Bibliography of American Editions of Robinson Crusoe to 1830*.
Exman, E. (1965), *Brothers Harper*.
Johns, A. (2010), *Piracy*.
Joshi, P. (2002), *In Another Country*.
Leaffer, M. (2009), "American Copyright Law since 1945," in *History of the Book in America*, ed. D.P. Nord, J. Shelley Rubin, M. Schudson, and D.D. Hall.
Matthews, B. (1889), *American Authors and British Pirates*.
McGill, M.L. (2003), *American Literature and the Culture of Reprinting, 1834–1853*.
Nowell-Smith, S. (1968), *International Copyright Law and the Publisher in the Reign of Queen Victoria*.
Putnam, G. (1891), *Question of Copyright*.
Raven, J. (2000), "Historical Introduction," in *English Novel, 1770–1829*.
St. Clair, W. (2004), *Reading Nation in the Romantic Period*.
Williams, S.S. (1997), *Confounding Images*.

Reversal *see* Closure

Reviewing

SCOTT ELLIS

In 1831, the *Edinburgh Review* published "Characteristics," in which Thomas Carlyle declared: "Nay, is not the diseased self-conscious state of Literature disclosed in this one fact, which lies so near us here, the prevalence of Reviewing!" Throughout its long history, reviewing has served many different roles, often simultaneously, and whether or not one accepts Carlyle's complaint about it as a diseased state of literary self-consciousness, reviewing has impacted the writing and reception of the novel from its development in the eighteenth century to the present. Among its many effects, reviewing advertised new books, it served as a medium for partisan and personal attacks and praise, it fostered the shift from patronage to professionalism, it positioned itself as a cultural mediator for morality, and perhaps most importantly, it created a public forum that allowed reviewers to speak about and evaluate literature in general and the novel in particular. This entry will address these aspects of reviewing and examine its impact on novel writing and reading practices over time.

REVIEWS AND PERIODICALS

Reviewing as a public practice took shape in England during the mid-eighteenth century. England's *Monthly Review* and *Critical Review*, while not the first periodicals to publish reviews or notices of new books, became the most prominent forums for reviewing. Offered to their eighteenth-century readers monthly, these journals established a model of reviewing, expanded upon and refined by their numerous successors, that both evaluated books from a variety of genres and also used them to explore the books' topics over several paragraphs or pages. Like most that followed this format, these periodicals sought a readership whose interests were diverse enough to read reviews about books exploring such topics as mineralogy, poetry, and foreign travel, all within the same issue. Readers of the Dec. 1763 issue of the *Critical Review*, for instance, encountered an analysis of "some sensible and judicious observations obscured and encumbered by a laboured, turgid, and affected stile" in Edmund Burton's *Antient Characters Deduced from Classical Remains* before reading an account of Frances Chamberlaine Sheridan's play *The Dupe*, which "would have met with deserved success" had she "carefully revised . . . some particular parts."

While book reviews have appeared in a variety of print media, the majority were published in periodicals that followed the general model set forth by the *Monthly Review* and *Critical Review*. Subsequent periodicals containing reviews were published in weekly, monthly, or quarterly formats. The length of reviews varied according to the publication, from one-sentence notices of recent publications to reviews that extended to more than seventy-five pages, in which the reviewed books were used as the basis for critical commentary on particular issues.

While some periodicals, like the two noted above, devoted all of their pages to reviews, others would include them in one section, where they would accompany general news about current events, original articles, and reprinted excerpts from miscellaneous works. At the end of the eighteenth century, for instance, New York's *Monthly Magazine*, edited by the novelist Charles Brockden Brown (who also wrote much of material in its pages), included original and reprinted reviews as one component of its format. These reviews tended to be brief, usually occupying no more than two pages each. Many other periodicals followed a similar format in their review sections. Brief reviews allowed writers and editors to introduce new books alongside news of the day and were particularly popular in publications distributed weekly, where the object was not to analyze extensively a book and its subject but to offer readers a glimpse of recently published works.

Other editors, though, believed that a less frequent publishing schedule would allow reviewers more time for thoughtful and critical consideration. In the early nineteenth century, the *Edinburgh Review*, for instance, appeared quarterly, its editors insisting that this schedule gave them more time to examine only the best literature and ideas in a more careful manner than its weekly and monthly counterparts. The prefatory advertisement to the first issue explains that this periodical will "decline any attempt at exhibiting a complete view of modern literature; and to confine their notice, in a great degree, to works that either have attained, or deserve a certain portion of celebrity." With such a focus, each issue of the *Edinburgh Review* included fewer reviews than its counterparts, but those published were much more extensive than brief synopses, often extending for more than seventy pages per article.

Similarly, the *Quarterly Review* might only run eight reviews in a single issue, but that issue would be more than 250 pages long. These longer reviews allowed the writer to evaluate books, but these books also functioned as the focal point for a broader discussion about a topic or idea. In the Jan.–Apr. 1857 issue of England's *Quarterly Review*, for instance, a writer discusses American slavery in its twenty-eight-page review of Harriet Beecher Stowe's *Dred* and one of Charles Sumner's speeches. The reviewer offers advice for Stowe: cut out Nina's (the main character's) comments about herself and slow the pace of the story (329). But this analysis of Stowe's novel segues into an investigation of slavery itself, particularly in slavery's effects on the union of the U.S. After examining Sumner's speech—"The substance of the speech is as generally good as the style is frequently detestable"—and a variety of articles in American newspapers on slavery and the Fugitive Slave Law, the reviewer presciently concludes, "Every election approaches nearer and nearer to a civil war.... [I]t does appear to us that a bond which every four years is on the point of separating must eventually snap" (352).

Along with editors' differing goals for their publications, the length of reviews and periodicals was also determined by material conditions of publication and distribution as well as reader demands. Thus, readers in the mid-nineteenth century witnessed the proliferation of competition for the quarterly, as weekly and daily newspapers and magazines, often bolstered by declining stamp rates and the removal of trade restrictions, regained their popularity and began to compete for readers' attention. Great Britain's the *Athenaeum* and *Saturday Review*, for instance, popularized shorter reviews in a weekly format, using readers' increasing appetite for literary knowledge to boost their sales and influence.

CREATING AND DISTINGUISHING A LITERARY MARKETPLACE

By fostering a public discussion about books and ideas, reviewing created a market for books and a desire to read. Summarizing the ascendancy of periodical reviews in the eighteenth century, Samuel Miller, a member of New York's intellectual elite, notes that while seventeenth-century criticism was mired in Latinized reflections directed only toward an educated few,

> the Reviews of the last age, besides being multiplied to an unexampled extent, have received a popular cast, which has enabled them to descend from the closets of philosophers, and from the shelves of polite scholars, to the compting house of the merchant, to the shop of the artizan, to the bower of the husbandman, and, indeed, to every class of the community, excepting the most indigent and laborious. In fact, they have contributed to give a new aspect to the republic of letters, and may be considered as among the most important literary engines that distinguished the period under consideration. (238)

Reviewing was therefore instrumental in the proliferation of books and book publishing, as readers of reviews became book consumers, either through book sales themselves or through circulating libraries. Indeed, these libraries, along with reading rooms and bookstores, often depended upon reviews to determine which books to order. Dublin's *Literary Journal* (1744–49), for instance, explicitly sought to introduce Irish readers to foreign books and ideas, thereby fostering a wider reading public. Similarly, the *North American Review* begins its first issue (1815) by noting that the periodical would publish extracts of the editor's catalogue of books relating to the history of North America, and that "where the works noticed are scarce, several extracts from them will be made, which may at once serve to give a more complete idea of the books, and to relieve the dryness of a mere catalogue."

Reviewing not only shaped a literary marketplace, but it also helped periodicals target specific segments of the reading population. Whereas the formative years of reviewing fostered the emergence of an increasingly literate public, reviewing in the nineteenth century often went further and shaped its writing to address different economic and cultural classes within this literate population. England's *Academy* and *Saturday Review*, influential mid-century periodicals, targeted a culturally sophisticated readership, one who was well versed in the literary and intellectual debates of the day. Similarly, England's *Nineteenth Century* served the interest of the highly educated and elite. Scholars have argued that by targeting specific socioeconomic classes, periodicals reflected increasing social divisions and brought such divisions to the very core of the literary marketplace.

Moreover, although editors and reviewers consistently argued for their own objectivity and impartiality, reviews and the periodicals in which they appeared often positioned themselves for specific audiences according to religion and politics. Liberal and conservative arguments, for instance, infiltrated even the most mundane book review, an act that not only served to support or challenge a particular perspective, but also effectively determined its readership. England's liberal *The Spectator*, for example, would often lend favorable reviews to those authors—Charlotte Brontë, Anthony Trollope, and others—whose storyworld and characters reflected the editors' and reviewers' ideas of morality. Similarly, the introductory essay to the first issue of the *American Whig Review* asserts that "to support freely and openly the principles and measures of the Whig party, is one great object of this review." As Frank Luther Mott notes, the very content of reviews in the U.S. during the mid-nineteenth century was often shaped by social positions of writers and reviewers and even by geography. As Mott demonstrates, the *New Englander*, for instance, was biased against Boston authors, while the *Southern Literary Messenger* dismissed writers with abolitionist leanings (407). The reviews of these and similar publications therefore went beyond a basic examination of books by targeting readers with particular cultural, political, religious, and intellectual beliefs. This approach often polarized the literary marketplace, but it also fed into the core concerns of many readers, whose literary appetites demanded a steady supply of reviews.

REVIEWING CRITERIA AND THE NOVEL

In the 1852 essay "Bird's-Eye View of English Literature in the Nineteenth Century" published in *Hogg's Instructor*, an Edinburgh weekly, a writer argues that "the age of Victoria is the age of the novel," and that poetry, drama, and the essay have fallen in status. In their place, "the novel alone, or prose fiction, as we call it, retains its former honours, and has even usurped the province of history and philosophy." While the novel, even in the nineteenth century, occupied only a small portion of the total publishing output, its emergence as a legitimate element of print culture demanded an increasing need among reviewers to establish criteria with which they could evaluate the genre. In a review of Mrs. (Agnes Maria) Bennett's novel, *Ellen, Countess of Castle Howel* (1794), for example, one reviewer in Philadelphia's *American Monthly Review* (1795) reflects upon the rise of novels and the need for critical evaluation: "Flowing and correct language, polished wit, sportive humour, the pathos of sensibility, and the charms of elegant simplicity, have introduced novels into the closets of the statesmen, of the grave divine, and of the careful father of a family, who best know how to appreciate their merits and defects:—but the young and gay require some assistance, and the *sanction* of these performances, in the schools, demands attention" (172). This desire to facilitate intellectual discussions about the novel while simultaneously establishing identifiable standards for evaluation stimulated the reviewing industry, and while evaluative criteria was not uniform across all periodicals, we can identify certain qualities that many reviewers shared.

Until the modernist period, reviews tended to favor novels that were realistic, with probable characters, events, and speech, and reviewers often challenged novels that deviated from mimetic representation of common, recognizable characters and situations. Many reviews of Nathaniel Hawthorne's and Herman Melville's novels, for example, criticized their allegorical tendencies and fanciful plots. Similarly, reviewers repeatedly rebuked the "romance" novel, one whose exaggerated romantic intrigues and seductive (usually male) characters would corrupt the minds of young (women) readers. These novels, allegorical or romantic, betrayed the expectations of the reader by not providing a realistic mirror of everyday life. As one writer evaluating *Monima, or the Beggar Girl* in the *American Review* (1802) noted, "Some of the circumstances are too improbable to admit of easy belief, and others too preposterous to be reasonably imagined." Furthermore, "The circumstances of this tale seem so little to correspond with the natural course of things in Philadelphia, or any where [*sic*] else . . . that to bestow encomiums on this production would be considered as a most inordinate sacrifice to the vanity of authorship." This is not to say that every review condemned any novel that was purported to be unrealistic, but the general tendency of reviews as they sought to shape novel writing and reading practices was to encourage authors to reproduce as faithfully as possible a storyworld that readers could envision as their own.

Similarly, reviewing in every era examined the morality of the novel and consistently exalted or condemned works according to a "proper" moral stance. In 1830, a writer for the *Edinburgh Review* noted simply that "we require from the novel that it shall be moral in its tendency, it shall be amusing, and that it shall exhibit a true and faithful delineation of the class of society which it professes to depict." Characters in each era were to behave in a manner that conformed to social and religious codes, and when writers had their characters break those codes, reviewers were quick to condemn the novel. In a review of Charlotte Brontë's *Jane Eyre*, for instance, a writer for the *Rambler* notes that the novel "is, indeed, one of the coarsest books which we ever perused. . . . There is a tendency to relapse into that class of ideas, expressions, and circumstances, which is most connected with the grosser and more animal portion of our nature; and that the detestable morality of the most prominent character in the story is accompanied with every sort of palliation short of unblushing justification." Such approaches to morality were very common in reviews. Nina Baym notes that of the more than 2,000 reviews she explores in her book about antebellum book reviewing in the U.S., only one—written by Edgar Allan Poe—claims that morality should not be examined in a review (173). Novelists as diverse in time and style as William Godwin, Henry James, and James Joyce had their novels criticized on moral grounds, and while negative reviews based on morality did not necessarily force writers to alter their craft—indeed, Joyce and other modernists would take such criticism as justification for their art—reviewers nonetheless continued to try to uphold moral standards in their reviews.

The standards that the reviewers trumpeted, though, were often tinged with assumptions about gender, both for readers and authors. Novel-readers were often considered, implicitly and at times explicitly, to be young women, and reviews often shaped its evaluative criteria with this audience in mind. Thus, a reviewer in *Graham's Magazine* (1853) evaluating Stowe's *Uncle Tom's Cabin* asserted: "Our female agitators have abandoned Bloomers in despair, and are just now bestride a new hobby—an intense love of black folks, *in fashionable novels!*" Similarly, as Nicola Thompson (1996) explains, the works of such authors as Emily Brontë and Anthony Trollope were often reviewed according to cultural assumptions of male- and female-appropriate topics, whereby such writers were often chastised in reviews for transgressing unwritten codes about what novelistic fare is appropriate for men and women writers. Reviewers therefore both reflected and shaped public assumptions about gender in novels, and writers were forced to contend with such limiting assumptions.

REVIEWING AND WRITERS

By making public a critical language that readers could use when evaluating the novel, reviewing was able to shape public discourse about literature, but its influence often went beyond that of readers to the writers themselves. Understanding the growing influence of reviewing in public consciousness, writers quickly became attuned to the comments about their work. As "Candidus" argued in New York's *Monthly Magazine* in 1799:

> Reviewers are to be considered as auditors who comment on our discourse in our presence, and likewise as men who employ themselves in diffusing their opinions of our merits in as wide a circle as possible. . . . No wonder, therefore, that we are anxious for the *good word* of reviewers, that we eagerly investigate their verdict, and are dissatisfied or pleased in proportion to the censures or praises conferred.

In pursuing the good word of reviewers, many writers therefore shaped their work, consciously or not, to accord with critical opinions.

During the eighteenth century, reviewers spent more time examining poetry, history, and other topics than the novel, but nonetheless those reviews of fiction served to shape the style, content, and morality of much subsequent fiction. If the reviewers rather than the writers were taking charge of a public literary discourse, many novelists recognized the need to listen to their advice. For instance, Frank Donoghue argues that in responding to reviews critical of *Tristram Shandy*, Laurence Sterne altered his writing style in his subsequent novel, *A Sentimental Journey* (1768), which became one of the most formative works in the genre of the sentimental novel.

Melville, moreover, received a warm reception in many reviews for *Moby-Dick*

(1851), but he tended to focus on the prominent scathing comments. A reviewer in London's *Athenaeum* asserted: "the style of this tale is in places disfigured by mad (rather than bad) English; and its catastrophe is hastily, weakly, and obscurely managed"; one in Boston's *Post* argued that Melville's novel "is not worth the money asked for it, either as a literary work or as a mass of printed paper"; and another in the New York *Independent* calls this and other Melville novels "a primitive formation of profanity and indecency . . . which makes it impossible for a religious journal heartily to commend any of the works of this author which we have ever perused." These and other reviews coincided with a weak reception for *Moby-Dick*, and when Melville submitted part of a manuscript for his follow-up novel *Pierre*, his publisher reduced the terms of Melville's contract, events that led the writer to significantly alter the story by adding details about Pierre as a failed writer abused by the literary community. For this novel, Melville, in turn, received even worse reviews than for *Moby-Dick*, forcing the writer to reassess his work as a novelist. Many scholars go so far as to suggest that the reviews of *Moby-Dick* and *Pierre* may have caused Melville to suffer an emotional breakdown.

If novelists frequently responded to reviews of their work, so too did novelists themselves take up the pen and review others' books. Writers as diverse as Sir Walter Scott, Edgar Allan Poe, William Makepeace Thackeray, Virginia Woolf, John Updike, and Italo Calvino honed their critical skills in book reviews, using their own approaches to writing as a lens through which they evaluated the work of their contemporaries. The reciprocal nature of novelist-as-reviewer at times fostered competition and even animosity, but such work was just as likely to spur attention to fellow novelists. Sir Walter Scott, for instance,

exemplifies both possibilities. On the one hand, Scott helped to establish the *Quarterly Review* (1809) in order to counteract the scathing reviews of his writing and that of Robert Southey (1774–1843) in the *Edinburgh Review*, a move that led to open competition and animosity between the two periodicals. On the other hand, Scott was often judicious and even generous in his reviews of contemporaries. In his review of Jane Austen's *Emma* in the *Quarterly Review*, for example, Scott writes that she copies "from nature as she really exists in the common walks of life, and present[s] to the reader, instead of the splendid scenes of an imaginary world, a correct and striking representation of that which is daily taking place around him" (192).

BOOK REVIEWERS

Reviewing as a practice and occupation varied widely depending upon the periodical, and there is no uniform experience for all reviewers. While some writers used their reviews to strengthen their reputation and, at times, their fame, the identity of other writers was never known to the public. In the eighteenth century, the *Monthly Review* and *Critical Review* published reviewers' comments anonymously, and many subsequent periodicals followed suit. The *Edinburgh Review* reinforced the status of the anonymous review, and this practice was followed by most nineteenth-century reviews. Many editors believed that ideas gained more credence if they were not assigned to a particular reviewer but instead were unsigned, thereby reflecting the opinions of many. Moreover, anonymity allowed reviewers the freedom to criticize or laud the work of a friend or prominent writer without fear of reprisal or public cries of favoritism. Anonymity therefore gave reviewers the freedom to offer honest commentary about any novel, regardless of the author. Women writers also benefited from anonymity, allowing them to participate in public discussions without incurring the rebukes of those who dismissed their capability of doing so. George Eliot, for instance, honed her critical tongue in anonymous reviews, which led to her later work at the *Westminster Review* before writing novels of her own. Similarly, Margaret Oliphant wrote prolifically and anonymously for *Blackwood's Magazine*, work that gave her an important public voice on contemporary fiction and ideas during the second half of the nineteenth century.

Of course, anonymity also worked against honest reviewing, as the absence of one's name at times fostered "puffery," in which an anonymous reviewer extolled the virtues of a novel written or published by a friend. For instance, the success of *Pamela* (1740), Samuel Richardson's first novel, was due in part to a favorable anonymous review by William Webster of the *Weekly Miscellany*, who had a personal debt of ninety pounds forgiven by Richardson; and Mary Shelley anonymously penned for *Blackwood's* a glowing account of *Cloudesley* (1830), a novel by her father William Godwin (Mullan). Similarly, anonymity effectively concealed the identity of writers—Sir Walter Scott and John Davis, among others—who positively reviewed their own work.

This practice, however, was not without its detractors. Many writers and editors understood the deception that often occurred behind the veil of anonymity and sought to change this practice. In his periodical, the *London Review*, Richard Cumberland challenged conventions of anonymity and stated in the first issue (1809): "A piece of crepe may be a convenient mask for a highwayman; but a man that goes upon an honest errand, does not want it and will disdain to wear it" (Vann and VanArsdel, 124). While Cumberland's periodical did

not last long, one of the most influential periodicals, the Parisian *Revue des deux mondes*, begun in 1829 and published biweekly, assigned names to nearly all of its writers. Printing reviews as well as serialized fiction, drama, and other miscellaneous articles, the *Revue* published the work of such authors as Dumas and Balzac and led to many periodicals around the world to try to copy its style and format, one component of which was to identify its writers. In the following decades such periodicals as the *Fortnightly Review, Contemporary Review, The Academy,* and *Nineteenth Century* affixed identities to their writers, including reviewers, as a way to challenge the conventional understanding of the necessity of anonymity.

The coexistence of anonymous and attributed reviewers also coincided with differing practices of remuneration. The pay scale for reviewers ranged from no compensation other than self-satisfaction to rates that would enable a reviewer to make a modest living. In the latter category, reviewers for the *Edinburgh Review* and the *Quarterly Review* were sometimes paid up to £100 for extensive reviews, which often grew to seventy pages or more (Shattock). However, many other reviewers found payment for reviews very low, even for elite journals, with the hope that the contributors would consider adding their voice to the public sphere payment enough. The *Saturday Review*, for instance, paid its contributors two to three guineas per article in the late 1850s, although this payment rose to three pounds and ten shillings per article by 1869 (1941, M. M. Bevington, *Saturday Review, 1855–1868*, 37–38). We also see that the pay for reviewers became an element of competition. In the final decades of the nineteenth century, reviewers in the U.S. were getting paid five to ten dollars a page for the *Atlantic Monthly*, whereas competitors such as the *Century*, boasting a larger number of subscriptions, were offering reviewers double that amount (1994, E. Sedgwick, *Atlantic Monthly*, 178).

Whatever the remuneration, reviewing has offered the reading public an influential yet contentious voice in the public sphere. Its best and worst impulses were perhaps described best by William Dean Howells, who wrote, edited, and felt the sting of reviews for more than five decades. In his 1866 essay entitled "Literary Criticism," published in the *Round Table,* a New York weekly, Howells challenged the poor state of literary reviews. The function of proper reviewing, he wrote, "is entirely distinct from the mere trade-puff of the publisher, the financial comments of the advertiser, or the bought-and-sold eulogium of an ignorant, careless, or mercenary journalist. It is equally removed from the wholesale and baseless attacks of some rival publication house, or from the censure which is inspired by political, personal, or religious hatred." Instead, Howells desired to read and practice a better style of reviewing: "True criticism, therefore, consists of a calm, just, and fearless handling of its subject, and in pointing out in all honesty whatever there is hitherto undiscovered of merit, and, in equal honesty, whatever there has been concealed of defect."

Such comments and approaches to reviewing have shaped reading and writing practices for nearly three centuries, and this impact continues to be felt today. Although the publishing industry as a whole is struggling with declining revenue and readership, as evidenced by cuts to reviewing departments in many major newspapers at the beginning of the twenty-first century, reviewing continues to affect the writing, reception, and sales of novels. Major review publications such as the *Times Literary Supplement* and the *New York Review of Books,* together with an increasing number of online book-review venues, give reviewing a forum that allows it to flourish and develop alongside the contemporary novel.

BIBLIOGRAPHY

Baym, N. (1984), *Novels, Readers, and Reviewers.*
Demata, M. and D. Wu, eds. (2002), British Romanticism and the *"Edinburgh Review."*
Donoghue, F. (1996), *Fame Machine.*
Graham, W.J. (1930), *English Literary Periodicals.*
Gross, J. (1969), *Rise and Fall of the Man of Letters.*
Miller, S. (1803), *Brief Retrospect of the Eighteenth Century.*
Mott, F.L. (1957), *History of American Magazines,* vol. 1.
Mullan, J. (2007), *Anonymity.*
Roper, D. (1978), *Reviewing before the Edinburgh, 1788–1802.*
Shattock, J. (1989), *Politics and Reviewers.*
Thompson, N.D. (1996), *Reviewing Sex.*
Vann, J.D. and R.T. VanArsdel, eds. (1989), *Victorian Periodicals.*
Waters, M.A. (2004), *British Women Writers and the Profession of Literary Criticism, 1789–1832.*

Revolutionary Romance *see* China

Rhetoric and Figurative Language

AARON McKAIN AND TREVOR MERRILL

Defining a 2,500-year-old literary tradition in 2,000 words is a difficult task; doubly so when that tradition has spent so much of its time haggling over its own meaning. But that is the task of this entry, and "rhetoric," despite its wide and narrow definitions, does provide many, more or less agreed upon, talking points and touchstones. The first—and it is a first that, as is the case throughout this entry, comes first conceptually, not chronologically—is Aristotle's (384–324 BCE) *On Rhetoric*, the treatise which provides the definition of rhetoric now familiar to two millennia of students, "the art of seeing the available means of persuasion in any given situation" (bk. I).

So what is this "art" of persuasion? For Aristotle, it is an investigation into how to move and convince audiences, both within the context of political occasions (e.g., the law courts, legislative assemblies, and official ceremonies) and with the use of particular types of evidence (particular appeals to emotion, or logic, or credibility). How do audiences come to accept or reject a speaker? How do speakers persuade or dissuade their audiences? What are the aesthetic, affective, and ideological consequences of speakers' rhetorical choices and audiences' judgments of them? These are the questions an Aristotelian approach to rhetoric asks. And they are the questions (though not necessarily the terminological methods) at the heart of the rhetorical approach to literature, an approach made most overt, and most famous, in the twentieth century by Wayne C. Booth with his *Rhetoric of Fiction* (1961), and by the work of Kenneth Burke and Mikhail BAKHTIN. This approach was carried forward most forcefully into the twenty-first century by the "third generation" of Chicago School rhetorical critics, most notably James Phelan and Peter Rabinowitz. But how do we get from the *polis* of ancient Greece to contemporary English Studies? What are the nuances of a rhetorical approach to literature? How do we account for the ever-expanding (and contracting) role of rhetoric within the field of literary studies? Exploring these questions requires us to treat the study of rhetoric *itself* rhetorically. So, with a nod to Stephen Mailloux's "rhetorical hermeneutics"—which advocates using "rhetoric to practice theory by doing history"—the short synopsis that follows will consider how and when the rhetorical approach to literature (and its evolving methodological and epistemological presuppositions) became persuasive within

particular intellectual and material moments in the history of English Studies.

Our "rhetorical hermeneutics" of rhetoric begins with a thorny binary central to rhetorical scholarship: the longstanding (and, in contemporary departments of English, still standing) distinction, if not outright division, between the study of rhetoric and the study of literature. This is a complex relation with ancient roots. Aristotle himself separates the study of dramatic texts (dealt with in his *Poetics*) from "rhetorical" texts (the civic communication outlined in *On Rhetoric*), despite the distinction failing to hold in his actual readings of texts (e.g., his examination of tragedy turns upon its ostensible emotional effect on the audience). Moreover, literature has been instrumental to rhetoric, and vice versa, since the emergence of rhetoric as a field of study: the speeches in Homer served as an early model for Greek scholars, and classical literature remained a centerpiece of rhetorical instruction through the Roman and medieval periods (Kallendorf, xx). For Quintilian (35–ca. 96 CE) (and for Cicero), the study of rhetoric was the pursuit of *vir bonus,* the "good man," speaking well, a commitment to civic humanism pursued via science, philosophy, art, and literature. But as the centuries progressed, epistemological critiques began to diminish the importance of rhetoric. Though it had been conceived by Aristotle (and to an even greater extent, the Sophists) as a means to discover or "invent" knowledge, in the sixteenth century Petrus Ramus (1515–72) reopened Plato's ancient criticism of rhetoric—housed in a critical distinction between rhetoric and dialectic—and thereby reasserted rhetoric's status as a degraded form of logic. The scientific revolution and the Enlightenment further diminished rhetoric's intellectual status and scholarly role, positing language as—at best—an ineffective tool to *transmit* scientific fact rather than a means to probe "probable" truths and discover knowledge (see the philosophical works of Francis Bacon and John Locke). Rather than a holistic understanding of ethics, common wisdom, and how to encourage people toward virtuous civic action (a broad educational project that would necessarily include the study of literature), rhetoric became subsidiary: a superfluous study of the eloquence and style that supplemented true knowledge.

In the twentieth century, two things about rhetorical study were clear. First, despite remaining at the heart of formal education in Europe through the eighteenth century, and in the U.S. until the late nineteenth, rhetoric, as a mode of epistemological inquiry, had been substantially downgraded (Bizzell and Herzberg). Within the newly formed departments of English, rhetoric had become reduced primarily to the teaching of grammar and expository writing, with investigation of persuasion and probabilistic knowledge pushed into the social sciences and, eventually, communication studies (R. J. Connors, 1991, "Rhetoric in the Modern University," in *The Politics of Writing Instruction*, ed. R.H. Bullock et al.). What remained within English Studies was the study of literature *as* literature, as a unique form of poetic language aesthetically and intellectually distinct from rhetoric, and deserving of its own particular modes of inquiry (J. A. Berlin, 1996, *Rhetorics, Poetics, and Cultures*). This method was provided by the New Criticism.

To best understand how the rhetorical study of literature eventually emerged from, and reacted to, the intellectual conditions of the New Criticism (a theoretical school which remained the dominant intellectual strain of literary analysis from the 1930s through the 1960s), it is useful to couch its theories in rhetorical terms. The work of W. K. Wimsatt and Monroe Beardsley, though coming in the middle of the New Criticism movement, provides the clearest example. In the "Intentional Fallacy" and the "Affective Fallacy" (1946), Wimsatt and Beardsley advocate excising the author (an entity whose true intentions can never be objectively discovered) and the audience (an entity whose subjective opinions about a work of literature are beneath scholarly consideration) from literary analysis. What remains in this decidedly *a-rhetorical* mode of inquiry is the text itself, an autonomous unit which can then be read—closely—to determine its forms, structure, nuance, and aesthetic quality (see FORMALISM). Though some New Critics adhered to these *a-rhetorical* strictures more tightly than others (a case in point is I. A. Richards, whose *Practical Criticism*, 1929, used readers' responses to seek out the cause of incorrect readings), what New Critical approaches generally presumed was that (1) literature, considered in its own right, was a unique form of language and (2) it should be considered by audiences in a detached and ahistorical manner, two points where the rhetorical approach to literature—defined by attention to a text's actual persuasive effects and the means by which an author created them—push back, most notably in the work of Burke and Booth.

Starting from the position that man is a "symbol-using animal," Burke's conceptualization of rhetoric as the means by which humans identify with each other not only erodes the distinction between poetic and rhetorical language (a position he argues in *Counter Statement*, 1931, and *The Philosophy of Literary Form*, 1941), but makes all language use necessarily a form of rhetorical discourse. For Burke, language *is* symbolic action (just as literature is "equipment for living"), and insofar as our symbol use touches on every facet of our lives—from war, to newspaper advertisements, to "Rime of the Ancient Mariner," to this encyclopedia entry—all of these texts should be opened up to a rhetorical method that can help probe the mysteries of human motivation and mutual understanding. Burke provides such a method in *Grammar of Motives* (1945), which outlined his analytical program of *dramatism*, a "pentadic" heuristic for dissecting a rhetorical artifact by (1) always considering rhetorical acts to be "molten," able to be approached by any number of interpretive angles and by (2) providing five, always refracting and mutually reinforcing, *ratios* of interpretation (*act, scene, agent, agency*, and *purpose*) and then extrapolating from them the ideological and philosophical consequences of their perspective on human conduct. Burke's notion of *ratio* was later to be taken up by Harold Bloom in his investigations on the anxiety of influence.

Though seen today as a viable critique of the New Critics (as well as an intellectual and methodological precursor to the poststructuralist rhetorical project), Burke's influence was not as apparent at the time of his writing (Bizzell and Herzberg). Another contemporary rhetorical challenge to the prevailing New Critical orthodoxies was more successful—one launched by the so-called Chicago School, founded by R. S. Crane (influenced by Richard McKeon, including Sheldon Sacks and Ralph Rader). These University of Chicago scholars engaged with Aristotelian techniques to rethink the rhetorical relationships inherent in literary communication. Rather than treat dramatic and poetic texts as sterilized and self-contained objects, the neo-Aristotelian method contemplated the effects (or affects) a work of literature produces and then reasoned back from those effects to determine, and typologize, the "means" (the method of craft or art) that produced them. The Chicago School's version of rhetorical poetics failed to unseat the prevailing orthodoxy of the New Critics. But a member of its second generation, Booth, innovated

upon their methods—pushing beyond both poetry and poetics and in a more overt form of rhetorical analysis—substantively redefining both the rhetorical criticism of literature in general, and the novel in particular, for American scholars in the mid-twentieth century.

Conceived as a critique of the "dogmas" of New Criticism—that literature, to achieve its exalted status, should be "objective"; that "REALISM" (a novelistic instinct to "show" and not "tell") should be the dominant aesthetic; that the audience should remain impartial in its deliberation upon a work—Booth's *Rhetoric of Fiction* reinserted rhetorical considerations into fiction in order to consider the efficacy of particular novelistic techniques in achieving particular literary—and ethical—effects. For Booth, literature is not only a communicative act between authors and readers, but one between authors, narrators, and readers, with the tacit understanding that an author is attempting to persuade her audience to assent to a particular set of judgments about the presented fictional world. Booth's expanded model of literary communication allowed him to assess and triangulate the potential consequences of authors' and audiences' "distance" (see SPACE) from narrators and characters (and from one another), leading to a host of still influential heuristics, including his views on narrators as unreliable and reliable; and dramatized and undramatized. *The Rhetoric of Fiction* also found Booth, in the book's most controversial innovation, advancing the proposition that an author's rhetorical presence, her craft in constructing the text, is never—despite the New Critics' claims—absent. Rather, it always emerges as the "implied author," the "sum total" of the author's choices ("the intuitive apprehension of a completed artistic whole ... to which *this* implied author is committed"), choices which are made precisely to create—rhetorically—a hypothetical reader "suited to appreciate such a character and the book he is writing" and to persuade the real reader to join in that appreciation (Booth, 89).

The raison d'être of Booth's rhetorical approach was developing criteria from which readers could make their own judgments about the ethics and efficacy of literary works, and from which they could understand the unique, and complex, relationships forged between authors and readers, a project continued in *A Rhetoric of Irony* (1974) and *The Company We Keep* (1988). Ironically, however, it was English Studies' eventual embrace of rhetorical study—or, more precisely, its embrace of the epistemologically robust, and arguably radical, theorizations of rhetoric heralded by poststructuralism's "linguistic turn"—that put the rhetorical approach to literature, as exemplified by Booth and the Chicago School, methodologically at odds with the field (see STRUCTURALISM).

Explained in the briefest of terms, the poststructuralist project begins with an echo of the ancient Sophists' understanding of the non-referentiality of language. Language—linguistic signs—is neither a transparent nor a degraded medium of access to a more knowable world; rather, language—rhetoric, the text—is all there is. Two paradigm-shifting implications for the rhetorical study of literature quickly arise. First, as articulated most famously by the mid-career work of Stanley Fish, this anti-foundationalist approach to text is both hyper-rhetorical and unmoored from the typical anchors of rhetorical interpretation: if neither authorial intention nor audience response can be presumed or appealed to in literary analysis (if, following Fish's penchant for quoting Protagoras, "man is the measure of all things"), then the validity of any interpretation of text (or even the *existence* of a particular text) is basically a matter

of the "interpretive community" one belongs to—an interpretive community, it must be pointed out, that one *always already* belongs to by virtue of acquiescing to a particular textual interpretation. Fish's interrogation of theories of intention and reader-response (coinciding with Roland Barthes's arguments against authorial intention and Jacques Derrida's deconstruction of authorship) necessarily changed the rules of the rhetorical approach to literature. The second impact of poststructuralism on the rhetorical study of literature, however, was to expand—and, as an intellectual, practical, and disciplinary matter, arguably explode—the very category of literature within English Studies. On this point, Michel Foucault is (ironically) the central organizing figure. Drawing upon the linguistic insights of Friedrich Nietzsche (1844–1900), and rolling back the Enlightenment's epistemological critique of rhetoric, Foucault sought out the complex relationships between rhetoric (in Foucault's parlance: *discourse*) and the development of particular regimes of knowledge, exploring the discursive constructivism inherent in SEXUALITY, science, psychology (see PSYCHOLOGICAL), power, and prisons, and helping to pave the way for an expansive, epistemic cultural studies approach to rhetoric and literature.

As is the case with any history, we must take care to acknowledge that there is no certain way to determine why trends in literary analysis come and go. That said, in the wake of the poststructuralist turn—with its emphasis on the ideological effects of discourse and its acknowledgment of the politics underpinning any particular interpretive community—the next analytical step would seem to be embracing a method able to trace out the ideological implications of literary discourse (see IDEOLOGY). And by the 1980s, the rediscovery and translation of the works of Bakhtin provided a rhetorical inroad to these queries. In his seminal early twentieth-century works—"Discourse in the Novel" and *The Problems of Dostoyevsky's Poetics* (1963)—Bakhtin moves beyond his Russian Formalist roots to consider more fully how all words and discourse, far from being sterilized and univocal, are "shot through with intentions and accents": no language is "neutral," or rather, "each word tastes of the context and contexts in which it has lived its socially charged life" (282). In other words, no word's meaning can ever be fully contained—completely cauterized from its social context—regardless of an author's appropriation and manipulation of it. The best approach to literary works, then, is to approach them dialogically: putting authors and readers into conversation via their mutual (though not necessarily non-competing) engagement—ideological, sociological, political—with language. And for Bakhtin, the best genre from which to consider these multiple, and often competing, social contexts of discourse ("heteroglossia") is the novel, a genre whereby an author acts as an orchestrator, bringing into conversation the competing discourses of the day—the church, the street, the court of justice, the bar, the home, the factory—via a panoply of narrative forms (hybrid, double-voiced, parodic, *skaz*, etc.) that do not allow the author to "monologically" overpower his characters.

Bakhtin's identification of particular narrative techniques, and the ways in which they engage readers in considering their aesthetic and ideological judgments of fictional work, brings us to the most prominent contemporary proponents of the rhetorical approach to literature, the "third generation" of Chicago School critics. Represented by the work of Phelan and Rabinowitz (though also including scholars such as Harry Shaw, David Richter, and Dorothy Hale), this continuation of the

Chicago School project takes as its starting point the communicative transactions between authors, narrators, and audiences in order to refine rhetorical heuristics that can enable evaluations of them. Working primarily from the perspective of readers, Rabinowitz has both explored the implications of how readers situate themselves among interrelated audience positions—the "flesh-and-blood" audience (the actual audience reading a text); the "authorial" audience (the ideal reader who understands the implied author's communication perfectly); and the "narrative audience" (the role, and assumptions, readers take on within a narrative world)—and investigated the conventions that typically guide readers' interpretations of narratives. Phelan, working from his 1996 redefinition of narrative as a form of rhetoric ("*the telling of a story by someone to someone on some occasion for some purpose*") considers the ethical and aesthetic calculations implicated in the multiple layers of rhetorical communication inherent in narrative acts (8). Beginning with *Reading People, Reading Plots* (1989), which considers how narrative progressions are catalyzed via an audience's responses to textual dynamics, and extending most recently to *Experiencing Fiction* (2007), which continues the exploration of three interlocking mechanisms for rhetorical judgment of fictional texts (the mimetic, thematic, and synthetic levels), Phelan's concern—whether dealing with character narration, authorial technique, or reader judgments—is the interrogation of narrative as a rhetorical activity with ideological, ethical, and affective implications.

This synopsis of current research into rhetorical literary criticism returns us to our original question: what is the status of the rhetorical study of literature in our present context? It has been nearly thirty years since Terry Eagleton, speaking on the state of literary theory (and attempting to clear the air of postmodern sensibilities and the treatment of literature as a "privileged object" "separate from the social"), lobbied for a return to the "oldest form of literary criticism in the world," rhetoric, the study of the effects of discourse and how to produce them in particular audiences. Now, in the early twenty-first century, English Studies has begun to see the return, and mainstreaming, of both ethical and aesthetic concerns, and their treatment—whether explicitly or implicitly—in rhetorical ways (see Berube and Hale, respectively) as well as a turn away from the poststructuralist "dogmas" against agency and intentionalism (see COGNITIVE). Put into rhetorical terms, the question then remains: in such an intellectual climate, and in an economic moment where the material conditions of the modern university have made Rhetoric and Composition Studies an increasingly powerful pedagogical and political influence within English departments (M. Bousquet, 2008, *How the University Works*), are we in another moment of rhetorical resurgence? Or merely another brief footnote in the 2,500-year-old relationship between rhetoric and literature?

FIGURATIVE LANGUAGE AND THE NOVEL

If the first part of this entry approaches the matter of rhetoric in terms of its broad conceptual and institutional history, it is also important to address figurative language, which is a fundamental element in the art of rhetoric and also plays an important role in the language of the novel.

Figurative language generally refers to any language that departs from ordinary usage or diction, although rhetoricians have noted that it frequently appears in everyday speech. Tropes such as *metaphor* ("a device for seeing something *in terms of* something

else," as Burke defines it in his 1945 *Grammar of Motives*), *litotes* (a form of understatement in which one states something by negating its opposite: "not bad," "not unattractive," etc.) or *hyperbole* (exaggeration, "the lecture went on *forever*") affect the meaning of words, while figures (or schemes) such as *anaphora* (the repetition of a word or phrase at the beginning of a series of clauses, used for force and emphasis), *hyperbaton* (change in syntax or word order), or *aposiopesis* (breaking or trailing off so as to call attention to what is left unsaid) affect their placing or repetition.

In *Classical Rhetoric in English Poetry* (1989) Brian Vickers notes that recent scholarship privileges tropes, especially metaphor, a complaint reiterated elsewhere by scholars such as Gérard Genette and Jeanne Fahnestock. Indeed, the deconstructionist critic Jonathan Culler has referred to metaphor as the "figure of figures, a figure for figurality" (1983, *The Pursuit of Signs*, 189), while Hayden White has called it the master of the four so-called master tropes singled out by Burke (metaphor, metonymy, synecdoche, and irony; 1973, *Metahistory*, 33). Many figures, by contrast, have been dismissed as technical curiosities, antiques better left to molder in dusty handbooks of rhetoric, yet Vickers and others argue that they have received short shrift: figures are vehicles for emotion. To give but two examples: a change in syntax can signify powerful feeling—a fragmented sentence, for example, could communicate the strain or stress of emotional disturbance, while by leaving the essential unsaid, *aposiopesis* may express grief or suspicion more powerfully than any explicit statement.

Classical Hellenic and Roman rhetoric divides style into four chief components: correctness, clarity, appropriateness, and ornamentation. It also accords great importance to the figures of speech. In his 1593 treatise *The Garden of Eloquence*, regarded as one of the greatest books in English on the subject, Henry Peacham defines figurative language as forms of speech that lend grace and strength to language, enabling orators to sway their listeners.

What role does figurative language play in literature, and more specifically in the novel? As noted above, in *The Rhetoric of Fiction*, Booth argues that authors intervene in their narratives to provide the reader with information about the otherwise inaccessible inner lives of their characters. Since Gustave Flaubert, who recommended that the author disappear behind his work, one of the guiding principles of modern fiction has been "show, don't tell." The novelist is supposed to become a *deus absconditus* who is absent from his creation: no authorial intrusions allowed. Booth counters that even deliberately self-effacing narrators continue to fulfill their age-old role of rhetorical persuaders, manipulating us into siding with this character or that one, coming at the fictional material from a particular angle, even skewing or distorting the facts, as is the case with the notorious "unreliable narrator." According to Booth, authors of fiction cannot shrug off their role of rhetors so easily.

It remains to determine the role of figurative language in this enterprise of rhetorical persuasion. One answer is that devices such as metaphor increase the reader's sense that the fictional world exists palpably and concretely. In his study, *Proust's Binoculars* (1963), an exploration of the author's optical imagery, Roger Shattuck writes that Marcel Proust provides us with "an image combined out of many images," and suggests that his prodigious layering of metaphors contributes to our sensation that the author has actually succeeded in re-creating the world (107). Booth's work suggests another possibility: tropes offer a glimpse into the recesses of characters' minds. One of the most famous

figures in Proust is the extended metaphor of the water gods in *Le Côté de Guermantes* (1920–21, *The Guermantes Way*), in which the prestigious aristocrats ensconced at the theater in their boxes (in French *baignoires*, or "bathtubs," hence the aqueous imagery) appear to look down upon the groundlings in the orchestra like divinities in a watery realm. Here the metaphor becomes an expression of the protagonist's anguished desire for inclusion in elite aristocratic society.

In *The Art of the Novel* (1988), Milan Kundera offers a contrast between metaphors from Rainer Maria Rilke's *Die Aufzeichnungen des Malte Laurids Brigge* (1910, *The Notebooks of Malte Laurids Brigge*) ("Already his prayer drops its leaves and juts out of his mouth like a dead shrub") and Hermann Broch's *Die Schlafwandler* (1932, *The Sleepwalkers*) ("He wanted unambiguous clarity: he wanted to create a world of such clear simplicity that his solitude might be bound to that clarity as to an iron post"; Kundera, 140). He argues that the former serves primarily an ornamental function while the latter reveals the character's existential attitude and furthers the phenomenological vocation of the novelistic genre. While novelists often employ the same rhetorical devices as orators or lyrical bards (or, for that matter, as advertising copywriters), the constraints and traditional parameters of the novel lead them to orient those devices toward ends germane to the genre. In *How Fiction Works* (2008), James Wood argues that the use of metaphor in a narrative fiction sums up the essence of imaginative writing. Every metaphor or simile is "a little explosion of fiction within the larger fiction of the novel or story" (202). For Wood, the leap toward the counterintuitive is the secret of powerful metaphor. Figurative language that defamiliarizes packs the greatest punch, though straining for flashy effects does little but draw unnecessary attention to the author's rhetorical gymnastics.

Some figures of speech (or patterns thereof) bring to mind the usages of a particular author. *Aposiopesis*, or "breaking off" (often typographically rendered with a dash), is a trope favored by Laurence Sterne, who uses it to particularly effective comic purpose at the conclusion of *A Sentimental Journey* (1768):

> —But the Fille de Chambre hearing there were words between us, and fearing that hostilities would ensue in course, had crept silently out of her closet, and it being totally dark, had stolen so close to our beds, that she had got herself into the narrow passage which separated them, and had advanc'd so far up as to be in a line betwixt her mistress and me— So that when I stretch'd out my hand, I caught hold of the Fille de Chambre's—("The Case of Delicacy")

Translation can also highlight how specific rhetorical strategies underpin an author's style. The translator runs the risk of either hewing too closely to the syntactic structure of the original or attempting to iron out its idiosyncrasies. The critic André Aciman has pointed out that recent attempts to improve upon existing translations of Proust have fallen into the latter trap. He notes one such error in the translation of the opening sentence of the second volume of Proust's *À la recherche du temps perdu* (1913–27, *Remembrance of Things Past*), which employs *anacoluthon*, an abrupt change of syntax within a sentence, in order to wind its way sinuously to a sharp, unexpected comic conclusion. In trying to smooth out the difficulties of Proustian prose, the translator avoids grammatical solecisms but transforms Proust's distinctive style and hijacks his underlying literary intentions. Aciman's gripe with Proust's translators

highlights our tendency to fall into predictable linguistic and rhetorical ruts. Paradoxically, as Richard Lanham has observed, clichés, which he characterizes as "petrified metaphors," stem from discontent with plain, everyday utterance. Lanham argues that we invent tautological and periphrastic ways of saying what could be said more plainly simply as a means of relieving tedium. But the sum total of these whimsical individual efforts turns out to be more tedious still. Echoing age-old ideas about art's role in renewing language, Lanham suggests that we need literature to shake us out of our bad habits by doing things with words that are truly fresh and creative.

BIBLIOGRAPHY

Aciman, A. (2005), "Proust's Way?" *New York Review of Books*, 1 Dec.

Bakhtin, M. (1981), "Discourse in the Novel," in *Dialogic Imagination*, ed. M. Holquist, trans. C. Emerson and M. Holquist.

Barthes, R. (1977), "The Death of the Author," in *Image, Music, Text*, trans. S. Heath.

Berube, M. (2005), "Engaging the Aesthetic," in *Aesthetics of Cultural Studies*, ed. M. Berube.

Bizzell, P. and B. Herzberg (1991), *Rhetorical Tradition*.

Booth, W. (1983), *Rhetoric of Fiction*.

Burke, K. (1969), *Rhetoric of Motives*.

Eagleton, T. (1983), *Literary Theory*.

Fahnestock, J. (2002), *Rhetorical Figures in Science*.

Fish, S. (1989), "Rhetoric," in *Doing What Comes Naturally*.

Genette, G. (1982), "Rhetoric Restrained," in *Figures of Literary Discourse*, trans. A. Sheridan.

Hale, D. (2009), "Aesthetics and the New Ethics," *PMLA* 124(3):896–905.

Kallendorf, C., ed. (1999), *Landmark Essays on Rhetoric and Literature*.

Lanham, R.A. (1974), *Style*.

Mailloux, S. (2001), "Interpretation and Rhetorical Hermenuetics," in *Reception Study*.

Phelan, J. (1996), *Narrative as Rhetoric*.

Rabinowitz, P. (1977), "Truth in Fiction," *Critical Inquiry* 4:121–41.

Rabinowitz, P. (1987), *Before Reading*.

Shaw, H. (1983), *Forms of Historical Fiction*.

Wimsatt, W.K. and M.C. Beardsley (1946), "The Intentional Fallacy," *Sewanee Review* 54:468–88.

Rogue Novel *see* Iberian Peninsula; Picaresque Novel

Roman *see* Romance

Roman à clef *see* Copyright/Libel

Romance

LORI H. NEWCOMB

The history of the novel, as the preeminent fiction form of the modern world, is so inextricable from the longer history of romance that most languages except English use a single word for all extended prose fictions. In Spanish that single word is *novela*, but many other languages still draw on the older tradition: *der Roman, le roman, il romanzo*. This entry, treating "romance" in an encyclopedia of the "novel," necessarily reflects English-language usage in distinguishing the two. However, it resists an Anglocentric model of fiction history, dominant in the nineteenth and twentieth centuries, that defined "novels" as ambitious, avowedly realist, fictions by modern authors (along with a few precursors), while implying that romances were not just formally distinct but developmentally inferior. Today, genre theorists recognize that the line drawn between novel and romance was and is provisional. Romance, then, includes much of the West's non-novelistic prose fiction, but not just *pre*-novelistic prose fiction, for romance did not become an atavism upon the novel's conception. Romances are written and read today not merely as ancestors of the novel; although often set in a version of the past, they are living kin. The romance space outside novelistic norms—timeless and boundless, deliberately conventionalized, idealized, even fantastic—remains compelling to writers and audiences.

Romance "as a *genre* is impossible adequately to define" in more positive terms (Saunders, 1–2), because its texts live in exchange between languages and cultures, authors and translators, past and present, verse and prose. That fluidity reflects the term's origins in cultural juncture. Early in the twelfth century, *romanz* named the vernaculars, such as old French and Anglo-Norman, derived from Latin by lay speakers. By the century's end, "romance" was applied metonymically to the secular texts most widely translated into, or produced in, those vernaculars: idealized adventures of historical heroes and their imagined courts. Audiences fluent in French or Anglo-Norman consumed metrical romances gathered from three distinct traditions: the "matter of Rome," or *romans antiques*, treating Troy, Thebes, or Alexander the Great; the "matter of France," featuring Charlemagne and Roland; and the "matter of Britain," Celtic legends of Arthur. A fragmentary fourth "matter of England" can be glimpsed in Anglo-Norman romances with northern ties: *Havelok the Dane, Guy of Warwick*. All four matters were intercultural, syncretizing old verse forms and epic values with Christian virtues in the European aristocracy's defining chivalric code. The matter of Britain, with its greater interest in the supernatural and in heterosexual love, grew most in scale and sophistication. Prose versions outstripped the verse romances and originated the influential technique of "interlace," the interweaving of multiple plots; by 1485, Malory's *Le Morte d'Arthur* compassed the Arthurian tradition in 507 chapters.

The last wave of chivalric prose romances came from Iberia. *Amadís de Gaula*, first published in 1508 in Castilian by Garci

Rodríguez de Montalvo, furthered romance's tendencies toward erotic frankness, magic, and length. Its many volumes, translations, and imitators profited from the expansion of the print market to reach a massive audience across Europe. New works in the Peninsular mode were written in seventeenth-century England, long after the continental vogue had faded. Writers ranging from the masters of the Spanish Baroque to English spiritual autobiographers cited the romances, or later chapbook redactions, as their earliest reading. Romance, in other words, continued to exceed the boundaries of national traditions, literary fashions, and authorial names. It was a Spaniard who indelibly satirized its excesses: Miguel de Cervantes Saavedra in *Don Quixote* (1605, 1615) portrayed an old man so addled by romances that he believes himself a knight. *Don Quixote* was an expanding text too, but newly aware of its print medium: in pt. 2, Don Quixote meets characters who have read pt. 1. That material self-reflexivity recurred in the eighteenth-century novel.

By 1600, many of romance's present senses were clearly established: its roots in the new Romance languages, its historical grounds, its characteristic quest structure—and its audience appeal across boundaries of era, nation, class, and gender. The vernacular and secular romance did not merit formal analysis by monastic scholars; nor was it clearly distinguished from "history." Even today, the breadth of romance defeats genre theory: it includes tales of adventure and/or love and/or the supernatural, in prose and/or verse, set in distant and/or past lands, centered on protagonists who are male and/or female, invented and/or historical, written for the pleasure and/or instruction of an aristocratic and/or popular audience. Not surprisingly, some contemporary critics have argued that romance is not a genre but a mode of heroism (Northrop Frye),

a language of multiplicity (Parker), a set of memes like shipwrecks and transposed birth (Cooper), or strategy for cultural translation (Fuchs). In the Renaissance, the unclassifiability of romance spurred distrust. Humanist writers condemned romances as immoral love stories especially pernicious to youth, foolishness for women, falsifications of history, or Romish trickery. The fear that romances were lies for the ignorant raised the bar for early modern romance writers.

A retrospective definition of romance can identify two dynamics of diversification in the early modern era, two ways for writers to use romance while evading formal or moral disapprobation. First, romance exchanged its memes and strategies with longer-established genres, such as verse epic. Second, romance itself proliferated subgenres, with new forms sometimes called "novel," at first simply meaning "new." The modern era resolved these dynamics by splitting fiction into the two genres that the English call novel and romance, and the French (for instance) *roman* and *roman moderne*. Of course this split was not uniform, inevitable, or final; the modern novel continued to absorb romance resources.

In the first dynamic, romance strategies enlivened the verse epics and allegories that grounded Europe's emerging national literatures. Interlace supported the complexity of Ludovico Ariosto's Roland epic, *Orlando Furioso* (1516); Torquato Tasso's epic of the Crusades, *Gerusalemme liberate* (1581, *Jerusalem Liberated*); and Edmund Spenser's unfinished Arthurian *Faerie Queene* (1590, 1596). These verse epics raised the stakes for prose romance, too. Sir Philip Sidney insisted in his *Defense of Poesie* (wr. 1579) that a true poem could be written in prose and still offer "notable examples" of virtue, powerfully asserting fiction's superiority to history. Sidney demonstrated his claim only partially in the revision of his romance *The Countess of Pembrokes Arcadia*, left incomplete on his death in 1589. Still, his revision joined continental humanists in devising the romance theory that Aristotle lacked: Sidney's models included Jacopo Sannazaro's Italian pastoral *Arcadia*, Jorge de Montemayor's *Diana*, and Heliodorus's *Aethiopica*. The latter (ca. 300 CE) was one of five Greek love-fictions rediscovered in the Renaissance and thenceforward attached to the Western romance tradition (suggesting that romance germinated as epic's counter-narrative). Romance even structured the Puritan allegory that was, for two centuries, the most influential English book after the King James Bible, John Bunyan's *Pilgrim's Progress* (1678). Chapbook versions of chivalric tales were the only books in Bunyan's hardscrabble village. After his conversion, he was inspired to treat the road to salvation as a very humble chivalric quest. The everyman Christian must escape the Giant Despair and fight the dragon Apollyon in order to win a golden crown beside God. Romance memes guided the autodidact writer and gripped his earnest readers.

Ambivalence about romance also led to a second dynamic, the constant assertion of new fiction subgenres. Some genres were named as subsets of "history"; other genres had names like "novel" that signified new literary decora. There was no consistent evolution, however. Since fiction was still theorized as offering exemplary ideals, the new romance subgenres primarily sought verisimilitude, which had more to do with the lifelike depiction of the best human actions than the pursuit of documentary truth. Verisimilitude was seen to vary with stories' framing, length, or narratorial embellishment. As early as the sixteenth century, short tales called *novellas* or *nouvelles* were gathered in framed collections imitating the manuscript *Decameron* of Giovanni Boccaccio from the 1350s, among them Matteo Bandello's *Novelle* (1554); the

Heptaméron (1558), attributed to Marguerite de Navarre; William Painter's translated sampler, *The Palace of Pleasure* (1566); and Cervantes's *Novelas Exemplares* (*Exemplary Novellas*, 1613).

A more recognizable "novel" was opposed to "romance" in William Congreve's polished *Incognita, or, Love and Duty Reconcil'd*, still in length a novella. Congreve's preface (1692) anticipates definitions hammered out a century later:

> Romances are generally composed of the Constant Loves and invincible Courages of Hero's, Heroins, Kings and Queens, Mortals of the first Rank, and so forth; where lofty Language, miraculous Contingencies and impossible Performances, elevate and surprize the Reader into a giddy Delight.... Novels are of a more familiar nature; Come near us, ... delight us with Accidents and odd Events, ... such which not being so distant from our Belief bring also the pleasure nearer us. ("Preface to the Reader")

Yet only forty years before Congreve, romance had peaked in prestige in the enormous *romans héroïques* produced in the French salons. As before, gentlemen and ladies passed historical fictions across the Channel; since these now ran to ten volumes, the readers themselves were heroic. It was an open secret that titles published under the name of M. de Scudéry, such as *Ibrahim ou l'Illustre Bassa* (1641–42, *Ibrahim: or the Illustrious Bassa*) and *Artamène ou le Grand Cyrus* (1649–53, *Artamene, or the Grand Cyrus*), were written by his sister, and that European current events were legible in these Orientalist settings. England's royalist exiles borrowed the strategy for manuscript romances about the Civil War.

The name of innovation then reverted to "history," with a more compressed ideal achieved in the French *petite histoire*, most notably Madame de Lafayette's psychologically penetrating *Princesse de Clèves* (1678,

The Princess of Cleves). In England, a new generation of professional women writers offered works on the boundaries of fiction called "secret histories" or, if short, "novels." Aphra Behn, England's signal professional woman author, exploited a Grub Street gray area by asserting that her *Oroonoko, or, the Royal Slave* (1688) was an eyewitness history. In fact, the text mixes accurate colonial observation, romance idealization of her African protagonist, and disturbing sensationalism. In the eighteenth century, "secret histories" by Mrs. Manley clearly were political allegories, while the "novels" of Eliza Haywood unleashed romance's dark secret, wronged female desire. The moralizing male writers of England's mid-eighteenth century, whose domestic realism would soon define the modern novel, were uncomfortably aware that many "romances" and "novels" were erotic; in *The History of Tom Jones, a Foundling* (1749), Henry Fielding mocked "foolish Novels" and "monstrous Romances" (bk. 9, chap. 5).

In 1785, Clara Reeve's *Progress of Romance* asserted that after romance declined into heroic monstrosity, "the modern Novel sprung up out of its ruins" (8). Longer retrospect shows that even the canonical novels depended on romance subtexts for their reality effects. In 1740–41 Samuel Richardson's Mr. B. threatened that he and Pamela could "make out between us, . . . a pretty Story in Romance" (*Pamela; or, Virtue Rewarded*, vol. 1, letter 15). Mr. B. implies that Pamela's fears are romance-fanned desires. The hint that romance is the novel's antagonist was taken up in Charlotte Lennox's *Female Quixote* (1752). (By 1801, the naïve American girl in Tabitha Gilman Tenney's *Female Quixotism* was misled by *novels*.) Yet Richardson's writing sometimes encodes his youthful affection for chivalric romances, as when he names Mr. B.'s Swiss manservant, feared by Pamela as a hairy monster, after Colbrand—the romance giant defeated by Guy of Warwick, a squire of low degree, in winning the lady Felice.

Nineteenth-century England claimed Fielding and Richardson as fathers of the modern novel, its realism a clean break with romance. Realism firmly appropriated literature to a nationalist agenda: fiction's lessons were no longer delivered from placeless idealizations but from individuals' lived, national particularities. Non-English-speaking literatures continued to call their new prose productions *romans*, yet their equation of realism to modernity tacitly followed England's disowning of romance. Our growing sense of the novel's transnationalism reveals a material difference between romance and novel: while romance was "effortlessly" translated for international traffic, the novel pursued authorial style and national identity so deliberately that it resisted translation (McMurran, 9).

A corollary was that romance was now relocated in time: a genre constantly reborn at the crossroads of history and fiction was reduced to dead, idealized past-ness. So misunderstood, romance became newly productive for the novel, and for modernity, as a literary license for fictive alternatives to the present. Hence writers rehabilitated "romance" for certain kinds of nonrealistic writing, not least romanticism. On a hint from Coleridge, Victorian Shakespeare critics called the late plays "romances" while suppressing their ties to early prose fictions. In a positivist age, Sir Walter Scott licensed his historical fictions by calling them romances. In America, Nathaniel Hawthorne claimed that the subtitle of *The House of the Seven Gables: A Romance* (1851) gave the work "a certain latitude, both as to fashion and material," not available in "writing a Novel" ("Preface by the Author"). As Henry James confirmed, such romance was sternly repressed in New England; Europe was romance's ancient and natural home. However, one mid-twentieth-century literary theory held that America's outsize experience grew its novels into "American romances." Increasingly, romance was a lost sense of the mythic that high modernism could filch from any culture's early literature. The 1925 English translation of the great Ming Chinese tale *Three Kingdoms*, a rigorous historical fiction, was dubbed *Romance of the Three Kingdoms*. Jessie L. Weston's reading of the Grail cycle in *From Ritual to Romance* (1920) shaped T. S. Eliot's *The Waste Land* (1922). In *Anatomy of Criticism* (1957) and *The Secular Scripture* (1976), Northrop Frye elaborated romance as a transcultural mode of lost heroism. Sigmund Freud's theory of *Familienroman* ("family romance"), first published in 1909, reads the romance meme of transposed birth as a formative stage in psychological development. These revivals and extensions prove that romance remains a powerful resource for fantasy in a world constrained by realism.

Romance still enriches modern novels in several registers. Romance as enfolded storytelling, creating a complex but otherworldly world, became the basis for the modern fantasy genre. The world of medieval romance is transposed in fantasy's first masterpiece, J. R. R. Tolkien's *Lord of the Rings* trilogy (1954–55), and its youngest blockbuster, J. K. Rowling's Harry Potter cycle. Ironically, the contemporary formula genre known as "romance" hews closer to the novel than romance in insisting that its likable female protagonist and her initially repellent wooer are developing characters. The readers of formula romance are intensely active in shaping their genre, in response to their changing wishes and even to literary critique. The readership of formula romance demonstrates that the long habit of defining romance by its audience has

a positive basis. Granted, the serious novel disowned audiences' pleasure in the inchoate and formulaic, and literary authorship cannot revert to the nameless collaborations that first circulated romance. Yet today's novelists still need romance's capacity to engage audiences in counterfactual, border-crossing narratives. The contemporary transnational novel embraces many strategies—historical layering, embedded and infolded tales, quests and cycles, intertextual ties to multiple national traditions—from among the endless resources of romance.

BIBLIOGRAPHY

Aravamudan, S. (2005), "Fiction/Translation/Transnation," in *Companion to the Eighteenth-Century Novel and Culture*, ed. P. R. Backsheiderr and C. Ingrassia.
Ballaster, R. (1998), *Seductive Forms*.
Cooper, H. (2004), *English Romance in Time*.
Fuchs, B. (2004), *Romance*.
Heng, G. (2003), *Empire of Magic*.
McMurran, M.H. (2010), *Spread of Novels*.
Parker, P.A. (1979), *Inescapable Romance*.
Pearce, L. (2007), *Romance Writing*.
Reeve, C. (1785), *Progress of Romance, through times, countries, and manners*.
Saunders, C., ed. (2004), *Companion to Romance*.
Warner, W.B. (1998), *Licensing Entertainment*.
Whitmarsh, T., ed. (2008), *Cambridge Companion to the Greek and Roman Novel*.

Romans héroïques *see* Romance
Romantic Novel *see* France (19th Century)

Russia (18th–19th Century)

ILYA KLIGER

The rise of the Russian novel in the middle of the eighteenth century coincides with a period of intense interest in and TRANSLA-

TION of narrative works from Western Europe. In the period from the 1730s to the 1760s, *précieux* ROMANCES and PICARESQUE and politico-PHILOSOPHICAL novels appeared in translations from French and English in handwritten and printed editions. Along with translations came the first attempts to defend the novel against the attacks of the neoclassical literary establishment. Most of these defenses reiterated Pierre Daniel Huet's celebrated argument in *Traitté de l'origine des romans* (1670, Treatise on the origin of romances) which claimed that the novel can serve as a powerful tool for communicating and inspiring virtuous principles through pleasurable entertainment.

However, dominant views on the value of the novel did not start shifting to its advantage until the last decades of the century. In the period between 1769 and 1794, a new wave of translations brought attention to masterpieces of the sentimentalist and preromantic novel. Jean-Jacques Rousseau's *Julie, ou la Nouvelle Héloïse* (1762, *Julie, or the New Héloïse*), Samuel Richardson's *Pamela* (1740) and *Clarissa* (1747–48), Henry Fielding's *Tom Jones* (1749), Oliver Goldsmith's *The Vicar of Wakefield* (1766), and perhaps most influentially Laurence Sterne's *A Sentimental Journey* (1768)—all were translated at this time. Translations of the English novel, less readily accessible in the original to the French-speaking members of the aristocracy, made a particularly strong impact. It was no longer possible to think of the "good novel" as, by virtue of its genre, an exception.

The elevation of the status of the novel as a GENRE did not immediately result in increased esteem for its native manifestations. As late as 1809, in his account of the novel, professor of Russian eloquence and poetry Aleksei Merzliakov (1778–1830) provides a long list of respectable novelists without mentioning a single Russian name.

1763–90: THE RISE OF "SERIOUS REALISM"

The first original Russian novel appeared in 1763. Written by Fyodor Emin, it was a quasi-autobiographical adventure narrative entitled *Pokhozhdeniia Miramonda* (*Adventures of Miramond*). *Miramond* presents the life of a virtuous nobleman from Constantinople, sent abroad by his father to study the "science of politics." The novel is marked by generic eclecticism, combining a politico-philosophical premise with an adventure plot, endowed with lengthy ethno-geographical digressions, studded with inserted novellas of the fairytale variety and unified by a love intrigue, in which the protagonists' love is tested through ordeals.

After *Miramond*, Emin went on to write the first Russian politico-philosophical novel as well as the first original EPISTOLARY sentimental novel. In the next two decades, a number of Russian original novels appeared, most following the generic topography traced out by Emin. A significant innovation was introduced by Mikhail Chulkov, whose novel *Prigozhaia povarikha* (1770, *The Comely Cook*) treats the picaresque adventures of Martona, an officer's widow, forced by circumstance to become a prostitute. Written in the first person, the novel takes place in recognizable Russian locales and is motivated by something like a "historical realist" premise: Martona's sad predicament results from her husband's death during the Russo-Swedish war (see HISTORICAL).

A qualitative leap past the formal and generic limitations of the earliest instances of the Russian novel is achieved by Aleksandr Radishchev in his seminal *Puteshestvie iz Peterburga v Moskvu* (1790, *Journey from Petersburg to Moscow*). Superficially modeled on *Sentimental Journey*, the novel is broken up into chapters, containing episodes that invoke in the sensitive and thoughtful traveler-narrator a feeling of dissatisfaction with the state of affairs in the country, followed by more abstract considerations on the proper form of political and social organization. The novel thus accomplishes a synthesis of previously unmixable narrative genres, combining elements of the politico-philosophical novel with close attention to the concrete conditions of contemporary Russian life. Here, for the first time, the "low" material of contemporary life deserves to be treated in "high," neoclassical generic codes. *Journey* can thus be said to inaugurate, in Russia, the practice of what Erich Auerbach has called "serious REALISM."

NIKOLAY KARAMZIN: STYLISTIC REFORM AND THE CREATION OF THE AUTHOR

To a mid-nineteenth-century Russian reader, however, Radishchev's *Journey* would sound antiquated. This is largely due to a revolution in literary language consummated in the work of his younger contemporary, Nikolay Karamzin. Karamzin's reform, accomplished primarily in the early 1790s, modeled the language of prose narrative on the conversational conventions of "polite" aristocratic society (see DIALOGUE). The Karamzinian style avoided the intricacies of the Church-Slavonic sentence, minimizing syntactic subordination in favor of rhythmic parallelism with clear intonational schemes. Lexically, it displayed a penchant for alliteration and assonance. It also avoided "high," neoclassical Slavonicisms as well as the "common" language of the people and professional jargon. In his sentimental short stories, Karamzin and his followers achieved a "middle style," creating an elegant, "polite" Russian to replace the French that was used by default in high society.

In addition to elevating the "middle style" to respectability, Karamzin developed a highly individualized figure of the narrator. His *Pis'ma russkogo puteshestvennika* (1791–92, *Letters of a Russian Traveler*) represents, like Radishchev's *Journey*, a mixture of empirical observation and lyrico-philosophical evaluation. But while Radishchev's narrator is projected as "man in general," pained by how far contemporary Russian life falls short of the ideal implanted in him by Nature, the authorial figure in Karamzin appears to the reader as more intimately connected with the biographical author himself. Karamzin, the person known in polite society, and K*, the author of the *Letters*, thus merged, creating the figure of a Russian writer as a sensitive, enlightened individual and a full-fledged contemporary of the political and intellectual life of Western Europe.

Throughout the nineteenth century, following Karamzin (as well as Radishchev), Russian novelists would continue to transcend their narrowly professional limitations, aspiring to the status of (and received as) social commentators, moral visionaries, political activists, and martyrs.

THE 1820s AND 1830s: PUSHKIN

The literature of the first two decades of the nineteenth century was dominated by smaller literary forms—elegies, ballads, epigrams, short fiction—fit for presenting in polite society and published in elegant, illustrated almanacs. Prominent among longer narrative genres was the long romantic poem, most gloriously represented by Alexander Pushkin's four so-called "Southern poems." Pushkin's romantic narrative poems (following and building on Lord Byron's (1788–1824) trailblazing use of the genre) were characterized by an intense focus on the inner life of a superior hero, on an elaboration of his mysteriously motivated estrangement from the social world, and on his tragic adventures in the exotic "South."

It is largely against the horizon of expectations established by this genre that the first canonical Russian novel was written and received. Pushkin's "novel in verse," *Evgenii Onegin* (1823–30, *Eugene Onegin*), frustrated these expectations, inserting the eponymous Byronic hero into the concrete and prosaic world of contemporary Russia, enveloping him in friendly but consistent narratorial irony and granting other character perspectives status at least equal to that of the hero.

The great literary critic of the 1830s–1840s, Vissarion Belinsky (1811–48), the great literary critic of the 1830s and 1840s, famously referred to Pushkin's novel as "an encyclopedia of Russian life." Indeed, the novel represents a wide range of concrete geographic locales, social classes, and cultural institutions, achieving through such sociohistorical concretization the deflation of the hero from the status of a representative of the universal human condition of Damnation and Exile to that of a more modest type— a disenchanted modern Russian nobleman.

More than an encyclopedia of Russian life, however, the novel is an almanac of contemporary sociohistorical discourses, serving as the first example of what Mikhail BAKHTIN has called the "polyphonic novel" in Russia. Coming together here, within the highly dynamic space of the "Onegin stanza" (iambic tetrameter; rhyme scheme aBaBccDDeFFeGG), are multiple discursively embodied worldviews: neoclassicist, sentimentalist—Karamzinian, German romantic, Byronic, etc. The hero's actions and worldview are thus ironized or rendered relative to other, competing worldviews represented or implicit in other characters' behavior and speech.

Finally, unlike the romantic poem out of which this "novel in verse" appears to have grown, the figure of the author is here highly individuated, playfully close to the biographical Pushkin and resolutely distinct from the romantic hero. In fact, it is ultimately the author-narrator of the novel who occupies center stage with his *salonnier* virtuoso capacity to switch codes, tones, and moods, as well as with his whimsical treatment of the plot (see NARRATIVE TECHNIQUE). The narrator of *Eugene Onegin* continues the traditions of the Karamzinian author, rejecting a strict demarcation between literature and life, staging their reciprocal involvement in, and dependence on, each other.

THE EARLY 1840s: LERMONTOV, GOGOL

The *"Onegin* line" of the Russian novel found its most immediate and significant development in Mikhail Lermontov's fragmentary novel, *Geroi nashego vremeni* (1839–40, *Hero of Our Time*).

Throughout the 1830s, the novel in Russia had an easier time accommodating great historical events than contemporary Russian life. This was evidenced by the surge of original historical novels, influenced by the works of Walter Scott on the one hand and French novelistic historiography (Comte de Vigny, Victor Hugo) on the other. Pushkin's only other completed novel, *Kapitanskaia dochka* (1836, *Captain's Daughter*), set during the great peasant uprising under the leadership of Yemelian Pugachev, represents the culmination of that movement.

Meanwhile, contemporary Russian life— apparently offering little material for a dramatic intrigue in which particular events might have universal resonance— was treated in shorter prose tales or cycles of tales. Lermontov's novel took its shape in sublating precisely the form of such a cycle. It is made up of five novellas, representing the major short narrative genres of the 1830s (a physiological sketch, an adventure tale, a slightly ironized GOTHIC novella, a society tale, and a philosophical tale) and unified through the figure of a single protagonist, Pechorin, an officer in the Caucasus and the "hero of his time."

Three of these tales appeared separately in a journal, and two more were added for the separate edition. The tales were arranged concentrically rather than chronologically (see TIME), narrowing in on the mysterious and fascinating personality of the hero. First Pechorin's adventures are given to us in the voice of his simple-minded roommate in the Caucasus; next we get the perspective of the more insightful narrator, and finally that of Pechorin himself: the last three tales are narrated under the subtitle "Pechorin's Journal."

A heightened, more thoroughly psychologized and historicized version of Onegin, Lermontov's protagonist harkens both back to the Byronic narrative poem and forward to the practices of PSYCHOLOGICAL realism in Ivan Turgenev, Fyodor Dostoyevsky, and Leo Tolstoy. He also both foreshadows and precipitates the crucial position of the figure of the fascinating hero as the unifying principle in the nineteenth-century Russian novel form.

Nikolay Gogol's *Mertvye dushi* (1842, *Dead Souls*) completed the triumvirate of early canonical Russian novels. It, too, is symptomatic of a certain looseness of contemporary Russian society, which made it difficult to find a dramatic unifying principle for the long narrative form and rendered early experiments in novelistic realism fragmentary and episodic (see NARRATIVE STRUCTURE). *Mertvye dushi* recounts the story of a former civil servant and crook who manages to wheedle from a number of landowners the legal titles of their deceased serfs (referred to as "souls" in pre-emancipation Russia) in order to use them as collateral for a loan. In the course of his journey from estate to estate, he

encounters a number of memorably grotesque landowners, whose estates are represented as their proper milieu.

While *Evgenii Onegin* draws on minor salon genres as well as on the long romantic poem, and Lermontov's *Geroi nashego vremeni* pushes off of the tale cycle, *Mertvye dushi* (projected as the *Inferno* of a Dantean trilogy and subtitled "*poema*" or "narrative poem") owes much to the picaresque tradition from *Gil Blas* to Fielding's "comic epic poems in prose" to the most prominent nineteenth-century Russian practitioner of the genre to date, Vasily Narezhnyi.

"THICK JOURNALS," THE NATURAL SCHOOL, AND THREE DEBUTS

The three works that jump-started the Russian novelistic tradition in the nineteenth century were written for a small audience of highly educated and mostly aristocratic readers. Each projected a cultivated image of the narrator, who would address the reader directly over the heads of the characters and who might meet that reader on any given night in society. In the late 1830s and into the 1840s this intimate relationship between author and reader began to dissolve. The institution of literature became more spacious; readership grew and became increasingly variegated. Reflecting and promulgating this development, the institution of the *tolstyi zhurnal* ("thick journal") came to the foreground of Russian literary life. In these, installments of serialized novels (see SERIALIZATION) would appear together with essays on current events, history, philosophy, the natural sciences, fashion, etc.

The thick journal, with fiction as its lifeblood and literary criticism at its heart, would play a major role in the development of the public sphere in Russia. In the environment of strict governmental censorship, literary criticism often served as a clandestine forum for the explication of political views implicit in literary texts. Heading the criticism section of the foremost thick journal of its time, *Otechestvennye zapiski* (*Fatherland Notes*), Belinsky promoted the figure of the literary critic to the status of a public intellectual, instructing his readers not merely on how to read but also on how to think and live.

The most prominent non-noble member of the nineteenth-century literary institution, Belinsky took up the struggle, in the 1840s, for a "poetry of the real" that would treat the various aspects of Russian life previously considered unworthy of artistic representation. With Belinsky's encouragement, the genre of the "physiological sketch" thrived, taking its name from the contemporary genre of the French *physiologie*. Keeping plot to a minimum, the sketch described the lower strata of St. Petersburg and Moscow society, focusing on petty clerks, prostitutes, indigent artists, and their determining milieus: garrets, poor neighborhoods, back streets, and marketplaces. In large part through Belinsky's efforts, two collections of such sketches came out, canonizing the literary practice of what came to be known as the Natural School (see NATURALISM).

The acknowledged master of the Natural School was Gogol, whose stories and novel, brilliantly elaborating relations between individual and environment, served as a source of inspiration to its younger practitioners. Extending the principles of the Natural School, three of them made significant contributions to the history of the Russian novel. In his novelistic debut, Dostoyevsky drew in particular on Gogol's sketch "Shinel" (1842, "The Overcoat"), adopting the type of a lowly copy-clerk, dim, inarticulate, and so immiserated that a new overcoat becomes an object of his deepest yearning, for an epistolary novel quite "physiologically" entitled *Bednye liudi* (1845, *Poor Folk*). In the process

of this generic mutation, the civil servant acquires many of the well-known characteristics of a Dostoyevskian hero: sensitivity, self-reflexivity, and a deeply dialogic speech, which constantly anticipates others' words and resists their finalizing accents (Bakhtin).

Ivan Goncharov drew on the principles of the Natural School to create the first (and perhaps only) classical Russian BILDUNGSROMAN in his *Obyknovennaia istoriia* (1847, *Common Story*). The novel depicted the disappointments of a naive, idealistic provincial in St. Petersburg, interspersing accounts of his experiences in the world with conversations about the legitimacy of the modern age as guided by the principles of bureaucratic-industrial mastery of existence.

Aleksandr Herzen took the preoccupation with the relation between hero and milieu in the opposite direction, developing an early version of the important and specifically Russian narrative form, the "superfluous man" novel. His *Kto vinovat?* (1847, *Who Is to Blame?*) endows the plot of a love triangle with historico-philosophical and political significance, staging it as a tragic conflict between gifted, ideal-bearing individualities and the suffocating world of contemporary Russia in which they are condemned to live.

THE NOVEL OF THE "SUPERFLUOUS MAN"

The 1850s were a productive period in the history of the Russian novel. During that time, Tolstoy appeared on the literary scene with some striking short stories and a quasi-autobiographical trilogy, *Detstvo, Otrochestvo, Iunost'* (1852–57, *Childhood, Boyhood, Youth*). Dmitry Grigorovich, author of some of the first short narratives on peasant life, expanded his scope in two full-size novels on the subject. Aleksey Pisemsky wrote a novel of disillusionment not unlike Goncharov's earlier one, but less schematic and less sympathetic to "the modern age." Some of the first female novelists made their debuts: the conservative society-novelist Evgeniia Tur, the hostess of a literary salon and prolific author of family novels Avdotya Panaeva, and the progressive novelist critical of bureaucracy and high society Nadezhda Khvoshchinskaia were the most prominent of these.

But the decade came to be dominated by the novel of the "superfluous man," whose most celebrated practitioner was Turgenev. The "superfluous man" is a specifically Russian sociopsychological type, congealing as a symptom of a tragic non-contemporaneity between the increasingly compelling bourgeois ideals of democracy, reason, and free human activity on the one hand and sociopolitical and economic retardation enacted by the state in fear of a bourgeois revolution on the other. The superfluous hero came to typify the "men of the '40s," progressively-minded Russian noblemen condemned to live in the heavy shadow of the official IDEOLOGY of "Orthodoxy, Autocracy, and Nationality."

Though the word *lishnii* ("superfluous") was already used by Pushkin to refer to Onegin in an early draft of the novel, and though it was used in a similar sense on other occasions, the expression forcefully entered Russian literary discourse with Turgenev's first novel, *Rudin* (1856). A brilliant thinker and speaker, the novel's eponymous hero proves incompetent when it comes to "real life," bringing only confusion and pain to those who are drawn to him.

The discourse of the "superfluous man," originating with Turgenev, retroactively created a tradition for itself, recruiting Onegin, Pechorin, Beltov (from *Who Is to Blame?*), and others, and thus solidifying the hero-centrism of the Pushkin–Lermontov novelistic line into a literary-critical and historico-philosophical category. Turgenev himself wrote two more novels about "superfluous men," but the tradition can be said to culminate with Goncharov's second novel, *Oblomov* (1859). Compared with Turgenev's enlightened failures, Oblomov represents a degenerate version of the "superfluous man," unable to raise himself from his feudal slumber to face the realities of an increasingly bureaucratized modernity. With Oblomov, a particular kind of landowner protagonist became outdated, retreated into what became known in contemporary criticism as *Oblomovshchina* (*Oblomov-ism*), in the face of which the question ending Turgenev's last novel from the 1850s rang all the more urgently: "Will there be men among us?"

THE EARLY 1860s AND THE NOVEL OF THE "NEW PEOPLE"

The 1860s in the history of the Russian novel open with a controversy regarding the change of guard at the forefront of Russian sociopolitical life. The death of the reactionary Nicholas I in 1855 and the end of the Crimean War in 1856 inaugurated a period of political liberalization and reform that would eventually lead to the abolition of serfdom in 1861. In the situation of relaxed censorship, journal polemics intensified, much of it focusing on the question of who should stand at the avant-garde of the political process. A heated exchange flared up in 1858 in response to Turgenev's novella *Asya* of the same year. Nikolai Chernyshevsky, literary critic, materialist philosopher, and the leading figure of the progressive St. Petersburg journal *Sovremennik* (*Contemporary*), reviewed the novella, arguing that the time of the "superfluous man" was up. What Russia needed now, in the days of great historical promise, were active, decisive people, more socially conscious, less preoccupied with themselves. A debate ensued in which prominent critics spoke out defending or condemning the superfluous "men of the '40s."

Written in large part as an intervention in this debate, Turgenev's most celebrated novel *Ottsy i deti* (1862, *Fathers and Children*) was thus a product of the unique proximity in which fiction and JOURNALISM were produced within the literary environment dominated by the institution of the thick journal. By contrast with Turgenev's earlier protagonists, Bazarov, the hero of *Fathers*, is a *raznochinets* (literally "a person of various or indeterminate rank") rather than a nobleman, a naturalist rather than a humanist, active rather than reflective. He dismisses speculative philosophy, scorns art and good manners, and pledges undivided allegiance to utility. He thus enters into an ideological and ultimately personal conflict with members of the older generation, the landowning idealists of the 1840s. Bazarov is characterized by his friend as a "nihilist," launching the term on a glorious career throughout the 1860s and 1870s as it came to signify an adherent of particular views (naturalist, materialist, utilitarian, democratic) as well as a practitioner of a certain ethos (direct, anti-hierarchical, provocatively uncouth).

The novel was badly received among both progressive and conservative critics. The majority of the former believed that Bazarov was a caricature, while the latter thought that Turgenev was too sympathetic to his hero. As was so often the case within the Russian novelistic field of the nineteenth century, critical attention soon gave way to novelistic response.

The first and most consequential of these was Chernyshevsky's novel *Chto delat'?* (1863, *What Is to Be Done?*), written in political imprisonment and published only thanks to a series of comic blunders committed by the censors (see CENSORSHIP). To the sullen Bazarov, Chernyshevsky's novel opposes a number of more cheerful protagonists, the genuinely "new people," espousing the principles of social justice, women's emancipation, and enlightened self-interest. Unlike the earlier, exclusively male and largely isolated "superfluous men," "the new people" was a GENDER- and number-neutral category: they could be men or women, and they could come together in groups. The events depicted in the novel were called upon to illustrate the possibility of fair and rational organization of life even in the spheres which had seemed to Chernyshevsky's predecessors from Pushkin to Turgenev the least tractable (especially intimate relations).

Chernyshevsky's novel was thus well suited to be retrospectively perceived as inaugurating the tradition of the socialist-realist novel of the 1930s–1950s. But in the meantime it appears to have galvanized two distinct novelistic lines, which flourished throughout the rest of the 1860s and 1870s: the "new-people" novel on the left of the political spectrum, focusing on the political education of a *raznochinets* hero and on his activism in the world; and the "anti-nihilist" novel on the right, frequently exploring the fate of an innocent victim (especially a pure-hearted young woman) seduced and misled by the cynical forces of destruction. These two lines of political novels about contemporary life were fueled by both contemporary events (discovered insurrectionary plots, trials of progressive activists, political assassination attempts) and their coverage in journalistic polemics. While few significant novelistic achievements came out of the progressive line, the anti-nihilist novel attracted important novelists such as Pisemsky (1863, *Vzbolomuchennoe more*; *Troubled Seas*), Nikolay Leskov (1864, *Nekuda*; *No Way Out*), Goncharov (1869, *Obryv*; *Precipice*), and perhaps most famously Dostoyevsky (1862, *Besy*; *Devils*).

A more immediate and highly noteworthy fictional retort to Chernyshevsky's novel came from Dostoyevsky, whose *Zapiski iz podpol'ya* (1864, *Notes from Underground*) was written from the point of view of a modern "underground man," mixing the genres of journalistic polemics and confession while addressing the burning socio-philosophical issues of the day: freedom, consciousness, reason, and social harmony. Staging, in his very style, the process whereby enlightened individualism turns against itself and reason turns into unreason, the underground man takes up Chernyshevsky's expressions and images, questioning the viability and desirability of a world organized according to enlightened self-interest. This journalistic-confessional critique of Chernyshevsky's "new people" is complemented, in Pt. 2 of the novel, by a more straightforwardly narrative rebuttal of the earlier generation of the 1840s with its "bookish" attempts to engage with the world. Thus, to the "new people" as well as to "superfluous men," Dostoyevsky opposes the figure of an underground man as the true (anti)hero of Russian modernity.

This cluster of strikingly different novelistic attempts to specify the socio-psychological makeup of the contemporary Russian *raznochinets* displays an impressive variety of views on the nature of novelistic realism. In Turgenev, the realist plot is conceived as an inexorably unfolding resistance of the pre-given world to higher ideals, producing the closest the Russian novel would come to the Western European novel of disillusionment. In Chernyshevsky, it is understood as a progressive actualization of pre-given reason in the contemporary world. And in Dostoyevsky, a new conception of realism dawns, one that the author will repeatedly put to work and articulate. Here, the actual is understood as the irrational: neither "science" nor "bookishness" can help stabilize the flux within and outside

the hero; both the hero and the world are in constant movement and thus inexhaustibly mysterious.

THE MID-1860s AND THE MULTI-PLOT NOVEL: *CRIME AND PUNISHMENT, WAR AND PEACE*

If according to the underground man neither the superfluous men of the 1840s, with their idealism and bookishness, nor the "new people," of the 1860s, with their reason and progress, rise to the status of a true Russian hero, then who does? *Prestuplenie i nakazanie* (1866, *Crime and Punishment*) is explicitly preoccupied with this question. An odd detective novel, where the identity of the criminal, Raskolnikov, is revealed from the very beginning and yet, in a deeper socio-psychological sense, remains mysterious until the very end, it crowns the forty-year-long tradition of hero-centrism in the history of the Russian novel. Here, throughout the novel, the *raznochinets* hero-criminal is offered a multiplicity of alternative plots to follow, each related to a particular social CLASS and ideology, each retrospectively emplotting the crime, giving it meaning. Building on Mikhail BAKHTIN's celebrated formulation, we can say that the novel presents the hero with a polyphony of plots, all carrying with them implicit worldviews, each representing a possible trajectory offered by contemporary Russian life.

Overlapping with the publication of *Crime* is another great multi-plotted novel of the mid-1860s, Tolstoy's *Voyná i mir* (1865–69, *War and Peace*). Tolstoy's first full-fledged novel follows the trajectories of several aristocratic families during the time of great historical events around the Napoleonic Wars. Each of these families possesses a set of stable characteristics, shared by most of its members and connected to its position in the Russian society of the time. If in

Dostoyevsky, as much as in Turgenev, Lermontov, and Pushkin, it is always easy to identify the protagonist, here at least five characters occupy center stage and ten or fifteen more frequently merit the narrator's exclusive attention. The best candidate for a more traditionally conceived protagonist is Pierre Bezukhov, who, being orphaned, fabulously rich, and intellectually restless, emerges as the most mobile character in the novel. Like Raskolnikov, Pierre represents the space of potentiality confronted with the choice between the historically available forms of life.

Tolstoy's decision to write a historical novel at a time when the efforts of the vast majority of novelists were directed at comprehending contemporaneity was an act of literary-historical defiance. But, as Boris Eikhenbaum authoritatively demonstrates, this defiance was also a strategic detour back to the burning questions of the day. In fact, Tolstoy can be said to launch at least a threefold polemic against the dominant concerns of the present—first in his focus on the aristocracy and peasantry to the exclusion of the emerging "new people"; second, in his explicit rejection of the possibility of conscious intervention in history; and third, in his attack on women's emancipation. Still, the form of the novel as a whole owes much to the structure of the specifically contemporary Russian experience: the rootless protagonist's passionate search for a meaningful place in the midst of available socio-ideological and chronotopic possibilities.

THE NOVEL OF DISINTEGRATION IN THE 1870s: SHCHEDRIN, DOSTOYEVSKY, TOLSTOY

A decade after the abolition of serfdom, journalistic and novelistic production—spurred on by increased peasant destitution,

a surge in political violence, and continued impoverishment and disorientation among the gentry—displayed a distinctive concern for the problem of social disintegration. Anti-nihilist novels continued to explore the consequences of modernization on the educated youth and the emancipated peasantry. At the other end of the political spectrum, the "new people" novel was accommodating itself to the emergence of *narodnichestvo*, or populism, a movement of the progressive youth from the cities to the villages with a view to improving the lot of the newly emancipated peasants. But the most successful novelistic experiments in staging and comprehending social disintegration were conducted in the more traditional genre of the family novel (see DOMESTIC).

The three novels that merit particular attention here were written in a literary environment in which the suitability of the novel for registering the swiftly changing contemporary scene was being contested. In the polemical frame of his novel *Podrostok* (1875, *Adolescent*), Dostoyevsky argued that the beautiful forms of a historical novel such as *War and Peace*, while they may have been effective in representing the "extremely pleasant and delightful details" of the family life of the old aristocracy, were insufficient for capturing the flux of contemporary Russian life. A new novel would be necessary for that, one that would sacrifice architectonic perfection and aesthetic "seemliness" to the project of capturing the truth of familial and social disintegration.

This is in fact what *Podrostok* attempted to do, substituting confused and confessional first-person "notes" for Tolstoy's epic omniscience, a tortuous series of unseemly episodes for Tolstoy's providential plot guiding the lives of nations and families, the progeny of an illicit affair between a superfluous man and his married serf for Tolstoy's children of noble houses.

Thus, Russia appears before us as an "accidental family," where anyone might come together with anyone, and the novel emerges as an equally accidental form, where characters, situations, and events fall together according to the unseemly logic of chance.

Dostoyevsky's bitter journalistic opponent, the great satirical writer Mikhail Saltykov-Shchedrin, shared his concern for the ability of the novel to stay abreast of the radical dynamism of contemporary Russian life (see PARODY). Arguably his only full-fledged novel, *Gospoda Golovlyovy* (1875–80, *The Golovyov Family*), took shape as a series of stories depicting three generations of degradation in the life of an aristocratic family. Through indolence, wastefulness, gambling, alcoholism, squabbles over inheritance, disease, suicide—story by story, the Golovlyov offspring ruin themselves and squander the estate. The novel's only unifying principle is the family itself; and yet it is the family which is falling apart, making it possible to dispose of the novel form.

The aristocratic family in dissolution is the opening theme and overarching motif of Tolstoy's second novel, *Anna Karenina* (1875–77). The opening passages of the novel describe the disintegration of the noble "house of Oblonsky"—a condition that is revealed in its full synecdochal significance as the novel explores contemporary life in the two capitals, the impoverishment of gentry estates, the conditions of agricultural labor, and the loss of ethical and epistemological absolutes. Thus, Tolstoy's second novel, whose serialization overlapped with that of *Podrostok*, renders Dostoyevsky's critique anachronistic. Here, the omniscient, epic tone of *War and Peace* has disappeared; events are narrated through the prism of irreconcilable character perspectives; characters find it impossible to understand each other; meaning is rendered radically private; providence is either malevolent or altogether in doubt. Formally, the most striking symptom of disintegration is the novel's own parallel plotting, with two protagonists following chronotopically distinct paths. The bracing narrative of happy marriage and ethical quest gravitates toward the feudal estate, while the tragic tale of adultery and death unfolds primarily in the capitals. Thus modernity itself is shown to have split off from Russia's wholesome pre-modern past, and the novel dedicated to the exploration of this break internalizes it as a refusal to bring these two stories into a single shape.

THE END OF THE CENTURY: AWAY FROM THE NOVEL

Starting in the 1870s, the center of gravity of Russian prose starts shifting away from the monumental genre of the novel and back toward smaller narrative forms. From literary-theoretical discussions of the time one might conclude that just as contemporary Russian life appeared to be too rarefied for the novel in the 1820s and 1830s, so it seemed too dense, too dynamic in the 1870s and 1880s. Prominent practitioners of the short story began to emerge: Gleb Uspensky, Vsevolod Garshin, Anton Chekhov, and others. Meanwhile, the last two great novels of the nineteenth century, Dostoyevsky's *Brat'ya Karamazovy* (1879–80, *The Brothers Karamazov*) and Tolstoy's *Voskresenie* (1899, *Resurrection*) can be understood as transitional works in the history of the Russian novel. Bringing much generically "archaic" material (folk and Christian legends, biblical apocrypha, hagiographic plots and motifs) to bear on the contemporary situation, they anticipate the modernist novel's subsumption of realist details under insistent patterns of frequently otherworldly structures of meaning (see MODERNISM).

SEE ALSO: Figurative Language and Cognition, Formalism, Gothic Novel, Intertextuality, Life Writing, National Literature.

BIBLIOGRAPHY

Bakhtin, M.M. (1973), *Problems of Dostoyevsky's Poetics*.
Bushmin, A., et al. (1962–64), *Istoriia russkogo romana v dvukh tomakh*.
Eikhenbaum, B. (1982), *Tolstoy in the Sixties*, trans. D. White.
Eikhenbaum, B. (1998), *Lermontov*, trans. R. Parrott and H. Weber.
Holquist, M. (1977), *Dostoyevsky and the Novel*.
Lotman, Yu. (1995), *Pushkin*.
Todd, W. (1986), *Fiction and Society in the Age of Pushkin*.

Russia (20th Century)

EDITH W. CLOWES

While in the twentieth century English-language critics proclaimed the death of the novel, in twentieth-century Russian literary culture this genre enjoyed a dominant position. The novel, as defined by its most famous Russian theorist, Mikhail BAKHTIN, is a polyphonic genre characterized by the ideological and stylistic counterpoint of multiple "speaking voices," "centrifugal" and generally freer of the clear "monological" authorial control that the three classical GENRES display. In the 1930s, even as Bakhtin was developing his theory of the novel, the Bolshevik revolution of 1917 and the eventual dictatorship of Joseph Stalin (1928–53) forced the split of the Russian novel into three sociopolitical avenues of development: the novel in exile, the highly censored officially published "Socialist Realist" novel, and, eventually, the underground novel (later known as samizdat, "writing for the drawer" e.g., self-publishing). This arrangement continued, though eventually with some loosening, until 1986, when the last Soviet leader, Mikhail Gorbachev, announced *glasnost*, or the freedom to express one's opinion publicly.

Beyond the political changes brought by the revolution, the twentieth-century Russian novel developed under rapidly changing social conditions. In the early twentieth century increasing literacy led to a new diversity of readership and divisions of novelistic production into the popular, the middlebrow, and the esoteric, experimental novel. After the fall of the tsarist regime and the Bolshevik revolution some traits of the esoteric novel were tolerated for another decade and thereafter existed only abroad or in the underground. In the 1930s, under High Stalinism, middlebrow and popular novels disappeared, replaced by centrally controlled mass literature.

In Russia both journal culture and the near-omnipresent CENSORSHIP led to a variety of ways of producing novels. In the Soviet era, as in the nineteenth century, editors, censors, and political leaders were often the novelist's most important readers, and the text of the novel could and often was altered to suit their taste. Traditionally a novel first appeared serially in a journal and only then in book form, thus making the novel cheaper and more accessible to the public (see SERIALIZATION). This practice continues even today, though it is no longer the rule. In the underground, banned novels were ever more frequently typed with multiple carbon copies. Some copies were entrusted to friends for safekeeping or sent abroad for publication (*tamizdat*). Others were lent to a trusted circle for rapid overnight reading. In the post-Soviet era, which thus far has been free of censorship, novels sometimes (e.g., those of Viktor Pelevin) appear on the internet for downloading free of charge.

The stylistic history of the twentieth-century Russian novel can be divided into the following broad, overlapping periods:

(1)   The modernist novel (1890–1930), also known as the Russian Renaissance or the Silver Age. Modernist novels are marked by meta-aesthetic discourse and mythopoetic experiment. Subcategories include: the DECADENT novel (based on realist descriptive and NARRATIVE TECHNIQUES); the Symbolist novel (rejecting realist technique for experiment with narrative voice, visual and musical structures, and mystical seeking); the post-Symbolist novel (playing with both realist and symbolist stylistic features). The modernist period also encompasses the middlebrow, neorealist, or expressionist novel as well as the popular serial novel.

(2)   The socialist-realist novel (1923–91): a form of didactic novel epic strongly controlled by the interests of the Communist Party. This form soon bred both (underground) satire and the critical realist novel, as well as documentary fiction, both semi-official and underground (see REALISM).

(3)   The post-Soviet/postmodernist novel (late 1960s to the present), until 1986 appearing in samizdat and tamizdat (see p. 723), characterized by parody, play with intertextual reference, and meta-aesthetic consciousness.

MODERNISM (1890–1930)

In the modernist period the Russian novel branched into an array of different forms, including the esoteric experimental novel (decadent, Symbolist, post-Symbolist), the first politically engaged revolutionary novel, the popular serial, and the middlebrow neorealist novel.

Although the decadent, or first-generation symbolist, novel was based on the established realist aesthetic (precise description, socioeconomic setting, third-person narration, a world knowable to reason and the senses), it added a meta-aesthetic consciousness of the creative process, including changing frames of human perception, effective parody of realist forms and experiment in narration, and ritualistic use of the novel world to apprehend and play out myths of cosmic and social renewal. The Symbolists were first of all poets, and that practice certainly shaped their use of language, voice, and perspective. Although quite traditional in his narrative style and imitative of the Polish novelist Henryk Sienkiewicz, Dmitry Merezhkovsky, in his popular trilogy Khristos i Antikhrist (Christ and Antichrist)—Smert' bogov: Yulian Otstupnik (1896, The Death of the Gods), Voskresshiye bogi: Leonardo da Vinci (1901, The Forerunner), and Antikhrist: Pyotr i Aleksey (1905, Peter and Alexis)—sought through voluntarist religious feeling the roots of cultural renewal in the three historical eras of late Rome, the Italian Renaissance, and early Enlightenment Russia.

Valery Briusov also wrote historical novels: Ognennyi angel (1908, The Fiery Angel), set in the German late Renaissance, and Altar' pobedy (1913, The Altar of Victory), set in ancient Rome. Prud (1908, The Pond), by Aleksei Remizov, deals with Russian merchant life, pursuing Dostoyevskian motifs of moral searching and adding lyrical techniques to convey dreams and meditations. The outstanding decadent novel Melkii bes (1907, The Petty Demon), by Fedor Sologub, undermines psychological realism in the absurdist character Peredonov, who, like Anton Chekhov's protagonist in the story "The Man in a Case," is obsessed with ambition and paranoid angst. One of several European coming-of-age novels of the early twentieth century, the novel also explores the Dionysian myth of cosmic renewal, suggesting that the novel's boy protagonist, Sasha Pylnikov, is a new incarnation of the god, who through festival and sacrifice will deliver the world from Peredonov's mental and emotional paralysis.

The second-generation Symbolist novel features much bolder experiment with narrative voice, perspective, lyrical and musical forms, linguistic destructuring, and mystical rituals of renewal, again typically by writers better known for their poetry. Certainly the best-known novelist among the younger Symbolists is Andrei Bely, whose first three novels are all highly experimental. The first, *Serebriannyi golub'* (1910, *The Silver Dove*), explores sound symbolism and the disintegration of language, consciousness, and self in the context of sectarian rituals of rebirth. *Peterburg* (1916, *Petersburg*), one of the greatest parodies in the history of the novel, looks for cosmic rebirth in the musical, phonemic, anthroposophical play behind the matrix of narratives associated with the city of St. Petersburg. *Kotik Letaev* (1922) explores earliest consciousness and memory and their relation to language. Belyi's novelistic technique and his rhythmic prose exerted a powerful influence on the post-Symbolist and later generations.

The post-Symbolist novel kept some of the experimental and mythical aspects of the Russian modernist tradition while functioning among emigrants or in the Soviet underground. *Kozlinaia pesn'* (1928, *Goat's Song*), by Konstantin Vaginov, plays on the roots of the Greek word for tragedy as a "goat song," heralding the death of Great Russian culture. Living in emigration after 1919, Vladimir Nabokov (pseud. Sirin) wrote in Russian until moving to the U.S. in 1940. Nabokov's early novels focus on aesthetic artifice. His most famous—*Zashchita Luzhina* (1930, *The Defense*), *Otchaianie* (1934, *Despair*), and *Priglashenie na kazn'* (1938, *Invitation to a Beheading*)—combine constructed parallel worlds with highly structured and stylized plots, play with consciousness and

unreliable narration, and mix paradox with brilliant verbal play. His best Russian-language novel, *Dar* (1937–38, *The Gift*), parodies the foundational Russian ideological novel, *Chto delat'?* (1863, *What Is to Be Done?*) by Nikolai Chernyshevsky. *Doktor Zhivago* (1957) by Boris Pasternak is the last echo of the Russian post-Symbolist novel. A parody of the Tolstoyan epic, it layers—over a meager skeleton of epic narrative about the revolutions of 1905 and 1917 and the ensuing civil war—other, more powerful lyrical, musical, philosophical, and mythopoetic structures.

Two important but often unnoticed aspects of the modernist era are the rapid growth of literacy and the widening gap between levels of readership and varieties of accessibility in the novel. The esoteric novel of the Symbolists and post-Symbolists was what Roland Barthes would call a writerly novel, meant for the initiated reader's active cooperation. Much more successful among the broader public were middlebrow, neorealist novels, which mimicked commonly recognizable actuality. Many of these works dealt with topical themes, from critique of the Russian military to sexual liberation. *Poedinok* (1905, *The Duel*), by Aleksandr Kuprin, is a traditionally realist short novel that became famous for its incisive critique of the Russian military just at the time of the Russian defeat in the Russo-Japanese War (1904–05). Mikhail Artsybashev's scandalously "pornographic" *Sanin* (1907), a novel in a somewhat popularized Turgenevian style, explores the free-sex movement and features a vulgarized superman protagonist. *Derevnia* (1910, *The Village*) and *Sukhodol* (1912, *Dry Valley*), by Ivan Bunin, Russia's first winner of the Nobel Prize for literature (1933), deal with the downward spiral of the Russian countryside in richly evocative prose. Bunin's *Zhizn' Arsen'eva* (1952,

The Life of Arsen'ev) is perhaps the most significant treatment of the Russian émigré experience, weaving the autobiography of a young artist.

The early twentieth century also saw the grassroots emergence of the potboiler and the truly popular novel-romance that were accessible to virtually every level of reader. The most famous of these serial novels, Anastasia Verbitskaia's *Kliuchi schast'ia* (1909–13, *The Keys to Happiness*), published in a series of six volumes, created a liberated heroine and is a virtual catalogue of political and artistic life, fashions, scandals, and celebrities of the years leading up to WWI.

After the revolution of October 1917, the new Soviet government attempted to curb the taste for real grassroots popular literature through a hybrid propaganda-popular novel; these included the Red Pinkerton novels; the series by Marietta Shaginian(pseud. Jim Dollar) combining adventure, sleuthing, and proletarian heroism; *Mess-mend, ili Ianki v Petrograde* (1924, *Mess-Mend, Yankees in Petrograd*); and Aleksey Tolstoy's immensely popular science-fiction novel and subsequent film, *Aelita* (1923), about a scientist's and a Red Army soldier's flight to Mars, the scientist's love affair with the princess Aelita, and the soldier's fomenting of a workers' revolt. The early 1920s also saw the emergence of the mass novel based on Lenin's call for "party literature," featuring the leadership of the Communist Party and the genre of the Tolstoy-inspired didactic EPIC novel. Various revolutions of 1905 and 1917, as well as the civil war (1918–21), gave ample material for such epics. Among the best were *Chapaev* (1923), by Dmitry Furmanov—whose historical hero, the commander Chapaev, became a genuinely popular hero in film and anecdote—and *Razgrom* (1927, *The Rout*), by Aleksandr Fadeev.

THE NEW ECONOMIC POLICY, 1921–28

The six years following revolution and civil war saw the novel develop relatively unencumbered by censorship. During the revolution many middlebrow writers emigrated or alternated between Russia and Europe. Many works were published both in Germany and in the Soviet Union, something that was legal only in the 1920s and then after 1986. Writers who remained in Russia but were undecided or unwilling to join the Party became what Leon Trotsky (1879–1940) and the new regime termed "fellow travelers." These writers accepted the revolution but did not typically adhere in their literary practice to the Leninist concept of party literature, which called on revolutionary art to serve the interests of the party. Some novels were highly experimental, while others retained a realist aesthetic. *Golyi god* (1922, *The Naked Year*), by Boris Pilniak (Boris Vogau), presented a collage of people and episodes in the Russian province during the civil war. Virtually plotless, it shows a Bely-inspired, highly stylized treatment of characters and moods. Like many modernist novels this one often engages in what formalists would call "baring the device," showing the artifice of novel writing, e.g., the frequent incursion of the author into the text.

Evgeny Zamyatin, a neorealist writer and teacher in the politically autonomous literary group, the Serapion Brothers, wrote the famous experimental dystopia *My* (*We*) in 1920–21, which could not be published in Russia until 1988. An English translation appeared in 1924 and the Russian original in New York in 1952. Written as a diary of D-503, an aeronautical engineer living in the totalitarian One State, centuries in the future, *My* builds on Dostoyevsky's parody of 1860s utilitarianism in *Zapiski iz podpol'ya* (1864, *Notes from Underground*), and Bely's experimental constructions of the city of St. Petersburg. It parodies contemporary avant-garde utopias of the Futurists, Suprematist and Constructivist artists, and the new proletarian poets.

The last permitted experimental novel, *Zavist'* (1927, *Envy*), by Yury Olesha, enjoyed a *succès de scandale* and confounded ideological critics who could not agree on its stylistic achievements and its meaning. In essence a "Symbolist fantasy," *Zavist'* rebels absurdly against all systems of meaning (Maguire, 344). It parodies the conventions of the novel of manners, although it can also be superficially read as a black-and-white novel pitting old attitudes against the fresh, youthful views of the new order. Konstantin Fedin, a member of the Serapion Brothers, wrote *Goroda i gody* (1924, *Cities and Years*), the first large-span novel to be published in Soviet Russia, best known for its experimental treatment of narrative TIME, starting the novel with the death of the protagonist, Andrei Startsov, who proves tragically unable to take a moral stand during the civil war. *Belaia gvardiia* (1925, *The White Guard*), by Mikhail Bulgakov, was a realist novel by an author known for his fantastic satire; it gave one of the few truly sympathetic and politically daring treatments of the educated Russian—Ukrainian elite in Kiev during the civil war. This novel made a stronger impression as a play, *Dni Turbinykh* (1926, *The Days of the Turbins*), supported by Stalin himself through a long tour at the Moscow Art Theater.

In the 1920s the middlebrow novel developed particularly successfully in satirical forms. A new wave of Ukrainian writers, particularly from the Jewish community in Odessa, enjoyed popularity. Among these were the satirical PICARESQUE novels coauthored by Ilya Ilf (I. Fainzil'berg) and Yevgeni Petrov (Evgenii Kataev): *Dvenadtsat' stul'ev* (1928, *The Twelve Chairs*), which enjoyed multiple film versions both in Russia and the U.S., and *Zolotoi telenok* (1931, *The Golden Calf*). Both feature the crafty rogue Ostap Bender and two of his get-rich schemes. Valentin Kataev satirizes the period's greed in his novel *Rastratchiki* (1926, *The Embezzlers*).

Andrei Platonov (Klimentov), by far the most innovative novelist of the 1920s, emerged from the Proletkult (Proletarian Culture) movement. His two greatest works, *Chevengur* (wr. 1929; pub. Paris 1972) and *Kotlovan* (*The Foundation Pit*, wr. 1930; pub. U.S. 1973), just missed acceptance for publication at the end of the New Economic Policy. Like many experimental novels of the 1920s they had to wait until the 1980s to appear domestically. Both novels at once participate in and satirize the utopian novel, creating more than the traditional dystopian vision. Both distort ideologically colored language and explore the link between language and consciousness.

HIGH SOCIALIST REALISM (1934–56)

During the period of Stalin the true popular novel disappeared, co-opted by the Stalinist government as the didactic mass novel, which was completely scripted and controlled by Party policy. Known also as the literature of "social command," Socialist Realism was codified as a method in 1934 at the first congress of the newly created Union of Writers. Socialist Realism featured the epic novel as the genre best suited to constructing and conveying the myth of Soviet success— the victory of the revolution, the success of Stalinist industrialization, and the promise of the coming Communist utopia. The notion that Soviet writers served as the "engineers of human souls" (Andrei Zhdanov) conveys the didactic purpose of the Socialist Realist novel. Writers were ordered to express the "truthful, historical depiction of reality in its revolutionary development" (Terts, 402). A fixed form with required ingredients, the Socialist Realist novel features *partiinost'* — the celebration of mass spontaneity and energy guided by the wisdom and political consciousness of Party leaders. The novel must also portray *narodnost'* (a "positive hero" who embodies the energy and character of the masses) and *ideinost'* (ideological correctness; see IDEOLOGY).

The roots of the Socialist Realist novel lie in nineteenth-century utopianism (such as Chernyshevsky's *Chto delat'?*), Tolstoyan realism, and the revolutionary romanticism of the 1905 period. Its direct precursor is *Mat'* (1907, *Mother*), by Maksim Gorky (Aleksei Peshkov), the story of a mother's switch from a figure of suffering passivity to the icon of the revolution. The epics of the civil war era — Furmanov's *Chapaev*, *Zhe-leznyi potok* (1924, *The Iron Flood*), by Aleksandr Serafimovich, and *Tsement* (1925, *Cement*), by Fedor Gladkov — comprised the instant Socialist Realist canon. Among these were genuinely fine novels, e.g., the Cossack epic, *Tikhii Don* (1928–40, *Quiet Flows the Don*), purportedly by Mikhail Sholokhov, and the strongly Dostoyevskian *Vor* (1927, *The Thief*), by Leonid Leonov. Some of these novelists became the leaders of the Writers' Union and the enforcers of the Socialist Realist method.

The Socialist Realist novel of the 1930s built on the civil war experience, the production novel of collectivization and industrialization, and the HISTORICAL novel. Kataev's *Vremia, vpered!* (1932, *Time, Forward!*) represents the Socialist Realist novel of "social command," dramatizing the building of a huge steel plant at Magnitogorsk. Shaginian's novel *Gidrotsentral* (1931, *The Hydroelectric Station*) is a well-researched production novel dealing with building a hydroelectric dam in Armenia. Blind and

ill, Nikolai Ostrovsky part-wrote and part-dictated *Kak zakalialas' stal'* (1932–34, *How the Steel Was Tempered*), an autobiographical fiction about the making of a true communist, the hero of which, Pavel Korchagin, became one of the icons of Soviet male consciousness. Aleksey Tolstoy wrote two well-received historical novels, the trilogy *Khozhdenie po mukam* (1921–42, *The Road to Calvary*), about an educated Russian family before, during, and after the revolution, and the unfinished *Petr pervyi* (1929–45, *Peter the Great*), in which Tolstoy recast modern Russian history and Russia's first modern emperor, Peter, as the prefiguration of Stalin. The tribulations of WWII fed more grist into the Socialist Realist mill. Most famous and idiosyncratic was *Vokopakh Stalingrada* (1946, *In the Trenches of Stalingrad*), by Viktor Nekrasov, which celebrated the decisive Soviet victory over the Nazis. A keen war journalist, Nekrasov delivered precise descriptions of sometimes unheroic characters and their heroic behavior and sidestepped the required Socialist Realist ingredients, *partiinost'* and *ideinost'*. Another readable war epic that touches upon, among other things, the normally taboo subject of the Holocaust on Soviet soil is *Buria* (1947, *The Storm*), by Ilya Erenburg.

THE "THAW PERIOD" (1953–66)

Following Stalin's death in 1953 and Nikita Khrushchev's "Secret Speech" in 1956, which called, among other things, for greater candor in art, the officially permitted possibilities for the novel opened somewhat, allowing the development of so-called "critical realism." The first Thaw-era novel was *Ne khlebom edinym* (1957, *Not by Bread Alone*), by Vladimir Dudintsev, which dealt with conflicts between an inventor and the administration of a research institute.

Critical realism was first to cross the boundaries of the permissible. Having taken seriously the call to expose the "mistakes" of Stalinism, realist writers were soon perceived to have written much too openly on topics that compromised living leaders. Vasily Grossman's *Zhizn' i sud'ba* (wr. 1961, pub. U.S. 1980, *Life and Fate*), a vast epic dealing with the Soviet resistance to the Nazi invasion, featured characters discussing the similarities between Nazi and Stalinist forms of totalitarianism. Aleksandr Solzhenitsyn successfully published *Odin den' iz zhizni Ivana Denisovicha* (1962, *One Day in the Life of Ivan Denisovich*), a short novel dealing with the survival of a simple man in the Gulag. Two of his novels, *V kruge pervom* (1968, *The First Circle*) and *Rakovyi korpus* (1968, *Cancer Ward*), were slated for publication, only to be rejected because they explored in detail the system of Stalinist police control and the prison system.

The critical realist novel, which emerged during the 1960s and 1970s, can be divided into the "urban" and "village" novel, since they re-create the experiences of various social groups, including the peasantry and the urban intelligentsia, without the falsely optimistic window-dressing typical of Stalin-era Socialist Realist writing. Among the finest is *Dom na naberezhnoi* (1976, *The House on the Embankment*), by Yury Trifonov, which deals with the children of the Stalinist elite and their privileged life. Another is *Khranitel' drevnostei* (1964, *The Keeper of Antiquities*), by Yury Dombrovsky, the first "museum novel" to deal with the Terror of 1938–39. Structurally and stylistically the novel abandons Socialist Realist ingredients and uses a much more ambiguous variety of voices, memories, and temporal frames. Among critical realist novels, the officially permitted village novel became prominent in the Thaw period and remained so to the end of the Soviet era, in part because of fine writing, in part because

of its claims to express true Russian national identity. Prominent examples are *Brat'ya i sestry* (1958, *Brothers and Sisters*), by Fedor Abramov, and *Zhivi i pomni* (1974, *Live and Remember*), by Valentin Rasputin. Abramov's novel is the first novel of an epic trilogy, *Priasliny* (1958–78, *The Priaslin Family*), dealing with several generations of an Old Believer clan in the far northern village of Pekashino. Rasputin's novel makes Siberia the locus of true Russian character. Few of these novels have been translated into English, although their spare, precise prose and their narrative closeness to rural consciousness have literary merit, and their bold treatments of the destruction of the Russian peasantry through collectivization were major historical achievements of the Thaw period.

Another important facet of the critical realist novel is the emergence of significant Russophone, non-Russian ethnic voices. *Belyi parakhod* (1970, *The White Steamship*) and *I dol'she veka dlitsia den'* (1981, *The Day Lasts More than a Hundred Years*), by the Kyrgyz writer Chingiz Aitmatov, are examples of successful novels written by a Central Asian. Aitmatov was Communist, yet openly and without repercussion alluded to the depredations of Stalinism and Soviet bureaucracy. The 1970s saw the emergence of Fazil Iskander, an Abkhazian writer, as a major novelist. Parts of his satirical trilogy, *Sandro iz Chegema* (1973, 1979, 1981, *Sandro of Chegem*), appeared in Soviet print, while others were available only in *samizdat* and *tamizdat*. The Kazakh writer Olzhas Suleimanov aroused official ire with his Turkic-nationalist novel, *Az-i-ia* (1975), which plays on the word "Asia" and two Russian words for "I."

Although Socialist Realism as a method started to fade soon after Stalin's death, censors still held control of official Soviet literary culture and enforced political and Party correctness. The subject matter and experimental style of many of the novel genres that developed during and after the Thaw quickly expanded beyond the bounds of what censors and editors viewed as politically acceptable. Among the array of novels published in the underground and abroad were experimental, parodic, satirical, documentary, and science-fiction novels. During the Thaw these novels were often first submitted for official publication and rejected. They then found their way to publication abroad (*tamizdat*). From the early 1970s onward innovative novels were first published underground (*samizdat*) or abroad.

Novelistic experiment and true ideological "polyphony" were discouraged until *glasnost*, and the still-heavy censorship led to the development of vital *samizdat* and *tamizdat* publishing of innovative novels. The first example is Pasternak's *Doktor Zhivago*, which was pulled after being accepted for publication in 1956 in the relatively permissive journal *Novyi mir* and published in Italy the following year. The 1960s saw the official publication of works banned through the Stalinist era, including Pasternak's poetry from *Doktor Zhivago* and the least corrosive of Platonov's fiction. The most intriguing novel of the Stalinist underground is Bulgakov's *Master i Margarita* (wr. 1928–40, pub. U.S.S.R. 1967, *The Master and Margarita*), which operates on multiple narrative layers as a brilliant satire of 1920s venality, a romance, political commentary, and a meta-aesthetic novel. It contains a novel within the novel that features a typically post-Symbolist interest in religious philosophy and mythopoesy.

Another genre that emerged as a result of the Thaw period's call to be "honest" and "sincere" was the documentary novel. Of those published in the official media, *Babii iar* (1966, *Babi Yar*), by Anatoly Kuznetsov, is certainly the most important. Based partly on interviews with witnesses and his own autobiography, Kuznetsov tells the story of a 14-year-old boy who experienced the Nazi murder of Kiev's Jews in the ravine known as Babi Yar. This work's thematically bold comparisons of Stalinist and Nazi terror disappeared under the censor's red pencil. Particularly famous is Solzhenitsyn's trilogy, *Arkhipelag GULag* (1973–75, pub. France, *The Gulag Archipelago*), which he called "an experiment in fictional investigation." These vast tomes investigated and documented life and death in the Soviet prison camp system.

The satirical novel, another genre that soon found a home in the literary underground and abroad, was among the first victims of the Soviet censor's red pen. Planned for publication, *Zhizn' i neobychainye prikliucheniia soldata Ivana Chonkina* (1969, *The Life and Extraordinary Adventures of Private Ivan Chonkin*), by Vladimir Voinovich, appeared first abroad. Influenced by Czech writer Jaroslav Hasek's popular anti-Austrian mock-epic, *Osudy dobrého vojáka Svejka za svetové války* (1923, *The Good Soldier Schwejk*), this novel parodies the Stalinist WWII epic, making broad use of slapstick humor and puns. Voinovich's *Moskva 2042* (1987, *Moscow 2042*) renders a "meta-utopian" parody of post-Soviet totalitarianism that satirizes a number of different views of the ideal society.

SCIENCE FICTION continued to enjoy popularity after the 1920s, when it bloomed partly under the influence of Jules Verne and H. G. Wells. The Strugatsky brothers (Arkady and Boris) were the leading representatives of Soviet science fiction during and after the Thaw period. Although their first works, e.g., *Strana bagrovykh tuch* (1959, *The Country of the Maroon Clouds*), adhere to the strictures of Socialist Realism, they introduced fresh characters and expanded the possibilities of science to alter the world. The novel *Piknik na obochine* (1972, *Roadside Picnic*) became the basis for the famous experimental film by Andrei Tarkovsky, *Stalker* (1987). With *Gadkie lebedi* (1972, pub. W. Germany, *Ugly Swans*) the Strugatsky brothers also crossed the boundary into novel writing that explored the ideologically unacceptable parallels between Stalinism and Nazism and challenged readers to think more critically.

THE LATE SOVIET AND POST-SOVIET NOVEL (1966–)

The late 1970s and 1980s saw a broadening array of themes openly aired under the rubric of critical realism. Historical novels on formerly taboo topics saw the light of day. *Tiazhelyi pesok* (1978, *Heavy Sand*), by children's writer Anatoly Rybakov, treated several generations of a Jewish family that suffered during the Holocaust. His novel *Deti Arbata* (1987, *The Children of the Arbat*) exposed the complicity of young people in the Stalinist repressions of the Great Terror in the late 1930s.

After the end of the Thaw younger writers parodied all claims to literary realism, let alone Socialist Realism. They pushed the novel in genuinely new directions from the edges of Soviet culture. To paraphrase the novelist Andrei Bitov the least well treated in literature—and thus offering perpetual sources for new creativity—are the worlds of the child, the drunkard, and the "inauthentic person lacking talent" (1978, *Pushkinskii dom*; *Pushkin House*, 72–73). Sasha Sokolov, who was brought up in a privileged family in the diplomatic service, wrote his "surreal" novel, *Shkola dlia durakov* (1975, pub. U.S., *A School for Fools*), from the point of view of a retarded child. Rejecting the life of an official litterateur, Venedikt Erofeev wrote a brilliant short novel, *Moskva-Petushki* (1969, excerpts pub. U.S.S.R., *Moscow to the End of the Line*), that made ingenious fun of every aspect of Soviet mass culture, told from the point of view of an unsalvageable alcoholic. Bitov published his "museum novel," *Pushkinskii dom*, in the U.S. Set in Leningrad, the novel treats the interface between genuine Russian culture destroyed in the Stalinist camps and the inauthentic culture of both the Stalinist 1930s and the 1950s and 1960s of the Thaw period.

Toward the final years of the neo-Stalinist government, a younger generation of writers exposed the oppressiveness of the literary power structure and rejected the strictures of Socialist Realism. In 1979 they openly published a compendium of experimental literature, entitled *Metropol'*. It was immediately confiscated and the minor contributors arrested. Two of the organizers were Bitov and Vasily Aksenov. Forced to emigrate from the Soviet Union in 1980, Aksenov wrote a number of fine novels, including the historical fantasy, *Ostrov Krym* (1984, *The Island of Crimea*), which imagines a Crimea free of Soviet rule, and *Ozhog* (1980, *The Burn*), about the jazzy, fast-paced life of the new, freer-thinking generation of 1960s Moscow. *Glasnost'*, announced in 1986, brought the first-time domestic publication of an enormous backlog of great twentieth-century Russian novels. Beyond novels well known abroad, such as *My*, *Kotlovan*, *Doktor Zhivago*, and *Rakovyi korpus*, new riches now emerged, such as Yury Dombrovsky's *Fakul'tet nenuzhnykh veshchei* (1978, *The Faculty of Superfluous Things*) and the works of Nabokov. Although for a few years contemporary novelists appeared stunned by the tidal wave, experimental trends already at work in Erofeev and others eventually regained their hold.

In this experimental turn away from all kinds of realism is what might be called the postsocialist novel, which adds a whole new dimension to the familiar postmodernist novel. This novel is characterized by literary play and PARODY, though with the material of

Stalinist culture and Socialist Realist art, rather than popular Western forms. *Vremia–noch'* (1992, *The Time–Night*), by Liudmila Petrushevskaia, parodies the Russian matriarchal myth. Boris Akunin (Grigory Chkhartishvili) has reintroduced subgenres of the DETECTIVE novel and the thriller with a parodic twist. His novels feature a family of detectives, the forebear (E. Fandorin) serving in the late nineteenth century, for example, in *Azazel'* (1998, *The Winter Queen*), and the grandson (N. Fandorin) in the Stalin secret police of the 1930s, for example, in the generic *Shpionskii roman* (2005, *Spy Novel*).

The most popular and prolific novelist of the post-Soviet era since 1991 is Viktor Pelevin. In the 1990s he wrote three outstanding novels. *Zhizn' nasekomykh* (1993, *The Life of Insects*) draws on the premise of Czech writer Karel Čapek's *Insect Play* (1921) but with a post-Soviet, postcolonial overlay. In this world where all characters transform into insects, the main character is Sam Sucker, an exploitative American businessman who becomes a mosquito and sucks the blood of a variety of locals. Pelevin's finest novel, *Chapaev i Pustota* (1996, *Chapaev and the Void*, also trans. as *Buddha's Little Finger*), building on Ken Kesey's *One Flew over the Cuckoo's Nest* (1962), is set partly in a Moscow mental hospital in which an oppressive psychiatrist assumes that mental illness is merely a reflection of tumultuous social change. Pelevin's style may be called "neo-baroque" in that its witty intertextual trompe l'oeil masks the deep pain of the post-imperial Russian psyche. His third major novel, *Generation P* (1999), satirizes the transition from Soviet-era ideology and propaganda to the post-Soviet commercialist culture of advertising.

Probably the best example of the post-socialist, postmodernist meta-utopian novel is *Kys'* (2000, *Slynx*), by Tatiana Tolstaia. Set two hundred years after a cataclysm that destroys Moscow, this isolated community is populated by part-human, part-animal mutants who rediscover and try to interpret the debris of Soviet civilization and culture. Another line of development in the post-Socialist Realist novel springs in part from the South American tradition of MAGICAL REALISM and the postcolonial experience. Liudmila Ulitskaia uses her novel to deconstruct the historiography of the Stalinist era. For example, her first novel, *Medea i ee deti* (1996, *Medea and Her Children*), traces the history of a clan of Greek heritage from the Black Sea area, thus replacing the debilitating "Great Family" myth of Stalinist culture with their and other minority cultures, including Jewish and Tatar.

Although the twentieth-century Russian novel survived powerful cataclysms, some forced by the nature of cultural discourse, some forced by political events, it has remained a vital form of Russian literature. The popularity of the playful, multilayered post-Soviet novel attests to the increasing sophistication of the general Russian readership. In world literature the impact of the Russian novel has remained powerful.

SEE ALSO: Modernism, Narrative Perspective, Narrative Structure.

BIBLIOGRAPHY

Brooks, J. (1985), *When Russia Learned to Read*.
Brown, D. (1978), *Soviet Russian Literature since Stalin*.
Brown, D. (1993), *Last Years of Soviet Russian Literature*.
Clark, K. (1981), *Soviet Novel*.
Clowes, E.W. (1988), *Revolution of Moral Consciousness*.
Clowes, E.W. (1993), *Russian Experimental Fiction*.
Cornwell, N., ed. (2001), *Routledge Companion to Russian Literature*.
Dunham, V.S. (1976), *In Stalin's Time*.

Freeborn, R. (1982), *Russian Revolutionary Novel*.

Garrard, J.G., ed. (1983), *Russian Novel from Pushkin to Pasternak*.

Gillespie, D.C. (1996), *Twentieth-Century Russian Novel*.

Jones, M.V.and R.F. Miller, eds. (1998), *Cambridge Companion to the Classic Russian Novel*.

Maguire, R. (1968), *Red Virgin Soil*.

Parthe, K. (1992), *Russian Village Prose*.

Peterson, N.L. (1986), *Fantasy and Utopia in the Contemporary Soviet Novel, 1976–1981*.

Shneidman, N.N. (2004), *Russian Literature, 1995–2002*.

Terts, A. [A. Siniavskii] (1957), *Chto takoe sotsialisticheskii realism* [1960, *On Socialist Realism*, trans. G. Dennis].

Weiner, A. (1998), *By Authors Possessed*.

Weir, J. (2002), *Author as Hero*.

Russian Formalism *see* Formalism; Novel Theory (20th Century)

S

Saga *see* Northern Europe
Samizdat see Russia (20th Century)
Satire *see* Parody/Satire

Science Fiction/Fantasy

PHILLIP E. WEGNER

Darko Suvin defines science fiction as a genre whose "necessary and sufficient conditions are the presence and interaction of estrangement and cognition, and whose main formal device is an imaginative framework alternative to the author's empirical environment" (1979, *Metamorphoses of Science Fiction*, 7–8). Science fiction estranges or denaturalizes the world that currently exists, showing its apparently immutable foundations to be contingent and changeable. If high modernist fiction accomplishes this through formal experimentation (see FORMALISM, MODERNISM), science fiction does so through the portrayal of "other" worlds: the future, different planets, or a version of our own world into which has been introduced a *novum* or new element in the form of an event, alien, or technology. (Each of these worlds corresponds to one of Mark Rose's four coordinates of the genre: time, space, monster, and machine; 1981, *Alien Encounters*.) However, unlike both older fantastic literatures *and* modern fantasy, science fiction portrays worlds bound by the scientific, historical, or "cognitive" laws of our own.

Although significant precursors are to be found in the GOTHIC novel, nineteenth-century utopias and dystopias, and Jules Verne's "*voyages extraordinaires*," it is the great "scientific romances" of H. G. Wells—in particular *The Time Machine* (1895) and *The War of the Worlds* (1898)—that establish the genre. Wells's work also demonstrates science fiction's critical potential, as *The Time Machine* uses its allegorical capacity to attack Great Britain's contemporary social inequities, while *The War of the Worlds* unveils the brutalities of European colonialism.

Thus, science fiction, as an original narrative form, is as modernist as film, the two coming together early on in Georges Méliès's (1861–1938) pioneering *Voyage dans la lune* (1902, *A Trip to the Moon*). There is also an interesting parallel between the two forms, as both have two distinct modernist moments. The first occurs for science fiction in the early twentieth century, in the work of writers who acknowledge their debt to Wells while also expanding the GENRE's possibilities. Significant figures from this first modernist efflorescence include the Russian and Soviet writers Alexander Bogdanov, Aleksey Tolstoy, Evgeny Zamyatin, and Andrei Platonov; the Czech novelist and dramatist Karel Čapek, whose play *R.U.R.* (1920) introduced the term *robot*; and the British authors E. M. Forster, Olaf Stapledon, and C. S. Lewis.

This first wave was interrupted in the late 1920s by the Soviet Union's growing intolerance for artistic experimentation and the rise in the U.S. of popular "pulp" magazine fiction. Examples of the latter include the

The Encyclopedia of the Novel   Edited by Peter Melville Logan
© 2011 Blackwell Publishing Ltd

"space operas" of E. E. "Doc" Smith and Philip Francis Nowlan (the creator of Buck Rogers), and the fantasy of Edgar Rice Burroughs (Tarzan and John Carter of Mars) and Robert E. Howard (Conan). These works presented tales set in intergalactic space, exotic worlds, or the imagined past, and offered their readers simplistic moral visions, with the critical estrangements of earlier modernist science fiction kept to a minimum. The heyday of pulp science fiction occurred under the editorships of Hugo Gernsback and John W. Campbell, the latter, in the 1930s, inaugurating science fiction's "Golden Age." Writers Campbell brought to prominence—among them Isaac Asimov, Robert Heinlein, and A. E. Van Vogt—remain some of the genre's best known. Campbell demanded a more rigorous grounding of science fiction in contemporary scientific knowledge—and thus created the basis for the subgenre of "hard" science fiction exemplified by writers such as Arthur C. Clarke and Hal Clement in the 1950s and today by Gregory Benford and Kim Stanley Robinson—as well as a more careful exploration of the implications of their estranging hypotheses. Moreover, most of these writers expressed a deep faith in the possibilities of science, rationality, and technology, values shared by much of the genre's early audience.

The conclusion of WWII saw the emergence of a new generation of writers—among them Alfred Bester, James Blish, Ray Bradbury, Fritz Leiber, Walter Miller, Jr., and Cordwainer Smith—whose confidence in science and technology was far less sure. Following the 1949 publication of George Orwell's *Nineteen Eighty-Four*, the early Cold War period also witnessed the resurgence of the sociopolitical subgenre of dystopia, exemplified by Bradbury's *Fahrenheit 451* and Frederick Pohl and C. M. Kornbluth's *The Space Merchants* (both 1953). Meanwhile, the genre's attention increasingly turned to the social and PSYCHOLOGICAL impact of modernity and to the development of complex character psychology, giving rise to "soft" science fiction. The single most important writer to emerge from this context was Philip K. Dick, whose rich visions of near future worlds, especially in the series of novels that begins with *Time Out of Joint* (1959) and culminates with *Ubik* (1969), would influence both the subsequent development of the genre and popular culture as a whole.

This was also the moment of the development of modern "heroic" fantasy, a subgenre that rejected science fiction's rationalism and can be characterized by a nostalgic longing for the distant past, the binary ethical imaginaries of older ROMANCE, and the presence of "noncognitive" wish-fulfillment devices such as magic. In this way, modern fantasy participated in a larger cultural reaction to the horrors of world war. The form's central practitioner was J. R. R. Tolkien, and his work encouraged later writers—such as Anne McCaffrey, Ursula K. Le Guin, Samuel R. Delany, and, later, Gene Wolfe, Philip Pullman, and China Miéville—to further develop the genre. Moreover, the contemporary dominance of popular fantasy is evidenced by the bestselling novelist J. K. Rowling.

The work of Bester, Dick, and these others set the stage for science fiction's second "modernist" moment, a period often referred to as the New Wave. These works reflected the political upheavals of the time, and often offered critiques of state and corporate bureaucracies, consumerism, the Vietnam War, environmental despoilage, and GENDER and racial inequality (see RACE). New Wave writers in the U.S. would include Harlan Ellison, who also edited the landmark *Dangerous Visions* anthologies (1967, 1972); Frank Herbert, whose most celebrated novel, *Dune* (1965), placed ecological concerns centrally within the genre; Thomas Disch, author of the acclaimed dystopias *Camp Concentration* (1968) and *334* (1972); and the prolific Robert Silverberg. Science-fictional elements also began to be more prominent in "literary" fictions by writers such as William Burroughs, Thomas Pynchon, and Kurt Vonnegut. The British magazine *New Worlds*, especially under the editorship of Michael Moorcock, showcased new works, including the experimental fictions of J. G. Ballard and Brian Aldiss. Meanwhile, John Brunner emerged as an important author of contemporary dystopian fiction. Major science fiction would again appear from the Soviet bloc, most prominently in the work of Stanislaw Lem (Poland) and Arkady and Boris Strugatsky (USSR).

Finally, this period would see an increasing diversity among the genre's authors. Although a handful of women—including Leigh Brackett, Carol Emshwiller, Judith Merril, C. L. Moore, and James Tiptree, Jr. (Alice Sheldon)—did publish memorable fiction in the 1940s and 1950s, it would not be until the later 1960s that women writers would take up a new prominence in the genre, often explicitly thematizing gender and sexuality. Some of the best known of these writers are Margaret Atwood, Doris Lessing, Suzy McKee Charnas, McCaffrey, Vonda McIntyre, Marge Piercy, Joanna Russ, and, most significantly Le Guin, whose masterpieces include *The Left Hand of Darkness* (1969), a tale of an alien race whose sexual biology and gender identities are radically different from our own, and *The Dispossessed* (1974), a work that heralded a full-scale revival of the literary utopia. Delany was another path-breaking figure, as one of the first AFRICAN AMERICAN and, later, openly gay writers in the field (see QUEER). Delany would be followed by other major African American science-fiction authors, such as Octavia Butler, whose *Xenogenesis* trilogy (1987–89) and *Parable* novels (1993, 1998) became some of the

genre's most discussed, and more recently by the Canadian Caribbean novelist Naola Hopkinson.

By the end of the 1970s, the energies of the New Wave had been exhausted, and the subsequent conservative counter-assault created an environment less hospitable to science-fiction experimentation and dangerous visions. A significant change in the genre was signaled by the emergence of "cyberpunk" in the early 1980s. Although Bruce Sterling took on the role of the movement's spokesperson, it was William Gibson who emerged as its leading practitioner. Gibson's novel *Neuromancer* (1984) rejected both the optimism of the Gernsback–Campbell era and the radicalism of the previous generation. Moreover, in its celebration of new information technologies, its suspicion of Fordist welfare state policies, and its poaching from and pastiche of different genres, including *noir* fiction, cyberpunk was seen as exemplary of postmodern sensibilities. Other prominent writers associated with the movement include Pat Cadigan, Rudy Rucker, and Neal Stephenson.

Many of the science-fiction writers who rose to prominence in the late 1980s and 1990s—including Iain M. Banks, Terry Bisson, Butler, Orson Scott Card, Hopkinson, Gwyneth Jones, Ken MacLeod, Miéville, Robinson, Stephenson, and Sheri Tepper—signal a further eclecticism in the genre as they draw upon the resources of hard science fiction, utopias and dystopias, cyberpunk, and heroic fantasy. There has also been a resurgence among these writers of the critical political energies that were in abeyance in the heyday of postmodern cyberpunk, signaling another turn in the genre's rich history.

SEE ALSO: Adaptation/Appropriation, Definitions of the Novel, Graphic Novel, Mythology, Time.

BIBLIOGRAPHY

Aldiss, B. (1986), *Trillion Year Spree*.

Attebery, B. (1992), *Strategies of Fantasy*.

Barr, M. (1993), *Lost in Space*.

Broderick, D. (1995), *Reading by Starlight*.

Clute, J. and J. Grant, eds. (1999), *Encyclopedia of Fantasy*.

Clute, J. and P. Nicholls, eds. (1995), *Encyclopedia of Science Fiction*.

Freedman, C. (2000), *Critical Theory and Science Fiction*.

Jameson, F. (2005), *Archaeologies of the Future*.

Moylan, T. (2001), *Scraps of the Untainted Sky*.

Seed, D. (2000), "Considering the Sense of 'Fantasy' or 'Fantastic Fiction,'", *Extrapolation* 43(3): 209–47.

Seed, D., ed. (2005), *Companion to Science Fiction*.

Wegner, P. (2002), *Imaginary Communities*.

Yaszek, L. (2008), *Galactic Suburbia*.

Self-Reflexivity *see* Narration
Sensation Novel *see* British Isles (19th Century); Melodrama
Sentimental Novel *see* British Isles (18th Century); Domestic Novel

Serialization

PATRICIA OKKER AND NANCY WEST

For many, the idea of a "novel" conjures up associations with an individual book, an individual reader, an individual pleasure. Neatly contained within its bindings, the novel affords a book lover both private and personal pleasures. She can carry an entire novel wherever she goes, and the very neatness of its containment ensures that she decides when to take a break or when to read voraciously through the night, perhaps with a flashlight in hand to avoid detection.

While this link between novel and book can seem immutable, millions of readers, especially in the nineteenth century, have enjoyed consuming their fiction through serialized installments apportioned over weeks, months, and sometimes years. Novels were issued in parts or numbers, each wrapped separately for distribution and purchase, or in monthly, weekly, or daily periodicals. Regardless of which type, part-issue or periodical publication, the serialized novel requires a prolonged reading experience, which brings different delights than the bound novel. A commentator in *Harper's New Monthly Magazine* (Dec. 1855) compared the serial reader to a gourmand slowly digesting a multi-course meal: "Readers who complain of serials have not learned the first wish of an epicure—a long, long throat. It is the serial which lengthens the throat so that the feast lasts a year or two years. You taste it all the way down" (128).

Although a global history remains to be written, serialized fiction has long been an international phenomenon, exhibiting striking similarities across nations. The rise of the serial novel corresponded with specific technological developments, the advent of a consumer culture, urbanization, increased literacy rates, and increased leisure. The basic narrative of the genre's evolution remains constant whether one considers Japanese newspapers during the 1800s, British periodicals in the 1840s and 1850s, or Shanghai magazines during the early 1900s. Publishers experimented with serialization to reduce initial expenses and disperse the prohibitive cost of books to consumers over time. As reading became measured by the clock and calendar of the workweek, the serial novel provided an ideal way to spend leisure time.

Given its extraordinary popularity, range, and longevity, serialization has generated a rich body of scholarship, especially within the field of British literature. Early criticism was largely devoted to recovering the history of serial publication by major authors such as Charles Dickens and William Makepeace Thackeray. By the late 1980s, critics began turning their attention to social and cultural issues, with an increasing emphasis on both theoretical concerns and the community of readers created by serialization. Some scholars, such as Jennifer Hayward, have addressed the commercial strategies of serialization. Richard Hagedorn, Linda K. Hughes and Michael Lund, and Laurie Langbauer have taken a more philosophical and theoretical look at serialization, examining its relation to capitalism, nineteenth-century conceptions of time, and the meaning of the "ordinary." Recent critics have devoted considerable effort toward uncovering the less prominent authors and more marginalized audiences of serial novels. Other critics are now looking at serialization within the context of specific magazines. This latter group of scholars—Susan Belasco Smith, Deborah Wynne, and Patricia Okker, among others—draw attention to the materiality of the periodicals in which the novels appeared and highlight the juxtaposition of serial installments with magazine features, including cartoons and advertisements. Yet, despite this breadth of scholarship, much work on the serial novel remains to be done.

SERIALIZATION IN ENGLAND AND THE U.S.: BEGINNINGS THROUGH THE 1870s

Often associated with the nineteenth century, serialization originated much earlier. In England, books of all sorts (including the Bible, John Milton's *Paradise Lost*, and *A Compleat History of Executions*) were serialized as early as the seventeenth century. Initial attempts at serializing fiction in separate parts or in periodicals emphasized short texts and/or reprinted texts. Samuel Johnson's slender novel *Rasselas*, for example, was reissued in various forms in four separate magazines—the *Edinburgh Magazine and Literary Miscellany*, the *Grand Magazine of Universal Intelligence*, the *London Magazine*, and the *Universal Magazine of Knowledge and Pleasure*—during 1759. Serializing original long fiction emerged with Tobias Smollett's *The Life and Adventures of Sir Launcelot Greaves* in the illustrated *British Magazine* between 1760 and 1761 and then in the U.S. with Jeremy Belknap's *The Foresters* in the *Columbian Magazine* between 1787 and 1788.

Despite these occasional examples, however, the serial novel did not begin to flourish until the mid-nineteenth century. Dickens's *The Posthumous Papers of the Pickwick Club* (published in twenty monthly parts, 1836–37) and Eugène Sue's *Les Mystères de Paris* (*The Mysteries of Paris*, published serially in *Journal des débats*, 1842–43) are credited with galvanizing the spread of serialization in the 1840s and 1850s in the U.S. and Europe. The French *roman feuilleton*, or serial story, inspired this international phenomenon, its influence still apparent in the Swedish term for serial, *följetonger*. Serialization's tremendous popularity in America forced more than one commentator to recant earlier defamations of the genre. A *Ladies' Magazine* editor who proclaimed in 1828 that there was not "so dull a phrase in the English language, as ... 'to be continued'" was serializing novels by the 1840s (Jan. 1828, 45). A decade later, serial novels like Harriet Beecher Stowe's *Uncle Tom's Cabin* (serialized 1851–52) became national bestsellers. Most fiction appeared in newspapers or magazines, although Dickens is a good reminder that independent monthly publications remained an option from the 1840s through the 1870s, especially in England. But the serial novel made its most significant advance in periodicals, including elite literary monthlies, middle-class family papers, and inexpensive weeklies for working-class readers that sometimes boasted circulations as high as a quarter-million. Because of this range of periodicals, the serial novel extended to readers of virtually every social class.

Early scholarship on serialization focused on its deployment by writers, many of whom were quite attentive to installment structure during the composition process. Anthony Trollope crafted parts of the same length, and Dickens specialized in cliffhanger endings that almost always corresponded with an installment break. Authors who favored the popular double- and sometimes triple-plot novel could extend readers' suspense by alternating between plots. Extended digressions from the protagonists sometimes prompted authorial apologies. After shifting the plot of *The Hidden Hand* (serialized 1859) away from the heroine Capitola for two straight weeks, E.D.E.N. Southworth commiserated with readers: "How glad I am to get back to my little Cap; for I know very well, reader, just as well as if you had told me, that you have been grumbling for two weeks for the want of Cap. But I could not help it, for, to tell the truth, I was pining after her myself" (chap. 60). Other writers fashioned installments as accompaniments to upcoming news articles and features. Readers of *All the Year Round* would have noticed a close correspondence between developments in Wilkie Collins's *The Woman in White* (serialized 1859–60) and the journal's coverage of various murder cases.

Scholars have demonstrated that the form of the installment as well as its content was not always an authorial choice. Editors frequently dictated a serial novel's appearance in a magazine or newspaper. Some editors favored the kind of craftsmanship Trollope developed, but others inserted breaks in the middle of chapters, paragraphs, sentences, and even words. In these cases, the installment unit had nothing to do with the writer's intentions; it was a matter of available columns. Other problems faced novelists publishing in periodicals. Writing in parts, especially for weekly magazines, also subjected an author to intense pressure to meet deadlines or even to an editor's presumptuous rewriting. Much to her frustration, Elizabeth Gaskell complied with Dickens's wholesale revisions to *North and South* (1854–55) when the novel was serialized in his *Household Words*.

Yet whatever assaults were waged on artistic integrity, the serial novel attracted many a literary luminary, including Mark Twain, William Dean Howells, Thackeray, Dickens, George Eliot, Gustave Flaubert, Leo Tolstoy, Fyodor Dostoyevsky, Stowe, Collins, Henry James, and Thomas Hardy. Many of these novels became sensations, as in the legendary case of Dickens's *The Old Curiosity Shop* (serialized 1840–41). So gripped were its readers that when the heroine fell sick, in the penultimate installment, thousands of fans dashed off letters to the novelist and implored him not to let Little Nell die. Upon learning that Dickens had killed her off, many were thunderstruck. Even Thomas Carlyle, who made a point of pooh-poohing Dickens's sentimentalism whenever he could, admitted to being overcome with grief at Little Nell's demise. Legend also has it that one famous Parliamentarian, having read the last chapter on the train, burst into tears and threw the book out the window, exclaiming, "He should not have killed her!" (E. Johnson, 1952, *Charles Dickens*, 1:303–4).

THE SERIAL READER

The audience's often intense engagement with serialized fiction has prompted scholars to consider the ways that readers serve as collaborators in serialization. Countless tales exist of authors changing course based on audience responses and actual sales. Dickens penned additional scenes for the inimitable Mrs. Gamp, in *Martin Chuzzlewit* (serialized 1843–44), when she proved a favorite among readers. Trollope exterminated a character in *The Last Chronicle of Barsetshire* (1866–67) because of a conversation overheard at the Athenaeum Club. Lamenting Trollope's penchant for recycling characters, two male readers expressed their worry that Mrs. Proudie, with whom they had "fallen afoul," would return in another book. Finding the conversation unbearable, Trollope walked up to the two men, introduced himself as the "culprit," and promised to "go home and kill her before the week is over" (*Autobiography*, chap. 15). And so he did. When enthusiasm and promising sales greeted Yusheng Sun's Chinese novel *Haishang fanhua meng* (1898–1903, *Dreams of Shanghai Splendor*), he expanded his initial plan for thirty chapters to sixty, and still later to a whopping one hundred (A. Des Forges, 2003, "Building Shanghai, One Page at a Time," *Journal of Asian Studies* 62: 783, 802).

Capturing the experience of these readers remains an elusive goal, but scholars have successfully characterized the readership of serial fiction. Some have documented the fact that serial reading was not limited to women, as many early critics of the form assumed. Critics working on British serials have likewise determined the changing demographics and practices of serial readers. In the 1840s and 1850s, middle-class readers tended to borrow books from circulating LIBRARIES or to buy them in monthly parts. Working-class readers, on the other hand, consumed novels in cheap magazines. Changes in newspaper and paper tax laws in 1859 and 1860 led to the creation of family magazines that appealed to the middle class, such as *All the Year Round*, *Macmillan's Magazine*, and *Cornhill*. For other periodicals, more detailed analysis of their readers is needed. Indeed, the demographics of serial readers varied considerably across different periodicals, based on class, gender, region, race and ethnicity, religion, and even profession.

The serial reader tended to imagine the novelist as far less remote than writers today are thought to be. In "A Box of Novels," Thackeray observed that installment publishing fostered a "communion between the writer and the public . . . something continual, confidential, something like personal affection" (*Fraser's Magazine*, Feb. 1844, 167). When the American novelist Ann Stephens embarked on a European trip, her "state-room was filled with bouquets . . . some from individuals to whom she was known only by her writings" (*Peterson's Magazine*, June 1850, 270). For many Victorians, the serial novel was woven into the ordinary and extraordinary moments of life. A single woman beginning Dickens's *Bleak House* in March 1852 might have been watching her first baby crawl by the time she finished the last number in August 1853. Serialized novels helped readers assuage loneliness, depression, even physical suffering. For example, the editor of *Macmillan's Magazine* recounts the apocryphal story of an old woman who, suffering from a fatal illness, "took much delight" in reading Collins's *No Name* (serialized 1862–63) during her final days. Though she was "content enough to die when the appointed time came," she whispered on her deathbed, "I am afraid, after all, I shall die without ever knowing what becomes of Magdalen Vanstone" (Dec. 1865, 156). Interweaving one's personal life with the serial's plot took place on the other side of the divide as well. At the beginning of chap. 10 of *Palaces and Prisons*, Stephens announced to her readers that "between this chapter and the last" her brother had died. She continued her narrative, explaining that, "like his young life," her work "must not be broken off in the middle" (*Peterson's*, Oct. 1849).

In addition to reinforcing the bond between reader and author, serial fiction encouraged a sense of community among readers. Unlike readers of bound novels, who proceed at different paces, readers of serial fiction must experience the narrative together, reading installments and anticipating subsequent ones as a group. The common practice of reading installments aloud among family or neighbors also bolstered the sense of reading within a community (see READING). Howells, for instance, recalled reading *Uncle Tom's Cabin* "as it came out week after week," and remarked, "I broke my heart over *Uncle Tom's Cabin*, as every one else did" (*My Literary Passions*, chap. 11).

Initial scholarship on serialization focused on literary lions such as Dickens and elite venues like *Harper's Monthly*, but the form was widespread and varied. Lesser-known novelists, such as Scottish writer David Pae and American author Southworth, dominated the field. Some authors produced more than fifty novels. Serial novels appeared in every conceivable kind of periodical: general newspapers, illustrated weeklies, women's magazines, political papers, children's periodicals, and of course literary journals. The "story papers" in America consisted almost entirely of serialized fiction and sometimes included as many as eight different serials at a time. Even more astonishing are the so-called mammoth papers, like *Brother Jonathan* and the *New World*, which offered Americans original and pirated serials in a cheap, gargantuan format, with pages upward of four feet long.

Because one could launch a periodical with relatively few resources in comparison to starting a book-publishing firm, serialization was crucial in the African American press. Martin R. Delany's *Blake: Or, the Huts of America* debuted in the *Anglo-African Magazine* in 1859, though was not completed. It was reissued to completion in the *Weekly Anglo-African* in 1861–62. Written for African American readers and published in African American-owned periodicals,

Delany's *Blake* opposed slavery vociferously, making it one of the most radical novels of its day. While white abolitionists like Stowe preferred childlike African American characters, Delany's protagonist leads an insurrection and is willing to kill those who oppose his missions. The fact that Delany's novel was not published in book form until 1970 is hardly accidental; indeed, were it not for the African American press it is hard to imagine that *Blake* would ever have been published.

1880s AND 1890s

Near the end of the century, serialization began to change, owing to the rise of newspaper syndicates in the U.S. and U.K., and in some circumstances to wane. Some magazines began to include entire novels in single issues. Others, like *Munsey's* in the U.S., pronounced the short story, not the serial novel, the "one form of literary work of which the public never has enough" (July 1893, 466). The same was true in England. In the 1880s and 1890s, new magazines like *The Strand* and *Tit-Bits* boasted of "short fiction, easily read on train or omnibus" (*Strand*, July 1891, 1). One explanation for this shift was that serialized novels became more difficult to publish when mass-market periodicals, like *Ladies' Home Journal*, began to flood the magazine industry and eclipse publications with smaller circulation rates but steadier readerships, like the *Atlantic Monthly*. The form that had attracted readers only decades before was now a liability. Editors could no longer be sure that audiences were reading their periodicals month by month. Some magazines navigated this new terrain by offering a creative hybrid of sorts. *The Strand* was lucky enough to get Arthur Conan Doyle, who, through his Sherlock Holmes stories, realigned serialization with the short story. In his autobiography, Doyle explained how he came upon the idea: "Considering these various journals with their disconnected stories, it had struck me that a single character running through a series ... would bind that reader to that particular magazine" (1924, *Memories and Adventures*, 95). His hunch was a prophesy. After the first Sherlock Holmes story, "A Scandal in Bohemia," appeared in the July 1891 issue of *The Strand*, circulation skyrocketed. When Doyle had the audacity to kill his detective two years later, many readers, some wearing black armbands, refused to read the magazine—until Holmes made his miraculous return in 1901.

1900–1970

The advent of mass-market publications cannot fully explain the serial novel's declivity in the early twentieth century. The form helped insure the success of the German periodical *Berliner Illustrirte Zeitung*, which boasted a readership of close to two million in the late 1920s and whose circulation increased by 200,000 because of a single novel, *Stud. Chem.: Helene Willfüer*, by bestselling author Vicki Baum (serialized 1928–29; L. J. King, 1988, *Best-Sellers By Design*, 12). Possible explanations for the decline of the serial novel in the U.K. and U.S. include competition from other media, like motion pictures (invented in the mid-1890s), and innovations in the novel itself. Rather than sprawling and social, early twentieth-century novels tended to be telescoped and introspective. Violent and sexual content was judged unsuitable for magazines designed mainly for family reading. Some writers, like James, found that the pursuit of psychological subtlety in their fiction made it less marketable. In 1900 the business manager of the *Atlantic*, which had serialized several of James's stories, begged

Perry Bliss, the editor, "with actual tears in his eyes, not to print another 'sinker' by James lest the *Atlantic* be thought a 'highbrow' periodical" (P. Bliss, 1935, *And Gladly Teach*, 178). The poet Evan Shipman declared serialization to be "an unnatural kind of publication for anyone with an idea of form" (L. J. Leff, *Hemingway and His Conspirators*, 90). Many modern novelists bristled at the idea of catering to what they perceived as the crass commercialism of the magazine industry.

A fascinating example of the apparent incompatibility between serialization and the modernist novel (see MODERNISM) is the magazine publication of Ernest Hemingway's *A Farewell to Arms* in 1929. By all accounts, Hemingway was ambivalent about serialization. He knew that it would give him greater visibility, but he feared that it might compromise his status as a writer and siphon off dollars from clothbound sales. This latter concern was less pronounced in the nineteenth century, since the extravagant cost of bound volumes made serialization the best means of attracting a wide audience. Because *Scribner's* was known for its "intelligent readers" and subdued use of advertising (all advertisements appeared in the back pages), Hemingway agreed to serialize the novel. He reasoned that even if his artistic integrity suffered, passages of his book would at least not jostle alongside Kotex advertisements (Leff, chap. 3). Unbeknownst to him, *Scribner's* editor censored the first installment (see CENSORSHIP). Hemingway persuaded him to use a gentler hand on the second installment, but as soon as it reached newsstands in June, the Boston superintendent of police, horrified by such words as "balls" and "cocksucker," banned *Scribner's* that month. And yet, despite these seeming incongruities between modernist fiction and serialization, the list of major novels first appearing in serial form is quite long. Joseph Conrad's *Heart of Darkness* and *Lord Jim* appeared in *Blackwood's* (1899, 1899–1900); Edith Wharton's *The House of Mirth* (1904–1905) and F. Scott Fitzgerald's *Tender Is the Night* (1934) both appeared in *Scribner's*; and most surprising of all, James Joyce's *Ulysses* was published in the *Little Review* (1918–20). This list tells us that serialization did not die in the early twentieth century, but it was no longer the polestar of years past. Once the best insurance for gaining a wide readership, serialization now became a supplement to book sales. Given the much shorter length of modernist novels, serial runs spanned a few months instead of years. Authors like Dickens once valued the opportunity serialization gave them to amend their novels to better please their audiences, but writers like Hemingway objected to such give-and-take, preferring a more detached relationship with the reader.

While serialization held lukewarm appeal for the twentieth century's most "literary" wordsmiths, it remained a mainstay for popular novelists. Romances and adventure novels appeared in the *Saturday Evening Post*, and crime novelists, including the influential Dashiell Hammett, published in pulp magazines like *Black Mask* and *Dime Detective*. Pitched at working-class male readers, who were among the publishing industry's most elusive audience, pulp magazines capitalized on crime fiction's use of suspense to sustain their readers' attention over a long serial run (see DETECTIVE). During the 1920s and 1930s, popular novelists serialized their work in tabloid papers whose literary quality was astonishingly good, like the *New York Daily News* and the *New York Daily Mirror*. These tabloids relied heavily on serial fiction. Editors commissioned guest authors to write novellas of criminal cases that the papers were currently covering. Thus Russell J. Birdwell's *Ruth Snyder's Tragedy: The Greatest True Story*

Ever Written was published weekly in the *Daily Mirror* between April and September 1927 as Snyder and her corset-salesman lover were being tried for the murder of her husband. (They both got the electric chair.)

Meanwhile the serial novel was flourishing in periodicals for the U.S.'s many immigrant populations. Serialization had been an essential part of the German, French, and Spanish press in the U.S. throughout the 1800s, but in the early twentieth century the range of languages and circulation broadened. During this period Swedish American periodicals published close to seventy serials each week, reaching nearly half a million readers. Because of the diasporic nature of immigrant populations, high circulations were possible even when the papers were published in small towns. A Norwegian-language newspaper from Decorah, Iowa, which featured a popular trilogy between 1919 and 1922, reached an estimated forty-five thousand readers by 1925, even though the town's population was only four thousand (see J. B. Wist, 2005, *Rise of Jonas Olsen*, trans. Øverland). And while Scandinavian periodicals declined in the later half of the twentieth century, during the 1960s the popularity of serial fiction in Jewish, Chinese, and other immigrant communities rivaled that of its nineteenth-century counterpart.

THE POST-1970 ERA

Since the 1970s, the serial novel has undergone a revival. Relaxed restrictions on newspaper and magazine content inspired writers to offer frank, fictionalized treatments of contemporary social problems, as Armistead Maupin did with *Tales of the City*, first serialized in the *San Francisco Chronicle* before moving to the *San Francisco Examiner* between the mid-1970s and the late 1980s. Inspired by Honoré de Balzac and Dickens, Maupin used San Francisco as a backdrop to explore a wide range of current events and social problems, including homophobia and drug addiction. The *Tales* were adapted for television and serialized in 1993, 1998, and 2001 (see ADAPTATION). Another celebrated example is Tom Wolfe's version of *Bonfire of the Vanities* for *Rolling Stone* (serialized 1984–85). Multiple plotlines, diverse characters, and a harsh look at New York's class divide made the novel ideal for serialization. Wolfe later admitted that its original publication in *Rolling Stone* provided him with the opportunity to write "a first draft in public. I have a feeling I never would have written Bonfire without it" (K. Pryor, 1990, "Serials: Making a Comeback," *Entertainment Weekly*, 16 Mar.). In the mid-1990s, *New York Newsday* hired crime novelist and reporter Soledad Santiago to write a serialized novel in order to increase the newspaper's Latino readership. The result was a sixty-four-part serial entitled *Streets of Fire* (1994), which explored the life of a Puerto Rican female cop in New York. Readers, especially women, loved the novel, and the newspaper had to create a special telephone line to handle inquiries and provide recorded plot summaries of past issues.

Within the past few years, more and more writers and editors have experimented with the serial novel. Professional and amateur novelists alike are serializing novels online via email lists. At the same time, some newspapers have turned to installment fiction as a way of boosting circulation. One editor remarked, "Many newspapers have become … almost staccato in their effect, with more news items and shorter stories. I think people quite like something more substantial to get their teeth into" (S. Ohler, 2006, "The Life and Times of the Serial Novel," *Edmonton Journal*, 8 Sept.). Between Dec. 2008 and Feb. 2009 the *Daily Telegraph* published installments of Alexander McCall Smith's *Corduroy Mansions* daily, providing free email delivery in both its written form and as audio chapters. In one of the most fascinating of these experiments, the *Los Angeles Times* published *Money Walks* over the course of twenty-eight days in Apr. 2009, with each installment written by a different author. This experiment echoes an earlier one, when in 1907–8, *Harper's Bazaar* published *The Whole Family* in twelve monthly installments, written collaboratively by twelve authors, including Howells, James, and Mary Wilkins Freeman. Readers were invited to guess the authorship of the individual chapters.

The history of serialization, including its downslides and permutations, tells us that the serial novel has tremendous resilience. While many reasons account for its indefatigability, perhaps the most important is that serialization allows for social binding; serial readers—despite whatever geographical and cultural differences separate them—are encouraged to feel that they are part of a community. As experiments in serialization keep evolving via television, the internet, and new media, serialization retains its power to create readerly communities even in a culture where the act of sustained reading, of devoting oneself to a single piece of literature and staying with it until the end, is becoming more and more of a rarity.

One place where we can still see serialization's power to create communities is in the BBC's production of classic Victorian serials in televised installments. When an adaptation of Dickens's *Bleak House* aired in the U.K. over Oct. and Nov. 2005, nearly five million television viewers, or 27 percent of the available TV audience, tuned in every Thursday and Friday night. According to Amazon.UK, sales of Dickens's *Bleak House* went up by 290 percent that October. When the show aired over a five-week period in the U.S. a few months later, audiences were equally rapturous. Stephanie Zacharek, a critic for *Salon*, commented: "For these next four Sundays, I'll be turning the pages, figuratively speaking, with many other viewers, and on Feb. 26, I'll close the cover at last. And then, instead of feeling confident that I already know the story backward and forward, I anticipate reading the novel for real—alone, as we always are with a book, and yet not alone at all" (2006, "Refuge in *Bleak House*," *Salon*.com, 4 Feb.). With a notable air of gratitude and wistfulness, Zacharek describes how the BBC series, an abbreviated approximation of the Victorian serialized novel, has reawakened in her the desire for a prolonged, absorbing interest in a story. The serialized novel may thus not be what it once was in 1852–53, when Dickens's *Bleak House* was first released to audiences in installments. But in this instance, as in others, we can see how the *dream* of it, if not always the actuality, still survives.

SEE ALSO: Illustrated Novel, Reprints.

BIBLIOGRAPHY

Brake, L. (2001), *Print in Transition, 1850–1910*.
Brantlinger, P. (1998), *Reading Lesson*.
Denning, M. (1987), *Mechanic Accents*.
Feltes, N.N. (1986), *Modes of Production of Victorian Novels*.
Hagedorn, R. (1988), "Technology and Economic Exploitation," *Wide Angle* 10(4):4–12.
Hayward, J. (1997), *Consuming Pleasures*.
Hughes, L.K. and M. Lund (1991), *Victorian Serial*.
James, L. (1963), *Fiction for the Working Man, 1830–1850*.
Johanningsmeier, C. (1997), *Fiction and the American Literary Marketplace*.
Langbauer, L. (1999), *Novels of Everyday Life*.
Law, G. (2000), *Serializing Fiction in the Victorian Press*.
Lund, M. (1993), *America's Continuing Story*.
Martin, C.A. (1994), *George Eliot's Serial Fiction*.
Mayo, R.D. (1962), *English Novel in the Magazines, 1740–1815*.
Okker, P. (2003), *Social Stories*.
Payne, D. (2005), *Reenchantment of Nineteenth-Century Fiction*.
Price, K.M. and S.B. Smith (1995), *Periodical Literature in Nineteenth-Century America*.
Queffélec, L. (1989), *Le Roman-feuilleton français au XIXe siècle*.
Wiles, R.M. (1957), *Serial Publication in England before 1750*.
Wynne, D. (2001), *Sensation Novel and the Victorian Family Magazine*.

Sexuality

DALE M. BAUER

Sexuality in novels can refer either to the history of sex (as action or being) appearing in novels or, as literary narratology has proposed, a style of sexuality displayed in novels. Characters either are sexual or act sexually, but one can also argue that plots are charged with sexuality. The difficulty in tracing sexuality in novels depends on whether one considers "sexuality" as a history (the amount of sexuality in novels) or as a theory (the possibilities of sexuality as a political praxis, of repression, or of liberation). For some theorists, sexuality is more of a discipline than a form of liberation. For others, literary sex marks a moment of confusion of normative behavior more than a reaction or rebellion (see Dollimore). Often, sexual battles are played out in novels, such as in the domain of Henry James's *The Portrait of a Lady* (1881), where Isabel Archer debates with herself about conventional marriage and liberal affect.

Michel Foucault inspired an examination of the modes by which novels would produce a new kind of sexual norm. His *History of Sexuality* included analyses of how sexuality became a source of biopower, and he offered a rejection of the "repressive hypothesis," which contended that humans had repressed their sexual desires in favor of knowledge and power. He argued, rather, that the nineteenth century introduced a new hegemony of sexuality, including one that named the self as a kind of sexual being. Foucault called "bodies and pleasures" as representative of genderless moments of resistance from the reigning power of sex-desire. This claim for the counter-discursive function of resistant pleasures may allow particular queer sexual acts to be considered oppositional practices (see Berlant and Warner). PSYCHOANALYSIS, too, influenced a literary theory that analyzed what Sigmund Freud and Jacques Lacan (among others) suggested was the symbolic nature of sexuality (see PSYCHOANALYTIC).

Histories of sexuality in novels were originally published as topical histories, like Tony Tanner's monumental study of adultery. Following Tanner, many critics charted sexual pleasure as a subversion of patriarchy or capitalism. With the rise of FEMINIST theory and QUEER studies, theorists saw the novel as a great democratic form that opened up questions about sexuality. For example, D. A. Miller and Eve Sedgwick argued that novels represent homosexuality through various modes as "between men," a theory of the novel about male homosocial relations that begins to mark the territory of erotic homosexuality. Most recently, the social critic Bruce Burgett has argued that in the nineteenth century the creation of categories such as "heterosexual" and "homosexual"—along with "Sapphist," "sexual invert," "intermediate sex," and "homogenic"—urged writers to use the terms as part of a policing of pleasure. In this light, some novels were infused with "sexology": a judgment about the "normalcy" of sexual relations and powers. As Burgett writes, "Here and elsewhere, the pressing historical question is not how 'sex' and 'race' have intersected in various historical conjunctures, but how, to what ends, and in what contexts we have come to think of the 'two' as separable in the first place"

(2005, 94). Arguments such as Burgett's have led to the examination of the confluence of these categories—along with CLASS and ethnicity (see Berlant; Haag; Horowitz).

Other critics of sexuality in the novel include Judith Roof, who argues that lesbianism was figured in "coming-out narratives" as conservative modes of queer visibility that actually reinforced the heteronormative mode of the novel. Another major critic of sexuality, Joseph Boone, incisively details how male sexualities informed narratives. Since the late 1990s, the advances of feminist and queer theory have opened up topics such as bisexuality and queer erotics, as well as public sex.

HISTORIES OF SEXUALITY IN THE NOVEL

Some of the earliest novels about sexuality concerned the use of personal desire as pleasure. "Fallen woman" fiction—like Susanna Rowson's *Charlotte Temple* (1791) and Hannah Webster Foster's *The Coquette* (1797)—included women who acted upon their sexuality only to be cast as fallen creatures who must be spiritually saved or literally killed as lessons about female desire. In Stephen Crane's *Maggie: A Girl of the Streets* (1893), Maggie dies by the end of this narrative, either having taken her own life or been killed by some attacker. In any case, Crane is careful not to take sides against Maggie, since his naturalistic tone suggests that the environment in which she lives and works may be responsible for her choices and her drift toward prostitution (see NATURALISM). By the 1920s, more and more middle-class novels, like Viña Delmar's *Bad Girl* (1928), would position female sexuality as blasé, addressing premarital sex as a way to domestic—and marital—bliss.

The representation of male sexuality in eighteenth-century novels might be said to start with Daniel Defoe's *Robinson Crusoe* (1719–22), in which *homo economicus* curbs his appetites in order to structure his own material world. Samuel Richardson's Loveless in *Clarissa* (1747–48) represents the rake as a figure of pure appetite. Henry Fielding's *Tom Jones* (1749) gives us a happier medium of male sexuality in the service of conviviality and honor.

In American fiction, Charles Brockden Brown made an early contribution to the discussion of men's and women's equality with his *Alcuin: A Dialogue* (1798). James Fenimore Cooper's Leatherstocking Tales (1823–41) document Natty Bumpo's asceticism and his polite, even diffident, relations to women. More appetitive males appear in the Southwestern tradition as witnessed in the works of William Gilmore Simms and Robert Montgomery Bird. Nathaniel Hawthorne follows the divided male self in configuring pairs like Chillingworth and Dimmesdale in *The Scarlet Letter* (1850) or Hollingsworth and Coverdale in *The Blithedale Romance* (1852). Even Holgrave in Hawthorne's *The House of the Seven Gables* (1851) has a dual sexual identity that needs to be resolved before he takes his place in the heterosexual concluding fantasy. Herman Melville's men often follow the twists of this mainstream divided logic. That division was famously codified in Leslie Fiedler's study of homoeroticism in the American novel in which he argued that pairings such as Bumpo and Chingachgook, Ishmael and Queequeg, and Huck and Jim reveal a dominant pattern in American culture where white males identify their erotics in their close relations with men of color (see Chap. 94 of *Moby-Dick*). In REALISM, we begin to see U.S. authors presenting men in their masculine fullness in Bartley Hubbard (William Dean Howells, 1885, *The Rise of Silas Lapham*) and Basil Ransom (Henry James, 1886, *The Bostonians*).

One could trace such a debate about gender roles even further back to Jane Austen's sentimental fictions. *Pride and Prejudice* (1813) argues that CLASS-based marriage and sexuality controlled by the "invisible hand" of markets conflict with an image of marriage as companionship, transcending the rules of class and status. Austen's Elizabeth Bennet and Fitzwilliam Darcy stage this debate in code-embedded rules of dancing, walking, and card playing, since these events have social rules that define how they are played, like lovemaking itself. Yet Elizabeth's blushing is an involuntary reaction, one that gives the lie to the social codes and expresses her sexual desire. By the same token, Darcy's confessions of love to Elizabeth reveal his sense of violating the market-driven pairing of his social class. A novel like Austen's poses questions to its audience about what counts as sexuality: conscious or unconscious motives, playing by social rules or giving up on all sexual rules entirely.

POPULAR FICTIONS ABOUT SEXUALITY: FROM MIDDLEBROW TO MIDDLE-CLASS DESIRE

The novel corresponded with the political and cultural arenas of the bourgeoisie in the nineteenth and early twentieth centuries. Sexuality in the novel also coincided with capitalist growth and the rise of the reading public. Sexuality in both normative and non-normative forms illustrated the relationship between public and private spheres, as well as between colonies and empires. As Nancy Armstrong has argued, the function of the novel was to form the discursive power of sexuality, particularly for the middle-class woman whose domesticity made her a powerful female subject, especially in sex relations. Armstrong contends that gendered power— particularly in DOMESTIC novels—earned women power through their represented subjectivity. For Armstrong, the female was constituted as the modern individual, a subject ready to consent to sexuality. That is, modern women gain power through their gender and class as consensual subjects. For instance, among the sixty works of nineteenth-century U.S. novelist E.D.E.N. Southworth, several, such as *The Discarded Daughter* (1852), are chronicles of domestic abuse, and *Self-Raised* (1876) illustrates what happens when one mistress denies her would-be lover sexual intercourse until after his divorce.

By the mid- to late nineteenth century, novels did not play by these rules so much as offer stories that broke those rules. Elizabeth Stoddard's *The Morgesons* (1862), for example, documents love that exceeds social rules and norms. The two women whose lives are at the central of the novel, Cassandra and Veronica, must get past dangerous health issues to consummate their marriages. Cassandra loves one brother, who must be absent from her for two years to prove he can overcome his passions, especially inebriation. Veronica's lover dies from drinking, but not before they marry and reproduce. In this way, so much about sexuality concerned what biological or biosocial issues might impair a marriage or a reproductive couple. In "social gospel" novels such as Elizabeth Stuart Phelps's *The Silent Partner* (1871), minor characters might find sex pleasurable, but the two main characters eschew their sexual possibilities to remain spinsters and thus to serve as social guides.

By the beginning of the twentieth century, there were a number of fictions published on both sides of the sexuality question, in one of the first "sex battles" of the modern era. Intellectual critics like Charlotte Perkins Gilman—called a feminist humanist in her day—wrote social-reform novels about the dangers of sexuality as pleasure, arguing instead that sexuality as reproduction was women's major contribution to sexual selection. At the same time, hundreds of New Woman novelists, in both Britain and the U.S., advocated sexual pleasure. For example, Grant Allen's *The Woman Who Did* (1895) developed ideas about free love, New Womanhood, and eugenic offspring as a result of independent and unmarried women giving birth.

Historically, the idea of sexuality as a form of a person's identity—and later as a kind of expression—took hold in modern culture. The beginning of the twentieth century inaugurated a new range of terms for sexuality, devoted to detailing a person's choice of sexual activity. By 1922, James Joyce's novel *Ulysses* opened up greater space for discussions of homosexuality or, in Molly Bloom's "yes I said yes," of sexual consent. In fact, the 1920s ushered in a Marxist-inspired debate about "sex expression" as a way out of the bourgeois restriction of sexuality. This influence of "sex expression" in literature, espoused by V. F. Calverton, made bourgeois sex regulation outdated, and instead celebrated the liberation of sexuality.

In premodern and modern texts, stories of "inversion," where one sex expressed the other gender's "qualities," were suggestive of alternative sexualities. In her exploration of inversion in *The Well of Loneliness* (1928), Radclyffe Hall contended for a new social recognition of lesbianism. As Laura Doan argues, this novel and its "insistent demand for social tolerance" was "*the* crystallizing moment in the construction of a visible modern English lesbian subculture" (xii, xiii). In Gale Wilhelm's lesbian fictions of the American 1930s, *We Still Are Drifting* (1935) and *Torchlight to Valhalla* (1938), the heroines in the first novel admit to each other's love, but they cannot deny the younger girl's parents, who want her to go on vacation with her betrothed and the mothers of the lovers. By the end, the older lover, an artist, has to say goodbye to her lover and express her sense of a "drifting" sexual life. This notion of sexual "drifting" was earlier represented in Theodore Dreiser's *Sister Carrie* (1900) and *Jennie Gerhardt* (1911), signaling "women adrift" in culture, their sexuality unconnected to domestic rites. By the 1940s, Mary McCarthy explored female sexuality in such works as *The Company She Keeps* (1942) and, twenty years later, her famous novel *The Group*. The first book is a collection of linked stories about a divorcee-in-waiting and her sexual play in a train to Nevada. The latter explores the sexual lives of six college graduates, with a focus on their gradual opening up to sexual adventures.

Nineteenth-century gay male novelists, such as Marcel Proust, André Gide, and Oscar Wilde, challenged conventional narratives of sexuality by introducing those that illustrate what Jonathan Dollimore calls the "terrifying mutability of desire" (56). By the turn of the century, masculinity enjoyed the cult of strenuousness, as espoused by President Teddy Roosevelt. His fear of "race suicide" influenced a number of American realists to write about a middle-class masculinity and reproductivity. An *élan vital* about masculinity was soon to be compromised by the experience of WWI, most notably in F. Scott Fitzgerald's *The Great Gatsby* (1925) and Ernest Hemingway's *The Sun Also Rises* (1926). Indeed, through the 1930s beleaguered American males seldom found vital expression, and were often seen as diminished by historical circumstances. Examples of such men are Charley Anderson in John Dos Passos's *U.S.A.* (1930–36) and Tom Joad in John Steinbeck's *The Grapes of Wrath* (1939).

It remained for Richard Wright to imagine Bigger Thomas in *Native Son* (1940), whose full-fledged racialized sexuality demanded punishment. Ralph Ellison's *Invisible Man* (1947) narrates Truman Blood's rape of his daughter to signify fear of black male sexuality. Through the 1950s and 1960s, in works like Sloan Wilson's *The Man in the Gray Flannel Suit* (1955) and Richard Yates's *Revolutionary Road* (1961), men have to find accommodation in a corporate world, where exertions of will are usually squashed. Perhaps the three most influential U.S. novelists in the post-WWII era—Saul Bellow, John Updike, and Philip Roth—have put the assertion of male sexuality and its complexities at the very center of their career-long projects.

SEXUALITY AS IDENTITY

Eventually, sexuality became part of the multivalent ways of identifying one's self. Other interstices of human identity—such as RACE, ethnicity, CLASS, RELIGION, and DISABILITY—helped to sharpen the notion of the privilege of one's sexuality or its alternative debility in a culture that promoted an essential heterosexuality. Second-wave feminists argued for sexual liberation, and their novels did the same: Pat Barker's *Blow Your House Down* (1984) details the sexuality of England's prostitutes, a sexual emotion that often leaves them feeling more for each other than for any heteronormative arrangement. Barker's language is key to her commitment to sexuality as a crucial marker of identity: her heroines are lodged in sexual capitalism, but they find themselves more in their female communities and lesbianism than in making money through sex. Later, QUEER fiction would become legion. In this context, the role of the Naiad Press's commitment to the lesbian novel from the 1970s to the 1990s cannot be underestimated. Twentieth-century gay male fiction, such as John Rechy's *City of Night* (1963) and Colm Tóibín's *The Master* (2004), glorified the new visibility of gay sexuality and the revisions of history about queer passions.

Thus, the history of sexuality in novels can be traced from early versions of eighteenth-century seduction novels to twentieth-century challenging fictions like Kathy Acker's *Blood and Guts in High School* (1984). GRAPHIC novels treat sexuality across the spectrum of responses: *Stuck Rubber Baby* (1995), by Howard Cruse, is a coming-out narrative/memoir about the civil rights movement in the South; *Potential* (1999), written by Ariel Schrag when she was in high school, is about queer sexuality and educational institutions; *Blankets* (2003), by Craig Thompson, is a straight romance that addresses teen sexuality, religion, disability, and childhood sexual abuse.

Alison Bechdel's *Fun Home* (2006), a graphic novel/memoir, has a rich historical dimension. A girl's father is closeted after WWII. His repression is a palpable vestige in the girl's life, especially after he walks in front of a truck and is killed. This death occurs right after the girl has confessed to her parents that she came out in college. Bechdel, the cartoonist of *Dykes to Watch Out For* (1986), took seven years to write and draw *Fun Home* because of the care she took in illustrating the historical difference between her father's gay identity and her own.

One might say that any narrative that changes the "Reader, I married him" plot (this from Charlotte Brontë's *Jane Eyre*, 1847) has its own sexuality—it resists the normative marriage plot. Plots that suggest a narrative challenge to normative sexuality might be called resisting fictions. In the twenty-first century, critics have addressed sexuality in novels through episodes, moments where sex, race, or class have worked together to change ideas of sexuality, such as during abolition and emancipation in the U.S., or in the "sex wars" of the 1980s and 1990s.

SEE ALSO: Gender Theory, Queer Novel

BIBLIOGRAPHY

Armstrong, N. (1987), *Desire and Domestic Fiction*.
Bechdel, A. (2006), *Fun Home*.
Berlant, L. and M. Warner (1998), "Sex in Public," *Critical Inquiry* 24(2):547–66.
Boone, J. (1998), *Libidinal Currents*.
Burgett, B. (2005), "On the Mormon Question," *American Quarterly* 57:75–102.
Burgett, B. (2007), "Sex," in *Keywords for American Cultural Studies*.
Doan, L. (2001), *Fashioning Sapphism*.
Dollimore, J. (2001), *Sex, Literature and Censorship*.
Fielder, L. (1960), *Love and Death in the American Novel*.
Foucault, M. (1990), *History of Sexuality*.
Haag, P. (1999), *Consent*.
Horowitz, H.L. (2003), *Rereading Sex*.
Miller, D.A. (1988), *The Novel and the Police*.
Sedgwick, E.K. (1985), *Between Men*.
Sedgwick, E.K. (1990), *Epistemology of the Closet*.
Tanner, T. (1981), *Adultery in the Novel*.

Shōsetsu see Japan
Simile *see* Figurative Language and Cognition
Siuzhet see Formalism; Narrative Structure
Socialist Realist Novel *see* Russia (20th Century)
Sosŏl see Korea

South Asia

CHELVA KANAGANAYAKAM

As a category within the larger corpus of postcolonial literature, the South Asian novel has become increasingly significant in the past few decades, particularly in the West. In general terms, the corpus refers to fiction written by all writers whose origins can be traced to South Asia. It would, for instance, include writers from the Caribbean, the Fiji Islands, South Africa, Malaysia, and Singapore who were part of the Indian and Sri Lankan diaspora from the eighteenth to the early part of the twentieth century.

Writers such as V. S. Naipaul (Trinidad) and K. S. Maniam (Malaysia), for example, would be considered part of this larger corpus. Apart from the fact that such a classification becomes too unwieldy for critical analysis, it is hardly possible to arrive at anything resembling a conceptual frame while dealing with such multiplicity. For the purpose of the present entry, the term "South Asian" refers to novels written by authors who either live in South Asia or are a part of the recent diaspora from South Asia. While there is a significant body of fiction written in various South Asian languages such as Hindi, Marathi, Tamil, and so forth, the present entry focuses specifically on novels written in English.

The South Asian novel, then, brings together the work of authors who are often identified nationally rather than regionally (see NATIONAL). Indian, Sri Lankan, Pakistani, and Bangladeshi authors, for example, make up the majority of this body. Some of them left their countries after independence, and are now part of the diaspora. Referring to them as a composite group has both advantages and obvious problems. In historical terms, India and Sri Lanka have had a long colonial history. Their literary traditions in English go back to the nineteenth century, if not earlier. Pakistan came into existence in 1947 with the partition of India. Bangladesh is of more recent origin in that it was created when East Pakistan broke away from West Pakistan in 1971. Diasporic authors from South Asia now live in various metropolitan cities, such as London, New York, and Toronto, and while they are often identified in relation to their hyphenated status, they too are very much a part of this corpus. Their novels have, for the most part, insistently located themselves in their ancestral lands, and that alone brings them within the fold of South Asian literature. The frame that encloses all these authors is a common Indian origin, although Sri Lankan migration goes back too far to be a natural fit. The divisions are often based on RELIGION, ethnicity, and NATIONAL history. South Asian novels do have a family resemblance, but even while one asserts commonalities, one should be aware of striking differences. Religion and secularism are useful markers to establish intersections, although any generalization tends to quickly become a simplification.

Unlike writing from the Caribbean, these various literatures have no clear originary moment or historical context to connect them. Apart from the chronological disjunctures that separate one nation from another, the novels produced by these authors are far too diverse in relation to thematic focus to fit easily in any mold. At some level it might be more meaningful to trace their literary histories nationally rather than regionally (see REGIONAL). A South Asian literary history remains a daunting task. Diasporic writing, one might argue, functions within its own discursive framework, although these texts too tend to fall naturally into national models. It is possible to assert that the experience of exile forms a common thread in all South Asian diasporic novels, but that does not completely overshadow national or hyphenated affiliations.

That said, it might be possible to claim that the South Asian novel in English has not been, for the most part, anticolonial in its orientation. Even the novels that were written in the decades immediately before or after independence do not concern themselves with colonialism or with the struggle for freedom. A case in point is G. V. Desani's groundbreaking novel *All About H. Hatterr* (1948), which, despite its date of publication, has very little to do with anticolonial struggle in India. To say this is not to deny that novels written during this time do not entirely eschew nationalist concerns. Raja Rao's famous work *Kanthapura* (1938) is about a village transformed by Mahatma

Gandhi's (1869–1948) nonviolent struggle against the British. The politics of colonialism is not totally absent from South Asian fiction, but it remains marginal to the overall body of literature.

The reasons for this lacuna are not entirely clear, since anticolonial struggle in India and Sri Lanka has a long and illustrious history. The reluctance among authors writing in English to focus on this struggle could well have something to do with the particular trajectory of colonial history in South Asia. Although English was introduced to India long before the nineteenth century, it was really in the first half of the nineteenth century that English came to be foregrounded as the language of governance, and an elaborate system of education in English was created by the East India Company. The famous Minute of Thomas Macaulay (1800–59) produced a class of people whose nationalist aspirations were combined with a commitment to the values of modernity. Although acts of resistance against the British gathered momentum in the twentieth century, there was also a measure of accommodation that made anticolonial sentiments less intense than in other parts of the world. This particular ambivalence, together with other factors, may have shaped literary history in ways that were not especially anticolonial. When South Asian authors began to write in the 1930s, the end of colonialism was already in sight and modernity had blunted the force of anticolonial sentiment.

While modernity is a central element in the South Asian novel, it is also true that any conceptual framework for understanding this corpus needs to acknowledge the presence of an ontology that has been shaped by RELIGION. If there is one element that distinguishes the South Asian novel as a whole, that would be its religiosity. The South Asian novel is not overtly religious, however, in that gods and temples do not figure prominently in fiction. Apart from Raja Rao's *The Serpent and the Rope* (1960) and a few other novels, one might be hard pressed to find texts that are overtly concerned with religion. But the majority of novels are framed by a religious sensibility in that a religious ontology forms a subtext in this writing. The social and cultural dimension of religion is quite central to the South Asian novel. The precolonial world in South Asia was shaped by religion in that the temple, in the medieval period, became a node for organizing social and economic structures. Relations among people at the level of family and community were determined by the presence of the temple and its conventions of purity and pollution. All aspects of human life were organized in relation to the temple, although the social connections were not always apparent or fully acknowledged. A temple-based culture is very different from a culture that is fundamentally religious. It is the former that remains a strong presence in shaping the ethos of the South Asian novel. Religiosity takes different forms, depending on context and national or diasporic affiliation, but it continues to exert a powerful influence. Contrary to the assumptions of Orientalist thought, what is central to South Asia and its literature is not institutionalized religion but a particular way of life that is framed by religion. Although Hinduism may have triggered this particular kind of religiosity, the presence of religion can be traced to the novel in Pakistan and Sri Lanka as well.

Colonialism brought with it ideas of modernity, secularism, democracy, liberalism, and so forth. While these were central to South Asian society, the precolonial ontology was never entirely erased. The precolonial survived and coexisted with modernity. It is the combination of these two that one encounters most often in the South Asian novel. Depending on circumstances, the emphasis could fall on different events and historical conditions, but often the texture of the novels accommodates a combination of the precolonial religious ontology and the British secular worldview. The phrase "tradition and modernity" has often been used to define much postcolonial fiction, but in South Asia it takes on a complex role. That said, each nation evolved its own literary history, with India being the dominant player in South Asian fiction.

INDIA

Serious writing in English in India began in the 1930s, although it is possible to claim that *Rajmohan's Wife*, written in 1864, was the first novel. The novels of the latter part of the nineteenth century and the early part of the twentieth were often imitative, and while they are of historical interest, they do not come across as significant writing. The one exception might be the novella *Sultana's Dream*, which appeared in 1905. Closer to a short story than a novel in its length, it demonstrates a control over form and a preoccupation with gender that are remarkable for the time.

After this the actual originary moment in the Indian novel was in the 1930s with the work of Raja Rao, R. K. Narayan, and Mulk Raj Anand. The three authors represent three different strands in the Indian novel, with Rao expressing the mystical, religious dimension, Narayan the fusion of the religious and the secular, and Anand the downtrodden and the subaltern. All three authors' first novels appeared in the 1930s—Rao's *Kanthapura* in 1938, Narayan's *Swami and Friends: A Novel of Malgudi* in 1935, and Anand's *Untouchable* in 1933. All three continued to write novels for the next five decades, and they remained the pioneers of the Indian novel. Rao's frame of reference is deeply religious and mystical, and his major work, *The Serpent and the Rope* (1960),

demonstrates a deep engagement with what it means to be a Hindu. Although the novel concerns itself with exile and hybridity, the major thrust is to establish the idea of Indianness as fundamentally religious and mystical. Of particular interest is the preface that Rao wrote for *Kanthapura*, which remains a precise statement about the distinctiveness of South Asian writing and the role of authors in expressing a different sensibility. Narayan, in most of his novels, focused on his imagined town called Malgudi, a place where the secular world of colonialism coexisted and sometimes collided with religion. His vision was benign, and he paved the way for a whole group of writers who molded his style to suit their own purposes. A more recent novel such as Kiran Desai's *Hullaballoo in the Guava Orchard* (1998) is a direct descendant of the Narayan mode of social comedy. Anand was more insistently a social critic, and his novels are often a strong indictment of caste and class in Indian society. He too has been deeply influential in shaping a particular strand of the Indian novel. Many of the recent novels that focus on marginalized groups can be considered direct descendants of the Anand mode.

The next phase in the Indian novel begins with the Partition of India, an event that involved violence on an unimaginable scale. On the eve of independence, the animosity between Hindus and Muslims became increasingly pronounced, resulting in widespread violence and the displacement of millions of people. Among the novels that were written about this moment, the best known is Khushwant Singh's *Train to Pakistan* (1956), a short but powerful work about the polarization of a once-peaceful village along religious lines. The conflict itself has continued to preoccupy novelists, and even a more recent novel such as the Pakistani writer Bapsi Sidhwa's *Cracking India* (1991), first published under the title *Ice-Candy Man* in 1988, is concerned with the complexity and violence of the Partition.

The one anomaly in a chronology of the Indian novel is the 1948 publication of G. V. Desani's *All About H. Hatterr*, a wonderfully irreverent and comic text that deals with the life of an Anglo-Indian who decides to "go native." The style of the book is decidedly modernist, and his work is probably closer than that of any other Indian novelist to the spirit of James Joyce (see MODERNISM). Written very much along the lines of a PICARESQUE work, this novel remained almost unnoticed until the 1980s. Arguably a major work, it had no followers until Salman Rushdie picked up Desani's style in 1980.

The three decades that followed the Partition were a period of exciting activity, with a number of writers carving out their own areas of interest but mainly concerned with issues of social dislocation, personal identity, political instability, and so forth. The worlds they created are largely secular and ostensibly modernist, but a religious sensibility informs their work. The best-known writer of this period is possibly Anita Desai, whose novels combine an awareness of social and political conditions with a deep understanding of psychological concerns. Her *Clear Light of Day* (1980), for instance, is at once about the breakup of a family and about class, religion, and the role of MYTHOLOGY in personal and collective lives (see DOMESTIC). Kamala Markandaya is equally important, and her more overt realism in novels such as *Nectar in a Sieve* (1954) deals with the collapse of traditional ways of life and the gradual migration of people to the cities. Ruth Prawer Jhabvala's *Heat and Dust* (1975) won the Booker Prize and remains a major work that deals with issues of identity and exile that are germane to Indian writing. A quest novel of

sorts, it embraces the colonial and post-colonial in remarkable ways.

The watershed moment in the South Asian novel occurred in 1981 with the publication of Salman Rushdie's *Midnight's Children*. A diasporic author, he produced with this novel a very different mode of literary representation. Not only is he overtly political and quite radical in his novel, he produced a work that was far more self-conscious and skeptical about grand narratives than anything written before. Rushdie has been a shaping influence for many writers, and even those who choose not to adopt his experimental style are much more sensitive to the difficulty of asserting absolute truths about nations or groups. With Rushdie, the South Asian novel became much more cosmopolitan, political, and experimental. In the post-1980 phase there is a much greater preoccupation with "public" events.

The period from Rushdie to the publication of Arundhati Roy's *The God of Small Things* (1997) forms another distinctive phase in the Indian novel. This period saw the rise of the international novel, with Indian authors being published and receiving recognition in the West. The more significant writers of this period include Allan Sealy, Amit Chaudhuri, Upamanyu Chatterjee, and Vikram Seth (see PUBLISHING). All these writers have their own styles, from the picaresque mode of Sealy to the Victorian triple-decker mode of Seth. Sealy's *The Trotter-Nama* (1990) is probably the first major novel after *All About H. Hatterr* to focus its narrative on the history of Indo-Anglians. Seth's *A Suitable Boy* (1993) goes back to the mode of nineteenth-century realism but shapes it to capture to multiplicity of India in the 1950s. Chaudhuri is among the finest of contemporary writers, and his *Afternoon Raag* (1993) has a lyrical and subtle texture that is distinctive. This was one of the most productive periods for Indian authors, both local and diasporic, and the work they produced is as impressive for its range as it is for its depth and complexity.

Roy's *The God of Small Things* is clearly a product of the Rushdie phase, but the novel goes a step further in that it combines irreverence and comedy with a real concern for exploring alternative social and cultural structures. If Rushdie's intention is to take things apart, Roy is more concerned with picking up the fragments and putting them back together in a different way. Many of the recent writers, again local and diasporic, have demonstrated a similar stance.

The burgeoning of the Indian novel is now best seen in the West, where a number of major authors live and write. Among the best-known authors, Rushdie, Amitav Ghosh, Manil Suri, Anita Desai, Rohinton Mistry, Shashi Tharoor, David Davidar, Suniti Namjoshi, Jhumpa Lahiri, and Bharathi Mukherjee have been prolific. All are important in their own right, and the novels they produce do not conform easily to any model. It is possible to argue that their distance, spatially and temporally, from India has given them a particular perspective. In general—and this can be seen very clearly in Ghosh's *The Hungry Tide* (2005) and Kiran Desai's *The Inheritance of Loss* (2006)—there is skepticism about grand narratives and a desire to look at historical forces from the perspective of the downtrodden and the marginalized. *The Hungry Tide* is a fine example of the kind of work that shows a deep commitment to understanding the lives of the downtrodden while moving beyond tendentious writing. Particularly among diasporic Indian authors, the quest novel has become increasingly common. There is clearly a distinction between the conventional realism of Mistry and the overt experiment of Namjoshi, but in general the thrust has been to create complex structures that would enable

a depiction of "home" and belonging from a diasporic perspective. Namjoshi occupies a unique niche in having chosen a fabulist mode that is deceptively simple. Her *Conversations of Cow* (1992) is a short but impressive novel that reads like a children's story but deals with complex issues of sexuality, migration, and religion.

Contrary to expectations, second-generation novelists who were born in the West or grew up there have chosen, for the most part, to write about an imagined India rather than the world that is most familiar to them. While the reasons for this decision may well be complex, the fact is that they gravitate naturally to the world that they have heard about rather than the one they have experienced. Lahiri's *The Namesake* (2003) is not entirely set in India, but its preoccupations remain very Indian. Padma Viswanathan's *The Toss of a Lemon* (2008) is a more typical case in point; Viswanathan goes back to the history of a family of Brahmins in South India. The sensibility that informs these authors' work is subtly different from that of the first-generation authors, but they too insist on seeing the old world from a new perspective.

SRI LANKA

Compared to Indian writing, the Sri Lankan novel is smaller in scope. The beginning of this corpus can be traced to the 1930s, but it really came into its own in the 1960s with the work of James Goonewardene, Punyakante Wijenaike, and Rajah Proctor. The first two have been particularly prolific, and novels such as Goonewardene's *A Quiet Place* (1968) and Wijenaike's *The Waiting Earth* (1966) continue to be read. In retrospect, however, the novels of the 1960s appear to be essentialist in their constant recourse to the rural world as a source of strength and beauty. The novels of this period are competent, but they do not convey a sense of authenticity. It was after the Insurgency of 1971 that the Sri Lankan novel came into its own, with several authors finding a new niche for their novels. The ethnic conflict between the Tamils and the Sinhalese which intensified in the 1980s added a further dimension of uncertainty and urgency to literature, with the consequence that several authors now produced a number of complex novels. Rajiva Wijesinha, Carl Muller, and Tissa Abeysekara are probably the best-known novelists who wrote from Sri Lanka. Wijesinha is easily the most experimental of the three, but all of them have written with a strong sense of a changing era. The majority of Sri Lankan novelists are part of the diaspora.

Among diasporic authors, the best known are Romesh Gunesekera and A. Sivanandan (England), Michael Ondaatje and Shyam Selvadurai (Canada), and Chandani Lokuge (Australia). Gunesekera's *Heaven's Edge* (2002), one of his finest works, not only explores the mindless violence in Sri Lanka but also demonstrates the difficulties of writing about this world with objectivity and accuracy. Equally political, Selvadurai's *Funny Boy* (1994) was acclaimed in the West for its frank and valuable treatment of both politics and sexuality. Predominantly a realist, Lokuge, in novels such as *Turtle Nest* (2003), writes about the experience of exile and the emotional consequences of return. Sivanandan's single novel, *When Memory Dies* (1997), brings together several generations to explore the complex path that led to the conflict between the Tamils and the Sinhalese.

The best-known Sri Lankan novelist is Michael Ondaatje, whose *The English Patient* won the Booker Prize in 1992. In *Anil's Ghost* (2000) he locates the narrative in a turbulent period of recent Sri Lankan history. A remarkable narrative about mindless violence and repression in Sri Lanka, Ondaatje's novel, despite all its pes-

simism, is framed by a commitment to a Buddhist vision. Like the Indian diasporic novel, Sri Lankan fiction continues to be preoccupied with politics, although notions of belonging and dislocation figure prominently. If some form of Hindu thought and ontology shapes much of Indian fiction, it is equally true that Buddhism frames much of Sri Lankan literature. In that sense, many of the recent novels that are ostensibly about politics are shaped by a sense of religion.

PAKISTAN

The notion of Pakistani writing is not easy to chart, particularly because some of the early writers lived in India before moving to Pakistan after the Partition. That said, among the early works Ahmed Ali's *Twilight in Delhi* (1940) is significant for its range and depth. It is the first novel to deal with Muslim life in colonial India with real sensitivity. Adam Zameenzad is another writer whose works combine formal experiment (see FORMALISM) with a real concern for the conditions in Pakistan. During its first three decades, however, Pakistan did not produce much fiction in English. This could well be a consequence of a national policy that established Urdu as the sole official language. In addition, Pakistan's political history has been very different from India's, and that might well explain the relative paucity of literary production specifically in the novel in English. While writing from Pakistan has begun to flourish in recent years, the majority of Anglophone novels by Pakistani writers are written in the diaspora.

The most accomplished writer from the earlier phase is Zulfikar Ghose, whose *The Murder of Aziz Khan* (1967) is set in Pakistan during the early days of independence. Many of his subsequent novels have been set in South America, although the subject matter appears to suggest that the reality of Pakistan is not far from his mind. Bapsi Sidhwa's novels are more centrally concerned with Pakistan, although she tends to look at this world from the perspective of the Parsi community. She is best known for her novel *Ice-Candy Man*, a powerful novel about the violence of the Partition, told through the perspective of a young Parsi girl. Another writer of note is Tariq Ali (England), whose *Shadows of the Pomegranate Tree* (1992) is a moving evocation of Muslim Spain, told through the intersecting lives of several characters.

In the last two decades the novel from Pakistan has experienced a growth spurt, and now there is a substantial corpus that can be considered significant. Hanif Kureishi's *The Buddha of Suburbia* (1990) provides a sensitive and sometimes disturbing depiction of the South Asian experience in England. More recently, several diasporic authors from Pakistan have published notable works, each one distinctive in its own way, but all concerned with issues of nationalism, belonging, marginality, and the representation of Pakistan. Politics continues to play a dominant role in Pakistani writing, although it is woven into the lives of a broad spectrum of characters. Kamila Shamsie's *Kartography* (2002), Nadeem Aslam's *Maps for Lost Lovers* (2004), Mohsin Hamid's *The Reluctant Fundamentalist* (2007), and Mohammed Hanif's *A Case of Exploding Mangoes* (2008) provide a good sampling of contemporary Pakistani fiction. Many of these have been controversial, but all of them are significant works that attempt to grapple with the local conditions and international profile of Pakistan.

BANGLADESH

Bangladesh has been relatively slow in its literary output. The only author to gain international recognition is Monica Ali, whose *Brick Lane* (2003) created considerable controversy over its depiction of Bangladeshis in London.

As a corpus, the South Asian novel in English has now become increasingly visible in South Asia and in the West. The increase in readership has resulted in greater sophistication and range among authors, and there is a much greater acceptance of this body of writing in South Asia than ever before. Within the broad framework of contemporary or postcolonial fiction, the South Asian novel remains distinctive in its evocation of a particular ontology.

SEE ALSO: Ancient Narratives of South Asia, Comparativism.

BIBLIOGRAPHY

Gopal, P. (2009), *Indian English Novel*.
Kanaganayakam, C. (2002), *Counterrealism in Indo-Anglian Fiction*.
Mukherjee, M. (1971), *Twice Born Fiction*.
Paranjape, M. (2000), *Towards a Poetics of the Indian English Novel*.
Rahman, T. (1991), *History of Pakistani Literature in English*.
Salgado, M. (2007), *Writing Sri Lanka*.

Southeast Asian Archipelago

RAZIF BAHARI

The Southeast Asian novel has come to be regarded as a problematic category, and justifiably so. Questions of critically representing and talking about the Southeast Asian novel have to ineluctably negotiate a series of issues relating to insider/outsider binaries of SPACE, perspective, voice, and representation that trouble the languages of literary creation and criticism. What constitutes a Southeast Asian novel: one written about or set in Southeast Asia, or one written by a Southeast Asian (with all the complexities that that appellation entails)? If we agree on the former, then works such as C. J. Koch's *The Year of Living Dangerously* (1978), Anthony Burgess's *The Malayan Trilogy* (1972), and Noel Barber's *Tanamera: A Novel of Singapore* (1981) would fall under the Southeast Asian category. It is unlikely that any one formulation will do justice to the longstanding concern about who and what should be regarded as Southeast Asian; therefore, when from time to time reference is made to the Southeast Asian novel, this is simply by way of shorthand to mark off writing by Southeast Asians—specifically from the maritime Southeast Asian nations of Indonesia, Singapore, and the Philippines, as well as Malaysia—from that by non-Southeast Asians. Two other nation-states in the region, Brunei and Timor-Leste, are not discussed in this entry as they do not have autonomous traditions in the novel.

Although a Western form, the novel in the Southeast Asian archipelago is by no means a direct and unmitigated borrowing from the West but is the product of a long and varied ancestry. The genesis of the novel in the archipelago has been traced to traditional literary forms that have existed in both local and REGIONAL literatures of the area. The HISTORY of the novel in Indonesia traces the moment of its birth to the late nineteenth and early twentieth centuries and identifies the Javanese *pakem* or prose summaries of shadow-play stories, travelogues, and novelistic literature in Dutch, Chinese, and Malay languages as its literary progenitors (Quinn). In Malaysia, the novel is regarded as an extension and transformation of the *hikayat* (a traditional form of Malay epic written in prose and verse) that has existed since the early seventeenth century (Wahab Ali), while in the Philippines it

is said to have developed from the nineteenth-century metrical romance known as the *awit* and *corrido*, moral tracts written in narrative form, and beyond these, the *pasyon*, or religious epic depicting the passion of Jesus Christ, in the eighteenth century as well as folk narrative traditions going back to pre-Spanish times (Kintanar).

The critical move toward local adaptation, cultural re-creation, and indigenized use of the novelistic genre cannot be ignored in any account of the genesis of the novel in Southeast Asia. Though European in origin, the novel, even early on, has shown its own practice of appropriation with recognizably "postcolonial" textual tactics of hybridized performance: the fusion of native orature and primordial mythology with the stylistic protocols of a new Western discursive GENRE. Indeed, the novel was shaped by the material and ideational changes associated with the rise of print technology, secular education, and contact with European sources, as much as it was, as Wahab Ali contends, a manifestation of "local response to these phenomena and how they were understood and imitated" (261).

RESPONDING TO MODERNITY

The idea of the modern, as contrasting or interacting with the traditional, is firmly embedded in the Southeast Asian novel. This is evidenced by early novels addressing the culture clash during the colonial period, e.g., Indonesian writers Merari Siregar's *Azab dan Sengsara* (1920, Torment and Misery) and Marah Roesli's *Sitti Noerbaja*; Malaysia's Ahmad Rashid Talu's *Iakah Salmah?* (1929, Is It Salmah?); and Filipino nationalist José Rizal's *Noli Me Tangere* (1887, Touch Me Not) and its sequel, *El Filibusterismo* (1891, The Filibustering). In these works, the collision of Western values with traditional ones is depicted through tracing the development and experiences of particular individual characters who personify the polarities of cultural authenticity and the rejection of traditional communalism. Extraordinary individuals set the tone of some early novels, and it is possible to see the significance and the pivotal position of the individual as a signifier of the core of ideas relating to modernity (see MODERNISM). This affirmation of individuality—in the form of exceptional individuals who stood apart from the masses and had a clearer vision: the nationalist revolutionary, the iconoclast, the educated reformer who gave voice to the hopes of those who were unable to articulate a different political future— both reflects and facilitates the transformation of other values relating to, for example, authority and community, national consciousness, and freedom of the individual.

The emphasis on characterization is thus expressive of the novelist's general orientation to the extent to which the traditional has been permeated by the modern. It must be said, of course, that the novel is hardly a neutral medium in this regard. As a Western literary form, the novel was shaped by the material and ideational changes associated with the rise of capitalism and Western form of education which privileged the individual over society. Yet in the hands of pioneering Southeast Asian novelists such as Rizal, Merari, and Ahmad, it proved adaptable enough to the needs of presenting a different consciousness. The tendency to acclaim characters that are pulled both ways—seen as representative of the masses, adhering in large part to traditional ideas and values and often rooted in village life or at least retaining rural ties, on the one hand; on the other, as fierce critics of their indigenous culture and defiant of tradition, cosmopolitan and unconventional, whose outlook is shaped by being brought up in the capital cities of Europe and being given a privileged education—became a stock-in-trade for these early novels. The elevation of the individual, however, need not involve any wholesale rejection of tradition-bound social practices and customary law or a continued communal consciousness. Though the rise of individualism in Southeast Asia seems to suggest an openness to modernity, the novelistic response to other forms of modernity has been more divided and has involved considerable hesitancy and ambivalence (Teeuw).

The city is a symbol of the modern, counterpoised to the village with its old-established rhythms and customs, and the dichotomy between the two is evident, for example, in Singaporeans Lim Boon Keng's *Tragedies of Eastern Life* (1927), Goh Poh Seng's *If We Dream Too Long* (1972), Filipino F. Sionil Jose's *My Brother, My Executioner* (1973), Indonesian Toha Mohtar's *Pulang* (1958, Homeward), and Malaysians A. Samad Said's *Salina* (1961, Salina) and Shahnon Ahmad's *Rentong* (1965, *Rope of Ash*). In these novels, the city is represented as the zone of contact between the old Southeast Asia and the world outside, as the hub of those processes of change concerned with revolution, commodity, and cultural exchange, or as the primary site of infection of the barren, exploitative, and depersonalized nature of modern life. Rural enclaves, on the other hand, remain a storehouse of indigenous spiritual sensibilities and traditional communalism. Recognition of the city as a fact of contemporary Southeast Asian life does not necessarily involve an emotional acceptance; in fact many of the narratives are resistant. Time and time again, as in the novels of Jose and Shahnon, we find a preference for the individual who has clung to his or her cultural roots, who is at home or yearns to be at home in the village, and whose strength is derived from connectedness with the past. If there is some duality in a character's makeup—elements of the traditional and elements of the modern, of the simple and the sophisticated, of the country and the city—invariably it is the former that are privileged.

The question of Southeast Asia's response to modernity, of how and in what ways a merger could be negotiated between the traditional and the modern, though incidental to the novels' main themes, continues to play out in East Kalimantan author Korrie Layun Rampan's *Api, Awan, Asap* (1998, Fire, Cloud, Smoke), Filipino Bienvenido Santos's *The Praying Man* (1982), Malaysian Abdul Talib Mohd Hassan's *Saga* (1976, Saga), and Singaporean Isa Kamari's *Memeluk Gerhana* (2007, Embrace the Eclipse). The picture that emerges from these novels is not so much a portrait of development as a collage of the conditions of urban life, deracination, displacement, breakdown of traditional values and social units, the human dislocation of structural change. Yet their more enduring value lies in their implicit endorsement of a modern future while at the same time insisting that the past must not be discarded, forced out by the juggernaut of modern technology and processes. The traditional and the modern are not seen as binary opposites but as shading into each other, even organically linked. Nor are they seen as separated in time but as existing contemporaneously. The clash between the indigenous and the foreign worlds is present, but so is the idea that modernization does not mean Westernization, nor should it take place under the tutelage of the West.

The literary response to modernity in Southeast Asian novels is arguably historically and culturally conditioned, though history and culture themselves are not separate and self-contained worlds. Clearly, over time socioeconomic developments intersect with culture. The emergence of the novel in Southeast Asia was, after all, itself the result of developments in education and technology and changing social relationships. It is certainly true that the evolution of the novel in Southeast Asia was responsive to the processes of social and economic change that had taken root. As a result of, e.g., the spread of globalization, the movement of people across national boundaries, and the wider circulation of ideas about modernity and development, the Southeast Asian novel has come increasingly to reckon with the individual grappling with this phenomenon. Instead of characters being the embodiment of their societies, we see them moving between different social worlds, usually struggling to arrive at some accommodation between them. The diasporic writings of Tash Aw, Shirley Lim, Fiona Cheong, Dewi Anggraeni, and Bienvenido Santos, for example, are representative of this dilemma, which brings to our attention individuals situated in the crossfire of cultural exchange, and hence emplaces debates about the negotiation of difference.

MAKING SENSE OF THE PAST

The Southeast Asian novel's characteristic concern with the past must be contextualized against the history of colonialism in the archipelago. For a century or more Southeast Asians had played little part in shaping the dominant ideas about themselves and the archipelago. Colonial evaluations had deeply permeated Asian consciousness—European literature, historical accounts, and political thought of the time rendered the natives as peoples without significant intellectual or cultural attainment. They were told they had no history. Given this imposed heritage, the Southeast Asian novel became an instrument of correction and a means of self-affirmation (Hooker; Martinez-Sicat). From its earliest days, the novel has been seen as a way of recovering a sense of self, expressing the hopes of decolonization, and imagining alternative futures. For reasons both of personal emancipation and social responsibility, Southeast Asian writers took upon themselves the task of undermining European representations of their respective peoples and establishing new ones. Led by writers such as Sutan Takdir Alisjahbana, Pramoedya Ananta Toer, and Mochtar Lubis in Indonesia; Lazaro Francisco, F. Sionil Jose, and Nick Joaquin in the Philippines; Ishak Haji Muhammad, Lee Kok Liang, and Lloyd Fernando in Malaysia; and Harun Aminurrashid in Singapore, the novelists became historians, anthropologists, and sociologists, as well as fabulists, in order to reclaim a national identity.

The nub of the novel's engagement with the past lies in the novelist's presentation of history as a space within which to search for meaning, open up new ways of seeing and patterning, and posit suggestive connections between then and now. This may be done by revisiting the past in the form of conventional realistic fiction—as is the case in Utuy Tatang Sontani's *Tambera* (1949), Harun Aminurrashid's *Panglima Awang* (1958, Commander Awang), Abdul Kadir Adabi's *Acuman Mahkota* (1988, Lure of the Crown), and Edilberto K. Tiempo's *More than Conquerors* (1964). Alternatively, it may take the form of presenting the past through symbols, cultural fragments, or personal remembrances conveyed as metafiction, pastiche, parody, irony, and other such characteristics associated with the postmodern—as in Y. B. Mangunwijaya's *Durga/Umayi* (1991), Eka Kurniawan's *Cantik itu Luka* (2002, Beauty Is a Wound), Faisal Tehrani's *1515* (2003), and Eric Gamalinda's *Empire of Memory* (1992) (see PARODY).

Characteristically, there is a felt need among some Southeast Asian novelists to draw on the past and show how it infuses the present, certain in their belief that narrative could propose an alternative social world to those which had existed or which now exist. On a postcolonial account, the process of retelling the colonial encounter from a counter-hegemonic standpoint undermines the constructs of Western universalism and creates a space within which previously subordinate peoples of the archipelago can take control of their own destinies (Razif). The reinterpretation of the past is crucial to Pramoedya Ananta Toer's purposes in his novels *Bumi Manusia* (1980, This earth of mankind), *Anak Semua Bangsa* (1980, Child of all nations), *Jejak Langkah* (1985, Footsteps), and *Rumah Kaca* (1988, House of glass), collectively known as the Buru Tetralogy. Pramoedya depicts the past both directly through authorial commentary and by means of the remembrances and reflection of his characters. In *Bumi Manusia*, for example, Minke's narration is interspersed with accounts (in the form of retelling, letters, and court testimony) by other characters modeled after figures from fin-de-siècle East Indies history, which gives a kind of interconnected fragments of narration within narrations of Indonesia's colonial history, much of it sharpened by recollections of his own involvement in the struggle both against Dutch colonialism and Javanese feudalism. Pramoedya's narrative starkly depicts the dangers of representing the past in the kind of essentialized terms that could be appropriated by a new imperium as bad as the old. His twin targets are feudalism and colonialism, and the one tends to reinforce the other. He is also concerned with highlighting elements of Indonesian culture received through history which he believes must be swept away if Indonesians are ever to be free. More than any other Indonesian writer, he sees the past as a mixed inheritance that can be deployed in very different ways. In this respect, Pramoedya's tetralogy is revelatory.

THE ISSUE OF LANGUAGE

There has been some debate about how far Southeast Asian novels in English are representative of the totality of Southeast Asian fiction, and also about whether they are less "authentic" than novels written in Bahasa Indonesia, Malay, Tagalog, or other indigenous languages. A fundamental site of contention concerns the nature and politics of language as resistance. The case for writing in the vernacular is framed in terms of resistance to the outside, commonality on the inside. By embracing a sense of relatedness, recognizing some elements of a shared past, and espousing values taken to be characteristically autochthonous—which writing in the indigenous language is perceived as epitomizing—the vernacular novel serves as a renewed instrument of affirmation against an imposed imperialist tradition and the colonial language that is its medium. In part this draws on the belief that the liberation from colonial domination presupposes liberation from the colonial language. There is also the stigma attached to the English language in the post-independence era as a neo-imperialist global language and that it is the language of a Western educated elite (see NATIONAL, REGIONAL).

The problematic status of English in the Philippines, Malaysia, and Singapore can be traced to their respective colonial legacies. Indonesia, which, as Benedict Anderson observes, was the only major exception in the overall imposition of the colonial language as the language of state in the colonial empires, never had a native modern literature in Dutch. The Dutch did not institutionalize the language of the metropole in its colony. On the contrary, Dutch colonial language policy has been one of racist segregation. The natives of the East Indies were forbidden to use the Dutch language for fear that—to use the words of a Dutch teacher of the time—Dutch education was "likely to increase the misdeeds of the natives. They will be less obedient because they are more acquainted with the norms and the way of life of the white man" (Ahmat, 76). Instead, Malay (the lingua franca of traders throughout the archipelago since as early as the seventh century) was adopted by the natives as the new national language and later, in 1928, named Bahasa Indonesia, or "the language of Indonesia." It was this language that was developed and became the primary literary medium in Indonesia.

The English language occupies an ambivalent place in Malaysia. Introduced by British colonial presence at the turn of the nineteenth century, English represented, for a long time, the language of the ex-colonizer, and is even now regarded as the language of Western capitalism. Though it is seen in its omnipresence as the international language of modernity, it was subsumed by the Malay language (nationalistically renamed Bahasa Malaysia, or "Malaysian language") which was, and still is, privileged by the state narratives as a key element in constituting Malaysian-ness in the postcolonial era (after 1957). One line of thinking that promotes the ideal of a postcolonial Malaysian consciousness derives primarily from a kind of reverse discrimination in the literary sphere, broadly coterminous with policies in the political and sociocultural domains. This is the demand that Malaysian writing should have a Malaysian (read: Malay) content, a Malay(sian) form, and be judged by distinctively Malay(sian) criteria. In addition, it is sometimes argued that for a work to come within the canon of Malaysian literature it must be written by a Malay, be committed to a political vision—even a particular ethnocentric vision—of Malaysia's future, and be written in the Malay language. This privileging of Bahasa Malaysia creates, as Quayum intimates, a "prevailing cleavage between Malaysia's national literature, written in the national language of Bahasa Malaysia, and those dubbed as 'sectional literatures,' written in its minority languages such as Chinese, Tamil and English" (1960, 2). It is emblematic of this cleavage that the recipients of the *Anugerah Sasterawan Negara* (National Literary Laureate award), conferred by the Malaysian government since 1981, have all been Malays writing in the Malay language. The hostile political attitude toward English, regarded as an "alien" language, "rooted neither in the soul nor in the soil" (Quayum, xii), bore serious implications for Malaysian writers like K. S. Maniam, Lloyd Fernando, and Lee Kok Liang, whose choice of English as their medium of expression meant, *ipso facto*, that their work would never be admitted into the Malaysian literary canon. Such views, although extreme, suggest a tendency in Malay(sian) texts to cultivate the distinctively Malay-(sian) and insulate the Malay(sian) experience from its intra- and international milieus.

In the Philippines, English became the medium of instruction in schools and communication among the populace when the Philippine Commonwealth became an American colony (1901–41). It subsumed Filipino, the national language (based on Tagalog, a dialect spoken by those who live in the capital city, Manila, and its immediate surrounds), in terms of prevalence. Though there is a strong tradition of novels written in the major vernaculars such as Tagalog, Hiligaynon, Cebuano, and Illocano—e.g., the early Tagalog novels of Lope K. Santos, such as *Banaag at Sikat* (1901, From Early Dawn to First Light), hailed as a milestone in the development of the socially conscious Tagalog novel, and Faustino Aguilar's broadside of the clergy's hypocrisy in *Busabos ng Palad* (1909, Slaves of Circumstance), Tagalog itself is often seen as a hegemonic construct of the nation-state, privileging those who reside in the seat of economic and political power in the capital. Consequently, as Philip Holden argues, "English

remained, partly because speakers of regional languages in the Philippines preferred the neutrality of English to what they perceived as the hegemony of Tagalog-based Filipino" (161). There has been some debate about how far this body of literature in English is representative of the totality of Filipino fiction, and also about whether it is less "authentic" than novels written in Tagalog, Illocano, or other indigenous languages. While these issues cannot be pursued here, it is useful to note that fiction written in the regional languages exceeds that in English in the Philippines. Novelists whose writings in English have been awarded the Magsaysay Award—Asia's equivalent of the Nobel Prize—for literature, include Nick Joaquin, F. Sionil Jose, and Bienvenido Lumbera. Works by a younger generation of novelists writing in English who have achieved prominence, such as Charlson Ong, Krip Yuson, Jose Dalisay, Vicente Groyon, and Dean Francis Alfar, also deserve a mention here.

The existence of important novelists writing in the ethnic vernacular languages in Singapore—the likes of Isa Kamari, Suratman Markasan, Rohani Din, and Peter Augustine Goh (Malay); Soon Ai-Ling, Yeng Pway Ngon, Huai Ying, and Wong Meng Voon (Mandarin); and Ma Elangkannan, Rama Kannabiran, Mu Su Kurusamy, and S. S. Sharma (Tamil)—seems to dislodge the notion that Singaporean writing is dominated by fiction in English, and in fact fosters an appreciation of the nation's vibrant, multiple cultural constitution. Despite ethnic literature's unique status as a repository for the otherwise forgotten and neglected realms of inwardness, sensuousness, cultural mooring, historicity, memory, and ethnic solidarity, there are valid concerns expressed by the writers themselves of the difficulties they faced in achieving recognition locally and at large, winning readerships and wider publication, and funding their own labors. Indeed, the fractured community of its writers is exemplary of the general experience of neglect, prejudice, lack of sustainable audience, and the short shrift given to them by international publishers experienced by writers writing in the local vernaculars. In part, this can be attributed to the language situation in Singapore, where English has become an entrenched lingua franca used by its multiethnic society of Chinese, Malay, Indian, and other communities. This is due to the colonial policy pertaining to the use of English, first adopted by the East India Company and later direct British colonial rule, as well as the post-independence government's introduction of English-medium education since the 1980s. Though English is officially promoted as "a language facilitating trade and technological development," and invested with a sense of social prestige—an attitude that stems from the fact that, historically, the English language (with its colonial origin) has functioned as a tool of power, domination, and elitist identity—it is not considered a language of "cultural belonging" (Holden, 161). In fact, an early generation of English-language writers struggled with their elite status. On the one hand, they were "identified with a colonialist heritage," being seen and indeed seeing themselves at times as "working in a second tongue, alien from Asian identity," and yet they also strove, through English, to connect with Asian literary traditions (Lim, 2002, 48). A policy of bilingualism introduced in schools from the 1960s—which privileges English as the "first language," and the study of Chinese (Mandarin), Malay, or Tamil, now termed mother tongues, and deemed crucial to the preservation of "traditional values," as a "second language"—has produced a new crop of writers more proficient in English than their own mother tongues. The works of contemporary Singapore writers such as Catherine Lim, Suchen Christine Lim, Philip Jeyaretnam, and Hwee Hwee Tan, while exposing the dead ends and the circularities of this postcolonial condition, and touching so profoundly upon many of the salient contemporary artistic and political issues—issues of identity and indifference, self and other, alterity and conformity, public and private—is thus best described as a kind of "postmodern realism" of present-day Singapore.

BIBLIOGRAPHY

Adam, A.B. (1995), *The Vernacular Press and the Emergence of Modern Indonesian Consciousness*.

Anderson, B. (1991), *Imagined Communities*.

Foulcher, K., and T. Day, eds. (2002), *Clearing a Space*.

Hau, C.S. (2000), *Necessary Fictions*.

Holden, P. (2008), "Colonialism's Goblins," *Journal of Postcolonial Writing* 44:159–70.

Hooker, V.M. (2000), *Writing a New Society*.

Kintanar, T.B. (1990), "Tracing the Rizal Tradition in the Filipino Novel," *Tenggara* 25:80–91.

Lim, S. (1991), "Malaysia and Singapore," in *Commonwealth Novel since 1960*, ed. B. King.

Lim, S. (2002), "The English-Language Writer in Singapore," in *Singapore Literature in English*, ed. M. A. Quayum and P. Wicks.

Martinez-Sicat, M.T. (1994), *Imagining the Nation in Four Philippine Novels*.

Quayum, M.A. (2006), "On a Journey Homeward," *Postcolonial Text* 2(4):13.

Quinn, G. (1992), *Novel in Javanese*.

Razif Bahari (2007), "Piecing the Past," in *Pramoedya Postcolonially*.

Singh, K., ed. (1998), *Interlogue: Vol. 1: Fiction*.

Teeuw, A. (1967), *Modern Indonesian Literature*.

Wahab Ali, A. (1991), *Emergence of the Novel in Modern Indonesian and Malaysian Literature*.

Southeast Asian Mainland

DAVID SMYTH

Mainland Southeast Asia refers to the countries of Burma, Thailand, Laos, Cambodia, and Vietnam. The national language of each is written in its own distinctive script, and with the exception of Thai and Lao, which are closely related, they are mutually unintelligible. In the past these countries have often been at war with one another and, even today, many citizens of the region have grown up with attitudes of indifference, suspicion, or hostility toward the countries which border their own. TRANSLATIONS of novels from one Southeast Asian language to another are almost nonexistent; the novel has developed separately in each of the five countries, responding to literary influences from outside the region more than from within.

There are, however, some similarities to be observed across the region, especially in the patterns of literary production, distribution, and consumption. Before the twentieth century the literature of most of mainland Southeast Asia was generally composed in verse, recorded by hand on palm-leaf manuscripts, and transmitted by oral recitation. The huge technological and social advances that took place in Europe during the nineteenth century spread quickly to the countries of mainland Southeast Asia and helped to create the environment in which the novel emerged. The capital cities grew rapidly, trade increased, and internal communication routes improved; the arrival of printing technology paved the way for the birth of JOURNALISM and print capitalism (see PAPER AND PRINT); educational expansion created a reading public and a new middle CLASS with the money and leisure to be able to afford newspapers, magazines, and books; and foreign novels, read by an elite minority in the original language, were then translated or adapted into the local language. When daily newspapers began to appear in the early decades of the twentieth century, a significant number of pages each day were devoted to serialized novels, and the majority of readers bought newspapers to find out what was happening in the more immediate fictional world rather than in the distant real world. The SERIALIZATION of novels in newspapers and magazines remains widespread in the twenty-first century, sometimes followed by publication in book format (see PUBLISHING).

The demand for new fiction in the early years of the newspaper created opportunities for aspiring writers. When newspapers became less reliant on fiction, many writers switched from fiction to journalism, political commentary, and EDITING. Making a living exclusively from writing fiction has always been difficult. Today, the financial rewards tend to lie in writing serialized novels for bestselling women's magazines, or film and television scripts. The market for "serious" fiction remains small and confined largely to the national capitals. Print runs, even for an established writer, are typically between two and three thousand copies, and with publishers often unwilling to risk reprinting, many books disappear after the first edition (see REPRINTS). Even the works of nationally recognized authors can be unobtainable for years before a publisher feels that a reissue might be financially viable, and with few public LIBRARIES in the region, can become almost impossible to track down. Some enterprising writers publish and distribute their own works, both to keep them in print and to maximize their own financial gain.

Thailand (formerly Siam) is the only country in mainland Southeast Asia to have escaped colonial rule by a European power. Nevertheless, the early HISTORY of the novel in Thailand reflects a strong British influence. In the 1890s Thai aristocrats who had recently returned from their studies in England founded the first literary magazines. It was in the pages of one of these magazines, in 1901, that Thais were introduced to the novel genre through *Khwam phayabat*, a serialized translation of Marie Corelli's *Vendetta* (1886). During the first two decades of the century translations and adaptations of the works of Western writers, including those by Alexander Dumas, H. Rider Haggard, Anthony Hope, A. Conan Doyle, and Sax Rohmer, were popular. The first original Thai novel was *Khwam mai phayabat* (Non-vendetta), a lengthy work of more than seven hundred pages, written by "Nai Samran" (Luang Wilat Pariwat) in 1915.

In the early 1920s silent foreign serial films had an impact on the novel. Writers were hired by cinema owners to write "film books" which explained the plots of the weekly episodes to cinemagoers and provided translations of the onscreen inter-title dialogues (see ADAPTATION). Producing these cheap paperbacks provided authors with experience in writing for a commercial market, but also awakened them to the possibilities of creative writing, unconstrained by the limitations of events unfolding on screen. Many went on to make a name for themselves among the first generation of Thai novelists. The film books also encouraged the public in the habit of buying and reading books.

By the late 1920s popular taste in reading had shifted away from translations and adaptations of Western fiction to original Thai stories. Most popular were romantic tales with a realistic, contemporary setting, where the hero and heroine faced some obstacle to their love, be it disapproving parents, prearranged marriage to another person, or a difference in social status (see ROMANCE, REALISM). Such themes recur throughout mainland Southeast Asian fiction. In the next decade novels that commented on wider social issues appeared. Siburapha used the correspondence between the hero and the heroine in the EPISTOLARY novel *Songkhram chiwit* (1932, The war of life) to portray social injustice, religious hypocrisy, corruption, and inadequate health care. Ko' Surangkhanang's *Ying khon chua* (1937, The Prostitute) dealt

with a controversial subject for a female author. Her sympathetic portrayal of the plight of prostitutes and her criticism of polite society's double standards created a considerable stir.

During the liberal climate of the early post-WWII years, a small number of writers, of whom Siburapha was the most famous, wrote MARXIST-influenced "literature for life" which aimed to highlight injustice and point the way forward to a fairer society. Their efforts were short-lived, and several were imprisoned in 1952 in a government purge of suspected communists. One of Thailand's most famous and popular novels, *Si phaen din* (1953, Four Reigns), appeared in the wake of this clampdown on progressive intellectuals. The author, M. R. Khukrit Pramoj, was a staunch royalist and drew on his own personal familiarity with palace life to provide a nostalgic portrayal of traditional court culture.

The 1970s were a turbulent period in the country's history. At the beginning of the decade the radical fiction of the 1950s was rediscovered and played a part in politicizing the student movement which toppled the military dictatorship in 1973. A violent military backlash in 1976 followed and heralded a brief dark age for writers and publishers. But by the 1980s, "literature for life" had had its day: society had become more complex, the political climate less oppressive, and the reading public more demanding. The country's most acclaimed contemporary writer, Chart Korbjitti, made his debut at this time, and while in works such as *Chon trok* (1980, No Way Out) and *Kham phiphaksa* (1981, The Judgment) he movingly portrays the plight of the disadvantaged and socially excluded, he does not preach an overt political message.

Burma, to the west of Thailand, was under British colonial rule from 1886 to 1948. The first important Burmese novelist was U Lat, whose novels *Sabe-bin* (1912,

Jasmine) and *Shwei-pyi-zo* (1914, Ruler of the Golden City) deal with the preservation of traditional Burmese values. They are written in an ornate, traditional style of language and represent a transition stage in the development of Burmese fiction. P. Monin adopted a more natural, economical style in *Bi-ei Maung Tint-hnin Ka-gyei-the Me Myint* (1915, Maung Tint B.A. and the Dancer Me Myint), which is regarded as the first "modern" Burmese novel. In the 1930s, as writers began to focus more on social issues, Thein Pe Myint created an outrage with his novel *Tet Hpon-gyi* (1937, The Modern Monk), which highlighted the sexual activities of monks.

In 1962 General Ne Win (1911–2002) staged the military coup that set the country on its isolationist "Burmese Path to Socialism." Writers were expected to play their part in the socialist revolution by producing works that glorified the triumph of peasants and workers over various hardships. Literary prizes were the potential reward for those who produced works of "socialist realism," imprisonment the potential fate of those who did not. Ma Ma Lay, author of *Mon-ywei mahu* (1955, Not Out of Hate) and modern Burma's most important female writer, was one of the many writers imprisoned by the regime. In 1988, massive rioting against the military regime, in which thousands of pro-democracy demonstrators died, led to Ne Win's resignation. But the military quickly reasserted its authority and has since maintained strict control over all forms of printed media, including literature.

To the east of Thailand lie Vietnam, Cambodia, and Laos, once collectively known in the West as French Indochina. Vietnam was invaded by the French in 1858 and became a French protectorate in 1884. The French colonial regime replaced the traditional character-based writing system with *quốc ngữ'*, a romanized system of writing devised by Catholic missionaries in the

seventeenth century. It was promoted in schools and newspapers, and because it was much easier to learn, it quickly became accepted. The new script, and a new generation of readers and writers who had passed through the French colonial education system and been exposed to French literature, were important factors in the process of literary modernization that began in the early years of the twentieth century. The first modern Vietnamese novels appeared in the South in 1910.

The polarization in Vietnam caused by thirty years of war (1945–75) and more than twenty years of partition (1954–75) is reflected in the country's literature. In the U.S.-supported South, writers enjoyed a degree of freedom to express their opinions, be they anticommunist sentiments, criticisms of the government, or portrayals of social upheavals brought by the intensifying war and the presence of large numbers of American soldiers in the country. In the Chinese/Soviet-supported North, the Communist Party required writers to spread the government's vision of a socialist future, which included the defeat of the foreign aggressors and the reunification of the country. For many writers who had wholeheartedly written stories glorifying the wartime struggle and sacrifices, peace brought with it a sense of disillusionment at the compromises that officially sanctioned literature demanded. But in 1986, in the wake of the liberalizing *glasnost* policy in the Soviet Union, the government introduced the *đổi mới* (renovation) program of political, economic, and cultural reforms that heralded a more liberal era. Established writers such as Lê Minh Khuê and Duong Thu Huong were able to broaden the scope of their work, while the freer climate saw the emergence of writers such as Nguyễn Huy Thiệp, Hồ Anh Thái-, and Phạm Thị Hoài-, whose works often reflect a disappointment with a postwar society that falls short of its heroic self-image. But even under *đổi mới* liberalization, there are unwritten boundaries beyond which a writer should not venture. Duong Thu Huong, author of *Tiểu Tuyết Vô Đề* (1991, Novel without a Name), has paid a heavy price for challenging those boundaries: her work is now banned in her native country, and she has been harassed, arrested, and subjected to travel restrictions.

Cambodia, once the center of an empire whose influence spread over much of mainland South East Asia from the tenth to the thirteenth centuries, was a French protectorate from 1863 until 1953. The first Cambodian novel, *Sophat* (1941, Sophat), by Rim Kin, appeared at a time when Cambodian printed material of any kind was very limited. Nou Hach is the most highly regarded of early Cambodian novelists for his novels *Phkā srabon* (1949, The Faded Flower), which attacks the convention of arranged marriages, and *Mālā ṭuoń citt* (1972, The Garland of the Heart), which portrays Cambodian society during WWII. He is assumed to be one of more than a million Cambodian citizens who died during the murderous Pol Pot period (1975–78). Kong Boun Chhoeun, whose works first appeared in the late 1950s, is one of very few Cambodian writers to have survived the Pol Pot years. Following the Vietnamese invasion of Cambodia in 1978 and the establishment of a new Vietnamese-backed Cambodian government, he and other writers produced state-published novels which portrayed the brutality of the Khmer Rouge and Cambodian—Vietnamese solidarity. Following the withdrawal of Vietnamese troops in 1989 and the move to a market economy, writers began to enjoy greater individual freedom.

From 1883 until 1953 Laos was a French colony. In 1963 the communist Pathet Lao movement launched an armed struggle against the constitutional monarchy, plunging the country into a decade of civil war and partition. Lao prose fiction dates back only

as far as the 1960s. Some writers aimed simply to entertain, while others were influenced by the spread of socially conscious literature in neighboring Thailand, and used fiction to criticize the corruption and moral decadence of the government. In areas of the country that were under the control of the Pathet Lao, revolutionary literature that celebrated the people's struggle against the Americans who heavily bombed the country—and the American-backed regime in Vientiane, was written under Party guidelines. After the Pathet Lao emerged victorious in 1975, Lao writers, like those in Vietnam, were expected to glorify the successful revolutionary struggle. In the late 1980s Laos, like Vietnam, saw the introduction of a liberalizing policy, the "New Imagination," which—within unwritten limits—permitted Lao writers to make constructive criticisms of government policy.

SEE ALSO: Historical Novel, Ideology, National Literature.

BIBLIOGRAPHY

Kratz, E.U., ed. (1996), *Southeast Asian Languages and Literatures*.
Lafont, P.-B. and D. Lombard, eds. (1974), *Littératures contemporaines de l'Asie du sud-est*.
Smyth, D., ed. (2000), *Canon in Southeast Asian Literatures*.
Smyth, D., ed. (2009), *Southeast Asian Writers*.
Tham Seong Chee, ed. (1981), *Literature and Society in Southeast Asia*.

Southeastern Europe
TATJANA ALEKSIĆ

Southeastern Europe is better known as the Balkans, although this name has historically been problematized and often acquired negative connotations. Maria Todorova's seminal study on the Balkans, *Imagining the Balkans* (1997), has, for example, analyzed both the category itself and the various negative connotations assigned to the region. The region is imagined as a more or less compact entity due to historical developments that marked it, primarily the Ottoman colonization, but also the many episodes of turbulent history since the formation of modern nation-states. Cultural development in the region that has, for the most part, been a polygon of conflicts for the world powers, has suffered a certain dose of "belatedness" relative to European mainstream influences, as Gregory Jusdanis controversially claims about modern Greek culture in *Belated Modernity and Aesthetic Culture* (1991). Most importantly, culture in the Balkans has rarely had the luxury of avoiding the grip of history and evolving with independent aesthetic attributes. The few periods of relatively unhindered literary and cultural developments created a sense of time compression that sometimes prevented literary styles that had almost run parallel courses from maturing to their full distinction.

With many nation-states comprising the region, the number of which has multiplied since the breakup of Yugoslavia in 1991, an attempt to give a general overview of the development of the novel seems an almost impossible task. There have been many arguments for and against the Serbo-Croatian linguistic designation, as well as attempts by nationalist linguists to emphasize the differences between Serbian and Croatian languages (see NATIONAL, REGIONAL). This entry will not emphasize the question of language, but will instead focus on both Yugoslav and post-Yugoslav literatures. In terms of its temporal arc, this discussion will be delineated by the appearance of the first modernist and avant-garde novels. The overview begins with the innovations in the field of poetics, language, and the subject of the novel,

followed by early attempts to dismantle the genre altogether. Geographically, it is concerned with what for most of the twentieth century existed as the Yugoslav cultural space, Greece, and to a certain extent Bulgaria. Finally, this typology follows certain historical frameworks.

FIRST MODERNIST NOVELS

Symbolism that spills over from the nineteenth century transfers to prose some of the key tenets of MODERNISM, primarily the interest in the individual psyche and its subjective vision of the world. One of its important representatives in Greek fiction is Konstandinos Hatzopoulos, with *O pyrgos tou akropotamou* (1909, *The Manor by the Riverside*). Milutin Cihlar Nehajev introduces the character novel *Bijeg* (1909, *Escape*) to the Croatian public, the text not generated by external events but entirely situated within the psyche of the main protagonist. The year 1910 marks the appearance of the first truly modern Serbian novel, *Nečista krv* (*Bad Blood*) by Borisav Stanković, which breaks with the mimetic prose of the nineteenth century and instead introduces the symbolic style in which local folklore and tradition become a background for passionate love dramas and family tragedies.

The contrast between the city and the country emerges in the work of some writers in the form of folkloric realism or idealization of the country, its people, and their morals, while with others it leads to the creation of the first urban novels. Milutin Uskoković's *Čedomir Ilić* (1914) makes a statement on the alienation and psychological decay in the emerging Serbian bourgeois culture that became decadent even before fully maturing. His *Došljaci* (1909, Newcomers) explores the common subject of the time in the Balkans—the difficulties and moral qualms of the peasants newly arrived in the fledgling city. But the text also uncovers many poetic aspects of the new urban environment, presenting Belgrade as the true capital of Serbian culture of the time. Rapidly mutating social setting is the subject of Konstandinos Theotokis's novel *Oi sklavoi sta desma tous* (1922, Slaves in Their Chains), while others include Andreas Karkavitsas, Grigorios Xenopoulos, and Ioannis Kondylakis. However, perhaps the most radical representation of this schizophrenic condition on the societal level is Janko Polić Kamov's *Isušena kaljuža* (1909, pub. 1957, Dried Swamp). In this novel, social critique takes the form of exposing a whole spectrum of immorality, perversions, and absurdity— a veritable bestiary of the repressed psyche of the Croatian bourgeoisie. Ksaver Šandor Đalski establishes the tradition of the Croatian political novel with *U noći* (1913, In the Night). The champion of Slovenian independence, Ivan Cankar, published his social novels *Na klancu* (On the Hill) and *Hiša Marije Pomočnice* (The Ward of Our Lady of Mercy) in 1902 and 1904, respectively. In Bulgaria, the authors scathingly critical of the Sofya urban environment are Anton Strashimirov, with *Esenni dni* (1902, Autumn Days), and Georgi Stamatov.

THE INTERWAR NOVEL: WAR, SOCIAL REALISM, AND PSYCHOANALYSIS

The end of the Balkan Wars (1912–13 and 1913, respectively) and WWI saw the collapse of the two former empires occupying most of the peninsula and the emergence of new independent states. Croatia gained independence from Austro-Hungarian dominance and joined the Kingdom of Slovenes, Croats, and Serbs in 1918, the precursor of Yugoslavia. However, while the period 1941–91 in the cultures of Serbs and Croats is generally treated as the period of Yugoslav literary production, the two literatures still figure as separate entities in the interwar period. Since the breakup of the country, revisionist literary history tends to separate the authors on the basis of their nationality. This approach creates difficulty due to the fact that the majority of authors disregarded ethnic boundaries and many authors are appropriated by two, or even three, national traditions (e.g., Ivo Andrić is claimed by the Bosnian as well as the Serbian and Croatian traditions). A pivotal event in Greek history of the period was the 1922 collapse of the Megali Idea (the Great Idea) of the "liberation" of former Byzantine territories occupied by the Ottomans since 1453, resulting in the war and "population exchange" of over a million Orthodox and Muslim refugees between Greece and Turkey.

Writing in the interwar period is influenced by European modernism, and the themes that dominate the novel are those of the "lost generation" of modernists everywhere. The dissatisfaction with the order of the world is transferred onto the subjective sphere, which in the language of fiction translates into experimentation with the genre and language, as well as genuine attempts to deconstruct the novel.

Isidora Sekulić is one of very few Serbian women writers of the period whose work is considered to inhabit the space outside "trivial literature," with her *Đakon Bogorodičine crkve* (1919, The Novice of Notre Dame). Influenced by Zenithism, the only authentic avant-garde movement in the Balkans, new voices in Serbian prose attempted to deconstruct or completely annihilate the genre of the novel with their "anti-novels": *77 samoubica* (1923, 77 Suicides) by Ve Poljanski and *Koren vida* (1928, The Root of Vision) and *Bez mere* (1928, Without Measure) by the surrealists Aleksandar Vučo and Marko Ristić, respectively.

The experience of war lies at the core of the interwar novel. *Dnevnik o Čarnojeviću* (1921, The Diary about Čarnojević), by Miloš Crnjanski, and *Dan šesti* (1932, Day Six), by Rastko Petrović, are considered the greatest achievements of Serbian interwar novelistic prose, written in innovative technique and grounded in the new philosophical and psychological trends, where the war represents the background for individual interrogations. Best known for the first part of his historical saga *Seobe* (1929, *Migrations*), it is in *Dnevnik* that Crnjanski achieves his highest lyrical expression in the form of fragmentary meditations. In *Dan šesti* Petrović depicts the unimaginable moral deterioration of human character in wartime that he witnessed firsthand. In Bulgaria the effects of war are covered in Yordan Yovkov's masterpiece, *Zemlyatsi* (1915, Countrymen), and in Greece in Stratis Myrivilis's gripping and meditative *I zoi en tafo* (1924, *Life in the Tomb*). Ilias Venezis, in *To noumero 31328* (1924, Number 31328), like Stratis Doukas in *Istoria enos aihmalotou* (1929, *A Prisoner of War's Story*), presents a semibiographical account of the situation of Anatolian Greeks in the months following the 1922 Disaster. Croatian literature of the period offers few direct reactions to the war, possibly because the Croatian nation's experience of WWI differed so much from that of the other Balkan states. Instead, we should note a few pieces of prose expressionism: the existential-psychological drama *Sablasti* (1917, Ghosts), by Ulderiko Donadini, and the visually rich dream-fantasy *Lunar* (1921), by Josip Kulundžić.

The interwar period in Greece is most emphatically marked by the "generation of the 1930s," or the true Greek avant-garde. Although Yorgos Theotokas called for a break with the past and the creation of a new type of fiction in his "manifesto" *Eleftihero pnevma* (1929, *Free Spirit*), the "generation of the 30s" is much better known for its poetry than prose. Three distinctive thematic divisions are recognizable: the "Aeolian School" of the writers concerned with the war, the new "urban realism," and "School of Thessaloniki" antirealist modernism (Beaton, 1988). Kosmas Politis's *Lemonodasos* (1930, Lemon Grove) and Angelos Terzakis's *Desmotes* (1932, Prisoners) belong to the urban category. Most of their texts deal with the deprivations of the proletarian classes and the immorality of the bourgeoisie, as well as the burgeoning leftist sentiment.

Social thematic, or "social realism," on the Serbo-Croatian scene produces a new type of literary hero, a member of the deprived Croatian social classes, in the novels of Vjekoslav Majer, or in the texts of leftist inclination, such as August Cesarec's *Careva kraljevina* (1925, Emperor's Kingdom). Ivan Dončević and the rare woman novelist Fedy Martinčić also belong to this circle. *Krv majke zemlje* (1935, Mother Earth's Blood) by Antun Bonifačić is of interest as the first Croatian novel employing metafictional documentation. Among Serbian novels of the urban/social thematic the three dominant ones are Anđelko Krstić's *Trajan* (1932), Branimir Ćosić's *Pokošeno polje* (1933, Reaped Field), and the joint work of Dušan Matić and Aleksandar Vučo, *Gluho doba* (1940, Deaf Times).

The writing of the antirealist modernists is primarily concerned with the psychological reflection of the dysfunctional world perceived as a spectrum of disorders, hallucinations, and nightmares. In Greece the most successful modernist experiments are Yannis Skarimbas's *To solo tou Figaro* (1938, Figaro's Solo), Politis's *Eroica* (1937), Nikos Gavrii Pentzikis's *O pethamenos kai i anastasi* (1938, The Dead Man and the Resurrection), and Melpo Axioti's *Thelete na horepsoume Maria?* (1940, Would You Like to Dance, Maria?). Miroslav Krleža, one of the foremost Croatian writers and an advocate of nonideological literature, produced his psychological masterpiece, *Povratak Filipa Latinovića* (*The Return of Filip Latinovitz*), in 1932, his sociopsychological drama *Na rubu pameti* (*On the Edge of Reason*) in 1938, and his *Banket u Blitvi* (*Banquet in Blitva*), tackling anarchism and terrorism, in 1939. *Španski zid* (1930, Spanish Wall), by Rade Drainac, and *Grozdanin kikot* (1927, Grozdana's giggle), by Hamza Humo, belong to this category of Serbian prewar literature. Strashimirov's *Robi* (1930, Slaves) is a Bulgarian work of this kind.

THE POSTWAR NOVEL: (SOCIALIST) REALISM

The fifteen years after WWII are characterized by a recurrence of realist fiction, even produced by writers of radically different positions in the previous decade. However, the first novels published in both Yugoslavia and Greece are historical: Ivo Andrić's *Na Drini ćuprija* (1945, *The Bridge on the Drina*), which won the Nobel Prize for literature in 1961, and Nikos Kazantzakis's *Vios Kai Politeia Tou Alexi Zorba* (1946, *The Life and Times of Alexis Zorbas*). Their early prose carries a distinct epic quality with a local flavor, as Andrić writes about Bosnia in his other historical piece, *Travnička hronika* (1945, *The Bosnian Chronicle*), and Kazantzakis praises the untameable Cretan spirit in *O kapetan Mihalis* (1950, *Freedom or Death*). Kazantzakis departs from historical existentialism and metaphysics with the controversial *O teleftaios peirasmos* (1951, *The Last Temptation of Christ*), a novel that led to his excommunication from the Orthodox Church, while Martin Scorsese's 1988 film based on the novel was banned in cinemas around the world. Bulgarian novelists of the period likewise show a strong interest in historical subjects. The most

notable are Stoian Zagorchinov, with *Praznik v Boiana* (1950, Feast in Boiana), and Dimitŭr Talev, whose tetralogy *Samuil* (1952–66) fictionalizes the Bulgarian struggle for independence from the Ottomans, and then from Greeks and Serbs in the Balkan Wars.

The postwar communist regimes of Yugoslavia and Bulgaria promoted "socialist realism" as the official cultural politics, a monumental genre devoid of aesthetic and literary values that insisted on concrete issues, a collective spirit, and the self-sacrifice of the individual for the creation of a socialist utopia. In the period immediately after WWII its main conceptual opponent was modernism, emphatically condemned by the cultural establishment as self-indulgent, antisocial, and morbid. Censorship was rife and undermined "suspicious" literary activity at its roots. Bulgarian Dimitr Dimov created his best work, *Osŭdeni dushi* (1945, *Damned Souls*), about the Spanish Civil War, but had to rewrite *Tiutiun* (1951, 1954, Tobacco) in order to get it published. Dobrica Ćosić, president of the fragmented Yugoslavia in 1992–93, wrote *Daleko je sunce* (1951, Distant Is the Sun) in the socialist-realist style, while in subsequent voluminous sagas he records a history of Serbia after WWI. Mihajlo Lalić depicts the psychological effects of war on people in his partisan story *Lelejska gora* (1957, *The Wailing Mountain*), while Vitomil Zupan departs from socialist-realist dogmatism in his vision of WWII, *Menuet za kitaro* (1957, Minuet for the Guitar). Notable novels not written in the socialist idiom are Vjekoslav Kaleb's social critique *Ponižene ulice* (1950, Humiliated Streets) and Vladan Desnica's stream-of-consciousness *Proljeća Ivana Galeba* (1957, The Springs of Ivan Galeb).

Recurrence of realism in Greece was brought about by the civil war between pro-communist and right-wing forces in 1946–49 and the reemergence of censorship.

Some of the finest novels of the period avoid the bleak political present through escapism into the 1930s: *Contre-Temps* (1947) by Mimika Kranaki, *O kitrinos fakelos* (1956, The Yellow File) by Mitia Karagatsis, and Terzakis's *Dihos theo* (1951, Without a God).

A coming-to-terms with the wars and the split in the Greek society was attempted through the renewal of folkloric realism and a historical novel that looks into the more distant past: Dido Sotiriou's *Matomena homata* (*Farewell Anatolia*), Politis's *Stou Hatzifrangou* (*In the Hatzifrangou Quarter*), and Kostas Tachtsis's *To trito stefani* (*The Third Wedding Wreath*), all published in 1962, return to the events of the 1922 Anatolian disaster. A certain amount of experimentation was again possible in the 1960s, before Greece lapsed into yet another episode of totalitarianism, with the dictatorship of the Colonels in 1967–74. Tatiana Gritsi-Milliex's *Kai idou ippos hloros* (1963, Behold a Pale Horse) and Stratis Tsirkas's trilogy *Akyvernites politeies* (1962–65, Drifting Cities) are good examples of such writing.

TOWARD THE POSTMODERN

In the 1960s and 1970s Yugoslavia underwent a significant period of liberalization. Meša Selimović created the existentialist *Derviš i smrt* (1966, The Dervish and the Death), Bora Ćosić his subversive *Uloga moje porodice u svetskoj revoluciji* (1969, The Role of My Family in the World Revolution), and Ranko Marinković the intertextual antiwar *Kiklop* (1966, Cyclops). Crnjanski, returning from exile in London, wrote his most important novels *Druga knjiga Seoba* (1962, The Second Book of Migrations) and *Roman o Londonu* (1972, A Novel about London). However, a new wave of realist prose brought to the surface a brutal metropolitan reality and socially undesirable phenomena: urban poverty, criminal underground activity, emigration, prostitution, alcoholism, and other social ills, as well as the subject of marginal groups that otherwise would remain off the radar for the majority of the population. Dragoslav Mihailović's *Kad su cvetale tikve* (1968, When Pumpkins Blossomed)—criticized for a contextual mention of the Goli Otok labor camp, where the author had been detained—Vitomil Zupan's *Leviathan* (1982), and Živojin Pavlović's *Zadah tela* (1982, Body Stench). Simultaneously, a different faction of realism directed its interests toward the taboo topic of crimes committed during WWII, the writing that became possible only in the next decade, such as Miodrag Bulatović's *Ljudi sa četiri prsta* (1975, People with Four Fingers).

Yet arguably the most influential fiction of the period was produced by the group whose writing anticipates postmodernist methods in Yugoslav literature, exerting an indelible influence on future generations of writers. The group includes Borislav Pekić, whose novels include *Kako upokojiti vampira* (1977, How to Quiet a Vampire), in which he traces the path of Western rationalism that leads to Nazism, and the 1981 science-fiction trilogy *Besnilo* (Rabies), *Atlantida* (Atlantis), and *1999*. To this group also belong Danilo Kiš, with his "Family Circus" trilogy, especially *Peščanik* (1972, Hourglass), and Mirko Kovač. Kiš's take on Stalinist totalitarianism, *Grobnica za Borisa Davidoviča* (1976, A Tomb for Boris Davidovich), is the best-known victim of the renewed process of regime control of the artistic freedoms in Yugoslavia following the 1971 Croatian nationalist revival movement, forcing the author into self-imposed exile. The local variant of the so-called "jeans prose" deserves a mention as a generational, if not exactly anti-establishment, revolt during the 1970s: Alojz Majetić with *Čangi off gotoff* (1970) and Zvonimir Majdak in *Kužiš, stari moj* (1970, Got It, Old Man).

In contrast to the isolation of postmodern literature since its introduction by Kiš and Pekić, the mid-1980s witnessed its enthusiastic embrace by cultural elites and broad audiences. The tremendous rise in popularity of postmodern literature following Milorad Pavić's international success with *Hazarski rečnik* (1984, *Dictionary of the Khazars*) manifests the postmodern paradox in the fragmenting Yugoslavia: the appropriation of the postmodern by writers whose orientation had a distinctly populist dimension as well as those whose writing resisted the prevalent nationalist mono-narrative. While the former approached history in a constructive manner, the efforts of the latter were directed at its subversion or parody: Svetislav Basara's *Fama o biciklistima* (1987, *The Cyclist Conspiracy*), Dragan Velikić's *Astragan* (1991), Radoslav Petković's *Sudbina i komentari* (1993, *Destiny and Comments*), Dubravka Ugrešić's *Muzej bezuvjetne predaje* (1996, *Museum of Unconditional Surrender*), David Albahari's *Mamac* (1996, *Bait*), Judita Šalgo's *Put u Birobidžan* (posthumous, 1996, *Trip to Birobidzhan*), and Mirjana Novaković's *Strah i njegov sluga* (2005, *Fear and Its Servant*).

The break with realism in Greek fiction, starting in the early 1960s, continued with a series of narratives that parody the mounting political tensions by transferring the Greek situation to a fantastic location. The Aesopian language of these novels only vaguely conceals the irony pervading Vassilis Vassilikos's 1961 trilogy, or Andonis Samarakis's prophetic *To Lathos* (1965, *The Flaw*), a text that anticipates the seizing of power by the junta. Yorgos Heimonas goes even further in *Oi htistes* (1979, *The Builders*), which dispenses altogether with a familiar Western setting or the language itself. Similar displacement is present in the Bulgarian Yordan Radichkov, who combines folkloric fantasy, parody, and the grotesque: *Vsichki i nikoi* (1975, *All

and Nobody*) and *Noev kovcheg* (1988, *Noah's Ark*).

Rather than rendering the past through fictional testimonies like previous generations of writers, Greek post-dictatorship narratives catalyze the events through the protagonists who then interpret them (Beaton, 1994, 283–95). Aris Alexandrou writes about the civil war in *To kivotio* (1974, *The Box*), while *I arhaia skouria* (1979, *Fool's Gold*) by Maro Douka and *I Kassandra kai o lykos* (1977, *Cassandra and the Wolf*) by Margarita Karapanou portray the Athens University massacre that preceded the fall of the dictatorship. The tendency throughout the 1980s was still the genre's deep involvement with history, as in Alki Zei's *I arravoniastikia tou Ahillea* (1987, *Achilles Fiancée*), and identity, both interrogated in relation to Greece's European present, as in Eugenia Fakinou's *To evdomo rouho* (1983, *The Seventh Garment*) or Rhea Galanaki's *O vios tou Ismail Ferik Pasha* (1989, *The Life of Ismail Ferik-Pasha*). Other writers employing metafictional documentation are Thanassis Valtinos, Thomas Skassis, and Pavlina Pampoudi.

THE NEW MILLENNIUM INTERNATIONAL NOVEL

Greece is increasingly seen as a safe haven from economic problems or political oppression, while Greeks themselves are now free to travel and explore the world. This two-way cultural exchange is frequently reflected in the new pattern of "centrifugal" literature that depicts the contact of the Greeks with the Other, both in and out of Greece (Tziovas, in Mackridge and Yannakakis). Sotiris Dimitriou's *N'akouo kalat'onoma sou* (1993, *May Your Name Be Blessed*) re-creates the oral mode of storytelling and plays out the tensions between Greeks and Albanian workers, while in Amanda Michalopoulou's *Oses fores antexeis*

(1998, As Many Times as You Can Stand It) a Greek goes on a love quest to Prague. Travel adventures and international themes abound in texts by Alexis Panselinos, Theodoros Grigoriadis, Alexis Stamatis, and Ioanna Karystiani.

A very similar tendency is visible in the post-Yugoslav novel, where after the crippling wars the newly independent states reinvented their former cultural affinities. Many new names in post-Yugoslav fiction still deal with the recent events, although the general tendency is extrovert, explorative, and unashamed of taboo subjects. Of particular interest are *U potpalublju* (1996, *In the Hold*) by Vladimir Arsenijević, and *Zimski dnevnik* (1995, Winter Journal), the novel by Srđan Valjarević that holds cult status in Serbia, as well as a novel on Belgrade nightlife by Barbi Marković. Zoran Živković belongs to a separate category with his much-translated science-fiction novels, as does the Bulgarian Evgeni Kuzmanov. Georgi Gospodinov was likewise internationally successful with *Estestven roman* (Natural Novel), while Teodora Dimova registers the post-socialist moral collapse in *Maikite* (Mothers), both 2005. On the Bosnian, Slovenian, and Croatian scene new texts continue to arrive from Ivančica Đerić, Aleksandar Hemon, Miljenko Jergović, Drago Jančar, Boris Dežulović, and the ever-controversial Vedrana Rudan.

BIBLIOGRAPHY

Beaton, R., ed. (1988), *Greek Novel AD 1–1985*.
Beaton, R. (1994), *Introduction to Modern Greek Literature*.
Cooper, H.R., ed. (2003), *Bilingual Anthology of Slovene Literature*.
Korać, S. (1974), *Hrvatski roman između dva rata*.
Korać, S. (1982), *Srpski roman između dva rata*.
Mackridge, P. and E. Yannakakis, eds. (2004), *Contemporary Greek Fiction in a United Europe*.
Nemec, K. (1998), *Povijest hrvatskog romana*.
Palavestra, P. (1986), *Istorija moderne srpske književnosti*.
Petković, N. (1995), *History of Serbian Culture*.
Šicel, M. (1982), *Hrvatska književnost*.
Tonnet, H. (1996), *Histoire du roman grec*.

Southern Africa

ANDREW VAN DER VLIES

The concerns and form of the novel in southern Africa have been determined largely by the region's cultural and social politics: for autochthonous communities as for settlers (mostly from Europe), writing served to mediate experiences of modernity, alienation, and ideological interpellation. Permanent European settlement began with the establishment by the Dutch East India Company of a refreshment station at the Cape of Good Hope in 1652; the diary of the settlement's first commander, Jan van Riebeeck, is often cited as the progenitor of an Afrikaans literary tradition in South Africa. Little creative writing was produced until the early nineteenth century, by which time the erstwhile Dutch settlement had expanded and come under British control (1795–1802, and from 1806): South Africa achieved measures of independence in 1910 and 1930, and became a white minority-ruled republic in 1961 and a multiracial democracy in 1994. Elsewhere in the region, British, Portuguese, and German colonial expansion ensured that the whole of southern Africa was directly or indirectly ruled by European powers, or by self-governing minorities of European descent, by the early twentieth century.

During the nineteenth century, southern Africa attracted ethnographers, scientists, and missionaries. The latter may be credited with the spread of printing and literacy and the development of orthographies for several African languages. Mission education altered belief systems and patterns of behavior amongst indigenous communities but also facilitated access to print technologies and networks of distribution, encouraging the growth of African elites who would spur the activities of anticolonial liberation movements in the twentieth century. Furthermore, literary genres encouraged by mission presses—including narratives of conversion or self-improvement—provided the basis for early black literary prose. Inevitably, however, the model for the novel in southern Africa has been a European one.

The novel, with its investments in post-Enlightenment conceptions of interiority and progress and its assumptions about leisure and the value of reading, offered diverging opportunities for authors to stake claims on local and global identifications, involving negotiations of European and African identities—invariably against the backdrop of actual dispossession for autochthonous communities. In relation to South Africa, Rita Barnard suggests that contests over physical and imaginary geographies continue to structure psychological and social experience in a country whose history is marked by successive attempts to regulate access to space on the basis of race and ethnicity. J. M. Coetzee's seminal *White Writing* dissected the legacies of European metaphysics and epistemologies in South Africa's culture of letters; Barnard cites atopia, utopia, dystopia, and the pastoral as among the most enduring imagined tropes still haunting its literary imagination. A similar argument might be made for the whole of southern Africa. Critics (including Van der Vlies) draw attention to the transnational nature of the region's literary cultures: authors looked to European and North American models of the novel, and construed metropolitan publication as cultural validation. Many also found most of their readers abroad until the end of the twentieth century. Conflicting expectations of the novel—as high art or popular entertainment, as realistic representation of social conditions or contribution to a global

literary field—continue to mark novelistic output from southern Africa in content, form, and in relation to the sites of publication and reception. Recent history, and unsettled narratives of cultural identity in the present, pose problems for literary historiography.

THE NOVEL IN SOUTH AFRICA

Anglophone novels

Most white English-speaking residents of the Cape Colony in the early nineteenth century read whatever arrived on the latest ship from England. By the 1870s, however, colonial romances and adventure narratives appeared as the number of settlers increased after the discovery of diamonds (1867) and gold (1886) in the interior. The imperial romance, Laura Chrisman argues, both articulates and works through the "socioeconomic contradictions brought on" by the ensuing capitalization of southern Africa (6). The expansion of capitalism and its attendant class tensions, migrations to the interior, and the displacement of black communities provided fit material for novelistic treatment, although most writing traded in stereotype and cliché: faithful native retainers and pets, as in J. Percy FitzPatrick's *Jock of the Bushveld* (1907); wise white masters; Western medicine triumphing over local superstition; the discovery of fertile land represented as having been misused by the natives. Plots often relied on accident, inheritance, and fortuitous discovery. The Anglo-Boer War (1899–1902) provided a backdrop for much adventure writing, like Ernest Glanville's *The Despatch Rider* (1901). Glanville, author of twenty novels, and Bertram Mitford, who wrote forty-five, were among the most prolific authors of imperial romance.

More critically interesting writing evidences a late nineteenth-century imperial discourse fusing a rhetoric of utilitarianism and belief in the value of modernization, with that of mysticism, chivalry, and romantic primitivism. Such impulses are especially evident in Henry Rider Haggard's *King Solomon's Mines* (1885) and *She* (1887), which draw on quest and rite-of-passage narratives, mystical motifs, and social Darwinism. Some critics trace to this strain of colonial adventure the writing of currently popular novelists like Zambian-born Wilbur Smith, author of international bestsellers like *When the Lion Feeds* (1964), whose work Michael Chapman characterizes as offering "endless safaris and seductions, big game, game women, an Africa where the approved politics are thoroughly conservative" (131).

It was against this widespread mode of adventure writing that what is arguably the region's first significant novel, written by a governess of German and English missionary parentage, was conceived. Olive Schreiner's *The Story of an African Farm* was published in London in two volumes by Chapman & Hall in Jan. 1883. Schreiner used the pseudonym "Ralph Iron," gesturing toward the influence of transcendentalist writing on her (characters in the novel are named Waldo and Em) and her desire not to have her work read as a simpering colonial romance for female patrons of the circulating libraries. With its "New Woman" character, Lyndall, Schreiner's novel was controversial; it remains a key reference point for Anglophone South African writing, particularly for its engagement with the pastoral, its generic inventiveness, and its negotiation of the twin demands of verisimilitude and the imagination. This negotiation, of demands that might be termed those of history and of the aesthetic, prefigures the agenda for the novel in South Africa in the ensuing century. Other novels by Schreiner are the parable-like *Trooper Peter Halket of Mashonaland* (1897) and two published posthumously: *From Man to Man* (1926) and *Undine* (1929).

Douglas Blackburn, a British immigrant on the Witwatersrand when gold mining was transforming the proto-Afrikaner Transvaal republic into a site of contestation in the new capitalist economy, also produced important early novels, including *A Burgher Quixote* (1903), in which a principled narrator comments on corruption in a deadpan manner, and *Leaven* (1908), perhaps the first important depiction of the effects of urbanization on rural black African society. This "Jim-comes-to-the-city" (specifically Johannesburg) trope would be explored most famously in English in Peter Abrahams's *Mine Boy* (1946) and Alan Paton's *Cry, the Beloved Country* (1948).

Land and language rights, cultural autonomy, race, and citizenship in a modern state (after 1910) within the British Empire—but with multiple cultures and traditions—form the overwhelming concerns of the early twentieth-century novel in South Africa. *Mhudi*, subtitled an "epic of South African native life a hundred years ago," by Solomon T. Plaatje, a mission-educated man of letters, newspaper proprietor, and politician, uses the story of a young Barolong couple in the 1830s to explore the roots of the post-Union dispossession of black South Africans by the Natives Land Act (1913), which reserved less than ten percent of the country for black ownership, in the incursions of the proto-Afrikaner *Voortrekkers* (migrant farmers) into central South Africa, and the contemporaneous migration of black African communities, known as the *mfecane* (occasioned by the expansion of the Zulu kingdom under Chaka).

The issue of race, whether in the form of tensions between English- and Afrikaans-speaking whites or the so-called "question" of the "native" population's rights, dominated much literary production. Sarah

Gertrude Millin's *God's Step-children* (1924), an indictment of miscegenation that plays on the "black peril" trope, became internationally known; it remains a point of reference for novels revisiting the hybrid nature of South African national identity. William Plomer, who left South Africa permanently in 1929, offered a scathing response to such conservative racialist discourse in his first—and only expressly South African—novel, *Turbott Wolfe* (1926), a first-person account by the dying eponymous narrator of his experiences in a thinly disguised Zululand.

Notable liberal realist novels in English, interrogating this dilemma to greater or lesser effect, include Laurens van der Post's *In a Province* (1934) and Jack Cope's *The Road to Ysterberg* (1959), although the most famous is undoubtedly Paton's internationally successful *Cry, the Beloved Country*. Imbued with a belief in humane cooperation and gradual amelioration (which struck critics as outdated paternalism), Paton's novel was received as a parable seeking to awaken South Africa's white population to their complicity in injustice, but also as a universal narrative of courage in adversity; its nonrevolutionary message resonated with white Cold War-era American readers. Its publication coincided, too, with the election victory of an Afrikaner nationalist party, which, under Prime Ministers D. F. Malan and H. F. Verwoerd, implemented the policy of apartheid (literally, separateness). The message of Paton's novel thus seemed immediately dated to many black readers. With the recognition of the hollowness of much white liberal rhetoric, the English novel in South Africa persisted in something of a crisis. Simon Gikandi suggests that Nadine Gordimer's *The Late Bourgeois World* (1966) is perhaps "the exemplary work of the liberal dilemma," its "rhetoric of failure" exposing a "failure of the liberal project that the novel,

nevertheless, espouses" (in S. Gikandi, ed., 2003, *Encyclopedia of African Literature*, 515). Gordimer, South Africa's first Nobel laureate for literature (in 1991), established herself as the apartheid era's most important—and most sophisticated—novelistic chronicler, with an impressive catalogue also including *A World of Strangers* (1958), *The Conservationist* (1974, joint winner of the Booker Prize), *Burger's Daughter* (1979), and *July's People* (1981). She refused to exile herself and believed it was, as she put it in a 1984 essay, "The Essential Gesture," "the white writer's task as 'cultural worker' ... to raise the consciousness of white people, who, unlike himself, have not woken up" (in S. Clingman, ed., 1988, *The Essential Gesture*, 293–94). Gordimer offered a sustained response to the country's politics through a blend of LUKÁCSIAN critical realism and elements of late modernist narration (often with implicated first-person narrators, and fractured, free-indirect discourse). She has continued to explore the complicated texture of post-apartheid life in recent work, including *The House Gun* (1998) and *The Pickup* (2001).

Black writers also experimented with critical realism. Most significant is Alex La Guma, whose novels appeared from publishers abroad and were banned inside South Africa. *And a Threefold Cord* (1964) is exemplary of his method: evoking a studied naturalism, it offers detailed descriptions of deprivation in a Cape Town shantytown, inviting readers to perceive the injustices suffered by characters who themselves only gradually identify their plight as political. Other novels include *The Stone Country* (1968) and *In the Fog of the Seasons' End* (1972). La Guma was one of the few novelists whom critic Lewis Nkosi was prepared to exclude from a charge—in his essay "Fiction by Black South Africans" (1966)—that the subservience of aesthetic form to the protest message had too often resulted in "journalistic fact parading outrageously as imaginative literature" (in U. Beier, ed., 1967, *Introduction to African Literature*, 212). Another might well, in due course, have been Bessie Head, whose complex work, including the novels *Maru* (1971) and *A Question of Power* (1973), has become more closely associated with Botswana, where she lived in exile from South Africa. Later "protest" writing included Miriam Tlali's *Amandla!* (1981), Mongane Wally Serote's *To Every Birth Its Blood* (1981), and Sipho Sepamla's *A Ride on the Whirlwind* (1981), which deal with the aftermath of the Soweto uprising of 1976. Tlali's semiautobiographical *Muriel at Metropolitan* (1975) is concerned with the everyday, exemplifying critic and novelist Njabulo Ndebele's suggestion that the "insensitivity, insincerity and delusion" of much protest writing should be superseded by a "rediscovery of the ordinary" (50) in which apartheid's spectacular narratives were eschewed and its effective authorship of every narrative of life in the country refused.

In an address at a book fair in Cape Town (1988, "The Novel Today," *Upstream* 6(1)), Coetzee spoke to a similar concern, arguing against what he called his historical moment's "powerful tendency ... to subsume the novel under history." History, Coetzee countered, was "not reality," but "a kind of discourse"; the novel did not need to answer to the dominant historical narrative. He had faced charges that his novels engaged insufficiently with the realities of his historical moment: his first, *Dusklands* (1974), offered twin narratives set in contemporary California and eighteenth-century South Africa; his second, *In the Heart of the Country* (1977), is a highly unreliable narrative by a woman in an apparently colonial-era setting. But his body of work is regarded by many as unparalleled in its ethical seriousness

(Attwell). *Waiting for the Barbarians* (1980), a sophisticated allegory pushing the limits of the form, responds to questions of torture and complicity in the South African context. *Life & Times of Michael K* (1983) won Coetzee his first Booker Prize; the second followed for *Disgrace* (1999), a controversial narrative set in post-apartheid South Africa. *Foe* (1986) offered a rewriting of Daniel Defoe's *Robinson Crusoe* (1719–22) and *Roxana* (1724), addressing issues of authority and the canon; *The Master of Petersburg* (1994) returned to similar issues. *Age of Iron* (1990) offered a self-reflexive and highly mediated meditation on ethics, writing, and the humanities in a time of political crisis. Coetzee has published three fictionalized memoirs: *Boyhood* (1997), *Youth* (2002), and *Summertime* (2009). Each, and especially the last, tests expectations of truth and fiction in autobiography, and they are sold in some markets as novels. Coetzee won the 2003 Nobel Prize for literature.

The work of several Anglophone novelists bridges the transition to democracy in South Africa. Damon Galgut's *The Beautiful Screaming of Pigs* (1991, rev. 2005) was well received, and *The Good Doctor* (2003) and *The Imposter* (2008) shortlisted for international and local prizes. Mike Nicol, known locally for novels like *The Powers That Be* (1989), expanded his audience with *The Ibis Tapestry* (1998), a postmodern thriller set in late apartheid South Africa. He has followed this success with detective fiction, including *Payback* (2008), the first of a contracted trilogy signaling his likely international success in a lucrative popular field. Lawyer Andrew Brown's *Coldsleep Lullaby* (2005) and academic Jane Taylor's *Of Wild Dogs* are examples of other recently successful—but more literary—DETECTIVE novels, a GENRE that seems likely to grow given the obsession shared by many South Africans with popular discourse about criminality, corruption, and violence in the postcolonial state.

Some writers whose work long reflected a felt obligation to represent the emergency in apartheid-era South Africa—like Zanemvula Kizito Gatyeni (Zakes) Mda, who established a reputation as an activist playwright during periods of exile—began publishing more inventive, less socially realistic work after 1994. Mda published *She Plays with the Darkness* and *Ways of Dying* in 1995, shortly after his return to the country, following with *The Heart of Redness* (2000), *The Madonna of Excelsior* (2002), *The Whale Caller* (2005), *Cion* (2007), and *Black Diamond* (2010). Mda's novels explore the claims of tradition and modernity in narratives that employ realism, magical realism, and satire. Anne Landsman also explored the potential of magical realism in *The Devil's Chimney* (1997).

Zoë Wicomb had only published short fiction until *David's Story* (2000), which challenges nationalist—Afrikaner and black South African—myths of gender and ethnic identity, established her as one of the most accomplished post-apartheid novelists. *Playing in the Light* (2006) is similarly concerned with race, language, memory, and writing. Wicomb's writing, in its concern with trauma and acts of witnessing, engaged with the one of the legacies of South Africa's Truth and Reconciliation Commission (TRC): the heightened profile of narrative, and a complex understanding of narrative "truth" (as opposed to forensic, or verifiable, truth). Other novels to respond to the potentialities suggested formally and thematically by the TRC include Achmat Dangor's *Bitter Fruit* (2001), Yvette Christiansë's *Unconfessed* (2006), and Njabulo Ndebele's formally experimental and politically provocative *The Cry of Winnie Mandela* (2003).

Ivan Vladislavić has produced adventurous and nuanced examinations of the late and post-apartheid urban landscape with a keen eye for the absurd, particularly in *The Folly* (1993), in *The Restless Supermarket* (2001), and in short fiction that aspires to the novelistic, especially *The Exploded View* (2004). Other "urban" fiction, grappling with the deprivations of street children, conditions of drug abuse and prostitution, and the devastation wrought by HIV/AIDS, include the small but powerful work of Phaswane Mpe (2001, *Welcome to Our Hillbrow*) and K. Sello Duiker (2000, *Thirteen Cents*; 2001, *The Quiet Violence of Dreams*). Kgebetli Moele's *Room 207* (2006) examines the textures of everyday life in urban South Africa, particularly for young black men; *The Book of the Dead* (2009) confronts issues of sexual behavior and social responsibility—and gives a voice (literally) to HIV/AIDS. Murhandziwa Nicholas (Niq) Mhlongo also explores urban life, in *Dog Eat Dog* (2004) and *After Tears* (2007).

African-language novels

There is a relatively long and robust novelistic tradition in South Africa's African languages. The publication of Tiyo Soga's isiXhosa translation of part of *Pilgrim's Progress* (as *uHambo Lomhambi*) in 1866 is often cited as a seminal moment in the development of a vernacular South African literature. It also bespeaks the significance of mission presses (particularly the Morija Press in Maseru, Marianhill in KwaZulu-Natal, and Lovedale in Alice in the Eastern Cape) which vetted writing for compliance with Christian orthodoxy by fostering a black southern African culture of letters (Attwell). Morija published Thomas Mofolo's 1907 Bunyanesque Sesotholanguage *Moeti oa Bochabela* (also *Moeti wa Botjhabela*, *The Traveller to the East*) and his masterful historical work *Chaka* (1925). The former revisits the hero-quest form and an allegory that tests as it examines the impact of Christianity on Basotho culture; Chapman suggests that *Chaka* might equally be regarded as epic and as romance (212). Mofolo's work features in early debates about whether the written word should be used to advance African nationalism, or serve the goal of Western—for which read Christian—modernity, and whether these goals are mutually exclusive.

A seminal debate about the use of English in developing a black national identity raged in print throughout the 1930s between isiZulu poet and critic Herbert Isaac Ernest Dhlomo (1903–56) and the novelist, poet, and academic Benedict Wallet Vilakazi. The latter's *Nje nempela* (1933, Really and truly) is among the first isiZulu novels to deal with contemporary life rather than historical subjects. John Langibalele Dube, writer, educator, and politician, wrote the first novel in isiZulu with *U-Jege: Insila kaShaka* (ca. 1930, *Jeqe, the Bodyservant of King Shaka*). Rolfes Reginald Raymond Dhlomo contributed a series of historical novels, including on kings Dingane (1936, *UDingane*), Chaka (1937, *UShaka*), and Ceteswayo (1952, *UCetshwayo*). He also authored the 1946 "Jim-comes-to-Jo'burg"-themed *Indlela yababi* (1946, Path of the Wicked). Also in this genre are Jordan Kush Ngubane's *Uvalo lwezinhlonzi* (1956, Fear of Authority) and James Nduna Gumbi's *Baba, Ngixolele* (1966, Father, Forgive Me) and *Wayesezofika ekhaya* (1967, He Was About To Go Home), novels tracing the implications for traditional community and family structures of the apartheid South African state's industrialization and urbanization.

The theme of the return of the prodigal son is treated in Deuteronomy Bhekinkosi Zeblon Ntuli's *Ubheka* (1962, The Watcher) and the prolific Kenneth Bhengu's *Baba Ngonile* (1971, Father, I Have Sinned). Each of these novels draws on oral traditions of storytelling, and on allegory and the structure of the morality tale—the latter showing the imbrication of Christian and older codes

of ethics and morality. In Cyril Lincoln Sibusiso Nyembezi's *Inkinsela yaseMgungundlovu* (1961, *The Rich Man of Pietermaritzburg*), an urban trickster hoodwinks rural folk. Christian Themba Msimang has published a number of novels, including *Akuyiwe emhlahlweni* (1973, Let Us Consult the Diviner) and *Buzani kuMkabayi* (1982, Ask Mkabayi), as well as a 1983 monograph, *Folktale Influence on the Zulu Novel*. According to the 2001 census, isiZulu was the home language of 23.8 percent of the South African population; it is thus the most-spoken home language. Samuel Edward Krune Mqhayi is regarded as having written the first novel, *U-Samson* (1907), in isiXhosa, home language of the second-largest proportion of South Africans (17.6 percent, according to the 2001 census). Mqhayi also authored a utopian fiction, *U-Don Jadu* (1929). Guybon Bundlwana Sinxo, an important translator of European literature into isiXhosa, himself wrote *UNomsa* (1922), *Umfundisi wase-Mthuqwasi* (1927, The priest of Mthuqwasi), and *Umzali Wolahleko* (1933, The prodigal parent), tackling issues such as the education of children, family structure, and the politics of race as it continues to affect even black Christian converts. James Ranisi Jolobe, chiefly known as a poet, wrote several novels—including *UZagula* (1923), dealing with witchcraft, and *Elundini loThukela* (1958, On the Tugela Hills). Victoria Nombulelo Mermaid Swaartbooi was a pioneering feminist writer whose 1934 novel, *U-Mandisa*, follows the career of a woman who seeks employment over marriage.

The flowering of isiXhosa prose fiction came with Archibald Campbell Jordan's celebrated *Ingqumbo Yeminyanya* (1940, *The Wrath of the Ancestors*), but the effect of so-called "Bantu" education, a policy of the apartheid government that, after 1953, deliberately impoverished the standard of education for black South Africans (who, it was held, should be raised only to work as laborers), had a deleterious effect on literary culture. Comparatively liberal mission presses were overtaken by Afrikaans publishing houses as the centers of publishing for black education, and little interesting vernacular literature was encouraged or allowed. IsiXhosa-language writers who came to the fore in this difficult period include Enoch Fikile Gwashu, Knobel Sakhiwo Bongela, Randall Langa Peteni, and the prolific Peter Thabiso Mtuze, an academic and man of letters whose novels include *UDingezweni* (1966), *Umsinga* (1973, A Tide), and *Indlel' ecand' intlango* (1981, The Road through the Wilderness).

In Sesotho, or Southern Sotho (spoken by 7.9 percent of South Africans, and the majority language of neighboring Lesotho), writers like Bennett Makalo Khaketla (1960, *Mosali a nkhola*; A Comforting Woman) and Kemuel Edward Monyatsi Ntsane (ca. 1967, *Bao Batho*; Those People) produced novels blending sociocultural concerns with a cautious note of political protest. Kgotso Pieter David Maphalla has published numerous prizewinning and much-prescribed short stories, poems, dramas, and novels, the latter including *Nna ke mang?* (1991, Who Am I?) and *Ha maru a rwalellana* (2007, The Clouds Eclipse One Another). The academic Nhlanhla Paul Maake's novels include *Ke Phethisitse Ditaelo tsa Hao* (1994, I Have Fulfilled Your Commands), *Kweetsa ya Pelo ya Motho* (1995, The Depth of the Heart of Man), and *Mme* (1995, Mother).

Amongst less widely spoken languages in South Africa are Setswana (the majority language of neighboring Botswana) and Northern Sotho (or Sesotho sa Leboa, sometimes called Sepedi, though this refers to a dialect in this group), with less than 10 percent of the population as home-language speakers, and Xitsonga (Shangaan in Mozambique), SiSwati (spoken, too, in Swazi-

land), Tshivenda, and isiNdebele, with less than 5 percent. Among contemporary Setswana novelists in South Africa, Kabelo Duncan Kgatea's *Monwona wa bosupa* (2008, The pointing finger) features a quest narrative, elements of pan-African transnationalism, and contemporary issues such as the legal custody of children.

Afrikaans novels

The "Boer" Republics established in the interior from 1854 onward (after the migration of many "Dutch" farmers—or Boers—from the British-ruled Cape Colony in the mid-1930s) were annexed by Britain after the Anglo-Boer War. Their spoken language differed from the Dutch used in the church and courts, and assimilated vocabulary from contact with autochthonous languages and the so-called "Malay" creole of slaves from the Indian Ocean rim. A concerted movement to recognize this as a new language began in 1874 and intensified in the early twentieth century, resulting in state recognition in 1925. The developing literary culture soon included significant novels by Johannes van Melle, Mikro (pseud. of C. H. Kühn), and C. M. van den Heever, whose pastoral novels in the *plaasroman* (farm novel) tradition (see Coetzee) included *Somer* (1935, Harvest Home) and *Laat Vrugte* (1939, Late Harvest). More complex representations of life in South Africa, including the dilemmas of racial politics, came with C. J. M. Nienaber's *Keerweer* (1946, Cul De Sac), which J. C. Kannemeyer regards as "the only novel written at this time showing any sign of genuine innovation" (61). F. A. Venter published a tetralogy in the 1960s—including *Geknelde land* (1960, Oppressed Land), *Offerland* (1963, Land of Sacrifice), *Gelofteland* (1966, Land of the Covenant), and *Bedoelde land* (1968, Intended [or Promised Land])—that explored Afrikaner struggles, in particular the mythology of the Voortrekkers, implicitly expressing optimism in the future of the white-ruled state. He is better known for his "Jim-comes-to-Jo'burg" novel about the supposed perils of urbanization, *Swart pelgrim* (1952, *Dark Pilgrim*). It is worth noting that some other Afrikaans novels in this genre were written by black Afrikaans authors—including Sydney Vernon Petersen's *As die son ondergaan* (1945, When the sun sets) and Arthur Fula's *Jôhannie giet die beeld* (1954, *The Golden Magnet*).

Anna M. Louw published historical novels, including *Die banneling: Die lyfwag* (1964, The Exile: The Bodyguard) and *Die groot gryse* (1968, The Great [or Honored] "Gray One" [or Old Man]; it was about Transvaal president Paul Kruger) in the 1960s, but is best known for books like *Kroniek van Perdepoort* (1975, The Chronicle of Perdepoort), a farm novel combining allegory, satire, and symbolism in a potent mix. Wilma Stockenström, better known as a poet, also engaged with the farm novel in *Uitdraai* (1976, Turn-off). Elsa Joubert published important work in the 1960s and 1970s, including, most famously, a novelized version of her black female employee's struggles (including with apartheid bureaucracy), *Die swerfjare van Poppie Nongena* (1978, *The Long Journey of Poppie Nongena*).

The 1960s saw the flowering of the "new" novel in Afrikaans, heavily indebted to existentialism, psychoanalytic theories, and the *nouveau roman*. Writers—many of whom spent time in France or the Netherlands—explored myth, deployed extensive symbolism, and were comparatively daring in representing sexuality and political dissent. Chief among this *Sestiger* (sixties) school are Jan Rabie, author of *Ons, die Afgod* (1958, We, the Idol), and Etienne Leroux (pseud. of S. P. D. le Roux), who is best known for the Silberstein trilogy: *Sewe Dae by die Silbersteins* (1962, *Seven Days at the Silbersteins*), recounting feckless

Henry van Eeden's week with his fiancée's family on a wine farm in the Western Cape, is a symbolically complex exploration of good and evil; *Een vir Azazel* (1964, *One for the Devil*) explores culpability and moral judgment, drawing on classical rhetorical patterns, detective-fiction formulae, and Greek tragedy; *Die Derde Oog* (1966, *The Third Eye*) is loosely patterned on the Hercules myth. They were published in English as *To a Dubious Salvation* (1972). The banning of Leroux's *Magersfontein, O Magersfontein* (1976) by the apartheid censors in 1977 was a *cause célèbre*, hastening changes in the restrictive censorship regime (discussed extensively by Peter McDonald).

Another *Sestiger*, André P. Brink, is perhaps the best-known Afrikaans novelist abroad, particularly for *'n Droë Wit Seisoen* (1979, *A Dry White Season*), later filmed. Highly prolific and eclectic, Brink has experimented with surrealism, social realism, political reportage, a version of magical realism, historical romance, confessional first-person narratives, and sweeping family sagas. The banning of his 1973 novel *Kennis van die Aand* (*Looking on Darkness*)—it was the first Afrikaans novel to be so censored—cast Brink as the spokesperson for enlightened Afrikanerdom. (Since the 1970s, he has prepared simultaneous English and Afrikaans versions of his novels). Post-apartheid fiction includes *Sandkastele* (1996, *Imaginings of Sand*) and *Donkermaan* (2000, *The Rights of Desire*).

Other significant novelists include John Miles. His *Donderdag of Woensdag* (1978, Thursday or Wednesday) and *Stanley Bekker en die boikot* (1980, Stanley Bekker and the Boycott) were both banned: the former featured artists planning to kidnap the president; the latter dealt with racial discrimination and school boycotts through a formal engagement with the children's story. Miles is best known for *Kroniek uit die Doofpot* (1991, *Deafening Silence: Police*

Novel), which was based on the case of the police killing of Richard Motasi—also recounted in Afrikaans poet Antjie Krog's creative nonfiction prose account of the TRC hearings, *Country of My Skull* (1998).

Karel Schoeman's many novels show a range of influences, including—unusually for an Afrikaner—conversion to Catholicism, and a later interest in Buddhism. A period as a novice in an Irish monastery informed *By fakkellig* (1966, By Torchlight), a historical novel about Irish nationalism in the late eighteenth century. Later novels included *Na die geliefde land* (1972, *Promised Land*), *Die hemeltuin* (1979, The Heavenly Garden), and a trilogy: *Hierdie lewe* (1993, This Life), *Die uur van die engel* (1995, The Hour of the Angel), and *Verliesfontein* (1998). Another writer who wrote historical novels, though in a more popular—and very successful—vein, is Dalene Matthee, whose series set in the southern Cape's Outeniqua forest (around present-day Knysna) includes *Kringe in 'n bos* (1984, *Circles in a Forest*), *Fiela se Kind* (1985, *Fiela's Child*; also filmed), and *Moerbeibos* (1987, *The Mulberry Forest*).

Significant voices in contemporary fiction include Jeanne Goosen, Marié Heese, Chris Pelser, Ingrid Winterbach, Christoffel Coetzee, and Eben Venter, whose well-received novels include *Ek Stamel Ek Sterwe* (1996, *My Beautiful Death*) and the dystopic *Horrelpoot* (2006, *Trencherman*). Mark Behr's *Die Reuk van Appels* (1993, *The Smell of Apples*), well received in the country and abroad, a tale of lost innocence, is also partially an example of *grensliteratuur* (border literature), engaging with the legacies of South Africa's costly covert military operations in Angola in the late 1970s and 1980s. Behr now writes in English (2009, *Kings of the Water*). Etienne van Heerden is prolific and highly regarded; his best-known novel is *Toorberg* (1986, *Ancestral Voices*). Marlene van Niekerk's harrowing 1994 novel *Triomf*

(*Triumph*), is named for the working-class white suburb built by the apartheid government on the ruins of the famed center of black Johannesburg culture, Sophiatown, and follows a trio of poor white siblings, the Benades, in the run-up to the first democratic elections of 1994. Van Niekerk's *Agaat* (2004, *The Way of the Women*), an ambitious revisioning of the *plaasroman*, has been received as amongst the most accomplished South African novels in any language in the new millennium.

OTHER COUNTRIES

In all countries of the South African Development Community (SADC), the usual delimitation of South Africa as a region, novelists have felt tensions between demands that writing act in support of projects of national self-definition in the postcolonial era, and concerns to interrogate the pitfalls of nationalist rhetoric or the disappointments of independence and neocolonialism. Attempts to write for a living in what are very small markets also pose dilemmas.

Southern Rhodesia became a self-governing colony in 1923. Early novels include colonial romances, although some work is critical of white racial attitudes and policies, including Arthur Shearly Cripps's *Bay Tree Country* (1913). Doris Lessing, the 2007 Nobel literature laureate, is sometimes regarded as a Rhodesian novelist; she spent the years 1925–49 in the colony, and *The Grass Is Singing* (1950), her first novel, is set there (as are parts of *The Golden Notebook*, 1962). The white minority Rhodesian government declared itself unilaterally independent of Britain in 1965, precipitating a protracted and bitter conflict with armed black nationalist guerrillas that culminated in the election of a majority government, and independence as Zimbabwe, in 1980.

Stanlake Samkange's *On Trial for My Country* (1966) is among the first significant proto-Zimbabwean novels, restaging the encounter between late nineteenth-century Ndebele/Matabele king Lobengula and Cecil Rhodes. Samkange also published *The Mourned One* (1968) and *Year of the Uprising* (1978). Charles Mungoshi's *Waiting for the Rain* (1975) compares earlier wars of liberation with the anticolonial struggle of the 1960s and 1970s, but was an indictment of the Rhodesian government's cultural policies, too, in that it was published in English in London, in the Heinemann African Writers series, so escaping Rhodesian censorship and defying the white government's attempts to corral black writers into writing in their vernaculars and being published by government-controlled presses (though Mungoshi did contribute greatly to the development of a literary Shona in his several novels in that language).

Much writing produced during the struggle (1966–79) is marked by a sense of psychic as well as spatial displacement, as writers attempted to balance aesthetic with political concerns. Nowhere is this more marked than in the work of Dambudzo Marechera, whose *The House of Hunger* (1978; strictly a short-story collection, but featuring an eponymous novella), *Black Sunlight* (1980), and *Mindblast* (1984) have earned him considerable regard as a high Modernist representing extreme alienation and psychological difficulties. Chenjerai Hove's *Bones* (1988) and *Ancestors* (1997) display striking formal inventiveness, including the use of Shona idioms and expressions. Like Shimmer Chinodya's *Harvest of Thorns* (1989) and *Chairman of Fools* (2005), Hove's writing engages with idealism and disappointment, solidarity, and the pitfalls of national identity. Chinodya's other novels include *Dew in the Morning* (1982) and *Farai's Girls* (1984).

Tsitsi Dangarembga's *Nervous Conditions* (1988), the narrative of a young rural Shona girl's education and coming to consciousness, and of her female family members' struggles with the twin burdens of colonialism and the chauvinism of traditional society, has received much critical attention. The much-anticipated second novel in a projected trilogy, *The Book of Not*, was published in 2006. Yvonne Vera published her first novel, *Nehanda*, in 1993, and followed it with four more, including the prizewinning *Butterfly Burning* (2000) and *The Stone Virgins* (2002). Vera has received praise for her poetic prose and sophisticated engagement with questions of gender identity. She died in Canada in 2005.

Vera's work is regarded as having been influenced by the form and style of the novel as it had developed in Shona, as well as of Shona oral culture. Important early work in Shona includes Bernard Chidzero's *Nzvengamutsvairo* (1957, Mr. Lazybones), published by the Rhodesia Literature Bureau and widely read in schools in the colonial period. Catholic clergyman Patrick Chakaipa's romances *Karikoga Gumiremiseve* (1959, Karikoga and His Ten Arrows) and *Pfumo Reropa* (1961, Spear of blood), and the didactic *Rudo Ibofu* (1961, Love Is Blind), which also draws on traditional storytelling, were influential. *Garandichauya* (1963, Wait, I Shall Return) deals with disruptions wrought by colonial intrusions into traditional life. Paul Chidyausiku produces mostly shorter work (and is also a poet). Raymond Choto's satirical novel *Vavariro* (1990, Determination) offered a departure from nationalist fictions. A journalist, he was arrested and tortured by Mugabe's regime in Dec. 1998. Ignatius Tirivangani Mabasa, a former senior editor of the *Herald* newspaper, has had great success with his novel *Mapenzi* (1999, Fools), a satire on post-independence

Zimbabwe drawing on aspects of Shona orature and contemporary urban slang.

A literary tradition in Sindebele (or Northern Ndebele) is less developed, as is the case in South Africa (where the variety of the language is isiNdebele, or Southern Ndebele, where, as a written language, it is one of the youngest in the region). In Zimbabwe, Barbara C. Makhalisa's *Qilindini* (1974, Crafty Person) won a Rhodesian Literature Bureau award and explores issues of tradition and modernity, although apparently endorsing mission schooling and colonial governance. She also published *Impilo Yinkinga* (1983, Life Is a Mystery).

Malawi, with a history of mission education and a literate elite, produced a more robust literary culture earlier than neighboring Zambia, which, as Northern Rhodesia, had developed economically primarily on the basis of colonial mining interests. A joint Northern Rhodesian and Nyasaland (Malawi) publications bureau, established in 1947, attempted to encourage literary production but too often promoted writing which endorsed colonial attitudes. Aubrey Kachingwe's *No Easy Task* (1966), about the anticolonial struggle, is regarded as the first Malawian novel in English. The first major Zambian novel was arguably Dominic Mulaisho's *The Tongue of the Dumb* (1971), while other significant writers include Gideon Phiri, Binwell Sinyangwe, and Andreya Masiye.

Angola and Mozambique achieved independence from Portugal in 1975. Despite economic difficulties and protracted civil conflicts that lasted into the 1990s, both countries have witnessed significant literary production, before and since independence, in Portuguese and in autochthonous languages. Among the better known are Angola's Pepetela (pseud. of Arthur Carlos Pestana), whose *Mayombe* (1971, pub. in Portugal 1980; *Mayombe: A Novel of the Angolan Struggle*) dramatizes debates about commitment and politics. Mozambican novelists include Paula Chiziane and António Emílio Leite (Mia) Couto, acclaimed author of, among other novels, *Terra Sonâmbula* (1992, *Sleepwalking Land*), *A Varanda do Frangipani* (1996, *Under the Frangipani*), and *O Último Voo do Flamingo* (2001, *The Last Flight of the Flamingo*). He is one of the best-known proponents of a regionally inflected magical realism. Angolan-born (now largely Lisbon-based) José Eduardo Agualusa (Alves da Cunha)'s *O Vendedor de Passados* (2004), translated as *The Book of Chameleons* (the translation won the Independent Foreign Fiction Prize in 2007), is rendered in a similarly fantastic—though lightly dazzling—style, featuring a character, Félix Ventura, who is a seller of pasts. *Nação Crioula* (1997, *Creole*) first won Agualusa notice as a leading young Lusophone writer; it followed *Estação das Chuvas* (1996, *Rainy Season*).

BIBLIOGRAPHY

Attridge, D. and D. Attwell, eds. (2010), *Cambridge History of South African Literature*.

Attridge, D. and R. Jolly, eds. (1998), *Writing South Africa*.

Attwell, D. (1993), *J.M. Coetzee*.

Attwell, D. (2005), *Rewriting Modernity*.

Barnard, R. (2007), *Apartheid and Beyond*.

Chapman, M. (2003), *Southern African Literatures*, 2nd ed.

Chrisman, L. (2000), *Rereading the Imperial Romance*.

Coetzee, J. M. (1988), *White Writing*.

Gérard, A. S. (1971), *Four African Literatures*.

Kannemeyer, J.C. (1993), *History of Afrikaans Literature*.

Kannemeyer, J.C. (2005), *Die Afrikaanse literatuur 1652–2004*.

Keenoy, R., ed. (1995), *Babel Guide to the Fiction of Portugal, Brazil and Africa in English Translation*.

McDonald, P.D. (2009), *Literature Police*.

Ndebele, N. (1994), *South African Literature and Culture*.

Ntuli, D.B., and C.F. Swanepoel (1993), *Southern African Literature in African Languages*.

Primorac, R. (2006), *The Place of Tears*.

Samuelson, M. (2007), *Remembering the Nation, Dismembering Women?*

Smith, M.v.W. (1990), *Grounds of Contest*.

van Coller, H.P., ed. (1998, 1999, 2005), *Perspektief en profile*, 3 vols.

van der Vlies, A. (2007), *South African Textual Cultures*.

Southern Cone (South America)

KELLY AUSTIN

Southern Cone narratives have captured the attention of readers around the world partly because of supremely talented writers such as Jorge Luis Borges, Julio Cortázar, José Donoso, Augusto Roa Bastos, Juan Carlos Onetti, and, more recently, Manuel Puig, Diamela Eltit, Luisa Valenzuela, Cristina Peri Rossi, and Roberto Bolaño. Then there is the unique notoriety of the region that inspires musicals, movies, documentaries, and histories about political upheaval. Critics, too, have accorded the Southern Cone novel greater attention than other novels in Latin America, with the exception of the Mexican novel. Popularity has shaped the region's narrative production, and critics have seen to it that these narratives receive special care and scrutiny.

Academic critics often stress the vicissitudes of the Southern Cone's novelistic production in terms of national and regional histories, especially political histories: for example, the nineteenth-century revolutionary struggles, the nineteenth-century dictatorship of Dr. José Gaspar Rodríguez de Francia, his enforcement of the official use of Guaraní in Paraguay, Perón's populism in Argentina, the struggle of the "common man," the rise of the Left, the

Pinochet and Perón dictatorships, the disappearance of tens of thousands of people, the Madres de la Plaza de Mayo, as well as the trials and triumphs of redemocratization. Academics write often of narratives of nation formation, DICTATORSHIP novels, and the novels of exile in the Southern Cone, although these genres are not peculiar to the region. Even as it is certain that Southern Cone novels respond to and are embedded in political histories, correlating the developments of these novels too closely with the geography and events of the nations that comprise the region—Argentina, Chile, Paraguay, and Uruguay—can easily obscure the intellectual and artistic independence of their extraordinary novelists. Exile, international travel, libraries filled with world literature, and cosmopolitan creativity—to name but a few—have contributed to Southern Cone novels of enormous import, just as political forces, local culture, and border-bounded intellectual arguments—to name but a few elements of the lives of Southern Cone novelists—have also contributed to Southern Cone novels of enormous import. Neither an aesthetic nor a political history alone can do justice to the developments of Southern Cone fiction. One might say, for purposes of introduction, that a history of the narratives spun in Southern Cone novels leads directly to questions concerning the literature and literary culture of newly forming (and constantly generated) nation-states.

This much may seem obvious, but the aesthetic positions taken by novelists and critics swirl, reverse, and rotate all around the eddies of individual national histories and of global intellectual priorities and preoccupations. To tie the novels of the Southern Cone closely to a unified history or even to differentiated histories of each nation would be as misleading as it would be to ignore the role of these histories in the founding of such a potent genre as the Southern Cone novel. What one wants is a way to see the political and social significance of these novels without attributing to such forces the very great artistic merit of individual novels.

From the mid-nineteenth century to the present, politics and art have been closely intertwined in the Southern Cone. In the 1840s, while Domingo Faustino Sarmiento was in exile, enforced by the Argentine Federalist government he criticized, he participated in what became a fundamental debate with Andrés Bello and José Victorino Lastarria about the formation and generation of language and literature in then-fledgling Latin American nations. As Efraín Kristal concludes:

> they set up the terms in which discussions about cultural emancipation of Hispanic America have been framed ever since: whether to apply the positive elements of Hispanic America's cultural and historical heritage in an original way (which is Bello's project), or to try to make a clean slate of the Hispanic cultural and historical heritage, viewed as a barrier to modernity (which is Sarmiento's position). (68)

Bello holds to the preservation of a common language as a foundation for and sign of shared human heritage across vast geographical spaces. Sarmiento envisions language as positively malleable: it expresses distinct ideas in locally established forms, and also exercises the freedom to alter and invent forms to encourage the development of a distinct art in Latin America. These arguments urge that the theoretical commitments that drive our choices about language use go far to determine the nature of civilization in the New World. The conflict between preservation and change resurfaces in later debates regarding the status of indigenous languages in relation to colonial language. For our purposes in describing the rise of the Southern Cone novel, it is important to highlight the fact that these thinkers' concern over a future Latin America and literature of the Americas reflects the notion that intellectual foundations should arise from open, public debate among persuasive individuals.

Sarmiento's highly influential *Facundo* (1845) in many ways sets ideological patterns that shape the development of the novel in the Southern Cone (especially in Argentina), although critics have argued whether and to what extent they should place this eclectic work within the literary genre of the novel. To understand Sarmiento's role in the literary history of the Southern Cone, one must remember that he was not only a prose writer but a head of state. First, in response to the political divisions between the Federalists and the Unitarians that then dominated Argentina, Sarmiento creates a narrative that establishes Buenos Aires as a civilized center opposed to the barbaric lands to the west, the Pampa. Second, he helps to construct and entrench a prehistory for the nation by artfully elaborating an account—from the eastern city, Buenos Aires—of the life of the Gauchos in the west. Between the city center of Arts and Letters and the unthinkable threat of the Indigenous or the Pampas as Wilderness, the Gaucho represents a middleman who adheres to neither pole but is necessary to enable civilization: to build society, to facilitate progress, and, eventually, to serve his passing part in founding a nation with boundaries worthy of its visionaries. Eventually, during Sarmiento's own presidency, he sought to realize the settlement of the Pampas, the extension of the railroad and telegraph westward, and the extermination of the Indigenous populations. His extermination policy was, in large part, an horrendous consequence of his understanding of the U.S. as a model for modern progress.

NINETEENTH-CENTURY ROMANTICISM, REALISM, AND NATURALISM

Critics on the whole agree that in the Southern Cone three modes of prose fiction take hold in the nineteenth century: Romanticism, Realism, and Naturalism. Doris Sommer has argued, based in part on representative samples from these three modes, that the romantic love plots in Latin America often signify, obliquely or forthrightly, the desires for unified countries and the resolution of social conflict. Among the novels she treats in *Foundational Fictions: The National Romances of Latin America* is the first novel published by an Argentine, *Amalia* (1855), written in exile from the Rosas government while its author, José Mármol, was in Montevideo. This novel blends the influences of Romanticism with polemics against the Rosas government. Daniel and Amalia pursue impossible love within a plot filled with intrigue, political violence, and dissidence. The failure of their relationship mirrors what Mármol sees as the national failures of the country to progress within the chaos engendered by a Federalist Argentina. Since Amalia fails to protect the life of pro-Unitarian Daniel from the Federalists who seek to murder him, under the Federalist government the doomed romance of Daniel and Amalia in this pro-Unitarian novel names violence as one of the main reasons that Argentina is unable to resolve intranational differences.

The rise of Realism in the Southern Cone does not, as often is the case in literary history, shake free of its Romantic precursors. *Martín Rivas* (1862), the most critically recognized novel by Chilean Alberto Blest Gana, is written on the heels of a decade of civil discord. It emphasizes national unity, consensus despite conflict between classes and regions in Chile. Set in Antofagasta, it portrays the social conditions brought about by class difference, social rank, and political division, yet a love is ultimately realized between Martín and Leonor, a woman of a social class above Martín's own. The optimistic union of Romanticism and Realism in this novel turns a socially blocked love to one that can represent reconciliation. Blest Gana consciously attempts to apply the Realist techniques of European authors such as Honoré de Balzac, whom he read during his four years in France, to fictional themes germane to Chilean history. His later work *Durante la reconquista* (1897, During the Reconquest), although remaining close to Realist roots, incorporates the methods of Naturalism more boldly to critique a squandering upper-class society.

Years earlier, Argentine Eugenio Cambaceres wrote the novel critics claim comes closest to Naturalism in Spanish America, *Sin Rumbo* (1885, *Without Direction*), and charts this familiar theme of upper-class decadence. The novel centers rather relentlessly on the *nausée* of a landed Argentine who, as the title implies, represents a man who appears to have been born without sufficient fortitude and stability to take seriously his responsibilities as a landowner, a representative of his class, or, ultimately, as an exemplar of the ideals of manhood. When the tide seems to turn as he takes on the care of his illegitimate daughter, her death proves too much for him, and he commits a gruesome suicide. His character leads to his own destruction, but Cambaceres points to the more general danger of carelessness in "the man of a certain class" that may lead to widespread financial destruction and moral corruptness in the nation as a whole.

EARLY TWENTIETH-CENTURY
MODERNISMO AND VANGUARDIA

The Southern Cone novel placed a premium on subjective experience, metaphysical questions, and aesthetic experimentation in its *modernista* and *vanguardia* incarnations. When Rubén Darío praises Francisco Contreras for his patriotism and cosmopolitanism in the prologue to *La piedad sentimental: Novela rimada* (1911, Sentimental Pity: A Rhymed Novel), Contreras's novel composed of poetry and prosaic verse advertises its ties with *modernismo*. Contreras follows the thoughts of the influential Uruguayan essayist José Enrique Rodó, who values both avant-garde experimentation and the maintenance of regional and local culture. Both are worthy of the aims of literature not only because innovation has at its foundation artifice rather than utility, but also because they encourage the enrichment of cultures along local lines. This is of special import to Rodó since he sees the pragmatism of the U.S. as encroaching on, and even threatening to, the diversity of Latin American habits. This similarity is striking since Contreras moved to and lived his entire life in Paris from 1905 onward. He shared this exile with a community of Latin American writers and intellectuals who hailed from such diverse places as Nicaragua, Guatemala, Mexico, Peru, Venezuela, and Argentina: Rubén Darío; Enrique Gómez Carrillo; Amado Nervo; Ventura, Francisco, and José García Calderón; Rufino Blanco Fombano; and Enrique Larreta. In fact, Contreras became a part of French intellectual life as the contributor to the *Mercure de France* of a column called "Lettres hispano-américaines" (Hispano-American Letters) for over twenty years (Weiss, 8–9). Although at a great distance physically from Latin America, in Contreras's *El pueblo maravilloso* (1927, The Wonderful Town), published first in French in 1924 as *La ville merveilleuse*, he named a movement that

proclaimed its subject to be based in community and history, focusing on land, tradition, and the people that would, like all superior literature, be interpreted by writers to reinforce through difference what he viewed as a shared primordial universality: *mundonovismo*.

Argentine Macedonio Fernández was a precursor of the *ultraísta* movement of the 1920s. His *Papeles de recienvenido* (1929, Papers of the recently arrived), although some would not strictly categorize it as a novel, later influenced the development of the novel in the 1960s and 1970s. The story consists in an accident in the street that leads a first-person narrator to a chain of apparently free associations that emphasize the absurdity, irrationality, humor, chanciness, and paradoxes of social and personal experience. Some of his most striking work was published posthumously: *Adriana Buenos Aires (Última novela mala)* (1974, Adriana Buenos Aires: The Last Bad Novel) and *Museo de la novela de la Eterna (Primera novela buena)* (1967, The Museum of Eterna's Novel: The First Good Novel). Only recently, seventeen years' worth of his correspondence with Jorge Luis Borges was published by Corrigedor. It reveals a meaningful literary bond of long mentorship and friendship that some critics believe inspired, developed, and refined Borges's opinions about issues many had previously believed to be largely particular to him (although Borges himself would likely disagree). The letters point especially to their shared preoccupation with how metaphysics (for example, the notion that our lives may be dreams) bears upon literary production.

It is widely known that Adolfo Bioy Casares collaborated closely with Borges. He began his career writing short fiction, and in 1937 he published his most significant work, *La invención de Morel (The Invention of Morel)*. Borges wrote the introduction to this novel that incorporates Modernist and

Surrealist aesthetic models. He draws upon avant-garde movements and cinematic technology to write a highly fragmented narrative that mimics filmic montage. It both undermines the notion of film's privileged relationship to reality and questions the ontological status of a novel. Further, he creates a protagonist who is also the narrator of the diary that largely comprises the text. Bioy Casares capitalizes on opportunities to destabilize the novel's referential truth value. For example, when the protagonist describes the island he fled to from Venezuela, he believes it is Villings, located in the archipelago Las Ellice (Ellis Islands). Bioy Casares turns editorial convention against itself by inventing an editor, N. del E., who writes his first footnote explaining that the identification is unlikely, since the island does not have the common characteristics of the islands of Las Ellice (Casares, 17). Bioy Casares innovates in order to turn the predominant literary themes of nation and local color toward cosmopolitanism.

Borges, it might be said, never penned a novel, yet in his own literary universe he just might have done so through translation. Borges fondly revised the fantastic, the detective genre, and the Gauchesque genre because of his faith and pleasure in human imagination and infinite libraries; he expressed gratitude for the accumulated art of the word, a glorious consolation for the writer who believes there is nothing new under the sun. In essays such as "Pierre Menard, el autor del *Quixote*" (1939, "Pierre Menard, the author of *Quixote*"), he reveals the ways that history creates readership. His ideas later appealed to the Boom writers, even though they would distance themselves from him politically. (The actions in question: Borges resigned from his position as the director of the Argentine National Library in 1973 when Perón was reelected, and he accepted an award from Augusto Pinochet, then dictator of Chile.)

In the first half of the twentieth century, Chilean María Luisa Bombal wrote two highly influential and beautiful narratives, *La amortajada* (1938, The shrouded woman) and *La última niebla* (1935, House of mist), that critique the national romance narrative in multiple ways. Her prose moves away from the dominant movements of the nineteenth century and toward more imaginative and experimental modes of writing: narrating a funeral from the point of view of an omniscient narrator and also from the perspectives of multiple characters in *La amortajada*, including that of the deceased woman. Bombal's French education, as well as her residence in Chile, Argentina, and the U.S., afforded her unique opportunities for contact with leading writers of the time, such as Borges and Pablo Neruda. Her unconventional aesthetic achievements were revisionary and forward-thinking, especially because she opened the category of gender to more varied representation than nineteenth-century national romance narratives had allowed.

Roberto Arlt, an Argentine, reoriented narrative on themes of the city, in his case Buenos Aires, with his first novel, *El juguete rabioso* (1926, *Mad Toy*), but with a difference. He turns away from the perils of social problems and policies and toward absurd characters. His character Silvio Astier not only feels degraded by the danger of the city (as Naturalism's characters regularly do), but contributes to his own degradation. He is a man who perpetrates random wrongdoing, yet remains impotent on the periphery of societal norms. He has not the full agency of a wicked person and thus is not held personally responsible for his offenses. Arlt's story hinges on both the senselessness of Astier's character and of his surroundings. This work influences Boom and post-Boom narratives, even as it reaches back to the concerns of Naturalist representation.

MID-TWENTIETH-CENTURY REALISM

Writers indeed took a backward glance as the Southern Cone novel developed in the mid-century. Beginning in the 1940s and 1950s, a Realist mode reemerged in order to express social protest. In Argentina and Paraguay, several works responded directly to living conditions during the Perón regime (1946–55) and the dictatorship of Alfredo Stroessner (1954–89). Argentine Bernardo Verbitsky found fame as a Socialist-Realist novelist. His *Un noviazgo* (1956, An Engagement) tells of working-class suffering during political upheaval in the 1930s and 1940s. Paraguayan Gabriel Casaccia wrote *La llaga* (1964, The Sore) and *Los exiliados* (1966, The Exiled) in part to denounce Stroessner's militarized strategies of political repression. Yet *La llaga* interprets an attempted coup of the government by using the intimacy of interior monologue; the thoughts of some characters, among them Atilio and his mother Constancia, open the public protest novel to personal stories of psychological complexity and sexual perversion. The Chilean generation of 1938 declared as their aims political and social reform in urban settings. Among these writers, the most critically recognized are Carlos Droguett and Fernando Alegría. Droguett's historical novel *Eloy* (1960) fictionally relates the last hours of the outlaw Eliodoro Hernández Astudillo's life from his own perspective, one that includes consciousness of his inevitable death. Droguett's *Patas de perro* (1965, Dog's Paws), on the other hand, pursues an unrealistic premise—a man born with dog's paws (Bobi)—to explore, through interior monologue and free indirect speech, the psychological and social consequences of an unwilled transgression of society's norms. Alegría's *Los días contados* (1968, The Counted Days) uses similar novelistic

techniques as he reveals in the life of a boxer the range and depth of human experience in Santiago's slums. In the final chapter, Alegría takes advantage of the literal meaning of his name when he writes himself as narrator and/or author into the plot. In the end, he implies that a character told him the story of his novel. She says, symbolically, "Adiós Alegría" (literally, "Goodbye Happiness"), and he replies, "Adiós Anita," ending his book with a melancholy metatextual flourish. Although Chilean Marta Brunet shares concerns and methods with Drogett and Alegría, her extensive body of work was considered controversial when it first appeared. Her most ambitious and appreciated novel, *Humo hacia el sur* (1946, Smoke toward the South), focuses on women's lives in a boom town in southern Chile in 1905. She explores how the individual is shaped by social dynamics, especially the forces of gender and class norms. The pressure of daily life in the mid-century was so great that even very talented writers reached back in the history of the novel to produce an art sufficiently rich in the representation of social life to express the political moment.

MID-TWENTIETH-CENTURY MODERNISMS

There was also a rejuvenation of Modernist aesthetics in mid-century. One sees plainly in a number of novels the main literary and intellectual currents of Europe moving through the literary culture in the Southern Cone. Leopoldo Marechal, Felisberto Hernández, and Ernesto Sábato all drew from and contributed to what is known as World Literature. Marechal's most important work was *Adán Buenosayres* (1948). He claimed a forefather in James Joyce's *Ulysses* that he adapted to his native Buenos Aires; instead of Homer, Genesis was his intertext.

Its eponymous hero makes his way through the city as Bloom did, in a mixture of modes, languages, and moods. Catholic and Peronist, Marechal thumbed his nose at what he saw as the liberal literary establishment.

The great Modernist lessons seemed to authorize some novelists' freedom from the political and social commitments of the preceding generation of intellectuals. For example, Uruguayan Hernández focuses his narrative works on unusual, surrealistic (not representative) scenes. He was admired by Julio Cortázar and known as a precursor of the neo-fantastic. Perhaps his most famous work, *Las hortensias* (1945, *The Daisy Dolls*), represents the power of a subject's psyche to animate empirical objects. Hernández creates a story of a man's obsession with dolls that borders on fetishism and pornography. And yet the narrative fosters sympathy by portraying the dolls as objects of love. The novella creates just enough narrative distance to make a reader feel complicit in these fantasies and to hold her at bay with the omission of crucial details.

Ernesto Sábato in particular is an Argentine artist to be reckoned with in post-WWII circles. His involvement with the canonical Argentine literary magazine, *Sur*, helped him to make an early mark. His novels *Sobre heroes y tumbas* (1961, On Heroes and Tombs) and *Abaddón, el exterminador* (1974, Abaddon, the Exterminator) are widely considered major works. Yet Sábato's *El túnel* (1948, The Tunnel) is perhaps one of the most popular Latin American novels that center on both city life and existentialist agency. The protagonist's perspective, that of Juan Pablo Castel (whose first names he shares with Jean-Paul Sartre), puts weight on the choices of the individual in this novel. The narration of his story from jail only heightens the sense that each of us is alone; Castel's misunderstanding of his lover and subsequent murder of her reveals the ways that

accidents and disorder set limits on reason vis-à-vis deliberative choice. Mid-century writers in the Southern Cone, then, resourcefully developed literary precedents within their own traditions as well as the literary and philosophical life of Europe and the U.S. at the time.

LATTER TWENTIETH-CENTURY SKEPTICISM AND THE BOOM

A general intellectual courage seemed accessible not to any one party or school of thought, but to several novelists in the 1950s. One sees in Southern Cone novels, then, a development of independent skepticism. Argentine David Viñas, for instance, was among those who questioned not only Perón populism, but the nation's institutions generally and its people of influence. His work reflects a neorealism, an effort to represent social life as it was actually experienced, rather than as it had been imagined. Although *Los años despiadados* (1956, The Ruthless Years) takes aim at a society virtually contemporary with its writing, Viñas was especially concerned with historical accuracy when he told this story about the friendship of a middle-class boy and a proletarian boy who is associated with *peronismo*. In one of his most critically acclaimed novels, *Cayó sobre su rostro* (1955, He Fell on His Face), Viñas layers multiple viewpoints in order to revise radically the official history of one of Argentina's acclaimed heroes: General and later President Julio A. Roca, the "Conqueror of the Desert." Roca's 1879 military attacks on the Indigenous in Patagonia are exposed in the novel as having been devastatingly violent and fraudulently rationalized.

Juan Carlos Onetti, who lived in Montevideo, Buenos Aires, and Paris, is considered the most important Urugayan novelist in the twentieth century; his work reflects an impressive intellectual integrity. His skeptical search for meaning through existentialist philosophies brought his novels to the attention of writers in the decade preceding the Boom of the 1960s. He deftly adapted European and American Modernist aesthetics in his major novels: *La vida breve* (1950, *A Brief Life*), *Los adioses* (1951, *The Goodbyes*), and *El astillero* (1961, *The Shipyards*). In these novels he employs doppelgängers, a narrator with multiple versions of the story, and a continual sense of alienation in his invented city of Santa María (placing him between the Yoknapatawpha County of Faulkner and the Macondo of García Márquez). In his final novel, *Dejemos hablar al viento* (1979, *Let the Wind Speak*), his skepticism moves as close as one may, while still writing, to nihilism. Medina, the protagonist of many Onetti novels, loses his battle to create a world for himself in Santa María. Many of the bases on which individuals and collectives may create meaning and value—capitalist success, romantic love, religion, psychoanalytic cures, and utopian politics—come to nothing in the novel; a reader inevitably arrives at the dark sense that all these means to satisfaction are equally empty. In 1980 Onetti received the Miguel de Cervantes literary prize.

Augusto Roa Bastos is the preeminent Paraguayan novelist, but this does not take one far in assessing his literary achievement. His 1959 *Hijo de hombre* (*Son of Man*) combines the use of the indigenous language Guaraní, virtually independent chapters, and highly metaphorical writing in a Modernist-inspired style that revises official histories of both the colonial period and the 1930s Chaco War. In his masterpiece, *Yo, el supremo* (1974, *I, the Supreme*), Roa Bastos offers a fictional autobiography and metafictional account of the nineteenth-century Paraguayan dictator José Gaspar Rodríguez de Francia. Written un-

der the dictatorship of Alfredo Stroessner, this novel is often read as a veiled attack on Stroessner's regime. The novel has achieved preeminence among dictatorship novels and New Historical novels, and has become one of the most comprehensive metatextual manuals since *Don Quixote*. As John King writes:

> It is impossible to summarize this extraordinary novel in a few lines. It incorporates the latest developments in linguistic theory and practice, talks of the arbitrariness and unreliability of language that purports to describe reality, rereads and comments upon the various histories and travelers' accounts of Paraguay, ranges across the breadth of Latin American history, implicitly condemning Stroessner and debating with Fidel Castro, and exploring once again the gap between writer and reader. (291–98)

The dictator and his secretary exemplify the Chinese boxes of interest in written and voiced multilingualism; the dictator pronounces and the secretary records truth and lies as autobiography is framed within the novel. Thus the aesthetic method creates and resists the novel as auto-verifiable.

Julio Cortázar—Argentine short-story writer, novelist, and translator—plays a central role in Latin American letters in the twentieth century, even though after 1951 he lived in exile in Paris. In addition to his highly influential collections of short stories (1951, *Bestiario*, *Bestiary*; 1956, *Final del juego*, *End of the Game*; 1962, *Historias de cronopios y de famas*, *Cronopios and Famas*; 1965, *Las armas secretas*, *The Secret Weapons*; and 1966, *Todos los fuegos el fuego*, *All Fires the Fire*), Cortázar wrote one of the most seminal and lauded novels of Latin America: *Rayuela* (1963, *Hopscotch*), a book as hip as its readers, and just as likely to send them up as itself. As his *lector cómplice* (complicit reader) we are free to read the novel chronologically, page after page, or in another order suggested by the text, even as this alternative reading leads us to an endless back-and-forth between two chapters. In this alternative reading, the progress of the text relies finally on the reader's effort, paralleled by that of the narrator, Morelli, an emblem of the novelist's desire for an active reader. On the other hand, La Maga advocates for a *lector hembra* or *lector pasivo* (passive reader), a position that is as easily defensible in the textual world of *Rayuela*, a turn as much toward happenstance as toward order. The novel establishes a dialectic of the narrated life of Horacio Oliveira between Paris and Buenos Aires, destinations of order and the annihilation of order: sex, alcohol, *mate*, and jazz. Between the narrator and his character lie the perils of existential freedom and literary liberation from tradition. One should recognize that the general literary success of the Southern Cone novel has, in some part, depended on translation. Cortázar in particular has been very well served by his collaborators. His *62; modelo para armar* (1968, *62; A Model Kit*) and *Libro de Manuel* (1972, *A Manual for Manuel*) have also attracted wide attention among literary critics, thanks partly to their masterful translation into English by Gregory Rabassa.

Chilean José Donoso became an integral part of the Boom, though he has been less recognized outside of Latin America. Unlike his Boom contemporaries, Donoso shied away from grand, explicitly historical novels about Latin America. An elite education at the Grange School led him to meet Carlos Fuentes, a lifelong friend, and to begin his practice as a writer. He eventually studied at Princeton, encountering R. P. Blackmur and Allen Tate. During the 1950s Donoso was stylistically bound neither to the Realist aesthetics of his contemporaries nor to those of the Modernists. He then wrote psychologically driven novels, such as *Coronación* (1957, *Coronation*). The criti-

cism this book expressed of the Chilean oligarchy was amplified in his novel *Este domingo* (1966, *This Sunday*). This stylistic tendency continued into what many consider his masterpiece, *El obsceno pájaro de la noche* (1970, *The Obscene Bird of Night*). Donoso concerned himself with creating surreal dreamlike states, the psychological and emotional conditions of characters who lie, for some reason or another, on the margins of society. The narrator Mudito, Humberto Peñalosa—a frustrated or aspiring writer—along with Jerónimo and Inés Azcoitía and their deformed son, whom they conceal on their estate, La Rinconada, may be the main players in *El obsceno pájaro*. Yet, the fact that the novel never settles on a consistent narrator, or on a main character, or even on a plot heightens the purposefully dizzying metadiscursive experiments of the novel. Donoso undermines the notion of a safe vantage point from which to construct stable hierarchies. *Casa de campo* (1978, *A House in the Country*) creates two worlds that exist simultaneously but cannot both be true. On the paradox of the adults of the Ventura y Ventura family enjoying a pleasant picnic day away from the manor while the children simultaneously endure the onslaughts of nature, attacks by the indigenous, political schisms, and more over the course of a year in the country manor, Donoso creates a novel that critiques the Pinochet dictatorship, the entire history of Chile, and various artistic and literary codes. For example, the famous entrance of the author as a character in the novel speaks to an awareness of reading models and expectations that heighten a reader's suspicion of his or her own practices. Donoso is also well known for other works: *El lugar sin límites* (1966, *Place without Limits*), *Historia personal del "boom"* (1972, *The Boom in Spanish American Literature: A Personal History*), and *El jardín de al lado* (1981, *The Garden Next Door*).

THE LATE TWENTIETH-CENTURY POST-BOOM

Argentine Manuel Puig's *La traición de Rita Hayworth* (1968, *The Betrayal of Rita Hayworth*) forthrightly shifts the art of the novel. He subtly uses popular culture, especially film, and employs a vertiginous narrative technique of multiple narrators and dialogue to disperse narrative authority. The absence of a controlling narrator undermines the stability of a world that shuns Toto's burgeoning sexuality. Puig especially trains a critical light on unjust principles that undergird the popular and the elite in equal measure. The novel that won Puig world acclaim was *El beso de la mujer araña* (1976, *Kiss of the Spider Woman*), which both undermines and recuperates mainstream gender and genre thoughts and practices. By layering low and high cultural elements in the context of a relationship between one man imprisoned for his politics and another for an affair with a young man, Puig constructs a critical perspective on civic and private autonomy in the 1970s.

The famous first words of Argentine Ricardo Piglia's *Respiración artificial* (1979, *Artificial Respiration*), "¿Hay una historia?" (Is there a history, a story?; *historia* means both history and story), indicate the multiple ambitions of this novel: to negotiate the strictures of official history imposed by political regimes and institutionalized narratives, the poststructuralist assault on the referential value of language, literature's capacity to intervene in social life, the ability of narratives to capture the heart, and, most of all, singularity. The novel is divided into two parts. The first concerns Emilio Renzi's collaboration with his uncle in telling the story of Juan Manuel Rosas and his private secretary, Enrique Ossorio. In the second, a Pole named Vladimir Tardewski, who lives in Argentina, narrates a conversation of some twenty hours' length about

Argentine political and cultural history. Taken together, the two parts of Piglia's novel forefront the collaborative construction of national histories and language.

Critics group Chilean Diamela Eltit with Piglia as prominent postmodern writers in Latin America. Their work reflects the influence of recent literary and political theory, and the alignment of the novel with the intellectuality of the academic sector. Because she remained in Chile throughout the Pinochet dictatorship, Eltit holds the status of an artist of "inner exile." Her first book, *Lumpérica* (1981), is a morbidly fascinating, ethically troubling book about the body, language, capitalism, commodities, public pressure, public display, exposure, and power—subjects well known to academic intellectuals. Her prose frames a multiply named woman vagabond as if through the lens of a camera. Through analysis of the sacred and the profane Eltit critiques a country under revised and, often, disorienting codes regarding the traditions of both in Chile. In truth, the most compelling hold her writing has over its reader comes from its density. The novel's title, perhaps the least example of its poetic prowess, provides an amazing neologism combining *lumpen* with *américa* where Eltit reaches for a wide audience for a subject below social boundaries and polite discourse. Some of her other acclaimed works are *Por la patria* (1986, *For the Mother Country*) and *Vaca sagrada* (1991, *Sacred Cow*).

Argentine Luisa Valenzuela writes one of the most complexly surreal and simultaneously allegorical and realist novels in all of Latin American history about the Dirty War in her homeland: *La cola de lagartija* (1983, *Lizard's Tail*). El Brujo, the protagonist of her novel, stands in for José López Rega, a Rasputin figure who became the Minister of Social Wellbeing when Isabela Perón was the regime's figurehead. Valenzuela's use of the doppelgänger, signifying fictional and real accounts, emancipates the confusing emotions of those living under the regime's control. When it is most important to distinguish the real from the fictional, beyond all poststructuralist accounts, she writes a provocative narrative about what one might believe as real and true. Her magnificent play with the acronym for the Alianza Anticomunista Argentina (Argentine Anticommunist Alliance), AAA; the attempts by La Bruja to auto-impregnate himself with his third testicle, Estrella, as a vesicle; and her devastating accounts of the rivers of blood all reveal amazing control of language, especially in the second part. She signs her name to the first part, announcing her authorial effort to transform the novel into a meta-testimonial account of her search for her missing lover. In the juxtaposition of the radically different discursive parts of the novel Valenzuela may make her most important intervention into the dictatorship novel, realizing in one book the power and persuasiveness for both oppressor and oppressed of diverse novelistic strategies. Her most striking novels include *Aquí pasan cosas raras* (1975, *Strange Things Happen Here*) and *Cambio de armas* (1982, *Other Weapons*).

For political reasons, Cristina Peri Rossi left Uruguay for Spain in 1972 and eventually became a citizen there. Her novel *Nave de los locos* (1984, *The Ship of Fools*) uses multiple narrators and an avant-garde pastiche travel narrative to explore the plight of exile, migration, and estrangement. The protagonist, Equis, points to her engagement with Foucault and other theorists (as the title suggests an allusion to *Madness and Civilization*). Not only does the ship of fools refer to the stories of medieval practices of exclusion, but also, in this novel, to a busload of pregnant women on their way from Spain to an abortion clinic in London and elusive concentration camps. One's inability to locate precisely the concentration camps

makes the horror extend, through displacement, across the world. She creates situations that push an openly universal agenda where the horror takes place in many locales, not only in the local one. These ethical dilemmas inevitably hit home. The final scene in the final chapter of the novel famously complicates performativity by portraying Equis finding Lucía (previously disappeared) in a transvestite club, in an act where she is dressed as a man, impersonating Charlotte Rampling, impersonating Helmut Berger, impersonating Marlene Dietrich in drag, dancing with a partner who wishes to be someone she desires to be, and who seems to be Dolores del Río (Kantaris, 74). Peri Rossi is thus a part of a wave of post-Boom writers who examine and engage contemporary philosophies of identity, language, and place.

TURN-OF-THE-CENTURY TRENDS

Indeed, since the late 1990s the Southern Cone narrative has engaged increasingly global themes and audiences. Chilean Isabel Allende is one of the most commercially successful writers to emerge from the Southern Cone. Her first novel, *Casa de los espíritus* (1982, *The House of the Spirits*), is widely recognized as a rewriting of Gabriel García Márquez's *Cien años de soledad* (1967, *One Hundred Years of Solitude*). Set in Chile, it blends historical fact with extravagant invention; Allende made a critical incursion into the genre of MAGICAL REALISM. She stays relatively true to the magical realist style as she chronicles four generations of the Trueba-del-Valle family, even as she focuses especially on the matrilineal: Nívea, Clara, Blanca, and Alba. Her most significant turn from the Boom is an alternative ethical gesture implied by the temporality of the final chapter. Although Allende's novel can be read as circular, since the last words echo the first, it proposes that telling and retelling are ethically progressive in combating forgetting. The worst injustice from this point of view is a life condemned to oblivion. Moreover, Alba's narration in the final chapter points to forgiveness rather than vengeance as a proper reaction to the atrocities of the military coup of 1973. Allende's second most acclaimed book about Chile is *De amor y de sombra* (1985, *Of Love and Shadows*), and she continues to write prolifically in the U.S.

Chilean Alberto Fuguet has written a series of novels in the wake of being among those who founded the influential literary group McOndo in 1996. His most widely read and acclaimed novel, *Mala onda* (1991, *Bad Vibes*), portrays the lives of teenagers in Santiago de Chile caught up in a globalized and fast-paced world unknown to previous generations. Its abundant use of slang and countercultural references explore youth culture alongside an increasingly open discontent with the Pinochet dictatorship in the early 1980s.

Roberto Bolaño became the darling and talented *enfant terrible* of many recent accounts of the Southern Cone novel. He was born in Chile but spent much of his life wandering through France, Mexico, and El Salvador, and he finally settled in Spain. Stories of his "vagabond" or "beatnik" life have fascinated contemporary critical accounts: was he actually detained by the forces of the 1973 Chilean coup? Was he truly a recovered heroin addict? One wonders whether these conjectures derive from a sensationalist journalist looking for the Romantic in the modern writer, or the author's efforts to show how stories and representations, even of the self, both reveal and conceal. Bolaño's career as a novelist is astonishingly dense in the ten years before his death in 2003: *La pista de hielo* (1993, *The Skating Rink*), *Literatura nazi en América* (1996, *Nazi Literature in the Americas*),

Estrella distante (1996, *Distant Star*), *Los detectives salvajes* (1998, *The Savage Detectives*), *Amuleto* (1999), *Monsieur Pain* (1999), *Nocturno de Chile* (2000, *By Night in Chile*), and *Amberes* (2002, *Antwerp*). The most highly acclaimed novel published during his lifetime was *Los detectives salvajes*. In this postmodern DETECTIVE novel, the array of voices describing the literary and adventurous ramblings of Ulises Lima and Arturo Belano lets the reader know she is on unstable ground. In the opening and final section, Juan García Madero describes his involvement with Ulises and Arturo, ever-promising writers who lead a literary group that espouses radical and erratic literary doctrine. In the end, the group is whittled down to these same three characters and a prostitute they are attempting to protect as they quixotically attempt to find a nearly forgotten poet of the 1920s avant-garde. Their only evidence of her work is a sheet of indecipherable writing. In the middle, various voices narrate the destinies of Ulises and Arturo. Contradictions and coincidences entice the reader to attempt to weave together the story of their lives while making it impossible to connect the warp and weft of their tapestry. The novel *2666* (2004) was unfinished and published posthumously, but critics concur that its dense allusions and postmodern devices identify ethical dilemmas of literature confronted by the world's horrors.

CONCLUSION

The push and pull between local and cosmopolitan communities needed thoughtful answers as Southern Cone political beliefs and national literatures evolved. Each novelist was called upon to write according to his conscience and to develop the gifts of Spanish in the Americas. The growth of the Southern Cone novel relied, like most literature, upon an individual mustering his widest resources to confront the most important dilemmas at hand.

BIBLIOGRAPHY

Bioy Casares, A. (1983), *Invención de Morel*.
Kantaris, E.G., (1995), *Subversive Psyche*.
King, J. (1987), "Augusto Roa Bastos," in *Modern Latin American Fiction*.
Kristal, E. (1993), "Dialogues and Polemics," in *Sarmiento and His Argentina*, ed. J.T. Criscenti.
Weiss, J. (2002), *Lights of Home*.

Space

JULIE O'LEARY GREEN

At least since Plato and Aristotle, space in narrative has often been seen as ornamental rather than functional, relegated disparagingly to the realm of the descriptive or the merely representational (as opposed to the artful or rhetorical) and subordinated to plot and character. It is often seen as nonpurposeful or as mere amplification, and within discourse on the novel it is considered unnecessary (although not useless): most definitions of narrative include tellers and events, but none includes any mention of or relation to space.

Despite this bias, the nineteenth century saw a new interest in narrative space on the part of both authors and scholars. Developments in sociology, biology, and ANTHROPOLOGY affirming the individual's dependence on his or her environment influenced aesthetic theories of fiction. These ideas about the role of space in the novel continued to develop throughout the twentieth century and into the twenty-first. Importantly, the human-centered bias remains: while there has been more interest in the ways in which narrative space functions, character still remains the nexus around which studies of space revolve.

Today, space is thought to function in the novel in significant ways: it is a frame of action (a place in which things happen), it conveys thematic information, it reveals information about characters and character relationships, it can influence reader expectations, and it is an active partner in the governing of how narrative progresses (i.e., certain spaces allow certain events to occur while other spaces prohibit events).

SPATIAL FORM

In 1766, eighteenth-century dramatist and philosopher Gotthold Ephraim Lessing (1729–81) characterized literature as a temporal art, opposed to spatial arts like painting and sculpture (see TIME). His argument centered on the assumption that an artwork's form is dependent on its manner of perception. Centuries later, the novel is still considered an inherently temporal medium. Objects and spaces must be incorporated into a temporal sequence in order to be represented in narratives; spatial structures must be transformed into temporal ones.

Beginning with his 1945 essay "Spatial Form in Modern Literature" and continuing for the next three decades, American literary scholar Joseph Frank broke new critical ground with his argument that a hallmark of modernist literature was that it was meant to be apprehended spatially rather than sequentially (see MODERNISM). He argued that because language proceeds in time and literature is naturally temporal, modernist writers like James Joyce, Gustave Flaubert, Djuna Barnes, and Marcel Proust had to find new ways to manipulate novelistic form in order to express their desired simultaneity. The result is that meaning, relationships, and references are arranged across the narrative without respect to temporal sequence and must be connected by a reader and viewed as a whole before meaningful patterns emerge.

Frank's essay drew responses from prominent literary scholars who returned to Lessing's claims and argued that the mode of perception (reading from beginning to end) makes modernist plots no less temporal than any others. Other critiques have centered on the fact that Frank's argument is not actually about space in the novel but rather an alternative reading process.

One frequently invoked theory of space in the novel that both contends with the temporal nature of narrative and focuses on literal spaces is Mikhail BAKHTIN'S (1981) theory of the chronotope, which states that space and time are mutually constitutive and interactive, comprising a single unit of analysis for studying literary texts. Chronotopes are narrative hubs where meanings are housed. They highlight the intrinsic connectedness of time and space. For Bakhtin, the road narrative, in which time spent means distance covered, is the clearest textual expression of the chronotope. It not only illustrates the interconnectedness of time and space but also provides narrative potential: potential for encounter, collision (i.e., of characters who might not have come in contact if they had not met at that exact time and place), and change across time and space.

The French philosopher Michel de Certeau makes a similar claim in "Spatial Stories" (1987), where he argues that every story is a travel story. He also argues for the necessity and ubiquity of boundaries, claiming that stories authorize the establishment, displacement, or transcendence of limits and that they set in opposition two movements that intersect.

All of these arguments about spatial form implicate plot. They all implicitly or explicitly argue that spatial form relates to the temporal organization of words and events in the novel, whether spatial form is created by temporal fragmentation (disjointed plots), as in Frank's understanding; is mutually constitutive of plots and meaning, as in Bakhtin's understanding; or is what actually drives the plot of a narrative forward toward climax and conclusion, as in de Certeau's understanding.

TYPOLOGIES OF SPACE

Analyses of spatial form tend to focus on the overall shape and progression of a novel. However, such analyses do not provide a way of studying and comparing specific representations of space in the novel. In other words, we must distinguish between spatial form and space as a formal element. Ruth Ronen has characterized two primary ways of classifying types of narrative space. In the first, space is understood in terms of its proximity to characters; in the second, it is understood according to its factuality.

Proximal and distant spaces

On this scale, spaces are classified according to how close and/or how accessible they are to characters in the narrative present. The most immediate narrative space is setting: the place where characters in the narrative present interact and where story-events take place. Setting is considered continuously relevant, capable of extending over a sequence of actions, events, and situations without needing to be rearticulated. As a result, setting is well suited to discussions of why certain authors, in certain texts or certain moments within texts, make widely differing choices about how, when, why, and how much to articulate setting.

Spaces near characters in the narrative present and accessible to them via their senses are called secondary spaces. In Toni Morrison's *Beloved* (1987), the narration follows Sethe in the kitchen as a group of women assemble within earshot outside; the kitchen is the setting, and outside is a secondary space. Secondary spaces allow myriad possibilities for overhearing, misunderstanding, misdirecting, etc., and thus can directly influence a novel's plot.

Fictional spaces might also be nearby but inaccessible to the characters in the narrative present. This inaccessibility may be provisional, thus linking inaccessible frames to narrative progression (meaning that something must happen for characters to gain access, and often gaining access causes other things to happen). In Charlotte Brontë's *Jane Eyre* (1847), the third floor of Mr. Rochester's mansion is an inaccessible space for most of the novel; the moment when it becomes accessible constitutes a significant climax, the result of which is a complete reorganization of the household and all of the relationships therein.

Fictional spaces might also be geographically or temporally distant from the present setting. When Marlow sits aboard the *Nellie* at the beginning of Joseph Conrad's *Heart of Darkness* (1902) and tells of his trip up the Congo River, that river is geographically distant. The events he retells are temporally distant.

Finally, narrative space can have an ambivalent degree of immediacy. Frequently, novels make reference to generalized or nonspecific spaces. Examples of this include references to "the world" or "the horizon."

Factual and counterfactual spaces

Fictional space can also be classified according to its degree of actuality, where actuality does not refer to the space's verisimilitude (see DECORUM) but rather to whether the characters in question are actually in those spaces. Actual spaces include all of the frames explained above; and non-actual spaces (these might be potential or hypothetical spaces, counterfactual spaces, and nonfactual spaces) are spatial articulations that are subordinated to future-tense sentences, imperatives, conditionals, questions,

negative sentences, predictions, or the subjunctive mood. In Leslie Marmon Silko's *Ceremony* (1977), the narrator explains Tayo's thought processes as he flees two men on horseback: "They were about a mile away when he first saw them, so he would try to find a deep grove of pine where he could stay until they passed" (198). He never does find a grove, so it remains a hypothetical space. Often, the non-actual space matters less than whether it remains non-actual or is eventually actualized.

Non-actual spaces have various relations to the actual space of the narrative. They can have ramifications for interpreting a novel's overall meaning or thematic bent by establishing binaries, by making or encouraging an evaluation, or by conveying emotion, for example.

SPACE AND CHARACTER

As these typologies reveal, what makes space interesting to most authors, readers, and scholars is its relation to narrative agents. Classifying a particular space depends on which characters the narrative follows in the narrative present.

Additionally, descriptions of fictional spaces are often used to provide information about character. In the novels of Henry James, as many have noted, the homes of main characters often function as metaphors for their owners. Miss Birdseye's apartment in *The Bostonians* (1886) articulates her identity with its refusal to conform to Victorian standards; her somewhat muddled and crowded home is seen as an expression of her character.

MOTIVATION AND FOCALIZATION

How descriptions of space are inserted can also tell us about character. Because setting and other narrative spaces do not require constant articulation, understanding the motivation for insertions of spatial descriptions can yield insight into characters and narrators. As Mieke Bal points out, the manner of description of a given fictional passage characterizes the rhetorical strategy of the narrator.

Bal lays out three primary motivations for spatial description in the novel. The most obvious (because it is voiced by a character) is motivation via speaking: these are spatial articulations that occur in DIALOGUE ("I went here" or "His house was very large"). Motivation via speaking can help us understand a character's attitude toward space.

Motivation via action occurs when an actor carries out an action with an object, e.g., a character rides a bicycle. The very act of riding that bicycle motivates a description of the bicycle and provides a justification for any related spatial description. This kind of spatial description can, but need not, reveal something about the character's relationship to his or her space.

Motivation via looking occurs when the narration (not the dialogue) describes what a character sees or saw. The narrator of Ian McEwan's *Atonement* (2001) follows Briony as she stands at a window and sees "a scene that could easily have accommodated, in the distance at least, a medieval castle. Some miles beyond the Tallises' land rose the Surrey Hills and their motionless crowds of thick crested oaks, their greens softened by a milky heat haze" (pt. 1, chap. 3). This description of the landscape is motivated by the act of Briony's looking.

Spatial articulations motivated by looking are the most common and often the least noticeable kinds of descriptions of space. They are also the motivations that, so far, have yielded the most significant understanding of the relationship between characters and the fictional spaces in which they interact. This is because spatial descriptions motivated by looking are often a case of focalization (see NARRATIVE PERSPECTIVE). Focalization refers to the perspective from which particular events or elements of the narrative are narrated. When fictional spaces are described via the narration (i.e., via looking), places are linked to certain points of perception: how space is articulated tells us about the ways in which characters bring their senses to bear on space, especially as they see, hear, and touch their surroundings. In the *Atonement* example, the narrator adopts the limited point of view of one character (Briony) not only to motivate a description of the scene she is about to witness but also to portray Briony's particular mindstyle. How she sees the landscape tells us about how she sees the world.

SPACE AND THE READER

Recent work in COGNITIVE narratology has explored other possible functions of space. Here, we find not only an interest in the relationships among places and agents in the narrative world but also an interest in the interaction between *readers* and the spaces of narrative. David Herman, Monika Fludernik, Marie-Laure Ryan, and others have suggested that space functions in narrative at the same time that narrative helps us create mental representations of space. Thus, story-telling necessitates modeling and enabling others to model spatially related entities.

The concept of deixis is important in this account of fictional space. Deixis is any reference to the context of the production of an utterance (as in the expression "come over *here*"). Herman argues that narratives, including novels, prompt readers to relocate from their own here and now to the here and now of the storyworld. Others, like Ryan, argue that paying attention to spatial deictics allows us to construct mental maps of the world inside the novel. These cognitive maps, which may be rudimentary or elaborate depending on both the reader and the amount of spatial data provided in the novel, can help readers orient fictional characters, places, and positions in terms of relational systems rather than geographically located points, which in turn can help them develop thematic readings of characters or places in spatial relationships. Recent research suggests that readers may construct cognitive maps of fictional space as background for understanding plot, character motivation, and moral or ethical issues articulated in the text. Furthermore, the extent to which readers compare their mental models of fictional spaces to their mental models of real-world spaces is also a focus of recent literary inquiry, particularly under the rubric of possible-worlds theory (see Ronen, 1994).

SEE ALSO: Metafiction, Narrative Structure, Rhetoric and Figurative Language, Story/Discourse.

BIBLIOGRAPHY

Bakhtin, M. (1981), "Forms of Time and the Chronotope in the Novel," in *Dialogic Imagination*, trans. C. Emerson and M. Holquist, ed. M. Holquist.

Bal, M. (2002), *Narratology*, 3rd ed.

de Certeau, M. (1984), "Spatial Stories," in *Practice of Everyday Life*, trans. R. Rendell.

Fludernik, M. (1996), *Towards a "Natural" Narratology*.

Frank, J. (1963), "Spatial Form in Modern Literature," in *Widening Gyre*.

Frank, J. (1978), "Spatial Form: Some Further Reflections," *Critical Inquiry* 5:275–90.

Herman, D. (2001), "Spatial Reference in Narrative Domains," *TEXT* 21(4):515–41.

Herman, D. (2002), *Story Logic*.

Lessing, G.E. (1962), *Laocoön*, trans. E.-A. McCormick.

Ronen, R. (1986), "Space in Fiction," *Poetics Today* 7.3:421–38.

Ronen, R. (1994), *Possible Worlds in Literary Theory*.

Ryan, M.-L. (2003), "Cognitive Mapping and the Representation of Narrative Space," in *Narrative Theory and the Cognitive Sciences*, ed. D. Herman.

Speech Act Theory

KIM EMERY

Speech act theory names a body of thought in which the use of language—a speech act—is conceived as a kind of action within the material world, rather than a description of or a reference to a discrete and exterior reality. Although anticipated in different ways by the works of Scottish philosopher Thomas Reid (1710–96), American pragmatist C. S. Peirce (1839–1914), and German phenomenologists Edmund Husserl (1859–1938) and Adolf Reinach (1883–1917), among others, speech act theory is most famously associated with Oxford philosopher J. L. Austin (1911–60). In a series of lectures delivered at Harvard in 1955 and published posthumously in a volume called *How to Do Things with Words*, Austin outlined what has since come to be considered the first systematic elaboration of speech act theory.

In these lectures, Austin begins his discussion of the speech act by distinguishing between two types of utterances that, despite their resemblance in grammatical form, may be seen to serve quite distinct functions. The statements studied by philosophers of language, on the one hand, are taken to describe an external reality or to report a fact. Such statements may be categorized as "descriptive" or, as Austin prefers, "constative," and are subject to evaluation on the basis of their truth or falsity.

However, a second type of utterance may also assume the first-person singular present-indicative active form of simple declarative sentences without submitting to such characterization. These utterances, which Austin terms "performative," do not make the kind of claim that can be tested against an external reality, and hence cannot be classified as simply true or false; instead, utterances of this sort perform an action, or are part of the performance of an action, that "is not normally thought of as just saying something" (7). Austin's examples include such actions performed in words as betting, bequeathing, promising, marrying, and christening. To say "I bet . . .," "I promise . . .," or "I christen . . .," in certain circumstances, is indeed to bet, promise, or name; the utterance itself accomplishes the act, rather than reporting on or referring to an act accomplished elsewhere or by other means.

Austin is careful to explain that the requirement of specific circumstances or, indeed, of correlative supporting actions does not vitiate the performative aspect of the utterance itself; hence, the bet must be accepted, the will must be signed and notarized, the minister officiating a marriage must be duly authorized and the participants eligible—but the fact remains that the words themselves are not only necessary to the act, but in an important sense are understood to themselves constitute the act. More importantly, he contends that the intention or inward state of the interlocutors is not critically at issue: the performative does not report on an inward act of, for example, committing to a marriage; one may be duly and legally married whether one "means" one's vows or not. A promise may be given in bad faith, but this does not mean that no promise has been made. Although such performatives may "misfire" in a variety of ways—on which Austin elaborates at some length—misreporting on an inward state is not among them, as the function of the performative is not to reflect an independent reality (either inward or exterior), but rather to act on the reality within which it is enmeshed. A performative is neither true nor false, but rather, in Austin's words, felicitous or infelicitous, happy or unhappy; it is evaluated not in terms of veracity, but in terms of performative force.

Austin further categorizes such explicit performatives as "I bet . . .," or "I promise . . .," as illocutionary acts, which he describes as actions accomplished *in* saying something and reliant on convention for their performative force. These he distinguishes from the more familiar sense in which saying something is already doing something: i.e., making sounds (the phonetic act) in a certain order (the phatic act) with a certain meaning (the rhetic act). This he calls the locutionary act, a concept that encapsulates "the full normal sense" of saying something (94) without excluding the possibility of the utterance exerting a further performative force. To these two categories Austin adds a third: the perlocutionary act, which is accomplished *by* saying something, or as an effect of saying something, but not performed in and of the utterance itself. Hence, the illocutionary act of a promise being made is accomplished in the utterance of promising, provided only that the most minimal conditions are met (e.g., that uptake is secured and the act is not voided by virtue of going unheard). The consequences of the promise, in contrast to the act itself, constitute its perlocutionary effect: the addressee may be thrilled by a promise, or unimpressed; this does not affect the illocutionary force of the promise, but it does make for a different perlocutionary act. There is in perlocution a certain gap or noncoincidence between utterance and effect that is not characteristic of illocution and its force. Although the coincidence of an illocutionary act and its performative force is merely prototypically and not necessarily temporal, it is in essence conventional and therefore inescapable; the relation of a perlocutionary act to its consequences, in contrast, is not in essence conventional and therefore not inevitable, however likely or predictable those consequences may be. Austin is clear that "there cannot be an illocutionary act unless the means employed are conventional"; however, as he also acknowledges, "it is difficult to say where conventions begin and end" (119).

Austin's method is to work from observations offered as "provisional, and subject to revision" (4n1). Just as the illocutionary act is revealed to have its locutionary and, inevitably, perlocutionary dimensions, the explicit performative that constitutes its prototypical appearance cannot in the end be cleanly separated from the constative. Illocutions involve reference and sense, and constative utterances exert performative force. Indeed, Austin concludes that "in general, the locutionary act as much as the illocutionary is an abstraction only: every genuine speech act is both" (147). The perlocutionary effects of a locution, moreover, are unpredictable and in theory infinite. In working through these mutual entailments so thoughtfully, Austin thoroughly undermines the "descriptive fallacy" for which he faults "both philosophers and grammarians" (2–3)—i.e., the idea that the primary function of language is mimetic or referential and its fundamental form, therefore, the declarative statement. By refusing to misrecognize abstraction for actuality, Austin reimagined the relation of language to the material world and offered a powerful model that would be taken up by deconstructionists, literary scholars, and GENDER theorists—as well as philosophers of language—in years to come.

LITERARY SPEECH ACTS

Despite his insistence on separating questions of inward states from the functional operation of illocutionary acts, Austin limited his discussion in these lectures to the "normal use" of language in "ordinary circumstances"—explicitly excluding from consideration, for example, theatrical and literary utterances, which he categorized here as "*parasitic*" (22). The grounds for this exclusion were soon questioned, however, by literary scholars concerned with the conventional, contextual, and social dimensions of literature. In a series of essays in the early 1970s for example, Richard Ohmann argued that literature comprises a kind of "quasi-speech-act," distinct from nonliterary language but dependent nevertheless on readers' immersion in sociality. In the late 1970s Mary Louise Pratt would reject categorical distinctions between ordinary and literary language altogether, contending that Ohmann's qualification itself relies on a misapprehension of ordinary language as lacking in ostensibly literary qualities on which it often depends. Drawing on the pragmatics of Austin's contemporary H. P. Grice (1913–88) and the work of sociolinguists including William Labov, Pratt offered a theory of literature as a linguistic activity continuous with oral narrative and imbedded in social interaction. Others, including Monroe C. Beardsley (1915–85), Seymour Chatman, and Marcia Eaton, have examined the use of speech acts within works of literature.

The engagement most important to contemporary theory, however, would come from philosopher Jacques Derrida (1930–2004), who proposed that the distinction between "normal" and "parasitic" uses is impossible to maintain because it is in the nature of language to be quoted. Against the "pure singularity" attributed to Austin's speech act proper—the illocution

SPEECH ACT THEORY 799

fully present to itself and fully congruent with its performative force—Derrida posits a principle of general iterability, contending that ordinary language is itself characterized by a "structural parasitism" (17). In this view, there can be no "pure" performative because each speech act relies for its success on the citation of an iterable (endlessly repeatable) model; only by invoking a recognizable formula—i.e., by citing a convention—can an illocution exert a performative force. Moreover, while convention must be cited, it can never be fully realized or exactly repeated; reiteration is required, but—strictly speaking—impossible. What Austin calls "the total speech act in the total speech situation" (52), the object of his study, can never be fully or finally defined, because the total speech situation—the act's salient context—is not "exhaustively determinable" (18). In citing an iterable model, the performative is not fully present to itself, but neither can it replicate in toto "the total speech act in the total speech situation" of any prior iteration or ideal model. Hence, Derrida concludes, citationality or parasitism is not a "special circumstance" to be held in abeyance or excluded from consideration, as Austin posits, but is instead integral to "'ordinary' language" as such—its "internal and positive condition of possibility" (17). Just as Austin decenters the constative, suggesting that language is not secondarily or peripherally performative, social, and materially situated, but fundamentally so, Derrida deconstructs the presumed primacy of so-called ordinary language, revealing the citationality at its core and arguing that Austin's a priori separation of normal use from special circumstances imputes to language "an ethical and teleological determination" in fact imposed by the assumptions of analytic philosophy (17).

Derrida's contention that this principle of iterability introduces a philosophically significant gap or "dehiscence" between the intention animating an utterance and the act of utterance has been strenuously challenged by American analytic philosopher John Searle, an important interpreter of Austin noted for his taxonomy of illocutionary acts, among other contributions. Searle maintains that iterability functions in service to intention, and he insists that the "parasitic" relation of literary speech acts to ordinary language is "fairly obvious" (1977, 204). Searle suggests that Derrida misreads Austin's merely strategic segregation of parasitic speech acts from normal use as a "metaphysical exclusion" (205). In maintaining that intention is the "heart" of the speech act (207–8), however, Searle has drawn the criticism that the role of intention is less central to Austin than he implies. Similarly, Derrida's decentering of intention does not entail an "essential absence" in the sense that Searle contends (207). Instead, "the category of intention will not disappear; it will have its place, but from that place it will no longer be able to govern the entire scene and system of utterance" (Derrida, 18).

Whereas Searle assumes that a relation of logical dependency obtains between literary language, on the one hand, and the ordinary uses of language on which it is presumably based, on the other, Derrida observes that the rules governing their relation are "not things found in nature," but human inventions—conventions "that, in their very normality as well as in their normativity, entail something of the fictional" (134). In an important amplification of this insight, psychoanalytic literary critic Shoshana Felman elaborates Searle's own focus on the promise as the prototypical illocution into an extended meditation on the role of seduction in language and literature. The speech act, she suggests, finesses the disjuncture between "the order of the act and the order of meaning, the register of pleasure and the register of knowledge" by creating a separate, self-referential linguistic space and sidestepping the entailments of absolute truth (31). Refiguring the performative as a ritual of desire, Felman restores to the act an intentional dimension while respecting the elements of fictionality and noncoincidence at its core.

For Felman, literary language comes to serve as "the meeting and testing ground of the linguistic and the philosophical, the place where linguistics and philosophy are interrogated but also where they are pushed beyond their disciplinary limits" (11).

GENDER THEORY AND PERFORMATIVITY

Speech act theory sketches both a slippage and an entanglement between language and the material world that has proven especially important to QUEER and GENDER theorists in recent years. Feminist philosopher Judith Butler famously observed that gender represents a copy for which there is no original (1991), an insight elaborated in her influential analyses of gender as performative (1990, 1993). Like Derrida, she suggests that the putatively parasitic, peripheral, and extra-ordinary performance may reveal an absence at the core of the "ordinary"— arguing, for example, that the practice of drag within queer subcultures points not to a derivative or imitative logical dependence of homosexuality on heterosexuality, but to the performative nature of gender as such (1990). Indeed, Butler contends that the sexed body itself is not the origin of gender expression, but a kind of back formation projected by the compulsory practice of gender performativity (1993). In undertaking to examine the social, pragmatic, and conventional dimensions of sex and gender, queer theorists such as Butler and Eve Kosofsky Sedgwick (1950–2009) have drawn extensively on speech act theory to sketch

the noncoincidence of intention—understood in the philosophical sense to encompass both will and meaning or referentiality—and actuality in the enactment and experience of gendered being. For Butler, it is the inevitable gap between performative citations and the ideal and iterable model that compels the endless reiteration of gender while simultaneously obscuring its normative and compulsory dimensions. For queer and gender theorists generally, speech act theory has provided a supple and productive model for thinking through the entanglements of language, knowledge, and materiality, while also revaluing marginal and non-normative realities. Perhaps most importantly, speech act theory acknowledges and helps to expose the ethical and teleological determinations conventionally obscured by "ordinary language" and the constative presumptions of philosophical traditions on which its identification has historically been predicated.

SEE ALSO: Dialogue, Discourse, Feminist Theory, Linguistics, Rhetoric and Figurative Language.

BIBLIOGRAPHY

Austin, J.L. (1962), *How to Do Things with Words*.
Butler, J. (1990), *Gender Trouble*.
Butler, J. (1991), "Imitation and Gender Insubordination," in *Inside/Out*, ed. D. Fuss.
Butler, J. (1993), *Bodies That Matter*.
Derrida, J. (1988), *Limited Inc*, trans. S. Weber and J. Mehlman.
Felman, S. (1983), *Literary Speech Act*, trans. C. Porter; reiss. 2002 as *Scandal of the Speaking Body*.
Ohmann, R. (1971), "Speech Acts and the Definition of Literature," *Philosophy and Rhetoric* 4:1–19.
Pratt, M.L. (1977), *Toward a Speech Act Theory of Literary Discourse*.
Searle, J. (1969), *Speech Acts*.
Searle, J. (1977), "Reiterating the Differences: A Reply to Derrida," *Glyph* 1:198–208.

Sedgwick, E. (1993), "Queer Performativity," *Gay and Lesbian Quarterly* 1:1–16.

Speech, Represented *see* Dialect; Dialogue; Discourse; Narration
Stacked Narrative *see* Frame
Stanzel, Franz *see* Narrator

Story/Discourse

RYAN KERNAN

The concepts of *histoire* (story) and *discours* (discourse) constitute the fundamental elements of the formalist (see FORMALISM) theory of narrative. Story resides in the content, the chain of events (the actions or happenings), and what is often labeled the "existents": the characters, settings, and the objects or persons that serve as a background for these events. Discourse refers to the means by which the content is communicated. In short, the story is that which is depicted, and the discourse is the actual narrative statements, the form of expression. While the distinction between story and discourse is most often associated with practitioners of narratology (the study of narrative) who can be classified as formalist, to a lesser extent it has also been incorporated into the arguments of structuralist and poststructuralist theorists of narrative (see STRUCTURALISM). Indeed, as Jonathan Culler emphasizes, most strands of narratology are united by the recognition that any theory of narrative requires a distinction between story and discourse.

Conventional theorizing about the story/discourse dichotomy is said to begin with the Russian formalists, and in particular with Boris Tomashevskii's *Theory of Literature* (1925) and Vladimir Propp's *Morphology of the Folktale* (1928). The Russian formalist employed the concepts of *fabula* (story) and *siuzhet* (discourse) to distinguish between the raw material of literature and its aesthetic rearrangement in narrative fiction. The basic difference between the two stems from their contrasting treatment of chronology (see TIME) and causality (see PLOT). Usually, the story is constituted of what is narrated as a chronological sequence of logically and causally related themes, motives, and plot lines that explain why its events occur. Discourse, in turn, describes the stylistic choices that determine how the text appears before the reader.

The Russian formalist articulation of this dualistic distinction has certain antecedents in Aristotle's *Poetics* as well as in the third book of Plato's *Republic* (ca. 380 BCE), but it came to the fore in continental narrative theory during the late 1960s in the work of Tzvetan Todorov and via the structural LINGUISTICS of Émile Benveniste. Nevertheless, it is most commonly associated with the work of the French literary theorist Gérard Genette and with the arguments contained in his 1976 essay "Frontières du récit" ("Boundaries of Narrative"). In the case of Genette, however, the double-tiered base structure of narrative levels becomes tripartite. In addition to the division between story and discourse, Genette employs the term "narration" to forefront the transaction between narrator and narratee. The *récit* (narrative discourse) is the actual text produced by the act of narration, and it conveys the story of the narrative. His categories of *temps* (tense) and *mode* (mood), in turn, describe the relationship between the levels of story and discourse on the surface level of the text. Here, past-tense verbs delivered by a third- or first-person narrator constitute story, while discourse is marked by the present tense of DIALOGUE or reported speech.

Given Genette's tripartite structure and the fact that story disappears—in his (markedly Hegelian) vision of the novel's future—leaving a fully emancipated discourse, it is somewhat curious that he is the theorist most commonly associated with the binary of story/discourse as it is rigidly employed elsewhere. This curiosity, though, is a testament to the enormous influence that his thought exerted over theorists writing both alongside him and in his wake. Several other influential narratologists, most notably Seymour Chatman, extrapolate the phenomenon of voice from the textual level and adhere to the aforementioned bipartite schema. These different uses of the terms story and discourse in narratology—the first where story and discourse correspond respectively to what the text is about and to how it is told—and the second, Genette's, has caused a considerable amount of confusion within the field itself.

The enduring importance of Genette's "Frontiers of Narrative" with respect to this dualistic binary is, in part, a function of the fact that his essay excavates Classical arguments concerning EPIC poetry, dramatic poetry, *mimesis* (imitation), and *diegesis* (narrative) not only to provide illustrative case examples of the differences between story and discourse, but also to qualify both as aspects of narrative. To support this bold assertion about the domain of narrative and to draw his readers' attention to the fact that, from time immemorial, the distinction between story and discourse has been of the utmost concern for theorists of literature, Genette points to two contradictory theorizations about the relationship between narrative and imitation that find their origin in Antiquity. The first frames narrative as the antithesis of imitation, and is exemplified by Aristotle's contention that narrative poetry (the poetry of *diegesis*) and dramatic poetry (the poetry of *mimesis* or the direct representation of events by actors speaking before the public) should be considered separate and distinct modes. The second frames imitation as one of the modes of narrative, and

originates in Plato's *Republic* wherein Plato makes the distinction between *logos* (that which is said) and *lexis* (the manner of speaking), which can be further divided into *mimesis* (imitation) and *diegesis* (instances where the narrator speaks in his own name).

Genette subscribes to neither of these traditions, but nevertheless turns to Plato's reading of bk. 1 of the *Iliad* to delineate story (or simple narrative) from discourse (or imitation). With respect to this distinction, Genette's example is canonical and worthy of full citation:

> By simple narrative Plato means all that the poet relates "in speaking in his own name, without trying to make us believe that it is another who speaks." Thus in Book I of the Iliad Homer tells us of Chryses: "He came to the Achaeans' great boats to buy back his daughter, bringing a tremendous ransom and bearing the bands of Apollo the archer on the golden staff in his hand. He entreated all the Achaeans, but especially Atreus' sons, two fine military leaders." In contrast, the next verses consist in imitation, because Homer makes Chryses himself speak, or rather Homer speaks, pretending to have become Chryses, and "strives to give us the illusion that it is not Homer speaking, but really the old man, Apollo's priest." Here is the text of the discourse of Chryses: "Descendents of Atreus, and you also, well-armed Achaeans, may the gods, dwellers on Olympus, allow you to destroy Priam's city and then to return without injury to your homes! But for me, may you also give me back my daughter! And for that, accept this ransom, out of respect to the son of Zeus, to Apollo the archer." But Plato adds that Homer could as well have continued his narrative in a purely narrative form by recounting the words of Chryses instead of quoting them. This would have made the same passage, in indirect style and in prose: "Having arrived, the priest implored the gods to allow the Achaeans to take Troy and to keep them from destruction, and he asked the Greeks to give him back his daughter in

exchange for a ransom and out of respect for the gods." (2)

For many critics who distinguish story from discourse at the surface level of the text, this citation from "Frontiers of Narrative" describes sufficiently the difference between them. What "Homer tells us of Chryses," or what the poet speaks "in his own name," comprises a structural level of the surface text that can be labeled the story or the narrative. The portion of the text where dialogue intrudes, or where "Homer makes Chryses himself speak," constitutes the elements of the text that can be identified as discourse. Indeed, Genette himself would concur with these designations.

What Genette finds troublesome about Plato's reading of the *Iliad* is Plato's assertion that what we have just labeled "story" and "discourse" (or, in Plato's lexicon, *diegesis* and *mimesis*, the elements of *lexis*) can be adequately distinguished from *logos* ("what is said"). This is the case because to assume a distinction between "that which is said" and "the manner of speaking" in a work of fiction is to conceive of "poetic fiction as a simulacrum of reality." Unlike a history or a landscape painting, a work of fiction does not necessarily have an event or landscape which is exterior to the artifact that represents it. The distinction between *lexis* and *logos* therefore posits a distinction between fiction and representation that is untenable, or—in Genette's words—the distinction reduces "the object of the fiction" to "a sham reality awaiting its representation." Hence, the very notion of imitation with regard to *lexis* is ephemeral at best—language can only perfectly imitate language. This, in turn, leads Genette to a startling, yet logical, conclusion that troubles both contradictory Classical theorizations of the relationship between narrative and imitation at their very core: in the literary realm, *mimesis* is *diegesis*.

Genette's dismantling of the Classical theorization between "what is said" and the "manner of speaking" neither leads him to cast aside the distinction between the content of expression (story) and the "mode of expression" (discourse), nor does it prompt him to deny the representational function of narrative altogether. Rather, it leads him to propose a new understanding of diegesis (narrative) that subsumes story and discourse and that locates both on the surface level of the text. The fundamental difference between "story" (narrative) and "discourse" is, for Genette, that the former is objective and the latter subjective, but only in strictly linguistic terms. *Récit* (story) makes use of the third person and *discours* (discourse) the first. Where the former in its most "pure" incarnation is marked—ever since the advent of realism in the novels of Honoré de Balzac—by a desire to efface all reference to a narrator and to arrange events in some type of chronological order, the latter—in the presentation of reported speech or dialogue—forefronts its speaker and defines the present as the instant in which the discourse is held. Hence, for Genette, story and discourse are distinguishable by *temps* (tense) and *mode* (mood), and constitute the "semiological existence" of the literary narration which—insofar as literary representation is concerned—has no concrete referent outside the text.

For Genette, both story and discourse are always present (to varying degrees) in narration. Story may be conceived without discourse, but any such conception does not exist in the real word of texts. The same can be said of an independently conceived narrative of pure discourse. This, however, is where the symmetry ends. Story is a very particular, restrictive mode marked by a number of exclusions and conditions, and any intrusion of discourse into story—in Genette's words—"forms a sort of cyst, easily recognized and localized." The slightest general observation, the slightest comparison, or even the tiniest adjective introduces an element of subjective discourse into story. In contrast, discourse does not have to answer to a concomitant demand of purity because it is, for Genette, "the natural mode of language" (12). Hence, although no novel of pure discourse yet exists, Genette sees it as a possibility for the novel's future.

For both Genette and for theorists like Seymour Chatman who adhere to the bipartite schema of story and discourse, time plays a key role in distinguishing one entity from the other. This is the case for Genette not only because he distinguishes discourse from story by making recourse to tense and mood, but also because of his understanding of *diegesis* (narrative) that posits the existence of two types of literary representation that use time in different manners, narrative and descriptive. These two types do not have what Genette labels a "semiological existence" (description is not its own mode but rather an aspect of narration), but they do bring to light how temporality differs in different modes of literary representation. Narration, insofar as it is tied to actions and events, puts an emphasis on what Genette labels "the temporal and dramatic aspects of narrative." Conversely, description suspends the flow of time because it "lingers over objects and beings considered in their simultaneity" (8). For theorists like Chatman, the analysis of narrative must also observe two time scales not because of the difference between description and narrative, but rather because the narratologist must distinguish between the inner time of the content (story time) and the outer time (discourse time), the time that it takes the audience to peruse the story. Chatman's theorization of temporality in story and discourse differs markedly from Genette's distinction between the temporality of narrative and

description. Nevertheless, it is worth noticing that here and elsewhere, the distinction between story and discourse consistently engenders questions about the different functions of time in the fundamental layers of narrative.

For many structuralists like Claude Bremond, story is distinguished from discourse as a layer of autonomous significance that can be isolated from the whole of the narrative message. This autonomous layer manifests in the same way regardless of the means of narrative conveyance, independent of the techniques that bear it along. Hence, story—in this formulation—may be transposed from medium to medium without losing its essential properties. For example, the subject of a novel may serve as the argument for a ballet. Whether it manifests in a novel, in a stage performance, in a piece of cinema, or even in a summary, it is the story that we follow. *Raconte* (that which is narrated) has its own *racontants* (story elements), and these elements do not correspond to words, images, or gestures but rather to the events, situations, and behaviors signified by them.

SEE ALSO: Metafiction, Narrative, Narrative Perspective, Narrative Technique.

BIBLIOGRAPHY

Bal, M. (1985), *Narratology.*
Benveniste, É. (1996), *Problèmes de linguistique générale.*
Bremond, C. (1973), *Logique du récit.*
Chatman, S. (1978), *Story and Discourse.*
Culler, J. (1981), *Pursuit of Signs, Semiotics, Literature, Deconstruction.*
Genette, G. (1976), "Boundaries of Narrative," trans. A. Levonas, *New Literary History* (1):1–13.
Genette, G. (1980), *Narrative Discourse.*
Miller, J.H., ed. (1970), *Aspects of Narrative.*
Prince, G. (2003), *Dictionary of Narratology.*
Todorov, T. (1965), *Théorie de la littérature.*

Stream of Consciousness *see* Psychological Novel

Structuralism/ Poststructuralism

DAVID HERMAN

Theorists working under the auspices of both structuralism and poststructuralism have developed ideas of broad relevance for the study of the novel. Although they evolved from a common heritage of concepts—in particular, those associated with Saussurean language theory, with its bipartite analysis of the sign into signifier and signified and its account of language as a system of differences—structuralist and poststructuralist approaches rely on different analytic procedures and set themselves contrasting investigative goals. Notably, whereas structuralism begins from the premise that cultural practices of all sorts are grounded in rule-systems that are subject to conscious scrutiny as well as unconscious mastery, poststructuralism is a version of antifoundationalism, i.e., skepticism concerning the existence (or accessibility) of ultimate foundations for knowledge, bedrock truths that subtend and guarantee the process of interpretation (Singer and Rockmore).

Having reached its heyday in the 1960s and 1970s, structuralism openly aims for explanatory reduction; it distinguishes between metalanguage and object-language, recasting ostensibly diverse textual phenomena (e.g., different novelistic genres, or novels originating from different periods and cultural traditions) as manifestations of a shared underlying code or structure (Jakobson). Thus, the early narratologists participated in a broader structuralist revolution when they sought to use Saussurean LINGUISTICS as a "pilot-science" for studying narrative in all of its many guises. Narratologists such as Tzvetan Todorov, Roland Barthes, Claude Bremond, Gérard Genette, and Algirdas Julius Greimas adapted Saussure's distinction between *parole* and *langue* to construe particular stories as individual narrative messages supported by an underlying semiotic code.

And just as Saussurean linguistics privileged code over message, focusing on the structural constituents and combinatory principles of the semiotic system of language rather than on situated uses of that system, structuralist narratologists privileged narrative in general over individual narratives, emphasizing the general semiotic principles according to which basic structural units (characters, states, events, actions, and so forth) are combined and transformed to yield specific narrative texts. In this context, Genette's work has been especially influential for research on the novel. In particular, *Narrative Discourse*—with its account of narrative temporality under the headings of order, duration, and frequency; its distinction between narration and focalization, voice and vision; and its taxonomy of narrative levels (extradiegetic, intradiegetic, hypodiegetic) and voices (homodiegetic, autodiegetic, heterodiegetic)—suggests that the distinctiveness of a given text can be captured by studying how it recruits from a common stock of narrative design principles (see DISCOURSE).

By contrast, poststructuralism makes a case for the irreducible specificity and heterogeneity of texts, their limitless semantic productivity or capacity for meaning generation, including their ability to generate incompatible interpretations. The goal for poststructuralists is not to partition the textual field into particular classes or kinds (e.g., narrative, argument, or instruction), each defined by a closed system of features and principles, but rather to demonstrate how a given text submits itself only more or less to the law of any particular genre

(Derrida), orienting itself to multiple generic norms at the same time. From this perspective the domain of novelistic discourse overlaps with those of philosophical, psychological, and other "nonliterary" discourses, jeopardizing the very opposition between literary and nonliterary texts, and for that matter between the object-language of fictional texts and the critical metalanguages that might be used to explicate them. Yet poststructuralist theorists, far from engaging in an anything-goes modus operandi, rely on specific, recurrent procedures for analysis. For example, deconstructionists working in the Derridean vein seek to reveal how texts signal the collapse of binary oppositions on whose force and integrity the texts simultaneously insist; those working in the tradition of Paul de Man highlight how a text's rhetorical profile (the tropes it deploys) can be at odds with its explicit themes or overt semantic content. Thus, in these and other varieties of poststructuralism (e.g., Jacques Deleuze and Félix Guattari's schizo-analytic account of literary and cultural phenomena in terms of de- and reterritorialized flows of desire), a species of explanatory reduction can be detected, however different in style or purpose from that informing structuralist analyses.

THE CASE OF ROLAND BARTHES: A SCIENCE OF THE TEXT?

As one of founding practitioners of structuralism in France, Roland Barthes, in his early writing, examined cultural phenomena of all sorts through the lens of Saussure's structural linguistics (Culler, Dosse). Barthes's *Mythologies* (1972) characterized diverse forms of cultural expression (advertisements, photographs, museum exhibits, wrestling matches) as rule-governed signifying practices or "languages" in their own right. In his classic 1966 essay "Introduction

to the Structural Analysis of Narratives," published as part of the special issue of the journal *Communications* that effectively launched structuralist narratology, Barthes adopted the same approach to narrative practices in particular. He used Ian Fleming's James Bond novels to explore the nature and distribution of fundamental narrative units, and more generally to outline a method of narrative analysis based on hierarchically arranged levels of description (spanning functions, actions, and, at the highest level, narration).

By the time he published "The Death of the Author" in 1968, however, Barthes had begun to speak about literary discourse in a very different way. Resisting the use of words like "code" and "message" as terms of art, and reconceiving texts as gestures of inscription rather than vehicles for communication and expression, he had come to embrace a Derridean view of the text as "a tissue of signs, an imitation that is lost, infinitely deferred" (147). The text is, as Barthes now put it, "not a line of words releasing a single 'theological' meaning . . . but a multi-dimensional space in which a variety of writings, none of them original, blend and clash" (146). The scientific decoding of messages has given way to the interpretative disentanglement of strands of meaning, "rendering illusory any inductive-deductive science of texts—no 'grammar' of the text" (1997c, 159). Barthes here disavows the possibility of a science of the text that just a few years earlier he had, if not taken for granted, assumed as the outcome toward which structuralist research was inexorably advancing.

Barthes's autocritique of structuralism, which would eventuate in the publication of *S/Z* (1974), was part of a broader reaction against structuralist assumptions and methods articulated by commentators as diverse as Hélène Cixous, Jacques Derrida, Michel Foucault, Julia Kristeva, Jacques Lacan, and

Jean-François Lyotard. Because of Barthes's uniquely double identity, as one of the world's foremost practitioners first of structuralism and then of poststructuralism, his revolution in thinking can be viewed as emblematic of this larger shift in critico-theoretical discourse. In particular, his 1971 essay "From Work to Text" can be read as a kind of internalized dialogue or debate, with Barthes adopting a persona who now embraces key tenets of Derridean poststructuralism, for example, and who thus takes issue with the author's own earlier, staunchly structuralist persona, champion of a classically semiolinguistic approach to literary and cultural analysis.

"FROM WORK TO TEXT": IMPLICATIONS FOR THE STUDY OF THE NOVEL

Though it articulates seven "principal propositions" about the nature of texts, Barthes's essay suggests that these statements should be construed less as "argumentations" than as "enunciations" or "touches" (156). The self-reflexivity, playfulness, and anti-exhaustive spirit of Barthes's proviso stems from the new, poststructuralist research paradigm that his essay goes on to outline. As Barthes puts it at the end of the essay, "a Theory of the Text cannot be satisfied by a metalinguistic exposition: the destruction of meta-language ... is part of the theory itself" (164). But what are the constructive, as opposed to critical, goals of Barthes's account? And how do those goals pertain to research on the novel?

TEXT VERSUS WORK

Since one of his major concerns is to distinguish between the classical concept of the work and the new, interdisciplinary notion of the text, Barthes's first proposition is that "the Text is not to be thought of as an object that can be computed" (156). (Throughout the essay Barthes uses the capitalized term "Text" as a mass noun, like "water" or "space," and the uncapitalized term "text" as a count noun, like "cat" or "pencil.") Barthes writes: "the work can be held in the hand, the text is held in language, only exists in the movement of a discourse," such that "the Text is not the decomposition of the work, it is the work that is the imaginary tail of the Text" (156–57). Hence, Barthes emphasizes, "*the Text is experienced only in an activity of production*" (157). This proposition echoes Barthes's emphasis, in *S/Z*, on readers' use of codes of signification to participate in the active structuration of texts, instead of merely passively appreciating works as pre-given, inert structures (18–21). Barthes's account thus points ahead to reader-response and other contextualist approaches to literary interpretation. More than this, structuralist methods of decomposing fictional narratives into their constituent features must be rethought when the basic unit of analysis becomes texts-in-contexts, as Barthes makes even more explicit in some of his other propositions.

GENRES AND FILIATION

Another proposition put forth in "From Work to Text" is that "the Text does not stop at (good) Literature; it cannot be contained in a hierarchy, even in a simple division of genres" (157). This statement or theme can be traced back to Mikhail BAKHTIN's investigations into the polygeneric origins and dialogic profile of novelistic discourse, but it also harmonizes with a broader deconstructive critique of evaluative hierarchies (Derrida, 1967, *Of Grammatology*). Further, the theme of genre is bound up with what Barthes terms "filiation." Whereas the idea of the work is caught up in an institution that bears striking similarities to that of patrilineal descent, originating from an author and relating to other works via principles of succession, the dominant "metaphor of the Text is that of the *network*; if the Text extends itself, it is as a result of a combinatory systematic" and "can be read without the guarantee of its father" (161). Discrete, autonomous works, linked to one another in a causal and chronological sequence, give way to the Text viewed as a network of reversible, multilinear, intertextual relations, only a small subset of which can be captured by classical concepts such as "genre," "allusion," and "citation." Such generalized intertextuality became not only a watchword of poststructuralist approaches to fiction but also the basis for Barthes's proposal to replace the notion of the author with that of the scriptor, who "is always anterior, never original" and whose "only power is to mix writings" 1977b, 146). Yet later analysts—e.g., those focusing on texts by women writers and others seeking to claim a voice for themselves—have taken issue with Barthes's attempt to evacuate the communicative intentions of writers, his embrace of a scriptor who functions merely as a kind of switch operator between (anonymous) discourses.

SIGNS AND PLURALITY

The idea of the sign and of plurality constitutes other dimensions along which work and Text can be contrasted. On the one hand, the work "closes on a signified," and insofar as modes of signification oriented around the signified involve either evident or hidden meanings, the work is the proper province of philology or hermeneutics, as the case may be. On the other hand, "the Text … practi[c]es the infinite deferment of the signified, is dilatory; its field is that of the signifier" (158). Hence terms like "undecidability" and "indeterminacy" take their place alongside "intertextuality" as hallmarks of a poststructuralist approach to interpretation, which foregrounds the process over the target of signification. Another way of talking about this infinite deferment of the signified is to talk about the Text's radical plurality. The Text is plural not because (like the work) it is ambiguous and can be assigned several candidate interpretations, but instead because it involves an explosion, or dissemination, of meanings. Here readers familiar with *S/Z* will recall Barthes's influential distinction between classical, "*readerly*" (lisible) works, which he characterized as only parsimoniously plural, and postclassical, "*writerly*" (scriptible) texts, which are limitlessly plural and thus "make the reader no longer a consumer, but a producer of the text" (4).

Barthes's account of the readerly and the writerly (like his opposition between work and text) leaves it an open question whether these terms are classifications of particular kinds of fictional texts or rather different stances toward the process of interpretation itself. The non-resolution of this issue may in turn reflect Barthes's understanding of the poststructuralist approach as fundamentally relativistic (1977c, 156). In contradistinction to structuralist methods, Barthes refuses to distance his own discourse from the research object—texts of all kinds—that he now construes as being shaped in part by the commentator's own interpretive practices.

SEE ALSO: Author, Genre Theory, Intertextuality, Narrative, Narrative Structure, Novel Theory (20th Century), Philosophical Novel, Reader.

BIBLIOGRAPHY

Barthes, R. (1972), *Mythologies*, trans. A. Lavers.
Barthes, R. (1974), *S/Z*, trans. R. Miller.

Barthes, R. (1977a), "Introduction to the Structural Analysis of Narratives," in *Image Music Text*, trans. S. Heath.

Barthes, R. (1977b), "The Death of the Author," in *Image Music Text*, trans. S. Heath.

Barthes, R. (1977c), "From Work to Text," in *Image Music Text*, trans. S. Heath.

Culler, J. (1975), *Structuralist Poetics*.

Derrida, J. (1991), "The Law of Genre," in *Acts of Literature*, ed. D. Attridge.

Dosse, F. (1997), *History of Structuralism*, vol. 1, trans. D. Glassman.

Genette, G. (1983), *Narrative Discourse*, trans. J.E. Lewin.

Singer, B. and T. Rockmore, eds. (1992), *Antifoundationalism Old and New*.

Style *see* Narrative Technique
Style indirect libre *see* Discourse
Superfluous Man Novel *see* Russia (18th–19th Century)
Supernaturalism *see* Gothic Novel; Magical Realism

Surrealism/Avant-Garde Novel

DEBORAH JENSON

Surrealism itself was conceptualized by its founder André Breton as an antidote to the novel. In the first *Manifesto of Surrealism* (1924), Breton described the novel, shaped by realist and positivist conventions (see REALISM), as hostile to the growth of the reader's intellect or ethical sense. The realist novel's informational and descriptive style, epitomized by the phrase "The Marquise went out at five" (7), had all the clarity of "a dog's life" (6) and fostered characters who represented the repetitive construction of a human type in the context of a prescriptive social logic. In the face of the novel's ready-made humans, Breton concluded: "The only discretionary power left to me is to close the book" (7). But although the Surrealists consistently aligned themselves against stasis, convention, and the psychosocial character formation that perpetuate them, they were also intrigued by the possibility of using NARRATIVE TECHNIQUES and literary character formation to cultivate alternative experiences of the world in authors and readers. The psychic revelations of the avant-garde novel associated with Surrealism were born of the imagination's encounter with the technology of narrative, inflected by the fields of psychiatry and neurology in which Breton had been trained.

The first published book of literary Surrealism, Breton and Philippe Soupault's *Les champs magnétiques* (1920, *Magnetic Fields*), has been called a novel, but its strict use of psychic automatism, displayed at three writing "speeds," deconstructs or avoids constructing virtually all temporal and spatial narrative continuity of character and story (see TIME, SPACE). Other Surrealist novels from the early 1920s include *Mort aux vaches et au champ d'honneur* (1923, *Death to the Pigs and to the Field of Glory*) by Benjamin Péret and, in Spain, *El Incongruente* (1922, *The Incongruent One*) by Ramón Gómez de la Serna.

The best-known example of a Surrealist avant-garde novel is Breton's 1928 *Nadja*. Nonlinear in its structure, this hybrid photo-narrative, anchored partly in the tradition of intimate or autobiographical writings, represents the Parisian trajectory of the author's brief relationship with a young woman who was a patient of the psychiatrist Pierre Janet (1859–1947). *Nadja* is an interrogation of the subjective relation to the enigma of the other's existence, mapped in urban space. The unpredictable female protagonist stimulated productive forms of non-knowing and experimental cognition for the author, who opens the text with the question "Who am I?" *Nadja* was preceded by *Le paysan de Paris* (1926, *Nightwalker*) by Louis Aragon and *La Liberté ou l'amour!*

(1927, *Give Me Liberty or Give Me Love!*) by Robert Desnos. It was contemporaneous with the composition of the novel *Aurora* by Michel Leiris and *Les Dernières Nuits de Paris* (*Last Nights of Paris*) by Soupault.

Visual artists figure strongly in the history of the Surrealist avant-garde novel also, showing its fundamentally transmedia approach to experimental narrativity. Giorgio de Chirico published *Hebdomeros* in 1929, and Salvador Dalí published *Hidden Faces* in 1945. Max Ernst innovated with the collage novel *A Week of Kindness or the Seven Deadly Elements* (1934), in which illustrations from pulp novels and catalogues were arranged in book form so as to stimulate unconscious or libidinal narratives in the viewer (see PSY-CHOANALYTIC THEORY). British painter and writer Leonora Carrington, born in 1917, wrote novels including *The House of Fear* (1938) and *The Oval Lady* (1939). Her fiction served as an inspiration to later avant-garde novels by women writers like Angela Carter and Kathy Acker, in which the hierarchies of gender and power that had been so evident in avant-garde works such as *Nadja* were destabilized.

The Surrealist avant-garde novel is related to novelistic experimentation in the Blooms-bury group and also to other areas of the modernist tradition, including novels such as *Nightwood* (1936) by expatriate Djuna Barnes (see MODERNISM). Raymond Queneau, who was briefly affiliated with Surrealism, later founded the avant-garde literary group OULIPO ("Workshop for Potential Litera-ture"), famous for its use of constrained writing techniques. Queneau's surrealist novel *Le Chiendent* (1933, *The Bark Tree*)

was a precursor to the avant-garde genre of the *nouveau roman* or "new novel," and shows a genealogy leading from the Surre-alist novel to later avant-garde fictional forms. In effect, despite the Surrealist rejec-tion of the novel as the emblematic form of bourgeois modernity, iconoclastic Surrealist revisions of the novel mark a lasting tension between the realist mode and the experimen-tal mode in fiction, rather than a disavowal of the novel per se. It is in this sense that Breton ultimately would claim the novel as one of Surrealism's lasting claims to the avant-garde. Maurice Nadeau notes that after the two world wars, Breton cited a Surrealist novel by Julien Gracq as a sign that in the absence of a "more emancipating move-ment," Surrealism remained in the front lines—"in the avant-garde" of experimental culture (216).

SEE ALSO: Adaptation/Appropriation, Decadent Novel, Definitions of the Novel, Intertextuality, Life Writing, Metafiction, Modernism.

BIBLIOGRAPHY

Biro, A. and R. Passeron (1982), *Dictionnaire général du Surréalisme et ses environs*.
Breton, A. (1960), *Nadja*, trans. R. Howard.
Breton, A. (1969), *Manifestoes of Surrealism*, trans. R. Seaver and H.R. Lane.
Breton, A. (1978), *What Is Surrealism?*, ed. F. Rosemont.
Breton, A. and P. Soupault (1985), *Magnetic Fields*, trans. D. Gascoyne.
Chadwick, W. (1998), *Mirror Images*.
Nadeau, M. (1989), *History of Surrealism*.

T

Tagged Discourse *see* Discourse

Temporality *see* Narrative Technique

Testimonial Novel *see* Central America

Textual Criticism and History *see* Editing

Thought, Represented *see* Discourse

Time

CATHERINE GALLAGHER

Paul Ricoeur tells us that a novel is a chronologically organized discourse ultimately referring (whatever its ostensible themes or subjects) to the passage of time. He also reminds us, though, just how complex and fractured that reference is, and especially in the case of fictional narratives, how far removed from our normal experience of time as comprising past, present, and future. Indeed, even as the novel takes place in time—as a linear sequence of signs in the consciousnesses of its readers—it nevertheless seems to suspend and displace the temporality of our daily existence, superimposing intricate, multilayered, and anachronistic time schemes of its own. This entry on the topic of time and the novel will survey various techniques for distinguishing, ordering, layering, interrupting, destabilizing, and suspending such temporal components of the form as story, plot, narrative, narrating, and reading. It will also discuss the historical facets of novels and their suspended time in textuality.

THE COMPONENTS OF NOVELISTIC TIME

Narrated and narrative times

Critics and theorists have made a number of crucial distinctions in the process of describing how novels organize time, but unfortunately there has been no general agreement about their terms. As Gérard Genette remarks in the introduction to *Narrative Discourse Reconsidered*, the most basic distinction is between the time of the narration (what he calls the *récit*) and the time of the events narrated (the *histoire*). A variety of other terms have been used to describe roughly the same division: the Russian formalists (see FORMALISM) distinguish between *fabula* (raw order of events) and *siuzhet* (order in which they are told); Émile Benveniste uses *énoncé* (the enunciated or said) and *énonciation* (the act of enunciating or saying, including *discours*, which consists of various linguistic markers placing the enunciator in time); Günther Müller differentiates between *Erzählte Zeit* (narrated time) and *Erzählzeit* (narrating time); Mieke Bal separates the *fabula* from the "text" by the intervening category of "story" (the order of events as told); while Ricoeur tends to use the hybrid pair of *énoncé* and *discours*. These pairs are by no means perfectly equivalent, but they might all be used to explain the difference between, e.g., (1) the time supposedly taken to write

Lockwood's diary in Emily Brontë's 1847 *Wuthering Heights*, and (2) the time of the story of the inmates of Wuthering Heights, which includes the introductory events of the diary and is largely told in the voice of the interpolated narrator, Nelly Dean (see FRAME). The narrative (or *récit, siuzhet, énonciation, Erzählzeit,* text, or *discours*) of the diary begins in 1801 and ends a year later in 1802, whereas the story (*histoire, fabula, énoncé, Erzählte Zeit*) of Heathcliff and the Earnshaws spans the period 1757–1802. The *fabula* of *Wuthering Heights* is constructed by the reader on the basis of over six hundred temporal allusions in the text, and it presupposes the existence of an "objective" and regularly proceeding calendar time as an external condition of the novel's temporality.

A double temporal order of the novel thus emerges in these two separate time-tracks, the short track of the narrative span and the long track of the narrated matter, and each of these tracks can be said to enclose and be enclosed by the other. The dates 1801–1802 in Lockwood's diary contain the whole of the story Nelly Dean tells, but inversely the events of 1801–1802 can be chronologically situated toward the end of her narrative. Furthermore, *Wuthering Heights*, like many novels following the epic model, takes full advantage of this doubleness by beginning *in medias res*; we first read Lockwood's diary entries describing his encounters with the mysterious world of Wuthering Heights, one of which contains a recollected portion of the dead character Catherine Earnshaw's diary, and only then, after Lockwood returns to his rented country house at Thrushcross Grange and seeks an explanation from the housekeeper, is the more linear, sequential story narrated. Thus, most of the novel consists of an extended analepsis (a flashback or time-shift backward) recounting previous events in more or less calendric sequence in order to answer the suspended question of how things came to be the way they are in 1801.

Story, narrative, and narrating times

To be sure, a frame narrative such as *Wuthering Heights* makes the distinction between the times of the narrative and the narrated unusually apparent by representing and dating the act of narrating. Indeed, I've chosen to use *Wuthering Heights* as an example because its temporal complexity requires the use of the full range of temporal analytical tools. For example, the novel's explicit representation of the narrative time, which makes the narrative/story distinction easy to see, also presents a problem for the division of *Wuthering Heights*'s time into merely two strands, for we might legitimately ask why the events surrounding the writing of the diary, which is every bit as fictional as the story of Heathcliff's life, should not themselves be included as part of the narrated matter, even though their temporality is distinct. The first narrated event we encounter in *Wuthering Heights* is Lockwood's initial short visit to *Wuthering Heights*, whereas the earliest chronological event is the arrival of Heathcliff at Wuthering Heights thirty-some years before. And thus, within the category of the narrated, another distinction emerges between the simple chronological line along which we might string all the events (the *fabula*) of the novel and the often quite different order in which the narration places them. Many critics use the term *siuzhet* to denote this ordering rather than to name any represented act of narrating. Other theorists, such as Ricoeur, have wanted to retain the pre-narratological term "plot" (rather than "narrative") to name this dimension, and Mieke Bal uses "story" as opposed to both the bare *fabula*, on the one hand, and the narrative "text," on the other. Genette also comes up with a third category to accommodate this complication; he uses *histoire* (story) for the mere chronology of the events, *récit* (narrative) for the temporal order in which they are arranged; and *discours* (narrating) for the act of telling as represented or implied in the fiction (e.g., the time in which Lockwood supposedly writes his diary). In English, Genette's terms have generally been rendered as story, narrative, and narrating, and many students of the novel acknowledge the usefulness of some such tripartite set of terms for separating out the layers of often simultaneous temporal patterning in a novel. For example, they allow us to see that the first analepsis of *Wuthering Heights*, in which Lockwood records (in chap. 3) Catherine's diary (supposedly written in 1777) is simultaneously proleptic; it shifts us backward in calendric or story time and might be said to interpolate an earlier narrating time, but in terms of the narrative order it also anticipates an incident that we will encounter three chapters later when Nelly's narrative reaches that same point in the story.

Represented and reading times

Even these three strands, however, have often not seemed adequate to the intricacy of novelistic temporality, and other dimensions of time have also been explored. Müller's concept of *Erzählzeit* (narrating time as opposed to narrated time), for example, refers less to the writing time of Lockwood's diary (which is a represented fictional entity) than to the time spent in reading the novel, as measured by its length. Since we do not confuse the time of our own reading with the represented time of Lockwood's diary writing, such a distinction would seem to be necessary. Müller implies, however, that in reading we unconsciously compare and contrast the two: in reading *Wuthering Heights*, for example, we register that the fictional time of Lockwood's writ-

ing is spread over a year, but the time that would normally elapse in reading the novel is merely a matter of hours. In such a complex novel, moreover, other such contrasts would be felt on every level: the thirteen-year span over which Catherine and Heathcliff grow into adults and are separated by Catherine's death may be measured against the five weeks of Lockwood's illness during which Nelly supposedly tells him the story intermittently, and that might in turn be measured against the time it takes us to read the chapters (perhaps an hour). Our experience of these different time values, according to Müller, constitutes the novel's temporal gestalt. Moreover, although narratologists have been reluctant to admit that they consider reading time in their analyses (because it seems too subjectively variable), even Genette acknowledges it under the guise of "duration" and requires it to describe the novel's complex and varying tempos.

Critics use these different temporal strands—we have so far identified four—not only to trace their organization in individual novels (as I have been doing with *Wuthering Heights*) but also to describe the techniques typical of various authors, nations, historical periods, aesthetic movements, and subgenres. Much of the scholarship on time and the novel, for example, has been devoted to the strong influence exerted on modernist narrative techniques by Henri Bergson's (1859–1941) philosophical writings on time (see MODERNISM). Within all of this great variety, though, we commonly find novelists handling the special temporal resources of their form in ways that at once reference our lived experience of time and create an experience apart from and even antithetical to lived time. A description of these effects will require us to look at some aspects of the novel (verb tenses and textuality, for example) that have not yet been mentioned.

ANACHRONY

For each of the main aspects of time—transience, sequence, and irreversibility—the novel's multiple temporalities, its tenses of fictionality, and its textual mode of being all supply counterweights. The novel, like music, is a diachronic art form, but it seems devoted to anachrony.

Anti-transience

To the transience of successive moments, especially as measured by the regular and unstoppable ticking of "objective" clock-time, the novel offers numerous techniques for slowing or suspending forward movement. I've been examining the compressions by which story time is reduced to narrating time, and narrating time to reading time, but the opposite effect is also in the novelistic repertoire. The reading time, the *Erzählzeit*, can be much longer than the moment narrated. As Henry Fielding's narrator declared in *Tom Jones* (1749), his story would "sometimes seems to stand still and sometimes to fly" (chap. 1). Recognizing that narrative rhythm is a relative matter and that the sensation of standing still is partly dependent on the opposite sensation of flying, we may nevertheless note that novelists since the seventeenth century have used descriptive pauses, discursive digressions, the represented reveries of characters, and other rhetorical ornaments to slow and stop the forward motion of narrative and to elongate or stretch reader's perception of time (see DESCRIPTION). With the invention of modernist narrative forms, other modes of time-suspension became available, such as James Joyce's "epiphanies" or Ford Madox Ford's purposeful *longueur*. The novelist's ability to slow the tempo by imposing a long reading time on a short incident, though, is not the form's only way of reacting against the transience of time.

Another is the suspension brought about by the very use of the past tense in fiction. As numerous theorists have noted, the traditional use of the preterite in the novel is unmoored from its normal meaning because there is no present situation of communication in relation to which the verb's tense deictically indicates pastness. Rather, to borrow Harald Weinrich's formulation, the past tense in narrative often signals not pastness but an ontological distance from actuality that induces a certain kind of aesthetic receptivity, which he calls "withdrawal" from the actual world. We could think of it as analogous to the "Once upon a time" of the fairy tale. And paradoxically, as the critic A. A. Mendilow noted in 1952, the past tense signaling fictionality allows for the engrossment in which readers translate "all that happens . . . into an imaginative present" unfolding as they read the novel (96–97). Other critics working on the phenomenon of free indirect discourse, such as Kate Hamburger and Ann Banfield, have similarly noted the distance between the uses of tense in fiction and the ordinary uses of tense, and they have especially stressed the anachronic layering of presentness and pastness. All of these methods of countering time's transience might be said to invoke our tacit knowledge that the various dimensions of fictional time only "happen" in actuality when someone reads the novel, which can also obviously be re-read repeatedly, so that its transience is suspended in its textuality. The most uncanny temporal aspect of the novel may, indeed, be this always available replaying of events that we know never occurred.

Anti-sequence

To the regular sequence of past—present—future that marks "objective" time, the novel counterpoises numerous anachronic concatenations. We have already identified instances of analepsis and prolepsis, for example, and *Wuthering Heights* also gives us a prominent instance of paralepsis or ellipsis, which Genette defines as the omission at the narrative level of a link in the story chain, leading to a noticeable gap in the sequence. Heathcliff leaves Wuthering Heights in 1780 as a poor farm boy and returns to the neighborhood in 1783 as a rich man, but there is no account of how this change occurred. Simultaneity is another anti-sequential device used repeatedly in *Wuthering Heights*; e.g., Lockwood's reading of Catherine's diary creates our awareness of the simultaneity of their two calendar times (1801 and 1777) in our reading experience, a simultaneity that is also made thematic in Catherine's ghostly appearance at the window of Lockwood's bed later that night. Through all of the disruptions, reversals, gaps, and layers of temporal sequences, the novelist suggests that some states of being manage to escape the constraints of time altogether, stepping out into a dimension of permanent endurance. Indeed, Mikhail Bakhtin identifies this quality of existence outside of sequenced time as the "chronotope" of the GOTHIC novel.

Anti-irreversibility

The ambition to retrieve past time, redeem it, recall it, and make it once again present, thwarting its unidirectional flow, is implicit in the trope of retrospection that so frequently motivates the narrating in novels, and temporal reversal operates also in many of the techniques we've already examined: backward ordering, time-shifting, layering, and rendering moments simultaneously. The repetition of plot elements might be seen as another method of reviving spent time. At Wuthering Heights, for example, we see Lockwood inhospitably left without the accommodation of a bed in chap. 2, then the newly arrived Heathcliff in chap. 4 (and thirty years earlier) wanders the same halls

with nowhere to sleep, and then in chap. 13 (and thirteen years later), Isabella Heathcliff (née Linton) finds herself in the same situation. We see a single pattern of struggle and oppression form itself repeatedly as the denizens of the Heights ascend and descend the structure of power. And, most obviously, Heathcliff's attempted revenge consists in forcing the children of his enemies to relive the experience of his own degradation at the hands of their parents.

Wuthering Heights may be a novel particularly haunted by such recurrences, but novelistic plots in general, as Peter Brooks has argued, redeem time as a "medium of meaning" through the patterning activity of repetition. The first time an event occurs it may seem locked in its context, but its recurrence both brings the earlier incidences back to mind, thereby unbinding them from their initial placement, and also creates the resonances we perceive as the work's themes and meanings. Time's direction can also be reversed by highly coincidental plots, which give the impression of having been teleologically arranged in order to bring about particular endings and thus create the effect of backward causation. Moreover, recent experiments in reversing time's course have included narrative exploitations of backward time-travel paradoxes, tales of people born old and growing young, and, in the singular case of Martin Amis's *Time's Arrow* (1991), a narrator telling an entire novel in reverse order, as if he were describing a film playing backwards.

NOVELS AND HISTORICAL TIME

Perhaps because the novel has invented such strong models for rescuing the past, it has been a favorite form of historicist critics. When it promises to be entirely up to date and portray the world of the author's times, it thereby also pledges to preserve that world for future generations. In the atmosphere of nineteenth-century historicism, it added the ambition of retrieving the subjective experiences of bygone eras. History could give both a record and an analysis of public events, but the historical novel would portray the nitty-gritty lived sensations and mentalities of private lives, which were only then coming to be understood as historically shaped. For these reasons, we often read novels with an intense sense of their historicity; indeed, we often read them as a way of dwelling mentally in a past made present.

But what is the time of this past? Partly, we think of it as the past in which the author composed the novel. Obviously, this would not be the intradiegetic time of the narrating persona (e.g., Lockwood) but rather an extradiegetic time (e.g., the 1840s in which Emily Brontë wrote) that can be placed in relation to the reader's historical moment. Part of what we seek when we read *Wuthering Heights* historically is the sense of that invisible but nonetheless characterizable sensibility, its period inflections, and also its miraculous singularity in contrast to all the other Victorian novelists we read. The historical embodied life that produced that sensibility came and went, but we nonetheless believe we can approximate an encounter with it in the act of reading the novel.

Since the 1970s, however, "new" historicists have mounted a critique of this view of the novel's historical being. Literary works, as theoreticians such as Jerome McGann, Hans Robert Jauss, and Stephen Orgel (in their different ways) insist, are not fixed by their authors at particular points in history and then retrieved in that form by later readers; instead they exist as a multitude of various versions and moments of reception. Their historical being consists in a series of events (writings, publications, editings, readings, performances, and other consummations). There is no historical gap between the Victorian *Wuthering Heights* and our

twenty-first-century readings of it but rather a continuous series of realizations in which readers appropriated and revised the meaning of the text. In these perspectives the text is either equated with the totality of the operations performed in realizing it or viewed as a kind of ghostly "potential" that might be actualized in myriad human actions, all of which can be situated historically as discrete events. We might say, therefore, that the historical time of the novel has been generously pluralized since the 1960s and is now an ever-renewing manifold of historical times.

This pluralizing, however, has by no means overcome the problems inherent in placing texts historically. As Jauss pointed out in 1970, they seem to lack the normal starting and ending dates we use for other kinds of historical phenomena. For example, we can ask (without speaking nonsense), "When was the French Revolution?" But we cannot ask, "When was *A Tale of Two Cities*? Or when is it? Or when will it be?" We need to specify further: When was it written, published, revised, made into a movie, or read by a particular person? The novel (or, for that matter, a history like Thomas Carlyle's *The French Revolution*, 1837) comes into being as a text and then, our ordinary language indicates, just is, in a kind of being without necessarily happening that characterizes all textuality but is particularly acute in the novel, which refers only obliquely to actual historical events.

Novels, we might say, are uncannily at once historical and atemporal, giving readers the sense of being delivered into an intimately known past and yet making that delivery in a stretch of time that has no specifiable termination. This is the quality of time-in-abeyance that Georges Poulet describes when he claims that all books in their merely physical form seem to "wait for someone to come and deliver them from their materiality" (41); the text, he reminds us, can only be brought out of this dormancy by a reader, "whose own life it suspends" (47). The richness and complexity of the novel's anachronic techniques, the subtle indicators of its fictionality, heighten our awareness of this state of suspension.

SEE ALSO: Closure, Metafiction, Narrative Structure, Serialization, Space, Story/Discourse.

BIBLIOGRAPHY

Bakhtin, M.M. (1982), *Dialogic Imagination*, trans. K. Brostrom and V.S. Liapunov, ed. M. Holquist and V.S. Liapunov.
Bal, M. (1985), *Narratology*.
Banfield, A. (1982), *Unspeakable Sentences*.
Benveniste, E. (1977), *Problems in General Linguistics*, trans. Marilynn Rose.
Brooks, P. (1984), *Reading for the Plot*.
Genette, G. (1980), *Narrative Discourse*, trans. J.E. Lewin.
Genette, G. (1988), *Narrative Discourse Revisited*, trans. J.E. Lewin.
Hamburger, K. (1973), *Logic of Literature*, trans. M.J. Rose.
Jauss, H.R. (1970), "Literary History as a Challenge to Literary Theory," *New Literary History* 2: 7–37.
Jauss, H.R. (1982), *Toward an Aesthetic of Reception*.
McGann, J. (1983), *Critique of Modern Textual Criticism*.
Mendilow, A.A. (1952), *Time and the Novel*.
Müller, G. (1968), *Morphologische Poetik*.
Orgel, S. (2002), *Authentic Shakespeare*.
Poulet, G. (1980), "Criticism and the Experience of Interiority," trans. C. Macksey and R. Macksey, in *Reader-Response Criticism*, ed. J. P. Tompkins.
Ricoeur, P. (1985), *Time and Narrative*, vol. 2, trans. K. McLaughlin and D. Pellauer.
Weinrich, H. (1973), *Temps*, trans. M. Lacoste.

Todorov, Tzvetan *see* Genre Theory
Tragedy *see* Comedy/Tragedy
Translation History *see* Arabic Novel (Mashreq)

Translation Theory

PETER CONNOR

Toward the end of his 1813 lecture "On the Different Methods of Translation," Friedrich Schleiermacher refers to "an inner necessity" that has driven the German people to "translating *en masse*" (28). Schleiermacher was thinking of the abundance of translations by contemporaries such as Friedrich Hölderlin, Wilhelm von Humboldt, and the brothers Wilhelm and August Schlegel, poets and scholars whose versions of Sophocles, Pindar, Aeschylus, Plato, and William Shakespeare promised to carry over into German culture "all the treasures of foreign arts and scholarship" (29). It is a noble and elevating vision of the role of translation and of the task of the translator. But another, much more authentically "mass" or "large-scale" form of translation activity escapes Schleiermacher's notice (it is beneath his notice): driven less by "inner necessity" than by commercial interest, carried out not by renowned poets but by anonymous journeymen, the translation of the novel marks the true beginning of mass literary translation in the nineteenth century. The popular appeal of novels outside of their country of origin created an increasingly lucrative international market for publishers, who were quick to capitalize on the growing literary reputations of certain authors abroad. Within a year of its publication in 1719, Daniel Defoe's *Robinson Crusoe*, taken by some (e.g., Ian Watt) to be the first novel in English, was translated into French, German, and Dutch; by the end of the nineteenth century, in addition to 277 imitations (arguably a form of translation), it had been translated 110 times, including into Hebrew, Armenian, Bengali, Persian, and Inuit (Fishelov, 343). Thanks to an army of translators, Defoe's novel reached a vast, worldwide audience for which it was not originally intended. Defoe's publishers might well have mused, along with Goethe, that "national literature is now a rather unmeaning term; the epoch of world literature is at hand" (qtd. in Damrosch, 1).

That the novel, the "most buoyantly migratory" of genres (Prendergast, 23), should so easily cross linguistic frontiers might appear somewhat paradoxical, given the important historical role it has played as a medium of national awareness. Literary historians and sociologists have argued that novel and nation evolved in tandem, in part because the novel was a capacious genre that accommodated the multiple and disparate voices or languages of large geographical units. Timothy Brennan, for example, argues that the novel "accompanied the rise of nations by objectifying the 'one, yet many' of national life, and by mimicking the structure of the nation, a clearly bordered jumble of languages and styles" (49), while Franco Moretti, adopting Benedict Anderson's thesis that the novel provided the nation-states of Europe with the symbolic form they needed in order to be understood by the people, stresses the crucial representational role of the novel in a period when new economic, political, and technological processes conspired to "drag human beings out of the local dimension and throw them into a much larger [national] one" (17). Yet, through translation, this narrative form, designed to integrate the local into the national and to transform disparate territories into nations, reached (and shaped) an international market the members of which had little immediate interest in the local dynamics of nation-building. Whatever its function at the regional and national level, the history of the translation of the novel shows that its appeal was, from an early stage, transnational.

Critical examination of the immense corpus of translations reveals that the translation of the novel, like translation in general, is a complex and often problematic cultural transaction involving "asymmetries, inequities [and] relations of domination and dependence" (Venuti, 1998, 4). Moretti's research into the holdings of a number of British circulating libraries as well as cabinets de lecture (commercial rental or circulating libraries) in France in the mid-nineteenth century reveals the presence of remarkably few translations in libraries on either side of the Channel. Moretti concludes from this that Britain and France, being the primary producers of novels in the nineteenth century, had less interest in importing them than had, say, Italy or Denmark (151, figs. 71, 72). His research also reminds us that translation policy and practices vary enormously from nation to nation, with some nations, notably those that are politically and economically powerful, translating less than others. On the basis of statistics covering the mid- to late 1980s, for example, Lawrence Venuti estimates the translation rate (the percentage of published books that are translations) in the Italian publishing industry to be 25.4 percent, the German 14.4 percent, the French 9.9 percent, and the British and American somewhere between 2 and 4 percent (1995, 11). Venuti attributes the relative paucity of translations into English to a "complacency in British and American relations with cultural others" which expresses itself in a profoundly nationalist and even chauvinistic philosophy of translation—"imperialistic abroad and xenophobic at home" (1995, 13).

The xenophobia and imperialism that Venuti detects in certain translation practices are aspects of a more general form of violence that is partly inherent in the act of translating (which perforce suppresses and replaces the original text) and partly contributed, more or less consciously, by the translator, who in addition to the external pressures of commodity capitalism must contend with personal cultural biases that may conflict with the source text, resulting in an ethnocentric rendering of the original. Venuti is particularly sensitive to the insidious violence of "domestication" in translating, meaning the tendency, in the interest of producing a "fluent" and "readable" translation, to assimilate the foreign text to the values and norms of the receiving culture. Current publishing and reviewing practices in the U.S., which valorize transparency and familiarity in translations, implicitly encourage this type of violence, perhaps especially in the case of the novel inasmuch as, if we except some important experimental fiction, intelligibility remains in this genre an entrenched readerly expectation. French theorist Antoine Berman sees in every culture an inbuilt resistance to the very notion of translation to the extent that it necessarily implies "the violence of *métissage* [crossbreeding]." The aim of translation—"to open at the level of writing a certain relation to the Other, to fertilize the Self through the mediation of the Foreign"—is an affront to "the ethnocentric structure of every culture," which would prefer to imagine itself as a self-sufficient entity (16). On Berman's view, this fundamental cultural resistance to the notion of translation produces a "systematics of deformation" which "conditions the translator, whether he wants it or not, whether he knows it or not" (18).

The translation of the novel is accordingly subject to distortion and deformation at both conscious and unconscious levels. A simple but forceful example of the conscious manipulation of an original is the English translation of the title of Victor Hugo's classic novel *Notre Dame de Paris*, which becomes, in both the 1941 and the revised 2002 editions for the Modern Library (of the World's Best Books), *The Hunchback of Notre Dame*. The effect of this operation is to prime the Anglophone reader for a novel dealing with a single character (Quasimodo) and to privilege from among the

multiple narrative strands in the work the theme of physical deformity (Hugo, 2002). As Hugo's original French title suggests, the cathedral itself is the "protagonist" of the sprawling novel, the major themes of which (architecture, the print medium, religious fanaticism, social justice, etc.) are tributaries of this symbolically invested space. The repositioning of the novel as a tragic or pathetic story of unrequited love is a strategic marketing ploy that shapes the reception of the work as well as the perception of the author in North America. By deemphasizing Hugo's historical role as a revolutionary social and political commentator, the shift in title paves the way for the wholesale dilution of Hugo's oeuvre via musicals and films based on his works, including the 1996 Disney film of *The Hunchback* (Grossman).

Not all forms of conscious textual manipulation are so apparent. Wen Jin, analyzing *The Lost Daughter of Happiness*, the English-language version of Yan Geling's Chinese novel *Fusang* (1985), in which a young woman (Fusang) is abducted from her village in China and sold into a Chinatown brothel in San Francisco, notes that the translation omits or abridges key descriptions concerning the main character's "unruly sexuality" (572). This has led to two almost diametrically opposed readings of the novel. Anglo-American readers, having access only to a bowdlerized version of the original, have seen Fusang as "opaque" and regard her as an example of the proverbial "inscrutable Oriental." Readers in mainland China, privy to explicit descriptions of Fusang's "effortless accommodation of forced sexual intercourse" (577), read her character in allegorical terms, recognizing in the young woman "the embodiment of a kind of feminine resilience that enabled China to hold its own against its Western enemies during the twentieth century" (573).

Unconscious interference in literary translation can take a number of different forms. Berman has attempted to classify the major "deforming tendencies" that beset translations; among these are "rationalization," "clarification," "expansion," and "ennoblement," as well as the "destruction" of the rhythms and signifying networks of the source text. Since these tendencies operate at the unconscious level, the ideal translator will have undergone a cathartic "ascesis" akin to a rigorous psychoanalysis (Berman recommends team-translation as a means to uncover and combat unconscious forces). Because the end result of these deforming tendencies is to suppress the alterity of the source text (rendering the original more transparent through rationalization, more aesthetically pleasing through ennoblement, more fluent or readable through clarification, etc.), Berman (following Schleiermacher and Wilhelm von Humboldt) advocates the "foreignizing" of literary translation through the use of literalisms, neologisms, and syntactical borrowings. The "foreignizing" method, witnessed mostly in the translation of poetry and drama by poets (e.g., Friedrich Hölderlin's translation of Sophocles, Pierre Klossowski's translation of Virgil, etc.), is rarely practiced in the case of the novel. This may reflect the novel's lowly position in the hierarchy of literary genres: of the many writers who also translate, few translate novels, work that is left to professional or amateur translators (often academics) who may feel uncomfortable with the degree of linguistic innovation such foreignizing entails. An exception, according to George Steiner, is the English translation of Hermann Broch's *Der Tod des Vergil* (1945) by Jean Starr Untermeyer. Carried out over five years in collaboration with the author, the "bilingual weave" of *The Death of Virgil* (1945) makes so few concessions to the "natural breaks and lucidities of English" that "English and German meet in a 'meta-syntax'" (337–38). Such a case remains rare, however, especially in the translation of novels into English, where the imbalance in the power relation between source and target languages often results in the obliteration of cultural difference. This risk is especially high in English translation of Third World literature, which, according to Gayatri Chakravorty Spivak, "gets translated into a sort of with-it translatese, so that the literature by a woman in Palestine begins to resemble, in the feel of its prose, something by a man in Taiwan" (182).

While translation scholarship has focused largely on the interlinguistic translation of literary forms, attention has turned recently to multilingualism and translingualism, phenomena that are particularly prevalent in the novel. In multilingual and translingual texts, a mode of translation becomes the motor of the creative enterprise; here translation is less "a process applied to a text than a process that takes place within it" (Levy, 107). Multilingualism refers to the presence of two or more languages in a given text: *Tristram Shandy* (1759), which mixes learned Latin digressions with the vernacular, is an example, as is Tolstoy's use of French in *Voyná i mir* (1869, *War and Peace*) or Mann's in *Der Zauberberg* (1924, *The Magic Mountain*). In recent times, multilingualism has emerged as a significant stylistic feature in bicultural, colonial or postcolonial novels. Chicano author Rudolf Anaya includes both Spanish and English in *Bless Me, Ultima* (1972), as does Dominican-American writer Junot Díaz in *The Brief Wondrous Life of Oscar Wao* (2007), while the Martinican Patrick Chamoiseau mixes French and Creole in *Texaco* (1992). The technique is often employed to thematize issues of (split) identity as it relates to language, the presence of two languages symbolizing "the failure to achieve cultural symbiosis" (Zabus, qtd. in Grutman, 159). Translingualism, likewise observed among writers employing an imposed or colonial language, refers to the presence of lexical or syntactic traces of an indigenous language in a writer's use of a hegemonic language (cf. Venuti, 1998, 174). Translingualism can be a strategy in the othering or foreignizing of a colonial language, as in Chinua Achebe's self-conscious Africanization of English ("the world language that history has forced down our throats") or Mário de Andrade's Brazilianization of Portuguese (Achebe, 431; Casanova, 258). Michael Cronin argues that such forms of "linguistic doubling" are subversive inasmuch as the embedding of indigenous words and phrases within an English-language text represents "the return of the linguistically repressed" (136). Recent studies have focused attention on the parameters and nature of various "other Englishes," "weird" or "rotten" forms of English that rely on various strategies of intralinguistic translation (Apter; Ch'ien). Ch'ien includes in the category of "weird-English authors" the novelists Arundhati Roy, Maxine Hong Kingston, Jonathan Safran Foer, and Irvine Welsh, writers whose espousal of linguistic hybridity challenges conventions of fluency, linguistic purism, and the hegemony of elite "educated English" (Crystal, 149).

Finally we might note the increased prominence of translators and translation as figures or an explicit theme in contemporary novels and other narrative forms. *The House on Moon Lake* (2000), by Italian Francesca Duranti, centers upon translator Fabrizio Garrone and his fascination with an obscure German author; Dai Sijie's partly autobiographical novel *Balzac et la petite tailleuse chinoise* (2001, *Balzac and the Little Chinese Seamstress*) dramatizes the importance of Chinese translations of Balzac and other Western classics during Mao's Cultural Revolution; Egyptian-born Leila Aboulela's *The Translator* (2005) portrays a Sudanese translator of Arabic living in Scotland; John Crowley has constructed a spy novel, *The Translator* (2002), around the motif of translation and betrayal, and so on. The publication of a number of "language memoirs," a term coined by Alice Kaplan to describe autobiographical accounts by bilingual subjects focusing on the forced or voluntary acquisition of a second language, complements and enhances the novelistic representations of the work of the translator. In addition to her own *French Lessons* (1993), this disparate category includes narratives generated by the experience of exile and war, such as Eva Hoffman's *Lost in Translation* (1989) and Daoud Hari's *The Translator* (2008). Such publications suggest that translation itself can be a valuable narrative and novelistic resource; they perhaps signal further that the translator has begun to combat the condition of invisibility that until recently was his or her lot (Venuti, 1995).

BIBLIOGRAPHY

Achebe, C. (1994), "The African Writer and the English Language," in *Post-Colonial Discourse and Post-Colonial Theory*, ed. P. Williams and L. Chrisman.

Anderson, B. (1991), *Imagined Communities*.

Apter, E. (2006), *Translation Zone*.

Berman, A. (1984), *Épreuve de l'étranger*.

Brennan, T. (1990), "The National Longing for Form," in *Nation and Narration*, ed. H.K. Bhabha.

Broch, H. (1945), *Death of Virgil*, trans. J.S. Untermeyer.

Casanova, P. (2004), *World Republic of Letters*, trans. M.B. Debevoise.

Ch'ien, E. (2005), *Weird English*.

Cronin, M. (2003), *Translation and Globalization*.

Crystal, D. (2003), *English as a Global Language*, 2nd ed.

Damrosch, D. (2003), *What Is World Literature?*

Fishelov, D. (2008), "Dialogues with/and Great Books," *New Literary History* 39:335–53.

Grossman, K. (2001), "From Classic to Pop Icon," *French Review* 74(3):482–95.

822   TURKEY

Grutman, R. (1998), "Multilingualism and
   Translation," in *Routledge Encyclopedia of
   Translation Studies*, ed. M. Baker.
Hugo, V. (1941), *Hunchback of Notre Dame*.
Hugo, V. (2002), *Hunchback of Notre Dame*, rev.
   trans. C. Liu, intro. E. McCracken.
Jin, W. (2006), "Transnational Criticism and Asian
   Immigrant Literature in the U.S.," *Contemporary
   Literature* 47(4):570–600.
Levy, L. (2003), "Exchanging Words," *Comparative
   Studies of South Asia, Africa and the Middle East*,
   23(1/2):106–27.
Moretti, F., ed. (2006), *Novel*.
Prendergast, C. (2004), "The World Republic of
   Letters," in *Debating World Literature*.
Schleiermacher, F. (1982), "On the Different
   Methods of Translation," trans. A. Lefevere, in
   German Romantic Criticism, ed. A.L. Willson.
Spivak, G.C. (1993), *Outside in the Teaching
   Machine*.
Steiner, G. (1998), *After Babel*, 3rd ed.
Venuti, L. (1995), *Translator's Invisibility*.
Venuti, L. (1998), *Scandals of Translation*.
Zabus, C. (1990), "Othering the Foreign
   Language in the West African Europhone
   Novel," *Canadian Review of Comparative
   Literature* 17(3/4):348–66.

Turkey

ERDAĞ GÖKNAR

The origins of Turkish literary modernity can be traced back to a mid-nineteenth-century Ottoman Muslim engagement with Enlightenment ideals. The literary form of the novel appeared during the Tanzimat era of modernization, first through translations (e.g., of François Fénelon's *Télémaque* and Victor Hugo's *Les Misérables* in 1862 and Daniel Defoe's *Robinson Crusoe* in 1864), then through imitations that merged local form and content such as traditional *meddah* storytelling with the European novel. Early novels such as Şemsettin Sami's *Taaşşuk-i Talât ve Fitnat* (1872, The Romance of Talât and Fitnat), Namık Kemal's *İntibah* (1874, The Awakening), and Ahmet Mithat Efendi's *Dürdane Hanım*

(1882, Miss Durdaneh) opened up a social space of self-examination with a moral intent to guide and instruct readers in the face of European cultural encroachment. The transition from a literary modernity to a fin-de-siècle aesthetic of literary modernism occurred through authors like Halit Ziya Uşaklıgil, who were able to emphasize aesthetic concerns and structure in novels like *Mai ve Siyah* (1897, Blue and Black) and *Aşk-ı Memnu* (1900, Illicit Love). In other words, the Ottoman novel itself was a medium of modernization. Its mediation, revision, and updating of narrative traditions in a new genre marked the beginnings of a literary modernity that persisted into the twentieth century and laid the foundation for an aesthetic of modernism that emerged more fully in the Republican era.

The process of Ottoman modernization did not prevent the failure of the Ottoman state. The historical oppositions of tradition and modernity, East and West, and Islam and Christianity found their way into literature through representative characters and tropes. These cultural oppositions were intensified by the occupation of the Ottoman capital of Istanbul (1918–23) by Allied armies after WWI and the Kemalist Cultural Revolution (1922–38) that responded to that occupation with a concentrated period of social engineering. Whereas the occupation ensured the partition of Ottoman territories into mandates, nation-states, and kingdoms, the Cultural Revolution, as if to sanction a European secular example, abolished the Ottoman Islamic sultanate, followed by the caliphate, and changed the written language, the legal system, dress codes, time, and the calendar. Perhaps owing to the intensity of events, a historiographic mode of novel-writing began to define literary modernity as in the novels of Halide Edib and Yakup Kadri Karaosmanoğlu. Literary realism dominated in the milieu of Republican social engineering that resulted in a cultural mapping of the opposition between tradition and modernity upon two distinct historical polities: the defunct Ottoman Islamic empire and the secular Republic of Turkey, respectively. As a result, the Tanzimat state of duality that dominated the formative period of Ottoman literary modernity became a trope of the "divided self" in the Republican period. The duality preoccupied Republican authors and intellectuals, constituting one of the major tropes of Turkish literary modernism observable in the novel from Ahmet Mithat Efendi to Orhan Pamuk.

The following tripartite periodization emphasizes the contingencies of a century and a half of literary development from modernity to modernism and postmodernism.

OTTOMAN LITERARY MODERNITY

Early Ottoman authors of modernization including Şinasi, Namık Kemal, Samipaşazade Sezai, Muallim Naci, and Recaizade Ekrem sanctioned "Westernization" only to the degree that it would preserve the Ottoman—Islamic order. They did not fully adopt Enlightenment epistemological foundations. The crises of modernization, as they affected Ottoman society, focused on a process of defensive modernization over the nineteenth and early twentieth centuries. This meant that novels were often socially instructive and didactic in their aim rather than literary.

Ottoman modernism (1876–1908)

This period is marked by two constitutional periods in late Ottoman history—beginning in 1876 and 1908, respectively—that might be read as part of a transnational movement of Modernist Islam stretching from Central Asia to North Africa. The late nineteenth-century Ottoman modern was an urban figure seduced by the trappings of European culture (including dress, the French language, and new modes of consumption). The dilemma, in short, was one of Ottoman Islam on the cusp of European colonization, and the response of Ottoman intellectuals preoccupied with reform and negotiating a synthesis between aspects of tradition and modernity. Though such themes are taken up in Recaizade Ekrem's *Araba Sevdası* (1896, Carriage Romance) and Hüseyin Rahmi Gürpınar's *Şıpsevdi* (1911, Love at First Sight), the representative novel of this era is Ahmet Mithat Efendi's *Felatun Bey ve Rakım Efendi* (1876, Felatun Bey and Rakım Efendi). This iconic novel describes positive and negative engagements in the late Ottoman modernization process through its display of the lives of two opposing characters: one representing passive mimicry of Europe and the other a strong work ethic steeped in traditional values. These two possible models of social change are contrasted as an object lesson against excessive "Westernization."

Ottoman Turkism (1908–22)

This time span reflects a period of almost constant warfare. The ideological changes brought about by the second constitutional revolution (1908), the Balkan Wars, WWI, and its continuation in Anatolia until 1922 resulted in a violent remapping of Ottoman territory based on ethno-religious categories that led to the transformation of the figure of the Ottoman modern. Turkism, the ideology of Turkish nationalism, provided an argument for self-determination in a limited territory that avoided the vagueness of Ottomanism, the expansiveness of Islamism, and the colonial cast of Westernism. "East vs. West" debates regarding tradition and reform are reflected in the works of Ottoman Turkist writers such as Ziya Gökalp, Ömer Seyfettin, Halide Edib Adıvar, and Müfide Ferit

Tek. Reşat Nuri Güntekin's *Çalıkuşu* (1922; *Autobiography of a Turkish Girl*, 1949), a popular novel of this era, is significant for its use of Anatolia as a setting, its identification of the challenges that await the "new" women of modernist Islam, and its implicit critique of Istanbul society for its ignorance of the lives of Anatolian peasants. Compromised in terms of gender and sexuality, the main character Feride becomes the focus of a dilemma of modernization; in short, as an educated woman she must struggle against the obstacles of Anatolian traditionalism.

REPUBLICAN LITERARY MODERNISM

The Kemalist Cultural Revolution instigated a new wave of Turkish literary modernity in the 1920s and 1930s. The intensity of the social engineering that occurred during these years caused a break between the Ottoman—Islamic past and national progress that affected literary production throughout the Republican era. Not only were the alphabet and language transformed, but Muslim traditions and symbols were pushed into the private sphere, and Sufi practices were outlawed. The tensions between Istanbul cosmopolitanism and Anatolia were reflected in the novel through realistic depictions that constituted the dominant conflict of literary modernism.

Republican Turkism (1922–50)

This era witnessed the proliferation of ideological novels supporting the Cultural Revolution, i.e., historically grounded representations of new "men" and new societies with a socialist, nationalist, and/or Turkist coloring. Often the main characters can be clearly read as didactic, allegorical figures. This period begins with the abolition of the Ottoman sultanate in 1922 and caliphate in 1924. Over the next few decades, the national allegories in novels written in the 1920s and 1930s by Yakup Kadri Karaosmanoğlu, Peyami Safa, and Halide Edib gradually give way to more nuanced accounts. In the work of Ahmet Hamdi Tanpınar, the reader is confronted *not* with object lessons, morality, or "party" novels espousing the Kemalist vision of society and history, but with a complex reckoning of the transition between Ottoman and Turkist worldviews. In the milestone novel *Huzur* (1949; *A Mind at Peace*, 2009), the historical traumas experienced in the establishment of the Republic have become psychological dilemmas that afflict the middle-class characters. The novel, set in 1939, dramatizes the mental breakdown of the main character, Mümtazm in the turmoil of the illness of his cousin and mentor İhsan, the ending of his relationship with his beloved Nuran, the suicide of his nemesis Suad (who also loves Nuran), and the impending WWII. In its depiction of Istanbul's streets, neighborhoods, Ottoman music, and the Bosphorus, the novel is an icon of modernist, cosmopolitan prose with leitmotifs of urban Turkish culture. *Huzur*, harkening back to the era of Ottoman modernism, is one of the first testimonies to the cultural limitations of national and social modernization projects.

Anatolian realism (1950–71)

The start of multiparty politics in 1946 and the election of the Democrat Party to power in 1950 contained an implicit critique of the Cultural Revolution that was reflected in literature through a move away from nationalist ideals focusing on elite intellectuals to socialist ideals focusing on the Anatolian peasant. The genre, often historically grounded and based on the use of actual documents, addresses bleak economic hardships, blood feuds, patriarchy, honor, outlaws, and the cruelty of gendarmes, petty officials, and exploitation by *ağas* (landowners). The 1960 coup and the new constitution established wide-ranging freedom of the press, an independent judiciary, and the right to form unions, and autonomy in universities reinforced a socialist context and kept alive the possibility of social freedoms and justice. Author-intellectuals including Orhan Kemal, İlhan Tarus, Talip Apaydın, Fakir Baykurt, and Tarık Buğra helped to establish the genre that advocated social justice for the dispossessed. But not until the work of Kemal Tâhir was this genre historicized and applied innovatively to the Ottoman past. In his famous novel *Devlet Ana* (1967, Mother State), Tâhir combines Anatolian realism, the Marxist belief in the Asiatic Mode of Production, and strains of Turkism, introducing a new understanding of historiography into the socialist novel. Drawing on the geographic, economic, and social conditions that gave rise to the Ottoman Anatolian (and by extension, the Turkish Republican Anatolian) state, *Devlet Ana* focuses on the establishment of the Ottoman state after the dissolution of the Seljuk state around 1300. It is, however, an allegory for the establishment of a socialist state accepting a variety of people, languages, and religions in the present.

Feminism and existentialism (1971–80)

The Anatolian socialist novel, which was meant to confront the realities of rural life, became formulaic and idealized, later leading to the emergence of individual concerns in the following generation, especially by women authors frustrated with marginalization. Strong women emerged to make social critiques of earlier eras, as exemplified by the narratives of Leyla Erbil, Sevgi Soysal, and Füruzan. Other writers retreated into isolation and alienation, such as Oğuz Atay (noted for his iconic novel *Tutunamayanlar*, 1972; The Good-for-Nothing), Bilge Karasu,

and Yusuf Atılgan. Futhermore, themes involving Islam and lived traditions began to appear with greater frequency, perhaps filling "spaces" evacuated by large-scale socialist movements that had failed to gain political power and transform society. At the same time, the *hidayet romanı* (Islamic novel) grew through the efforts of authors such as Şule Yüksel Şenler, Ahmet Günbay Yıldız, and Mustafa Miyasoğlu.

The "inter-coup" era was a socially fragile period that witnessed the removal of intellectuals from life, career, and family in society. Irony and sarcasm about ideological projects on the left and the right began to make their way into fiction, and depictions of alienation become prominent. Themes include the critique or indictment of national and socialist modernity from the perspective of its victims: women, alienated intellectuals, Islamicists, and other marginalized populations. Adalet Ağaoğlu's *Ölmeye Yatmak* (1973, Lying Down to Die) is a novel that represents this period with a female protagonist, Aysel, a professor who withdraws to a hotel room to commit suicide. The focus on the plight of one woman is set against a reckoning of Turkish history between 1938 (Atatürk's death) and the revolutionary upheavals of 1968 in Europe. Aysel has had an affair with one of her students, Engin, and believes she might be pregnant. The moral and ethical implications disrupt everything she has known about bourgeois life in Turkey. The reemergence of sexuality is an important theme here, and the novel represents the stirrings of second-wave feminism out of the first wave ("state feminism") in the Turkish context.

REPUBLICAN LITERARY POSTMODERNISM

The strong hold of committed literature of social engagement and realism delayed the acceptance of formal innovation in the novel that relied on metanarrative, metahistory, and deconstruction. Republican postmodernist writing focused on historiographic fiction, fantasy, and parodic genres that placed literary artifice over and above socialist concerns and Anatolian realism. The literary establishment reacted with animosity toward such cosmopolitan formal innovation, which also implicitly critiqued the narrative of national and social progress. Well-known practitioners of this trend include Oğuz Atay, Bilge Karasu, Hasan Ali Toptaş, and İhsan Oktay Anar.

Post-nationalism and neo-Ottomanism (1980–2002)

The leftist intelligentsia marks the 1980 coup as the beginning of "depoliticization," a first step in reorienting society toward neoliberalism. In literature, this led to drastic changes, as writers responded to the political transformations by moving away from social issues and realism in a manner that questioned grand narratives of nationalism/Kemalism and socialism through aesthetic experimentation with content and form. Though these trends could be more generally labeled part of postmodernism, their manifestation in the Turkish context can be further specified as expressions of literary post-Kemalism, post-socialism, and neo-Ottomanism (not to be confused with the political ideology).

A strong Marxist tradition led to a delay and resistance to the representation of postmodernism, a literary category that was suspect to the practitioners of engaged literature and the literature of witness. The novels of this period acknowledge the collapse of metanarratives of socio-national progress through the multiplication of perspectives, the ironic revisiting of Ottoman history, parody, formal experimentation, and the subversion of realism through fantasy or magical realism. Latife Tekin and Nobel laureate Orhan Pamuk define this generation of writers. Pamuk's ever-changing narrative style reached the first of many peaks with his third novel, *Beyaz Kale* (1985; *The White Castle*, 1990), a concise historical metafiction that subtly criticizes authoritarian nationalism while reintroducing the Ottoman past to a sophisticated, literary readership. Furthermore, the novel presents an allegorical challenge by subverting the self/other binary through a display of narrative finesse that marked Pamuk as a postmodern writer. In the novel, a Venetian slave and his Ottoman master reveal their worlds to each other until they begin to overlap. The Ottoman theme in Pamuk's work is picked up again with *Benim Adım Kırmızı* (1998; *My Name Is Red*, 2001), a complex and fragmented work that takes the flat, two-dimensionality of the Ottoman miniature painting and transforms it into a living, vital, aesthetic model pertinent to the present day. The novel, combing a number of genres, is a historical murder mystery focusing on the imperial miniaturists' guild and a mysterious book that the Sultan has commissioned. In its multiplicity of narrators and its aesthetic self-consciousness, the novel becomes Pamuk's "large canvas."

Cosmopolitical texts (2002–present)

There are a few hundred novelists writing in Turkish today. The novels of the youngest generation of Turkish writers, represented by Murat Uyurkulak, Şebnem İşigüzel, and Elif Şafak, are emotionally charged, cynical, and violent. They are political, yet promote distance from their immediate cultural affiliations. The novelistic claims by these authors are cosmopolitical in that they have multiple national and international affiliations that strive for transnational legibility and relevance. This is the generation of EU

accession politics and the rise of the Justice and Development Party, which won general elections in 2002 and 2007. The writers of the newest generation do not ascribe to any particular movement in the traditional sense. Their idiosyncrasies, experimental in terms of form and content, are, however, unified in one important respect: their work represents a mixing or crossing of traditional novelistic styles that might include DETECTIVE stories, underground fiction, youth subcultures, and fantasy. The boundaries that they cross in their fiction challenge the limits of national tradition through transgressions of taboo, history, gender, and GENRE. They have learned to live with contradictions rather than trying to resolve them. In the wake of the collapse of grand narratives of modernization, nationalism, and socialism, and in an increasingly consumerist culture, they explore new avenues of cynical narration that unsettle concepts of belonging.

Representing the first generation to grow up within the neoliberal system that was established after the 1980 coup, these writers are tacticians of resistance on an individual rather than social scale. They have little conviction in monolithic ideologies, but they do have an inkling of the market of identities and a multitude of sites of power influencing one's choices. In short, there is a new relationality in these works, a new way of seeing the regional and international world into which Turkey has increasingly become integrated. Importantly, these authors are redefining what it means to be Turkish.

Uyurkulak's *Tol* (2002, Revenge) is a reassessment, an unofficial history, of the previous fifty years of Turkey's history told from the perspective of poets, revolutionaries, and madmen from various generations. The fragmented plot revolves around an alcoholic poet ("Poet") and a proofreader, Yusuf, who has lost his will to live. The two are on a train journey from Istanbul to the heavily Kurdish region of Diyarbakır—two cities representing the opposing poles of modern Turkish modernity and oppression/dispossession. *Tol* conveys the perspective of frustrated leftist idealism that exacts its revenge against the state and a system of war, inhumanity, and capitalism through alternative narratives and ways of being.

This 150-year overview of Ottoman and Republican literary modernity reveals that the Turkish novel has not stayed within the confines of historically determined binaries of modernization such as "East and West" but has established contingent tropes and chronotopes of literary modernity, modernism, and postmodernism.

BIBLIOGRAPHY

Evin, A. (1983), *Origins and Development of the Turkish Novel*.
Göksu, S. and E. Timms (1999), *Romantic Communist*.
Gürbilek, N. (2010), *Return of Turkey*.
Güzeldere, G. and S. Irzık (2003), *Relocating the Fault Lines*.
Holbrook, V.R. (1994), *Unreadable Shores of Love*.
Moran, B. (1983), *Türk Romanına Eleştirel bir Bakış* [A critical look at the Turkish novel], 3 vols.
Ostle, R., ed. (1991), *Modern Literature in the Near and Middle East 1850–1970*.
Pamuk, O. (2007), *Other Colors*.
Rathbun, C. (1972), *Village in the Turkish Novel and Short Story 1920 to 1955*.
Seyhan, A. (2008), *Tales of Crossed Destinies*.

Typography
ROBIN KINROSS

Novels are written in prose rather than in verse. This simple insight promises to stimulate philosophical and historical investigations into the nature of the form. But any description of what the pages of almost every novel look like is so far largely missing. When a novel's typography is mentioned it is usually to point to pages that depart in some way from the norm. The normal page is one in which lines of text are arrayed under each other to form a rectangular block surrounded by sufficient margins of unprinted paper. Outside this block of text there will be page numbers and, often, headings or "running headlines" that give the title of the book and the chapter.

Unlike verse, a line of text in a novel does not contain meaning. The breaks at the end of a line happen more or less arbitrarily, governed only by whatever rules are being followed for where to break a word, if a word has to be broken. In a novel the lines of text will almost always be justified. By varying the spaces between the words they will have equal, constant length. A page will be brought to an end at its last line. The attention of the typesetter, or whoever is making the blocks of text into pages, is brought to bear only when one line of the prose-unit, typically a "chapter," is left stranded at the top of the following page. Computers now assist in these processes.

Pages made in this way become containers for the flow of text. The writer writes it; the typesetter pours it into these molds. The resulting page will be a fairly robust and unremarkable device that suits and, to some extent, makes the novel possible. Because the strict, unvarying visual form does not carry meaning, many things can happen in the imagination of the writer and the reader. Standardized pages accommodate both "large loose baggy monsters, with their queer elements of the accidental and the arbitrary," and the short, tight, slim texts of twentieth-century MODERNISM (Henry James, 1908, *Tragic Muse*, Preface).

Yet there is more to say, particularly about the ways in which a text is embodied in apparently mundane pages. As the historical bibliographer D. F. McKenzie argues convincingly (1999, 2002), the form of the book and of the text plays a constituent part in its meanings. Pour the text into another mold of different letterforms, different sizes, different spatial configurations, and the meanings of it will change. McKenzie's examples are mainly of poetic and dramatic texts in which typographic form is more meaning-charged than in the continuous text of the novel, but these ideas apply equally to prose works.

MEANINGS IN THE NORMATIVE PAGE

Printed text carries its history with it, visibly, and in its touch and smell. From picking up the book and looking into its pages, without reading a title or an imprint page, one will usually be able to tell by what processes the text was set and printed, and when and where it was made. Any published novel will have that particular embodiment.

Robinson Crusoe by Daniel Defoe helps make some of the necessary distinctions clear. Henry Clinton Hutchins established the early bibliographical history of this work in 1923. Compare the first four licensed English editions of *Robinson Crusoe*, all published in 1719 by William Taylor (see fig. 1), with two pirated editions of that same year: the so-called "Amsterdam" coffee-house edition and the "o" edition. The licensed editions are typographically unremarkable, normal products of the English printing and PUBLISHING trade of that time (see fig. 1). The unlicensed editions reveal the nature of their publication in the rougher quality of their typesetting and printing. In the case of the "o" edition, named after its misspelling on the title page, *The life, and strange surprizing adventures of Robeson Cruso, mariner*, the typesetting is wild, evidently done on the cheap and in a hurry.

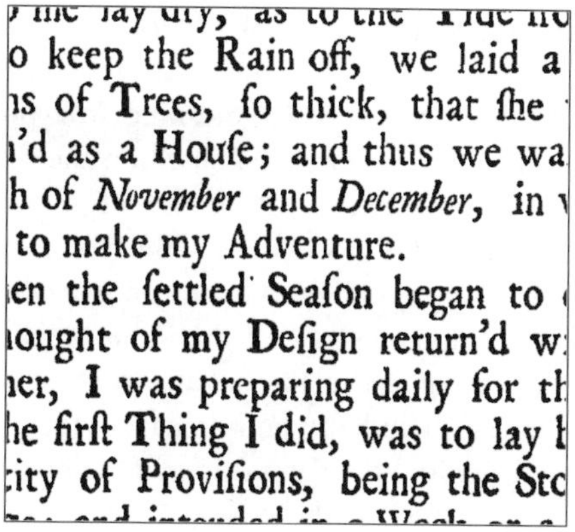

Figure 1 Typography in a 1719 edition of Daniel Defoe, *Robinson Crusoe* (London: William Taylor), illustrates the normal product of the English printing trade of the time

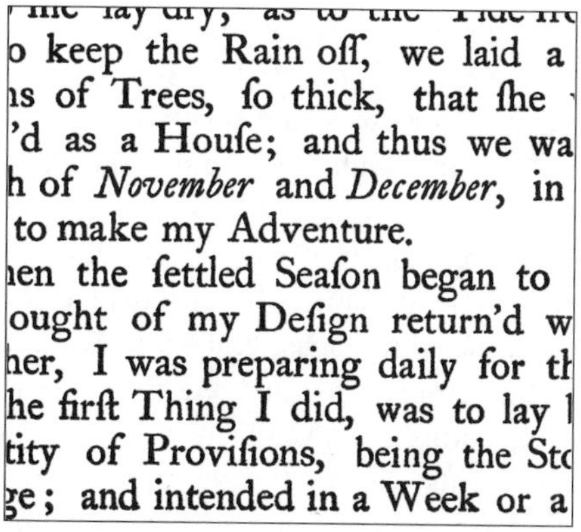

Figure 2 Typography in the 1883 "facsimile" edition of *Robinson Crusoe* (London: Elliot Stock) is similar, yet every character and every space is different

Type of different fonts and styles is set together, and there are parts of the text in which italic is used only because there can have been no roman to hand. The only meaning to read into the typography of these pages is "unlicensed."

In 1743 a French TRANSLATION of *Robinson Crusoe* was published in Amsterdam by Zacharie Chatelain. It looks different from the English editions of the time. This is partly, of course, because the language of the text is now different. Put the text into another language and the visual appearance of it must change, however well the meanings of the text have been captured by the translation. But further, the conventions of French typography (émigré French, in this case) were slightly different from those of English typography. The type is a little larger, the lines are a little shorter, and the title page is more grandiloquent.

In 1883 the London publisher Elliot Stock issued an edition described on its title page as "a facsimile reprint of the first edition published in 1719" (see fig. 2). On looking at these pages, someone familiar with the first edition might easily believe that the 1883 edition is indeed a reprint of the original

made by photographic methods. Its text matches the book of 1719 line for line, page for page, word break for word break. But a more careful look shows that, though the type used is a close match for the original—Elliot Stock used a revival of an eighteenth-century model similar to the Dutch type used by Taylor in 1719—the type is too smooth, too regular, too evenly printed to be the product of the worn type and wooden presses of seventeenth-century printing. This was a painstaking emulation of the original setting using the best tools of late nineteenth-century small-industrial production. The typesetting was almost certainly done by hand rather than by the powered machines that were just then being developed. The Elliot Stock edition is eerily reminiscent of the book of 1719. Its text seems to match its model in every detail of setting and spelling; the long *s*'s and ligatured characters are faithfully copied. Apart from a few inevitable errors, it can be considered the same as the text of the 1719 edition. And yet, it is quite distinct. Every character and every space is different. The paper is machine-made rather than handmade. The image of the characters is regular and light where the original image is ragged and imperfect. The book speaks of "England in 1883": of the attempts to recover and preserve historical artifacts by imitation, using the latest technologies.

How and to what degree one can copy an original are issues of constant concern to anyone editing historical texts. The line-for-line emulation practiced in the Elliot Stock edition is usually a step too far. Labor costs will hardly ever allow it. But how far should one go in copying orthography and spelling? In the University of Florida Press and Penguin Classics editions of Laurence Sterne's *Tristram Shandy* (ed. Melvyn New and Joan New, 1978, 2003)—a work that has come to be a primary instance of the typographically conscious novel—the different kinds of dashes used in the first printings of the book are faithfully copied. The nine volumes of the novel, issued over eight years (1759–67) by three different printer-publishers, use dashes of different lengths. It is hard to see any consistent system at work in their deployment by any of these printers. The first two volumes, printed by Ann Ward in York and thus near at hand to Sterne, are especially idiosyncratic in their use of a series of hyphens for a dash. Two, three, or four hyphens may be set this way, but elsewhere dashes of varying lengths are used. One can guess that a certain size of dash was employed ad hoc to help out with the justification of that particular line. If a long dash would not quite fit in a line without causing problems, then a shorter one might be used. If the modern edition is not following the word and line breaks of the original, the necessity behind that choice of dash is lost. The fact that the modern editions are set without any attempt at imitation of the original type or the original paper, as in late nineteenth-century facsimiles, further undermines this partial attempt at typographic emulation.

AUTHOR AND TYPESETTER

Any attempt to assign meaning to typographic effects in a novel based on the size or style of letters or the use of marks, symbols, or the spaces that are the repertoire of typography will need to be aware of what was within the scope of the writer at that time and in that place. What sort of communication did the author have with the publisher and the compositor of the novel? The liveliness of the pages of some eighteenth-century novels seems to derive from a number of factors.

During the eighteenth century, relations between authors and those making the books could be quite close. The publisher and printer were usually the same person. In the exceptional case of Samuel Richardson, the author was a printer and publisher by trade. Richardson would have been able to oversee the production of his own novels, though some editions were put out to other printers. In her work on English novels of this period, Janine Barchas treads carefully. She notices the graphic and typographic effects and considers what part they might play in the design of the novel, but she holds back from any historically unsupportable interpretation. In her study the term "graphic design retains its literal meaning as the intentional use of graphic effects for novelistic purposes. For example, the decorative pieces that are used to show a gap in the time of the novel could perhaps have been chosen to match the scene and characters of that moment in the story, or they could merely have been taken by the compositor from what was available in his case of ornaments on that day. These ornaments were, after all, stock devices, designed for a wide variety of uses and not made especially for the work in question.

As publishing and printing began to separate into two distinct practices, so an author's ability to take part in the design of pages diminished. The larger the publishing firm, the less input authors could have in how their books would be made. This widely recognized standardization of book design was reinforced by technical changes in text composition, above all the introduction of powered text composition, which began in the closing years of the nineteenth century in the U.S., Western Europe, and the territories of the British Empire. But already with handset type, in printing offices of even moderate size, the work process had to be split between compositors and thus needed to be governed by common standards and routines. Another less recognized factor in this process of normalization was the growing use of typewriting machines by writers, secretaries, and copyists. With the waning of the handwritten text, the possibilities for graphic effects decreased. Any special desires that an author or publisher might want would need to be drawn by hand in a "layout," a mimetic instruction for the printer's compositor to follow. Wytze Hellinga published a suggestive survey of over five hundred years of surviving material evidence of "copy," the author's text with any instructions for typesetting or layout, and "print," what this copy became.

In his discussion of what he calls "the revolution in the layout of books in the eighteenth century," Nicolas Barker reluctantly adopts the term "layout" in preference to "typography" to describe what others in and outside of France have sometimes called *mise en page* (127). He thus passes over the narrower specialist sense of layout as a plan used to convey instructions. (This short text was written as a lecture for the same 1977 conference at which McKenzie first gave his paper on typography and the meaning of words.) Barker of necessity uses a broad brush. He sketches the national styles of page design in France, Germany, and England to show

how simplification and standardization changed from Baroque elaboration of the display elements of a text to the plain, undecorated pages that we can now see as beginning the modern style. The prosaic pages of novels are hardly touched on in Barker's rapid survey, and his propositions have never been taken further. His analysis needs display pages, especially title pages, with which to work, while remaining silent on the rest of a book.

In the twentieth century, publishing and printing procedures became ever more routinized and divided. Publishers typically became parts of conglomerated firms, and printers became not much more than a means of duplicating the files of data that these publishers supplied. Although novels of eighteenth-century typographic exuberance have sometimes been attempted under these conditions, their effects have been hampered by the fact that the final process of producing pages has not been in the author's hands. The ease with which a Richardson or a Sterne could deploy such effects has gone; it cannot be re-created or emulated with the present materials of typography and book production. Some writers are now beginning to bypass conventional publishing and printing processes by preparing PDF (portable document format) files of their pages to be downloaded from websites or issued in the single copies or small runs of "print on demand" editions. The production of pages is in the hands of the writer as it never was before, though writers would do well to seek the help of typographers for advice and final execution. Whether the resulting pages carry plain prose or semantically shaped configurations, such routes to publication open the way for texts that would not otherwise be duplicated and distributed.

SEE ALSO: Author, Editing, Paper and Print Technology, Reprints.

BIBLIOGRAPHY

Barchas, J. (2003), *Graphic Design, Print Culture, and the Eighteenth-Century Novel*.

Barker, N. (1981), "Typography and the Meaning of Words," in *Buch und Buchhandel in Europa in achtzehnten Jahrhundert*, ed. G. Barber and B. Fabian.

Ginsburg, M.P. and L.G. Nandrea (2006), "The Prose of the World," in *Novel*, ed. F. Moretti, 2 vols.

Hellinga, W.G. (1962), *Copy and Print in the Netherlands*.

Hutchins, H.C. (1925), *Robinson Crusoe and Its Printing*.

McKenzie, D.F. (1999), *Bibliography and the Sociology of Texts*.

McKenzie, D.F. (2002), *Making Meaning*.

U

Unfinalizability *see* Bakhtin, Mikhail

United States (19th Century)

SHIRLEY SAMUELS

Writing about the nineteenth-century novel in the U.S. in 1957, a moment of the consolidation of the canon of American literature, Richard Chase drew a firm distinction between the novel and the romance: unlike the romance, he declared, the "novel renders reality closely and in comprehensive detail" (12). He cites the novelist Nathaniel Hawthorne in his preface to *The House of the Seven Gables* (1851): "When a writer calls his work a Romance, it need hardly be observed that he wishes to claim a certain latitude, both as to its fashion and material, which he would not have felt himself entitled to assume, had he professed to be writing a Novel" (18). The implication here is that the canonical works of nineteenth-century U.S. literature such as Hawthorne's are not, in fact, novels at all: just as it was held in the mid-twentieth century that the history of the U.S. was an "exceptional" case, so, apparently, was its literature. For all the influence Hawthorne has had on the form of the novel, such a distinction has not persisted in the critical analysis of nineteenth-century fiction. Rather, scholars have come to recognize a rich diversity of forms and genres of the novel in use in this period, and their engagement with the complex social and

political issues of this moment. They have also returned to a historical context in which questions of readership challenge conventional assumptions such as Chase's about literary value and canonicity.

Hawthorne, whose novel *The Scarlet Letter* (1850) had a limited readership at publication, later achieved canonical status, a detail that would have shocked professors in his New England college. In their moment, popular fiction was represented by, among other genres, the sensation fiction of George Lippard, George Thompson, and E. D. E. N. Southworth, exposés of urban crime that advanced the motif of class transgression, which also appeared later in the century in Horatio Alger's popular novels of newsboys who rose to riches from the streets of Boston and New York (see DETECTIVE). Some of the most popular novels of the nineteenth-century U.S. focused on RELIGION. Prime examples are *The Wide, Wide World* (1850) by Susan B. Warner; *The Gates Ajar* (1868) by Elizabeth Stuart Phelps; and *St. Elmo* (1866) by Augusta Evans. But the religious virtues these writers celebrated were not compatible with a later concept of great literature based on aesthetic values. Such values became separated from the polemical circumstances that influenced many nineteenth-century novels in the U.S.

The relation of polemics to the role of the novel in the nineteenth-century U.S. influences the approach taken in this entry. In particular, the claims authors make as they negotiate boundaries for the projects of the

The Encyclopedia of the Novel Edited by Peter Melville Logan
© 2011 Blackwell Publishing Ltd

novel appears here in my attention to the complexity of the novel's many claims on a believable relation to historical events. Specifically, the edge between historical realities and fictional constructions frequently becomes blurred and this entry pays close attention to the times when the novel crosses boundaries.

Writers in the nineteenth-century U.S. found themselves busy responding both to political changes in national boundaries and to market changes in producing fiction. Witnessing such dramatic historical shifts as the Civil War and the end of slavery, their fiction created a shift in the related concepts of the nation and the novel. Indeed, the formal construction that came to be known as the American novel emerged from an early attempt to document historical change in the new nation. To consider how the novel evolved during the nineteenth century, we must look at the formatting of GENRE within, for example, the EPISTOLARY, GOTHIC, sensation, sentimental, and HISTORICAL novel. The epistolary and gothic novel forms were fading by the early nineteenth century. Novels of sensation and sentiment held sway until mid-century, when the Civil War produced a gloomier reading public whose appetite for realist and naturalist fiction was honed through the rise of urbanization and industrial capitalism (see NATURALISM, REALISM). Historical fiction, however, remained popular throughout the nineteenth century.

THE PLACE OF POLEMIC IN THE NINETEENTH-CENTURY NOVEL

That nineteenth-century writers used fiction to compel action emerged from a history of significant public uses of narrative. In New England, for example, the earlier practices within a state-sanctioned church to publicly declare religious conversion in effect produced identity as the proper business of narrative. To tell a public story about private identity, within a community that presents the narrative formation of a self as fundamentally important, began as a condition for joining a religious community. The community of readers that emerged in the nineteenth-century U.S. began by reading novels that emphasized interiority. In relating private reading and public action, such novels also related reading and political mobilizing, transforming at once public spaces and interior spaces, the space of the mind and the heart, through narrative declaration. Conversion narratives were popular well into the nineteenth century, yet they were eclipsed by captivity narratives, typically depicting escape from an Indian raid. These accounts of compelled errands into the wilderness became transformed into origin stories for other forms of American identity. Stories about escape from captivity were joined by escapes from slavery, emancipation narratives that fused racial differentiation with the progressive enlightenment associated with Christianity (see AFRICAN AMERICAN). Learning to read in these accounts provides access to freedom. In the nineteenth century, such accounts overlap with the historical romance to forge national narratives into courtship dramas. These travels through time further supplement travel narratives that produce vicarious existence and also reinforce the concept of "home."

Fiction written before and after the U.S. Civil War presents different accounts of violence. In particular, nineteenth-century fiction refers to wars such as the American Revolution, the Mexican–American war, Indian warfare, and concepts of borderlands. Later in the century, realist and naturalist fiction describes the failure of reconstruction and the tactics associated with lynching, in novels such as *Contending Forces* (1900) by Pauline E. Hopkins. The very foregrounding of the color red in novels such as *The Scarlet Letter* and Stephen Crane's *The Red Badge of Courage* (1895) emphasizes the color of blood as the color of shame and belonging at once. These novels, long taken as markers of U.S. adolescent passages, as well as staples of the literature classroom, produce value through allusions to blood. Novels frequently use killing to motivate movement of characters and plot and mobilize identities through staving off interracial sex and, indeed, any chance of reproduction. Such tactics appear in almost all of James Fenimore Cooper's novels.

Although the Civil War continues to serve as a momentous dividing line between the understood antebellum and postbellum novels, it scarcely ever appears as a subject in the postbellum world of fiction. Before the war, troops declared themselves to be inspired by the bestselling *Uncle Tom's Cabin* (1852) by Harriet Beecher Stowe. During the war, Northern troops sang "John Brown's Body" and "Mine Eyes Have Seen the Glory" to the same tune. Southern troops read Augusta Evans's *Macaria* (1864), which was dedicated to the "Glorious Cause" (and secretly read in the North). A less known postwar exception to the great silence in fiction about the war experience is John DeForest's *Miss Ravenel's Conversion from Secession to Loyalty* (1867). DeForest was said to have issued the call for the great American novel and is credited as the first to use the term. Yet the major novel associated with the Civil War had to wait a generation. Crane's *The Red Badge of Courage* formulated for the warriors who survived an account of fear and cowardice, as well as heroism, that has seldom been equaled.

THE HISTORICAL NOVEL

Many of the novels most often associated with the nineteenth-century U.S. are historical novels, presenting episodes from U.S. history through the lens of the author's nostalgic retelling of past trauma. *Moby-Dick* (1851) by Herman Melville analyzes the whaling industry as it went into decline; *The Scarlet Letter* revisits Puritan judgments about sin two centuries later; and *Huckleberry Finn* (1884) by Mark Twain reenacts the crisis of slavery decades after the Civil War had ended the practice.

The best-known of the early practitioners of the historical novel was James Fenimore Cooper, whose Leatherstocking Tales—*The Deerslayer* (1841), *The Last of the Mohicans* (1826), *The Pathfinder* (1840), *The Pioneers* (1823), and *The Prairie* (1827)—were popular in his day, and remain canonical. Cooper was charged with imitating the famous historical novelist across the Atlantic, Walter Scott. Such an anxiety of influence makes it even more difficult to see early historical novelists such as the prolific southern author William Gilmore Simms, the Maine author John Neal, or the Border States' John Pendleton Kennedy as other than imitators of Cooper. Gestures of dominance and subordination recur in descriptions of women authors as well. Although ranked as a peer by her contemporaries, Catharine Maria Sedgwick wrote historical fiction whose reputation gradually dimmed in relation to that written by Cooper.

Anxieties about cultural value still pervade critical descriptions of authors such as Cooper, Sedgwick, Neal, or Lydia Maria Child. Some of this has to do with the difference in contemporary sensibilities toward the raw facts of American history, as when novels engaged readers (and citizens) in defending the atrocities of border warfare. In *Hope Leslie* (1827), for example, Sedgwick's prefatory remarks at once declare her reliance on original records and call attention to the domestic nature of her concerns. Sedgwick's narrator allows the historical record to speak tellingly; she cites the seventeenth-century Massachusetts governor John Winthrop, who called it a "sweet sacrifice" when his troops burned Pequod women and children. Nevertheless, this, and other historical romances like the Leather-stocking Tales, Neal's *Logan* (1822), and Child's *Hobomok* (1824), offered to do for America what Scott had done for Scotland: provide a heretofore colonized country with a history (see NATIONAL).

While these authors produce an American identity through historical romances patterned on classical or Shakespearean themes, they also produce dramas whose crises reach the most difficult edges of the American landscape. These dramas include controversial topics: Indian–white marriage or progeny, incursions or excursions west or south, and the sexual vulnerability of women. Delineating the boundaries of such topics provided the U.S. novel with its hardest challenge.

READERS AND WRITERS

The vicarious experiences that formed part of the novel's appeal depend in part on the development of a middle CLASS, that class of persons that emerged from the novel-reading practices of a leisure class once chided for the conspicuous consumption of idle time. The relation between class formation and the novel was affected by the changes in agriculture made possible by urbanization and industrialized labor. Increases in the production and consumption of novels in the early U.S. accompanied the emergence of the middling classes.

Novels display new understandings of what it is to have a separate and private identity that accompanies a desire for the privacy that might be necessary for reading them. That is, at the same time that they market and display this identity, novels encourage reading practices that will aid and abet it. In so doing, novels reinforced class stratification at a time when newspapers were available everywhere and novels initially an expensive reading pastime.

Many early novels are epistolary, presenting their plots through a series of linked letters, as in *The Coquette* (1797), by Hannah Foster, or through the conceit of an extended letter, as in *Wieland* (1798) or *Edgar Huntly* (1799), by Charles Brockden Brown. The essentially mobile quality of the letter as a device, as a piece of writing designed to be mobile, reflects the mobility of the population as well as the increasing mobility of the novel as an object. Early nineteenth-century novels could be carried around in pockets. The epistolary nature of these novels may also allude to the way they take up the private space in the home that might also have been occupied by letters and letter writing.

Novels in the early U.S. republic emphasized the training for citizenship that reading might confer. Novels that empowered forms of thinking were favored, whereas those that encouraged bodily sensations were viewed with suspicion. Like other guilty pleasures, however, they were nonetheless pursued. Contemporary critics expressed anxiety about corrupting young women by fiction, yet they also pressured writers to produce national romances (see DEFINITIONS). Some of these tensions were addressed by authors like Tabitha Tenney, who presented a burlesque of the novel-reading heroine Dorcasina Sheldon as a "true history" in *Female Quixotism* (1801). Similarly, writers of historical fiction such as Sedgwick and Child also wrote numerous domestic fictions and works for children. When he began to write, Cooper, the most famous creator of fictional men in the wilderness, still understood his audience to include women readers.

SPACE AND DOMESTICITY

Attention to the Americanness of fiction became blended with the staging of national drama through adventures of courtship and marriage. Historical romances thus energize the cultural work performed by the novel by engaging emotional attachment to a nascent nation. This attachment frequently operates through correlations between the destinies of women and the destinies of national movements. In many novels, romance and marriage are related to the transmission of property. Thus, while mid-twentieth-century critics celebrated the autonomous male "hero in SPACE" (Lewis) and the encounter with "virgin land" (Smith), plots of early novels frequently focus on women's bodies. In other words, issues of seduction, courtship, and marriage become ways to talk about the nation's destiny.

Enforcing as well as enacting relations between public and private spaces, the novels of the rapidly expanding U.S. bring landscapes home. For example, *A New Home, Who'll Follow?* (1839) by Caroline Kirkland critiques but also uses the language of opportunism as it promotes a class that could appreciate the landscape (as possible purchasers); hence, the novel works at once as a satire and as a sales pitch. Tracing domestic life at the frontier of Michigan, the novel asks how reading practices persist when readers must negotiate between romance and land contracts. The romance appears as various fantasies that have inspired new settlers; the contract intrudes as they try to survive collisions with corrupt land speculators.

As the popularity of novels increased and as methods of production and distribution improved, the contents of novels shifted. During the early national period, the nascent ideologies of the early U.S. nation were necessarily caught up with embodiments—such as the charged rendition of bodies in domestic spaces characteristic of the GOTHIC novel. To speak of how bodies appear in domestic spaces, whether in historical fiction or novels by women, also calls attention to the novel's investment in moving between interiors and the natural world. Whether looking at women at home or men in the wilderness, early republican novels produce attention to spaces that are at once gendered, classed, and racialized (see GENDER, CLASS, RACE). That is, through attention to the invasion or destruction or abandonment of homes, the question of who may be permitted to be at home in the new nation is repeatedly and dramatically lived out.

The texture and detail of being displaced from a home dominate the best early novels as they move from landscapes like the maze of wilderness facing Cora and Alice Monroe in Cooper's *The Last of the Mohicans* to the streets of Philadelphia wandered by Arthur Mervyn in Charles Brockden Brown's eponymous novel. Solitary bodies repeatedly stand out against these backgrounds. In Sedgwick's *Hope Leslie*, the Pequod Magawisca jumps from a great height to interpose her arm for the neck of her beloved Everett, the son of white settlers; in Cooper, the dark figure of Magua, felled by the rifle of the ambiguously white Hawkeye, topples over a precipice; in another eponymous Brown novel, the beleaguered Edgar Huntly crouches in a cave, gnawing the raw flesh of a panther.

And yet, though the plots of these novels often depend on what will happen to a woman alone in a house or a man alone in the woods, the protagonist is not merely alone. The spectatorial function of the reader and the presence of the author (often highlighted by asides) are mimetically engaged by a hidden observer, usually in the form of an alien presence. From the ventriloquist Carwin hidden in Clara Wieland's closet to the murderous lurking of Magawisca's father in *Hope Leslie*, from the malevolent vigilance of Magua in *The Last of the Mohicans* to the designs of the seducer in *Female Quixotism*, or even the comic bumbling of Teague O'Regan in the extended production of *Modern Chivalry* (1792–1815) by Hugh Henry Brackenridge, such lurking figures are usually Irish or Native American. The conspiracies these figures portend serve to highlight a whiteness at once vulnerable and inept (in contrast to the abilities of the onlooker) and yet resourcefully resilient (implicitly because American). The very vulnerability of the main characters might be said to produce Americanness as embodied. And even as they suggest equivalence between whiteness and vulnerability, these novels ruthlessly identify and exclude exceptions. But in excluding the alien from the newly constituted nation, novels like *Edgar Huntly* internalize alienation. After a dreamlike search through the wilderness, Edgar Huntly wakes assailed by a thirst so powerful that he imagines drinking his own blood. Instead, he first drinks the blood of a panther and then kills so many Native Americans that the blood soaks his skin and hair. He thus wakes to violence that makes the wilderness into a national home, the site of the incorporation and domestication of a savagery that can no longer be projected elsewhere.

CROSSING BORDERS

Anxieties about border crossings pervade the nineteenth-century U.S. novel: the boundary of the ocean, the nation, the alien territory. Even the boundary line between animal and human comes to seem a national border, possibly to be crossed, suspiciously and repeatedly to be named and described. Paragraphs appear in Cooper's frontier fiction to explain which appearances are human and which are animal for the benefit of confused interlopers from white settlements. The domestic enclosures or temples of rural retreat that appear in the fictions of Brockden Brown tend to be safest in England: transplantation to the new world means violation. In short, the business of America often appears as the violation of the

expected boundaries between animal and human, Indian and white (see RACE).

Such violations of boundaries include confusion about boundary crossing. Race and SEXUALITY, for example, often stand in for each other. If Cooper writes fictions that provide a wilderness foundation for the national sense of self, he also writes foundational nightmares that propose that to shed blood in the wilderness might enable certain forms of socially approved marriage. By producing a phenomenally engrossing figure like his hero Natty Bumppo, who repeatedly stalks into the wilderness in ambiguous relation to a male Native American companion, Cooper also opens the door to figures like Nick Slaughter, created by the southern novelist Robert Montgomery Bird. In *Nick of the Woods* (1837), the goal of avenging the death of his family motivates often indiscriminate and grotesque carnage against Native Americans.

This gothic tale, like Cooper's, also relies on a plotting of inheritance, stolen birthright, and courtship with a suspiciously dark heroine to resolve the matter of alien boundaries. And however much it may flirt with racial mixing, like *The Last of the Mohicans*, the novel ends with the marriage and retreat of the racially palest characters. Even in gothic fiction like Brown's *Wieland*, forms of miscegenation threaten national identification—of the nation or of citizenship as a racial category. Perhaps through the novel's preoccupation with the maintenance of order, sexuality becomes racialized. Moves to legislate the boundaries of race and identity subsume or merge with land claims that depend on courtship narratives. Notably, contests about identity seem to invoke a valorizing in which, for example, class trumps gender, sexuality trumps class, and race trumps sexuality. Each seems to gain ground, as it were, at the expense of another. The relation between possessive individualism and the individual's possessions—whether in land or in bodies—appears as part of the founding gesture of the republic.

In crossing the boundaries that the New World presented, the increasingly popular form of the novel provided an uneasy but enduring form for the romance of America. As the generation of the 1820s turned to writing the story of the American Revolution fifty years later, the romance of the nation and the romance of the family collided. The intangible business of locating national identifications through novels emerged through material questions of landownership and women's bodies. In novels, rewriting the revolution as a founding moment could subsume the tensions caused by expanding immigrant populations and the new territories claimed in the name of a coherent nation. At the same time, as a political investment in national narrative began to take form in the novel, the founding stories of families were uneasily located in the tense relation between property and women's bodies.

In addition to the novel's attention to transatlantic migrations and, famously, to the whale trade, the internal migrations, along the rivers and inland waterways of the U.S., preoccupy its characters. These internal migrations along the geographic terrain markers of such waterways accompany migrations internal to the body, such as that of blood. Concepts of sacrifice draw on a contract, a compact sealed with blood sacrifice, as in the story of Abraham and Isaac. The gesture of substitution also asks about the founding move of the nation as a city on a hill understood to be the compact, the "visionary compact" once proposed by John Winthrop that would allow other substitutions.

Such relations appear in the most prominent fiction writers of the mid-nineteenth century, Harriet Beecher Stowe, Nathaniel Hawthorne, and Herman Melville. Each published a momentous novel between 1850 and 1852. In Stowe's bestselling *Uncle Tom's Cabin*, the central concepts of property and bodies become a network shuttling in between the matters of slavery and reproduction. In short, the novel asks and answers, "What is it to have a child under a system of slavery?" It is to have offspring who are also property. The question of children born into a Puritanical New England addressed by Hawthorne's *The Scarlet Letter*, published the previous year, might appear far from the political crisis of *Uncle Tom's Cabin*. Yet the two works both investigate the close interweaving of religion and politics in determining what rights women have to their children.

Other Hawthorne novels, such as *The House of the Seven Gables* (1851), insist on the importance of inherited property in determining the identity of families. For Melville, the mobility of property separates it from women's bodies and reproduction in novels like *Moby-Dick*. Such attention to the relationship between property and women's bodies shows up throughout the nineteenth century, even in novels about the west, such as María Ámparo Ruiz de Burton's *The Squatter and the Don* (1885) and *Who Would Have Thought It?* (1872).

The pattern of increased urbanization later in the nineteenth century saw novelists turning to the structure of social class as they presented marital prospects. The formidably loquacious Henry James led the way for observers of social manners with novels like *The Bostonians* (1886) and *The Portrait of a Lady* (1881). In *Portrait*, the crisis faced by the new heiress Isabel Archer takes place on European soil, yet it becomes an American story by virtue of her American suitors and her American past. In *The Bostonians*, the quirky habits of an upper-class Boston culture formed in abolition and the movement for women's suffrage are observed from the perspective of Basil Ransom, a gentleman from the defeated South. The crisis of marital prospects is bound up in *Portrait* with the cultural conflicts between the elites of Europe and America; in *The Bostonians*, they serve to imaginatively resolve the conflicts among members of this class in the American North and South.

However, some topics could only begin to be addressed in the nineteenth century. The consequences of racial oppression appeared in novels such as *Our Nig* (1859) by Harriet Wilson. Wilson's subtitle, "Sketches from the Life of a Free Black, In A Two-Story White House, North," suggests its aims. When Wilson asserts that slavery's shadow falls in the North, she brings the entire country together in the question of race and sexuality. Similarly, in *Clotel* (1853), William Wells Brown explored the extreme misery of light-skinned women sold into sexual slavery, with the provocative assertion that his title character was the mixed-race daughter of the former president Thomas Jefferson. The popular humorist who called himself Mark Twain started out with a boy's book, *Tom Sawyer* (1876), and then complicated readings of race and identity in the U.S. with the problematic story of runaways—one a white boy and the other a slave—on a raft headed down the Mississippi River in *The Adventures of Huckleberry Finn*. Twain revisited the questions raised by *Clotel* about racially mixed children whose ability to control their own futures is fatally compromised by slavery in his dark comic novel *Pudd'nhead Wilson* (1894). Such novels view the U.S. as a country conceived in liberty but repeatedly caught up in the proposition that its dedications engage slavery. To view fiction as a path to freedom persuasively carries these novels toward the twentieth century.

BIBLIOGRAPHY

Baym, N. (1978), *Woman's Fiction*.

Chase, R. (1957), *American Novel and Its Tradition*.

Davidson, C. (1986), *Revolution and the Word*.

Fiedler, L. (1966), *Love and Death in the American Novel*.

Fisher, P. (1985), *Hard Facts*.

Harris, S. (1990), *19th-Century American Women's Novels*.

Lewis, R.W.B. (1955), *American Adam*.

Samuels, S. ed. (2004), *Companion to American Fiction, 1780–1865*.

Smith, H.N. (1950), *Virgin Land*.

Tompkins, J. (1985), *Sensational Designs*.

Wald, P. (1995), *Constituting Americans*.

Warren, J., ed. (1993), *(Other) American Traditions*.

United States (20th Century)

ROBERT SEGUIN

The history of the novel in the U.S. during the twentieth century can in many ways be charted in terms of a fundamental, interactive tension between, on the one hand, the idea or sense of the national SPACE and, on the other, local or REGIONAL specificities or densities that are in some fashion resistant to this idea. The "NATIONAL" in this context signifies essentially the rapid and expansive unfolding of capitalist modernity in America following the end of the Civil War in 1865, an era that saw the increasing unification of what had hitherto been a more loosely aggregated national realm (see MODERNISM). With the full advent of industrialization, along with the widespread implementation of railroads and the telegraph, a genuinely national commercial marketplace was established for the first time. The rhythms of wage labor and commodity production (and consumption) became increasingly the norm, and people, goods, ideas, and images could now circulate more widely and easily than ever before, all of which fostered a manifold set of overlapping and often contradictory perceptions and experiences and offered up a new social substance for literary reflection. Thus, modernity might be welcomed for its social dynamism and cosmopolitanism, or instead criticized for its rootlessness and cultural depthlessness; the local, meanwhile, might either be favored for its traditional values and sense of connectedness (to people, to the land) or shunned for its backwardness and refusal to embrace innovation. This multivalent, ongoing cultural dialectic of nation and region, intertwined with a tension between modernity and tradition, affords a productive framework for considering the course of the twentieth-century American novel.

One result of this dialectic was an efflorescence of so-called "local-color" writing during the late nineteenth century, to use the contemporary, somewhat condescending term—the condescension rooted in the fact that it was through local color that more and more women were writing themselves into the domain of literary fiction. These stories made of those regional folkways and sensibilities, before their subsumption within some overarching national culture, an object of frequently ambivalent representation. While first appearing before the Civil War (Harriet Beecher Stowe's story "Uncle Lot," from 1834, is often taken as an inaugural point of the genre), it is really from the 1870s onward that the GENRE develops fully. Local colorists paid particular attention to regional DIALECT and forms of speech, broadening the literary scope of American English. While the short story was the preferred form for regionalism, several important novels belong to the genre: Sarah Orne Jewett's *The Country of the Pointed Firs* (1896), Kate Chopin's *The Awakening* (1899), and George Washington Cable's *The Grandissimes* (1880), the last two both set in New Orleans, as intensely liminal a city as one might find in the U.S. A novel like Mark Twain's *Adventures of Huckleberry Finn* (1884), while often held up as the national

tale par excellence, is deeply indebted to the forms of local color, as is, to a lesser extent, the work of other realists of the period such as Frank Norris (in *McTeague*, 1899 and *The Octopus*, 1901) and Harold Frederic, whose remarkable *The Damnation of Theron Ware* (1896), while ostensibly about a crisis of faith, is at a deeper level an acute analysis of the sources of cultural and ideological authority. A common device in local-color writing was the use of an "outsider" NARRATIVE PERSPECTIVE—an urban visitor to some rural locale who in effect FRAMES the story and sets up at least the opportunity for a certain bidirectional estrangement or ironizing. This structural pattern has in turn helped fuel the longstanding critical debate about the genre, i.e., whether it represents a genuine effort of preservation and regional advocacy or rather a kind of literary tourism for urbanized readers, one that merely enfolds the local ever more surely within modernity's web.

AMERICAN NATURALISM

Regardless of this question of generic function, regionalism doubtless expanded the reach of REALISM, if we follow that account of realism which stresses its opening up to literary representation hitherto unrepresented social groups, CLASSES, and SPACES. Regionalism thus helped make way for the brief flowering of that variant of realism known as NATURALISM during the first years of the twentieth century. While some naturalist fiction toyed with Darwinian themes (notably Jack London's work, as in *The Call of the Wild*, 1903 and *White Fang*, 1906), naturalism is best grasped as a turning away from the more genteel realisms of William Dean Howells and Henry James (with their comfortable middle-class settings) toward working-class and ethnic subjects—rendered all too often through broad caricature—and a more frank consideration of themes of sexuality, violence, poverty, and prejudice.

With this came a strong emphasis on the determining influence of both the physical and social (chiefly economic) environments on individual behavior and destiny. Norris's work is central here, with its cast of vivid Californians enmeshed by greed and the railroad companies, as is that of the brilliantly unclassifiable Stephen Crane, whose *Maggie: A Girl of the Streets* (1893) is one of the earliest tenement or slum tales. Also important are Abraham Cahan, a Russian-born chronicler of the Jews of New York's Lower East Side and a pioneering figure in the coming wave of immigrant fiction— *Yekl* (1896), *The Rise of David Levinsky* (1917)—and the prolific journalist, social critic, and activist Upton Sinclair, whose novel *The Jungle* dramatized the deplorable conditions in the U.S. meatpacking industry. But it is Theodore Dreiser's *Sister Carrie* (1900) that stands as perhaps the central achievement of naturalism, offering a brilliant anatomy of money, desire, and commodity spectacle which, while rooted in a certain regional experience (in particular Dreiser's flight from the restrictions of small-town Indiana and his German Catholic family), in effect short-circuits the dialectic invoked above and develops an immanent presentation of the social forces of modern capitalism. The work of Edith Wharton, meanwhile, despite its generally more privileged settings, might plausibly be grouped with naturalism for its clear-eyed focus on the inexorable and destructive force of GENDER and class conventions on individuals—*The House of Mirth* (1905), *The Age of Innocence* (1920).

The season of naturalism was in some respects short-lived: *Sister Carrie* sold poorly and Dreiser did not really regain his writerly footing until the seldom-read Cow-perwood Trilogy of 1912–15; London became increasingly alcoholic and erratic; and both Crane and Norris died young, leaving the first two decades of the twentieth-century novel in the U.S. with a somewhat patchy record of achievement. One standout emerging in the teens is Willa Cather, a Virginia-born transplant to the Great Plains who brilliantly reenergized the regionalist dialectic with deceptively complex meditations on the passing of tradition, the growth of new wealth, new roles for women, and the fate of immigrant culture in the Plains and Southwest—*O Pioneers!* (1913), *My Antonia* (1918), *The Professor's House* (1925), *Death Comes for the Archbishop* (1927). Cather's work presages in part the fiction of the so-called "revolt from the village" movement, a set of mostly Midwestern writers who, far from casting the small town as a bulwark against modernity, see it as all too eager to embrace everything that is corrupting and spiritually deadening about bourgeois society. The novels of Sinclair Lewis—*Main Street* (1920) and *Babbit* (1922)—and Sherwood Anderson—*Winesburg, Ohio* (1919) and *Poor White* (1920)—while popular and critically acclaimed in their day (indeed, Lewis was the first American recipient of the Nobel Prize in Literature), have in recent years fallen into disfavor as readers have found their critique to be rather one-note.

THE 1920s

Lewis and Anderson were certainly not wrong, however, in training their attention on a rapidly modernizing capitalist system. With innovations such as Henry Ford's "five-dollar day" (the substantial, if conditional, wage increase given his workers starting in 1914), the layaway system and other forms of credit, and the rapid growth of advertising, modern mass consumerism was gradually though unevenly extended to certain sectors of the working- and lower-middle classes. The economy in the 1920s famously boomed (a misleading image, to the extent that inequalities of wealth were also increasingly exacerbated), and President Calvin Coolidge could declare, in a phrase that grates on the sensibilities of cultural workers to this day, that "the business of America is business."

The writers of the 1920s thus found themselves in a difficult situation: while passionately committed to the aesthetically and culturally New (spurred on, of course, by the twin thunderclaps of 1922, James Joyce's *Ulysses* and T. S. Eliot's *The Waste Land*, and by modernism more generally), the "new" as it manifested itself in other social domains often occasioned a good deal more uncertainty. Hence the choice of expatriation for so many of the central writers of the decade, or the renewed and intensified focus on specific locales for others, as ways of keeping alive a kind of imaginative tension or distance, or perhaps a paradoxically nourishing sense of marginality, in the face of both the increasingly exuberant materialism of American culture together with its still dominant Puritanical ways, as witnessed for example by the (in hindsight, remarkable) prohibition on the sale of alcohol between 1919 and 1933.

The impact of modernism on the novel in the U.S. was in most instances subtle rather than overt, inflecting the main realistic current rather than reshaping its course outright. The TIME shifts, lyrical density, and cinematic flourishes employed in F. Scott Fitzgerald's masterpiece of upward mobility and American mythmaking (chiefly the abiding American myth of transcending one's origins), *The Great Gatsby* (1925), are a good example of the distinctive yet accessible modernist elements writers began to use. Fitzgerald, for many the representative novelist of the decade, was a Midwesterner who went to Princeton and then Paris, and

whose sharp (if exaggerated) sense of class and regional marginality fuels much of his best work. Ernest Hemingway, meanwhile, under the influence partly of the journalism trade and partly of modernist doyenne Gertrude Stein, developed a lean, stripped-down (and much imitated) style designed to say little and imply much. The success of books like *In Our Time* (1925), *The Sun Also Rises* (1926), and *A Farewell to Arms* (1929), along with his assiduous cultivation of the Hemingway "brand," centered on the masculine pursuit of strenuous pastimes, made him for a long time the most famous American author in the world. Even Cather, a writer not generally known for formal innovation, began to speak, as the 1920s wore on, of the novel *demeublé* ("unfurnished"), a vision of clean, spare prose shorn of what were seen as the weighty encumbrances of older realisms.

The most exuberant modernisms appeared, first, with John Dos Passos's *Manhattan Transfer* (1925), whose fragmentary, jump-cutting style attempts to capture the rhythm of a city and which was directly inspired both by Joyce and the cinema (indeed, film and its techniques are an abiding source of fascination and inspiration for many writers during these decades; see ADAPTATION). Dos Passos amplified this approach in his epic *U.S.A.* trilogy—*The 42nd Parallel* (1930), *1919* (1932), and *The Big Money* (1936)—an admixture of glassy, depersonalized prose, news clippings, biographical pastiche, and subjective lyricism. Here Dos Passos attempts to "synthesize" the nation/region dialectic through a great totalization of all regions of the country and offers a grim panoply of political dreams crushed and ambitions of all sorts squelched by the routinized grind of profit making. Djuna Barnes, another expatriate, brought together female SEXUALITY and cultural decay in the dense and harrowing *Nightwood* (1936). But it is undoubtedly

William Faulkner who went furthest and most lastingly with the modernist enterprise in fiction. Faulkner chose to stay in the rural northern Mississippi of his childhood and make of its history and geography, and that of the South more generally, the stuff of an intricate and architectonic fictional world, over which hangs the GOTHIC curse of the South's history of defeat and the baleful aftereffects of slavery, inflected in turn by the belated modernization of the region. The elaborate stream of consciousness of *The Sound and the Fury* (1929) and the serpentine, multiclausal sentences of *Absalom, Absalom!* (1936) are only two instances of the many techniques he employed in the construction of his fictional mythos—see also *As I Lay Dying* (1930), *Light in August* (1932), and *Go Down, Moses* (1942).

Another key literary movement beginning in the 1920s, one centrally rooted in spatial and demographic processes, is of course the Harlem (or New Negro) Renaissance (ca. 1918–37). The Great Migration, beginning around 1910, brought tens of thousands of African Americans from the rural South to the urban, industrial North (see AFRICAN AMERICAN). Places like Harlem fostered strong social and cultural ferment as more settled, middle-class blacks lived cheek by jowl with new working-class arrivals. The Renaissance itself was a rather more loosely knit affair than its name might suggest, comprising writers with strong ties to Harlem as well as many others with more tangential affiliations. Harlem in that sense was less a stable geographic locale than a touchstone for a kind of imagined community, a space of flows serving to organize symbolically a disparate collection of cultural producers. Their striking social positionality, meanwhile—on the liminal cusp of North and South, modernity and tradition, all complicated by the fraught calculus of RACE—allowed them to ring intricate changes on the many facets of the cultural

dialectic we have been foregrounding, and to interrogate the bearing of African American culture with respect to American culture more generally. The outstanding novelists of the movement include Nella Larsen—*Quicksand* (1928), *Passing* (1929)—Claude McKay—*Home to Harlem* (1928), *Banjo* (1929)—Arna Bontemps—*Black Thunder* (1936)—and Zora Neale Hurston—*Their Eyes Were Watching God* (1937).

THE 1930S

The arrival of the Great Depression in 1930 began to change the literary landscape in the U.S. in many ways. The rapid economic deterioration (fully one-quarter of the workforce unemployed by 1932) led to a widespread leftward movement amongst writers and intellectuals and an often contentious reconsideration of the appropriate forms and purposes of literature. While this politicization was by no means consistent—with some joining the Communist movement, others remaining within a more liberal/progressive orbit, with many offshoots in between—nonetheless what Michael Denning has called a broad "cultural front" came into being in the 1930s, marked by a fellow-traveling sensibility at once critical of capitalism and engaged in advocating on behalf of the dispossessed. One early outgrowth of this was the set of novels, all by women, focusing on the textile strike in Gastonia, North Carolina, in 1929: Mary Heaton Vorse's *Strike!* (1930), Myra Page's *Gathering Storm* (1932), Grace Lumpkin's *To Make My Bread* (1932), and Fielding Burke's *Call Home the Heart* (1932).

More representative, however, of fiction in the 1930s is what Denning calls the "ghetto pastoral," portraits of largely ethnic working-class urban neighborhoods and the daily struggles of their inhabitants. Such work differs from earlier naturalistic excursions into this territory in that the later writers frequently shared this plebeian social background with their subjects. The ghetto, of course, was a region unto itself, caught between an ambivalently desired mainstream America on the one hand and the values of the Old Country on the other. Tonally, the ghetto pastoral was often an uncertain blend of tough, even brutal naturalism (conditioned in part by the cynical, often violent hardboiled detective fiction pioneered in the 1920s by writers like Dashiell Hammett), as in James T. Farrell's *Studs Lonigan* trilogy (1932–35), set in Irish Chicago, and lighter material, often drawing on youthful escapades and comic neighborhood tales and gossip, as in Mike Gold's *Jews Without Money* (1930) and Daniel Fuchs's *Williamsburg* trilogy (1934–37), both set in poor Jewish neighborhoods of New York. While versions of realism were the dominant stylistic strain in the ghetto pastoral, more modernist techniques feature in important works like Henry Roth's *Call It Sleep* (1934), Pietro DiDonato's *Christ in Concrete* (1938), set amongst immigrant Italian bricklayers, and Tillie Olsen's *Yonnondio* (wr. 1930s, pub. 1974).

The politicization of the decade energized the FEMINIST movement of the time as well, swelling the ranks of women writing literary fiction (as the above might already suggest). Other important works by women include *The Unpossessed* (1934) by Tess Slesinger and the *Trexler* trilogy (1933–39) by Josephine Herbst. The novel of migration, meanwhile, was a recurring form in the 1930s, as the economic crisis forced thousands onto the roads and rails in search of work: John Steinbeck's *The Grapes of Wrath* (1939) is easily the most famous—indeed, along with Margaret Mitchell's Civil War saga *Gone With the Wind* (1936), it is probably the most famous novel of the decade (these two texts themselves, of course, using a regional focus to mount a national

narrative). Nelson Algren's *Somebody in Boots* (1935) deserves mention here as well. Finally, while much of this writing is already grim enough, there are those writers who present a uniquely pessimistic portrait of American society, in that the political sensibility that animates so much of the foregoing is with them suppressed. Steeped more in European symbolism and SURREALISM than, say, the Chicago School sociology of Farrell and Algren, these novelists envision society as a *danse macabre* of people increasingly in thrall to powerful culture industries that stoke unfulfillable desires, inciting violence and madness, with only a shrinking world of private fantasy remaining with which to resist: Henry Miller— *Tropic of Capricorn* (1938)—Horace McCoy—*They Shoot Horses, Don't They?* (1935)—and, especially, Nathanael West— *Miss Lonelyhearts* (1933), *The Day of the Locust* (1939). In works like these we begin to see the emergence of black humor as a device for undermining the conventions of standard realism.

THE 1940s AND 1950s

The onset of WWII reoriented cultural priorities yet again, and the literary novel, while it did not cease production as did the automobile, nonetheless received less focused attention for a time. If the 1940s were the decade of the noir in cinema, much the same could be said for the novel, with the noir thriller being among the more vital genres of the decade, drawing the efforts of at least a few writers who had been poets and literary novelists in the 1930s. Raymond Chandler, James M. Cain, Kenneth Fearing, Edwin Rolfe, Chester Himes, and Cornell Woolrich are key figures in a genre that, thrills aside, offers an often complex set of reflections on the political aftermath of the Depression (the richly atmospheric Los Angeles locales frequently deployed are also of note). Richard Wright's *Native Son* (1940) occupies an ambivalent and important juncture: between high- and middlebrow fiction (Wright made several choices aimed at broadening his readership, and the novel became a Book-of-the-Month Club selection), and also in terms of genre. A late version of the ghetto pastoral (the story is set in Bronzeville, an African American district in Chicago), it is also something of a noir thriller in its own right, while also presaging the rise of the suburb in postwar fiction. The war itself, meanwhile, furnished the material for at least one major novel, Norman Mailer's *The Naked and the Dead* (1948); Mailer would later publish one of the more interesting fictional meditations inspired by the disastrous war in Vietnam, *Why Are We in Vietnam?* (1967), a scabrous dissection of machismo and the emotional investments in violence that never, title aside, mentions Vietnam. Nor does Joseph Heller's *Catch-22* (1961), a WWII novel whose satire on the absurdity and moral vacuity of warfare became increasingly resonant as the 1960s wore on and American involvement in Southeast Asia grew deeper. Distinguished work that does mention Vietnam of course exists, such as *The Things They Carried* (1990), by Tim O'Brien.

The novelists in the years following the war found themselves once more at a difficult aesthetic and political conjuncture. On the one hand, those realisms that had been the predominant novelistic modes for some eighty years, and had been so strenuously championed during the proletarian 1930s, were now, as the country moved into the era of Cold War conservatism, seen as critically suspect, as if encoding a certain Stalinism in their very heart. On the other hand, modernism was by and large felt to be reaching its limit, its dialectic of innovation having exhausted itself (a situation allegorized in John Barth's *The Floating Opera*, 1956). Apolitical irony was the new order of the day in criticism, and older works were refunctioned to fit the new dispensation: thus Faulkner (whose best work was well behind him) and Henry James (who had been dead for over forty years) emerge as in some ways the most important novelists of the 1950s. Those novelists who wished to craft something lasting in the fifties needed guile and determination beyond the usual. One strategy was to cleave to older modes in defiance of prevailing styles, an approach most often leading to failure but one that worked for Harriette Arnow, whose *The Dollmaker* (1954) is perhaps the last of the great ghetto pastorals. Or one might revive even older forms, now seen as a breath of fresh air, to great critical acclaim, as with the PICARESQUE fabulism and nineteenth-century pontificating of Saul Bellow—*The Adventures of Augie March* (1953), *Henderson the Rain King* (1959). But achieving the new in this context demanded once more a certain distance from the constricted literary horizon and related critical fashion, a distance provided, for instance, by the experience of exile, as with the Russian-American Vladimir Nabokov, whose *Lolita* (1955) stands as one of the few masterpieces of an authentically late modernist style. Another would be Ralph Ellison's *Invisible Man* (1952), which weds an irrepressible narrative drive to a layered, allusive allegory of African American marginality. For the Beats, immersion in the bohemian (for them) world of jazz and drugs afforded a space apart from the felt conformity of the age. Jack Kerouac's *On the Road* (1957) and William S. Burroughs's *Naked Lunch* (1959), in their freeform composition and often hallucinatory intensity, revivify prose in yet new ways. The road, in both *On the Road* and *Lolita* alike, is an ambivalent trope: for Nabokov, a pathway into the seductive realm of American popular culture, for Kerouac the sign of an always-on-the-cusp-of-vanishing freedom. In any case, it testifies yet again to the irreducibly spatial dimension of literary production in the U.S.

The regional dialectic takes another turn in these years by the emergence of the suburb as a fresh site of narrative investment. The economic boom of the postwar era, coupled with measures like the G.I. Bill (1944) for veterans and tax incentives, helped millions become homeowners for the first time, and the suburban areas of American cities underwent a phase of enormous growth. The phenomenon of so-called "white flight" from more racially mixed city centers, beginning around the early 1960s, only amplified this development. Despite the evident public enthusiasm for these new living spaces, the novelistic suburb is mostly a baleful place, a realm of thwarted dreams, cultural deprivation, and (typically male) anxiety and depression: middle-class privilege is here reimagined as a kind of impoverishment. This is the imaginary terrain treated with a certain sentimentality in John Updike's five Rabbit novels (appearing every ten years from 1960 to 2001), with rather more pungency in Richard Yates's Revolutionary Road (1961), through to the important work of Richard Ford—The Sportswriter (1986), Independence Day (1995)—and Rick Moody—The Ice Storm (1994).

AMERICAN POSTMODERNITY

At length we come to the matter of POST-MODERNISM and its place in the consideration of U.S. fiction of the last few decades. As with modernism, postmodernism comes in several versions, some more consequent than others. In perhaps its narrowest sense, we have here to do with an aesthetic of the signifier as such, devoted to the cunning free play of language. In an earlier age, such a strategy had more political content, as in the radical maneuvers of Dada, aimed at the repressive conventions of the bourgeois institutions of Art and Literature; under postmodernism this more often issues in elaborate, mazelike METAFICTION, such as that by Barth and Robert Coover, that displays great inventiveness but can seem rather self-absorbed, arguably possessing little in the way of deeper cultural resonance. When the difficult attempt is made to ground this aesthetic in some wider cultural experience, like the traditions of black signifying as in Ishmael Reed's Mumbo Jumbo (1972), Maxine Hong Kingston's meditations on Chinese mythology and the immigrant experience—The Woman Warrior (1976), Tripmaster Monkey (1989)—or Kathy Acker's explorations of alternative sexualities and the bodily sensorium, the results are rather more interesting and valuable (see QUEER). Works such as these typify the blending of genres often observed in post-1960s fiction, as nonfictional materials, poetic passages, elements of fantasy, other subgeneric modes, and so forth come together in an increasingly heterogeneous mixture.

The most consequent deployment of a postmodern strategy within the realm of the novel probably comes through the turn to history, what Linda Hutcheon has called historiographic metafiction. This is paradoxical, in that postmodernity has been characterized as a profoundly unhistorical era, but in a sense therein lies the key. The intention of this fiction is in no way to conjure some convincing representation of the past, or to make some case for its continuing claims upon us, as in older historical thinking. Rather, these narratives in effect refract and estrange the present through the past, using the intricate and unexpected juxtaposition of real and imaginary people and events to prize apart the highly compartmentalized social world of late capitalism. This, as Fredric Jameson has argued, is an essentially spatial exercise, that works by undermining the ideological cell walls between the many cultural and political subzones of our social formation, allowing a more synthetic narrative and conceptual process to take place (see IDEOLOGY). This would then be the latest (now second- or third-order) development in the socio-spatial dialectic with which we began. The central figures here are Thomas Pynchon (1973, *Gravity's Rainbow*; 1997, *Mason and Dixon*), Don DeLillo (1988, *Libra*; 1997, *Underworld*), and E. L. Doctorow (1975, *Ragtime*; 1989, *Billy Bathgate*). These writers also frequently evince themes of conspiracy and paranoia, another response to the increasingly systematic and all-pervasive character of the times (Pynchon's *The Crying of Lot 49*, 1966; DeLillo's *White Noise*, 1986). Toni Morrison's work (1987, *Beloved*; 1992, *Jazz*) figures in this context as well, though account must be made of the greater existential density of the historical within the African American context. In addition, the fiction of Richard Powers, such as *Gain* (1998) and *Plowing the Dark* (2000), juxtaposes scientific speculation, historical pastiche, and contemporary political events to probe the genesis and structure of the new global order.

CONTEMPORARY NOVELS

The general cultural fragmentation of postmodernity has clearly left its mark on the contemporary novel, making any attempt to survey the territory problematic. In some respects the realm of literary fiction has suffered as creative energies have moved into subgeneric territory: SCIENCE FICTION, for example, has developed remarkably in the last few decades, encompassing now the full range of so-called "soft" sciences and rich in political and anthropological speculation

(see ANTHROPOLOGY); DETECTIVE fiction, too, continues to map social space in ever more inventive ways. Still, staying within our working framework reveals several important recent developments. Thus alongside (often bombastic) calls for a new realism—directed against the perceived narrowness of "creative writing program" fiction—there persists strong work in a (sometimes deceptively) traditional realism, particularly that of Russell Banks, who has explored the conjuncture of America's racial stain and the injuries of class society with unflagging determination, frequently focusing on small-town New England and New York's Adirondack Mountains (1985, *Continental Drift*; 1995, *Rule of the Bone*; 1998, *Cloudsplitter*). Meanwhile, there is also a well-established new regionalism, as novelists once more turn to the byways and forgotten corners of the nation. Sometimes, this local is badly in need of a now global modernity, while at other times the local provides the resources to resist the force field of globalized economic and cultural flows, with the narratives seeking to explore an always troubled balance between value and rootedness on the one hand and drudgery and deprivation on the other. Work by Richard Russo, Carolyn Chute, Annie Proulx, Pat Conroy, Barry Hannah, Dorothy Allison, and Chris Offutt, among others, demonstrates once more the absolute centrality to the narrative imagination in the U.S. of the problems of cultural integrity versus cosmopolitanism, of the simultaneous fostering and curtailment of desire and freedom, all thought through a profoundly spatial frame.

Little by little, it seems, the themes that arose so often during the first half of the nineteenth century, as the nation was coalescing and its concept had yet to stabilize, inexorably return, as the uncertain solvents of the unfolding global dispensation increasingly exert their power, complicating and expanding the spatial dialectic. For example, the examination of both the idea and the reality of the border has drawn much interest from novelists as late capitalism slowly redefines the very notion of the nation state. Novelists such as Cormac McCarthy (1985, *Blood Meridian*; 1994, *The Crossing*) and Leslie Marmon Silko (1991, *Almanac of the Dead*) explore the creation and violation of borders and the violence that spreads forth from this, highlighting imperialism and Manifest Destiny, and underscore the unsettling shifts of identity endemic to the borderlands. Perhaps more crucially, the recent wave of writing by people of color is replete with signs and portents of future metamorphoses of American fiction. Taking initial impetus from the political energies of the 1960s, particularly as these shifted somewhat later into the set of debates and movements identified by the notion of identity politics, this literature frequently sets in motion a set of complex exchanges between an increasingly decentred American national space and ever-widening real and conceptual territories in the global South and Pacific Rim (not to mention the disruptive and unmappable terrain of the native reservation system). While varying widely in style, setting, and tone, work by Julia Alvarez, Sandra Cisneros, Sherman Alexie, Amy Tan, Jessica Hagedorn, Junot Diaz, Anita Desai, Ha Jin, Louise Erdrich, and Rolando Hinojosa, among many others, not only reinterrogates amid fresh circumstances the literary dialectic of ethnic and immigrant experience established earlier in the century, but also stays true to the fundamental impulse of realism to bring unexplored social spaces and subjects into the realm of narrative representation. The many ways in which American fiction goes global will continue to surprise.

SEE ALSO: Asian American Novel, Jewish American Novel, Latina/o American Novel.

BIBLIOGRAPHY

Bercovitch, S., ed. (1999), *Cambridge History of American Literature*, vol. 7.

Bercovitch, S., ed. (2002), *Cambridge History of American Literature*, vol. 6.

Denning, M. (1997), *Cultural Front*.

Hutcheon, L. (1989), *Poetics of Postmodernism*.

Jameson, F. (1991), *Postmodernism, or The Cultural Logic of Late Capitalism*.

Jurca, C. (2000), *White Diaspora*.

Kazin, A. (1942), *On Native Grounds*.

Lutz, T. (2003), *Cosmopolitan Vistas*.

McCann, S. (2000), *Gumshoe America*.

Michaels, W.B. (1993), *Our America*.

Seguin, R. (2001), *Around Quitting Time*.

Unreliable Narrator *See* Narrator

Utopian Novel *See* Science Fiction Fantasy

V

Verisimilitude *see* Decorum/Verisimilitude
Vision *see* Narration; Narrative Technique
Visual Arts *see* Illustrated Novel;
Photography
Voice *see* Narration; Narrative Technique
Vraisemblance *see* Decorum/Verisimilitude

W

Watt, Ian *see* Definitions of the Novel; History of the Novel; Novel Theory (20th Century)

Western Africa

KWAKU LARBI KORANG

The first known novel from Western Africa was serialized in a Gold Coast (colonial Ghana) newspaper between 1885 and 1889. In the next half-century, writers—mostly from the Gold Coast and Senegal—published a handful of titles. It was in and since the 1950s that the novel in Western Africa acquired the breadth, depth, and intensity of authorial productivity, readerly reception, and publishing sponsorship that have made novel writing in the region a sustainable intellectual enterprise.

Western Africa has been a zone of long-lived cultural contact and exchange between groups arriving from Europe and the peoples of the region. Between 1884 and 1960, this region was divided up into the colonial territories of Britain, France, and Portugal. These historic relations of culture, commerce, and power have generated necessities wherein the Europeans have either imposed on, or gifted to, the Western African peoples cultural institutions and technologies of Western literacy. Education, the alphabet, the European language, and the printing press: these are cultural and institutional transfers that, having taken root in Western Africa, would guarantee the emergence, and elevation into social prominence, of a literary culture in the region. Pioneer institutions of higher education in the region—preeminent among them the École William Ponty (Senegal), Fourah Bay College (Sierra Leone), the Achimota School (Ghana), and the University of Ibadan (Nigeria)—as well as countless lower-echelon schools, have contributed seminally to Western Africa's modern literary acculturation. The products of these schools, as authors and readers, are responsible for the novel's domestication and popularization in the region.

One cannot overlook either the role of international and local PUBLISHING houses in facilitating the rise of the novel in Western Africa. Heinemann and Longman stand out among the former, having vigorously promoted the literary writings of West Africans through their African Writers' Series and Longman African Writers, respectively. Présence Africaine and Editorial Caminho, catering to a French-speaking and Portuguese-speaking readership, respectively, are other international publishing houses of note. Of the many local, nationally based publishers sustaining the novel's growth in the region, we can name an important extant few: First Dimension, Malthouse, and Spectrum (Nigeria); Sub-Saharan and Afram (Ghana); Nouvelles Éditions Africaines du Sénégal and Per Ankh (Senegal); Nouvelles Éditions Ivoiriennes (Cote d'Ivoire); and Le Figuier (Mali).

The novel is, of course, a form of fictional NARRATIVE whose immediate sources and

The Encyclopedia of the Novel Edited by Peter Melville Logan
© 2011 Blackwell Publishing Ltd

foremost elaboration is, by and large, European. It traveled to Western Africa as part of the institutional package of literacy transferred to the region's inhabitants as they came into cultural contact with, or fell under the colonial hegemony of, Europeans. In its formal European elaboration, as Bakhtin has noted, what emerges as a distinctive and defining feature of the novel is its "heteroglossia," i.e., the novel definitively stands out in accommodating a (competing) heterogeneity of socio-ideological voices and expressive registers. A "dialogic imagination," Bakhtin points out in this connection, informs the novel: agreeing to cohabit in disagreement is, as it were, the condition under which different registers and voices share the novel's formal space. As a dialogic given, therefore, the novel is predisposed not to produce some ultimate unisonance or closure.

One might plausibly argue, then, that, by virtue of its heteroglossic and dialogic predisposition, the novel, as it has fallen into the hands of West Africans in cultural transfer, has offered them a literary form that, its immediate European sources notwithstanding, is not in cultural "foreclosure." The novel comes potentially "open," then, to being added to; to its socio-cultural relevance being extended in space and time; and to being competitively remade according to post-European conceptions. As is the case in other parts of the world, therefore, one finds in the Western African novel voices and expressive registers of a non-European variety belatedly, but not unoriginally, negotiating an opening—and competing in that to be recognized—within a narrative mode whose prior formal elaboration is European.

In Western African negotiation and appropriation, the novel has provided a major representational and expressive outlet for authors to be responsive to, and be responsible for, existences, experiences, and problems that are comparatively similar in being shared across their region. What novelists take on and respond to have commonly arisen for West Africans (a) within and after their encounters with, and then colonial domination by, Europeans; and (b) within and after their transition to postcolonial self-rule. Encounter has thrown up for West Africans a problematic of culture-contact. West Africans commonly contend with a heritage of overlapping "polarities": a "modern" heritage received via European acculturation and a "traditional" one of native provenance. In the circumstances, West African novelists have been recurrently compelled to imagine whether, and if so how, an alien modern may be "nativized" (Appiah, 1992); or nativity, for that matter, modernized. For other novelists, coming from a purist nativist perspective, it has been a matter of articulating the undesirability, if not the danger, of bringing into nativist reconciliation what for them must weigh, in Western Africa's shared contact experience, as an alienating and contaminating modern.

Colonialism furnishes a second regional problematic. Facing situations where their communities and peoples have been unethically deprived of a self-determining freedom, of human equality and dignity, West African novelists have felt compelled to express an allegiance to anticolonial resistance, to decolonization, and to ideals of nationhood. It has been a region-wide imperative to produce narratives that foreground acts of liberating the region's peoples from foreign control. Both during the era of decolonization and afterwards, West African novelists have tended to be literary nationalists (see NATIONAL literature) engaged ideologically—as negritudists, nativists, pan-Africanists, "cosmopolitan patriots" (Appiah, 1998)—in a search for the authentic bases and orientations to the world of national community in their region.

Finally, we can talk about Western African problematics that arise with the arrival of national independence and self-rule, and with concomitant projects of communal reformation and social transformation within the region after 1960. West Africans have confronted postcolonial tasks of fashioning equitable societies, viable communities, and ethical personal identities. In the face of obvious region-wide failures by national power elites to exercise state power responsibly, an enduring theme in Western Africa, recurrently submitted to novelistic exploration, has been degenerate power and its material and moral consequences for regional societies and subjects.

Beyond the power and people problematic, the internal relationships of Western African national societies—as societies of patriarchally structured inequality, of class exploitation, of rivalries between social factions, of different generational worldviews and orientations—have thrown up a number of postcolonial questions and ideological responses that have thematically fed the regional novel. Critiques of the social, and viewpoints on ethically reforming and materially transforming its internal relations, have emerged from various Western African perspectives: liberal-humanist, socialist, MARXIST, FEMINIST, ethical-universalist, etc.

Over regional time and space, significant novelistic variety has emerged to allow literary critics to identify different Western African "traditions" or "tendencies." Thus the novel is identified as either Anglophone, Francophone, or Lusophone in an acknowledgment of its production within distinct communities of transnationally shared language and culture in Western Africa. There are also a small number of novels in some of the region's vernacular languages, and regional writing is also identified by nation, GENDER, and generation. Furthermore, a typological distinction is made between the elite novel and the popular novel.

This brief entry cannot hope to effect anything but a partial representation of the regional trends. In what follows the focus will largely be on select examples of the elite and European-language novel, which has traditionally been where critics have derived a Western African canon.

THE COLONIAL ERA

The earliest known Western African novels are *Marita* (1885–89), by the Gold Coaster "A. Native," and *Guanya Pau: The Story of an African Princess* (1891), by the Liberian Joseph J. Walters. The two authors offer Western African prototypes of the nativist ("A. Native") and the cosmopolitan patriot (Walters). "Native," in *Marita*, mounts a strong cultural relativist defense of home-grown Gold Coast customary law and practices, doing so in protest against the colony's British rulers who are bent on replacing indigenous traditions with Anglo-Christian norms. On the other hand, as he trains an abolitionist eye on tyrannical patriarchal customs that he finds injurious to ethnic Vai women's wellbeing in Liberia, Walters is a Christian, a liberal-humanist, and a cosmopolitan advocate of modernizing reform.

The defense of cultural authenticity returns in the second Gold Coast novel, J. E. Casely Hayford's *Ethiopia Unbound* (1911), whose protagonist is seen successfully embarking on an allegorical journey of return to the source of the native soul. Loss of this soul is the subject of Kobina Sekyi's serial *The Anglo-Fanti* (1918), which tells the tragic story of an intellectual whose authentic native self (Fanti) has been irretrievably despoiled by his English acculturation.

If at the outset of the Anglophone novel in Western Africa we find Gold Coast novelists critical of an unreconstructed modernity for their societies, the Senegalese originators of the regional Francophone novel in the 1920s start on a contrary note. In the French colonies, the policy was that natives, after being successfully subjected to modern forms of tutelage, discipline, and acculturation, became assimilated into a French "universality." It is from within the ranks of the *assimilés* that the first Francophone novelists emerged, Senegalese pioneers betraying their intellectual, psychic, and affective conditioning as "French." Accordingly, Ahmadou Mapate Diagne in *Les Trois volontés de Malic* (1920, The three wishes of Malic) eulogizes French colonial modernity for its beneficial civilizing effects. Similar attitudes are to be found in Bakary Diallo's *Force-Bonté* (1926, Much goodwill).

French assimilationist modernity is represented in a dual aspect of promise and peril for the first time by the Senegalese Ousmane Soce in *Karim* (1935) and *Mirages de Paris* (1937, Mirages of Paris). Soce originally deployed a motif that would be repeated in Francophone autobiographical novels (see LIFE WRITING) that followed: the hero, having discovered Frenchness to be more a peril to his soul than a blessing, and unable to recover the nativity from which his modern upbringing has distanced him, is left perplexingly suspended in an ambiguous no man's land. The classic of the genre is the Senegalese Cheikh Hamidou Kane's *L'Aventure ambiguë* (1961, The Ambiguous Adventure). The Guinean (Conakry) Camara Laye's *L'Enfant noir* (1956, The African Child) offers a romantic variation on the motif. Even as he confronts the potential pitfall of modern alienation, the hero's nostalgic remembering is of sufficient power to keep his selfhood rooted in the idyllic native world of his childhood.

The inception of the Lusophone novel in Western Africa—a Cape Verdean affair—is marked by Baltasar Lopes's *Chiquinho* (1947). Lopes was part of the *Claridade* (cultural) movement which espoused a nativist ideology, and emerged in reaction to the universalism of an earlier literary school on the island whose writings were fed by an impulse "to flee the restricted environment of the islands, and to plug into the wider context of Western culture" (Brookshaw, 180). *Chiquinho* follows its eponymous hero growing up and endorses his arriving at a native Cape Verdean consciousness. Manuel Lopes would reaffirm *Claridade*'s nativist commitments in *Chuva Braba* (1956, *Wild Rain*) and *Os Flagelados do Vento Leste* (1960, The victims of the east wind).

DECOLONIZATION

In the 1940s, the call for decolonization was increasingly being sounded by the Western African intelligentsia: the region's peoples must cease to be colonial subjects and come into their own as citizens of nations. Decolonization also raised the question of the complementary role of culture in political struggle and in the imagining of the future (modern) community of the nation. In what modalities of expression was culture to appear if it was to inspire the march of West Africans toward the self-owned modernity of nationality and citizenship?

Literary representation would supply some inspirational answers by revisiting the times before imperial and colonial intervention, when West Africans independently created orderly, self-sustaining communities and ran self-determining polities. Such mythmaking is evident in two Francophone historical novels: Dahomeyan (Benin) Paul Hazoumé's *Doguicimi* (1938), which reconstructs the kingdom of Dahomey; and Nazi Boni's *Crépuscule de temps anciens* (1962, Twilight of ancient times), set in the past of his native Upper Volta (Burkina Faso). Nationalist vindicationism is also the purpose behind the Nigerian Chinua Achebe's classic *Things Fall Apart* (1958). The novel's documentation of the orderly institutions and dignified way of life of a small preco-lonial Igbo community modulates into a tragic swansong as colonial intrusion de-stroys this civilized community's well-wrought social order.

Achebe accomplishes an indigenizing of the language of the Anglophone novel, most notably in his *Arrow of God* (1964). The Ivorian Ahmadou Kourouma's *Les soleils des indépendances* (1968, *The Suns of Inde-pendence*) is a comparable pioneer Franco-phone achievement. Achebe's compatriots Amos Tutuola's *The Palm-Wine Drinkard* (1953), Gabriel Okara's *The Voice* (1964), and Flora Nwapa's *Efuru* (1966) are also notable Western African attempts at making an "oraliterature."

If one Western African novelistic strategy, indigenization, is to "acculturate" what is European and modern in language and form by infusing it with elements of oral tradition, another regional strategy—a de-fining characteristic of the vernacular nov-el—has been "inculturation." This has entailed infusing the region's indigenous languages with modern expressive modali-ties-such as the novel form affords—such that these languages will be expressively enriched, for their ethno-national commu-nity of speakers and readers, as producers of "literature." Vernacular cultural national-ism of this kind is what is at work in the Yoruba-language novels of D. O. Fagunwa, including the famous *Ògbójú Odè Nínú Igbó Irúnmalè* (1938, *The Forest of a Thousand Demons*). The Cape Verdean Manuel Veiga is able to use a "novelized" Creole to ex-press complex literary ideas in his *Oju d'Agu* (1974, The wellspring).

Still on culture's role and place in de-colonization, there were some in Western Africa for whom uncritical re-creations and nationalist endorsements of the feudal, tribal, or patriarchal glories of the region's distant pasts or surviving traditions were inadequate for the imagining of modern,

progressive national communities. There were writers in the decolonizing era and its aftermath, then, who sought alternative imaginings of the basis of national culture, an important one being Senegal's Sembene Ousmane. His *Les Bouts de bois de Dieu* (1960, *God's Bits of Wood*) stands out in its Marxist insistence that the basis of national culture was to be sought in contemporary working people's resistance culture—i.e., those traditions of political and moral sol-idarity which emerge out of working peo-ple's struggles against a capitalism which has taken historic form in Africa as colonialism.

WOMEN'S WRITING

Women's novelistic contribution to the cul-turalist discourse of a renascent Africa would not come until 1966, the year when Nwapa's *Efuru*, the first (non-serial) novel by a woman in Western Africa, was pub-lished. Typically, the female novel has moved between (anti-patriarchal) protest and (matriarchal) testimonial. As protest, the female novel portrays the tragedies in-flicted on women characters by patriarchal traditions—indigenous, Islamic, Christian, and secular-modern. Cases in point are the Nigerian Buchi Emecheta's *The Joys of Motherhood* (1979) and the Senegalese Ken Bugul's *Le Baobab fou* (1991, *The Aban-doned Baobab*).

On the other hand, as testimonial, the female-authored novel demonstrates and validates an altruistic female ethic—a set of "womanist" attributes often operating in the interests of communal creation, cohe-sion, and survival. This ethic stands out in the Ghanaian Ama Ata Aidoo's *Our Sister Killjoy* (1977) and in the Senegalese Mariama Ba's *Une si longue lettre* (1979, *So Long a Letter*). In the portrayals of historic and contemporary heroines by Nwapa,

Aidoo, Ba, Emecheta, and others who follow them, we see a womanist projection of the audacious, headstrong woman—at once fiercely defensive of her rights and fiercely committed to building sustainable community—as the iconic "new woman" of national culture. Heroines and women characters in the Nigerian Zaynab Alkali's *The Stillborn* (1984); the Ivorian Véronique Tadjo's *Le Royaume aveugle* (1991, *The Blind Kingdom*) and *Reine Pokou* (2005, *Queen Pokou*); and the Nigerian Chimamanda Adichie's *Half of a Yellow Sun* (2006) continue this womanist projection.

THE POST-INDEPENDENCE ERA

As an article of faith, West Africans leading the charge for decolonization had projected the imaginary, affective, purposive, and moral integrity of a collective self of decolonization—"the people." It had become apparent shortly after independence, however, that the national-popular idealism of decolonization had been betrayed by the emergent power elites. What had succeeded colonialism was degenerate power, now wielded by the governing classes in the emergent nation-states. Western Africa had entered the troubled postcolonial times that will generate the literary reflex called "the literature of disillusionment."

The titles of a number of Anglophone Western African novels written by the first generation of post-independence writers convey how dispiriting the new times had become: *The Beautyful Ones Are Not Yet Born* (1968) and *Fragments* (1970), both by the Ghanaian Ayi Kwei Armah; *This Earth, My Brother* (1971), by the Ghanaian Kofi Awoonor; *Season of Anomy* (1973), by the Nigerian Wole Soyinka. Francophone contributions include Kourouma's *Les Soleils des indépendances*; Malian Yambo Ouologuem's *Le Devoir de violence* (1968, *Bound to*

Violence); and Senegalese Boubacar Boris Diop's *Le Temps de Tamango* (1981, The time of the Tamango). Germano Almeida's *O meu Poeta* (1991, My poet) also portrays Cape Verde from a disenchanted perspective. These novels of disenchantment are notable for their outrage at hopes betrayed; their inclination toward tragic, absurdist, or baroque expression; their scatological imagery; and their pessimistic tone.

After pessimistically diagnosing the postcolonial condition, however, West African writers would also make monumental efforts to revive and re-enchant the mythology of nation and belonging. What we might group together as "novels of revival" include Armah's *Two Thousand Seasons* (1973) and Abdulai Sila's *Eterna Paixão* (1994, Eternal passion), Guinea Bissau's pioneer contribution to the Lusophone novel. Other novelists would re-enchant the mythology of nation and community by reaching for a visionary magic realism: Ghana's Kojo Laing in *Search, Sweet Country* (1986); Sierra Leone's Syl Cheney Coker in *The Last Harmattan of Alusine Dunbar* (1990); Nigeria's Ben Okri in *The Famished Road* (1991).

THE "THIRD GENERATION"

More recently, a third (post-independence) generation of West African novelists, spearheaded by Nigerian writers, is said to have arrived. For the most part, the novelists of this third generation, like those of the first two, have retained the nation as their focus as they conduct communal and social stock-taking in the variety of ways outlined above. Nevertheless these recent novels, often produced by expatriates and migrants, look beyond the nation, bringing to bear "cosmopolitan" norms and sensibilities and "transnational" forms of ethical critique. These "postnationalist" novels thus tend to uphold ways of self-fashioning, ways of knowing and judging that the nationalist discourse of an earlier period has more or less dismissed as "un-African"—hence incompatible with authentic national culture and national belonging. Thus, in Chris Abani's *Graceland* (2005), Sefi Atta's *Everything Good will Come* (2005), Unoma Azuah's *Sky High Flames* (2005), and Jude Dibia's *Walking with Shadows* (2006), we have some of the latest varieties of regional voice and expression exemplarily showing how, and the extent to which, novelistic heteroglossia and dialogism continue to be turned to Western African account.

BIBLIOGRAPHY

Adesanmi, P. and C. Dunton, eds. (2008), "Nigeria's Third Generation Novel," *Research in African Literatures* 39(2):vii–xii.

Anderson, B. (1991), *Imagined Communities*.

Appiah, K.A. (1992), *In My Father's House*.

Appiah, K.A. (1998), Cosmopolitan Patriots," in *Cosmopolitics*, ed. P. Cheah and B. Robbins.

Bakhtin., M.M. (1981), *Dialogic Imagination*.

Brookshaw, D. (1996), "Cape Verde," in P. Chabal, et al., *Postcolonial Literature of Lusophone Africa*.

Gerrard, A., ed. (1986), *European-Language Writing in Sub-Saharan Africa*, 2 vols.

Michelman, F. (1976), "The West African Novel Since 1911," *Yale French Studies* 53:29–44.

Newell, S. (2006), *West African Literatures*.

Padilha, L.C. (2007), "Tradition and the Effects of the New in Modern African Fictional Cartography," *Research in African Literatures* 38(1):106–118.

Porter, A.M. (2000), "New 'New' Jerusalem?" Jouvert 4(2), http://english.chass.ncsu.edu/jouvert/v4i2/porter.htm

Wehrs, D.R. (2001), *African Feminist Fiction and Indigenous Values*.

Wilson-Tagoe, N. (2003), "Representing Culture and Identity," Feminist Africa 2 http://wwWestfeministafrica.org/index.php/representing-culture-and-identity

Working-Class Novel *see* Class; Marxist Theory; Russia (20th Century)

World Literature *see* Comparativism

Worldview Making *see* Cognitive Theory

X

Xiaoshuo *see* China; Ancient Narratives of China

Y

Yiddish Novel

KEN FRIEDEN

A latecomer to the genre, the Yiddish novel was heavily influenced by Russian and English models. Satiric REALISM and PARODY characterize nineteenth-century Yiddish fiction, while twentieth-century authors explored a wide range of styles. With a few notable exceptions, Yiddish novels were directed to a popular audience.

Sholem Yankev Abramovitsh, who is sometimes known as Mendele Moykher Sforim (the central character in his fiction), greatly influenced the Yiddish novel. Five works form the core of his literary achievement: *Dos kleyne mentshele* (1864, *The Little Man*), *Dos vintshfingerl* (1865, *The Wishing-Ring*), *Fishke der Krumer* (1869, *Fishke the Lame*; 1888, expanded ed.), *Di klyatshe* (1873, *The Nag*), and *Kitser masoes Binyumin hashlishi* (1878, *The Brief Travels of Benjamin the Third*). In later years he revised and expanded these novels. Closely associated with the Jewish intelligentsia of Odessa after 1881, Abramovitsh developed a compelling satiric realism. Some characters appear typical, while others are comically distorted. His HEBREW adaptations of Yiddish works played a major role in the creation of modern Hebrew fiction (see ADAPTATION/APPROPRIATION).

Sholem Aleichem (the pen-name used by Sholem Rabinovitsh) was also a founder of modern Yiddish fiction. His best-known work is *Tevye der milkhiker* (1894–1914, *Tevye the Dairyman*), which could be considered a novel but is a collection of stories narrated by Tevye. Sholem Aleichem experimented with the novelistic form in the late 1880s, producing *Stempeniu* (1888, *Stempeniu: A Jewish Romance*) and *Yosele Solovey* (1889, *The Nightingale; or, The Saga of Yosele Solovey the Cantor*). He also employed a first-person, oral-style narrator, as in *Motl Peyse dem khazns* (1907–16, *Adventures of Mottel, the Cantor's Son*). Other works include the EPISTOLARY novel *Menakhem Mendel* (1892–1909, *Letters of Menakhem-Mendl, Sheyne-Sheyndl and Mot, the Cantor's Son*) and third-person narratives such as *Blondzhende shtern* (1912, *Wandering Stars*).

In the early twentieth century, the Warsaw center of Yiddish literature formed around I. L. Peretz, who excelled as an author of short fiction but never published a novel. Nevertheless, he inspired a generation of novelists, including David Pinski, Sholem Asch, Isaac Meir Weissenberg, I. J. Singer, and the poet and fiction writer Kadya Molodowsky.

David Bergelson became the master of the modernist novel in Yiddish (see MODERNISM). His work extends the form beyond the realm of his predecessors by employing innovative narrative techniques to create more ambiguous fictional worlds. His novel *Opgang* (1920, *Descent* or *Departing*) portrays the collapse of traditional values and the decline of the small town *shtetl*.

Following the Holocaust (ca. 1933–45), Yiddish fiction continued to be written in the Soviet Union, Israel, and the U.S. I. J. Singer's brother, I. B. Singer, became the only Yiddish writer to receive the Nobel Prize for literature, in 1978. Their sister Esther Kreitman also published Yiddish novels, including *Der sheydim tants* (1936, *The Dance of Demons*).

Several successful authors wrote first in Yiddish before publishing in another language. One example is Mary Antin's first draft of *From Plotzsk to Boston* (1899). Elie Wiesel first published his autobiographical novel *La nuit* (1958, *Night*) in Yiddish under the title *Un di velt hot geshvign* (1956, *And the World Remained Silent*).

Active Yiddish novelists in the later twentieth century include Chaim Grade, Chava Rosenfarb, and Boris Sandler. Because of the decline in the Yiddish-speaking population, through genocide and assimilation, few Yiddish novels are likely to be written in the twenty-first century.

SEE ALSO: National Literature, Religion.

BIBLIOGRAPHY

Frieden, K. (1995), *Classic Yiddish Fiction*.
Harshav, B. (1990), *Meaning of Yiddish*.
Miron, D. (1996), *Traveler Disguised*.
Roskies, D. (1995), *Bridge of Longing*.
Seidman, N. (1997), *Marriage Made in Heaven*.
Wisse, R. (1991), *I. L. Peretz and the Making of Modern Jewish Culture*.

Z

Zeugma *see* Figurative Language and Cognition

Index of Novelists

This index of novelists includes all novelists mentioned in the *Encyclopedia* as well as writers of other narrative forms that, while not themselves thought of as novels, played a significant role in the development of the novel. It is designed to be as generous as possible in determining which names to include. When questions arose, the editors generally chose to include writers rather than exclude them.

al-'Alim, Raja' (b. 1963)   63, 64
al-A'raj, Wasini (b. 1954)   63
al-'Arawi,' Abdallah (b. 1933)   63
Aba-enlil-dari   36
Abani, Chris (b. 1966): *Graceland*   857
Abd al-Qader, Ahmed Ben (b. 1941)   577
Abdel Malek, Smari (b. 1958)   580
Abdelqader, Ahmed Ould
  Al-asma' al-mutaghayyira   577
  Al-qabr al-majhoul   577
Abdelwahab, Hasan Hosni (1884–1968): *Amiratu*
  Gharnata   574
Abdolah, Kader (b. 1954)   498
Abdul Kadir Adabi (1901–44): *Acuman*
  Mahkota   754
Abdul Samad Said (b.1935): *Salina*   752
Abdul Talib bin Mohd. Hassan (b. 1947):
  Saga   753
Abdul-Baki, Kathryn (b. 1952)   63
Abe Kōbō (1924–93): *Kemonotachi wa kokyō*
  mezasu   441
Abeysekera, Tissa (1939–2009)   749
Aboulela, Leila (b. 1964)   63, 64
  The Translator   821
Abrahams, Peter (b. 1919): *Mine Boy*   770
Abramov, Fedor (1920–83)
  Brat'ia i sestry   722
  Priasliny trilogy   722
Abramovitz, Sholem Yankev (1835–1917)   379–80
  Fishke der Krumer   859
  Kitser masoes Binyumin hashlishi   859
  Dos kleyne mentshele   859

  Di klyatshe   859
  Dos vintshfingerl   859
Abu Shawir, Rashad (b. 1942)   64
Abu-Jaber, Diana (b 1960)   63
Accad, Evelyne (b. 1943)   63
Achebe, Chinua (b. 1930)   125, 230, 821
  Arrow of God   855
  Things Fall Apart   56, 131, 255, 854–5
Achilles Tatius (fl. 2nd cent. CE)   35, 44
  Leucippe and Clitophon   284
Acker, Kathy (1948–97)   810, 847
  Blood and Guts in High School   743
Ackroyd, Peter (b. 1949)   4–5
  Chatterton   514
  Dickens   4
  The Great Fire of London   5
Acosta, Oscar Zeta (1935–74): *The Revolt of the*
  Cockroach People   468
Adamson, Joy (1910–80)   269
Adán, Martín (1908–85)   50
Adichie, Chimamanda (b. 1977): *Half of a Yellow*
  Sun   856
Adiga, Aravind (b. 1974): *The White Tiger*   620
Adıvar, Halide Edib   824
Adnan, Etel (b. 1925)   63
  Sitt Marie Rose   64
Adoum, Jorge Enrique (b. 1926)   51
Afghani, A. M. (b. 1925)   429
Ağaoğlu, Adalet: *Ölmeye Yatmak*   825
Agee, James (1909–55)   614
  Let us Now Praise Famous Men   458, 614
Agnon, S. Y. (1888–1970)   381

General Index

Canada (*Continued*)
  Great Depression 140–2
  historical novelists 136
  hybrid forms 144
  identity 135
  immigrant novelists 143
  indigenous people 137, 140
  multiculturalism 143
  pluralism 142–4
  postmodernism 142
  provincialism 140
  Quebec's Quiet Revolution 135
  realism 136, 140
  Romance 135
  Romanticism 137
  roots 135–6
  separatist novels 139–40
  Union of Upper and Lower 135
  urbanization 140
  World Wars 135, 140–2
Canadian Bookman 140
The Canadian Forum 140
Candido, A. 101
canon
  censorship 156–7
  challenges/confirmations 3–4
  editing 272
  English literature 124, 128
  French literature 330–1
  German literature 362
  national 565
  and other novels 397
  revisions 276
  theater 6
  USA 833
Cantar de mio Cid 399
A Canterbury Tale (Powell) 6
cantigas 399
Cao Cao 382
Cape, Jonathan 157
Cape Verde 854, 856
capitalism
  class 191
  Enlightenment 672
  feudalism 35
  individual 592
  and Marxism 504
  merchant 47
  novel 592
  serialization 731
  sexuality 742
captivity narratives 834

Carby, Hazel 131, 296, 297, 351
Cardwell, S. 7
Caribbean 144–53
  Anglophone novels 150–1
  Cuban novel 147–9
  cultural identity 144–5, 151
  dialect 249
  Dominican Republican novel 149–50
  Francophone novels 151–2
  geography of 144
  languages of 145
  literary awards 145
  migration 146
  Puerto Rican novel 149–50
  racial themes 146–7
  Spanish-speaking 146
  writers 129
  see also specific islands
Caribbean Voices (BBC) 129
Carnegie, Andrew 477, 479
carnivalesque 85, 142
Carrithers, D. W. 667
Carroll, Joseph 200
Carthage 43
Cartmell, D. 8
Casanova, Pascale 501, 566
Case, Alison 553
Cassin, Barbara 303
Cassirer, Ernst 83, 359
Castilian literature 399, 401–2, 410–11
Castillo, Bernal Díaz del 517
Castle, Gregory 55
Castle, Terry 299
Castro, Américo 401
Catalonia
  literature 400–1, 404, 407
  Spanish Civil War 406, 408
catharsis 176
Catholic Church 493, 498, 672
  censorship 154
  corruption 161
  freedom of expression 161
  Quebec 141–2
  ultramontanism 139
  Western 87, 89
Caudwell, Christopher 506
Caxton, William 400, 638
cell-phone novel 449
Celtic cultural nationalism 55–6
Celtic legends 701
censorship 153–60
  activism 158–9